Persuasion

Now in its sixth edition, *Persuasion: Social Influence and Compliance Gaining* continues to boast an accessible voice and vibrant aesthetic that appeals to undergraduate students of communication, psychology, advertising, and marketing. In addition to presenting established theories and models, this text encourages students to develop and apply general conclusions about persuasion in real-world settings. Along the way, students are introduced to the practice of social influence in an array of contexts (e.g., advertising, marketing, politics, interpersonal relationships, social media, groups) and across a variety of topics (e.g., credibility, personality, deception, motivational appeals, visual persuasion). The new edition features an expanded treatment of digital and social media, up-to-date research on theory and practice, and enhanced discussions of topics such as political campaigning, emotional marketing, olfactory influence, and ethics. Instructors can also use the book's downloadable test bank, instructor's manual, and PowerPoint slides in preparing course material.

Robert H. Gass is Professor Emeritus of Communication Studies at California State University, Fullerton, USA.

John S. Seiter is Professor in the Department of Languages, Philosophy, and Communication Studies at Utah State University, USA.

Persuasion

Social Influence and Compliance Gaining

Sixth Edition

Robert H. Gass

John S. Seiter

Routledge
Taylor & Francis Group

NEW YORK AND LONDON

Sixth edition published 2018
by Routledge
711 Third Avenue, New York, NY 10017

and by Routledge
2 Park Square, Milton Park, Abingdon, Oxon, OX14 4RN

Routledge is an imprint of the Taylor & Francis Group, an informa business

First edition published by Pearson Education, Inc. 2002

Fifth edition published by Routledge 2016

Library of Congress Cataloging in Publication Data
Names: Gass, Robert H., author. | Seiter, John S., author.
Title: Persuasion : social influence, and compliance gaining /
Robert H. Gass, John S. Seiter.
Description: Sixth edition. | New York, NY : Routledge, 2018.
Identifiers: LCCN 2017042512| ISBN 9781138630598 (hardback) |
ISBN 9781138630611 (pbk.)
Subjects: LCSH: Persuasion (Psychology) | Influence (Psychology) |
Manipulative behavior.
Classification: LCC BF637.P4 G34 2018 | DDC 153.8/52—dc23
LC record available at https://lccn.loc.gov/2017042512

ISBN: 978-0-8153-5821-3 (hbk)
ISBN: 978-1-138-63061-1 (pbk)
ISBN: 978-1-315-20930-2 (ebk)

Typeset in Sabon
by Florence Production Ltd, Stoodleigh, Devon, UK

Visit the eResource: www.routledge.com/9781138630611

Printed and bound in the United States of America by Sheridan

Contents

Preface for the Sixth Edition

PERSUASION CONTINUES TO OCCUPY the attention of academics and non-academics alike. Not only scholars, but practitioners such as advertisers, lawyers, lobbyists, marketing firms, motivational speakers, politicians, public relations experts, social activists, syndicated columnists, and others have a vested interest in knowing how persuasion works. Therefore, students who aspire to careers in any of the "people professions" would be wise to acquire a basic understanding of how persuasion functions.

With each edition of this text, we marvel at how much persuasion changes over time, yet still remains the same. For example, controversies over "fake news" have altered the way people perceive facts and assess source credibility. Even so, credibility remains as central to the process of persuasion as ever. It is *perceived* credibility that counts. The credibility of news sources is in the eye of the beholder.

The observation that "the more persuasion changes, the more it remains the same" applies to almost every aspect of persuasion. Compliance-gaining strategies such as the "foot in the door" now occur in online settings. Audience analysis is key to persuasion, but rather than examining demographic data, persuaders can now use *microtargeting* to tailor their messages to niche groups. For example, in the 2016 presidential election, rumors swirled that Cambridge Analytica, a company that specializes in opinion mining and data analysis, identified low-information voters in key swing states and bombarded them with highly targeted messages (Confessore & Hakim, 2017). Product placement, once only found on television and in movies, is now prevalent in novels, pop music, and virtual environments such as computer games. Fear appeals, long a staple of persuaders, have moved online. In addition to being fearful of Ebola, terrorism, and clowns, we can now be worried about cyberstalking, cyberbullying, and whatever diet and nutrition advice Gwyneth Paltrow is about to post.

In this edition, we address the increasing importance of digital and online persuasion, while emphasizing the importance of traditional forms of persuasion as well. Since the last edition, digital persuasion has come into its own. On social media, pop-up ads and banners have given way to more sophisticated forms of marketing, such as *webtracking* (Avergin, 2016). Using third-party cookies, *canvas fingerprinting* (Kirk, 2014), and other techniques, Web marketers can follow users' activities across websites. "Like" a bluegrass video on YouTube, "follow" a fiddle player on Facebook, or post some banjo pictures on Instagram, and you'll start getting messages about hoedowns and honky-tonks in your area.

Persuasion on the Web also relies on *sentiment tracking* or *opinion mining*. For example, using natural language processing software, millions of tweets can be analyzed to see what topics, people, or brands are trending and what emotion-laden words or emojis are being used in connection with those topics or issues. Insights about political preferences, brand images, and economic trends can be gleaned from the results. As Bannister (2015) noted, "shifts in sentiment on social media have been shown to correlate with shifts in the stock market" (para. 3).

The widespread use of mobile technology has also been accompanied by increasing apps and techniques designed to influence. Texting, tweeting, and other apps disseminate word-of-mouth (WOM) messages. WOM is perceived by many as more genuine, authentic, and trustworthy than commercial advertising or expert opinions. Of course, marketers can sneak into these conversations via sponsored tweets and promoted posts. In many ways, social media has become a form of *mass interpersonal persuasion*. Posting a picture on Instagram may seem interpersonal in nature, but posts can be shared far beyond one's social network. Just ask Anthony Weiner.

Despite the advent of digital and social media, most of us still live in a face-to-face world, too. Traditional forms of influence still matter, and interacting "in person" is by far the most effective way to persuade other people. A retail salesperson talking to a customer has a much greater chance of success than a pop-up ad reminding you about the last item you viewed on Amazon.com. That said, we often underestimate our effectiveness in one-on-one-settings. For example, Roghanizad and Bohns (2017) found that when people were asked to judge their influence via email versus in person, they overestimated the former and underestimated the latter. Groups, too, exert enormous influence over people. Whether within a family, a classroom, a workplace, at a coffee shop with friends, or some other group setting, the pressure to conform or risk being isolated is potent. Mass persuasion has greater reach, but less effectiveness.

As long as humans occupy planet Earth, they will be engaged in persuading one another. If apes or machines do take over one day, who can say? For now, we believe a solid understanding of persuasion, social influence, and compliance gaining will be an asset in this world. With that in mind, we hope you catch our enthusiasm for this field of study and turn the pages of this book with a better understanding of how persuasion functions, an improved knowledge of ways to maximize your own persuasion efforts, and a greater ability to resist influence attempts, especially unscrupulous influence attempts, by others.

REFERENCES

Avergin, J. (2016, September 2). Internet tracking has moved beyond cookies. FiveThirtyEight.com. Retrieved on July26, 2017 from: https://fivethirtyeight.com/features/internet-tracking-has-moved-beyond-cookies/

Bannister, K. (2015, January 26). Understanding sentiment analysis: What it is & why it's used. Brandwatch.com. Retrieved on July 26, 2017 from: www.brandwatch.com/blog/understanding-sentiment-analysis/

Confessore, N., & Hakim, D. (2017, March 6). Data firm says "secret sauce" aided Trump: Many scoff. *The New York Times*. Retrieved on July 26, from: www.nytimes.com/2017/03/06/us/politics/cambridge-analytica.html

Kirk, J. (2014). Three devious ways online trackers shatter your privacy. *PCWorld, 32*(10), 38–40.

Roghanizad, M. M., & Bohns, V. K. (2017). Ask in person: You're less persuasive than you think over email. *Journal of Experimental Social Psychology, 69*, 223–226. doi:10.1016/j.jesp.2016.10.002

Acknowledgments

We would like to offer our heartfelt thanks to everyone at Routledge/Taylor & Francis for their support throughout the process of completing this edition of our text. They are a skilled and talented group. We are especially grateful to Laura Briskman and Nicole Salazar for their relentless graciousness in answering our many questions and guiding us through the requirements for completing this project. Their patience is officially legendary. We also want to thank Josh Curtis and members of his team for painstakingly proofreading and copyediting the drafts of all the chapters.

We are also extremely grateful to the graduate and undergraduate students who offered numerous illustrations of real-life examples of persuasion. In particular, we single out Taylor Halverson for her excellent work. Every time we think we have taught the brightest group of students ever, another sharp group comes along. We also want to thank the many instructors using our book who have sent comments and suggestions for this edition, as well as the many short-course participants who have offered ideas and insights leading up to this edition.

Finally, we are fortunate to be working alongside the best colleagues anyone could ever hope for. Thank you all for making "work" a fun and rewarding place to be!

ONE OF THE AUTHORS was enjoying a day at the beach with his family. As he sat in a folding chair, lost in a good book, he could hear the cries of seagulls overhead and the pounding of the surf. Nothing was bothering him. He was oblivious to the world around him. Or so he thought. As he reflected more on the situation, however, he became aware that he was being bombarded by persuasive messages on all sides. A boom box was playing a few yards away. During commercial breaks, various ads tried to convince him to choose a new cellphone provider, switch auto insurance companies, and try a hot, spicy cheeseburger. A nearby sign warned that no alcohol, glass objects, or smoking were permitted on the beach. A plastic bag in which a nearby family's children had brought their beach toys advertised Walmart on its side. The family picnic cooler proudly displayed its manufacturer, Igloo, as well.

And that was only the beginning. A plane flew overhead, trailing a banner that advertised a collect calling service. The lifeguard's tower displayed a Hurley logo. Their swimsuits were sponsored by Izod. The lifeguard's truck, a specially equipped Toyota, announced that it was the "official emergency vehicle" of "Surf City USA," a moniker trademarked by the city of Huntington Beach, California. Oh, the indignity of being rescued by an unofficial vehicle.

There were oral influence attempts, too. His son tried to lure him into the water by saying, "Come on, it's not that cold." But he knew better. His son *always* said that, no matter how cold the water was. "Would you mind keeping an eye on our things?" the family next to the author's asked. I guess our family looks trustworthy, he thought. His wife asked him, "Do you want to walk down to the pier? They have frozen bananas." She knew he would be unable to resist the temptation.

And those were only the overt persuasive messages. A host of more subtle messages also competed for the author's attention. A few yards away, a woman was applying sun block to her neck and shoulders. The author decided he'd better do the same. Had she nonverbally influenced him to do likewise? Nearby, a young couple was soaking up the sun. Both were wearing hats with the Nike "swoosh" logo. Were they "advertising" that brand? A young man with a boogie board ran by, headed for the water. His head was shaved and he sported a goodly amount of body art. Did his appearance advocate a particular set of values or tastes? Was he a billboard for an "alternative" lifestyle? A half dozen male heads turned in unison as a trio of bikini-clad women walked by. Were the males "persuaded" to turn their heads or was this simply an involuntary reflex? Two tan, muscular dudes were tossing a Frisbee back and forth. Both had six-pack abs. The author made a mental note to do more sit-ups. There seemed to be as many persuasive messages, or potentially persuasive messages, as there were shells on the beach.

The preceding examples raise two important issues. First, persuasion and social influence are pervasive. We are surrounded by influence attempts, both explicit and implicit, no matter where we are. As Cascio, Scholz, and Falk emphasize (2015):

> social influence is omnipresent, occurring through implicit observation of cultural norms, face-to-face and mediated interpersonal communication, as well as mass mediated communication. Even though individuals are often unaware of the power of social influence, research shows its effects on behavior in a wide variety of circumstances.

(p. 51)

Second, it is difficult to say with any certainty what is and is not "persuasion." Where should we draw the line between persuasion and other forms of communication? We address the first of these issues in this chapter. Here we examine the pervasive nature of persuasion and offer a rationale for learning more about its workings. In the next chapter, we tackle the issue of what constitutes *persuasion* and related terms such as *social influence* and *compliance gaining*.

AIMS AND GOALS

This is a book about persuasion. Its aims are at once academic and practical. On the academic side, we examine how and why persuasion functions the way it does. In so doing, we identify some of the most recent theories and findings by persuasion researchers. On the practical side, we illustrate these theories and findings with a host of real-life examples. We also offer useful advice on how to become a more effective persuader and how to resist influence attempts, especially unethical influence attempts, by others.

If learning how to persuade seems a bit manipulative, remember, we don't live in a society populated with unicorns and rainbows. The real world is brimming with persuaders. You can avoid learning about persuasion, perhaps, but you can't avoid persuasion itself. Besides, we can't tell you everything there is to know about persuasion. Nobody knows all there is to know about this subject. One of the points we stress throughout this book is that people aren't that easy to persuade. Human beings are complex. They can be stubborn, unpredictable, and intractable, despite the best efforts of persuaders.

Persuasion is still as much an "art" as it is a "science." Human nature is too complicated, and our understanding of persuasion too limited, to be certain which influence attempts will succeed and which will fail. Think how often you flip the channel when a commercial costing millions of dollars to produce and air appears on television. As one advertising executive put it, "half the money I spend on advertising is wasted . . . but I don't know which half" (cited in Berger, 2011, p. 1). Think how many candidates for public office have spent fortunes campaigning, only to lose their elections. Or think how difficult it is for the federal government to convince people to stop smoking, practice safe sex, or avoid texting while driving—behaviors that are in their own self-interest.

The science of persuasion is still in its infancy. Despite P. T. Barnum's axiom that "there's a sucker born every minute," people are uncannily perceptive at times. It is tempting to believe that if one only knew the right button to push, one could persuade anybody. More often than not, though, there are multiple buttons to push, in the right sequence, and the sequence is constantly changing. Even so, persuasion is not entirely a matter of luck. Much is known about persuasion. Persuasion has been scientifically studied since the 1940s.[1] Written texts on persuasion date back to ancient Greece.[2] A host of strategies and techniques have been identified and their effectiveness or ineffectiveness documented. Persuaders are a long way from achieving an Orwellian nightmare of thought control, but a good deal is known about how to capture people's hearts and minds. Before proceeding further, we want to address a common negative stereotype about persuasion.

PERSUASION IS NOT A DIRTY WORD

The study of persuasion has gotten some bad publicity over the years. Everyone seems to agree that the subject is fascinating, but some are reluctant to embrace a field of study that conjures up images of manipulation, deceit, or brainwashing. There is, after all, a sinister side to persuasion. Adolf Hitler, Charles Manson, Jim Jones, David Koresh, Marshall Applewhite, and Osama bin Laden were all accomplished persuaders—much to the detriment of their followers.[3] We, however, do not think of persuasion as the ugly stepsister in the family of human communication. Rather, we find the study of persuasion to be enormously intriguing. Persuasion is the backbone of many communicative endeavors. We can't resist the urge to learn more about how and why it works. Part of our fascination stems from the fact that persuasion is, on occasion, used for unsavory ends. It is therefore all the more important that researchers learn as much as they can about the strategies and tactics of unethical persuaders.

PERSUASION IS OUR FRIEND

Persuasion isn't merely a tool used by con artists, chiselers, charlatans, cheats, connivers, and cult leaders. Nobel Peace Prize recipients and Pulitzer Prize-winning journalists are also persuaders. In fact, most "professional" persuaders are engaged in socially acceptable, if not downright respectable, careers. They include advertising executives, bloggers, campaign managers, celebrity endorsers, clergy, congresspersons, diplomats, infomercial spokespersons, lawyers, lobbyists, mediators, media pundits, motivational speakers, political cartoonists, press secretaries, public relations experts, radio talk-show hosts, recruiters, salespersons, senators, social activists, syndicated columnists, and whistleblowers, to name just a few.

Let's focus on the positive side of persuasion for a moment. Persuasion helps forge peace agreements between nations. Persuasion helps expose corruption and open up closed societies. Persuasion is crucial to the fundraising efforts of charities and philanthropic organizations. Persuasion convinces motorists to buckle up when driving or refrain from driving when they've had a few too many. Persuasion is used to convince a substance-abusing family member to seek professional help. Persuasion is how the coach of an underdog team inspires the players to give it their all. Persuasion is a tool used by parents to urge children not to accept rides from strangers or to allow anyone to touch them inappropriately. In short, persuasion is the cornerstone of a number of positive, prosocial endeavors. *Very little of the good that we see in the world could be accomplished without persuasion.*

Persuasion, then, is a powerful and often prosocial force. Having highlighted the positive side of persuasion, we address the question of *why* the study of persuasion is so valuable. The next section, therefore, offers a justification for the study of social influence.

THE PERVASIVENESS OF PERSUASION: YOU CAN RUN BUT YOU CAN'T HIDE

We've already mentioned one of the primary reasons for learning about this subject: Persuasion is a central feature of every sphere of human communication. The same is true of social influence. We can't avoid it. We can't make it go away. Like Elvis impersonators in Las Vegas, persuasion is here to stay. Various estimates suggest that the average person is exposed to anywhere from 300 to 5,000 messages per day.[4] There are more ways to persuade than ever before. Indeed, traditional persuasion in the form of political speeches, television commercials, print ads, billboards, and product placements in movies and television is alive and well. So too are protest marches, demonstrations, sit-ins, and other forms of symbolic action. In the last two decades, social media has been added to the mix. You can submit online reviews of products and services, post a YouTube video advocating your message, engage in *hashtag activism*, advocate a cause via Facebook, Twitter, or Instagram, solicit funding via crowdfunding platforms such as Kickstarter or GoFundMe, or promote change through a website such as www.change.org or www.dosomething.org. Let's consider one of these pervasive strategies, known as *viral persuasion*, more closely.

Tipping Points, Buzz Marketing, and Word of Mouth

Key concepts and principles associated with viral persuasion were laid out by Malcolm Gladwell in his bestseller, *The Tipping Point* (2000). Gladwell likens word-of-mouth (WOM) to a virus through which a message is spread until the whole society is "infected." Based on what he calls *"the law of the few,"* a small number of influential people can generate a groundswell of support for an idea, brand, or phenomenon. If a message gains sufficient traction, it reaches a tipping point and becomes "contagious." In order to reach the tipping point, however, a number of things have to happen.

Über Influencers

First, the right kinds of people must be involved. Gladwell identifies three types of people who are essential to the process. *Mavens* possess specialized expertise. They are in the know. They may be celebrity chefs, fashionistas, fitness gurus, tech geeks, or wine snobs. Mavens needn't be rich or famous, but they must be ahead of the curve. They are the early adopters, opinion leaders, or what some call *alpha consumers*, the ones who hear about ideas and try out gadgets first. "One American in ten," Keller and Barry (2003) maintain, "tells the other nine how to vote, where to eat, and what to buy" (p. 1).

In addition to mavens, Gladwell states that *connectors* are also essential. Based on the viral metaphor, they are carriers. They have large social networks. When connectors learn from mavens what the "next big thing" is, they spread the word. Since social circles tend to be overlapping, forwarding messages spreads them increasingly outward from their epicenter.

The last type Gladwell identifies is *salespeople*. They receive the message from a connector and then talk it up within their own circle of friends. Salespeople tell their friends, "You must see this movie," "You've got to try this restaurant," or "You gotta read this book."

FIGURE 1.1
ALS ice-bucket challenge in New York City.

Source: Saklova/ Shutterstock.com

Orchestrating the Next Big Thing

In addition to having the right kinds of people, some additional conditions must be satisfied for an idea to go viral. *Context* is critical. The idea must come along at the right time and place. Twitter, for example, wouldn't have worked before there was widespread mobile access to the Internet. An idea also must possess *stickiness*, which means that it is inherently attractive. Without some sort of natural appeal, people won't gravitate toward the idea or pass it along (Heath & Heath, 2008). For example, in 2014, the ALS water bucket challenge, which dared people to dump ice water over their own or other people's heads, went viral, raising over $100 million in the USA alone (www.als.org). Its stickiness was based, in part, on its eye-catching appeal, its urgency (there was a 24-hour deadline to respond), and the fact that it was for a good cause.

Scalability is another requirement: It must be easy to ramp up production of the idea, product, or message to meet demand. The ice-bucket challenge met this requirement because almost everyone can find a bucket and some ice. Finally, *effortless transfer* is yet another ingredient in the recipe for an effective viral campaign. A viral campaign has to leverage free media. Ideas that can be spread by forwarding an email, including an attachment, or embedding a link are easy to disseminate. The more time, effort, or money it takes to spread the word, the less likely the idea will go viral. In the ice-bucket campaign, most challenges were issued from one friend to another via video.

Infectious or Inexplicable?

Although viral marketing holds considerable potential, it is often a hit-or-miss strategy, with far more misses than hits. What's more, evidence for the effectiveness of tipping points is largely anecdotal, and there is no guarantee that an idea will gain traction. If one does, its shelf life is often limited. The ice-bucket challenge, for example, came and went in a few months. And flash mobs, another approach to viral marketing, were a flash in the pan.

The Word of Mouth Marketing Association (WOMM) offers advice for conducting viral campaigns. The very concept of viral marketing, however, is something of an oxymoron. A viral campaign is planned to appear unplanned. It is contrived to seem genuine. As consumers grow wise to the strategy, it will become less effective. There are also ethical questions about using friends as shills. The FTC now requires any online endorsement that involves compensation to be disclosed (Sprague & Wells, 2010).

Nudges: Sometimes Less Is More

The ubiquitous nature of persuasion is also illustrated by *nudge theory*, developed by Richard Thaler and Cass Sunstein (2008). They maintain that subtle changes in the way choices are presented to people can influence, or "nudge," them to behave in certain ways. For example, when men use a public restroom, they aren't always neat and tidy. They often miss the mark, to put it mildly, which increases janitorial costs significantly. To address this, folks at Amsterdam's Schiphol international airport gave men a target of their own. Specifically, urinals were installed that included a stenciled image of a housefly near the drain. The result? Having a target made all the difference. The men's aim improved considerably (Thaler & Sunstein, 2008).

As another example, school cafeterias tried offering apples at lunch. Most of them wound up in the trash can. However, when kids were given sliced apples, as opposed to whole apples, they were 73 percent more likely to eat them (Schwartz, 2016). Similarly, when vending machines listed the calories in snack foods, people were more likely to make healthier choices.

Although some critics have accused nudge theory of being paternalistic (Pasquale, 2015), others (Sunstein, 2014) argue that people are free to resist nudges if they wish. Kids can still throw apple slices in the trash. They are simply being provided with options that encourage healthy behaviors (www.nudges.org). That said, some nudges may be perceived as more like shoves. To encourage organ donors, for example, some countries have adopted a "presumed consent" policy, meaning that a person must take the initiative to opt out if she or he does not want to be an organ donor.

NEW PERSUASION: DIGITAL AND ONLINE INFLUENCE

Some people seem to spend their every waking moment texting, tweeting, blogging, or posting their views on all matter of subjects large and small. That said, social media isn't just an entertaining diversion, it is an important tool for influence. Whenever someone likes, follows, posts, shares, tweets or retweets, forwards, or comments on a message, online influence is taking place. Let's consider a few forms of digital influence.

FIGURE 1.2
Persuasion is
everywhere—even in
the womb.
Source: Baby Blues ©
2001, Baby Blues
Partnership. King Features
Syndicate. Reprinted with
special permission.

eWOM: Digital Buzz

Earlier, we mentioned the importance of viral persuasion and word-of-mouth
(WOM). Like WOM, electronic word of mouth (eWOM) is all the rage. People
actively comment on brands, companies, political issues, and public figures via all
manner of social media. By way of illustration, Twitter alone accounts for 6,000
tweets per second or 500 million tweets per day (www.internetlivestats.com). Eighty
percent of Twitter users have mentioned brands in their tweets and 54 percent of users
report that they have acted based on tweets (Midha, 2014).

Like WOM, eWOM is most effective when it is perceived as genuine rather than
manufactured and peer driven rather than commercially sponsored. eWOM enjoys
several advantages over traditional advertising and marketing techniques (Erkan &
Evans, 2016). It operates largely through interpersonal channels (cellphone, email,
texting), lending it an air of authenticity. It is inexpensive compared to traditional
media. And it is self-perpetuating. Moreover, eWOM is far more effective than
traditional media at reaching younger audiences.

Sponsored Content: The Native Advertisers Are Getting Restless

The rise of social media has spawned a surge in advertising masquerading as genuine
peer-to-peer influence. For example, *sponsored content* includes promoted tweets
and Instagram posts, which are essentially paid advertisements. *Native advertising*
involves ads posing as news stories. Native ads function as "clickbait," luring in
readers with snappy headlines or provocative photos. Both approaches are effective
because many users have difficulty distinguishing such content from genuine material
(Wojdynski, 2016).

Opinion Mining and Sentiment Tracking: I Feel You

The Web is an opinion-rich environment. People constantly share their attitudes,
opinions, and values via social media. And marketers are listening. Many companies,
for example, now specialize in *opinion mining* and *sentiment tracking* by monitoring
social media to gauge the public's mood in nearly real time (Ravi & Ravi, 2015).
Sophisticated algorithms can track how a person, brand, or issue is trending based,
not only on the number of tweets generated, but also on how favorable, neutral, or
negative those tweets are (Kennedy & Moss, 2015; Lee, Yang, Chen, Wang, & Sun,
2016). As an example, after analyzing over 10,000 online mentions from auto-

enthusiast websites, the Ford Motor Company adopted a three-blink turn signal on all of its vehicles (Rosenbush & Totty, 2013).

As sophisticated as such methods seem, a problem with opinion mining is that the data is often "squishy"—that is, the people commenting aren't always articulate or coherent. Furthermore, the tone of a message—that is, whether it is ironic, satirical, or hyperbolic—can be hard for artificial intelligence to decipher. Nevertheless, programmers are getting better at analyzing and interpreting words related to feelings, emotions, and opinions.

Gamification: You've Got Game

Parents have known for decades that one way to get infants to eat their vegetables is by turning mealtime into a game. "Here comes the airplane," the parent says with each spoonful of strained peas. A modernized version of this approach, known as *gamification*, is being used to stimulate consumer interest and involvement (McGonigal, 2011). Gamification applies video-game methods to other contexts to increase consumer engagement. People like to play games. They enjoy the competition. Why else would they spend hours on end playing Angry Birds or Candy Crush? Games are entertaining, challenging, and rewarding. Transforming a mundane task into a game can make it more fun and exciting.

Games also can be used to influence. Take exercise, for example. Thanks to a shoe sensor that allows runners to post information about their running distance, time, and calories burned, Nike+ provides customers with a fun way to socialize, compete, and "play" with each other using downloadable apps (Are you game? 2011). What's more, through points, badges, leaderboards, and other incentives, gamification keeps people coming back for more. This approach has been used to enhance education, improve workplace productivity, increase voter turnout, and promote awareness and participation in social causes.

Gamification is not without its critics, however. Ian Bogost (2011), a professor and expert in video games as cultural artifacts, cautioned that "'exploitationware' is a more accurate name for gamification's true purpose" (para. 12). Critics charge that earning badges and points trivializes activities such as learning, working, exercising, or participating in social causes.

Crowdsourcing and Crowdfunding: Lending a Helping Hand

Moving a heavy object, like a piano, isn't easy. To accomplish such a task, you might invite some friends to pitch in. Similarly, *crowdsourcing* puts out an open call for anyone online to participate in completing a task or solving a problem. Wikipedia was one of the earliest crowdsourcing platforms (Lee & Seo, 2016). The online encyclopedia is collaborative. Content can be contributed and edited by anyone. Crowdsourcing is premised on the assumption that wisdom is not the exclusive province of experts, but is distributed throughout the commons (Kitter, 2010). As an example, Doritos invited consumers to participate in a "Crash the Super Bowl" contest by generating their own ideas for a 30-second commercial (for examples, got to www.youtube.com/watch?v=8vVIUBU1gZs). As another example, Starbucks's "White Cup Contest" contest solicited customers' suggestions for a graphic design for a limited edition coffee cup. Contestants posted their creations via #WhiteCupContest.

FIGURE 1.3
Persuasive messages must struggle to cut through the background of media clutter.

Source: Reprinted with permission: www.andysinger.com

While crowdsourcing has assisted in solving problems in astronomy, legislation, language translation, and urban planning, among many areas, it is not without its critics. Detractors complain that crowdsourcing is exploitative; it relies on the unpaid labor and efforts of others. Another complaint is that the wisdom of the commons isn't always so wise. For example, when NASA asked people to submit names for a new section of the International Space Station, the crowd chose "Colbert" (after the late-night comedian) over names like "Serenity," "Earthrise," and "Tranquility." NASA went with the name "Tranquility" anyway.

A related strategy, *crowdfunding*, involves raising money through online donations. Websites such as Kickstarter, GoFundMe, and Indiegogo allow people to ask for donations or start-up funds for a cause or business venture. On the plus side, crowdfunding gives "the little guy" or a good cause the chance to be noticed. On the downside, some of the requests are scams (Fredman, 2015) and most start-ups fail. The SEC recently adopted rules regulating crowdfunding practices online.

Persuasive Technology: My Heart Says Yes, but My Watch Says No

Persuasive technology focuses on devices "aimed at changing users' attitudes or behaviors through persuasion and social influence, but not through coercion or deception" (Persuasive Technology, 2016, para. 1). Smart devices and wearable technology "are not just persuasive but specifically aimed at forging new habits" (*MIT Technology Review*, p. 64). Smartwatches, for example, exhort wearers to take action via taps, vibrations, or other haptic cues (Gilmore, 2016). Got a big date coming up? An app developed by MIT can tell you if you sound boring, nervous, happy, or sad based on your speech pattern (Lee, 2017). As an alternative, you could always check to see if your date is asleep.

Fitness trackers not only track your daily step count, they also encourage you to exercise. For example, Fitbit's display shows a flower that grows or shrinks based on your activity level. Taking that concept one step further, Nissan Leaf owners can view an LCD display of a pine tree that grows as they drive more efficiently.

As part of the Internet of Things, smart pill bottles can remind people when to take their medicine (Orji & Moffat, 2016). Skip a dose and a light will glow or a chime will sound, followed by a text or phone-call reminder. For some patients, taking their medicine at the right time each day is a matter of life and death. As many as 125,000 deaths per year and $105 billion in medical costs are attributable to patients not taking medicine properly (Ruggerio & Wick, 2016).

Persuasion will continue to play a major role in traditional contexts, such as advertising and marketing. It is worth noting, though, that persuasion also plays a key role in a variety of not-so-obvious contexts. We examine two such contexts next: persuasion in the sciences, and persuasion in the arts.

PERSUASION IN THE SCIENCES

You may not think of them this way, but scientists are persuaders (Glassner, 2011). The ongoing debate about climate change illustrates the persuasive challenge facing climatologists. Despite widespread agreement among evolutionary biologists that evolution is a fact rather than a theory, there is a continuing social controversy over the teaching of creationism alongside evolution in public school curriculums. Even in fields such as chemistry, mathematics, or physics—the so-called hard sciences—persuasion plays a major role.[5] Scientists often have to convince others that their research possesses scientific merit and social value. They also have to argue for the superiority of their theories over rival theories. In this respect, Thomas Kuhn (1970) argues that all scientists employ "techniques of persuasion in their efforts to establish the superiority of their own paradigms over those of their rivals" (p. 151). Similarly, Mitroff (1974) comments that "the notion of the purely objective, uncommitted scientist [is] naïve. . . . The best scientist . . . not only has points of view but also defends them with gusto" (p. 120). Scientists must do more than conduct experiments and report their results. They also must persuade other scientists, funding agencies, and the public at large of the merits of their work.

PERSUASION IN THE ARTS

Another not-so-obvious context for persuasion is the arts. Not all art is created "for art's sake." Art serves more than an aesthetic or decorative function. Artists have strong opinions and they lend expression to their opinions in and through their work. Consider film as an art form, for example. Movies such as *12 Years a Slave, Life Is Beautiful*, and *Schindler's List* demonstrate the power of the camera to increase awareness, change attitudes, alter beliefs, and shape opinions. Other art forms have the capability to persuade as well. Playwrights, painters, muralists, sculptors, photographers, and dancers give voice to their political and social views through their art.

Think about painting for a moment. Many of the famous works hanging in museums were created out of a sense of social conscience. Using images rather than words, artists comment on social conditions, criticize society, and attempt to transform the social order. We examine this issue in more detail in Chapter 14, but for now let's consider one particular work of art, Pablo Picasso's *Guernica*. Through this painting, Picasso offered a moral indictment of war and man's inhumanity to man. The painting features people and animals, the victims of the indiscriminate bombing of a Basque town during the Spanish Civil War, in various states of agony, torment, and grief. As Von Blum (1976) notes, "the purpose of the painting is frankly propagandistic. The artist's intent was to point out the inhuman character of Franco's fascist rebellion" (p. 92). Picasso wasn't trying to paint a "pretty" picture. He was making a moral statement. The painting has been dubbed by one art historian "the highest achievement in modernist political painting" (Clark, 1997, p. 39). Not only Picasso, but also many other artists express persuasive points of view in and through their art.

OTHER NOT-SO-OBVIOUS CONTEXTS FOR PERSUASION

Persuasion operates in a variety of other contexts, some of which are not so obvious. We highlight a few here as illustrations. Social scientists have studied bumper stickers as a form of political expression and as an unobtrusive means of measuring attitudes (Endersby & Towle, 1996; Sechrest & Belew, 1983). Scholars have examined the effects of intercessory prayer (offered for the benefit of another person) on recovery from illness (Frank & Frank, 1991; Hodge, 2007). Studies have examined the military's use of social influence (Cialdini, 2011; King, 2010). Other researchers have focused on 12-step programs, such as Alcoholics Anonymous, and other support groups as forms of self-help and group influence (Kassel & Wagner, 1993). Some studies have investigated terrorism as a form of persuasion by examining how jihadists are radicalized and recruited and how effective the use of violence is on the groups who are targeted (Bhui & Ibrahim, 2013; Iyer, Hornsey, Vanman, Esposo, & Ale, 2015; Kydd & Walter, 2006). As Tuman (2010) observed, "the real goal of the communicated message in terrorism may be persuasion: to persuade audience members that chaos and fear will be their lot in life, to persuade them to pay attention to an issue they have ignored" (p. 37). One scholar has written about compliance-gaining tactics found in dramatic plays, such as Shakespeare's *Hamlet* and Ibsen's *A Doll's House* (Kipnis, 2001). One of the authors investigated various styles and strategies of panhandling to see which ones proved most effective (Robinson, Seiter, & Acharya, 1992). Research on the study of robotic persuasion is just beginning to emerge. One study found, for example, that having a robot whisper instructions to people increased their motivation to perform a boring task (Nakagawa, Shiomi, Shinozawa, Matsumura, Ishiguro, & Hagita, 2013). Another study focused on the effect of robot-to-human touch as a method of compliance gaining (Shiomi, Nakagawa, Shinozawa, Matsumura, Ishiguro, & Hagita, 2017).

WEIRD PERSUASION

Sometimes persuasion is downright weird. A case in point involved Kensington, Canada, where the police department threatened that any motorist arrested for drunk driving would be subjected to Nickelback music while riding in the police cruiser to the station (Zenteno, 2016). When the story went viral, Colin Jost, the news co-host of *Saturday Night Live*, joked, "Just make sure the crash kills you." Ultimately, the policy was rescinded because the seriousness of the message was obscured by the frivolousness of the strategy.

Yet another example of weird persuasion occurred in Mansfield, Nottinghamshire, UK. The citizens wanted to stop rowdy teens from loitering at an underpass at night. Their solution was to install street lights with a bright pink hue. Why pink, you ask? Pink light highlights acne. Teens with blemishes didn't want to be seen with bright, glowing acne. The plan worked: The teens moved on (Spotty teens, 2009).

Scholars sometimes investigate quirky aspects of persuasion, too. Did you know that participants in a study who consumed caffeine were more easily persuaded than participants who had no caffeine (Martin, Hamilton, McKimmie, Terry, & Martin, 2007)? Now you do. As long as the participants were motivated to pay attention to the message, caffeine consumption increased agreement. Here is another strange finding: Washing one's hands not only produces cleaner hands, it also reduces a person's sense of guilt (Kaspa, 2013). The explanation for this is related to a phenomenon called *embodied cognition*, wherein physical behaviors often affect higher mental states.

Other researchers found that mixed-handed people were more persuadable and more gullible than purely left- or right-handed people (Christman, Henning, Geers, Propper, & Niebauer, 2008). And Briñol and Petty (2003) discovered that asking people to nod their heads up and down (as if in agreement) made them more agreeable than shaking their heads back and forth (as if in disagreement). What is the point of such research, you ask? Such studies illustrate both the complexities and subtle nuances of persuasion.

Persuasion, then, can be found in obvious and not-so-obvious places. Before concluding this section, we examine one additional context in which persuasion occurs: the interpersonal arena.

PERSUASION IN INTERPERSONAL SETTINGS

The extent of influence exerted in the interpersonal arena should not be underestimated. Although we may think of Madison Avenue as all-powerful, face-to-face influence is far more effective. Yet people tend to underestimate the effectiveness of in-person influence compared to other communication contexts. One study, for example, found that people making requests underestimated how successful face-to-face requests would be, compared to email requests (Roghanizad & Bohns, 2017). Another study found that people tend to underestimate their influence on others when it comes to questionable requests. Participants were asked to estimate how successful they would be at convincing a stranger to commit a minor act of vandalism (writing the word "pickle" on a page in a library book). Overall, 87 percent of the participants underestimated how persuasive they would be. On average, they were twice as effective as they thought (Bohns, Roghanizad, & Xu, 2014).

Despite all the money spent on traditional advertising and the increasing amounts being spent on new media, most influence attempts still take place in face-to-face settings. Some 90 percent of word-of-mouth recommendations, for example, take place offline (Moore, 2011). On a daily basis we are bombarded with persuasive requests in the interpersonal arena. Your brother wants you to hurry up and get out of the bathroom. A homeless person asks if you can spare some change. Your parents try to talk you out of getting a tongue stud. Or worse yet, your significant other uses the "F" word to redefine your relationship: That's right; she or he just wants to be "friends." Aaahhh! Naturally, we persuade back as well, targeting others with our own entreaties, pleadings, and requests for favors.

Why is interpersonal influence so much more effective? Because it seems more genuine and less conspicuous. Consider the following scenario:

> *The bait:* Your friend calls up and says, "Hey, what are you doing Friday night?"

> *The nibble:* Anticipating an invitation to go somewhere, you reply, "Nothing much, why?"

> *You're hooked and reeled in:* "Well, I wonder if you could help me move into my new apartment then?"

At least when you watch a television commercial you *know* the sponsor is after something from the outset. In interpersonal encounters, others' motives may be less transparent. Most communication scholars agree that if you have a choice of mediums for persuasion, you should choose the interpersonal arena. Our advice: Next time you want to turn in a paper late, talk to your professor in person.

From our discussion thus far, it should be apparent that persuasion functions as a pervasive force in virtually every facet of human communication. Kenneth Burke (1966), among others, has written that humans are, by their very nature, symbol-using beings. One vital aspect of human symbolicity involves the tendency to persuade others. We are symbol users, and one of the principal functions of symbol usage is persuasion.

The recognition that social influence is an essential, pervasive feature of human symbolic action provides the strongest possible justification for the study of persuasion. Persuasion is one of the major underlying impulses for human communication. By way of analogy, one can't understand how an automobile works without taking a look under the hood. Similarly, one can't understand how human communication functions without examining one of its primary motives—persuasion.

FIVE BENEFITS OF STUDYING PERSUASION

Given that persuasion is an inevitable fact of life, we offer five primary benefits of learning about persuasion. We refer to these as the instrumental function, the knowledge and awareness function, the defensive function, the debunking function, and the well-being function. We examine each of these in turn.

The Instrumental Function: Be All That You Can Be

One good reason for learning about persuasion is so that you can become a more effective persuader yourself. We refer to this as the *instrumental function* of persuasion, because persuasion serves as an instrument, or a means to an end. We view the ability to persuade others as an important aspect of communication competence. *Communication competence* involves acting in ways that are perceived as effective and appropriate (Spitzberg & Cupach, 1984). Competent communicators possess the skills needed to achieve their objectives in fitting ways for the particular situation.

A competent persuader needs to know how to analyze an audience in order to adapt the message to the audience's frame of reference. She or he needs to be able to identify which strategies are appropriate and which will enjoy the greatest likelihood of success. A competent persuader also must know how to organize and arrange a persuasive message for maximum benefit. These are only some of the abilities required for successful persuasion.

But achieving the desired outcome is only one facet of communication competence. How one goes about persuading also matters. A competent persuader needs to be viewed as persuading in acceptable, appropriate ways. This means a persuader must be aware of social and cultural norms governing the persuasive situation. For example, a parent who publicly berates his or her child during a soccer match may be seen by other parents as engaging in boorish behavior.

We are confident that by learning more about persuasion you will become a more effective and appropriate persuader. Of course, not every influence attempt will succeed. By applying the principles and processes presented in this text, and by adhering to the ethical guidelines we offer, you should be able to improve your competence as a persuader.

The Knowledge and Awareness Function: Inquiring Minds Want to Know

Another good reason for learning about persuasion is because it will enhance your knowledge and awareness of a variety of persuasive processes. Knowledge is power, as the saying goes. There is value in learning more about how persuasion operates. You may not plan on going into advertising for a living, but simply knowing how branding operates is worthwhile in and of itself. You may not plan on joining a cult (who does?), but learning more about what makes persons susceptible to cult conversion is worthwhile nonetheless. Simply from the standpoint of an observer, learning about these topics can be fascinating.

An additional benefit of learning about how persuasion functions concerns overcoming *habitual persuasion*. Many people rely on habitual forms of persuasion, regardless of whether they are effective. They get comfortable with a few strategies and tactics that they use over and over again. A good deal of our communication behavior is "mindless," as opposed to mindful, meaning we don't pay much attention to how we communicate (Langer, 1978, 1989a, 1989b). Sometimes persuasion operates this way. Just as runners, swimmers, and other athletes need to learn to adjust their breathing in response to different situations, persuaders—to maximize their effectiveness—need to learn to adapt their methods to different audiences and situations. Persuasion isn't a "one-size-fits-all" form of communication.

"That's it, Henry—you've dialed your last mattress!"

FIGURE 1.4
A little persuasive acumen just might save you from yourself.
Source: © Lee Lorenz/The New Yorker Collection/www.cartoonbank.com

The Defensive Function: Duck and Cover

A third reason for learning about how persuasion operates is vital in our view: The study of persuasion serves a *defensive function*. By studying how and why influence attempts succeed or fail, you can become a more discerning consumer of persuasive messages, unlike the hapless fellow depicted in Figure 1.4. If you know how persuasion works, you are less likely to be taken in. It is worth noting that people tend to *underestimate* the influence of advertising on themselves and *overestimate* its effects on others, a phenomenon known as the *third-person effect* (Davidson, 1983; Jensen & Collins, 2008). Thus, you may be more defenseless than you realize.

Throughout this text, we expose a number of persuasive tactics used in retail sales, advertising, and marketing campaigns. For example, we have found in our classes that after students are given a behind-the-scenes look at how car salespeople are taught to sell, several students usually acknowledge, "Oh yeah, they did that to me." Admittedly, a huckster could also take advantage of the advice we offer in this book. We think it is far more likely, however, that the typical student reader will use our advice and suggestions as weapons *against* unethical influence attempts. Box 1.1, for example, offers advice on how to recognize various propaganda ploys. In later chapters of this book, we warn you about common ploys used by all manner of persuaders, from cult leaders to panhandlers to funeral home directors.

The Debunking Function: Puh-Shaw

A fourth reason for studying persuasion is that it serves a *debunking function*. The study of human influence can aid in dispelling various "common-sense" assumptions and "homespun" notions about persuasion. Traditional wisdom isn't always right, and it's worth knowing when it's wrong. Some individuals cling tenaciously to folk wisdom about persuasive practices that are known by researchers to be patently false. For example, many people believe that subliminal messages are highly effective and operate in a manner similar to that of post-hypnotic suggestion. This belief is pure poppycock, as we point out in Chapter 15.

Of considerable importance, then, are empirical findings that are *counterintuitive* in nature—that is, they go against the grain of common sense. By learning about research findings on persuasion, the reader can learn to ferret out the true from the false, the fact from the fiction.

Well-Being and Self-Worth: I Feel Good

A fifth benefit of learning about persuasion is that the ability to persuade others improves one's subjective sense of well-being. There is a sense of satisfaction that comes from persuading others. Researchers have found that influencing others satisfies five basic needs, which are accuracy, belonging, self-worth, control, and meaning (Bourgeois, Sommer, & Bruno, 2009; Sommer & Bourgeois, 2010). The first need, accuracy, refers to the desire to be right about one's beliefs and attitudes. One of the author's spouses likes to joke, "I married Mr. Right. Mr. *always* Right." Winning someone over is one way of validating one's own views.

The need for belonging reflects the desire for social inclusion. People value social connections. Persuading others is one means of establishing and maintaining relationships. People also strive to maintain a positive self-concept or sense of self-

BOX 1.1 | Persuasion Versus Propaganda and Indoctrination

What are propaganda and indoctrination and how do they differ from persuasion? To a large extent, it is a matter of perspective. People tend to label their own messages as persuasion and the other guy's as propaganda. The same applies to indoctrination: We tend to think that our government educates its citizens, but foreign governments, especially those we dislike, indoctrinate their citizens. Understood in this way, propaganda and indoctrination are largely pejorative terms used to describe persuasive messages or positions with which people disagree. Gun control advocates claim the NRA uses propaganda to thwart legislation that would place restrictions on gun sales. Opponents of school prayer think that requiring students to recite a prayer in class constitutes a form of religious indoctrination. When accused of propagandizing, the common defense is to state that one was only engaged in an education or information campaign. Thus, whether a given attempt at influence, such as the D.A.R.E. campaign, is persuasion, propaganda, or indoctrination is largely in the eye of the beholder.

Definitions of propaganda are many and varied, but we happen to think Pratkanis and Aronson's (1991) definition does a good job of capturing the essence of the term:

> Propaganda was originally defined as the dissemination of biased ideas and opinions, often through the use of lies and deception. . . . The word propaganda has since evolved to mean mass "suggestion" or influence through the manipulation of symbols and the psychology of the individual. Propaganda is the communication of a point of view with the ultimate goal of having the recipient come to "voluntarily" accept the position as if it were his or her own.
>
> (p. 9)

Different scholars have offered different views on the nature and characteristics of propaganda (see Ellul, 1973; Jowett & O'Donnell, 1986; Smith, 1989). However, there are some essential characteristics on which most scholars agree. These are as follows:

- Propaganda has a strong ideological bent. Most scholars agree that propaganda does not serve a purely informational function. Propaganda typically embodies a strong bias, such as that of a "left-wing" or "right-wing" agenda. The campaign of People for the Ethical Treatment of Animals (PETA) to promote animal rights would fall into this category. Propagandists aren't trying to be neutral or objective. They are working a specific agenda.
- Propaganda is institutional in nature. Most scholars agree that propaganda is practiced by organized groups, whether they happen to be government agencies, political lobbies, private corporations, religious groups, or social movements. For instance, the Anti-Defamation League is an organization founded to prevent libeling and slandering of Jewish people. Although individuals might use propaganda too (a parent might tell a child, "Santa only brings presents for good girls and boys"), the term usually is associated with institutional efforts to persuade.
- Propaganda involves mass persuasion. Most scholars agree that propaganda targets a mass audience and relies on mass media to persuade. Propaganda is aimed at large numbers of people and, as such, relies on mass communication (TV, radio, posters, billboards, email, mass mailings, etc.) to reach its audience. Thus, gossip that was shared by one office worker with another at the water cooler wouldn't constitute propaganda, but a corporate rumor that was circulated via email would.
- Propaganda tends to rely on ethically suspect methods of influence. Propagandists tend to put results first and ethics second. This characteristic is probably the one that laypersons most closely associate with propaganda and the one that gives it its negative connotation.

What are some of the questionable tactics used by propagandists? The Institute for Propaganda Analysis, which was founded in 1937, identified seven basic propaganda techniques, which still exist today (Miller, 1937). These include the plain folks appeal ("I'm one of you"), testimonials ("I saw the aliens, sure as I'm standing here"), the bandwagon effect (everybody's doing it), card-stacking (presenting only one side of the story), transfer (positive or negative associations, such as guilt by association), glittering generalities (idealistic or loaded language, such as "freedom," "empowering," "family values"), and name calling ("racist," "tree hugger," "femi-Nazi").

worth. The ability to persuade others enhances a person's self-esteem. The need for control, or perceived control, stems from a desire to shape our environment and exert influence over those with whom we interact. Some people like to be in charge, take over, and have things their way. Others are content to let someone else take the helm. Yet everyone seeks some degree of self-efficacy or a sense that she or he is in control of their life. Lastly, people want to believe there is meaning and purpose in their lives. One way of demonstrating one's value or importance is by influencing others.

We hope you'll agree, based on the foregoing discussion, that there are quite a few good reasons for studying persuasion. We hope we've persuaded you that the study of persuasion can be a prosocial endeavor. That brings us back to an earlier point, however: Not all persuaders are scrupulous. At this juncture, then, it seems appropriate that we address two common criticisms related to the study of persuasion.

TWO CRITICISMS OF PERSUASION

Does Learning About Persuasion Foster Manipulation?

We've already touched on one of the common criticisms of studying persuasion: the notion that it fosters a manipulative approach to communication. We address ethical concerns surrounding the study and practice of persuasion more specifically in Chapter 16. For the time being, however, a few general arguments can be offered in response to this concern. First, our principal focus in this text is on the *means* of persuasion (e.g., how persuasion functions). We view the means of persuasion not so much as moral or immoral, but rather as amoral, or ethically neutral. In this respect, persuasion can be likened to a tool, such as a hammer. Like any other tool, persuasion can be put to good or bad use. If this sounds like a cop-out, read what Aristotle had to say on this same point in his *Rhetoric*:

> If it is urged that an abuse of the rhetorical faculty can work great mischief, the same charge can be brought against all good things (save virtue itself), and especially against the most useful things such as strength, health, wealth, and military skill. Rightly employed, they work the greatest blessings; and wrongly employed, they work the greatest harm.
>
> (1355b)

Related to this idea is the fact that tools can be used in good or bad ways, depending on their user. We believe that first and foremost, a *persuader's motives* determine whether a given influence attempt is good or bad, right or wrong, ethical or unethical. We maintain that the moral quality of a persuasive act is derived primarily from the ends a persuader seeks, and only secondarily from the means the persuader employs. It isn't so much *what* strategies and tactics a persuader uses as *why* he or she uses them.

To illustrate, suppose you asked us whether the use of "fear appeals" is ethically justified. We would have to say, it depends. If a fear appeal were being used to warn sexually active teens of the risks of HIV infection from unprotected sex, we would tend to say the appeal was justified. If a fear appeal were being used by a terrorist who threatened to kill a hostage every hour until his demands were met, we would say the appeal was unjustified. In each case, the motives of the persuader would "color" the use of the fear appeal. Consistent with our tool analogy, fear appeals, like other persuasive strategies, can be used for good or bad ends.

A second response to this criticism was highlighted earlier. The study of persuasion performs a *defensive function* insofar as it educates people to become more discriminating consumers of persuasive messages. For instance, we believe our "Tips on Buying a New or Used Car" (see Box 1.2) are useful to any potential car buyer who wants to avoid being manipulated at a car lot. By increasing your awareness of the ploys of would-be persuaders, this text performs a watchdog function. You can use the information contained herein to arm yourself against the tactics of unscrupulous persuaders.

A third response that bears mentioning is that in denouncing the study of persuasion, antimanipulation types are also attempting to persuade. The message that persuasion is manipulative or exploitative is itself a persuasive appeal that advocates a position regarding the "proper" study of communication. When one group claims to know best how human communication should be studied, they are, in fact, standing on the persuasion soapbox themselves.

Are Persuasion Findings Too Inconsistent or Confusing?

An additional complaint is that the study of persuasion has led to findings that are overly qualified, or contradictory in nature. Empirical investigations of persuasion, it is argued, have not yielded clear and consistent generalizations. There is no "$E = mc^2$," no "second law of thermodynamics," no universal when it comes to persuasion.

First, the complaint that persuasion isn't worth studying because the findings are often inconclusive or contradictory makes little sense. Quite the opposite: We believe that persuasion warrants study precisely because it *is* so elusive. Underlying this criticism is the expectation that reality is, or should be, simple and uncomplicated. Like it or not, understanding reality is hard work. As we've already noted, human beings are complex creatures who rarely respond to messages for one and only one reason. Actually, we find this to be a redeeming feature of humanity. We rejoice in the fact that we aren't an altogether gullible, predictable, or controllable species.

A second response to this criticism is simply that persuasion research *has* revealed a number of significant, relevant generalizations. You'll find many such generalizations throughout this book. Newer techniques of statistical analysis, such

BOX 1.2 | Tips on Buying a New or Used Car

Given the current state of the economy and the economic fix in which car dealers find themselves, buying a car nowadays is easier than before. Car dealers are eager to sell cars. Nevertheless, car salespersons, especially used car salespersons, have a bad reputation. We've met some honest, upstanding sellers. We've also met some shady operators. Because a car is a major purchase, one would be well advised to err on the side of caution when negotiating with a car salesperson. Caveat emptor, as the saying goes: Let the buyer beware.

1. Be wary. Remember, buying a car is a ritual in which the car dealer has the upper hand. This is the prototype for high-pressure sales. They are professionals. They sell cars every day. You are an amateur. Who do you think has more experience with persuasion in this setting?

2. Do your homework before you go visit a car dealer. Read up on the makes and models in which you're interested. Find out about performance criteria, standard features, and options before setting foot on a car lot. Consumer Reports compares used cars on reliability, safety, and other criteria based on data from actual owners. Research shows that doing your homework can save you money (Seiter & Seiter, 2005).

3. Keep a poker face. If the salesperson knows you are eager or excited about the car purchase, he or she will smell blood. Once the salesperson knows you are emotionally attached to a particular car, you'll wind up paying more.

4. Take a calculator with you. Car salespersons like to pretend that the prices of things are entirely up to the calculator ("Hey, let's see how the numbers shake out"). The implication is that the numbers aren't negotiable or flexible. Everything is negotiable. Do your own figuring to see if the numbers "shake out" the same way. If not, ask why.

5. Once you are on the car lot, dealers will try to keep you there. They may put you in a cubicle, holding you "hostage" during the negotiations. Their psychological strategy is to wear you down. After hours of haggling, you'll become mentally drained and more likely to give in. They may ask for the keys to your trade-in, presumably to look it over and determine its value. Once they have your keys, you can't leave.

6. The car salesperson will want to avoid talking about the total price of the car, opting instead to discuss the monthly payment you can afford. You, however, should focus on four things: (a) the total purchase price, (b) the finance period, (c) the interest rate, and (d) the monthly payment. Don't discuss the monthly payment unless you are clear on the finance period involved (a 3-year loan, 4-year loan, 5-year loan, etc.). If you admit you can afford $300 per month, the salesperson may simply switch to a longer finance period—say, 4 years, instead of 3, thereby adding thousands of dollars to the total purchase price.

7. During the negotiations, the salesperson may leave the room a number of times to talk with the "sales manager." This is all choreographed. The salesperson can't agree to anything without checking with this mysterious figure, so the person with whom you are negotiating really can't commit to anything. You, however, will be asked to commit to a lot of things. Don't.

8. The salesperson will act like he or she is your best friend, even though you just met. The salesperson will look for ways to identify with you or ingratiate himself or herself to you to establish camaraderie ("You like fly fishing? That makes two of us." "Whaddya-know, my granddaughter is named 'Fifi' too!"). During the negotiations, the salesperson will pretend he or she is on your side and is willing to go out on a limb for you ("Well, my sales manager may

Continued

kick my butt for even taking him this offer, but hey, I like you"). Remember, these two are working as a team, against you. Don't be confused for a moment about where the salesperson's loyalties reside.

9. The car salesperson will do all kinds of things to get you to make a commitment to buy ("What would it take to get you to buy this car? Just tell me, whudda-I-godda-do to get you in this car?"). Often, the salesperson will ask you to write down any amount you're offering on a slip of paper or an offer sheet, even though it isn't legally binding (it does increase your psychological commitment, however). The car dealer wants you to sit in the car, take it for a test spin, smell the upholstery, because then you will become psychologically committed to owning the car.

10. If you get close to a deal, or alternatively, if a deal seems to be coming apart, don't be surprised if another salesperson comes in to take over the negotiations. Often a "closer" is sent in (sort of like a relief pitcher in baseball) to complete the sale.

11. Beware of "loss leaders" (advertised specials at absurdly low prices). These are come-ons designed to get you onto the lot. Once there, however, you'll be subjected to the "old switcheroo." You'll find there is/was only one car at that price. You will probably be told, "Sorry, it's already sold . . . but I can make you a honey of a deal on . . ."

12. The sale isn't over simply because you've agreed on a price. You still have to deal with the dreaded "finance person." You'll be given the impression that you're simply seeing the finance person to sign documents and process paperwork. Don't let down your guard. The finance person will try to add on thousands of dollars in the form of extended warranties, antitheft systems, and protective coatings.

13. The interest rate is just as important as the price of the car. Shop around for a car loan from a bank or credit union before you shop for a car. The rates may be lower and you can find out exactly how much you qualify for in advance.

14. Shop around for prices on options such as stereos before you go to a car dealer. People often bargain well on the purchase price, then give up everything they've gained by failing to bargain on the price of extras. The price of everything is negotiable.

15. Don't let the salesperson know in advance that you have a trade-in. Any bargaining gains you make on the purchase price of the new car will just be deducted from the trade-in value of your used car. Sell the used car on your own, if at all possible. If that's not possible, you can always mention your trade-in after you've negotiated the price of the new car.

16. Don't get a lemon. Buying a used car can be particularly risky. One of the authors bought a used sports car on eBay. How did he know from a mere picture and description whether the car was in good shape? He ran a CARFAX history on the car, easily available online (see www.carfax.com), which revealed that the car had had only one previous owner; had never been stolen, totaled, or repossessed; had correct odometer readings; and had passed a smog check each year when the vehicle registration was renewed. Since the car was coming from another state, the author went one step further and hired an independent mechanic to perform a "prepurchase inspection" on the car, at a cost of about $150. We strongly suggest you do the same for any used car. After all, how much can the average consumer tell about a car from looking under the hood and kicking the tires?

as *meta-analysis*,[6] have made it possible to reconcile some of the previous inconsistencies in the literature. In this text, we identify a number of noteworthy, albeit qualified, generalizations that are based on the most recent meta-analyses available.

You'll notice in this book that we've drawn on the people in the trenches themselves to learn how persuasion works in particular contexts and settings. We've talked to used car salespersons, funeral home operators, retail clothing clerks, advertising firms, former cult members, door-to-door salespersons, and telemarketers to find out—from the horse's mouth, so to speak—how persuasion operates.

ETHICAL CONCERNS ABOUT THE USE OF PERSUASION

We would be remiss if we concluded this chapter without emphasizing the importance of ethics in the persuasion process. We wish to underscore the point that the use of

---

BOX 1.3 | Ethical or Unethical Persuasion? You Decide

Instructions: For each of the following scenarios, indicate how ethical or unethical you perceive the persuader or the persuasive strategy to be, based on a five-point scale (with 1 being "highly ethical" and 5 being "highly unethical").

1. A student pretends to cry in a professor's office in an attempt to coax the professor into giving her a makeup exam. Is this ethical persuasion?
2. A persuader advances an argument he doesn't believe in, but that he thinks will be convincing to his listeners. The argument isn't untrue or invalid; it just happens to be one with that the persuader himself does not agree. Is this ethical persuasion?
3. A car salesperson emphasizes that the model of car a customer is considering has "more horsepower and better mileage than the competition." The salesperson fails to mention that the car has worse reliability and a worse safety record than the competition. Is this ethical persuasion?
4. A skilled attorney successfully defends a client she knows to be guilty. Is this ethical persuasion?
5. A minister tells his congregation that a vote for a particular candidate is "a vote for the Devil incarnate" and that the scriptures demand that the faithful cast their ballots for another candidate. Is this ethical persuasion?
6. A persuader sincerely believes in the arguments she is presenting, but the facts and information she cites are incorrect and outdated. Is this ethical persuasion?
7. Parents use a fear appeal to convince their child to clean her room. "Santa doesn't bring presents to children with dirty rooms," they warn. Is this ethical persuasion?
8. A children's cereal states on the box, "High in the vitamins kids need" but doesn't mention that the cereal is high in sugar, too. Is this ethical persuasion?
9. A newlywed husband is upset that his wife wants to go to a dance club with some of her single friends for drinks. "If you go," he warns, "I'm going to a strip club with some of my friends." Is this ethical persuasion?
10. A political campaign runs a series of negative attack ads against an opponent, not because the campaign manager prefers to but because voter surveys show that negative ads will work, whereas ads that take the political "high road" won't. Is this ethical persuasion?

persuasion is fraught with ethical concerns. We raise a number of such concerns in Box 1.3 for you to ponder. Our position is that in learning how to become a more effective persuader, you should strive to be an ethical persuader as well. In the final chapter, we address a number of ethical questions related to various strategies and techniques of persuasion discussed throughout the text. We wait until the final chapter to fully examine ethical concerns for two reasons: First, until you've learned more about persuasion, you may not fully appreciate all of the ethical issues that are involved. Second, after you've studied the full scope of persuasion as we present it in this text, you'll be in a much better position to place these ethical questions in perspective.

SUMMARY

We hope that we've convinced you of the ubiquity of persuasion in human interaction. The capacity to persuade is one of the defining features of humankind. This fact provides the strongest possible reason for studying persuasion. Given that learning about persuasion serves an instrumental function, a knowledge and awareness function, a defensive function, a debunking function, and a well-being and self-worth function, we believe there is ample justification for studying this topic. Finally, rejoinders to two current criticisms of the study of persuasion were offered. Hopefully, a persuasive case has been made for learning about persuasion.

One other thing: Did we mention that learning about persuasion can also be fun?

NOTES

1. The scientific study of persuasion dates back to the 1940s and 1950s, when Carl Hovland founded the Yale Attitude Research Program as part of the war effort. The government wanted to know how to counter enemy propaganda that could affect the morale of troops and how susceptible POWs were to brainwashing.
2. Aristotle's work *Rhetoric* is one such text that has survived the test of time. Written in the fourth century BCE, Aristotle's work has had a lasting influence on our understanding of persuasion. Many of his insights and observations are considered valid even today.
3. Note that with the exception of Hitler, these charismatic leaders enjoyed a limited following. The rest of us weren't taken in by their claims, suggesting that people, in general, aren't that gullible after all.
4. A *New York Times* article (Story, 2007) sets daily ad exposure at up to 5,000 ads per day. Rosseli, Skelly, and Mackie (1995) state, "even by conservative estimates, the average person is exposed to 300–400 persuasive messages a day from the mass media alone" (p. 163). Jones (2004) pegs the number of advertising messages at 300 to 1,500 every day, but indicates that some estimates are as high as 3,000 per day—a number Jones labels fanciful (p. 12). Without saying who says so, Berger (2011) reports that "some estimate that we are exposed to 15,000 commercial messages each day" (p. 101).

    We are suspicious of such estimates, however, because they may simply represent "unknowable" statistics. At the very least, estimates of the number of persuasive messages to which the average person is exposed involve extrapolations, and the criteria upon which the extrapolations are based aren't always provided. What's more, the estimates often contradict one another. By way of illustration, Berger (2011) maintains that "advertisers spend around $800 per person in the United States on advertising" (p. 101), whereas Dupont (1999) claims, "In the U.S., close to $400 for every man, woman, and child are invested in advertising each year" (p. 8). Which, if either, estimate is correct?

5. We don't have sufficient space to devote to this topic here, but suffice it to say that the traditional notion of scientific realism is under siege from the antirealism camp (see Kourany, 1998). The antirealists argue that science is neither purely objective nor impartial but heavily value laden (see also Laudan, 1984; Longino, 1990).

6. *Meta-analysis* refers to a statistical technique that allows a researcher to combine the results of many separate investigations and examine them as if they were one big super study. A meta-analysis is capable of revealing trends across a number of studies and resolving apparent inconsistencies among studies.

REFERENCES

Are you game? (2011, September 30). *B&T Magazine, 61*(2751), 16–22.

Aristotle. (1932). *Rhetoric* (L. Cooper, Trans.). Englewood Cliffs, NJ: Prentice Hall.

Berger, A. A. (2011). *Ads, fads, and consumer culture* (4th ed.). Lanham, MD: Rowman & Littlefield.

Bhui, K., & Ibrahim, Y. (2013). Marketing the "radical": Symbolic communication and persuasive technologies in jihadist websites. *Transcultural Psychiatry, 50*(2), 216–234. doi:10.1177/1363461513479329

Bogost, I. (2011, August 8). Gamification is bullshit. Retrieved on February 16, 2012 from: www.bogost.com/blog/gamification_is_bullshit.shtml

Bohns, V. K., Roghanizad, M. M., & Xu, A. Z. (2014). Underestimating our influence over others' unethical behavior and decisions. *Personality and Social Psychology Bulletin, 40*, 348–362. doi:10.1177/014616721351182

Bourgeois, M. J., Sommer, K. L., & Bruno, S. (2009). What do we get out of influencing others? *Social Influence, 4*(2), 96–121. doi:10.1080/15534510802465360

Brinol, P., & Petty, R. E. (2003). Overt head movements and persuasion: A self-validation analysis. *Journal of Personality and Social Psychology, 84*(6), 1123–1139.

Burke, K. (1966). *Language as symbolic action.* Berkeley, CA: University of California Press.

Cascio, C. N., Scholz, C., & Falk, E. B. (2015). Social influence and the brain: Persuasion, susceptibility to influence and retransmission. *Current Opinion in Behavior Sciences, 3*, 51–57. doi:10.1016/j.coheba.2015.01.007

Christman, S. D., Henning, B. R., Geers, A. L., Propper, R. E., & Niebauer, C. (2008). Mixed-handed persons are more easily persuaded and are more gullible: Interhemispheric interaction and belief updating. *Laterality, 13*(5), 403–426.

Cialdini, R. B. (2011). Roots, shoots, and fruits of persuasion in military affairs. *Analyses of Social Issues and Public Policy, 11*(1), 27–30. doi:10.1111/j.1530–2415.2010.01227.x

Clark, T. (1997). *Art and propaganda in the twentieth century.* New York: Harry N. Abrams.

Davidson, W. P. (1983). The third-person effect in communication. *Public Opinion Quarterly, 47*, 1–15.

Dupont, I. (1999). *Images that sell: 500 ways to create great ads.* Sainte-Foy, Quebec, Canada: White Rock.

Ellul, J. (1973). *Propaganda: The formation of men's attitudes.* New York: Knopf.

Endersby, J. W., & Towle, M. J. (1996). Political and social expression through bumper stickers. *Social Science Journal, 33*(3), 307–319.

Erkan, I., & Evans, C. (2016). The influence of eWOM in social media on consumers' purchase intentions: An extended approach to information adoption. *Computers in Human Behavior*, *61*, 47–55. doi:10.1016/j.chb.2016.03.003

Frank, J. D., & Frank, J. B. (1991). *Persuasion and healing: A comparative study of psychotherapy* (3rd ed.). Baltimore, MD: Johns Hopkins University Press.

Fredman, K. (2015). Fund me or fraud me? Crowdfunding scams are on the rise. *Consumer Reports*. Retrieved on April 6, 2017 from: www.consumerreports.org/cro/money/crowdfunding-scam

Gilmore, J. N. (2016). From ticks to tocks to budges and nudges: The smartwatch and the haptics of informatics culture. *Television and News Media*, 1–14. doi:10.1177/1527476416658962

Gladwell, M. (2000). *The tipping point*. Boston, MA: Little, Brown, & Company.

Glassner, B. (2011, March 14). How to help scientists and the public see eye to eye. *USA Today*, p. 9–A.

Heath, C., & Heath, D. (2008). *Made to stick: Why some ideas survive and others die*. New York: Random House.

Hodge, D. R. (2007). A systematic review of the empirical literature on intercessory prayer. *Research on Social Work Practice*, *17*(2), 174–187.

Iyer, A., Hornsey, M. J., Vanman, E. J., Esposo, S., & Ale, S. (2015). Fight and flight: Evidence of aggressive capitulation in the face of fear messages from terrorists. *Political Psychology*, *36*(6), 631–648. doi:10.1111/pops.12182

Jensen, K., & Collins, S. (2008). The third-person effect in controversial advertising. *American Behavioral Scientist*, *52*, 225–242.

Jones, J. P. (2004). *Fables, fashions, and facts about advertising*. Thousand Oaks, CA: Sage.

Jowett, G. S., & O'Donnell, V. (1986). *Propaganda and persuasion*. Newbury Park, CA: Sage.

Kaspa, K. (2013). Washing one's hands after failure enhances optimism but hampers future performance. *Social Psychological and Personality Science*, *4*(1), 69–73. doi:10.1177/1948550612443267

Kassel, J. D., & Wagner, E. F. (1993). Processes of change in Alcoholics Anonymous: A review of possible mechanisms. *Psychotherapy*, *30*, 222–233.

Keller, E., & Barry, J. (2003). *The influentials*. New York: Free Press.

Kennedy, H., & Moss, G. (2015). Known or knowing publics? Social media data mining and the question of public agency. *Big Data and Society*, *2*, 1–11. doi:10.1177/2053951715611145

King, S. B. (2010). Military social influence in the global information environment: A civilian primer. *Analyses of Social Issues and Public Policy*. doi:10.1111/j.1530-2415.2010.01214.x

Kipnis, D. (2001). Influence tactics in plays. *Journal of Applied and Social Psychology*, *31*(3), 542–552.

Kitter, A. (2010). Crowdsourcing, collaboration, and creativity. *XRDS*, *17*(2), 22–26. doi:10.1145/18869086.1869096

Kourany, J. A. (1998). *Scientific knowledge: Basic issues in the philosophy of science*. Belmont, CA: Wadsworth.

Kuhn, T. S. (1970). *The structure of scientific revolutions* (2nd ed.). New York: Springer-Verlag.

Kydd, A. H., & Walter, B. F. (2006). The strategies of terrorism. *International Security*, *31*(1), 49–80.

Langer, E. J. (1978). Rethinking the role of thought in social interaction. In J. H. Harvey, W. J. Ickes, & R. F. Kidd (Eds.), *New directions in attribution research* (Vol. 2, pp. 35–58). New York: John Wiley.

Langer, E. J. (1989a). *Mindfulness*. Reading, MA: Addison-Wesley.

Langer, E. J. (1989b). Minding matters. In L. Berkowitz (Ed.), *Advances in experimental social psychology* (Vol. 22, pp. 137–173). New York: Addison-Wesley.

Laudan, L. (1984). *Science and values*. Berkeley, CA: University of California Press.

Lee, T. (2017, February 1). MIT has a smartwatch app that detects emotions. *Ubergizmo*. Retrieved on February 13, 2017 from: www.ubergizmo.com/2017/02/mit-smartwatch-app-detect-emotions/

Lee, J., & Seo, D. (2016). Crowdsourcing not all sourced by the crowd: An observation on the behavior of Wikipedia participants. *Technovation*, *55–56*, 14–21. doi:10.1016/j.technovation.2016.05.002

Lee, A. J. T., Yang, F., Chen, C., Wang, C., & Sun, C. (2016). Mining perceptual maps from consumer reviews *Decision Support Systems*, *82*, 12–25. doi:/10.1016/j.dss.2015.11.002

Longino, H. (1990). *Science as social knowledge: Values and objectivity in scientific inquiry*. Princeton, NJ: Princeton University Press.

Martin, P. E., Hamilton, V. E., McKimmie, B. M., Terry, D. J., & Martin, R. (2007). Effects of caffeine consumption on persuasion and attitude change: The role of secondary tasks in manipulating systematic message processing. *European Journal of Social Psychology*, *37*, 320–338.

McGonigal, J. (2011). *Reality is broken: Why games make us better and how they can change the world*. New York: Penguin Press.

Midha, A. (2014). Study: Exposure to brand tweets drive consumers to action—both on and off Twitter. Retrieved on February 6, 2017 from: https://blog.twitter.com/2014/study-exposure-to-brand-tweets-drives-consumers-to-take-action-both-on-and-off-twitter

Miller, C. P. (1937). How to detect propaganda. *Propaganda analysis*. New York: Institute for Propaganda Analysis.

MIT Technology Review (2016). Technology and persuasion, *118*(3), 64–65.

Mitroff, I. I. (1974, November 2). Studying the lunar rock scientist. *Saturday Review World*, pp. 64–65.

Moore, J. (2011, May 10). Bringing SEXY back to offline word of mouth. Presentation at the WOMMA School of WOM, Chicago. Retrieved on February 9, 2012, from: http://womma.org/schoolofwom/attachments/presentations/tue/genochurch.pdf

Nakagawa, K., Shiomi, M., Shinozawa, K., Matsumura, R., Ishiguro, H., & Hagita, N. (2013). Effects of a robot's whispering on people's motivation. *International Journal of Social Robotics*, *5*, 5–16. doi:10.1007/s12369–012–0141–3

Orji, R., & Moffatt, K. (2016). Persuasive technology for health and wellness: State-of-the-art and emerging trends. *Health Informatics Journal*, 1–26. doi:10.1177/1460458 21665097

Pasquale, F. (2015, December 4). Why "nudges" hardly help. *The Atlantic*. Retrieved on February 19, 2017 from: www.theatlantic.com/business/archive/2015/12/nudges-effectiveness/418749/

Persuasive Technology (2016). 11th conference on persuasive technology. Salzburg, Austria, April 2016.

Pratkanis, A. R., & Aronson, E. (1991). *Age of propaganda: The everyday use and abuse of persuasion*. New York: W. H. Freeman.

Ravi, K., & Ravi, V. (2015). A survey of opinion mining and sentiment analysis: Tasks, approaches, and applications. *Knowledge-Based Systems*, *89*, 14–46. doi:10.1016/j.knosys.2015.06.015

Robinson, J. D., Seiter, J. S., & Acharya, L. (1992, February). *I just put my head down and society does the rest: An examination of influence strategies among beggars*.

Paper presented at the annual meeting of the Western Communication Association, Boise, ID.

Roghanizad, M. M., & Bohns, V. K. (2017). Ask in person: You're less persuasive than you think over email. *Journal of Experimental Social Psychology*, *69*, 223–226. doi: 10.1016/j.jesp.2016.10.002

Rosenbush, S., & Totty, M. (2013, March 10). How big data is changing the whole equation for business. *Wall Street Journal*. Retrieved on February 6, 2017 from: http://search.proquest.com.lib-proxy.fullerton.edu/docview/1315454301/fulltext/B02C996E7F8745D3PQ/2?accountid=9840

Rosseli, F., Skelly, J. J., & Mackie, D. M. (1995). Processing rational and emotional messages: The cognitive and affective mediation of persuasion. *Journal of Experimental Social Psychology*, *31*, 163–190.

Ruggerio, G., & Wick, J. Y. (2016, March 28). Telling technology: Increasing adherence, telling triggers. *Pharmacy Times*. Retrieved on February 12, 2017 from: www.pharmacytimes.com/news/telling-technology-increasing-adherence-tagging-triggers

Schwartz, E. (2016, May 20). Why we eat sliced apples. *Econlife*. Retrieved on February 19, 2017 from: http://econlife.com/2016/05/behavioral-nudges-and-apple-consumption/

Sechrest, L., & Belew, J. (1983). Nonreactive measures of social attitudes. *Applied Social Psychology Annual*, *4*, 26–63.

Seiter, J. S., & Seiter, D. L. (2005). Consumer persuasion: The use of evidence when negotiating the price of a new automobile. *Journal of Applied Social Psychology*, *35*(4), 1197–1205.

Shiomi, M., Nakagawa, K., Shinozawa, K., Matsumura, R., Ishiguro, H., & Hagita, N. (2017). Does a robot's touch encourage human effort? *International Journal of Social Robotics*, *9*, 5–15. doi:10.1007/s12369–016–0339-x

Smith, T.J. (Ed.). (1989). *Propaganda: A pluralistic perspective*. New York: Praeger.

Sommer, K. L., & Bourgeois, M. J. (2010. Linking the perceived ability to influence others to subjective well-being: A need-based approach. *Social Influence*, *5*(3), 220–224. doi:10.1080/15534510903513860

Spitzberg, B. H., & Cupach, W. R. (1984). *Interpersonal communication competence*. Beverly Hills, CA: Sage.

Spotty teens (2009, March 25). Spotty teens deterred from underpasses by acne light. *The Telegraph*. Retrieved on March 29, 2009, from: www.telegraph.co.uk/news/uknews/law-and -order/5049757/Spotty-teens-detered-from-underpasses-by-acne-light.html

Sprague, R., & Wells, M. E. (2010). Regulating online buzz marketing: Untangling a web of deceit. *American Business Law Journal*, *47*(3), 415–454.

Story, L. (2007, January 15). Anywhere the eye can see, it's likely to see an ad. *The New York Times*. Retrieved on February 20, 2017 from: www.nytimes.com/2007/01/15/business/media/15everywhere.html?pagewanted=all&_r=0

Sunstein, C. R. (2014). *Why nudge? The politics of libertarian paternalism*. New Haven, NJ: Yale University Press.

Thaler, R. H., & Sunstein, C. R. (2008, April 8). Easy does it: How to make lazy people do the right thing. *New Republic*. Retrieved on February 17, 2016 from: https://newrepublic.com/article/63355/easy-does-it

Tuman, J. S. (2010). *Communicating terror: The rhetorical dimensions of terrorism* (2nd ed.). Thousand Oaks, CA: Sage.

Von Blum, P. (1976). *The art of social conscience*. New York: Universe Books.

Wodjynski, B. W. (2016). The deceptiveness of sponsored news articles: How readers recognize and perceive native advertising. *American Behavioral Scientist, 60*(12), 1475–1491. doi:10.1177/000276421666014

Zentino, R. (2016, November 30). Canadian cops to punish drunk drivers with Nickelback tunes. *CNN*. Retrieved on February 20, 2017 from: cnn.com/2016/11/30/americas/police-canada-nickelback-dui-trnd/

CHAPTER 2

What Constitutes Persuasion?

WHAT IS PERSUASION? How broad or narrow is the concept? Is persuasion a subset of human communication in general, much like baseball is a subset of sports? Or is persuasion an element found in all human communication in the same way that coordination plays a role in every sport? Not surprisingly, different authors view the concept of persuasion in different ways and have adopted different definitions of the term. In this chapter, we explore some of the ways that persuasion has been defined. We offer our own rather broad-based, far-reaching conceptualization of persuasion based on five limiting criteria. We also present our own model of what persuasion is (Gass & Seiter, 1997, 2000, 2004) and examine three additional models (Chaiken, 1979, 1987; Eagly & Chaiken, 1993; Petty & Cacioppo, 1986a, 1986b; Kruglanksi & Thompson, 1999a, 1999b) of how persuasion functions.

You may have encountered some unusual uses of the term *persuasion*. For example, we have a friend in the construction industry who refers to his sledgehammer as his "persuader." He tends to err on the side of cutting a 2 × 4 board too long, rather than too short, and then "persuading" it into place. As another example, you may recall seeing an old gangster movie in which a mob boss orders his henchman to take somebody out back "for a little gentle persuasion," meaning a beating. Although we don't normally associate persuasion with pounding lumber or pummeling people, even in ordinary usage the term does have a wide variety of meanings. Consider each of the hypothetical situations in Box 2.1, "What Constitutes Persuasion?" Which of these scenarios do *you* consider to be persuasion?

BOX 2.1 | What Constitutes Persuasion?

1. Muffin notices a grubby-looking weirdo in one of the front seats of the bus she is boarding. She opts for a seat toward the rear of the bus. Did the man "persuade" her to sit elsewhere?

2. Benny Bigot is the principal speaker at a park rally to recruit more members to the American Nazi party. Many of the people who hear Benny are so turned off by his speech that they are more anti-Nazi than they were before they attended the rally. Did Benny "persuade" them?

3. During a dramatic pause in his lecture for his three-hour night class, Professor Hohum hears a student's stomach growling. The professor then decides it would be a good time for the class to take a break. Did the student "persuade" Professor Hohum?

4. Babbs is standing at a street corner, watching passersby. The first three people she sees are wearing sweatshirts with political and/or social slogans emblazoned across the front. The fourth person to pass by is wearing a plain white T-shirt. Are the first three people "persuading" Babbs? Is the fourth?

5. Sheldon makes a new year's resolution to go on a diet. To remind himself not to snack, he sticks a picture of a male model with "six pack" abs on his refrigerator. Later, when he has an ice-cream craving, he sees the picture and decides to have an apple instead. Did Sheldon "persuade" himself?

6. Bubba is at the supermarket, pondering which of two brands of beer to purchase. After studying both brands attentively, he opts for an imported brand. Unbeknown to him, another shopper observed his deliberations. That shopper then walks over to the display and selects the same brand. Did "persuasion" take place?

7. Trudy is an impressionable freshperson who is in a jam. She has just realized a term paper is due in her philosophy class. Desperate, she asks Rex, who is the captain of the debate squad, if he will help her. Rex offers to give her an "A" paper he submitted when he had the same class 2 years prior if Trudy will sleep with him. Is Rex using "persuasion"?

Adding to the difficulty of defining persuasion is the fact that persuasion also goes by a variety of other names. Some of its aliases include terms such as *advising, brainwashing, coercion, compliance gaining, convincing, education, indoctrination, influence, manipulation,* and *propaganda.* Of course, whether these terms are considered synonyms for persuasion, or simply related terms, depends on one's definition of persuasion.

Defining a concept is analogous to building a fence. A fence is designed to keep some things in and other things out. In the same way, a definition encompasses some elements or aspects of a concept while excluding others. Which "species" of human communication is to be found inside the "barnyard" of persuasion depends on the size and shape of the fence a particular author builds. Fortunately, the differences in various definitions can be clarified, if not resolved, by focusing on two key considerations. We turn to these next.

PURE VERSUS BORDERLINE CASES OF PERSUASION

The first consideration is whether one is interested in pure persuasion or borderline cases of persuasion. By *pure persuasion*, we mean clear-cut cases of persuasion, on which most people would agree. Everyone would agree that a presidential debate, or a television commercial, or an attorney's closing remarks to a jury are instances of persuasion. Such examples represent "paradigm cases" (O'Keefe, 2016; Simons, 1986) because they are at the core of what we think of when we envision persuasion at work. Other instances, though, lie closer to the boundary or periphery of what we normally think of as persuasion. These instances we refer to as *borderline cases* of persuasion. Not everyone would agree that a derelict's mere appearance "persuades" passersby to keep their distance. Nor would everyone agree that involuntary reflexes such as burps, blinking, and pupil dilation constitute "persuasive" phenomena. These cases are less clear-cut, more "iffy." Much of the disparity in definitions is rooted in the fact that some authors are concerned with pure persuasion, whereas other authors are concerned with borderline cases as well. It isn't so much a matter of being right or wrong as it is a matter of how wide a net each author wishes to cast. The preliminary model of the scope of persuasion (Figure 2.1) illustrates this distinction in approaches.[1] As the shading in the model suggests, the dividing line between pure and borderline persuasion is fuzzy, rather than distinct.

Although we don't think there is a single, correct definition of persuasion, we do think there are some things that a functional, contemporary definition of persuasion ought to do. A contemporary definition should take into account the rich complex of verbal, nonverbal, and contextual cues found in interpersonal encounters. A contemporary definition also should acknowledge the many subtle, implicit cues that accompany face-to-face influence attempts. By implicit cues, we mean communication that occurs at a very low level of awareness, or even unconsciously. As an example, cultural factors might influence a person's choice of compliance-gaining strategies, without the person even realizing it (Wiseman et al., 1995). Such implicit communication is, in fact, quite common (Langer, 1978, 1989a, 1989b; Roloff, 1980) and an important ingredient in persuasion. The definition and model of persuasion that we offer later in this chapter take these features into account.

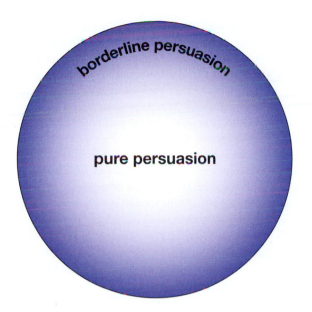

FIGURE 2.1
Preliminary model of
persuasion.

LIMITING CRITERIA FOR DEFINING PERSUASION

A second consideration in defining persuasion involves the limiting criteria that form the basis for a given definition. Different scholars apply different litmus tests when defining persuasion. Five basic criteria can be gleaned from the various definitions offered in the literature (Gass & Seiter, 2004). We examine each of these criteria in turn.

Intentionality

Is persuasion necessarily conscious or purposeful? Is there such a thing as "accidental" persuasion? Many who write about persuasion adopt a source-centered view by focusing on the sender's intent as a defining feature of persuasion. Perloff (2013) adopts this view, stressing that "persuasion does involve a deliberate attempt to influence another person. Persuaders must intend to change another individual's attitude or behavior and must be aware (at least at some level) that they are trying to accomplish this goal" (p. 18). For some authors, intentionality is the litmus test that distinguishes *persuasion* from *social influence* (Gass & Seiter, 2004).

Certainly, pure persuasion would seem to be intentional. When we think of obvious cases of persuasion we tend to think of situations in which one person purposefully tries to influence another. But what about borderline cases of persuasion? We believe that many influence attempts take place without any conscious awareness on the part of the persuader.

As just one instance, parents quite commonly instill beliefs, impart values, and model behavior for their children, a phenomenon known as *social modeling* (Bandura, 1977). Yet they may not realize how much of what they say and do is absorbed by their young-uns. As any parent will attest, many of the lessons parents "teach" their children are completely unintended. Another form of unintentional influence involves *socialization* processes. From the moment children are born, they are socialized into their respective gender roles, cultural customs, religious practices, and socioeconomic habits. Some socialization processes are mindful, but many are not.

A second way in which an intent criterion is problematic is that people do not always know what specific outcome they are seeking. Face-to-face encounters, in particular, are laden with spontaneity. Social influence may arise in and through our interaction with others, rather than as a result of planning and forethought. Sometimes persuasion just happens.

A third problem with relying on an intent criterion involves situations in which there are unintended receivers. Imagine a scenario in which two people are discussing which bets to place on a horse race. One tells the other about an inside tip on a horse that's a "sure thing." A third party overhears the conversation and places a wager on the horse. In such situations, persuaders don't intend for third parties to be influenced, yet they often are. Two studies (Greenberg & Pyszczynski, 1985; Kirkland, Greenberg, & Pyszczynski, 1987) clearly demonstrate the operation of the *unintended receiver effect*. In these studies, the researchers created a situation in which third parties overheard an ethnic slur directed against an African American. The results of both studies revealed that the overheard ethnic slur led to lower evaluations by the third parties of the individual at whom the slur was directed. Notice that a reliance on an intent standard for defining persuasion tends to make senders less accountable for the consequences of their unintended communication. If a message has harmful effects, the source can disavow any responsibility by claiming "that's not what I intended."

A fourth limitation lies in the difficulty of ascertaining another's intent. There can be a difference between a persuader's *stated* intent versus his or her *actual* intent. Who makes the determination in such cases? The sender? The receiver? A third party?

Finally, resolving the issue of intent is particularly difficult in interpersonal contexts, in which both parties may be engaged simultaneously in attempts at influence. When there are two interactants, whose intent counts? Intent-based definitions, we believe, are ill suited to modern conceptualizations of human interaction as a two-way venture. The linear view of persuasion that such definitions imply, from sender to receiver, ignores opportunities for mutual influence.

Effects

The effects criterion poses the question: Has persuasion taken place if no one is actually persuaded? Some authors adopt a receiver-oriented definition of persuasion by restricting its use to situations in which receivers are somehow changed, altered, or affected. Daniel O'Keefe (2016) underscores this perspective when he writes:

> The notion of success is embedded in the concept of persuasion. Notice, for instance, that it doesn't make sense to say, "I persuaded him, but failed." One can say, "I *tried* to persuade him, but failed," but to say simply, "I persuaded him" is to imply a successful attempt to influence.
>
> (pp. 2–3)

Although we recognize the attraction of this point of view, we believe there are problems with limiting the definition of persuasion in this way. We take the position that even if a person is communicating badly, he or she is *still* communicating. Similarly, we believe that a person can be engaged in persuasion even if it is *ineffective* persuasion. The same can be said for most other activities. A salesperson might fail to close a deal but would still be engaged in selling. A dancer might dance badly, stepping on his or her partner's toes, but would still be engaged in dancing. In short, a person can be engaged in an activity whether the person is doing it well or not.

An effects criterion emphasizes persuasion as a *product*. Such an orientation, however, bears little fidelity to current conceptualizations of human communication as a *process*. If we think of persuasion only as an outcome or a thing, then an effects orientation makes perfectly good sense. We maintain that persuasion is better understood as an activity in which people engage. This is more than semantic quibbling. By approaching persuasion as a process, scholars and researchers are more likely to gain insights into how it functions, or what makes it tick, because they are focusing on *what's going on*, not simply on how things turn out.

A second weakness is the same as that already associated with an intent criterion: An effects criterion embodies a linear view of persuasion, from source to receiver. In face-to-face encounters, however, there isn't simply *a* source and *a* receiver. Both parties may be simultaneously engaged in persuasion. They shape, adapt, and adjust their strategies in response to one another (Prislin et al., 2011).

A third problem with relying on an effects criterion is that it is often difficult, if not impossible, to measure persuasive effects. Rotzoll and Haefner (1996), for example, concluded that only 20 to 40 percent of advertising is effective. The other 60 to 80 percent is also persuasion—it's just ineffective persuasion. In fact, the ability to measure persuasive outcomes may hinge entirely on the sensitivity of one's measuring instruments (scales, surveys, sales figures, etc.). Furthermore, what constitutes the threshold for a successful versus unsuccessful attempt at persuasion? How much attitude or behavior change must take place to say persuasion has occurred? And what about the occasional odd circumstance in which persuasion "boomerangs"— that is, a persuader achieves an effect that is *contrary* to his or her intended purpose? Such questions, we believe, highlight the many vagaries inherent in relying on an effects criterion.

We do agree that, as with an intent criterion, pure cases of persuasion can usually be evaluated by their overall effectiveness. Even then, persuasion is rarely an all-or-nothing venture. If one also wishes to focus on borderline cases of persuasion, one must accept the fact that partial persuasion is more the rule than the exception. Notice, too, that there is some tension between relying on intent and effects as limiting criteria: What is achieved isn't always what is intended, and what is intended isn't always what is achieved.

Free Will and Conscious Awareness

Many authors endorse the view that there is a distinction between persuasion and coercion. This view is also receiver based, but it focuses on whether a person is aware that she or he is being persuaded and how much freedom the person has to accept or reject the message. Persuasion, these authors suggest, is noncoercive. As Herbert Simons (1986) puts it, "persuasion is a form of influence that predisposes, but does not impose" (p. 22). Richard Perloff (2013) also makes this point when he states that persuasion requires "an atmosphere of free choice" (p. 27).

"I insist."

It naturally follows that if a person is unaware that an influence attempt is taking place, she or he can't consciously resist it. Thus, mindfulness is a prerequisite for free choice. Nevertheless, we believe that persuasion can and does occur without the conscious awareness of receivers. For example, Ackerman, Nocera, and Bargh (2010) found that evaluations of job applicants can be shaped in important yet unconscious ways. Participants in an experiment were asked to evaluate resumes of job applicants. Some participants read resumes attached to heavier clipboards, while others read resumes attached to lighter clipboards. The results were intriguing. Applicants whose resumes were attached to heavier clipboards were rated higher overall and as being more serious than their "lightweight" counterparts. The physical weight of the clipboards translated into judgments about whether the applicants themselves were more substantial. Our advice, if you want to be seen as having more "gravitas": print your resume on a heavier bond of paper or, better yet, chisel it in stone.

In fact, many influence attempts succeed precisely because they operate at a low level of awareness. For example, consumers generally may be aware that product planting (placing products in movies and TV shows) is common, but they may not know how prevalent the practice is, let alone recognize each and every instance of product planting that occurs. Persuasion that relies on social networking, such as word of mouth (WOM), is designed to seem spontaneous rather than planned. A person might receive a link to a funny website from a friend, not realizing that the site was developed as a marketing tool by a commercial entity.

You may think of persuasion and coercion as being separate and distinct, but in our view, they aren't so much polar opposites as close relatives. Powers (2007) agrees when she asks:

Does a coercion claim have to show that another choice was in fact available? Just how available does the other choice have to be? Is it necessary to present all possible alternatives in order to avoid a charge of coercion? How equal do the choices have to be and how aware does the receiver have to be of those choices, and who decides what *available* means?

(p. 128)

In fact, we would suggest that most influence attempts we encounter in daily life include both persuasive and coercive elements. Rarely in life is one free to make a completely unfettered choice. There are almost always strings attached. This is particularly true of face-to-face encounters. If a friend asks to borrow 20 bucks, we can say "no," but there may be relational consequences for declining.

Rarely, too, are influence attempts completely coercive. For example, holding a gun to another person's head would seem to be an obvious example of coercion. We readily admit that this situation is *primarily* coercive. But what if the victim doesn't believe the gun is loaded? Or what if the victim thinks the threatener is bluffing? To be successful, a threat—even a threat of violence—must be perceived as credible. Thus, even in what might seem like a clear-cut case of coercion there are persuasive elements at work. And conversely, even in what appear to be cut-and-dried cases of persuasion, there may be coercive features operating. In our view, the issue isn't so much *whether* a situation is persuasive or coercive as *how* persuasive or coercive the situation is.

Symbolic Action

A number of authors maintain that persuasion begins and ends with symbolic expression, which includes language as well as other meaning-laden acts, such as civil disobedience and protest marches. This approach focuses on the means, or channel, of persuasion as a limiting criterion. Timothy Borchers (2013) endorses this view, noting that "our definition of persuasion uses the phrase 'language strategies and/or other symbols' to indicate the content of persuasion" (p. 19). Similarly, Gerald Miller (1980) maintains that "in most instances, language is an integral aspect of the persuasive transaction" (p. 5). Richard Perloff (2013) also adheres to this point of view, noting that "Persuasion is a symbolic process" (p. 17).

Authors who limit the scope of persuasion to symbolic action fear that without such a limitation, all human behavior could be construed as persuasion. Their point is well taken. However, restricting the medium for persuasion to words or symbols leads to a rather disjointed view of persuasion. We believe that a definition that limits persuasion to words and clearly codified symbols leaves out too much. Most magazine ads emphasize pictures rather than words. In fact, one study suggests that the text of a typical ad is read by fewer than 10 percent of the readers (Starch, cited in Dupont, 1999). The same is true of television commercials. It seems arbitrary to limit persuasion to the words contained in an ad or a commercial, without considering the role of the images as well. We think that the *whole* ad or the *whole* commercial persuades.

We also believe that some of the most intriguing aspects of persuasion can be found in nonverbal behavior, which lies on the periphery of symbolic action. For example, research on the physiological correlates of deception demonstrates that a variety of involuntary nonverbal cues (such as blinking, smiling, and pupil dilation) are positive indicators of lying (DePaulo, Stone, & Lassiter, 1985). We focus on deception as a form of persuasion in Chapter 12. Research on source credibility reveals that physical attributes, such as height or attractiveness, influence judgments of source credibility (Chaiken, 1979). We examine such factors in Chapter 4.

We also can think of situations in which pure behavior—for example, nonsymbolic actions—are nevertheless persuasive. When a basketball player makes a head fake to fool a defender, we would maintain that the player is *persuading* the defender to go the wrong way. The fake is all behavior, but the player has to *sell* the fake to get the defender to "bite" on it.

We believe that restricting the study of persuasion exclusively to symbolic expression leads to a fragmented understanding of the subject. Persuasion involves more than language usage or symbol usage. A whole host of factors are at work. Interestingly, many authors who profess an adherence to symbolic action nevertheless treat a variety of nonsymbolic aspects of behavior, such as those just mentioned, in their texts.

Interpersonal Versus Intrapersonal

How many actors are required for persuasion to take place? A last limiting criterion that deserves mention is whether persuasion can involve only one person or whether persuasion requires the participation of two or more distinct persons. Some scholars adopt the view that engaging in persuasion is like dancing the tango: it takes two (Bettinghaus & Cody, 1994; Johnston, 1994). We agree in the case of the tango, but not in the case of persuasion. In fact, we maintain that attempts at self-persuasion are quite common (Aronson, 1999; Perloff, 2013). A person might search for a rationalization to do something he or she wants to do, such as blowing the rent money on front-row concert tickets. In such cases, people talk themselves into whatever they wish to do.

We are sympathetic to the "two or more" perspective but suggest that, once again, the issue comes down to whether one wishes to focus exclusively on pure cases of persuasion or borderline cases as well. We heartily agree that when we think of pure cases of persuasion, we conjure up an image of one person persuading another. When we include borderline cases, we imagine instances in which individuals sometimes try to convince themselves.

A MODEL OF THE SCOPE OF PERSUASION

In light of the five limiting criteria just discussed, we can now offer an enhanced model (see Figure 2.3) that encompasses both pure and borderline cases of persuasion (Gass & Seiter, 2004). As with the preliminary model, the inner circle represents pure persuasion—that is, what we think of as the core of persuasion. The outer circle represents borderline persuasion. Superimposed on top of these two circles are five wedges, each representing one of the five limiting criteria previously discussed. The inner portion of each wedge represents the pure case for that criterion. The outer portion represents the borderline case. Once again, the shading between the inner and outer circles reflects the fuzzy dividing line that exists between pure and borderline persuasion.

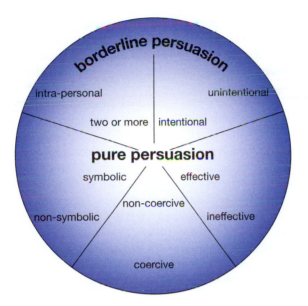

FIGURE 2.3
Enhanced model of persuasion.

Based on this enhanced model, you can appreciate the fact that different definitions feature different wedges of the inner and outer circles. Source-oriented definitions restrict persuasion to the inner circle of the "intentional–unintentional" wedge. Receiver-based definitions limit persuasion to the inner circle of the "effects–no effects" wedge. Other receiver-based definitions favor the inner circle with respect to the "free choice–coercion" criterion, and so on.

As you can also see from the enhanced model, some definitions concern themselves with several wedges at the same time, whereas other definitions are based on a single limiting criterion. It's worth noting that all definitions of persuasion— including our own, which we present shortly—are linguistic constructs. They exist in the world of words. Whether a given situation involves persuasion is not a matter of fact but of judgment.

Our own preference is for an expanded view of persuasion that includes borderline cases as well as pure persuasion. We tend to side with the view that persuasion is sometimes unintentional; that it sometimes has no discernible effects; that people aren't always aware of when it is occurring; that it often includes at least some coercive features; that it needn't be conveyed exclusively via symbols; and that humans do, on occasion, engage in self-persuasion. Many of the topics discussed in later chapters reside in the outer ring of our model. As we've already indicated, we believe that some of the most intriguing aspects of persuasion can be found there. We firmly believe we must look at both the inner and outer rings to fully understand the phenomenon of persuasion.

THE CONTEXT FOR PERSUASION

Consistent with current conceptualizations of persuasion, we view social influence as a process. Thus far, however, our model has remained relatively static. A final feature must be incorporated into our model to reflect the nature of persuasion as a process.

That feature is the *context* for persuasion. The context in which persuasion occurs— for example, within a small group, via mass media, in an organizational setting, and so forth—is crucial because it is the context that determines the nature of the communication process. In a face-to-face setting, for example, influence is a mutual, two-way process. In an advertising setting, influence tends to be more linear, from the advertiser to the consumer (there may be feedback from consumers, but it is delayed). Each context imposes its own unique set of constraints on the options available to persuaders.

By context, we don't simply mean the number of communicators present, although that is certainly one key factor. The context for communication also includes how synchronous or asynchronous communication is. Synchronous communication refers to the simultaneous sending and receiving of messages. Such is the case in face-to-face interaction. Asynchronous communication refers to a back-and-forth process that involves some delay, such as email or texting.

Another contextual factor is the ratio of verbal to nonverbal cues that are present. A print ad consisting entirely of text would rely exclusively on verbal cues (words) to persuade. A poster featuring only an image would rely exclusively on nonverbal cues to persuade. Most persuasive messages involve both verbal and nonverbal cues. The ratio of verbal to nonverbal cues available in any persuasive situation imposes particular constraints on the persuasion process.

An additional contextual factor is the nature and type of media used in the persuasion process. Television commercials, radio ads, magazine ads, and telemarketing are traditional media for persuasion. New media include blogs, Facebook, Twitter, and YouTube, among many others. Face-to-face encounters, such as door-to-door sales and panhandling, are unmediated. As with the other contextual factors, each medium imposes its own constraints on the persuasion process.

Yet another contextual factor involves the goals of the participants. Often, but not always, participants enter into communication encounters with specific objectives in mind (Dillard, 1990, 1993, 2004; Dillard, Segrin, & Harden, 1989). Canary and Cody (1994) break down these goals into three types—self-presentational goals, relational goals, and instrumental goals. *Self-presentational goals* have to do with identity management. People want to project a favorable image of themselves to others. *Relational goals* have to do with what people want out of their relationships— how to develop them, improve them, change them, and so forth. *Instrumental goals* involve attempts at compliance gaining. People's goals may be thwarted or may change during a persuasive encounter.

A final contextual variable involves sociocultural factors that affect the persuasion process. People from different cultures or subcultures may persuade and be persuaded in different ways (Ma & Chuang, 2001). For example, research suggests that some cultures prefer more indirect approaches to compliance gaining (hinting, guilt, reliance on group norms), whereas other cultures prefer more direct approaches to compliance gaining (direct requests, demanding) (Wiseman et al., 1995). Different cultural traditions can dramatically affect what is expected or accepted in the way of influence attempts.

Note that all of these contextual factors are operating at once in a given persuasive situation. Each of the contextual factors constrains the process of persuasion in one way or another. The context involves the totality of the relationships among all these factors. The final version of our model, depicted in Figure 2.4, illustrates how persuasion is shaped by context (Gass & Seiter, 2004). Context, then, is what determines the nature of the process involved in a given persuasive situation.

A WORKING DEFINITION OF PERSUASION

At last we arrive at our own definition of persuasion. Our view is that *persuasion involves one or more persons who are engaged in the activity of creating, reinforcing, modifying, or extinguishing beliefs, attitudes, intentions, motivations, and/or behaviors within the constraints of a given communication context*. The advantage of our definition is that it encompasses the full scope of persuasion, both pure and borderline cases. Our definition also emphasizes persuasion as an activity or a process; it is something people do. Our definition encompasses the notion that in face-to-face encounters, persuasion is a two-way street. Each party has an opportunity to influence the other. With respect to our definition, we also wish to stress that persuasion doesn't involve simply changing one's own or another's mind, though that is the most typical connotation (Miller, 1980). Persuasion also can involve creating new beliefs or attitudes, where none existed before. It also can involve reinforcing, strengthening, or solidifying attitudes already held by receivers. And persuasion also can involve attempts to extinguish or eliminate beliefs and attitudes. The latter approach is exemplified by Alcoholics Anonymous's position that alcoholics must abandon the belief that other people are responsible, or circumstances are to blame, for their dependency.

If our definition seems expansive, it is because we believe the topic of persuasion itself is rather far ranging. We wish to examine not only the core of persuasion in this text but its periphery as well. The majority of our examples focus on pure cases of persuasion. However, from time to time we dabble on the fuzzy outer edges. We find some of the borderline cases of persuasion quite interesting, and we believe you will too.

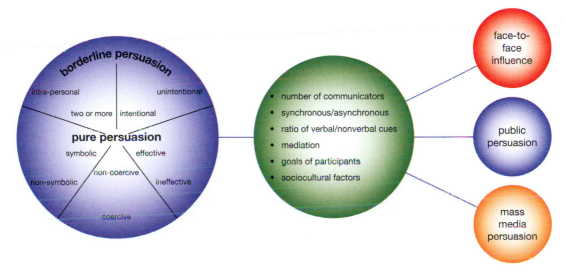

FIGURE 2.4
Completed model of persuasion. This figure illustrates three of many possible persuasive situations.

SO WHAT ISN'T PERSUASION?

Given the breadth of our definition, you're probably wondering, "What *isn't* persuasion?" We address this concern now. Our position is that the ingredients for persuasion can be found in most, if not all, communication transactions. The degree to which these persuasive ingredients are present is what matters. We think most human communication involves at least the *potential* to influence. Of course, one may choose not to focus on the persuasive, or potentially persuasive, elements in a communication situation. One can concentrate on some other aspect of communication instead. The potential for persuasion remains nonetheless. What matters, then, is how persuasive a given communication situation is, not whether a communication situation is persuasive.

Many other features of communication besides persuasion can command one's attention. For example, one can examine the role of self-disclosure and relationship satisfaction without discussing persuasion. One can study effective listening skills, regardless of whether the message listened to is persuasive or not. One can study nonverbal cues and liking without focusing on persuasion. One can look at how people try to save face during conflicts without involving persuasion. Persuasive elements needn't comprise the focus of attention even if they are present. One can focus on other relevant features of human communication to the exclusion of persuasive processes.

Although we believe that nearly all human communication is potentially persuasive, we don't believe the same about all human behavior. The mere act of breathing, in and of itself, doesn't seem like persuasion to us—although under the right circumstances it could be (such as pretending to be out of breath). Tripping over a rock, by itself, doesn't seem like a persuasive act to us, although, again, under certain conditions it could be (such as feigning clumsiness). Biological functions, such as sneezing, coughing, or vomiting don't strike us as being persuasive, though, again, a person could fake having allergies, a cold, or a hangover to influence someone else. A good deal of human behavior, then, we don't consider to be persuasion, unless and until some additional conditions are met. We don't think everything humans do is persuasive.

There are also some forms of communication that we've excluded from consideration in this text for purely practical reasons. We don't discuss torture as a form of persuasion, although some, like Abbott (2016) call it persuasion at its most gruesome. We also don't address the possibility of human-to-animal persuasion, or vice versa, though such a case probably could be made. Furthermore, we don't consider a whole range of studies on how plants, such as willow trees or sugar maples, can warn other trees about insect infestations. There are biologists, though, who study "talking trees" (McGowan, 2013). We don't examine the power of hypnotic suggestion as a form of influence. We don't examine attempts to persuade via telepathy, paranormal, or psychic activity either. We've heard that some people with cancerous tumors try to "talk to" their cancer and "persuade" it to go away. We don't deal with that topic here, except insofar as it may constitute a form of self-persuasion. We also don't address a host of other intriguing topics, such as the role of genetics and neuropsychology in persuasion. We simply don't have the space to devote to those topics here. Thus, as big as the fence that we've built is, there is a lot of human communication we've left out.

DUAL PROCESSES OF PERSUASION

Now that we've clarified what we think persuasion is, we want to take a look at how it functions. To this end, we present a brief explanation of two prevailing models of persuasion. Both are known as *dual process* models (Chaiken & Trope, 1999) because they postulate that persuasion operates via two basic paths. The two models share many similarities and, in our opinion, both do an excellent job of explaining how persuasive messages are perceived and processed.

The Elaboration Likelihood Model of Persuasion

Richard Petty and John Cacioppo's (1986a, 1986b) *elaboration likelihood model of persuasion* (ELM), is one of the most widely cited models in the persuasion literature.[2] Their model proposes two basic routes to persuasion that operate in tandem. The first of these they call the *central route*. The central route, or *central processing*, as they sometimes refer to it, involves *cognitive elaboration*. That means thinking about the content of a message, reflecting on the ideas and information contained in it, and scrutinizing the evidence and reasoning presented. The second route to persuasion is known as the *peripheral route*. The peripheral route, or *peripheral processing*, as it is sometimes called, involves focusing on cues that aren't directly related to the substance of a message. For example, focusing on a source's physical attractiveness, or the sheer quantity of arguments presented, or a catchy jingle as a basis for decision making would entail peripheral processing. According to the ELM, the two routes represent the ends, or anchor points, of an elaboration continuum (Petty, Rucker, Bizer, & Cacioppo, 2004). At one end of the continuum, a person engages in no or low elaboration. At the other end, a person engages in high elaboration.

To illustrate the two basic routes, imagine that Rex and Trudy are on a date at a restaurant. Trudy is very health conscious, so she studies the menu carefully. She looks to see whether certain dishes are fatty or high in calories. When the food server arrives to take their order, she asks, "What kind of oil is used to prepare the pasta?" She might sound picky, but Trudy is engaging in central processing. She is actively thinking about what the menu says. Rex, however, is smitten with Trudy's good looks. He hardly looks at the menu, and when the food server asks for his order, he says, "I'll have what she's having." Rex is engaging in peripheral processing. He's basing his decision on cues that are unrelated to the items on the menu.

Petty and Cacioppo acknowledge the possibility of *parallel processing*—that is, using both routes at once (Petty, Kasmer, Haugtvedt, & Cacioppo, 2004). For example, when people judge the credibility of websites, they consider the look and layout of a website (peripheral cue) and the content of the website (central processing) (SanJosé-Cabezuo, Gutiérrez-Arranze, & Gutiérrez-Cillán, 2009). However, Petty and Cacioppo (1986a, 1986b) suggest that there is usually a trade-off between central and peripheral processing, such that a person tends to favor one route over the other. Whether a person emphasizes the central or the peripheral route hinges on two basic factors. The first of these is the individual's *motivation* to engage in central processing. Because central processing requires more mental effort, a person with greater motivation is more likely to rely on central processing. Typically, this means the person has *high involvement* with the topic or issue. That is, the topic or issue matters to him or her, or affects him or her personally. If a person has *low involvement* with a topic or issue, he or she will be less inclined to engage in central processing, and more likely to resort to peripheral processing. For example, voters with little knowledge are more likely to be swayed by politicians' looks than voters who are informed about the candidates' positions (Lenz & Lawson, 2011).

The second factor that determines whether a person will rely on central or peripheral processing is his or her *ability* to process information. A person must not only be willing but also able to engage in central processing. Some people are more adept at grasping ideas, understanding concepts, and making sense of things. Some people also have more knowledge of or expertise in certain topics or issues than others. Thus, receivers are more likely to process a persuasive message via the central route if they have the motivation and ability to do so. If they lack the motivation or the ability, they will tend to rely on peripheral processing instead.

Aside from ability and motivation, a variety of other factors can tilt the balance in favor of central or peripheral processing. These include distractions, such as background noise, time constraints, a person's mood, or a personality trait called *need for cognition*. Need for cognition has to do with how much a person enjoys thinking about things. We discuss this trait in more detail in Chapter 5.

The type of processing affects the persistence of persuasion. Researchers have found that persuasion via the central route tends to be more long lasting, whereas persuasion via the peripheral route tends to be more short-lived (Carpenter, 2015; Petty, Haugtvedt, & Smith, 1995). This seems sensible: When we think about ideas,

FIGURE 2.5
Peripheral processing in action.

Source: © Joe Martin. All Rights Reserved. Reprinted with permission.

they are more likely to be absorbed. Similarly, persuasion that takes place via central processing also tends to be more resistant to counterinfluence attempts than persuasion via peripheral processing. This also makes sense: If you've thought through your position, you're less likely to "waffle." Researchers also have found that if receivers disagree with the content of a message, using central processing causes them to generate more counterarguments. That is, they mentally rehearse their objections to the message. If receivers disagree with a message and rely on peripheral processing, however, they will generate fewer counterarguments or other unfavorable thoughts about the message. A useful generalization when persuading, then, is that to make persuasion last, you've got to make people think.

The Heuristic Systematic Model of Persuasion

Another model of persuasion that bears many similarities to the ELM is Shelley Chaiken and Alice Eagly's *heuristic systematic model*, or HSM (Chaiken, 1987; Chaiken, Liberman, & Eagly, 1989; Chaiken & Trope, 1999; Eagly & Chaiken, 1993). As with the ELM, the HSM operates on the assumption that individuals rely on two different modes of information processing. One mode, called *systematic processing*, is more thoughtful and deliberate. Systematic processing in the HSM is roughly analogous to central processing in the ELM. The other mode, called *heuristic processing*, relies on mental shortcuts. Heuristic processing is based on the application of *decision rules* or *heuristic cues* that help simplify the thought process. An example of a decision rule would be buying a TV based on its brand name ("Sony televisions are reliable"). An example of a heuristic cue would be choosing one wine over another because the bottle is prettier. Heuristic processing in the HSM is roughly equivalent to peripheral processing in the ELM.

Chaiken and Eagly's model also maintains that *simultaneous processing* of messages is commonplace. Messages travel the heuristic and systematic routes concurrently. As with the ELM, the HSM states that *motivation* and *ability* are two primary determinants of the extent to which heuristic or systematic processing will be used. A problem for both models is that, to date, there is limited empirical evidence of simultaneous processing, at least in laboratory studies of persuasion (Booth-Butterfield et al., 1994; Chaiken et al., 1989).

Another feature of the HSM is the *sufficiency principle*, which states that people strive to know as much as they need to when making a decision, but no more or less. On one hand, people want to devote the time and attention to issues that they deserve. On the other hand, people can't afford to spend all their time and mental energy worrying about every little thing. Therefore, people balance their heuristic and systematic processing to create the best "fit" for the issue at hand.

By way of illustration, suppose Irwin is thinking of buying a digital camera. If Irwin didn't know much about such devices, he could take one of two approaches. He could rely on systematic processing by reading up on digital cameras. He would likely adopt this route if he thought he really needed a digital camera (motivation) and he lacked the necessary knowledge about them (sufficiency principle). He also would need time to gather information and be able to understand it (ability). Alternatively, he could opt for heuristic processing. He could base his decision on a friend's advice using a simple decision rule ("Lance knows his cameras") He could base his decision on a heuristic cue, such as the brand ("Canon is the best brand"). He would be more

"I have no idea what gluten is, either, but I'm avoiding it, just to be safe."

likely to resort to heuristic processing if he didn't really need a digital camera—it was only an electronic toy (low motivation)—or if he didn't think he could make sense of the information about cameras anyway (lack of ability).

Both the ELM and HSM are useful for explaining and predicting people's reactions to persuasive messages. Literally dozens of studies devoted to testing the explanatory and predictive power of these two models have been conducted. These studies have generally upheld the models' utility. Although both models have their critics (see Kruglanski & Thompson, 1999a, 1999b; Mongeau & Stiff, 1993; Stiff & Boster, 1987), it is safe to say that they enjoy considerable support in the literature. We develop and amplify principles related to the ELM and HSM throughout this text. Because we refer to both models repeatedly, it would be worth your while to familiarize yourself with their basic concepts for later reference.

THE UNIMODEL OF PERSUASION

An alternative to dual process models of persuasion is the *unimodel* developed by Arie Kruglanski and Erik Thompson (Kruglanski & Thompson, 1999a, 1999b). Kruglanski and Thompson posit that, rather than two distinct modes of information processing, there is a single route to persuasion. Central processing isn't qualitatively different from peripheral processing, according to the *unimodel*; there is simply more or less of it. Kruglanski maintains that the alleged differences in processing based on the ELM and HSM merely reflect differences in the messages themselves. Longer, more complex messages require more thought, while shorter, simpler messages require less thought (Erb, Pierro, Mannetti, Spiegel, & Kruglanski, 2007; Kruglanski et al., 2006; Pierro, Mannetti, Erb, Spiegel, & Kruglanski, 2005).

Despite the simplicity of the *unimodel*, we believe there are cases in which persuasive messages are processed in fundamentally different ways (Petty, Wheeler, &

Bizer, 1999). For example, a consumer who responded to a fear appeal emotionally or reflexively would be quite different from a consumer who responded to a fear appeal rationally or reflectively. Even so, the *unimodel* raises important questions about whether and how dual processing occurs. Some scholars have questioned whether dual processing has ever been empirically documented (Booth-Butterfield et al., 1994).

SUMMARY

We began this chapter by presenting a preliminary model of persuasion that distinguishes pure from borderline cases of persuasion. We identified five limiting criteria for defining persuasion that are reflected in our own model of persuasion. We followed our model with our own broad-based, far-reaching definition of persuasion. Finally, we provided a brief explanation of Petty and Cacioppo's *elaboration likelihood model* (ELM) of persuasion and Chaiken and Eagly's *heuristic systematic model* (HSM) of persuasion. An alternative to dual-process models, the *unimodel*, also was presented.

NOTES

1. More than two decades ago, Simons (1986, p. 116) introduced a model of persuasion having concentric circles, representing pure persuasion, peripheral persuasion, and non-persuasion. Our preliminary model (Figure 2.1) draws on his work.
2. Not all scholars are enamored with Petty and Cacioppo's model. Among others, Mongeau and Stiff (1993) and Stiff and Boster (1987) have criticized the ELM for its theoretical and empirical limitations. Petty, Wegener, Fabrigar, Priester, and Cacioppo (1993) and Petty, Kasmer, Haugtvedt, and Cacioppo (2004) have responded to many of the criticisms directed against their model.

REFERENCES

Abbot, G. (2016). *Torture: Persuasion at its most gruesome*. Chichester, UK: Summersdale.

Ackerman, J. M., Nocera, C. C., & Bargh, J. A. (2010). Incidental haptic sensations influence social judgments and decisions. *Science, 328*, 1712–1715.doi:10.1126/science.1189993

Aronson, E. (1999). The power of self-persuasion. *American Psychologist, 54*(11), 875–884.

Bandura, A. (1977). *Social learning theory*. Englewood Cliffs, NJ: Prentice Hall.

Bettinghaus, E. P., & Cody, M. J. (1994). *Persuasive communication* (6th ed.). Fort Worth, TX: Harcourt Brace.

Booth-Butterfield, S., Cooke, P., Andrighetti, A., Casteel, B., Lang, T., Pearson, D., & Rodriguez, B. (1994). Simultaneous versus exclusive processing of persuasive arguments and cues. *Communication Quarterly, 42*, 21–35.

Borchers, T. A. (2013). *Persuasion in the media age* (3rd ed.). Long Grove, IL: Waveland Press.

Canary, D. J., & Cody, M. J. (1994). *Interpersonal communication: A goals–based approach*. New York: St. Martin's Press.

Carpenter, C. J. (2015). A meta-analysis of the ELM's argument quality × processing type predictions. *Human Communication Research, 41*, 501–534. doi:10,1111/hcre.12054

Chaiken, S. (1979). Communicator physical attractiveness and persuasion. *Journal of Personality and Social Psychology, 37*, 1387–1397.

Chaiken, S. (1987). The heuristic model of persuasion. In M. P. Zanna, J. M. Olson, & C. P. Herman (Eds.), *Social influence: The Ontario symposium* (Vol. 5, pp. 3–39). Hillsdale, NJ: Erlbaum.

Chaiken, S., Liberman, A., & Eagly, A. H. (1989). Heuristic and systematic information processing within and beyond the persuasion context. In J. S. Uleman & J. A. Bargh (Eds.), *Unintended thought* (pp. 212–252). New York: Guilford Press.

Chaiken, S., & Trope, Y. (Eds.). (1999). *Dual-process theories in social psychology.* New York: Guilford Press.

DePaulo, B. M., Stone, J. I., & Lassiter, G. D. (1985). Deceiving and detecting deceit. In B. R. Schlenker (Ed.), *The self and social life* (pp. 323–370). New York: McGraw-Hill.

Dillard, J. P. (1990). Primary and secondary goals in interpersonal influence. In M. J. Cody & M. L. McLaughlin (Eds.), *Psychology of tactical communication* (pp. 70–90). Clevedon, UK: Multilingual Matters.

Dillard, J. P. (1993). A goal-driven model of interpersonal influence. In J. P. Dillard (Ed.), *Seeking compliance: The production of interpersonal influence messages* (pp. 41–56). Scottsdale, AZ: Gorsuch, Scarisbrick.

Dillard, J. P. (2004). The goals-plans-action model of interpersonal influence. In J. S. Seiter & R. H. Gass (Eds.), *Perspectives on persuasion, social influence, and compliance gaining* (pp. 185–206). Boston, MA: Allyn & Bacon.

Dillard, J. P., Segrin, C., & Harden, J. M. (1989). Primary and secondary goals in the interpersonal influence process. *Communication Monographs, 56,* 19–39.

Dupont, L. (1999). *Images that sell: 500 ways to create great ads.* Sainte-Foy, Quebec, Canada: White Rock.

Eagly, A. H., & Chaiken, S. (1993). *The psychology of attitudes.* New York: Harcourt, Brace, Jovanovich.

Erb, H. P., Pierro, A., Mannetti, L., Spiegel, S., & Kruglanski, A. W. (2007). Biased processing of persuasive evidence: On the functional equivalence of cues and message arguments. *European Journal of Social Psychology, 37,* 1057–1075.

Gass, R. H., & Seiter, J. S. (1997, November). *On defining persuasion: Toward a contemporary perspective.* presented at the annual convention of the Western Communication Association, Monterey, CA.

Gass, R. H., & Seiter, J. S. (2000, November). *Embracing divergence: A reexamination of traditional and nontraditional conceptualizations of persuasion.* Paper presented at the annual convention of the National Communication Association, Seattle, WA.

Gass, R. H., & Seiter, J. S. (2004). Embracing divergence: A definitional analysis of pure and borderline cases of persuasion. In J. S. Seiter & R. H. Gass (Eds.), *Perspectives on persuasion, social influence, and compliance gaining* (pp. 13–29). Boston, MA: Allyn & Bacon.

Greenberg, J., & Pyszczynski, T. (1985). The effect of an overheard ethnic slur on evaluations of the target: How to spread a social disease. *Journal of Experimental Social Psychology, 21,* 61–72.

Johnston, D. D. (1994). *The art and science of persuasion.* Madison, WI: William C. Brown.

Kirkland, S. L., Greenberg, J., & Pyszczynski, T. (1987). Further evidence of the deleterious effects of overheard derogatory ethnic labels: Derogation beyond the target. *Personality and Social Psychology Bulletin, 13*(2), 216–227.

Kruglanski, A. W., Chen, X., Pierro, A., Mannetti, L., Erb, H.-P., & Spiegel, S. (2006). Persuasion according to the unimodel: Implications for cancer communication. *Journal of Communication, 56,* S105–S122.

Kruglanski, A. W., & Thompson, E. P. (1999a). Persuasion by a single route: A view from the unimodel. *Psychological Inquiry, 10,* 83–109.

Kruglanski, A.W., & Thompson, E.P. (1999b). The illusory second mode or, the cue is the message. *Psychological Inquiry, 10*(2), 182–193.

Langer, E. J. (1978). Rethinking the role of thought in social interaction. In J. H. Harvey, W. J. Ickes, & R. F. Kidd (Eds.), *New directions in attribution research* (Vol. 2, pp. 35–58). New York: John Wiley.

Langer, E.J. (1989a). *Mindfulness.* Reading, MA: Addison-Wesley.

Langer, E. J. (1989b). Minding matters. In L. Berkowitz (Ed.), *Advances in experimental social psychology* (Vol. 22, pp. 137–173). New York: Addison-Wesley.

Lenz, G. S., & Lawson, C. (2011). Looking the part: Television leads less informed citizens to vote based on candidates' appearance. *American Journal of Political Science, 55*(3), 574–589.

Ma, R., & Chuang, R. (2001). Persuasion strategies of Chinese college students in interpersonal contexts. *Southern Communication Journal, 66*(4), 267–278.

McGowan, K. (2013, December 20). How plants secretly talk to each other. *Wired.* Retrieved on March 19, 2017 from: www.wired.com/2013/12/secret-language-of-plants/

Miller, G. R. (1980). On being persuaded: Some basic distinctions. In J. P. Dillard & M. P. Fau (Eds.), *Persuasion: New directions in theory and research* (pp. 3–16). Thousand Oaks, CA: Sage.

Mongeau, P. A., & Stiff, J. B. (1993). Specifying causal relationships in the elaboration likelihood model. *Communication Theory, 3,* 65–72.

O'Keefe, D. (2016). *Persuasion: Theory and research* (3rd ed.) Thousand Oaks, CA: Sage.

Perloff, R. M. (2013). *The dynamics of persuasion: Communication and attitudes in the 21st century* (5th ed.). New York: Routledge.

Petty, R. E., & Cacioppo, J. T. (1986a). The elaboration likelihood model of persuasion. In L. Berkowitz (Ed.), *Advances in experimental social psychology* (Vol. 19, pp. 123–205). New York: Academic Press.

Petty, R. E., & Cacioppo, J. T. (1986b). *Communication and persuasion: Central and peripheral routes to attitude change.* New York: Springer-Verlag.

Petty, R. E., Haugtvedt, C., & Smith, S. M. (1995). Elaboration as a determinant of attitude strength: Creating attitudes that are persistent, resistant, and predictive of behavior. In R. E. Petty & J. Krosnick (Eds.), *Attitude strength: Antecedents and consequences* (pp. 93–130). Mahwah, NJ: Erlbaum.

Petty, R. E., Kasmer, J. E., Haugtvedt, C. P., & Cacioppo, J. T. (2004). Source and message factors in persuasion: A reply to Stiff's critique of the elaboration likelihood model. *Communication Monographs, 54,* 233–249.

Petty, R. E., Rucker, D., Bizer, G., & Cacioppo, J. T. (2004). The elaboration likelihood model of persuasion. In J. S. Seiter & R. H. Gass (Eds.), *Readings in persuasion, social influence, and compliance gaining* (pp. 65–89). Boston, MA: Allyn & Bacon.

Petty, R. E., Wegener, D. T., Fabrigar, L. R., Priester, J. R., & Cacioppo, J. T. (1993). Conceptual and methodological issues in the elaboration likelihood model of persuasion: A reply to the Michigan State critics. *Communication Theory, 3*(4), 336–362.

Petty, R. E., Wheeler, S. C., & Bizer, G. Y. (1999). Is there one persuasion process or more? Lumping versus splitting in attitude change theories. *Psychological Inquiry, 10,* 156–163.

Pierro, A., Mannetti, L., Erb, H. P., Spiegel, S., & Kruglanski, A. W. (2005). Informational length and order of presentation as determinants of persuasion. *Journal of Experimental Social Psychology, 41,* 458–469.

Powers, P. (2007). Persuasion and coercion: A critical review of philosophical and empirical approaches. *HEC Forum, 19*(2), 125–143. doi:10.1007/s10730-007-9035-4

Prislin, R., Boyle, S. M., Davenport, C., Farley, A., Jacobs, E., Michalak, J., Uehara, K., Zandian, F., & Xu, Y. (2011). On being influenced while trying to persuade: The feedback effect on persuasion outcomes on the persuader. *Social Psychological and Personality Science, 2*(1), 51–58.

Roloff, M. E. (1980). Self-awareness and the persuasion process: Do we really *know* what we're doing? In M. E. Roloff & G. R. Miller (Eds.), *Persuasion: New directions in theory and research* (pp. 29–66). Beverly Hills, CA: Sage.

Rotzoll, K. B., & Haefner, J. E., with Hall, S. R. (1996). *Advertising in contemporary society: Perspectives toward understanding.* Urbana, IL: University of Illinois Press.

SanJosé-Cabezudo, R., Gutiérrez-Arranze, A. M., & Gutiérrez-Cillán, J. (2009). The combined influence of central and peripheral routes in the online persuasion process. *CyberPsychology & Behavior, 12*(3), 299–308. doi:10.1089=cpb.2008.0188

Simons, H. W. (1986). *Persuasion: Understanding, practice, and analysis* (2nd ed.). New York: McGraw-Hill.

Stiff, J. B., & Boster, F. J. (1987). Cognitive processing: Additional thoughts and a reply to Petty, Kasmer, Haugtvedt, and Cacioppo. *Communication Monographs, 54*, 250–256.

Wiseman, R. L., Sanders, J. A., Congalton, K. J., Gass, R. H., Sueda, K., & Ruiqing, D. (1995). A cross-cultural analysis of compliance-gaining: China, Japan, and the United States. *Intercultural Communication Studies, 5*(1), 1–17.

Attitudes and Consistency

I F SOMEONE SAID, "Mabel has an attitude," you might think she was being irritable. However, the word *attitude* doesn't have the same meaning for social scientists that it does in everyday parlance. Social scientists have long been fascinated with the study of attitudes on all manner of subjects. Prislin and Crano (2008) went so far as to say that social scientists have carried on an "unremitting romance with attitudes over the past half-century" (p. 3). The honeymoon isn't over. Attitudes remain a vital element in understanding how persuasion works today.

Just why are attitudes so important to understanding persuasion? The reason is that attitudes help to predict, explain, and modify behavior. Just as a baker uses yeast as a catalyst in baking bread, persuaders rely on attitudes as a means of bringing about changes in receivers. An understanding of attitudes is, therefore, a key ingredient in any recipe for persuasion. For this reason, this chapter is devoted to a discussion of attitudes. We begin by considering what an attitude is.

WHAT IS AN "ATTITUDE" IN 20 WORDS OR LESS?

There is now general agreement among social scientists that an attitude is a "psychological tendency that is expressed by evaluating a particular entity with some degree of favor or disfavor" (Eagly & Chaiken, 1993, p. 1). Let's examine some key aspects of this definition more closely. First, attitudes reflect *tendencies* or *predispositions* to respond to things in predictable ways. We don't have time to reflect on each and every action we take in life, so attitudes provide us with mental templates that guide our behavior.

This is not to say that there is a one-to-one correspondence between attitudes and behaviors. A person may have a favorable attitude toward losing weight but may not stay on a diet. To a large extent, though, our attitudes do correspond with our behaviors. For example, people who favor gun-control laws are less likely to own guns than people who oppose such laws. Attitudes have been shown to predict environmental behavior, consumer behavior, voting behavior, contraceptive use, marijuana use, discrimination based on race, and numerous other behaviors (Holland, Verplanken, & van Krippenberg, 2002).

A second feature of attitudes is that they represent favorable or unfavorable evaluations of things. This *evaluative dimension* is, perhaps, the most central feature of attitudes (Dillard, 1993). If a person says, "I can't stand Marmite" or "I love Vegemite," the person is expressing his or her attitudes toward the two sandwich spreads. Along with their valence, attitudes *vary in degree or intensity*. Not all attitudes are equal. Stronger attitudes, whether positive or negative, tend to be better predictors of behavior and less subject to change.

A third aspect of attitudes is that they are always directed toward an *attitude object*. Attitudes may be held in memory or formed on the spot (Argyriou & Melawar, 2011), but people hold attitudes *about* things or *toward* things. The attitude object can be another person, an idea, a policy, an event, or a situation. Attitudes toward a complex issue may be composed of multiple attitudes toward a variety of sub-issues.

SO HOW DO YOU MEASURE THE DURN THINGS?

If you want to know how much you weigh, you can stand on a scale. If you want to know how tall you are, you can use a tape measure. But what if you want to measure someone's attitudes? Attitudes can't be observed directly. They are inside people's heads. As such, social scientists have developed a number of methods—both *explicit* and *implicit*—for measuring attitudes.[1] Let's take a look at each of these approaches.

Explicit Measures: Self-Report Scales

The old saying, "Straight from the horse's mouth" suggests that whatever is being shared comes directly from the source. With that in mind, *self-report scales* might be thought of as "straight-from-the-horse's-mouth" measures. That's because self-report scales measure attitudes by directly asking people to reveal their attitudes. Because people know their attitudes are being measured, self-reports are considered to be *explicit measures* of attitudes (Petty, Fazio, & Briñol, 2009). Two widely used self-report scales are *Likert* scales and *semantic differential* scales.

Likert Scales

Rensus Likert's (1932) "equal appearing interval" scales are among the most popular in use today. You've probably already completed a number of them yourself. A Likert scale consists of a series of statements about some attitude object, followed by a continuum of choices ranging from "strongly agree" to "strongly disagree" (see Figure 3.1). A respondent's attitude is represented by the average of his or her responses to all the statements in the scale. The scales are easy to construct and administer and enjoy widespread acceptance in academia, government, and industry.

Semantic Differential Scales

Although its name may be unfamiliar, you are probably already acquainted with the *semantic differential* scale (see Figure 3.2), developed by Osgood, Tannenbaum, and Suci (1957). This scale is based on the *connotative* meanings that words have for people. It consists of a series of bipolar adjective pairs or, more simply, opposites, such as light–dark, fast–slow, happy–sad, and so on. In completing the scale, a respondent checks the "semantic" space between each adjective pair that best reflects his or her overall attitude toward the concept in question. The respondent's overall attitude is represented by the average of the spaces checked on all of the items.

"The media has a liberal bias."

_____   _____   _____   _____   _____
strongly   agree   neutral/   disagree   strongly
agree   no opinion   disagree

or

"Illegal immigrants should be allowed to get a driver's license"

_____ strongly agree

_____ agree

_____ neutral/no opinion

_____ disagree

_____ strongly disagree

FIGURE 3.1
Examples of Likert-type scale items.

Rush Limbaugh

expert   _____ _____ _____ _____ _____ _____ _____ inexpert

relaxed   _____ _____ _____ _____ _____ _____ _____ tense

bold   _____ _____ _____ _____ _____ _____ _____ timid

FIGURE 3.2
Examples of semantic differential scale items.

Visually Oriented Scales

Other visually oriented methods of measuring attitudes via self-reports also have
been developed. Visual scales make it easier for respondents to conceptualize their
attitudes, because they can "see" where their attitudes fit on a scale or continuum.
The *visual analog scale* or VAS (Flynn, van Schaik, & van Wersch, 2004), for
example, simply asks respondents to place a mark along a continuum. A Web tool
for creating such a scale can be found at www.vasgenerator.net (Reips & Funke,
2008). Other visual scales include simple drawings of facial expressions. The
expressions represent different degrees of favor or disfavor toward the attitude
object, ranging from smiling to frowning (see Figure 3.3).

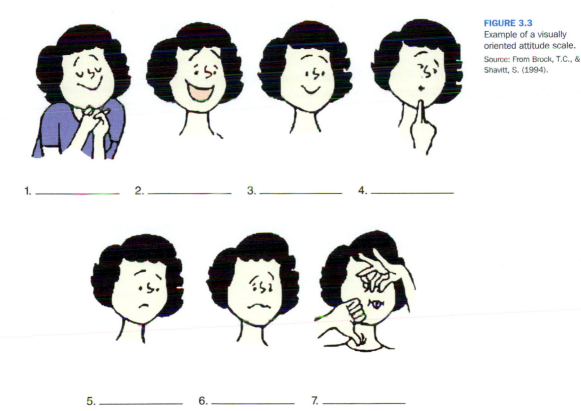

FIGURE 3.3
Example of a visually oriented attitude scale.
Source: From Brock, T.C., & Shavitt, S. (1994).

1. _____   2. _____   3. _____   4. _____

5. _____   6. _____   7. _____

Pitfalls in Measuring Attitudes

Although explicit measures are fairly easy to administer, they have drawbacks. A reliance on self-reports presumes that people are aware of their attitudes and that they are willing and able to report them. One limitation of self-reports is known as *social desirability bias*. When people know that their words or actions are on display, they may exhibit what they perceive to be socially acceptable norms of conduct. During a job interview, for example, a person might express "politically correct" attitudes to win favor with the interviewer.

A second pitfall involves the problem of *non-attitudes*. People don't want to appear uninformed or unintelligent. So quite often, when they are asked for their attitude on a particular issue, they simply make one up—on the spot! They fear that saying "I don't know" or "I don't care" will make them look uninformed. For example, when late-night host Jimmy Kimmel asked passersby who won a "First Lady/Man" debate between Bill Clinton and Melania Trump, a number of people expressed strong opinions. No such debate ever took place, however (www.youtube.com/watch?v=vG8lVhyWPmI).

A third drawback has to do with *mindfulness*. In order for a person to mark the space on any self-report measure, the person must be aware of what his or her attitude is. Unfortunately, respondents often, quite literally, don't know their own minds. For example, a person could harbor racist, sexist, or homophobic attitudes, without consciously realizing it.

Implicit Measures: What's Rattling Around Inside Your Brain?

To avoid the pitfalls just described, social scientists utilize *implicit measures* of attitudes (Goodall, 2011; Wittenbrink & Schwartz, 2007). Such measures assume that unconscious attitudes can be accessed, thereby reducing conscious bias on the part of respondents (Petty, Fazio, & Briñol, 2009). We discuss these measures next.

Implicit Association Test (IAT)

The best known implicit measure is the *Implicit Association Test* or IAT (Greenwald, McGhee, & Schwartz, 1998). Respondents are asked to press keys on a computer keyboard in a series of rapid-fire word-association tasks. The snap judgments reveal their underlying attitudes. To illustrate, let's say you wanted to find out whether managers harbor negative stereotypes toward employees with disabilities. On the IAT, managers with negative attitudes would be faster at classifying word pairs, such as "disabled/unpleasant" or "able-bodied/happy" compared to word pairs, like "disabled/pleasant" or "able bodied/sad" (Wilson & Scior, 2014). The speed at which respondents press the keys signifies the strength of association for their stereotypes. Variations of the IAT have been developed to measure implicit attitudes toward gender, age, weight, religion, race, disability, and many other topics.

Other Implicit Measures

A variety of other implicit measures have been developed, including the *affect misattribution procedure* or AMP and *evaluative priming* (Fabrigar, Krosnick, & MacDougall, 2005; Fazio & Olson, 2003). We don't have sufficient space to examine them all here. What all these measures have in common, though, is that they tap into attitudes that people may be unable or unwilling to divulge. Not surprisingly, implicit measures do not always produce the same results as explicit measures, prompting some to ask, "So which is the *real* attitude?" (Greenwald, Poehlman, Uhlmann, & Banaji, 2009). The answer is both. For judgments that are made reflexively or impulsively, implicit measures tend to be more reliable. For judgments that are made more thoughtfully or deliberately, explicit measures tend to yield better results.

More Roundabout Ways of Measuring Attitudes

In addition to explicit and implicit measures, a variety of other, less scientific means can be used to infer people's attitudes. These include inferring attitudes from appearances, from associations, and from behavior.

Judging a Book by Its Cover—Appearances

Attitudes may be inferred from appearances. In fact, people do this all the time. Take, for example, the ability to spot homosexuals, known by the slang term *gaydar*. In controlled studies, observers were able to judge the sexual orientation of females and males at greater than chance odds, based on facial cues, posture, gestures, and gait (Rule, Ambady, & Hallett, 2009). As another example, observers correctly guessed which political parties candidates belonged to, based solely on photographs, at a much higher rate than chance would predict (Rule & Ambady, 2010; Rule, Ambady, Adams, & Macrae, 2008).

FIGURE 3.4
It is often possible to infer attitudes from clothing and other artifacts.

Source: Heidi Besen/ Shutterstock.com

The danger of relying on such appearance-based cues, however, is that the person may commit a "sweeping generalization." Not every black teen wearing a hoodie is a thug, nor is every white teen with a shaved head a skinhead.

Birds of a Feather—Associations

"You can tell a person," so the saying goes, "by the company he or she keeps." A person who enjoys hunting, for example, may well belong to the NRA. A cancer survivor might participate in a bike ride for the Livestrong Foundation. It makes sense that people enter careers, join organizations, and establish affiliations with groups of like-minded people. Politicians rely on the fact that people who share similar attitudes tend to form memberships. This enables politicians to curry favor with "voting blocs."

How does all of this relate to persuasion? By knowing that members of unions, professional associations, churches, and other organizations tend to share similar attitudes, politicians can tailor their messages to each group's frame of reference. Marketers use a technique called *segmentation analysis* to target their advertising campaigns to specific groups of consumers, such as soccer moms, NASCAR dads, or Millennials. We focus more on this topic in Chapter 5.

Note that the approach of inferring attitudes based on associations is not without limitations. People may join organizations for all kinds of reasons, some of which have little or nothing to do with the group's avowed purpose. We know of a "fun run," for example, that was created to celebrate health and individuality. We also know someone planning to run it. Why? There's a unicorn medal awarded at the finish line.

You Are What You Do—Behavior

Inferences about other people's attitudes are often based on brief glimpses or "thin slices" of their behavior (Ambady, 2010). A person's overt actions, mannerisms, habits, and nonverbal cues can be used to infer his or her attitudes. If a person participates in a "Resistance March," it's a pretty good indication that he or she holds anti-Trump attitudes. If a person buys season tickets to the philharmonic orchestra, it's a fairly safe bet that he or she likes classical music. Indeed, concealing one's attitudes can be difficult, precisely because one's actions tend to give one away. Actions speak louder than words, as the saying goes.

Of course, inferring attitudes from behavior can be fraught with difficulties. A meta-analysis (Kim & Hunter, 1993) of more than 100 attitude–behavior studies sheds some light on the extent to which attitudes reflect behavior and vice versa. Kim and Hunter found that in many cases, researchers made poor choices about which attitudes to examine in relation to particular behaviors. They found that when the attitude measures employed were *truly relevant to the behaviors in question,* attitude–behavior consistency (ABC) was quite high. Past studies that found weaker ABC may have been looking at the wrong attitudes. The bottom line is that behavior can be extremely revealing of attitudes, but care must be exercised in determining which attitudes are germane to which behaviors. Some ways of improving ABC are identified in Box 3.1.

Physiological Measures of Attitude

Affect or emotion is often accompanied by physiological reactions. To date, however, efforts to identify biological markers of affect have produced "iffy" results (Fabrigar, Krosnick, & MacDougall, 2005; Petty & Cacioppo, 1983). Researchers have studied pupil dilation, which can signify arousal and galvanic skin response (GSR), which measures changes in the electrical conductivity of the skin. The problem with these measures is that they are *bi-directional indicators* of attitude, meaning that they can signal positive *or* negative responses. For example, your heart rate might increase upon seeing someone you like, a positive reaction, or upon seeing someone you dislike, a negative reaction.

Micromomentary facial movements have also been examined as signs of emotion. Such movements are involuntary and last for only a fraction of a second (Porter & ten Brink, 2008). They are, therefore, hard to detect. Furthermore, although microexpressions indicate that an emotion is being suppressed, they don't reveal what emotion or why (Ciolacu, 2014).

More recently, researchers have turned to neuroscience to study attitudes (Cacioppo, Cacioppo, & Petty, 2017). Through the use of techniques such as *functional magnetic resonance imaging* (fMRI), neural activity in different regions of the brain can reveal different reactions to stimuli (Cacioppo, Berntson, & Decety, 2012; Falk, Berman, Mann, Harrison, & Lieberman, 2010; McDermott, 2009). While offering considerable promise as a tool for measuring attitudes, however, fMRI is not there yet (see Jack & Appelbaum, 2010; Tingley, 2006). One neuroimaging study of swing voters, for example, predicted the wrong candidates as the likely winners in the 2008 presidential election (Iacoboni et al., 2007; Mind Games, 2007).

BOX 3.1 | When Do Attitudes Coincide With Behavior?

Just because a moviegoer tends to prefer action-adventure movies over comedies doesn't mean that he or she will always insist on seeing the former instead of the latter. So when can we expect attitudes to coincide with behavior? There tends to be greater attitude–behavior consistency (ABC) when:

1. Stronger as opposed to weaker attitudes are involved. Stronger attitudes are better predictors of behavior. When attitudes are weaker, people may use the reverse approach; they infer their attitudes from their behavior (Holland, Verplanken, & Van Knippenberg, 2002). If a woman's last three boyfriends had long hair, she might decide, "I guess I like shaggy guys."

2. Multiple attitudes aren't confused with single attitudes. A person doesn't have one attitude toward "immigrants," for example. Immigrants from one country might be preferred over those from another country. ABC is greater when a single attitude is measured within a specific situation, place, and time.

3. "Multiple act criteria" are employed. Giving people different opportunities to manifest their attitudes improves the "fit" between attitudes and behavior. One-shot measures aren't as reliable. If you want to assess a person's attitudes toward homeless people, for example, you should examine her or his behavior toward more than one homeless person in more than one setting.

4. The attitudes are based on personal experience. Attitudes formed as a result of direct personal experience tend to correspond more closely with actual behavior. Secondhand attitudes, shaped by the media or based on what others have told us, do not predict behavior as well.

5. Attitudes that are central to the belief system are involved. Attitudes that are central to a person's core beliefs tend to be better predictors of behavior than attitudes that are tangential to the person's belief system. A person's attitudes about "marital fidelity" would be more revealing of his or her behavior in relationships than his or her preferences regarding pineapple on pizza.

6. Attitude certainty is high. The more certain a person is about the correctness of an attitude, the greater the effect on the person's behavior. As Tormala and Rucker (2015) note:

> people who are certain of their beliefs are more likely to buy, buy sooner, and spend more. They're more likely to sign petitions and to vote. They're more willing to express their opinions, endorse products, advocate for causes, and try to persuade others to adopt their views.
>
> (p. 98)

Bear in mind that the more complex the attitudes are, the more difficult the task of reducing them to purely physiological terms. At present, physiological measures appear to be less reliable, and more difficult to administer, than other "low-tech" measures of attitude.

THE REASONED ACTION APPROACH (RAA)

Up to this point, we've seen that attitudes often lead to behaviors. That said, there are other factors involved. To illustrate, consider Martin Fishbein and Icek Ajzen's (2010) *reasoned action approach* (RAA), which views *intention* as the best predictor of behaviour. That is, a person's intention to perform a behavior is the best indicator of whether or not the person will actually carry out the behavior. Keep in mind, however, that intentions don't always correspond with behavior, as anyone who has set an alarm clock for an early wake up, then hit the snooze button, well knows. One way to improve the correspondence between intention and behavior is to be specific about the behavior in question. Thus, rather than asking whether someone intends to exercise more often, you could ask whether he or she intends to walk more often. Better yet, you could ask whether he or she intends to walk at least 20 minutes per day, three days per week, starting next Monday, which is more specific still. Bottom line? The more specific the intention is to a particular behavior, the more accurate your prediction will be.

Behavioral Beliefs and Attitudes: Believe It or Not

Not only that, your accuracy will improve even more if you can figure out what forms a person's intentions. According to the reasoned action approach, three key elements are involved. The first is a person's *behavioral beliefs and attitudes*. Suppose you wanted to convince your friend, Minnie, to wear a helmet when riding her bicycle. You could start by discovering her beliefs and attitudes toward wearing a helmet. Is she aware of specific dangers? Does she believe that helmets can protect her? You may have to convince Minnie that cyclists are at risk and that wearing a helmet is essential to her safety. "I care more about your brain than your hair," you might say. "Besides, if you're a vegetable, you'll have bed head anyway."

Normative Beliefs: It's What the Cool Kids Are Doing

Second, *normative beliefs*, based on what significant others think or do, also shape intentions. Two types of normative beliefs are involved. *Descriptive norms* refer to what people generally or typically do. Does Minnie think helmet wearing is a common practice among her friends, family, or cyclists in general? *Injunctive norms*, on the other hand, refer to what people should or ought to do. Does she face social pressure to wear a helmet, or conversely, social sanctions for wearing one? If Minnie perceives that her friends think helmets are dorky, you may have to convince her otherwise. You might point out that professional cyclists, snowboarders, or BMX riders, look snazzy when sporting a helmet. "Hey," you might say, "Matt Damon, an avid cyclist, always dons a helmet. So do Jake Gyllenhaal and Pink. Daft Punk wear helmets when they aren't even riding!"

Perceived Behavioral Control: I Got This

The third element in forming intentions is *perceived behavioral control*. Behavioral control involves a person's confidence that she or he is capable of performing a given behavior. Wearing a helmet isn't that difficult, but Minnie may need help picking one out and making sure it fits. Some behaviors, like riding 100 miles on a bike, are harder to perform. Minnie might want to do a centennial ride, but she may believe that she is not capable of riding that far. You might have to convince her that she can build up to a longer ride. You could tell her "Try a 20 mile ride. As you build up your stamina, you can go for longer rides. All it takes is willpower."

In combination, these three elements, behavioral and attitudinal beliefs, normative beliefs, and perceived behavior control, shape a person's behavioral intention, which, in turn, guides his or her behavior (see Figure 3.5). The stronger the intention, the more likely a person is to perform a given behavior. A few qualifications to the RAA are worth mentioning. First, past behavior strengthens the intention–behavior correlation. In other words, if a person has already performed a behavior, like donating to a specific charity, it is more likely that she or he will perform it again. Second, *actual control*, not just perceived behavior control, matters too. A person may overestimate or underestimate her or his ability to perform a behavior. Despite the best intentions, for example, not every yoga enthusiast can do an Eka Hasta Vrksasana (one-handed tree pose) or a Pungu Mayurasana (wounded peacock pose). These caveats notwithstanding, the RAA has proven to be reliable and accurate in predicting intentions and behaviors (Fishbein, 2008).

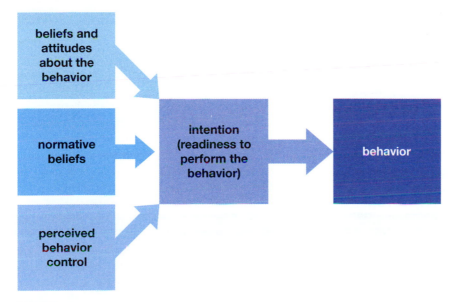

The Reasoned Action Approach

FIGURE 3.5
The reasoned action approach.
Source: Adapted from Fishbein & Ajzen (2010).

THE PERSISTENCE OF ATTITUDES

A final feature of attitudes we wish to address is their persistence. Attitudes are malleable and change over time. They aren't as fleeting as moods or emotions, but neither are they etched in stone. Sometimes a person's attitude will change in response to a single, brief exposure to a persuasive message. Sometimes a person's attitude will endure for years. What makes some attitudes so durable and others so transitory?

Petty and Cacioppo's (1986a, 1986b) *elaboration likelihood model* (ELM), discussed in the previous chapter, provides a useful answer to this question. Attitudes formed via central processing—for example, those involving thought and deliberation—are more persistent and resistant to change than attitudes formed via peripheral processing, which rely on mental shortcuts (Petty, Cacioppo, Strathman, & Priester, 2005). The reason is because actively thinking about an issue seems to "plant" the attitude more firmly. Because peripheral processing requires little mental effort, attitudes formed as a result of peripheral processing tend to be more short-lived.[2]

What does this mean for you as a persuader? If you want a message to have a lasting effect on receivers' attitudes, you should design and deliver it in such a way as to promote central processing (i.e., active thinking). How can you encourage central processing? Increasing receivers' involvement is one way of promoting central processing. Explaining why a topic or issue is relevant to receivers and how it affects them personally will increase their *motivation* to use central processing. Adapting your message to the receivers' levels of understanding will increase their *ability* to engage in central processing. In short, if you can get your listeners to actively think about your message, you are more likely to change their attitudes for the long term, not just the short term.

ATTITUDES AS ASSOCIATE NETWORKS: YOUR MIND IS A WEB

Our attitudes are interrelated. In some ways, our attitudes, beliefs, and values can be likened to a spider's web. Like the fine silky threads of a spider's web, they are connected to one another in a delicate balance. Attitudes, therefore, exist in elaborate *associative networks* (Tesser & Shaffer, 1990). An individual may or may not be consciously aware of all these connections. To a large extent, these associative networks operate implicitly—that is, without the individual's conscious awareness. A change in one attitude affects other attitudes, beliefs, opinions, and values. Like jiggling a spider's web, a vibration in one attitude can trigger reverberations in other cognitive structures. These mental reverberations may be quite minor, or they can be of major consequence to the individual.

MANUFACTURING FAVORABLE ASSOCIATIONS: JIGGLING THE WEB

Why would anyone buy automobile insurance from a company whose spokesperson is an animated gecko with an Aussie accent? Or, for that matter, why would anyone buy a laundry detergent because its logo is emblazoned on a race car? The associative networks in which attitudes exist are critical to such influence attempts. Persuaders actively seek to create connections among these networks. They want to link their messages with favorable attitudes and avoid associations with unfavorable attitudes.

Brands and Branding: That's the Life

A clear case of manufacturing favorable associations can be found in *branding*. The point of branding is to create a distinctive product image that is linked to favorable qualities. These may be tangible or intangible in nature. Different brands conjure up different images in the minds of consumers. Walmart's appeal is based on value or low prices. Nordstrom's appeal is based on quality and customer service.

Let's examine how these associations are created. Consider the energy drink Red Bull. When you think of Red Bull, what associations come to mind? Do you think of speed, danger, or risk taking? One study (Brasel & Gips, 2011) found that consumers used descriptors such as *hyper*, *speed*, *extreme*, and *dangerous* in relation to the energy drink. A look at the kinds of events Red Bull sponsors helps explain why. Red Bull sponsors "extreme" sports, such as adventure racing, mountain biking, cliff diving, and other "gravity" sports. If downhill "street luging" is your thing, you might want to down a Red Bull beforehand. Thanks to branding, the drink "goes with" the sport.

As another illustration, consider beer commercials. The spots almost always depict people, usually males, in pairs or groups (never drinking alone) socializing and having a good time. What is the image or association the ads are projecting? *Beer = fun.* It's a simple formula. Drinking beer is equated with good times and camaraderie. So strong is the association that some people might find it hard to imagine a Super Bowl Sunday

FIGURE 3.6
Source: BIZARRO © by Dan Piraro. Reprinted with permission. Universal Press Syndicate. All Rights Reserved.

party, St. Patrick's Day gathering, *Cinco de Mayo* celebration, Labor Day shindig, or Fourth of July revelry that didn't include beer. No suds, no buds.

Who Are You Wearing? Brand Personality

Some brands have their own personality. They are imbued with human qualities with which consumers identify. Brands may be perceived as honest, fun, exciting, cool, sophisticated, sexy, or nerdy. Aaker (1997) developed the brand personality scale, which rates brands on the basis of characteristics such as perceived sincerity, excitement, competence, sophistication, and ruggedness. What's more, a brand's personality tends to "rub off" on consumers (Park & John, 2010). After shopping at Victoria's Secret, for example, females might see themselves as more attractive, sexy, or glamorous.

Modern branding includes cultivating *brand relationships*. Some consumers may regard a brand as they would a best friend (Fournier, 1998), while others may view brands as extensions of themselves (Belk, 1998). As Halloran (2014) observes, "we don't just consume or interact with brands. We engage in relationships with them. With some brands, we have wild, short-term flings. Others stay with us for a lifetime" (p. 3). Brands also serve as vehicles for self-expression (Swaminathan, Stilley, & Ahluwalia, 2009). Some consumers go so far as to get brands tattooed on their bodies (Orend & Gagné, 2009).

Branding occurs in other ways. *Aspirational brands* are those that consumers admire and aspire to own one day. They represent the ideal. Rolex watches, Viking stoves, and Gucci handbags fall into this category. The Martha Stewart brand is aspirational. Few women will actually make the complicated recipes featured in her magazine, but they like to think that they could. Aspirational brands may be so expensive that consumers settle for knock-off versions instead.

Authenticity: Keeping It Real

Another approach is brand *authenticity*, which emphasizes genuineness, integrity, and down-to-earth values. The website Etsy is devoted to such goods. Authentic brands may be hand crafted, like craft beers and artisanal cheeses. They may be ecofriendly, like "farm-to-table" restaurants and boutique bicycles. They often have a story to tell. They emphasize the values of the person or company behind the brand. Ben & Jerry's ice cream is a case in point. Authentic brands may try to build a community around the brand. Dove's "real beauty" campaign exemplifies this theme.

Cause-Related Marketing: The Feel-Good Factor

Many consumers want to make the world a better place. Corporations want to sell things. So why not align consumers' purchases with doing good deeds? *Cause-related marketing* (CRM) makes consumers feel good about themselves by feeling good about their purchases. They aren't just shopping. They are contributing to the greater good. The expression "think globally, shop locally" reflects this trend.

Suppose you are a conscientious consumer seeking an upscale cup of coffee. Why not buy a Fair Trade cup of joe? It comes with a psychological pat on the back for doing a good deed. TOMS Shoes, Product (RED), the Livestrong brand, and the Susan G. Komen Foundation's pink ribbon products employ this strategy.

Cause-related marketing is part of a larger trend toward *corporate social responsibility* (CSR). Corporations want to be seen as good citizens, giving back to communities, and engaging in philanthropy. Although "shopping as philanthropy" (Einstein, 2012) may seem like a win–win–win for the consumer, the company, and the charity, there is a downside as well. A concept called *moral licensing* suggests that if a person buys a cause-related product, she or he may be less likely to make an actual donation to that cause (Krishna, 2011a, 2011b). "I've already done a good deed" the person reasons. Yet the amount that actually goes to the charity may be a few cents on the dollar. Sending even one dollar directly to the charity might do far more good.

Sloganeering

Another means of fostering favorable associations is through *sloganeering*. The importance of slogans in persuasion is underscored by Sharkansky (2002), who observes, "politics would be poorer without them, advertising could not exist, and religion would be in trouble" (p. 75). Consider the following advertising taglines. Notice the positive associations they are designed to instill with respect to each product.

"When you're here, you're family." (Olive Garden)

"Breakfast of champions." (Wheaties)

"Like a good neighbor, State Farm is there." (State Farm)

"We'll leave the light on for you." (Motel 6)

"Because you're worth it" (L'Oréal)

The slogans imbue the products with positive qualities that, over time, become embedded in receivers' minds. If you feel like "eatin' good in the neighborhood," where would you go for dinner?

Sponsorship

Another way of linking products and services with favorable attitudes is through *sponsorship*. Earlier, we mentioned Red Bull's sponsorship of extreme, gravity sports. Most major sporting events now have corporate sponsors who provide funding in return for the right to associate their products with the event. Almost every stadium and ballpark in America now has a corporate sponsor.

Naturally, advertisers aren't the only ones who try to tie themselves to favorable associations. When candidates for political office kiss babies, eat home cooking, and stand next to the flag, they are trying to link themselves to positive, patriotic values. Negative political campaigning, or "mudslinging," serves the same purpose in reverse: A candidate seeks to link his or her opponent with negative associations.

A major tenet of persuasion thus involves establishing favorable connections between attitudes and attitude objects. Persuaders try to establish these connections by selling an image or lifestyle. When you buy a product, you are buying into the image as well (Fournier, 1998). But do you really need to have a relationship with your credit card ("My card, my city" [American Express])? Do you really want brands to define you ("Do you speak Prada?")? Sometimes it is important to break the connections that advertisers are trying to create.

PSYCHOLOGICAL CONSISTENCY

People strive to be consistent. This simple principle forms the basis for a whole host of theories, variously known as "cognitive consistency" theories (Festinger, 1957; Heider, 1958; Osgood & Tannenbaum, 1955). Consistency was originally conceived of as a "drive-reduction" theory. More current thinking suggests that consistency is also socially motivated and is as much an attempt to manage face and project a favorable self-image as it is an internal drive (Greenwald & Ronis, 1978; Matz & Wood, 2005; Scher & Cooper, 1989). Although the individual theories differ somewhat in their approaches, we've integrated the tenets of several theories here in order to present a more coherent perspective. Though this principle is fairly basic, the recognition that most people strive to remain consistent in their thoughts, words, and deeds reveals a good deal about processes of social influence.

The Inner Peace of Consistency

When harmony exists among our attitudes, beliefs, values, and behavior, life is ducky. When there are inconsistencies in what we think, say, or do, however, we tend to experience psychological discomfort. A classic example is that, for smokers, the knowledge that they smoke and that smoking causes cancer is psychologically uncomfortable. Another example involves children whose parents are undergoing a divorce or separation. The children often experience psychological conflict because they can't understand why two people, whom they love, don't want to remain married.

The amount of psychological discomfort that results from holding incompatible attitudes is not the same in all situations. The degree of discomfort depends on the *centrality* of the attitudes involved. If the issue is relatively minor (for example, a person prefers plastic grocery bags but knows paper bags are better for the environment), the amount of psychological discomfort will be small. If the issue is major, as when attitudes involve core beliefs or values, then the psychological consequences can be enormous (for example, the mother of a teenage girl is fervently pro-life but learns that her daughter has just had an abortion).

To understand the nature and effects of psychological consistency, attitude theorists have developed a means of graphically depicting compatible and incompatible attitude states. For example, suppose that Muffin thinks of herself as a firm believer in animal rights. However, while out shopping, she finds a leather jacket that looks "totally cool." Her attitudes toward animal rights and owning the jacket are in conflict. Her psychological dilemma is depicted in Figure 3.7.

According to consistency theory, Muffin will experience psychological stress no matter what decision she makes. If she buys the jacket, she'll sacrifice her principles; if she doesn't buy the jacket, she'll forgo an opportunity to look cool. Muffin's case is not unique. We are all confronted with dilemmas involving our attitudes, beliefs, and behaviors on a daily basis. Because psychological inconsistency is unpleasant we are motivated to avoid it, deny it, reduce it, or eliminate it when it occurs.

Methods of Maintaining Consistency

How do people go about reconciling incompatible attitudes when they occur? People don't necessarily preserve or restore psychological consistency in logical ways. They do so in psychological ways—that is, ways they find psychologically satisfying or comfortable but that may or may not be strictly logical. Using the example of Muffin, scholars suggest a number of possible routes for resolving inconsistency:

1. *Denial:* Denying or ignoring any inconsistency. "I really don't like that jacket after all" or "I don't really need a jacket now."
2. *Bolstering:* Rationalizing or making excuses. "That cow is already dead, so what difference can it make?" or "Sooner or later someone will come along and buy that jacket anyway."
3. *Bargaining:* Striving to reach a compromise between the conflicting attitudes. "I'll buy the jacket and volunteer to work at an animal shelter."
4. *Differentiation:* Separating or distinguishing the attitudes in conflict. "The jacket is cowhide. Cows aren't an endangered species. It's not as if I'm buying a jacket made from a baby harp seal or a spotted owl."
5. *Transcendence:* Focusing on a larger or higher level. "No one is perfect. We all give in to temptation every once in a while."
6. *Modifying one or both attitudes:* Altering the attitudes themselves to become more consistent. "I need to be more practical and keep my concern for animals' rights in perspective."

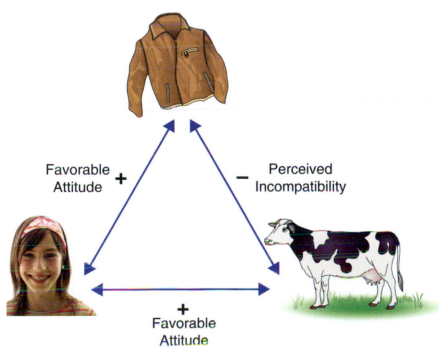

FIGURE 3.7
Muffin's dilemma: an illustration of consistency theory.

7. *Communicating:* Trying to convince others to change or convince others one did the right thing. "I'll just have to convince my friends that I'm not a hypocrite when they see me in my new jacket."

Of course, these are only some of the ways people go about maintaining consistency. In trying to gauge which approach a person will use, a good rule of thumb is that people follow an *efficiency principle*; they tend to reduce dissonance in the most efficient way possible—that is, they tend to follow the path of least resistance in finding a way to restore consistency. Changing an inconsequential attitude to restore consistency, for example, is much more likely than changing a core attitude.

Marketing Strategies: How to Have Your Cake and Eat It Too

Now that you understand the basic nature of consistency theories, let's look at how neatly consistency theories apply to persuasion. Imagine that you are at the supermarket. You have a craving for ice cream, but you're on a diet. No problem. You can buy a "light" brand with reduced fat and fewer calories. In fact, thanks to modern technology, you can choose from a veritable array of frozen desserts including ice milk, frozen yogurt, diabetic ice cream, fruit sorbet, or a nonfat, nondairy product. Think how many other products at the grocery store rely on the principle of "having your cake and eating it too." There are "light," "fat free," "cholesterol free," "high fiber," "low sodium," "calcium enriched," and "natural" food products on every shelf. The marketing strategy behind such products is to allow consumers to make food purchases that are consistent with their beliefs regarding health and nutrition.

Brand Loyalty: Accept No Substitute

The concept of *brand loyalty* offers another useful illustration of psychological consistency. Advertisers want us to experience psychological discomfort if we change brands. By instilling brand loyalty in us, advertisers hope to discourage product switching. We are trained by Madison Avenue to remain faithful to one motor oil, be true to one long-distance provider, stay devoted to one pain reliever, or cherish a particular make of car. Consider the following slogans:

"Don't leave home without it." (American Express)

"Like nothing else." (Hummer)

"Only in a Jeep." (Jeep)

"The best, or nothing." (Mercedes)

"When you care enough to send the very best." (Hallmark cards)

All of these slogans are designed to foster brand loyalty on the part of the consumer and feelings of psychological inconsistency if consumers betray their usual brands.

Write and Tell Us Why You Love This Book in 24 Words or Less

Yet another means of reinforcing brand loyalty is through active participation on the part of the consumer. Viewers can text in their votes on a variety of reality shows. Sometimes a prize is offered for calling a radio station or writing an essay about a product. Win or lose, the mere act of calling, writing, or texting is bound to increase one's allegiance. Active participation increases commitment.

Brand loyalty can also be encouraged through merchandising. People who wear branded clothing (a Cubs jersey, a Pink hoodie, a Fender T-shirt) are paying for the right to serve as walking billboards—and engaging in self-persuasion to boot.

An example of how consumers succumb to merchandising pressure involves one of this book's ever-gullible authors. He liked the Indian maiden logo on Land O'Lakes butter. So when he learned he could order two Land O'Lakes mugs for only $7.95, plus three proof-of-purchase seals from any Land O'Lakes product, he couldn't resist. He switched from margarine to butter. He bought only Land O'Lakes butter for the next three months (the amount of time it took to accumulate three proof-of-purchase seals). When he found he'd lost one of the proof-of-purchase seals he was despondent. Did he give up? Nay, nay! He went out and bought another package of Land O'Lakes butter *he didn't even need,* just to complete the trio of proof-of-purchase seals. The author is now the proud owner of a pair of Land O'Lakes mugs, complete with Indian maiden logo, but let's examine what can be learned from this lesson:

- The merchandising offer got the author actively involved in the process of reinforcing his own brand loyalty. Because the mugs themselves cost little to manufacture, the author was paying Land O'Lakes for the privilege of becoming a loyal consumer.
- The merchandising offer secured the author's brand loyalty for a period of 3–4 months. In fact, the author still buys the Land O'Lakes brand whenever he purchases butter (after all, he has the mugs to remind him where his loyalty lies).

"Remember, the enemy of your enemy is your friend."

FIGURE 3.8
Source: © Leo Cullum/
The New Yorker. Collection/
www.cartoonbank.com.
All Rights Reserved.

- The author bought and used far more butter than he otherwise would have without the mug offer. In fact, as he was closing in on that elusive third proof-of-purchase seal, he was searching high and low for ways to use butter.

Admittedly, the author got a little carried away, but that's the beauty of brand loyalty. We don't necessarily think or act rationally when our allegiance to a particular brand takes over.

Marketing Inconsistency

Of course, other advertising campaigns, typically those for newer products or products with a smaller market share, use just the opposite strategy. These ads encourage us to switch brands. They realize that consumers can be set in their ways. These advertisers try to create psychological imbalance. They want us to have second thoughts about the products and services on which we've been relying unquestioningly year after year. Consider the following advertising slogans:

"Think different." (Macintosh computers)

"Think outside the bun." (Taco Bell)

"Switch and play." (Nintendo)

"I could have had a V8!" (V8 vegetable juice)

Such slogans are based on the recognition that consumers can be set in their ways and seek to overcome this inertia by encouraging brand switching. Many other types of advertising campaigns are based on creating a state of psychological inconsistency.

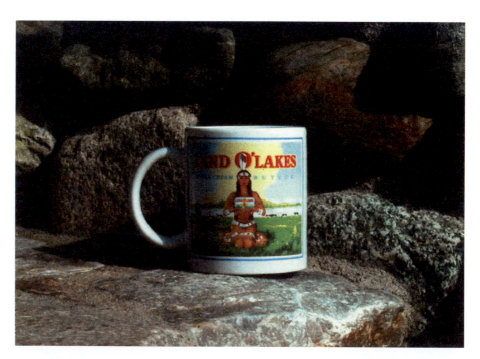

FIGURE 3.9
Merchandising can increase consumer commitment.
Source: Photo by Robert Gass.

Capitalizing on Inconsistency

The use of consistency theory isn't only for advertisers, marketers, and other "professional" persuaders. You, too, can incorporate the principles of consistency theory in your own persuasive messages. One way you can accomplish this is to align your message with your audience's frame of reference. It is much easier to tailor a suit to fit a person than it is to change a person's figure to fit a suit. Similarly, successful persuasion isn't so much a matter of shifting receivers' attitudes over to your position as it is a matter of adapting your message to the attitudes of your audience. A child who suggests to her mother, "Let's play hooky and go to the zoo today. Zoos are very educational!" is adapting her message to the mother's value system. Such adaptation is key to persuasion, which is why we discuss this strategy in more detail in Chapter 5.

Another way you can apply principles of consistency theory is to highlight potential inconsistencies in receivers' attitudes. If you can demonstrate that some of the attitudes held by your receivers are incompatible, you may motivate them to change their attitudes in the direction you are advocating. Be cautious, however, when employing this strategy. If you attempt to drive too big a psychological wedge between your receivers' attitudes, they may simply change their attitudes and come to dislike you.

COGNITIVE DISSONANCE THEORY (CDT)

Suppose you are a fan of Apple products. You are also aware that Chinese workers who assemble them work in deplorable conditions. Would you throw away your iPod, iPhone, or iPad? If you think of yourself as an honest person, would it bother you to download music illegally, or would you find a way to justify your piracy and disregard for copyright laws? People often hold contradictory positions on issues. Their talk doesn't match their walk. For example, many voters say they are opposed to "Big Government" and federal handouts, even though they are receiving government assistance. According to a nationwide survey (Mettler, 2011), 44 percent of Social Security recipients and 40 percent of Medicare recipients reported they did not receive any government assistance!

How can people hold such seemingly contradictory views? Why do they engage in what appears to be hypocritical behavior? Leon Festinger's *cognitive dissonance theory* (CDT) does a nice job of explaining how people rationalize contradictory decisions and behaviors in their own minds and to other people (Cooper, 2007; Festinger, 1957, 1964; Festinger & Carlsmith, 2007; Harmon-Jones & Harmon-Jones, 2008). The basic idea is that after making a decision or performing a behavior, a person worries about whether she or he made the right decision or did the right thing. The person is therefore motivated to reduce the resulting dissonance. For this reason, CDT is often referred to as a "post-decision theory." The anticipation of having to make a tough choice, however, also can produce dissonance. People sometimes say it "hurts" or it's "painful" to make a difficult decision. In fact, researchers found that taking acetaminophen reduced the pain of decision making (DeWall, Chester, & White, 2015). The researchers concluded that "the pain of decision making is not a mere metaphor" (p. 119). Cognitive dissonance, it turns out, involves some of the same neural pathways associated with physical pain.

Aside from popping Tylenol, how else can people reduce cognitive dissonance? An intriguing aspect of CDT is the variety of ways in which people try to reconcile their angst. For example, they may employ a "sour grapes" strategy. Like the fox in Aesop's fable who tried repeatedly but failed to reach some grapes, they conclude, "They were probably sour anyway."

Cognitive Dissonance and Buyer's Remorse

The theory of cognitive dissonance is closely connected to the phenomenon known as *buyer's remorse.* Imagine that a consumer shelled out a lot of money for a big, flat-screen TV, only to find out a few weeks later that a newer, better model was available for less money. To assuage their lingering doubts, buyers engage in dissonance-reduction strategies. One method, known as *selective exposure,* involves seeking out consonant information and avoiding dissonant information. The TV buyer might reread ads and articles recommending the brand he or she purchased and avoid ads and articles for other brands. Cognitive dissonance isn't an all-or-nothing phenomenon. It occurs in varying degrees. The amount of dissonance one experiences is known as the *magnitude of dissonance.* Spending $8,000 on a plasma TV that wasn't very reliable would produce more dissonance than spending $8 on a movie that wasn't very good.

Polarization of Alternatives

When making a tough decision, a person tends to *polarize* the attractiveness of the alternatives once the decision is made. Suppose Lola has to decide between an iPhone and an Android. It is a close call. Each model has its pros and cons. Once Lola makes her choice, she will tend to disparage the unchosen brand and value the chosen brand even more. What was formerly a tough choice becomes a "no brainer." The tendency to spread the alternatives is a form of self-justification (Tavris & Aronson, 2007). It is easier to see choices in terms of "black and white" than shades of gray. This explains why voters who are initially torn between two candidates solidify their preference once they cast their ballot (Besley & Joslyn, 2001).

Cognitive Dissonance, Self-Image, and Culture

Cognitive dissonance can be largely internal in nature, such as when a person is confronted with a moral dilemma. Dissonance also can arise when one's self-image is inconsistent with one's beliefs, attitudes, or behaviors. For instance, a person who thinks of himself or herself as unprejudiced but who laughs at a racist, sexist, or homophobic joke might experience cognitive dissonance. There is a cultural component to dissonance as well. For Americans and others from individualistic cultures, dissonance tends to be more internally motivated, while for Asians and others from more collectivistic cultures, dissonance tends to be more socially motivated (Hoshino-Browne, Zanna, Spencer, Zanna, Kitayama, & Lackenbauer, 2005; Kitayama et al., 2004). While some studies suggest that Asians have a greater tolerance for inconsistency (Aaker & Sengupta, 2000; Nisbett, 2003), others suggest just the opposite (Xie, Jang, & Cai, 2007). There is also evidence that dissonance is a culturally universal phenomenon (Egan, Santos, & Bloom, 2007).

Factors That Affect the Magnitude of Dissonance

Four paradigms that moderate cognitive dissonance have been studied by researchers (Beauvois & Joule, 1999; Harmon-Jones & Mills, 1999). One of these, known as the *free choice paradigm,* states that the greater the choice one has in making a decision, the more dissonance one will suffer. Cooper (2007) emphasizes that dissonance occurs *only* if the negative outcome of a freely chosen decision was foreseeable at the time the person made the choice. Otherwise the person can say, "How was I to know?" A second paradigm, known as *belief disconfirmation,* argues that dissonance is aroused when a person encounters information contrary to his or her beliefs. The person engages in denial and resorts to *selective exposure* by ignoring or distorting information that contradicts his or her belief system. A third paradigm is called *induced compliance.* When a person is forced to do something, little dissonance is aroused because the person can rationalize the action by saying "I had no choice." The fourth paradigm, called the *effort justification paradigm,* centers on the amount of effort or sacrifice required: the greater the effort, the greater the dissonance.

Dissonance and Persuasion: Putting It All Together

Persuasive messages can be tailored to either increase or decrease dissonance in receivers. A persuader might want to arouse dissonance in a target audience to get people to rethink their position on an issue. Or, conversely, a persuader might seek to allay people's doubts by reassuring them that their decision or action was justified. In this case, the persuader would want to convince receivers that they did the right thing and they had no other realistic alternative. Recent research shows that attitude change brought about by CDT can have lasting effects (Sénémeaud & Somat, 2009).

FORBIDDEN FRUIT: PSYCHOLOGICAL REACTANCE

In 2003, Barbra Streisand filed a lawsuit against a photographer for taking aerial photos along California's coastline, including her Malibu home, and posting them on the Web. Prior to the lawsuit, few people had bothered to look at the photos. After the publicity surrounding the lawsuit, however, people flocked to the website in droves (Arthur, 2009). Half a million viewers logged on to see what the fuss was about. A judge subsequently dismissed the suit. Similarly, when the MPAA filed a lawsuit against The Pirate Bay for facilitating illegal downloading of movies, the website became more popular than ever (Sullivan, 2009). Attempts to muzzle information on the Web often backfire, a phenomenon Mike Masnick termed the *Streisand effect* (2005).

When people believe that their freedom is being threatened, they tend to rebel. Tell a little kid not to play with a particular toy and the kid won't be able to keep his grubby little hands off it. Tell your teenage daughter that you disapprove of her new boyfriend and she'll like him even more. The tendency to react defensively to perceived encroachments on our freedom is called *psychological reactance* (Brehm, 1966; Brehm & Brehm, 1981). You may also know of it as "reverse psychology."

Psychological reactance can help or hinder persuasion. Suppose a mother wants to get her picky 3-year-old to eat her broccoli. The mother could use a controlling message such as, "You are going to sit there until you finish your broccoli." This approach might backfire, however, if the daughter is willing to sit and pout for an hour. Instead, the mother could use psychological reactance to her advantage by saying, "Mabel, there is no way you can eat that broccoli in less than a minute. No way." Now the daughter may want to prove she's up to the challenge.

A wealth of studies on littering behavior reveal that a negative or punitive message ("No littering!" or "Don't you dare litter.") actually *increases* littering compared to a polite message ("Please pitch in.") (Hansmann & Sholz, 2003; Horsley, 1988; Huffman, Grossnickle, Cope, & Huffman, 1995). Stated simply, asking is a more effective strategy than ordering. Psychological reactance also has been examined on a variety of other topics, including alcohol consumption (Dillard & Shen, 2005), condom use (Quick & Stephenson, 2007), drug use (Burgoon et al., 2002), promotional health messages (Miller, Lane, Deatrick, Young, & Potts, 2007), and smoking (Miller, Burgoon, Grandpre, & Alvaro, 2006). The tendency to react negatively to perceived threats varies from person to person. These individual differences can be measured with the *psychological reactance scale* (Hong, 1992; Hong & Faedda, 1996).

To avoid a boomerang effect, a persuader should be cautious about using controlling language. A politician who says "You must vote for this proposition. It is the only way" is practically daring voters to reject the measure. To use psychological reactance to his or her advantage, a persuader should acknowledge listeners' personal autonomy. A politician who says "I favor this measure, but you'll have to make up your own minds" is less likely to provoke resistance. A persuader also can use psychological reactance against an opponent. For example, a candidate might argue "My opponent wants to limit your health care options, but I want you to be able to choose your own health care provider." We return to the subject of psychological reactance in Chapter 8 when we discuss the *scarcity principle*, and in Chapter 11 when we discuss the *evoking freedom technique*.

COUNTERATTITUDINAL ADVOCACY: PLAYING DEVIL'S ADVOCATE

An even better approach to changing people's attitudes is to get them to persuade themselves. This can be accomplished by having them engage in what is called *counterattitudinal advocacy* (CAA). CAA involves having people create and present (orally or in writing) a message that is at odds with their existing attitudes—for example, claiming they favor capital punishment when, in fact, they oppose it. Research demonstrates that after engaging in CAA, people's attitudes will tend to shift in the direction of the position advocated (Festinger, 1957; Kelman, 1953; Preiss & Allen, 1998; Sénémeaud & Somat, 2009). Mind you, their attitudes won't undergo a complete reversal. Some degree of attitude change takes place, such that the initially counterattitudinal position becomes somewhat more favorable in the people's minds.

The explanation is that CAA causes psychological conflict within people. They are aware of the inconsistency between their privately held beliefs and attitudes, and their public behavior. One means of resolving the conflict is to make their private beliefs and attitudes more consistent with their public behavior—hence, the resultant shift in attitudes. This suggests an effective way of getting other people to persuade themselves. Simply try to get them to speak or act in a manner that is contrary to their attitudes. This can be accomplished by asking them to role-play for a few minutes, or to play devil's advocate for a while. The research demonstrates that attitude change should follow in the direction of the counterattitudinal position. When using this technique, however, it is important that the other people *choose* to engage in CAA, as opposed to being forced to do so. A meta-analysis by Preiss and Allen (1998) revealed that voluntarily engaging in CAA is the key to this strategy's effectiveness.

I'M ALL IN: INCREASING COMMITMENT

Commitment goes hand in hand with persuasion. When people become committed to ideas, groups, causes, or decisions they find it difficult to change their minds. By way of example, did you know that once horse-racing fans have bet on a horse, they become even more convinced their horse will win (Knox & Inkster, 1968)? Individuals who volunteer their time to work for political campaigns tend to overestimate the prospects of their candidate winning. The more public the nature of the commitment, the more psychologically entrenched people become.

Many social customs and rituals are designed to increase a person's sense of psychological commitment to an idea, group, cause, or decision. Wedding engagements do so. Fraternity initiation rituals do so as well. Boot camp in the military serves this purpose. Baptism achieves this goal. This also explains why people often announce their New Year's resolutions publicly. Doing so binds them all the more to their commitments. Political rallies, protest marches, and demonstrations accomplish this function for the participants. Whenever we make public statements or engage in public actions, we tend to become bound by our words or deeds. Yes, we can renege on what we've said or done, but we will pay a psychological price for doing so. The greater the public commitment, the greater the toll paid.

Commitments Can "Grow Legs"

In the movie *Tin Cup* (1996), Roy McAvoy is a gifted golfer who makes his own bad luck. In a heroic comeback bid, he finds himself in contention to win the U.S. Open. He refuses to play it safe, however. On an over-water approach shot to the 18th hole, he goes for the flag. The ball lands in the water. Rather than cut his losses, he takes the same shot again and again, each time with the same result. On his 12th try, and down to his last ball, he finally clears the water and the ball rolls in the cup. He loses the tournament, but proves something to himself. Let's face it, we all behave a bit like Roy from time to time. Robert Cialdini (1993) makes the interesting point that commitments sometimes "grow legs." By this he means that once we become committed to a given course of action, we tend to remain steadfast in our determination, even if the reason for selecting that course of action is diminished, altered, or eliminated.

Getting Carried Away

A story involving one of the authors illustrates this phenomenon. The author wanted to build a retaining wall in his backyard. He was planning on spending $1,000. Once he got several bids for the job, he discovered it would cost $3,000 to $4,000 for a stone wall rather than a block wall. He signed a contract with the lowest bidder for a $3,000 retaining wall made of river rock. A few days before the work was to begin, the author had another idea. As long as he was going to all the trouble and expense, why not build in a recessed bench for reading? And, his wife added, why not add some steps, so it would be easy to get up and down? The $3,000 wall soon became a $4,000 wall.

But it didn't end there. Once the wall was completed, the author sprang for sprinklers and landscaping. After all, the wall looked so good, it was worth a little extra to make it a focal point of the backyard. In the end, the $1,000 wall became a $4,500 wall. Once the author got started, his commitment to build the rock wall of his dreams grew legs. He loves the wall, of course. He has to. It cost him a bundle.

Throwing Good Money After Bad

We all engage in similar behavior from time to time. The owner of an unreliable car keeps spending money on repairs, hoping this brake job or that muffler repair will finally be the last. The repair bills keep mounting, until they may eventually exceed the car's resale value. Does the owner throw in the towel? Nope. The owner becomes even more resolute the next time something breaks. "I've already poured two grand into that car. I can't give up now." A gambler bets on a football team that loses. The next week, he doubles the bet, feeling confident that he will win the next time around. He loses again. Does he wise up and cut his losses? No way. He becomes more determined than ever that the team will win. His resolve actually increases with each loss.

Once we've invested our time and energy or poured our hearts and souls into a cause, a person, an idea, a project, or a group we find it difficult to let go. We may have second thoughts, but we repress them. We build up layers of rationalizations for remaining true to our original convictions.

Keep in mind, a large initial commitment isn't required in order for persuaders to take advantage of us. Even relatively simple acts, such as raising your hand, signing a petition, or filling out a form, can be enough. The fact that commitments can grow legs means that we are vulnerable to self-persuasion as well. Remember, we manufacture the additional reasons for bolstering our commitment ourselves. Once we become committed, we may become blind to alternative ways of seeing, thinking, or acting. Thus, we need to remain on guard, not only from others seeking to extract commitments from us but also from ourselves.

Before concluding this section, we wish to note that several worthwhile lessons can be learned from our discussion of commitment and consistency. First, don't allow persuaders to "box you in" by getting you to commit to something when you really don't want to. Feel free to say, "I want to think it over" or "I want to consider some other options first" or "You're not trying to rush me into a hasty decision, are you?" Second, don't paint yourself into a corner by making public commitments you really don't want, or intend, to keep. Be willing to say, "Sorry, I'd rather not" or "I have to say 'No' this time." Third, if you do happen to make an ill-advised commitment, admit it and see what you can do to correct it. Don't double-down on a bad decision. Avoid becoming so preoccupied with saving face that you follow through on a really bad idea. When buying anything, ask about a return or refund policy in advance.

SUMMARY

The concept of *attitude* is central to the study of persuasion. Attitudes can't be directly observed. They can, however, be inferred and measured through a variety of explicit and implicit means, most commonly via standardized scales. The theory of reasoned action provides a useful, rational model of how attitudes and intentions guide behavior. People's attitudes tend to correlate with their behavior, more so when the attitudes are formed via central processing than peripheral processing. Attitudes formed via central processing are also more persistent and resistant to change. We discussed the fact that attitudes exist in associative networks, and that advertisers use these connections to foster favorable images and associations with their products and services. People have a tendency to strive for consistency among their attitudes, beliefs, and behaviors. Persuaders can adapt their messages either to reinforce consistency or to create inconsistency. Cognitive dissonance, a specialized form of consistency theory, explains how people go about rationalizing decisions after they have made them. The phenomenon of psychological reactance can be used to a persuader's advantage. Engaging in counterattitudinal advocacy or making commitments, especially public commitments, are two important means of facilitating influence, based on the theory of cognitive dissonance.

NOTES

1. The implicit–explicit distinction is not a hard-and-fast distinction. Some explicit attitudes may be activated in a nearly automatic, spontaneous manner. Some implicit attitudes may not be beyond a person's conscious awareness.
2. This explanation is highly consistent with findings based on *inoculation theory*, which we discuss in Chapter 9. Inoculating receivers against opposing arguments (e.g., giving them a small dose of the arguments they are likely to hear, along with answers to those arguments) requires that they actively think about message content. This increased mental effort makes them more resistant to opposing arguments presented at a later date.

REFERENCES

Aaker, J. L. (1997). Dimensions of brand personality. *Journal of Marketing Research*, *34*(3), 347–356.

Aaker, J. L., & Sengupta, J. (2000). Additivity versus attenuation: The role of culture in the resolution of information incongruity. *Journal of Consumer Psychology*, *9*, 67–82.

Ambady, N. (2010). The perils of pondering: Intuition and thin slice judgments. *Psychological Inquiry*, *21*, 271–278. doi:10.1080/1047840X.2010.524882

Argyriou, E., & Melewar, T. C. (2011). Consumer attitudes revisited: A review of attitude theory in marketing research. *International Journal of Management Reviews*, *13*, 431–451. doi:10.1111/j.1468-2370.2011.00299.x

Arthur, C. (2009, March 19). The Streisand effect: Secrecy in the digital age. *The Guardian*, p. 6.

Beauvois, J. L., & Joule, R. V. (1999). A radical point of view on dissonance theory. In E. Harmon-Jones & J. Mills (Eds.), *Cognitive dissonance: Progress on a pivotal theory in social psychology* (pp. 43–70). Washington, DC: American Psychological Association.

Belk, R. W. (1988). Possessions and the extended self. *Journal of Consumer Research*, *2*(2), 139–168.

Besley, R., & Joslyn, M. (2001). Cognitive dissonance and post-decision attitude change in six presidential elections. *Political Psychology*, *22*, 521–540.

Brasel, S. A., & Gips, J. (2011). Red Bull "give you wings" for better or worse: A double-edged impact of brand exposure on consumer preference. *Journal of Consumer Psychology*, *21*, 57–64. doi:10.1016/j.jcps.2010.09.008

Brehm, J. W. (1966). *A theory of psychological reactance*. San Diego, CA: Academic Press.

Brehm, J. W., & Brehm, S. S. (1981). *Psychological reactance: A theory of freedom and control*. San Diego, CA: Academic Press.

Brock, T.C., & Shavitt, S. (1994). *Persuasion: Psychological insights and perspectives*. Boston, MA: Allyn & Bacon.

Burgoon, M., Alvaro, E. M., Broneck, K., Miller, C., Grandpre, J. R., Hall, J. R., & Franck, C. (2002). Using interactive media tools to test substance abuse prevention messages. In W. D. Crano & M. Burgoon (Eds.), *Mass media and drug prevention: Classic and contemporary theories and research* (pp. 67–87). Mahwah, NJ: Lawrence Erlbaum.

Cacioppo, J. T., Berntson, G. G., & Decety, J. (2012). A history of social neuroscience. In A. W. Kruglanski & W. Stroebe (Eds.), *Handbook of the history of social psychology* (pp. 97–110). New York: Psychology Press.

Cacioppo, J. T., Cacioppo, S., & Petty, R. E. (2017). The neuroscience of persuasion: A review with an emphasis on issues and opportunities. *Social Neuroscience*, January 9, 1–44. doi:10.1080/17470919.2016.1273851

Cialdini, R. B. (1993). *Influence: Science and practice* (3rd ed.). LaPorte, IN: HarperCollins.

Ciolacu, M.V. (2014). Theoretical approaches regarding the psychophysiology of emotions, facial expressions and emotion regulation. *Procedia—Social and Behavioral Sciences*, *127*, 748–752. doi:10.1016/j.sbspro.2014.03.348

Cooper, J. (2007). *Cognitive dissonance: Fifty years of a classic theory*. Los Angeles, CA: Sage.

DeWall, N. C., Chester, D. S., & White, D. S. (2015). Can acetaminophen reduce the pain of decision-making? *Journal of Experimental Social Psychology*, *56*, 117–120. doi:10.1016/j.jesp.2014.09.006

Dillard, J. P., & Shen, L. (2005). On the nature of reactance and its role in persuasive health communication. *Communication Monographs*, *72*, 144–168.

Dillard, P. (1993). Persuasion past and present: Attitudes aren't what they used to be. *Communication Monographs*, *60*(1), 90–97.

Eagly, A. H., & Chaiken, S. (1993). *The psychology of attitudes*. New York: Harcourt, Brace, Jovanovich.

Egan, L. C., Santos, L. R., & Bloom, P. (2007). The origins of cognitive dissonance: Evidence from children and monkeys. *Psychological Science*, *18*(11), 978–983.

Einstein, M. (2012). *Compassion, Inc.: How corporate America blurs the line between what we buy, who we are, and those we help*. Berkeley, CA: University of California Press.

Fabrigar, L. R., Krosnick, J. A., & MacDougall, B. L. (2005). Attitude measurement: Techniques for measuring the unobservable. In T. C. Brock & M. C. Green (Eds.), *Persuasion: Psychological insights and perspectives* (2nd ed., pp. 17–40). Newbury Park, CA: Sage.

Falk, E. B., Berkman, E. T., Mann, T., Harrison, B., & Lieberman, M. D. (2010). Predicting persuasion-induced behavior change from the brain. *Journal of Neuroscience*, *30*(25), 8421–8424. doi:10.1523/JNEUROSCI.0063–10.2010

Fazio, R. H., & Olson, M. A. (2003). Implicit measures in social cognition research: Their meaning and use. *Annual Review of Psychology, 54*, 297–327.

Festinger, L. (1957). *A theory of cognitive dissonance.* Stanford, CA: Stanford University Press.

Festinger, L. (1964). *Conflict, decision and dissonance.* Stanford, CA: Stanford University Press.

Festinger, L., & Carlsmith, J. M. (2007). Does cognitive dissonance explain why behavior can change attitudes? In J. A. Nier (Ed.) *Taking sides: Clashing views in social psychology* (2nd ed., pp. 74–91). Dubuque, IA: McGraw-Hill.

Fishbein, M. (2008). A reasoned action approach to health promotion. *Medical Decision Making, 28*(6), 834–844. doi:10.1177/0272989X0832609

Fishbein, M., & Ajzen, I. (2010). *Predicting and changing behavior: The reasoned action approach.* New York: Psychology Press.

Flynn, D., van Schaik, P., & van Wersch, A. (2004). A comparison of multi-item Likert and visual analogue scales for the assessment of transactionally defined coping function. *European Journal of Psychological Assessment, 20*, 49–58.

Fournier, S. (1998). Consumers and their brands: Developing relationship theory in consumer research. *Journal of Consumer Research, 24*, 343–373.

Goodall, C. E. (2011). An overview of implicit measures of attitudes: Methods, mechanisms, strengths, and limitations. *Communication Methods & Measures, 5*(3), 203–222. doi:10. 1080/19312458.2011.596992

Greenwald, A. G., & Ronis, D. L. (1978). Twenty years of cognitive dissonance: Case study of the evolution of a theory. *Psychological Review, 85*(1), 53–57.

Greenwald, A. G., McGhee, D. E., & Schwartz, J. K. L. (1998). Measuring individual differences in implicit cognition: The implicit association test. *Journal of Personality and Social Psychology, 74*, 1464–1480.

Greenwald, A. G., Poehlman, T. A., Uhlmann, E. L., & Banaji, M. R. (2009). Understanding and using the implicit association test: III. Meta-analysis of predictive validity. *Journal of Personality and Social Psychology, 97*(1), 17–41.

Halloran, T. (2014). *Romancing the brand: How brands create strong, intimate relationships with consumers.* San Francisco, CA: Jossey-Bass.

Hansmann, R., & Scholz, R. W. (2003). A two-step informational strategy for reducing littering behavior in a cinema. *Environment and Behavior, 35*(6), 752–762.

Harmon-Jones, E., & Harmon-Jones, C. (2008). Cognitive dissonance theory: An update with a focus on the action-based model. In J. Shaw & W. Gardner (Eds.) *Handbook of motivation* (pp. 71–83), New York: Guilford Press.

Harmon-Jones, E., & Mills, J. (Eds.). (1999). *Cognitive dissonance: Progress on a pivotal theory in social psychology.* Washington, DC: American Psychological Association.

Hashino-Browne, E., Zanna, A. S., Spencer, S. J., Zanna, M. P., Kitayama, S., & Lackenbaur, S. (2005). On the guises of cognitive dissonance: The case of easterners and westerners. *Journal of Personality and Social Psychology, 89*(3), 294–310. doi:10. 1037/0022–3514.89.3.294

Heider, F. (1958). *The psychology of interpersonal relations.* New York: John Wiley.

Holland, R. W., Verplanken, B., & Van Knippenberg, A. (2002). On the nature of attitude–behavior relations: The strong guide, the weak follow. *European Journal of Social Psychology, 32*, 869–876.

Hong, S. M. (1992). Hong's psychological reactance scale: A further factor analytic validation. *Psychological Reports, 70*, 512–514.

Hong, S. M., & Faedda, S. (1996). Refinement of the Hong psychological reactance scale. *Educational and Psychological Measurement, 56*, 173–182.

Horsley, A. D. (1988). The unintended effects of a posted sign on littering attitudes and stated intentions. *Journal of Environmental Education, 19*(3), 10–14.

Hoshino-Browne, E., Zanna, A. S., Spencer, S. J, Zanna, M. P., Kitayama, S., & Lackenbauer, S. (2005). On the cultural guises of cognitive dissonance: The case of easterners and westerners. *Journal of Personality and Social Psychology, 89*, 294–310.

Huffman, K. T., Grossnickle, W. F., Cope, J. G., & Huffman, K. (1995). Litter reduction: A review and integration of the literature. *Environment and Behavior, 27*, 153–183.

Iacoboni, M., Freedman, J., Kaplan J., Jamieson, K. H., Freedman, T., Knapp, B., & Fitzgerald, K. (2007, November 11). This is your brain on politics. *New York Times,* Sec. 4, p. 14. Retrieved on March 30, 2009, from: www.nytimes.com/2007/11/11/opinion/11freedman.html?pagewanted=all

Jack, J., & Appelbaum, L. G. (2010). This is your brain on rhetoric': Research directions for neurorhetorics. *Rhetoric Society Quarterly, 40*(5), 411–437.

Kelman, H. C. (1953). Attitude change as a function of response restriction. *Human Relations, 6*, 185–214.

Kim, M-S., & Hunter, J. E. (1993). Attitude–behavior relationships: A meta-analysis of attitudinal relevance and topic. *Journal of Communication, 43*(1), 101–142.doi:10.1111/j.1460-2466.1993.tb01251.x

Kitayama, S., Snibbe, A. C., Markus, H. Z., & Suzuki, T. (2004). Is there any "free choice"? Self and dissonance in two cultures. *Psychological Science, 15*(8), 527–533.

Knox, R. E., & Inkster, J. A. (1968). Postdecision dissonance at post time. *Journal of Personality and Social Psychology, 3*, 319–323.

Krishna, A. (2011a). Can supporting a cause decrease donations and happiness? The cause marketing paradox. *Journal of Consumer Psychology, 21*(3), 338–345. doi:10.1016/j.jcps.2011.02.001

Krishna, A. (2011b, October 16). Philanthropy and marketing: Buying products linked to good causes makes us feel better, but who really benefits? *The Toronto Star,* p. A–15. Retrieved on April 4, 2012 from Lexis-Nexis Academic search engine.

Likert, R. (1932). A technique for the measurement of attitudes (special issue). *Archives of Psychology, 22*, 1–55.

Masnick, M. (2005, January). Since when is it illegal to just mention a trademark online? *Techdirt.* Retrieved on March 10, 2009, from: www.techdirt.com/articles/20050105/0132239.shtml

Matz, D. C., & Wood, W. (2005). Cognitive dissonance in groups: The consequences of disagreement. *Journal of Personality and Social Psychology, 88*(1), 22–37.

McDermott, R. (2009). The case for increasing dialogue between political science and neuroscience. *Political Research Quarterly, 62*(3), 571–583. doi:10.1177/10659 12909336273

Mettler, S. (2011). *The submerged state: How invisible government policies undermine American democracy.* Chicago: University of Chicago Press.

Miller, C. H., Burgoon, M., Grandpre, J., & Alvaro, E. (2006). Identifying principal risk factors for the initiation of adolescent smoking behaviors: The significance of psychological reactance. *Health Communication, 19*, 241–252.

Miller, C. H., Lane, L. T., Deatrick, L. M., Young, A. M., & Potts, K. A. (2007). Health messages: The effects of controlling language, lexical concreteness, and the restoration of freedom. *Human Communication Research, 33*, 219–240.

Mind games: How not to mix politics and science. (2007, November 22). *Nature, 450*(7169), 457.

Nisbett, R. E. (2003). *The geography of thought.* New York: Free Press.

Orend, A., & Gagné, P. (2009). Corporate logo tattoos and the commodification of the body. *Journal of Contemporary Ethnography, 38*(4), 493–517.

Osgood, C. E., & Tannenbaum, P. H. (1955). The principle of congruity in the prediction of attitude change. *Psychological Review, 62*, 42–55.

Osgood, C. E., Tannenbaum, P. H., & Suci, G. J. (1957). *The measurement of meaning.* Urbana, IL: University of Illinois Press.

Park, J. K., & John, D. R. (2010). Got to get you into my life: Do brand personalities rub off on consumers? *Journal of Consumer Research, 37*(4), 655–669.

Petty, R. E., & Cacioppo, J. T. (1983). The role of bodily responses in attitude measurement and change. In J. T. Cacioppo & R. E. Petty (Eds.), *Social psychophysiology: A source-book* (pp. 51–101). New York: Guilford Press.

Petty, R. E., & Cacioppo, J. T. (1986a). The elaboration likelihood model of persuasion. In L. Berkowitz (Ed.), *Advances in experimental social psychology* (Vol. 19, pp. 123–205). New York: Academic Press.

Petty, R. E., & Cacioppo, J. T. (1986b). *Communication and persuasion: Central and peripheral routes to attitude change.* New York: Springer-Verlag.

Petty, R. E., Cacioppo, J. T., Strathman, A. J., & Priester, J. R. (2005). To think or not to think: Exploring two routes to persuasion. In T. Brock & M. C. Green (Eds.), *Persuasion: Psychological insights and perspectives* (pp. 81–116). Thousand Oaks, CA: Sage.

Petty, R. E., Fazio, R. H., & Briñol, P. (Eds.). (2009). *Attitudes: Insights from the new implicit measures.* New York: Psychology Press.

Porter, S., & ten Brinke, L. (2008). Reading between the lies identifying concealed and falsified emotions in universal facial expressions. *Psychological Science, 19*(5), 508–514. doi:10.1111/j.1467–9280.2008.02116.x

Preiss, R. W., & Allen, M. (1998). Performing counterattitudinal advocacy: The persuasive impact of incentives. In M. Allen & R. Preiss (Eds.), *Persuasion: Advances through meta-analysis* (pp. 231–239). Cresskill, NJ: Hampton Press.

Prislin, R., & Crano, W. D. (2008). Attitudes and attitude change: The fourth peak. In W. D. Crano & R. Prislin (Eds.), *Attitudes and attitude change* (pp. 3–15). New York: Taylor & Francis.

Quick, B. L., & Stephenson, M. T. (2007). Further evidence that psychological reactance can be modeled as a combination of anger and negative cognition. *Communication Research, 34*(3), 255–276.

Reips, U.-D., & Funke, F. (2008). Interval-level measurement with visual analogue scales in Internet-based research: VAS Generator. *Behavior Research Methods, 40*(3), 699–704.

Rule, N. O., & Ambady, N. (2010). Democrats and Republicans can be differentiated by their faces. *PLoS ONE, 5*(1), e8733.

Rule, N. O., Ambady, N., & Hallett, K. C. (2009). Female sexual orientation is perceived accurately, rapidly, and automatically from the face and its features. *Journal of Experimental Social Psychology, 45*, 1245–1251.

Rule, N. O., Ambady, N., Adams, R. B., Jr., & Macrae, C. N. (2008). Accuracy and awareness in the perception and categorization of male sexual orientation. *Journal of Personality and Social Psychology, 95*, 1019–1028.

Scher, S. J., & Cooper, J. (1989). The motivational basis of dissonance: The singular role of behavioral consequences. *Journal of Personality and Social Psychology, 56*, 899–906.

Sénémeaud, C., & Somat, A. (2009). Dissonance arousal and persistence in attitude change. *Swiss Journal of Psychology, 68*(1), 25–31.

Sharkansky, I. (2002). Slogan as policy. *Journal of Comparative Policy Analysis: Research and Practice, 4*, 75–93.

Sullivan, T. (2009, April 22). The Pirate Bay case: Not necessarily a victory for Hollywood. *Christian Science Monitor*, p. 6.

Swaminathan, V., Stilley, K. M., & Ahluwalia, R. (2009). When brand personality matters: The moderating role of attachment styles. *Journal of Consumer Research*, *35*(6), 985–1002.

Tavris, C., & Aronson, E. (2007). *Mistakes were made (but not by me)*. New York: Harcourt.

Tesser, A., & Shaffer, D. R. (1990). Attitudes and attitude change. *Annual Review of Psychology*, *41*(1), 479–523.

Tingley, D. (2006). Neurological imaging as evidence in political science: A review, critique, and guiding assessment. *Social Science Information*, *45*(1), 6–33. doi:10.1177/0539018406061100

Tormala, Z. L., & Rucker, D. D. (2015). How certainty transforms persuasion. *Harvard Business Review*, 93(9), 96–103.

Wilson, M. C., & Scior, K. (2014). Attitudes toward individuals with disabilities as measured by the implicit association test: A literature review. *Research in Developmental Disabilities*, *35*, 294–321. doi:10.1016/j.ridd.2013.11.003

Wittenbrink, B., & Schwartz, N. (2007) *Implicit measures of attitudes*. New York: Guilford Press.

Xie, X., Jang, A., & Cai, D. A. (2007, November 15). *Are Asians really okay with contradictions? Using dissonance to explain cultural differences in responding to contradictions*. Paper presented at the annual meeting of the National Communication Association, Chicago.

Credibility

BARACK OBAMA AND DONALD TRUMP have it. So do astrophysicist Neil deGrasse Tyson and media mogul Oprah Winfrey. John F. Kennedy, Ronald Reagan, Dr. Martin Luther King, Jr. and Princess Diana had it. So did Adolf Hitler, unfortunately. Depending on whom you ask, Dwayne Johnson, Narendra Modi, Ellen DeGeneres, and Sir Richard Branson have it. What all these people have, or had, is *charisma*. *Charisma* is a lay term used to describe someone who possesses a certain indefinable charm or allure. Such a person may be said to have a magnetic personality or possess a sense of *savoir faire* (Riggio, 1987, 2010).

There is a problem with describing people as charismatic, however. The term has no clear, precise meaning. Because charisma is a fuzzy concept, persuasion researchers tend to rely instead on a different but related concept called *ethos,* or *source credibility.* Ethos bears some similarity to charisma. However, whereas charisma represents an elusive, ineffable quality, ethos can be defined and measured with much greater precision. In this chapter, we examine the concept of ethos, or source credibility, and its relationship to persuasion. First we examine credibility as it relates to celebrity endorsers and spokespersons. Next we offer a definition, discuss the basic features, and explore the underlying dimensions that make up credibility. Then we consider how credibility functions according to Petty and Cacioppo's (1986a, 1986b) *elaboration likelihood model* of persuasion, and we examine a phenomenon known as the *sleeper effect.* Finally, we discuss credibility as it applies to both institutions and interpersonal settings.

CELEBRITY SELLING POWER: THE ANSWER IS IN THE STARS

Did you know that roughly one in four advertisements features a famous person (Elberse & Verleun, 2012; Spry, Pappu, & Cornwall, 2011)? Were you aware that approximately 10 percent of all advertising expenditures go to pay celebrity endorsers (Agrawal & Kamakura, 1995)? Nike alone spends about $500 million per year on celebrity endorsements (Bruno, 2011). Celebrities and athletes with a high *Q-Score* (their selling quotient)[1] can command salaries in millions of dollars. No wonder Berger (2011) claims we now live in a *celebritocracy.*

Considering all the money that is spent on celebrity endorsements, you might be wondering whether they actually work. When asked, most consumers claim they would never buy a product based on a celebrity endorser's say-so (Study finds . . . , 2000). However, consumers may be more susceptible than they think. Indeed, a phenomenon known as the *third-person effect* reveals that people underestimate the effect advertising has on themselves and overestimate its effect on others (Jensen & Collins, 2008; Shin & Kim, 2011).

A recent meta-analysis (Knoll & Mathis, 2017) found that celebrity endorsements improved consumers' attitudes toward endorsed products, but not necessarily their intentions to purchase those products. Another study found that endorser credibility has a significant effect on *brand equity*, which refers to the value attached to a particular brand (Spry, Pappu, & Cornwall, 2011). According to one study (Elberse & Verleun, 2012), endorsers boost sales by about 20 percent on average. Celebrity endorsers appear to be most effective at promoting new products and services rather than established brands (Djafarova & Rushworth, 2017; Kumkale, Albarracín, & Seignourel, 2010). If celebrities didn't yield profits, advertisers wouldn't use them.

That said, some people argue that celebrity endorsers are losing their clout. Why? Consumers are relying more and more on social networks than spokespersons (Weir, 2011). In fact, some people rate bloggers as more credible than traditional news media (O'Neil & Eisenmann, 2017). Even so, celebrities with large numbers of followers, such as Kim Kardashian, Taylor Swift, and Justin Bieber, have considerable online clout.

FIGURE 4.1
Source: © David Sipress/
The New Yorker Collection
www.cartoonbank.com

"Which celebrities do this type of yoga?"

The Match-Up Hypothesis: Why Jonah Hill Should Not Be Revlon's Spokesperson

The *match-up hypothesis* suggests that an endorser must be a good "fit" for the brand being endorsed (Kamins & Gupta, 1994; Koernig & Boyd, 2009; Till & Busler, 2000). As such, Usain Bolt, the "world's fastest man," is a natural choice for Gatorade. Likewise, Justin Bieber's huge fan base of young "Beliebers" makes him a good choice for Proactiv skin-care products.

One explanation of why celebrities should fit the brands they endorse stems from the *meaning transfer perspective*. According to this view, an endorser's public persona is projected onto a brand. The brand's image is then incorporated into the consumer's self-concept (McCracken, 1986, 1989). By way of illustration, Ellen DeGeneres danced her way through one of American Express's "My Life, My Card" commercials. Independent-minded consumers who see themselves as "dancing to their own tune" can identify with DeGeneres, whom they see as successful while doing her own thing.

Catch a Falling Star

Of course, there can be a downside to relying on well-known celebrities, athletes, or other famous figures. What happens if a famous person becomes embroiled in a scandal or a legal proceeding? When former Subway pitchman, Jared Fogle, was charged with distributing kiddie porn, the company tossed him like wilted lettuce. After it was revealed that celebrity chef Paula Dean made racist remarks off air, Home Depot and other sponsors dumped her like a pan of hot grease. Following news reports that Olympian Ryan Lochte falsely claimed that he was robbed at gunpoint during the 2016 Olympics, the swimmer's stock with Speedo and Polo Ralph Lauren sunk like a stone.

As these examples clearly show, if a celebrity, athlete, journalist, or politician is tainted by scandal, it can rub off on the sponsor's credibility (Till & Shimp, 1998). To avoid the risk and expense of actual endorsers, many companies rely on fictional spokespersons. Aunt Jemima would never engage in insider trading. The Geico gecko will never be arrested for sexual assault. Mr. Clean won't ever test positive for steroid use, and the Keebler elves won't be charged with child pornography in an undercover sting operation. Having examined the downside of relying too heavily on credibility as a tool of persuasion, let's consider more carefully what it actually is and how it actually works.

WHAT IS CREDIBILITY?

O'Keefe (2002) defines credibility as "judgments made by a perceiver (e.g., a message recipient) concerning the believability of a communicator" (p. 181). We suggest that this definition should be extended to institutions as well. Private companies and governmental agencies also have images to protect. They want to be viewed favorably, too. In addition, it should be recognized that in face-to-face encounters there are really *two* sources whose credibility is at stake, because each party to the interaction is simultaneously a sender and a receiver of messages.

Credibility Is a Receiver-Based Construct

An important feature of O'Keefe's definition is the recognition that credibility is a *receiver-based construct*. Credibility exists in the eye of the beholder. For example, Edward Snowden may be perceived as a heroic whistleblower by some, and as a publicity-seeking traitor by others. A celebrity who takes a strong political stand may be cheered by some and jeered by others. In short, if these folks are credible, it is because we bestow credibility on them. Modifying a time-worn philosophical question, one might ask, "If a source stood in the middle of a forest and there were no one around to perceive him or her, would there be any credibility?" Our answer is no. Different sources possess different abilities and attributes, but the value assigned to these abilities and attributes resides in the receiver, not in the source. Credibility is a perceptual phenomenon.

Credibility Is a Multidimensional Construct

A second important feature of credibility is that it is not a unidimensional construct —that is, it is not made up of only one element. Credibility represents a composite of several characteristics that others perceive in a source. Credibility is a *multidimensional construct*. An analogy may serve to clarify. Imagine that you were trying to define *athleticism*. It would be difficult to single out only one thing that makes an individual athletic. Athleticism requires strength, coordination, stamina, and quick reflexes, among other things. Similarly, credibility isn't a single characteristic, but a combination of qualities a source is believed to possess. We discuss these qualities shortly.

Credibility Is a Situational/Contextual Phenomenon

A third feature of credibility is that it is a *situational* or *contextual phenomenon*. A persuader's credibility is subject to change from one audience or setting to another. The very qualities that are admired in a communicator in one setting may be derided in another setting. The president of the National Rifle Association might be well received when speaking before an audience of hunting and fishing enthusiasts. The same source might encounter a hostile reception, however, if he spoke before a group of animal rights advocates. Your own credibility is subject to such situational changes too. You may enjoy more credibility in one context—for example, work, family, friends, school—than in another.

Credibility Is Dynamic

Credibility can change over time. For example, in his first 100 days in office, the public's disapproval of President Donald Trump increased 11 percent, from 41 to 55 percent (https://projects.fivethirtyeight.com/trump-approval-ratings/). It is important to recognize, then, that credibility is *dynamic:* It fluctuates over time. A source's credibility can change even during the course of a single speech, sales pitch, or boardroom presentation.

THE FACTOR ANALYTIC APPROACH TO CREDIBILITY

Just as chefs are interested in what ingredients go into award-winning recipes, persuasion researchers have tried to determine the "ingredients," or underlying dimensions, of credibility. In fact, as long ago as 380 BCE, Aristotle proclaimed in *The Rhetoric* that the ingredients "which inspire confidence in the orator's character . . . that induce us to believe a thing apart from any proof of it . . . [are] good sense, good moral character, and good will" (1378). Aristotle wasn't far off the mark.

In the 1960s and 1970s researchers began to use a statistical technique known as *factor analysis* to uncover the underlying dimensions or ingredients of credibility. Controversy emerged during this period over how many credibility dimensions there were and what they should be called (Cronkhite & Liska, 1976; Pornpitakpan, 2004). Subsequent investigations, though, have clarified the situation considerably, if not completely.

Primary Dimensions of Credibility

There is now fairly solid evidence that there are three *primary dimensions* of credibility that almost always apply to the evaluation of sources. There are also multiple secondary dimensions that are more situation specific. To enhance your own credibility, you should focus on these primary dimensions. The secondary dimensions may or may not matter depending on your particular situation. The scale items used to measure these dimensions can be found in Box 4.1.

Expertise

The first primary dimension of credibility is *expertise* (McCroskey, 1966; Pornpitakpan, 2004). To be credible, a persuader must know his or her stuff or, at least, *appear* to know his or her stuff. Sometimes a title alone, such as MD, PhD, or CPA, can confer credibility on a source. You have to be careful, though; not all

BOX 4.1 | Bipolar Adjectives Used to Measure Credibility With a Semantic Differential Scale

PRIMARY DIMENSIONS

Expertise
(also called competence or qualification)
- experienced/inexperienced
- informed/uninformed
- trained/untrained
- qualified/unqualified
- skilled/unskilled
- intelligent/unintelligent
- expert/inexpert
- competent/incompetent
- bright/stupid

Trustworthiness
(also called character, safety, or personal integrity)
- honest/dishonest
- trustworthy/untrustworthy
- open-minded/close-minded
- just/unjust
- fair/unfair
- unselfish/selfish
- moral/immoral
- ethical/unethical
- genuine/phony

Goodwill
- cares about me/doesn't care about me
- has my interests at heart/doesn't have my interests at heart
- not self-centered/self-centered
- concerned with me/not concerned with me
- sensitive/insensitive
- understanding/not understanding

SECONDARY DIMENSIONS

Extroversion
- timid/bold
- verbal/quiet
- meek/aggressive
- talkative/silent

Composure
- poised/nervous
- relaxed/tense
- calm/anxious
- excitable/composed

Sociability
- good-natured/irritable
- cheerful/gloomy
- friendly/unfriendly

Source: Adapted from McCroskey, J. C., & Young, T. J. (1981). and McCroskey, J. C., & Teven, J. J. (1999).

titles mean what they say. For example, a person who uses the prefix Dr., may not be a medical doctor or an academic. Honorary doctoral degrees are sometimes awarded by universities, but only as a form of recognition. Kermit the Frog, for instance, received an honorary doctorate of "amphibious letters" from South Hampton College. What's more, it isn't difficult to buy a doctoral degree online from a non-accredited institution (Bartlett & Smallwood, 2014). And, of course, some "doctors," like Dr. Dre, Doc Rivers, and Doc Marten are simply nicknames.

To be regarded as experts, sources needn't possess advanced degrees, specialized training, licenses, or credentials, however. For example, at an Alcoholics Anonymous meeting, members who had been alcoholics for 20 years, and who had been sober for the past 10 years, would likely be perceived as having expertise. Such members would know what they were talking about, because they had "been there" (Denzen, 1987; Robertson, 1988). Even astrologers, fortune-tellers, and psychics make attempts to establish their expertise. "Don't pay for advice from phony psychics," a psychic website proclaims, "We have *genuine, certified psychics* waiting to chat with you online."

Interestingly, a source's expertise doesn't always have to be in the field in which he or she is attempting to persuade. LeBron James and Cristiano Ronaldo, for example, aren't experts in electronics. Yet they are effective endorsers for Samsung. Endorsements by famous persons enjoy a *halo effect* that allows them to carry their credibility to new, unrelated fields. The halo effect isn't limited to famous people. In one study (Rind, 1992), a confederate working with the experimenter approached shoppers in the food court of a mall and asked them to buy raffle tickets. In one of the experimental conditions, he amazed the shoppers with his calculating ability (the confederate used a hidden transmitter, through which he received the correct answers). In another condition, he made a fool of himself by exhibiting poor calculating skills. In a third control condition, the confederate didn't profess to have any amazing skills. Shoppers bought significantly more raffle tickets when the confederate demonstrated astonishing calculating skills than in either of the other two conditions. It mattered not that the purpose of the raffle was unrelated to the confederate's amazing talent. Expertise, even unrelated expertise, then, can be an asset in persuasion. Bear in mind, however, that purchasing a raffle ticket is a fairly trivial act. We suspect that on a more involving issue, relevant expertise would be valued more highly by receivers.

Although we tend to think of expert sources as being highly confident, this is not always the case. Sources who already possess high credibility may be more influential when they express their opinions with less certainty, whereas sources who have lower credibility are more persuasive when they express their opinions with greater certainty (Karmarkar & Tormala, 2010).

Trustworthiness

The second primary dimension of credibility is *trustworthiness* (McCroskey, 1966; Pornpitakpan, 2004). A source may appear knowledgeable, but what if you don't think he or she is being truthful or can be trusted? If your car needs a brake job, you not only want a qualified mechanic, you want an *honest,* qualified mechanic. To be successful, persuaders must, therefore, convey an impression of honesty and integrity.

Perhaps you've noticed that some advertisements in magazines or newspapers carry the logo "As Seen On TV." The purpose in displaying this logo is to instill trust. Many consumers unthinkingly presume that only reputable companies can afford television commercials. The same applies to *Yellow Pages* ads that feature the ichthys logo, the Christian sign of the fish. Consumers may assume that an electrician, plumber, or carpenter who is a Christian is less likely to rip them off. Such "sign reasoning" may have merit. But then again, couldn't an unscrupulous tradesperson simply use the ichthys logo to dupe customers into believing that he or she is trustworthy? Bernie Madoff, a stockbroker and investment advisor, seemed trustworthy, until he was exposed for operating a Ponzi scheme. He defrauded investors out of $65 billion.

Goodwill

The third primary dimension of credibility is *goodwill*. McCroskey and Teven (1999) suggest that goodwill is synonymous with *perceived caring*. That is, a source who seems to care about and take a genuine interest in the receiver is displaying goodwill. Goodwill can be demonstrated by displaying understanding for another person's ideas, feelings, or needs. Goodwill can also be demonstrated by displaying empathy—that is, identifying with another person's feelings or situation. Goodwill can be displayed by responsiveness as well, by being open and receptive to another's communication attempts. A source who said, "I hear where you are coming from" or "I can relate to that" or "I sympathize with how you feel" would be displaying this quality.

Of the three primary dimensions just discussed, expertise seems to have the greatest effect on persuasion. Wilson and Sherrell (1993) revealed in a meta-analysis that the effect of expertise was greater than that of trustworthiness, attraction, or similarity on persuasion. The importance of the dimensions on persuasive outcomes, however, may depend on the particular topic or context for persuasion.

Secondary Dimensions of Credibility

Researchers have uncovered several other dimensions of credibility that tend to be more situation specific. One of these, termed *dynamism* by some (Berlo, Lemert, & Mertz, 1969) and *extroversion* by others (Burgoon, 1976; McCroskey & Young, 1981), has to do with how energetic, animated, or enthusiastic the source appears. Obviously, it wouldn't do for a fitness trainer like Jillian Michaels, or a dancer like Julianne Hough, to appear sluggish or lethargic. Certain situations call for the source to be "peppy" and full of energy. However, a person who is too bubbly and effervescent, especially at the wrong times, may lose credibility (Burgoon, 1973). The trick is for a source to match his or her level of dynamism to the demands of the situation.

Another secondary dimension of credibility is *composure* (Miller & Hewgill, 1964). In some situations, we expect a source to remain calm, cool, and collected. The character of James Bond, secret agent 007, exudes this quality. Captain Chesley "Sully" Sullenberger, who safely landed US Airways flight 1549 on the Hudson River, retained his composure during the entire ordeal. The flight recordings released by the FAA revealed that Sully was "the epitome of composure under life-threatening pressure" (McShane, 2009, p. 12). On the flip-side of the coin, a source who loses composure, or who seems nervous or ill at ease, may lose credibility. When Tom

FIGURE 4.2
Perceived expertise
is a prerequisite for
credibility.

Cruise jumped up and down on Oprah's couch while proclaiming his love for Katie Holmes, viewers felt he had lost it.

An additional secondary dimension of credibility has been dubbed *sociability*. This dimension refers to a source's friendliness or outgoingness. To us, Paul Rudd, Emma Thompson, Rashida Jones, Tom Hanks, Reese Witherspoon, and Magic Johnson possess this quality, as do others who relate to people easily. Sanders (2006) emphasizes that friendliness, empathy, and authenticity go a long way in trying to persuade people. Sociability is particularly important in the "people professions," such as sales, law, education, social work, and the like.

THE FACTOR ANALYTIC APPROACH AND THE REAL WORLD

Given the extraordinary amount of attention devoted to the study of credibility, how do these dimensions hold up in the real world? The answer is, remarkably well. More than three decades of research by Kouzes and Posner (2017) involving thousands of people in leadership positions verify that admired people display competence, exhibit honesty, are inspiring, and forward-looking. Kouzes and Posner highlight the overlap with several of the dimensions described above. "For trustworthiness, you can say *honest*. For expertise, you can say *competent*. For dynamism, you can say *inspiring*. In other words . . . what has been reaffirmed . . . is that above all else, people want leaders who are credible" (2011, p. 16).

CREDIBILITY AS A PERIPHERAL CUE

Now that we've explained what credibility is, we turn our attention to how and why it facilitates persuasion. To do so, we return to Petty and Cacioppo's (1986a, 1986b) *elaboration likelihood model* of persuasion (ELM), which was introduced in Chapter 2. According to the ELM, there are two distinct routes to persuasion; a *central route* and a *peripheral route*. The central route, involves thinking or *cognitive elaboration*. The peripheral route relies on mental shortcuts or *heuristic cues*.

Petty and Cacioppo conceptualize credibility as a peripheral cue to persuasion. When receivers have little at stake, their motivation to pay attention to a message is lower. They therefore tend to favor the peripheral route. As a general rule, source credibility exerts more influence on receivers who aren't highly involved in an issue. Credibility matters far less if receiver involvement is already high. Instead, credibility tends to work its magic when receiver involvement is low (Benoit, 1987). Receivers with low involvement are more likely to defer to sources, because doing so requires less mental effort than concentrating on the substance of a message. To put it bluntly, low-involved receivers are cognitively lazy. This limitation notwithstanding, we mustn't underestimate the importance of credibility. Credibility may be conceptualized as a peripheral cue, but it is still a big peripheral cue.

You can use this information to your advantage if you are trying to persuade receivers who perceive you as having low credibility. You should do everything you can to increase their involvement in the topic or issue. Explain why the issue is relevant to them. Emphasize how the topic or issue affects them directly. If you can increase your target audience's involvement in the topic or issue, they'll pay more attention to the message and less attention to your credibility.

IT'S WHAT'S UP FRONT THAT COUNTS

When should a source's expertise be identified—at the beginning or end of a persuasive message? Research findings strongly suggest that credibility tends to work only if the source is identified *prior* to the actual presentation of a persuasive message (Benoit & Strathman, 2004; Nan, 2009; O'Keefe, 1987). If the source is identified after the fact, credibility has little or no effect. Several studies, for example, found no differences in the persuasiveness of high- versus low-credibility sources when the sources were identified after the messages were presented (O'Keefe, 1987; Ward & McGinnies, 1974). Benoit and Strathman (2004) suggest that this is because credibility affects the way receivers process a message. For credibility to do any good, therefore, receivers must consider the source's credibility as they process a persuasive message.

THE SLEEPER EFFECT

The traditional view is that the impact of a persuasive message wanes over time (Hovland, Lumsdaine, & Sheffield, 1949; Stiff, 1994). Receivers forget what was said or who said it. Persuasion wears off. The *sleeper effect*, however, suggests that under the right circumstances, the delayed impact of a message may be more effective than its initial impact (Kumkale & Albarracín, 2004)—that is, the message might grow on receivers. Specifically, the sleeper effect posits that a message from a low-credibility source may increase in persuasiveness as time passes, compared to a message from a high-credibility source. Sound unlikely? It is, to some extent. Yet the sleeper effect has been documented by researchers, dating back more than 50 years (Hovland et al., 1949). How the sleeper effect works requires some explanation.

Imagine that one audience is exposed to a persuasive message from a source with high credibility. A second audience is exposed to the same persuasive message, but from a source with low credibility, by means of a *discounting cue*. A discounting cue consists of a disclaimer containing negative information about the source, the message, or both. For example, let's say the first group heard a message in favor of irradiating fruits and vegetables to kill bacteria before they are shipped to market. The second group would hear the same message, plus a disclaimer saying the message was drafted by a lobbyist for the agricultural industry whose real concern was agricultural profits, not consumer safety. The discounting cue would thus serve as an impediment to the effectiveness of the second message, a "ball and chain," so to speak. Afterward, each group's attitudes toward irradiated produce would be measured.

Initially, the first group's attitudes should be much more favorable toward the topic than the second group's. After all, the first group heard the message from the high-credibility source. With the passage of time, however, things might change. The first group's attitudes would gradually decay over time. The second group's attitudes, however, might undergo a process known as *disassociation,* whereby the message is separated from its source in the minds of receivers. The second group might remember the message, but forget the discounting cue. If you've ever heard someone say, "I heard somewhere that . . ." or "I read somewhere that . . ." you've observed disassociation in action. Once the message was decoupled from its source, the ball and chain would be removed. The result would be that as the first group's attitudes diminished, the second group's attitudes would become more positive. *Voilà*! The sleeper effect.

Although the sleeper effect has been demonstrated in laboratory studies (Kumkale & Albarracín, 2004), it is difficult to produce on a consistent, reliable basis. Only a few studies have demonstrated an *absolute* sleeper effect (see Figure 4.3) of the type we've been discussing (Gruder et al., 1978; Watts & Holt, 1979; Watts & McGuire, 1964). An absolute sleeper effect occurs when a message from a high-credibility source loses favor over time, whereas a message from a low-credibility source gains favor over time. Other studies have demonstrated a *relative* sleeper effect (see Figure 4.3), meaning that both messages lose favor over time, but the high-credibility message loses more favor than the low-credibility message (see reviews by Allen & Stiff, 1989, 1998). Some studies have failed to find a sleeper effect at all (see reviews by Allen & Stiff, 1989, 1998). The sleeper effect, then, can be pretty fickle.

There is evidence, however, that fictional narratives can induce the sleeper effect (Appel & Richter, 2007). Over time, a person may forget what was fact and what was fiction, and come to believe a fictional storyline. What implications does this hold for you as a persuader? In practice, it would be very difficult for an ordinary persuader,

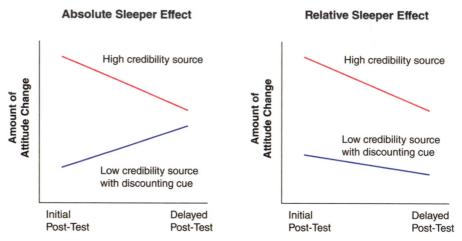

Absolute Sleeper Effect

High credibility source

Low credibility source
with discounting cue

Amount of
Attitude Change

Initial
Post-Test

Delayed
Post-Test

Relative Sleeper Effect

High credibility source

Low credibility source
with discounting cue

Amount of
Attitude Change

Initial
Post-Test

Delayed
Post-Test

FIGURE 4.3
Illustration of an absolute and a relative sleeper effect.

as opposed to a laboratory researcher, to satisfy all of the requirements for obtaining a sleeper effect. We believe there are far too many "ifs" associated with this strategy to recommend it to an ordinary persuader. Our advice is that you would be much better off trying to enhance your credibility as much as possible in the first place.

CREDIBILITY AND IMAGE MANAGEMENT

Thus far, we've discussed credibility strictly in connection with people. We believe the concept of credibility can be extended to corporations, organizations, governmental agencies, social movements, and other institutions as well. Such group entities care about how they are perceived by the public and other constituencies. They want to project positive images. And to a large extent, their power and ability to influence are linked to their images and their reputations. For these reasons, we maintain that the credibility construct applies equally well to institutional entities and individuals. Britain's slogan, "keep calm and carry on," for example, embodies the dimension of composure for an entire nation.

As further illustration, consider the charitable activities of major corporations. McDonald's established Ronald McDonald House to provide assistance to hospital-bound children and their families. The National Football League donates generously to the United Way. Other companies contribute to the Make-A-Wish Foundation. In so doing, these corporations are demonstrating that they are good citizens in their communities. Doing good deeds enhances public perceptions of goodwill. We aren't suggesting that corporations are disingenuous when they sponsor causes or that corporate altruism is based solely on the profit motive. We do wish to point out, however, that philanthropic acts make for good public relations.

So important is image management for corporations, institutions, government agencies, and the like that entire departments, divisions, and staffs exist for just this purpose. They may be called publicists, press agents, mouthpieces, or spin doctors, but their goal is the same: to generate favorable publicity and avoid unfavorable media coverage. Even the military employs public relations officers, because good PR is part of good military strategy. Whatever the title of these types of positions, one of their primary missions is to maintain the credibility of the host institution.

On occasion, corporations, institutions, and government agencies commit blunders that damage their credibility. For example, the oil spill in the Gulf of Mexico made BP the poster boy for evil oil companies. William Benoit (1995) refers to this process as *image restoration* and notes that such efforts are highly persuasive in nature (p. 6). Examples in which circumstances have forced corporations and other institutions to engage in image restoration abound. Volkswagen's credibility took a hit when it admitted that 11 million of its diesel engine cars were fitted with software designed to defeat emissions tests. Thus far, the automaker has paid out $20 billion in fines, with more in the offing. VW ran a series of ads apologizing to customers and promising to make things right. Wells Fargo piqued consumers' ire when it created 3.5 million bogus accounts without their customers' permission. Soon after the company launched a "make things right" campaign. United Airlines suffered a public relations nightmare when airport security forcibly removed a passenger from one of its airplanes.

Benoit (1995) notes that such defensive campaigns are commonplace. They are undertaken out of a necessity to restore the credibility of the corporation, institution, or agency whose image has been tarnished. Benoit highlights a variety of strategies aimed at image restoration. The specific strategies employed, of course, depend on the nature of the difficulty in which the institution finds itself and the range of available defenses.

We can see, then, that corporations and other institutions, not only individuals, possess credibility in varying amounts. We suspect that the same primary dimensions of credibility that apply to individuals apply equally well to corporations. We suspect that the secondary dimensions of credibility discussed previously, however, might differ. After all, the secondary dimensions don't always appear in studies of individuals' credibility. This would appear to be a fruitful topic for future scholarly inquiry.

INTERPERSONAL CREDIBILITY, IMPRESSION MANAGEMENT, FACEWORK, AND ACCOUNTS

Ordinary folks can't hire their own public relations firm or employ a publicist to maintain a positive public image. They do engage in public relations campaigns, nonetheless. Ordinary persons tend to function as their own PR departments through impression management and facework.

Impression management theory (Tedeschi & Reiss, 1981) seeks to explain how persons go about trying to project a positive self-image.[2] Individuals want others to form favorable impressions of them. In short, individuals want to be perceived as credible and likable. The importance of likability, specifically, is featured in Box 4.2. Individuals attempt to manage others' impressions of themselves by trying to say and do the right things. Engaging in "politically correct" behavior is an example of impression management at work.

Our position is that when an individual is engaging in impression management, he or she is engaging in persuasion. He or she is attempting to influence others'

BOX 4.2 | Icing on the Cake: The Benefits of Likability

Suppose you are choosing which of two tour guides to hire. Both are equally knowledgeable and experienced. Their tour prices are the same and include the same itinerary. One guide, however, is more friendly and likable, the other more distant and aloof. Which one would you choose? If you are like us, you would rather spend your day with the more likable guide. As Gitomer (2015) observes, "all things being equal, people prefer to do business with people they like. All things being not so equal, people still prefer to do business with people they like" (p. 10).

Lovas and Holloway (2009) explain that "likability is a combination of characteristics including (but not limited to) interest, empathy and genuineness. In a professional context, likable people tend to be interesting to us, interested in us, empathetic, positive, non-judgmental, and genuine" (p. 40). Sanders (2006), who refers to likability as the "L-factor," defines likability as "an ability to create positive attitudes in other people through the delivery of emotional and psychological benefits" (p. 33). Interestingly, Donald Trump and Hillary Clinton were the two most unlikable presidential candidates since modern polling began (Holyk & Langer, 2016). In contrast, Bernie Sanders was rated the most likable candidate in 2016. Other likable public figures include Ellen DeGeneres, Tom Hanks, Chris Pratt, and Taylor Swift.

While important, likability only goes so far. If you were having brain surgery, would you prefer the best surgeon available or a lesser surgeon with a great bedside manner? For women in politics or the business world, Cooper (2013) argues that being likable and competent entails a double standard. Strong, successful women may be labeled as "aggressive," "abrasive," or "difficult." She suggests that, for women, success and likability are often negatively correlated.

Sample "Likability scale" items

1. This person is friendly

Very Strongly Disagree	Strongly Disgree	Disagree	Neutral	Agree	Strongly Agree	Very Strongly Agree

2. This person is likable

Very Strongly Disagree	Strongly Disgree	Disagree	Neutral	Agree	Strongly Agree	Very Strongly Agree

3. This person is approachable

Very Strongly Disagree	Strongly Disgree	Disagree	Neutral	Agree	Strongly Agree	Very Strongly Agree

Source: Reysen (2005)

impressions of him or her. At the same time, he or she is vulnerable to influence attempts by others. This is because persons are highly susceptible to persuasive appeals aimed at enhancing their own self-image. By way of illustration, a common preoccupation of teenagers, especially younger teens, is "looking cool." If one teen can convince another that dressing or acting a certain way will make him or her look "cool," the other teen is likely to conform to that style of dress or behavior. Most of us need look no further than our high school yearbooks to realize that we, too, were susceptible to the fads, trends, and fashions of our day.

Impression management also requires that people engage in *facework,* a term coined by Erving Goffman (1967, 1974). A person's "face" refers to his or her social standing in the eyes of others. Facework involves negotiating one's social standing and social worth with others (Ting-Toomey, 1988, 1994; Ting-Toomey & Kurogi, 1998). For example, committing a social faux pas could result in the loss of one's own face. Facework would be required to restore one's face. Threatening or challenging another person could cause the other to lose face. Facework would again be required for the other to regain face.

As with identity management, we suggest that facework is inherently persuasive in nature. Facework involves goal-oriented communication that seeks particular outcomes or ends—namely, "satisfying one's own face wants and the face wants of one's interlocutor" (Cupach & Imahori, 1993, p. 117). For example, consider the related social rituals of asking someone out on a date and declining someone's invitation for a date. Both rituals, asking and declining, are persuasive in nature, and both are laden with face-saving implications. Although not synonymous with credibility, we see the concepts of face and facework as being closely related to the credibility construct. Maintaining one's face, we believe, is akin to maintaining one's credibility in the eyes of others.

STRATEGIES FOR ENHANCING CREDIBILITY: GET YOUR MOJO WORKING

Having gained a better understanding of what credibility is and how it works, what can you do to enhance your credibility when persuading? A number of general guidelines are offered for improving your credibility. Keep in mind that because credibility is a receiver-based construct, what works on one listener or audience may not work on the next.

1. *Heed the Boy Scout motto: "Be prepared."* Before making your case, be as well prepared and well organized as possible. Think through your position beforehand and anticipate likely objections to your position. If you don't seem to know what you are talking about, your credibility will suffer. Research shows that unorganized messages are far less convincing than organized ones (McCroskey & Mehrley, 1969; Sharp & McClung, 1966).
2. *Cite evidence for your position and identify the sources of your evidence.* In a review of the effects of evidence usage, Reinard (1988) concluded that in almost all cases, citing evidence and sources significantly enhanced speaker credibility. This advice applies especially to low-credibility sources.

3. *Cite your own or your sources' qualifications and expertise on the topic or issue up front.* Remember, expertise is one of the primary dimensions of credibility. For credibility to enhance persuasion, however, the source's credentials must be identified prior to presenting the message. If you have expertise on a topic or an issue, let your listener(s) know. If you lack expertise on an issue, don't dwell on your deficiencies. Instead, explain how you came to develop an interest in the subject. Also, consider this: If, in fact, you know little or nothing about a topic, then you have no business trying to persuade others about that topic in the first place.

4. *Attempt to build trust by demonstrating to your listener that you are honest and sincere.* One approach is to demonstrate that you possess good moral character. Another is to acknowledge that although compliance would benefit you, it would benefit the other person as well; compliance would be in both parties' mutual interest.

5. *Display goodwill toward your audience.* Don't seem aloof or indifferent. Show that you care about others, that you understand their ideas and their situation, that you empathize with their feelings and views, and that you are attentive and responsive to their communication attempts. For example, if a listener asks you a question, begin your answer by saying, "If I heard you correctly, you want to know . . ." and end by asking, "Does that address what you were asking?"

6. *Improve your likability, or L-factor.* Likability affects how you and your message are received. Some view likability as a form of emotional intelligence (Sanders, 2006). You can improve your L-factor by conveying warmth and immediacy. Smile often. Remember people's names. Listen. Thank people and accept compliments sincerely. Being genuine and authentic goes a long way.

7. *Adopt a language and delivery style appropriate to the listener(s), topic, and setting.* Your style of speech should be tailored to your particular receiver(s). Different receivers have different needs. In general, nonfluencies, pauses or gaps, and a choppy style of delivery hinder credibility (Berger, 1985, 1994; Miller & Hewgill, 1964). A reliance on "uhms," "ahs," and other fillers impairs credibility as well. An overreliance on slang, colloquialisms, or trite expressions can also compromise credibility.

8. *Avoid a powerless style of communication. Use an assertive style of communication instead.* A powerless communication style involves using tag questions ("That was a good movie, don't you think?"), hesitations ("uhm," "uh"), qualifiers ("kind of," "sort of," "perhaps," "maybe"), and negative preambles ("This will probably sound really dumb, but . . ."). A reliance on powerless language signals to the other party that you perceive yourself as occupying a lower status position in the relationship. For more about this topic, refer to Chapter 7, in which we examine the role of language in persuasion.

9. *Emphasize your similarity to another to indirectly enhance your credibility.* Listeners find it easier to identify with sources they perceive as similar to themselves. O'Keefe (2002) points out two important caveats regarding similarity and influence. First, he emphasizes, the similarities must be relevant to the topic or issue. Commenting, "Hey, I'm a Libra, too!" will probably get you nowhere unless the topic happens to center on astrology, horoscopes, and other similar topics. Second, O'Keefe notes that the perceived similarities must involve positive,

rather than negative, qualities. Stressing, "I was arrested for shoplifting once, too" may not enamor you to a new acquaintance, even though he or she may have confessed to a similar mistake.

10. If you think you are perceived as having low credibility, try to increase receiver involvement and emphasize the central route to persuasion. Remember, receivers who are highly involved in a topic place less emphasis on source credibility and more emphasis on the substance of a message. If you suspect your target audience is skeptical of your credibility, explain how the topic or issue is directly relevant to them and then focus on the substance of the message. That will tend to encourage central processing on the part of your audience.

11. Have another source who is already perceived as highly credible introduce or endorse you. This is a common strategy used in election campaigns. Salespersons also use this strategy when they rely on referrals. The technique allows a source to piggyback on the established credibility of the person making the introduction or endorsement. Acquiring credibility via endorsements and introductions emphasizes the peripheral route to persuasion.

SUMMARY

As we've seen, credibility is a complex construct. Yet there is one overriding generalization about credibility that persuaders can "take to the bank": *Credibility is a good thing to have if you are a persuader.* As long as we keep in mind that credibility is a perceptual phenomenon, the generalization that high-credibility sources are more influential than low-credibility sources is as close as one can come to a universal "law" of persuasion.

In advancing this generalization, however, we believe it is important to underscore the point that credibility is a complex, multidimensional, situational communication phenomenon. Credibility can't be bought in a bottle or purchased out of a vending machine. In many persuasive settings, a source who has low or no initial credibility can do little or nothing about it. Low-credibility sources tend to be dismissed out of hand; receivers simply fail to attend to their messages. There is an old joke about how to become a multimillionaire: "It's simple: First, get a million dollars, then . . ." Much the same advice can be offered for using credibility to enhance persuasion: "It's simple: First, get a lot of credibility, then . . ."

NOTES

1. Q-scores are calculated by Marketing Evaluations, Inc. (www.qscores.com), a company that rates over 1,800 personalities.
2. Impression management theory also has been referred to as identity management theory (IMT for short) by William Cupach and Todd Imahori (1993).

REFERENCES

Agrawal, J., & Kamakura, W. A. (1995). The economic worth of celebrity endorsers: An event study analysis. *Journal of Marketing, 59*(3), 56–62.

Allen, M., & Sriff, J. B. (1989). Testing three models for the sleeper effect. *Western Journal of Speech Communication, 53*(4), 411–426.

Allen, M., & Stiff, J. B. (1998). An analysis of the sleeper effect. In M. Allen & R. W. Preiss (Eds.), *Persuasion: Advances through meta-analysis* (pp. 175–188). Cresskill, NJ: Hampton Press.

Appel, M., & Richter, T. (2007). Persuasive effects of fictional narratives increase over time. *Media Psychology, 10*, 113–134.

Aristotle (1954). *Rhetoric* (W. R. Roberts, Trans.). New York: Random House.

Bartlett, T., & Smallwood, S. (2014, June 25). Psst. Wanna buy a Ph.D.? *The Chronicle of Higher Education*. Retrieved on May 9, 2017 from: www.chronicle.com/article/ Psst-Wanna-Buy-a-PhD-/24239

Benoit, W. L. (1987). Argumentation appeals and credibility appeals in persuasion. *Southern Speech Communication Journal, 52*, 181–187.

Benoit, W. L. (1995). *Accounts, excuses, and apologies: A theory of image restoration strategies*. Albany, NY: State University of New York Press.

Benoit, W. L., & Strathman, A. (2004). Source credibility and the elaboration likelihood model. In J. S. Seiter & R. H. Gass (Eds.), *Readings in persuasion, social influence, and compliance gaining* (pp. 95–111). Boston, MA: Allyn & Bacon.

Berger, A. A. (2011). *Ads, fads, and consumer culture* (4th ed.). Lanham, MD: Rowman & Littlefield.

Berger, C. R. (1985). Social power and interpersonal communication. In M. L. Knapp & G. R. Miller (Eds.), *Handbook of interpersonal communication* (pp. 439–499). Newbury Park, CA: Sage.

Berger, C. R. (1994). Power, dominance, and social interaction. In M. L. Knapp & G. R. Miller (Eds.), *Handbook of interpersonal communication* (2nd ed., pp. 450–507). Newbury Park, CA: Sage.

Berlo, D. K., Lemert, J. B., & Mertz, R. J. (1969). Dimensions for evaluating the acceptability of message sources. *Public Opinion Quarterly, 33*, 563–576.

Bruno, C. (2011, October 11) The perfect job to deal with disgrace: Advertising. *Ad Nauseum*. Retrieved on April 18, 2012 from: www.adnauseumblog.org/the-perfect-job-to-deal-with-disgrace-advertising/

Burgoon (Heston), J. K. (1973, April). *Ideal source credibility: A reexamination of the semantic differential*. Paper presented at the International Communication Association Convention, Montreal, Quebec.

Burgoon, J. K. (1976). The ideal source: A reexamination of source credibility measurement. *Central States Speech Journal, 27*, 200–206.

Cooper, M. (2013, April 30). For women leaders, likability and success hardly go hand in hand. *Harvard Business Review*. Retrieved on May 12, 2017 from: https://hbr.org/ 2013/04/for-women-leaders-likability-a

Cronkhite, G., & Liska, J. (1976). A critique of factor analytic approaches to the study of credibility. *Communication Monographs, 43*, 91–107.

Cupach, W. R., & Imahori, T. T. (1993). Identity management theory: Communication competence in intercultural episodes and relationships. In R. L. Wiseman & J. Koester (Eds.), *Intercultural communication competence* (pp. 112–131). Newbury Park, CA: Sage.

Denzen, N. K. (1987). *The recovering alcoholic*. Newbury Park, CA: Sage.

Djafarova, E., & Rushworth, C. (2017). Exploring the credibility of online celebrities' Instagram profiles in influencing the purchase decisions of young female users. *Computers in Human Behavior, 68*, 1–7. doi:10.1016/j.chb.2016.11.009

Elberse, A., & Verlun, J. (2012). The economic value of celebrity endorsers. *Journal of Advertising Research, 52*(2), 149–165. doi:10.2501/JAR-52-2-149–165

Gitomer, J. (2015). *The sales bible, new edition: The ultimate sales resource*. Hoboken, NJ: Wiley.

Goffman, E. (1967). *Interaction ritual essays on face-to-face behavior*. Garden City, NY: Anchor Books, Doubleday.

Goffman, E. (1974). *Frame analysis: An essay on the organization of experience*. Cambridge, MA: Harvard University Press.

Gruder, C. L., Cook, T. D., Hennigan, K. M., Flay, B. R., Alessi, C., & Halamaj, J. (1978). Empirical tests of the absolute sleeper effect predicted from the discounting cue hypothesis. *Journal of Personality and Social Psychology*, 36, 1061–1074.

Holyk, G., & Langer, G. (2016, August 31). Poll: Clinton unpopularity at new high, on par with Trump. *ABC News*. Retrieved on May 12, 2017 from: http://abcnews.go.com/Politics/poll-clinton-unpopularity-high-par-trump/story?id=41752050

Hovland, C. I., Lumsdaine, A., & Sheffield, F. (1949). *Experiments on mass communication*. Princeton, NJ: Princeton University Press.

Jensen, K., & Collins, S. (2008). The third-person effect in controversial product advertising. *American Behavioral Scientist*, 52(2), 225–242. doi:10.1177/0002764208321353

Kamins, M. A., & Gupta, K. (1994). Congruence between spokesperson and product types: A match-up hypothesis perspective. *Psychology & Marketing*, 11(6), 569–586.

Karmarkar, U. R., & Tormala, Z. L. (2010). Believe me, I have no idea what I'm talking about: The effects of source certainty on consumer involvement and persuasion. *Journal of Consumer Research*, 36(6), 1033–1049. doi:10.1086/648381

Knoll, J., & Matthes, J. (2017). The effectiveness of celebrity endorsements: A meta-analysis. *Journal of the Academy of Marketing Science*, 45, 55–75. doi:10.1007/s11747–016–0503–8

Koernig, S. K., & Boyd, T. C. (2009). To catch a tiger or let him go: The match-up effect and athlete endorsers for sport and non-sport brands. *Sport Marketing Quarterly*, 18, 25–37.

Kouzes, J. M., & Posner, B. Z. (2011). *Credibility: How leaders gain and lose it, why people demand it*. San Francisco, CA: Jossey-Bass.

Kouzes, J.M., & Posner, B.Z. (2017). *The leadership challenge* (6th ed.). Hoboken, NJ: Wiley.

Kumkale, G. T., & Albarracín, D. (2004). The sleeper effect in persuasion: A meta-analytic review. *Psychological Bulletin*, 130(l), 143–172.

Kumkale, G. T., & Albarracín, D., & Seignourel, P. J. (2010). The effects of source credibility in the presence or absence of prior attitudes: Implications for the design of persuasive communication campaigns. *Journal of Social Psychology*, 40(6), 1325–1356.

Lovas, M., & Holloway, P. (2009). *Axis of influence: How credibility and likeability intersect to drive success*. Garden City, NY: Morgan James.

McCracken, G. (1986). Culture and consumption: A theoretical account of the structure and movement of the cultural meaning of consumer goods. *Journal of Consumer Research*, 13, 71–84.

McCracken, G. (1989). Who is the celebrity endorser? *Journal of Consumer Research*, 16, 310–321.

McCroskey, J. C. (1966). Scales for the measurement of ethos. *Speech Monographs*, 33, 65–72.

McCroskey, J. C., & Mehrley, R. S. (1969). The effects of disorganization and nonfluency on attitude change and source credibility. *Speech Monographs*, 36, 13–21.

McCroskey, J. C., & Teven, J. J. (1999). Goodwill: A reexamination of the construct and its measurement. *Communication Monographs*, 66(1), 90–103.

McCroskey, J. C., & Young, T. J. (1981). Ethos and credibility: The construct and its measurement after three decades. *Central States Speech Journal*, 32, 24–34.

McShane, L. (2009, February 6). Caught on tape! Super-cool Sully. *Daily News*, p. 12.

Miller, G. R., & Hewgill, M. A. (1964). The effect of variations in nonfluency on audience ratings of source credibility. *Quarterly Journal of Speech*, *50*, 36–44.

Nan, X. (2009). The influence of source credibility on attitude certainty: Exploring the moderating effects of source identification and individual need for cognition. *Psychology and Marketing*, *26*(4), 321–332.

O'Keefe, D. J. (1987). The persuasive effects of delaying identification of high- and low-credibility communicators: A meta-analytic review. *Central States Speech Journal*, *38*, 63–72.

O'Keefe, D. J. (2002). *Persuasion: Theory and research* (2nd ed.). Thousand Oaks, CA: Sage.

O'Neil, J., & Eisenmann, M. (2017). An examination of how source classification impacts credibility and consumer behavior. *Public Relations Review*, *43*(2), 278–292. doi:10.1016/j.pubrev.2017.02.011

Petty, R. E., & Cacioppo, J. T. (1986a). The elaboration likelihood model of persuasion. In L. Berkowitz (Ed.), *Advances in experimental social psychology* (Vol. 19, pp. 123–205). New York: Academic Press.

Petty, R. E., & Cacioppo, J. T. (1986b). *Communication and persuasion: Central and peripheral routes to attitude change*. New York: Springer-Verlag.

Pornpitakpan, C. (2004). The persuasiveness of source credibility: A critical review of five decades' evidence. *Journal of Applied Social Psychology*, *34*(2), 243–281.

Reinard, J. C. (1988). The empirical study of the persuasive effects of evidence: The status after fifty years of research. *Human Communication Research*, *15*, 3–59.

Reysen, S. (2005). Construction of a new scale: The Reysen likability scale. *Social Behavior and Personality*, *33*(2), 201–208. doi:10.2224/sbp.2005.33.2.201

Riggio, R. E. (1987). *The charisma quotient*. New York: Dodd, Mead.

Riggio, R. E. (2010, February, 15). Charisma? What is it? Do you have it? *Psychology Today*. Retrieved on April 16, 2012, from: www.psychologytoday.com/blog/cutting-edge-leadership/201002/charisma-what-is-it-do-you-have-it

Rind, B. (1992). Effects of impressions of amazement and foolishness on compliance. *Journal of Applied Social Psychology*, *22*(21), 1656–1665.

Robertson, N. (1988). *Getting better: Inside Alcoholics Anonymous*. New York: Morrow.

Sanders, T. (2006). *The likeability factor: How to boost your L-factor and achieve your life's dreams*. New York: Three Rivers Press.

Sharp, H., & McClung, T. (1966). Effects of organization on the speaker's ethos. *Speech Monographs*, *33*, 182–183.

Shin, D.-H., & Kim, J. K. (2011). Alcohol product placements and the third-person effect. *Television & New Media*, *12*(5), 412–440. doi:10.1177/1527476410385477

Spry, A., Pappu, R., & Cornwall, T. B. (2011). Celebrity endorsement, brand credibility, and brand equity. *European Journal of Marketing*, *45*(6), 882–909. doi:10.1108/03090561111119958

Stiff, J. B. (1994). *Persuasive communication*. New York: Guilford Press.

Study finds ads induce few people to buy. (2000, October 17). *Wall Street Journal*, p. B10.

Tedeschi, J. T., & Reiss, M. (1981). Identities, the phenomenal self, and laboratory research. In J. Tedeschi (Ed.), *Impression management theory and social psychological research* (pp. 3–22). New York: Academic Press.

Till, B. D., & Busler, M. (2000). The match-up hypothesis: Physical attractiveness, expertise, and the role of fit on brand attitude, purchase intent, and brand beliefs. *Journal of Advertising*, *29*(3), 1–13.

Till, B. D., & Shimp, T. A. (1998). Endorsers in advertising: The case of negative celebrity information. *Journal of Advertising, 27*(1), 67–82.

Ting-Toomey, S. (1988). Intercultural conflict styles: A face-negotiation theory. In Y. Y. Kim & W. Gudykunst (Eds.), *Theories in intercultural communication* (pp. 213–235). Newbury Park, CA: Sage.

Ting-Toomey, S. (1994). *The challenge of facework: Cross-cultural and interpersonal issues.* Ithaca, NY: SUNY Press.

Ting-Toomey, S., & Kurogi, A. (1998). Facework competence in intercultural conflict: An updated face negotiation theory. *International Journal of Intercultural Relations, 22,* 187–225.

Ward, C. D., & McGinnies, E. (1974). Persuasive effect of early and late mention of credible and noncredible sources. *Journal of Psychology, 86,* 17–23.

Watts, W. A., & Holt, L. E. (1979). Persistence of opinion change induced under conditions of forewarning and distraction. *Journal of Personality and Social Psychology, 37,* 778–789.

Watts, W. A., & McGuire, W. J. (1964). Persistence of induced opinion change and retention of inducing message content. *Journal of Abnormal and Social Psychology, 68,* 223–241.

Weir, T. (2011, January 17). Endorsers lose influence. *USA Today,* p. 3C.

Wilson, E. J., & Sherrell, D. L. (1993). Source effects in communication and persuasion research: A meta-analysis of effect size. *Journal of the Academy of Marketing Science, 21,* 101–112.

CHAPTER 5

Communicator Characteristics and Persuasion

DO YOU HAVE A CELEBRITY CRUSH? Have you ever dreamt of Kerry Washington or Zac Efron? Spent hours on the Internet stalking Harry Styles or Jessica Alba? Retweeted or liked posts by Scarlett or Channing? Better yet, have you ever wondered whether your celebrity crush would like you back? Fortunately, for Spencer Morrill of Knoxville, Tennessee, the answer to that last question was "no!" Indeed, his celebrity crush—the megastar pop singer, Katy Perry—told him that she loved him . . . or so he thought. Sadly, after "dating" Katy online for six years, after making her an engagement ring out of his great-grandmother's emerald, and after blowing 25 percent of his savings, Spencer learned that "Katy" was really a woman named Harriet from England. Spencer, it turns out, had been duped in what is commonly known as an online "catfish scheme," in which the scammer pretends to be someone he or she is not. His ordeal was later featured on the MTV series *Catfish* (Delbyck, 2016).

If you're at all like us, you might be wondering how anyone could fall for such a hoax, especially for such a long period of time. But then again, when you consider all possible people, it's likely that someone would be gullible enough to fall for such a scheme.

However, although it seems that some people are more persuadable than others, the search for a single underlying trait or characteristic that makes people persuadable has not been successful. Persuasion is more complicated than that. And so are people. Even so, the characteristics of the people in a persuasive interaction cannot be ignored. All communicators are unique in terms of gender, age, personality, and background, and such characteristics are important to understanding the nature of social influence.

In this chapter, we explore the role communicator characteristics play in the process of persuasion. Although we don't have room to cover the immense number of characteristics that have been studied, we discuss several that past research has identified as being important to social influence. Then we discuss ways in which a communicator might analyze and adapt to an audience when trying to be persuasive. Before we begin, however, we note, as we have in earlier chapters, that persuasion is a two-way street. Thus, when we use the term *communicator characteristics,* we are not limiting our discussion to one person. The characteristics of all the interactants in a persuasive encounter are part of the equation.

DEMOGRAPHIC VARIABLES AND PERSUASION

If someone asked you to use 10 words to describe yourself, there is a good chance you would use demographic information to do so. Demographics include characteristics such as age, gender, ethnicity, and intelligence, which we discuss in the following sections.

Age and Persuasion: Pretty Please With Sugar on Top

The expression "It's like taking candy from a baby" suggests that children are easy targets for persuasion, and research indicates that this is generally true: Children tend to be especially vulnerable to persuasive trickery because they lack the ability to understand the nature and intent of persuaders (McAlister & Cornwell, 2009).

The implications of such research can be frightening. Indeed, we've all heard stories of children who have been tricked or lured away by criminals (for more on this issue, see Box 5.1).

What we may be less aware of, however, are other types of messages that may be persuading our children, or, for that matter, our fetuses! As Lindstrom (2011, p. 15) noted, because strong tastes and aromas (such as garlic and vanilla) pass through a mother's amniotic fluid and are actually "tasted" by a fetus, even unborn kids may be influenced to develop tastes inside the womb. He reported, for example, that Kopiko, a candy brand in the Philippines, supplied doctors with coffee-flavored candies to give away to pregnant mothers. Some time later, Kopiko introduced a new product—coffee—which was phenomenally successful, particularly among children in the Philippines.

Once outside the womb, it doesn't take long before kids are bombarded by the world of advertising. According to Lindstrom (2011), for example, by three months, 40 percent of all infants watch screen media regularly, and by two years, 90 percent of all children do. What's more, in the United States, typical kids are exposed to 40,000 commercials a year (Kunkel, Wilcox, Cantor, Palmer, Linn, & Dowrick, 2004). These numbers become especially meaningful when you understand that advertisers do not always have children's best interests in mind. According to Lindstrom's sources (2011, p. 22), for instance, the clothing retailer Abercrombie

BOX 5.1 | "Never Take Candy From Strangers"

I was certain it could never happen. After all, I'm a very street-savvy, New York City parent. I write articles advising moms and dads on child safety. Needless to say, I've been so conscientious in teaching my own children that my husband insists I'm paranoid, and my daughter has more than once rolled her eyes heavenward at my often repeated warnings. Which is why I can hardly describe the sick feeling in my stomach as I watched my redheaded little boy and his friend Tahlor march right out of the park one spring afternoon with a total stranger.

(Rosen, 1994, p. 108)

Fortunately for Margery Rosen, this scene was only part of an informal experiment. To test how well she had trained her children, she had gotten Kenneth Wooden, an expert on the ways in which sex offenders lure children, to see if he could persuade her children to leave the playground with him. He didn't have much trouble. He told the boys he had lost a puppy and would give them money if they would help him find it. They went right with him, and so did several other children involved in the experiment (Rosen, 1994).

Many children aren't as fortunate as those involved in Rosen's experiment. Indeed, it's been estimated that one in four girls and one in six boys are sexually abused by age 18 (Wooden, 2014). Clearly, children are especially susceptible to persuasion, and sometimes the results are tragic. For that reason, Kenneth Wooden (1988) argued, "Teaching your kids about the tricks that molesters use could save them from grievous harm—even death" (p. 149).

In an effort to prevent children from being molested, Wooden interviewed convicted molesters, pimps, and murderers and discovered several lures that are commonly used on children. Of the lures he said, "Knowledge of them is so basic to a child's safety that they should be taught—indeed must be taught—by every parent" (Wooden, 1988, p. 149). With this in mind, if you know, are, or plan to be a parent, here is an abbreviated list of lures and prevention strategies that Wooden (1995; see also Dickinson, 2002; Rosen, 1994; Wooden, 1988; Wooden, Webb, & Mitchell, 2014) identified:

1. The assistance lure. The lost puppy example described previously is an example of this lure. In it, the pedophile asks kids for directions, for help carrying packages, or for some other type of assistance. Children should be advised to keep their distance from strangers in cars. Children should tell the assistance seeker to ask another adult for help.
2. The authority and hero lures. Some molesters lure children by posing as police officers, Santa Claus, or other figures that children trust. Children should be taught that bad people can play tricks on children and that real heroes won't do certain things.
3. The affection/love lure. Some pedophiles lure children by promising them love and affection. Parents should know that 75 to 80 percent of sex crimes are committed by someone a child knows and trusts. Children should beware of anyone who wants excessive time alone with them and be encouraged to tell their parents about improper advances. Parents should trust their instincts.
4. The bribery lure. Children are often offered gifts from molesters. Parents should be suspicious of any new toys their children have. The age-old saying "Never take candy from strangers" is still true today.
5. The ego/fame lure. Youngsters are sometimes lured by modeling jobs or beauty contests that should be kept secret from mom and dad. For that reason, parents should accompany kids to such events, encourage openness, and check the credentials of "would-be" modeling agencies.
6. The emergency lure. Molesters might trick children by claiming "a house is on fire" or "mommy had to go to the hospital." To prevent falling for this, parents and children should prearrange an emergency plan. Under no circumstance should a child ride with a stranger.
7. The fun and games lure. Molesters sometimes turn tickling, wrestling, and other games into intimate contact. Children need to be taught that there are good and bad touches. Bad touches (e.g., anywhere under a bathing suit) should be reported.
8. The pornography lure. Pedophiles have been known to use pornography to destroy their victims' inhibitions. Wooden, therefore, advises parents to keep pornography out of the home so it does not seem legitimate.
9. The jobs lure. Molesters sometimes lure children by promising high-paying jobs. When suspicious, parents should accompany children to interviews, especially if the interview is in a secluded or unusual place, and ask to see a business license.

Finally, parents and children need to be aware that the Internet has become a vehicle for strangers who prey on children. Parents should watch for warning signs, including pornography on a child's computer (often sent by sexual predators to desensitize victims) and telephone calls or mail from strangers ("Beware 'Net predators," 2001).

Although some psychologists have argued that teaching children about a potential molester only serves to terrify them and prevent the formation of friendships (for a discussion, see Teaching fear, 1986), Rosen (1994, 2014) and others have argued that teaching children to be cautious about potential molesters is little different from vaccinating them against a disease or teaching them to be safe around stoves or electrical sockets. Education should start at a young age, with the goal of making children cautious, not paranoid. As Wooden (1988) noted, children should be taught that most people are good and won't hurt them but should also realize that some people are bad and sick.

& Fitch marketed padded bikini tops to girls as young as eight, and Tesco, a retailer in the UK, released the "Peekaboo Pole Dancing Kit," marketed to females under 10, as something to help them "unleash the sex kitten inside."

Unfortunately, until age eight, children do not understand the persuasive nature of advertising. Instead, kids think that ads are just there to inform them (Oates, Blades, & Gunter, 2002). Worse yet, children may have an especially difficult time understanding the persuasive intent behind "gamification," which promotes brands through fun and interactive online games (see Vanwesenbeeck, Walrave, & Ponnet, 2016; Panic, Cauberghe, & De Palsmacker, 2013). Fortunately, however, at least two variables seem to decrease children's vulnerability to advertising: adult influence and getting older. First, research shows that if you interact with children during ads, you can increase their ability to critically examine the ads and provide them with a better understanding of the nature and purpose of advertising. One study, for example, found that when adults made factual (e.g., "Those ads aren't telling the truth. Those toys look different in real life.") or evaluative ("These ads are dumb. These toys aren't fun.") comments during advertisements, children were less persuaded by the ads (Buijzen, 2007). Second, as children become older, they become less susceptible to distorted claims (Mills & Elashi, 2014). Notice, however, we say *less* susceptible, not immune. For example, Morgenstern, Isensee, Sargent, and Harwinkel (2011) found that teenagers who were exposed to a greater number of alcohol advertisements consumed larger amounts of alcohol.

So far, we've made it clear that young people tend to be highly susceptible to persuasion. But what about older people? Although earlier studies indicated that elderly people may be more "set in their ways," and, thus, less persuadable than younger folks, a newer generation of research supports the *life-stages hypothesis* (Sears, 1981), which suggests that there is a curvilinear relationship between age and persuadability (for a review, see Eaton, Visser, Krosnick, & Anand, 2009). In other words, compared to youthful and elderly people, middle-aged people are less persuadable. Consistent with this hypothesis, Liao and Fu (2014) found that, compared to younger adults (19–26), older adults (58–80) were less skilled at judging the credibility of online health information. This is troubling, of course, considering that older people are frequent users of health information, even though the content of health-related websites is often rated as unsatisfactory (see Liao & Fu, 2014).

Gender Differences and Persuasion: The Times, They Aren't a-Changin'

Do men and women differ in their ability to influence others? Before you answer, we should warn you: This is a trick question. Although the lion's share of research reveals that men are more successful than women in their attempts to persuade others (see Carli, 2004), their success has little to do with ability but rather a double-standard in audiences' perceptions. This conclusion is supported by the work of Carli (2004), who demonstrated that gender stereotypes cause audiences to perceive males as more competent than females and to expect females to be warmer and more nurturing than males. As a result, women experience a double bind: They must perform better than men to be considered equally competent, and they are perceived negatively when they try to be direct, assertive, and forceful. In one study, for instance, when females adopted aggressive communication behaviors in debates, they were judged more harshly than males who adopted the same behaviors (Matthews, 2016). Similarly, a meta-analysis found that women were less persuasive when they used aggressive and assertive tactics than when they used more role-consistent, communal tactics (Smith, Watkins, Burke, Christian, Smith, Hall, & Simms, 2013).

Consistent with this finding is Klingle's (2004) *reinforcement expectancy theory,* which applies to persuasive encounters between doctors and patients. According to the theory, once a doctor has tried to persuade a patient to do something (e.g., take medication), the patient judges the appropriateness of the doctor's message. If the message is viewed as inappropriate, the patient rejects it. If it is viewed as appropriate, it guides the patient's future behavior. How does this relate to gender? According to Klingle (2004), because of certain norms, female doctors can't get away with using aversive strategies the same way that male doctors can. When female doctors use such strategies, they violate patients' expectations about what is appropriate, and, as a result, patients are less likely to comply. According to the theory, then, male doctors can increase compliance by using either positive (e.g., "Regular eating will make you feel so much better") or negative ("You have two choices—change your diet or spend the rest of your life wishing you had") influence strategies, but female doctors can increase compliance by using only positive strategies (Klingle, 2004).

In addition to having double standards about the use of various persuasive strategies, people also hold stereotypes about who seems better suited for selling certain products. In one study (Rodero, Larrea, & Vázquez, 2013), for example, people listened to various radio advertisements that featured male or female voices. Results indicated that people perceived the male voice as more appropriate for selling mechanical products and the female voice as more appropriate for selling body-hair removal products. No differences were observed for neutral products.

Up to this point, we've seen that men and women differ regarding how successful they are when trying to persuade other people. But how do men and women compare when it comes to being persuaded? Early research suggested that women were more easily persuaded than men (e.g., Chaiken, 1979). Later, however, researchers who examined and summarized large numbers of studies on the topic questioned the notion of whether women were any different from men when it came to being persuaded (e.g., Eagly, 1978). As a result, many researchers abandoned the idea of general gender effects and instead tried to explain *when* gender differences could be expected. For instance, in Eagly's 1978 study, 32 percent of the studies published before 1970 (generally regarded as the onset of the women's movement) found that women were more easily influenced than men, but only 8 percent of the studies published after 1970 found the same result. Thus, evaporating gender differences might be the result of changing times and the attitudes of and toward women. However, considering the research we have discussed on how gender stereotypes affect males' versus females' ability to persuade, we doubt that this explanation is correct.

Even so, there is another possible explanation for the change in research findings before and after 1970. Specifically, earlier studies used male rather than female sources (Ward, Seccombe, Bendel, & Carter, 1985), which means that male receivers were being persuaded by members of the same sex, whereas females were being persuaded by members of the opposite sex—that is, in the earlier studies, there may have been a *cross-sex effect,* by which people were more easily influenced by members of the opposite sex than by members of the same sex. This effect, however, may be stronger for males persuading females than for females persuading males (Ward et al., 1985).

From our review so far, it is clear that generalizations about gender and persuasion are hard to come by. As Cody, Seiter, and Montagne-Miller (1995) argue, "There is no simple model that links 'gender' or 'sex' to influenceability" (p. 312). Instead, these researchers argue that persuadability is not so much related to one's gender as it is to one's goals, plans, resources, and beliefs (Cody et al., 1995). For instance, imagine that you are in a shopping mall, looking at clothing. If you don't intend to buy anything (goal), have decided you will look now and buy later (plan), have very little money (resources), and think that all salespersons are dishonest (beliefs), you will probably be more difficult to influence than if you intend to buy now, have lots of money, and believe salespersons are honest. In other words, it may not matter so much whether you are male or female; how easy you are to influence depends on your goals, plans, resources, and beliefs. Gender matters only to the extent that males and females have different goals, plans, resources, and beliefs. For instance, Cody and colleagues (1995) found that when shopping for clothes, men and women tend to have different goals and that such goal differences were related to influenceability and the effectiveness of certain sales tactics. Likewise, Orji, Mandryk, & Vassileva (2015) found that males and females differed in their responsiveness to different persuasive strategies.

Ethnicity, Culture, and Persuasion: "Me" and "We" Perspectives

Cultural differences play a major role, both in terms of how people fashion influence attempts and how they respond to them. Perhaps the most commonly discussed dimension of cultural variability is known as *individualism–collectivism* (Hofstede, 1983). Whereas people in collectivist cultures (e.g., China) tend to value harmony, concern for others, and the goals of the group over the goals of the individual, people in individualistic cultures (e.g., the United States) tend to value independence and the goals of the individual over the goals of a collective.

With that in mind, consider the following list of slogans (see Han & Shavitt, 1994, p. 346) and imagine which you would use to appeal to people in a collectivistic culture and which you would use to appeal to people in an individualistic culture:

"The art of being unique."

"She's got a style all her own."

"We have a way of bringing people closer together."

"The dream of prosperity for all of us."

A study by Han and Shavitt (1994) found that advertisements, such as the first and second in the previous list, that appealed to individual benefits, personal success, and independence were used more in the United States (an individualistic culture) than in Korea (a collectivistic culture) and were more persuasive in the United States than in Korea. Ads, such as the third and fourth, that appealed to group benefits, harmony, and family were used more often and were more persuasive in Korea than in the United States.

Also consistent with the notion that people from collectivistic cultures focus on groups and relationships, Fu and Yukl (2000) found that Chinese managers rated "emphasizing coalitions" and "gift-giving" among the most effective influence tactics, whereas managers from the United States preferred rational persuasion. Similarly, a study by Wiseman and colleagues (2009) found differences between the persuasive strategies used by people from the United States, China, and Japan. For example, when trying to persuade roommates to be more quiet, people from the United States, who tend to be more individualistic and less concerned with saving face, preferred more direct strategies (e.g., "You are making too much noise. Please be quiet") and strategies with individually controlled sanctions ("If you don't quiet down, I'll be as noisy as possible when you are trying to study"). People from China, who tend to be more collectivistic, preferred indirect strategies (e.g., commenting on how they like quiet moments) and strategies with group-controlled sanctions (e.g., "Your noisiness shows a lack of consideration for others"). However, people from Japan hinted less than people from both the United States and China, leading Wiseman and colleagues (2009) to conclude that collectivism and individualism may not be opposite orientations. In fact, Agrawal (2015) suggested that people from individualistic cultures can sometimes be primed to behave in collectivistic ways and vice versa. For example, someone from an individualistic culture might be asked to think about family obligations (Agrawal, 2015). As such, sometimes culturally incongruent messages can be persuasive.

Finally, with regard to individualism–collectivism, Orji (2015) identified several additional cultural differences. Specifically, people from collectivistic cultures perceived appeals to authority (e.g., expertise), consensus (e.g., others are doing it, so you should too), liking, and reciprocity (e.g., you are obligated to give back) as more persuasive than did people from individualistic cultures.

Although individualism and collectivism are important values affecting cross-cultural differences in persuasion, they are not the only ones. For example, after conducting interviews with people from the People's Republic of China and Taiwan, Ma and Chuang (2001) identified three influence tactics reflecting additional values of importance. First, *anshi,* or "hinting" (e.g., telling a friend who loaned you money that you'd like to buy something if you weren't broke), compared to more direct strategies (e.g., demanding the money a friend borrowed), not only preserves harmony in a relationship, it is more respectful and seeks to save another person's face. Second, *yi shen zuo ze,* or "setting an example by one's own action" (e.g., a manager works exceptionally hard hoping her subordinates will do likewise), reflects the Chinese culture's mistrust of words. Third, *tou qi suo hao,* or "feeding people what they relish" (e.g., agreeing to do something another person loves before asking a favor), reflects a preference for indirectness, other-orientedness, and granting people "face" (Ma & Chuang, 2001).

Similarly, a study by Fitch (1994) found that distinctive cultural systems of beliefs, values, and symbols underlie differences in the influence messages used by people in the United States and Colombia. A recurring theme in the influence strategies used in the United States was "empowerment." For instance, a manager observed in Fitch's study argued:

A stumbling block to empowerment is the low self-esteem of people who have been told what to do. If we want them to make their own decisions, we have to build up their self-esteem. And that starts with asking, not telling people what to do.

(p. 194)

In contrast, Colombians' influence attempts centered on the concept of *confianza* (having trust or closeness in a relationship). For example, Colombians commonly ask intermediaries who have closer relationships with persuadees to deliver influence messages for them (e.g., "You know Dioselina better than I do. Will you ask her to put up the signs?").

Intelligence and Persuasion: Dumb and Dumber

Imagine you were offered a million dollars to persuade either Forrest Gump (if you haven't seen the movie, Forrest isn't known for his brains) or Albert Einstein to believe or do something. Who would you choose? Earlier work (e.g., McGuire, 1968) suggested that neither Forrest nor Albert—but rather someone with moderate intelligence—should be chosen. The idea was that Forrest would be difficult to persuade because he would be unable to comprehend a message, while Albert would be difficult because he would be better at scrutinizing a message. Later work, however, indicated that Forrest should be your choice. Indeed, a review of research by Rhodes and Wood (1992) indicated that less intelligent people are easier to persuade than people with a lot of smarts. Even so, we imagine that other variables may be important too. More intelligent people may be in a better position to process complex messages. Recall that when central processing is required, the ability to process a message is important. Less intelligent people may be more receptive to simpler messages or messages that encourage peripheral processing.

PSYCHOLOGICAL AND COMMUNICATION STATES AND TRAITS

Two common explanations for why people differ from one another centers on the notion of traits and states. A *trait* is a characteristic of a person presumed to be relatively stable across situations. A *state* varies from situation to situation. For instance, if we conceptualize anxiety as a trait, we would predict that a person possessing the trait would be anxious in practically all situations. On the other hand, if we conceptualize anxiety as a state, we would predict that there are certain situations in which a person becomes anxious. For instance, some people become very anxious when talking with authorities or when meeting members of the opposite sex. With these definitions in mind, we now turn to a discussion of some specific traits and states that have been the focus of research in the area of persuasion.

Self-Esteem and Persuasion: Feelin' Kinda Low

Are individuals with low self-esteem more susceptible to influence attempts than individuals with high self-esteem? Although this notion seems reasonable, it is not supported by research (Rhodes & Wood, 1992). This is because to be persuaded, a person must both receive and yield to a message. People with low self-esteem may be more likely to yield to a message because they lack confidence in themselves and their opinions. However, they may also be too concerned about their appearance and behavior to be receptive to a persuasive message. On the other hand, people with high self-esteem may be more receptive to persuasive messages. However, because they are more confident in themselves and their own opinions, they may be less likely to yield. Thus, research indicates that people with moderately high self-esteem are easier to persuade than people with either high or low self-esteem (Rhodes & Wood, 1992).

Anxiety and Persuasion: Living in Fear

Unless you've grown up in a closet, you've undoubtedly been exposed to messages about the dangers of global warming, secondhand cigarette smoke, gang violence, and so forth. How do you react to such messages? Do they make you overly nervous or tense? If so, you may be chronically anxious. Research suggests that anxiety, whether chronic or acute, may be related to persuadability, although the relationship is not clear. For instance, Nunnally and Bobren (1959) found that anxious people were more persuadable than nonanxious people, whereas Janis and Feshbach (1965) found just the opposite. Moreover, research by Lehmann (1970) indicated that anxiety is related to persuasion as much as self-esteem is. Specifically, anxious people, compared to the nonanxious, may be more likely to yield to a message. However, because they may be distracted or overly worried, they may be less likely to receive a message. On the other hand, nonanxious people, compared to the anxious, may be more likely to receive a message but less inclined to do something about it (Lehmann, 1970). Finally, Nai, Schemeil, and Marie (2016) found that anxiety increases people's motivation to be accurate. As such, anxious folks, compared to calm ones, are more open to messages that challenge their opinions, and, as a result, are more persuadable.

Whatever the relationship between anxiety and persuasion, one thing is clear: When trying to persuade anxious people, be sure to include specific recommendations for avoiding the harms, along with reassurances that if they follow the recommendations, everything will be okay. As you'll see in more detail in Chapter 13, without such reassurances, people who are anxious may not respond well to fear appeals.

Preference for Consistency: I Wouldn't Change a Thing

In Chapter 3, we stated that people are generally motivated to be consistent with their attitudes and behavior. As with most things, however, there are exceptions to this statement. It turns out that individuals differ in their *preference for consistency* (PFC). While "high PFCs" value and strive to be consistent, "low PFCs" have a preference for change, spontaneity, and unpredictability (see Guadagno & Cialdini, 2010). As such, several studies indicate that high PFCs are more susceptible to the effects of cognitive dissonance. For example, Sénémeaud, Mange, Fointiat, and Somat (2014) induced a group of French students to feel hypocritical, which, presumably, would cause dissonance. Specifically, after listing the dangers of excessive alcohol consumption, the students were asked to consider previous situations in which they had consumed too much alcohol. Not surprisingly, compared to students who had not undergone this procedure, the "hypocritical" students were more willing to spend time helping young adults avoid alcohol abuse. This was especially true for high PFCs who had been made aware of their desire for consistency (Sénémeaud et al., 2014) (for more on PFC, see Chapter 10).

Self-Monitoring and Persuasion: Periscope Up

In high school, a sister of one of the authors dated a guy who was a maniac on the dance floor. Out of context, you'd never have guessed he was dancing. He used to stomp his feet and flap his hands wildly and out of rhythm. Some said he looked badly wounded. Others simply stared. But whatever went on around him, he seemed oblivious, not caring what others thought of him.

The account you've just read is related to a personality trait called *self-monitoring* (Snyder, 1974, 1979). The wild dancer in the story is what people who study personality would call a *low self-monitor*. If you are a low self-monitor, you tend to be less sensitive than others to social cues. In addition, you are not that concerned about what others think of your behavior. You are individualistic and may not always act in ways that are considered socially appropriate. You honestly express your thoughts and feelings, even though you may not be conforming to other people's expectations.

However, if you are a *high self-monitor*, you tend to be very sensitive to social cues. You pay close attention to what's considered appropriate in a given situation and act accordingly. You watch other people's behavior and are good at adapting to different audiences because you have a large repertoire of social skills. You are concerned with appearances and try to "fit in" with others, even when such behavior may contradict what you believe.

As you might expect, high and low self-monitors are persuaded differently. For instance, White and Gerstein (1987) conducted a study to investigate how high and low self-monitors might be persuaded to offer help to people with disabilities. Because they knew that high self-monitors want to "look good," these researchers suspected that high self-monitors could be persuaded to help if they thought a social reward would result. To test this, high and low self-monitors heard lectures about Kitty Genovese, a woman who was murdered in New York City while many people watched but did not help. In one version of the lecture, subjects learned that people who help receive social rewards. In another version, subjects were told that helping others usually does not result in social rewards. Later, the subjects were phoned and asked to volunteer to help people who were visually impaired. Of those who'd been told that helping results in social rewards, 80 percent of the high self-monitors volunteered, but only 48 percent of the low self-monitors did. When subjects did not expect social rewards, 68 percent of the low self-monitors volunteered, and only 40 percent of the high self-monitors did. In other words, high self-monitors are influenced by situations that yield social benefits or enhance their images. Low self-monitors are more internally motivated and less susceptible to external rewards.

Similarly, several studies in advertising suggest that high self-monitors are more influenced by "image-based" advertising. In contrast, low self-monitors are more interested in "product-quality" advertising. For example, Snyder and DeBono (1989) found that high self-monitors were willing to pay more money for a product that promised to improve their image (e.g., an ad shows a bottle of Canadian Club resting on a set of house blueprints and reads, "You're not just moving in, you're moving up"), whereas low self-monitors would pay more for a product that suggests high quality (e.g., an ad for Canadian Club that reads, "When it comes to great taste, everyone draws the same conclusion"). Moreover, high self-monitors reported liking

FIGURE 5.1
High self-monitors:
Daffodil Queen
contestants
eavesdropping on
contestant interviews.
Source: Reprinted by
permission of Steven G.
Smith.

cheese more when they believed it was from France (an image-enhancing country) than from Kansas (DeBono & Rubin, 1995), liking perfume more when it was in an attractive rather than an unattractive bottle (DeBono, Leavitt, & Backus, 2003), preferring an energy drink when it was labeled "Fast Track" rather than "Energy Drink Enhancer" (Smidt & DeBono, 2011), and preferring champagne that was endorsed by four people rather than one person (Myers & Sar, 2013). In contrast, low self-monitors based their judgments on the actual taste of the cheese and smell of the perfume, and preferred the label "Energy Drink Enhancer." Finally, Evans and Clark (2012) found that low self-monitors were more confident in their thoughts about a persuasive appeal when the source of the appeal was described as being an expert (e.g., a doctor and researcher), while high self-monitors were more confident when the source was described as having an attractive image (e.g., an honor student, active in student government).

Ego Involvement: Not Budging an Inch

One of the most important explanations of the process by which people are persuaded, presented by Muzafer Sherif, Carolyn Sherif, and Robert Nebergall (Sherif & Sherif, 1967; Sherif, Sherif, & Nebergall, 1965), is known as *social judgment theory*. We present the theory here because it focuses on receivers and is particularly relevant to a psychological characteristic known as *ego involvement*.

According to the theory, on any topic, whether it be abortion, an advertised product, or a favorite movie, there are a range of possible opinions that a person can hold. For example, one topic is what should be done with people who have been found guilty of first-degree murder. Here are several positions, some extreme, some moderate, which you might embrace on this topic. Murderers should:

1.   Be pardoned if they have performed other good deeds during their lives.
2.   Be allowed to pay "blood money" to the victim's family to avoid prison.
3.   Receive a 5-year prison term.
4.   Receive a 20-year prison term.
5.   Receive a life sentence with a chance for parole.
6.   Receive a life sentence with no chance for parole.
7.   Be put to death.
8.   Be tortured to death, along with all other violent criminals.

Persuasion by Degrees

Social judgment theory argues that on this continuum of positions, we each have a most preferred position, called an *anchor*. For instance, imagine that two people, Muffy and Mort, both agree most with position 6, that murderers should spend their lives in prison with no chance for parole. In Figure 5.2, this anchor point is represented by an "X." Of course, the anchor position is not the only position a person might find acceptable. You can see in Figure 5.2, for example, that Muffy also would accept the death penalty as a fitting punishment. Together, with Muffy's anchor, these positions represent Muffy's *latitude of acceptance*. In other words, these are positions she finds tolerable. She would not, however, agree with all positions, for in addition to the latitude of acceptance, social judgment theory describes two other latitudes. The first, called the *latitude of noncommitment,* contains positions about

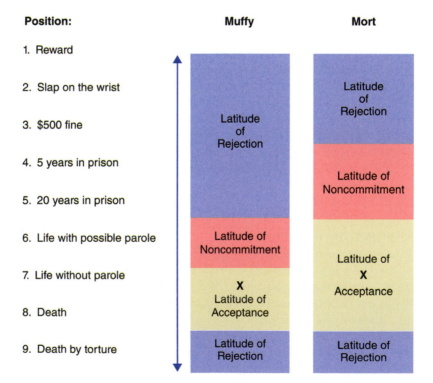

FIGURE 5.2
Illustration of social judgment theory.

which a person feels neutral or ambivalent. Muffy is neither for nor against murderers receiving life sentences with the possibility of parole; she is neutral. The second, called the *latitude of rejection,* contains positions that a person would reject. For example, Muffy rejects the idea that murderers be pardoned for good deeds, be allowed to pay blood money, spend 5 to 20 years in prison, or be tortured to death.

Changes in Attitude, Changes in Latitude

Notice in Figure 5.2 that the span of these latitudes is different for different people. Compared to Mort, Muffy has a larger latitude of rejection and narrower latitudes of noncommitment and acceptance. For this reason, Muffy is a good example of an ego-involved person. People are ego involved when an issue has personal significance to them and their sense of self. Thus, they become strongly committed to their stand on the issue and are more likely to reject other positions. A person might also be ego involved about one issue and not another. For instance, Muffy might have strong feelings about what happens to murderers, but care less about abortion, gun control, or gasoline prices.

Assimilation–Contrast Phenomenon: The Great Divide

Social judgment theory makes several important predictions about the process of persuasion. First, because people judge everything according to their anchor position, it is difficult, if not impossible, to persuade them to accept a position too far away from that anchor. For instance, if you tried to convince Mort that murderers should be pardoned for performing good deeds, you'd be wasting your time (see Figure 5.2); messages falling inside a person's latitude of rejection are bound to fail. In fact, the theory argues that when a message falls too far away from a person's anchor position, the person perceives the message to be farther away from the anchor than it really is. This is known as the *contrast effect.* However, the *assimilation effect* occurs when a message that falls within a person's latitude of acceptance is perceived to be closer to the anchor position than it really is. For example, although Mort would prefer that murderers be severely punished, if you told Mort that murderers should be moderately punished, he might decide that you basically agree and accept your position. Thus, whereas contrast leads to the rejection of a message, assimilation leads to successful persuasion.

You might have guessed by now that the contrast effect is more likely in ego-involved people than in people who are not ego involved. Indeed, it's difficult to persuade someone who is ego involved (e.g., Sherif, Kelly, Rodgers, Sarup, & Tittler, 1973). Because their latitude of rejection is so large (and their latitude of acceptance is so narrow), obviously, they will reject most persuasive messages.

Baby Steps: Nudging Someone Along

One of the things we like best about *social judgment theory* is how it suggests that persuasion is not a "one-shot deal." We think the theory does a good job of illustrating that persuasion may have to occur over time. For example, imagine trying to persuade Muffy that murderers should merely be pardoned for good deeds (see Figure 5.2). We've already seen that trying to convince her of that will lead to rejection. But aiming messages nearer the anchor point might meet with more success. You might try to persuade Muffy that life in prison with a chance for parole is a good position. Then, if she agrees to that, later you could try to convince her that 20 years in prison is justified; some murderers do repent and reform. Get the idea? Anchor positions need to be moved gradually.

Issue Involvement: What's This Have to Do With Me?

Although we just stated that involvement inhibits persuasion, in reality, things are more complicated than that. Indeed, the effect of involvement on persuasion depends on the type of involvement we're considering. Specifically, Johnson and Eagly (1990) argued that two types of involvement are ego involvement (a.k.a. *value-relevant involvement*), which is linked to enduring values embedded in a person's self-concept, and *outcome-relevant involvement* (a.k.a. *issue involvement*), which has to do with a person's current goals or outcomes (e.g., a cancer patient with the goal of using marijuana to minimize physical pain). Based on this notion, Johnson and Eagly analyzed a large number of studies and found that, consistent with social judgment theory, value-relevant involvement inhibited persuasion. Meanwhile, consistent with the *elaboration likelihood model* (see Chapter 2), issue involvement caused people to pay closer attention to arguments in persuasive messages. Issue involvement facilitated persuasion when arguments were strong but inhibited persuasion when arguments were weak (Johnson & Eagly, 1990). Another study found that when listening to messages promoting health, involved people were more persuaded by informational messages, while noninvolved people were more persuaded by testimonials (Braverman, 2008).

Dogmatism, Authoritarianism, and Social Vigilantism: You Can't Teach an Old Dog New Tricks

In the classic movie *A Few Good Men,* Tom Cruise and Demi Moore defend two Marines, who, while following orders from their superior officers, accidentally killed a fellow soldier. Their defense? "We were simply following orders."

History is replete with examples of this excuse. It was used by Nazi defendants at Nuremberg. It was repeated again during the Vietnam War by soldiers involved in the My Lai massacre, by Ollie North in the Iran-Contragate scandal, and by U.S. soldiers in charge of Iraqi detainees at Abu Ghraib. "We were following orders" is a timeworn excuse and a reflection of a personality trait known as *authoritarianism.*

Authoritarian people respect authoritative leadership and tend to follow authorities blindly (Adorno, Frenkel-Brunswik, Levenson, & Sanford, 1950; Allport, 1954). They condemn those who question and deviate from conventional norms, exhibit hostility toward out-group members, and help cause and inflame intergroup conflict (Altemeyer, 1999). They are less forgiving and more vengeful toward unrepentant transgressors (Khoury, Struthers, Santelli, & Marjanovic, 2012), and they raise children who are unaccepting of out-groups and who tend to associate with bullies (Knafo, 2003). They believe that power and rigid control are acceptable, and are likely to use physical punishment. Finally, if you are authoritarian, you may not have the self-insight to recognize it. According to Altemeyer (1999):

> If you tell people about authoritarianism, including the part about authoritarians being aggressive when backed by authority, and then ask them how willing they would be to help the federal government eliminate

authoritarians, then—you guessed it—High [authoritarians] will be more willing to volunteer than others, to hunt themselves down. . . . And yet, compared with most people, they think their minds are models of rationality and self-understanding.

(p. 159)

A personality trait that is very much related to authoritarianism is *dogmatism* (Rokeach, 1960). In fact, according to Christie (1991), dogmatism was introduced as a more general type of authoritarianism; although some argue that authoritarianism and dogmatism scales measure the same thing, others claim that the authoritarianism scale tends to identify closed-minded conservatives, whereas the dogmatism scale identifies closed-minded liberals and conservatives. Whatever the case, dogmatic people, like authoritarians, tend to be deferential to authorities. In addition, dogmatics are closed-minded, have difficulty being objective, and tend to believe there is only one right way to do things (i.e., their way).

With this in mind, you might think that such closed-mindedness makes authoritarian and dogmatic people difficult to persuade. Interestingly, however, a meta-analysis by Preiss and Gayle (1999) found just the opposite—that is, compared to their counterparts, dogmatic and authoritarian people were *easier* to persuade. The authors suggested that the rigid beliefs of people with such traits might interfere with the way they scrutinize messages, thereby resulting in greater agreement with a message.

Note, however, that although Preiss and Gayle's (1999) analysis is useful in some respects, we think it's too soon to conclude that dogmatic and authoritarian people are easy to persuade. Indeed, we suggest that more research needs to be conducted to determine *when* dogmatism/authoritarianism is positively related to persuasion and when it is not. By way of example, successfully persuading such people might depend on the nature of the source. Harvey and Beverly (1961), for instance, reported that high authoritarians, compared to low authoritarians, are more likely to be influenced by a person who is a high-status authority. Similarly, a study by DeBono and Klein (1993) found that when dogmatic people received persuasive messages from experts, they did not think much about the messages and, regardless of the quality of the messages, were more persuaded than people who were not dogmatic. However, when they received persuasive messages from nonexperts, dogmatics were more persuaded by strong arguments than by weak ones. Thus, it may be that authoritarians and "high dogs," as people who are highly dogmatic are called by researchers, are especially vulnerable to messages from authority figures.

A related trait is known as *social vigilantism* (Saucier & Webster, 2010). Like dogmatics, social vigilantes think their beliefs are superior to others' beliefs. Unlike dogmatics, who tend to dismiss those who disagree with them, social vigilantes try to impress their beliefs onto others. By way of example, when confronted with a contrary view, a social vigilante in one study stated, "Everyone does have a right to their own opinions. I just think you should know how ignorant you sound when you voice them" (Saucier & Webster, 2010, p. 19). Not surprisingly, research indicates that social vigilantes, compared to people measuring low on this trait, not only express more belief superiority, they also counterargue more (Saucier & Webster,

2010), and attempt to dominate conversations (Maki & Raimi, 2017). Finally, when trying to resist the persuasive attempts of others, social vigilantes use a variety of tactics, including getting emotionally upset and belittling their conversational partners (Saucier, Webster, Hoffman, & Strain, 2014).

Narcissism: How Do I Love Me? Let Me Count the Ways

In Greek mythology, Narcissus, who scorned those who loved him, saw his reflection in a pool of water and fell in love with himself. Not only that, he got a personality trait named after him. According to a review by Kausel and his colleagues (2016), narcissists have grandiose views of themselves, a lack of concern for others, and use a wide range of persuasive strategies to increase their self-concept and public image. What's more, narcissists are persuaded by messages that fuel their conceit. One study, for example, found that narcissists, compared to non-narcissists, were more likely to purchase high- versus low-distinctive merchandise (e.g., a "limited-edition" iPod case with personal name engraving rather than a $50 gift card) (Lee, Gregg, & Park, 2013). Another found that narcissists were fond of "virtual mirror," a popular application that allows consumers to experience products virtually. Specifically, narcissists, compared to non-narcissists, were more inclined to purchase clothing when their own images, rather than the images of professional models, were overlaid with the clothing (Baek, Yoo, & Yoon, 2016). Finally, when it comes to persuading potential sexual partners, narcissists are more likely to employ coercive tactics, including physical force, the use of alcohol, and manipulation (Blinkhorn, Lyons, & Almond, 2015). Given that, it's hard to see what they see in themselves.

Cognitive Complexity and Need for Cognition

How would you describe your best friend? Fun or boring? Intelligent or stupid? Superficial or disclosive? Even-tempered or moody?

According to a theory known as *constructivism* (Delia, O'Keefe, & O'Keefe, 1982), people attempt to make sense of their world by using constructs like the ones just mentioned. *Constructs* are perceptual categories (e.g., fat/thin, popular/unpopular, strong/weak) that we use when evaluating everything from professors, to textbooks, to music, to arguments. Constructs can be compared to eyeglasses: Just as the size, shape, and color of lenses affect the way you see things, the constructs you use to filter messages influence the way in which you perceive the world. For instance, someone who evaluates you on the sole basis of whether you are Christian or non-Christian will see you much differently than someone who uses more constructs (such as kind or cruel, shy or extroverted, happy or sad, playful or serious, emotional or stoic) to evaluate you. Obviously, everyone has a unique system of constructs, and some people clearly use more constructs than others. People who use a large number of different and abstract constructs that are well integrated are known as *cognitively complex,* whereas those who use fewer and less abstract constructs are *cognitively simple.*

People who are more cognitively complex, compared to those who are not, are better at seeing the world from their listeners' perspective. As a general rule, they are better at adapting their messages to their listeners and are much more persuasive (Waldron & Applegate, 1998).

When it comes to *being* persuaded, cognitively complex people may also differ from those who are cognitively simple. For instance, cognitively complex people may be more willing than people low in cognitive complexity to tolerate messages that are inconsistent with their cognitions (McGill, Johnson, & Bantel, 1994).

In addition to being different in the degree to which they are cognitively complex, research shows that people differ in their *need for cognition* (Cacioppo & Petty, 1982). People who are high in the need for cognition enjoy effortful thinking more than those low in the need. We also bet they like playing chess and torturing themselves with logic puzzles. According to some researchers, need for cognition is one facet of cognitive complexity (McGill et al., 1994). Whatever the case, compared to people who are low in the need for cognition, those high in the need for cognition are more tolerant of disagreement (Linvill, Mazer, & Boatwright, 2016) and are viewed by discussion partners as more effective persuaders who generate more valid arguments for their views (Shestowsky & Horowitz, 2004). Perhaps that is why research indicates that people who are high in the need for cognition are more effective salespeople than those who are low in the need for cognition (Sojka & Deeter-Schmelz, 2008).

Research also shows that people high in the need for cognition are persuaded differently than their brain-relaxing counterparts. Although people high in the need for cognition pay close attention to messages, evaluating and scrutinizing all the time, people low in the need for cognition are less motivated to attend to messages and are persuaded by peripheral cues instead (Cacioppo & Petty, 1982). Thus, if you're high in the need for cognition, you are persuaded by quality arguments. If you're low in the need for cognition, you may be persuaded by an attractive speaker (see Perlini & Hansen, 2001), a likable source (Reinhard & Messner, 2009), a celebrity spokesperson (Williams-Piehota, Schneider, Pizarro, Mowad, & Salovey, 2003), a lot of examples, or a snappy-sounding sales pitch, even if the arguments used are weak. For example, Kaufman, Stasson, and Hart (1999) found that when reading an article on evolution theory, the evaluations of people high in the need for cognition were not affected by the source of the article. In contrast, people low in the need for cognition rated the article favorably, but only if they thought it came from the *Washington Post* (a highly credible source). If they thought the article was from the *National Enquirer,* they did not rate it favorably. At least one implication is clear: If the ghost of Elvis Presley *really* wants a following, it should seek coverage in a more reputable publication.

Persuasion and Aggression: Sticks and Stones

Persuasion is not always pretty. Spouse abuse is rampant. Parents beating children as a way to get them to behave is all too common. And who hasn't been called "chicken," "wimp," "bitch," or "brat" by someone wanting to see a change in behavior? Clearly, aggression is the dark side of persuasion. On the other hand, Dominic Infante (1987) argues that aggression is not always bad; aggressive acts can be either constructive or destructive (or both), depending on the type of aggression and how it affects a relationship (Infante, 1987; Rancer, 2004). According to Infante, there are several forms of aggressive communication. We discuss two of them here.

First, *verbal aggressiveness,* a destructive form of aggression, involves the tendency to attack someone by using threats, profanity, insults, and teasing, and by insulting their character, competence, background, appearance, and so forth (Rancer, 2004). In short, verbal aggression is aimed at damaging another person's self-concept. As might be expected, compared to nonviolent marriages, violent ones are characterized by higher verbal aggressiveness (Infante, Chandler, & Rudd, 1989). In other contexts, verbally aggressive teachers are perceived as less credible than their counterparts (Mazer & Stowe, 2016), and verbally aggressive supervisors have less satisfied and committed employees (Madlock & Dillow, 2012).

In contrast, *argumentativeness,* a constructive form of assertiveness, involves the tendency to defend and refute positions on controversial issues. Argumentative people approach arguments while nonargumentative people avoid them (Rancer, 2004). Although we sometimes have negative connotations about the word "argument," research shows that argumentativeness is associated with employee satisfaction (Infante & Gordon, 1991) and success in college (Infante, 1982). Moreover, while students perceive verbally aggressive instructors as having low credibility, they perceive argumentative instructors as having high credibility (Edwards & Myers, 2007).

To us, perhaps the most interesting line of research on traits and influence examines the ways in which people "edit" their persuasive messages before they present them. Perhaps you've caught yourself doing this—you want to use a particular strategy, but something keeps you from doing it. A study by Hample and Dallinger (1987) explored the reasons people keep themselves from using certain influence strategies and found that verbal aggressiveness is associated with these reasons. For example, compared to verbally aggressive people, those who are not verbally aggressive tend to suppress arguments because the arguments violate their principles (e.g., threats may be seen as unethical) or for person-centered reasons (e.g., using certain strategies may harm a person's image or a personal relationship). (For more detail on this topic, see Hample, 2016.)

Finally, although we've painted a rather grim picture of verbal aggression, some of our own work (Seiter & Gass, 2010) argues that such aggression may be acceptable in certain situations. Take political contests as an example. Unlike many people we've heard grumbling about how negative and nasty political campaigns have become, we welcome political attacks. Don't get us wrong; we are not condoning all comments. Foes who labeled John Quincy Adams a tyrant and pimp, and Abraham Lincoln an ape and butcher were clearly out of line. On the other hand, we do not mind attacks, even those aimed at a politician's character, as long as the attacks are truthful, relevant, and appropriate. Voters should have the information they need to make tough choices, even if that information comes at a cost to potentially ineffective or unethical folks who are running for public office.

ANALYZING AND ADAPTING TO AUDIENCES

To us, the most entertaining part of Super Bowl Sunday is its television advertisements. This, of course, is not surprising when you consider that businesses spend billions of dollars every year analyzing their audiences, trying to determine what will pique interests and sell products. Despite the big bucks, however, when attempting to market products to different cultural groups, businesses have made some pretty big blunders: Here are some classic examples:

- The Swedish furniture company Ikea agreed on the name "Fartfull" for one of its desks (Cross cultural marketing blunders, 2012).
- When Kentucky Fried Chicken opened in China, its famous slogan "Finger lickin' good" was mistranslated into Chinese characters that meant "eat your fingers off" (Brooks, 2013).
- Imagine how those in the auto industry felt when they learned that, in Spanish, Nova means "It doesn't go"; in Portuguese, Pinto is slang for "a small male organ"; and Esso, pronounced phonetically in Japanese, means "stalled car" (Copeland & Griggs, 1985).

But wait! Corporations can still goof up, even when cultural differences are not involved. Take Target, for example. The mammoth discount store ran into trouble when a customer noticed that the same dress was listed as "Manatee Gray" in plus-sizes and "Dark Heather Gray" in regular sizes (Krupnick, 2013). Whoops!

The lesson here is simple: If you want to be influential, know whom you are talking to and adapt accordingly. Remember what we said earlier about cognitively complex people? Research shows that such people are more persuasive because they are able to see the world from other people's points of view. As a result, they tend to use person-centered influence tactics (i.e., tactics tailored specifically to the person they are trying to persuade; Waldron & Applegate, 1998). This, to us, seems to be what persuasion is all about: adapting a message so it coincides with the receiver's frame of reference. To be sure, a persuader doesn't move the receiver to the message, the persuader moves the message to the receiver. It's what's called being "market-driven" in business, "audience-centered" in public speaking, and "listener-oriented" in interpersonal communication. It may also be the most important lesson you can

"Most of these pelts were suicides."

FIGURE 5.3
Adapting the message to the audience's frame of reference.

Source: © Arnie Levin/
The New Yorker Collection/
www.cartoonbank.com.
All Rights Reserved.

learn about how to be a successful persuader. To influence other people, you should know as much as possible about them so you can appeal to their needs and wants, while at the same time avoid offending them. Of course, attempting to be too diplomatic can go too far. For example, we once heard a story of some people who asked a politician where he stood on a particular issue. So as not to alienate anyone, the politician replied, "Some of my friends are for it, some of my friends are against it, and I'm for my friends." If we'd been in the audience, we would not have been impressed. Thus, it's important to adapt to an audience without coming across as insincere, "smooth," or deceptive.

Entire books have been written on audience analysis (McQuail, 1997), and we cannot give full treatment to the topic here. However, to help you understand the types of issues involved, we discuss segmentation analysis, a special type of audience analysis, in Box 5.2. In addition, we list a few guidelines that might be useful if you're ever faced with an audience that needs to be analyzed.

Pay Attention to the Situation

Remember what we discussed earlier in the chapter: Communicator characteristics *and* situations affect how audiences respond to persuasive messages. Knowing details about some aspects of a situation can be useful when preparing to persuade someone. For instance, will you be talking to one person or to a large audience? Will the setting be noisy, hot, colorful? Will the persuasion occur in the morning or evening? Will you be inside or out, in a church, or on a football field? Might there be hecklers? Are you expected to talk for five minutes, or can you blab for hours?

Obviously, the number of possible situations is endless. Even so, knowing something about the situation can help you adapt. It's important to try to put yourself in the shoes of your audience. Try to figure out what would appeal to you if you were in their situation and then adapt your message accordingly. Of course, remember to be an ethical persuader. In our opinion, analyzing the situation can help you do this. We'll have more to say about this topic in Chapter 16.

Box 5.2 | Bull's-Eye! An Examination of Targeted Micromarketing

When you consider the billions of dollars that advertisers spend each year, it shouldn't surprise you to find out how much time they devote to learning "things" about their audience. But we have to admit—we were surprised, even scared a little, by some of the things these folks know, or at least claim to know. Did you realize, for example, that based on your zip code, market researchers claim to know what you eat for breakfast, what kind of car you drive, what you watch on television, and a whole lot more? They base these predictions on research showing that people who have the same zip codes tend to be remarkably similar. Not only that, based on your zip code, marketers have dubbed you with funny-sounding nicknames like "Blue-Blood Estates," "Money and Brains," and "Single City Blues." So, for example, if your zip code is 94117 or 15232, you are a "Bohemian Mix," you're probably 18 to 34 years old, you enjoy liberal politics and classical records, read *The New Yorker*, and eat frozen waffles (Berger, 2004). See? Spooky!

Using zip codes to categorize consumers is just one example of what is known as micromarketing or market segmentation, which involves "breaking a market down to definable, manageable segments and then tailoring your efforts to just one or two (Ogden, 2000, p. 29; Schewe & Meredith, 2004). It sounds complicated, but nowadays, it's necessary. Clearly, advertising, campaigning, and marketing are not as easy as they used to be. For example, Penn (2007) argued that a once-universal audience has fragmented into hundreds of small groups or niches. Examples include "Tech Fatales" (women prone to buying technological equipment), "30 Winkers" (people getting less than seven hours of sleep a night), and "Late-Breaking Gays" (gay people who have come out of the closet later in life due to more social acceptance of homosexuality). These small groups, if understood correctly, can be adapted and appealed to, thus starting "microtrends" that can affect business and society in profound ways.

Of course, it's not only zip codes that help marketers segment audiences. They have a large list of ways to categorize their consumers. Knowing your age, for instance, may help them design ads that appeal to you. But wait—it gets more complicated. For example, it is not enough to know that your main audience is composed of children. One marketing firm has argued that there are "six species of kids," each requiring a different approach (Gertner, 2004, p. 102). According to Debra Phillips (1999), it may sound funny, but there's a big difference between being 10 years old and being 14, and advertisements aimed at teens are different than those aimed at "the legions of 9- to 12-year-olds whimsically referred to as ''tweens'"(p. 126). Whereas 'tweens may scoff at the likes of Mickey Mouse and his pals (Phillips, 1999), younger children are still attracted to such characters.

If your head isn't spinning yet, just wait. We all know, for instance, that kids like candy, but different groups of kids (and adults) may have different tastes. If you're a marketer, here's when knowing the ethnicity of your target audience can come in handy. For example, market research suggests that while African Americans enjoy very sweet, hard candies in nonchocolate flavors like mint and coconut, Hispanic Americans like "aggressive" flavors like lollipops coated with chili powder and mixed with tamarind. Asian Americans, on the other hand, like the texture of chocolate ("Serving ethnic markets," 1999). When you consider this, along with the fact that African Americans, Hispanic Americans, and Asian Americans make up a large portion of the U.S. population, it is clear why marketers are targeting these groups with all sorts of appeals, including ethnic "aisles" in grocery stores and packaging that attracts certain ethnic groups (e.g., for many Asian Americans, candy packaged in tins connotes quality) ("Serving ethnic markets," 1999).

Of course, by now, we're sure you see that the number of ways that marketers can segment consumers is almost limitless. Indeed, in addition to using age, zip codes, and ethnicity, marketers design messages on the basis of gender, education, economic status, and career choice, just to name a few. As time goes by, consumer markets only promise to get smaller. This is especially true on the Internet, which, according to Bianco, Lowry, Berner, Arndt, and Grover (2004), is an interactive medium that enables marketers to personalize messages and products for each consumer. One of the authors, for example, is a member of Netflix, a company that lets you order movies online. After viewing a movie, you can rate it and, based on your ratings, the company provides you with personalized recommendations for other movies you might like. If you have ever purchased a product from Amazon.com, you might have noticed the same feature: Every time you make a purchase, you may be giving information that can be used to persuade you in the future. In fact, according to Lindstrom (2011), when you search Google, use Facebook, swipe your credit card, or download an iTunes song, data-mining companies are analyzing it and then selling your data to marketers. Even using those innocent-looking online coupons can help marketers target you. Specifically, those coupon's bar codes are encoded with information about you, which can be used by marketers later (Lindstrom, 2011).

Keep Your Audience's Mind in Mind

In the old movie *What Women Want,* Mel Gibson played a male chauvinist advertiser who, after a freak accident, was able to read women's minds. Not surprisingly, Mel not only became an expert at attracting the opposite sex but could also design advertisements that women couldn't resist. The movie illustrates how much easier persuasion might be if you had ESP. Indeed, if you could look into people's minds and know their attitudes, values, and needs, we imagine that adapting your persuasive messages would be a piece of cake.

Although we can't teach you to be psychic, we can give you a few tips about "reading" people's attitudes, values, and needs. First, as you already know from Chapter 3, there are a number of ways to measure or make guesses about people's attitudes (e.g., using scales, simply asking them, and so on). Once you know a person's attitudes, it is easier to show him or her how that attitude may be inconsistent with other attitudes, shifted to be stronger, and so forth.

Second, it may be possible to make guesses about a person's values based on other information. For example, values are often culturally determined. By learning the values of a culture, there's a reasonable chance you've learned the values held by an individual within the culture. For instance, earlier in this chapter, we saw that people from the United States tend to value individuals over collectives and that people from China tend toward the opposite. With that in mind, persuasive messages that highlight and promote these values in their respective cultures should be more influential than those that do not. Remember, though, that stereotypes are not always accurate. Keep in mind that cultural values serve as guidelines for developing persuasive messages. Even so, such messages might backfire on some individuals.

Finally, though different individuals' needs may vary drastically, some needs may be universal. Knowing about such needs could prove useful for designing persuasive messages. For example, do you think people who design and advertise smoke alarms know about basic security needs? You bet they do! If you've ever seen one of those advertisements with a family standing at the curb in their pajamas while their house burns down in the background, you know what we're talking about. Advertisers know how to appeal to people's needs.

To help you get a better handle on the types of needs that may be used to motivate people, consider the now-classic typology presented by the humanistic psychologist Abraham Maslow (1970). According to Maslow, human needs are hierarchical, with the most basic biological needs at the lowest level of the hierarchy and more complex needs at the top. Specifically, Maslow argued that human needs were arranged in the following order, from most basic to most complex: physiological (e.g., the need for food and water), safety (e.g., the need for stability and security), belonging (e.g., the need for acceptance and love), esteem (e.g., the need to feel important and unique), and self-actualization (e.g., the need to grow, create, and understand). According to Maslow, before people are motivated to satisfy higher-level needs, their lower-level needs must be met. Thus, a person who is starving to death will be more interested in obtaining food than in boosting his or her self-esteem.

Remember the Importance of Audience States and Traits

You know by now that communicator traits and states play a large role in persuasion. It's something to keep in mind if you're ever confronted by someone with traits or in the states we've discussed. For example, we noted that anxious people require specific recommendations and reassurances when using fear appeals and that high self-monitors respond well to messages that promise to help them "fit in." Previous research suggests that tailoring your appeals to the particular traits of your audience will make you more successful in your persuasive endeavors (Hirsch, Kang, & Bodenhausen, 2012; Kraichy & Chapman, 2014).

Don't Forget About Audience Demographics

A person who can adapt to people of different ages, genders, cultures, and so forth obviously will be more successful than a person who can't. For example, when speaking to small children, using lots of statistics would probably lead to lots of "ants in the pants." By the same token, a group of senior citizens would probably squirm or snooze if forced to listen to a speech about planning for pregnancy. Moreover, although we noted that there do not appear to be gender differences in persuadability, it doesn't mean a speaker can ignore the gender of her audience. Notice, for example, by using the word *her* in the previous sentence, we failed to address males who might be reading this book. In short, we're sure you get the point: Whenever possible, know about your audience's age, gender, socioeconomic status, and so forth. Then adapt.

SUMMARY

In this chapter, we discussed several communicator characteristics that affect the process of persuasion. First, we examined demographic variables, noting that some (e.g., age, ethnicity) influence the sending and receiving of persuasive messages, whereas others (e.g., gender) do not appear to be related to influenceability. Second, we showed how several psychological and communication states and traits (i.e., self-esteem, anxiety, preference for consistency, self-monitoring, ego involvement, dogmatism, authoritarianism, social vigilantism, narcissism, cognitive complexity, need for cognition, and aggression) influence persuasive communication. Finally, we examined the notion of audience analysis, indicating that persuaders, when possible, should attempt to adapt to the needs, wants, backgrounds, and so forth of their audiences.

REFERENCES

Adorno, T., Frenkel-Brunswik, E., Levenson, D., & Sanford, N. (1950). *The authoritarian personality*. New York: Harper.

Agrawal, N. (2015). Culture and persuasion. In S. Ng & A. Y. Lee (Eds.), *Handbook of culture and consumer behavior* (pp. 121–134). New York: Oxford University Press.

Allport, G. W. (1954). *The nature of prejudice*. Reading, MA: Addison-Wesley.

Altemeyer, B. (1999). To thine own self be untrue: Self-awareness and authoritarians. *North American Journal of Psychology, 1*(2), 157–164.

Baek, T. H., Yoo, C. Y., & Yoon, S. (2016). Augment yourself through virtual mirror: The impact of self-viewing and narcissism on consumer responses. *International Journal of Advertising*. Advance online publication. doi:10.1080/02650487

Berger, A. A. (2004). *Ads, fads, and consumer culture: Advertising's impact on American character*. Lanham, MD: Rowman & Littlefield.

Beware 'Net predators. (2001, March 7). *The Herald Journal, 92*(66), 1, 12.

Bianco, A., Lowry, T., Berner, R., Arndt, M., & Grover, R. (2004, July). The vanishing mass market. *Business Week*, *3891*, 60.

Blinkhorn, V., Lyons, M., & Almond, L. (2015). The ultimate femme fatale? Narcissism predicts serious and aggressive sexually coercive behaviour in females. *Personality and Individual Differences*, *87*, 219–223.

Braverman, J. (2008). Testimonials versus informational persuasive messages: The moderating effect of delivery mode and personal involvement. *Communication Research*, *35*, 666–694. doi:10.1177/0093650208321785

Brooks, C. (2013, October 7). Lost in translation: 8 international marketing fails. *Business News Daily*. Retrieved from: www.businessnewsdaily.com/5241-international-marketing-fails.html on January 6, 2017.

Buijzen, M. (2007). Reducing children's susceptibility to commercials: Mechanisms of factual and evaluative advertising interventions. *Media Psychology*, *9*, 411–430.

Cacioppo, J. T., & Petty, R. E. (1982). The need for cognition. *Journal of Personality and Social Psychology*, *42*, 116–131.

Carli, L. L. (2004). Gender effects on social influence. In J. S. Seiter & R. H. Gass (Eds.), *Readings in persuasion, social influence and compliance gaining* (pp. 133–148). Boston, MA: Allyn & Bacon.

Chaiken, S. (1979). Communicator physical attractiveness and persuasion. *Journal of Personality and Social Psychology*, *37*, 1387–1397.

Christie, R. (1991). Authoritarianism and related constructs. In J. P. Robinson, P. R. Shaver, & L. S. Wrightsman (Eds.), *Measures of personality and social psychological attitudes* (pp. 501–571). San Diego, CA: Academic Press.

Cody, M. J., Seiter, J. S., & Montagne-Miller, Y. (1995). Men and women in the marketplace. In P. J. Kalbfleisch & M. J. Cody (Eds.), *Gender, power, and communication in human relationships* (pp. 305–330). Hillsdale, NJ: Erlbaum.

Copeland, L., & Griggs, L. (1985). *Going international: How to make friends and deal effectively in the global marketplace.* New York: Random House.

Cross cultural marketing blunders. (2012). Kwintessential. Retrieved on June 14, 2012, from: www.kwintessential.co.uk/cultural-services/articles/crosscultural-marketing.html

DeBono, K. G., & Klein, C. (1993). Source expertise and persuasion: The moderating role of recipient dogmatism. *Personality and Social Psychology Bulletin*, *19*, 167–173.

DeBono, K. G., & Rubin, K. (1995). Country of origin and perceptions of product quality: An individual difference perspective. *Basic and Applied Social Psychology*, *17*, 239–247.

DeBono, K. G., Leavitt, A., & Backus, J. (2003). Product packaging and product evaluation: An individual difference approach. *Journal of Applied Social Psychology*, *33*, 513–521.

Delbyck, C. (2016, August 18). This poor unfortunate soul thinks he's been dating Katy Perry for 6 years. *The Huffington Post*. Retrieved from: www.huffingtonpost.com/entry/this-poor-unfortunate-soul-thinks-hes-been-dating-katy-perry-for-six-years_us_57b6205be4b0b51733a258cf on December 18, 2016.

Delia, J. G., O'Keefe, B. J., & O'Keefe, D. J. (1982). The constructivist approach to communication. In F. E. X. Dance (Ed.), *Human communication theory* (pp. 147–191). New York: Harper & Row.

Dickinson, A. (2002, April). What to say to your kids. *Time*, *159*(17), 48.

Eagly, A. H. (1978). Sex differences in influenceability. *Psychological Bulletin*, *85*, 86–116.

Eaton, A. A., Visser, P. S., Krosnick, J. A., & Anand, S. (2009). Social power and attitude strength over the life course. *Personality and Social Psychology Bulletin*, *35*, 1646–1660. doi:10.1177/0146167209349114

Edwards, C., & Myers, S. A. (2007). Perceived instructor credibility as a function of instructor aggressive communication. *Communication Research Reports, 24,* 47–53.

Evans, A. T., & Clark, J. K. (2012). Source characteristics and persuasion: The role of self-monitoring in self-validation. *Journal of Experimental Social Psychology, 48,* 383–386. doi:10.1016/j.jesp.2011.07.002

Fitch, K. L. (1994). A cross-cultural study of directive sequences and some implications for compliance-gaining research. *Communication Monographs, 61,* 185–209.

Fu, P., & Yukl, G. (2000). Perceived effectiveness of influence tactics in the United States and China. *Leadership Quarterly, 11*(2), 251–266.

Gertner, J. (2004, November 28). Hey Mom, is it OK if these guys market stuff to us? *New York Times Magazine, 154*(53047), 100–107.

Guadagno, R. E., & Cialdini, R. B. (2010). Preference for consistency and social influence: A review of current research findings. *Social Influence, 5,* 152–163.

Hample, D. (2016). Cognitive editing. In C. R. Berger, M. E. Roloff, J. P. Dillard, J. Caughlin, & D. Solomon (Eds.), *The international encyclopedia of interpersonal communication.* Wiley Online. doi:10.1002/9781118540190.wbeic0204

Hample, D., & Dallinger, J. M. (1987). Individual differences in cognitive editing standards. *Human Communication Research, 14,* 123–144.

Han, S., & Shavitt, S. (1994). Persuasion and culture: Advertising appeals in individualistic and collectivistic societies. *Journal of Experimental Social Psychology, 30,* 326–350.

Harvey, O. J., & Beverly, G. D. (1961). Some personality correlates of concept change through role playing. *Journal of Abnormal and Social Psychology, 63,* 125–130.

Hirsh, J. B., Kang, S. K., & Bodenhausen, G. V. (2012). Personalized persuasion: Tailoring persuasive appeals to recipients' personality traits. *Psychological Science, 23,* 578–581.

Hofstede, G. (1983). Dimensions of national cultures in fifty countries and three regions. In J. Deregowski, S. Dzuirawiec, & R. Annis (Eds.), *Explications in cross-cultural psychology* (pp. 335–355). Lisse, The Netherlands: Swets & Zeitlinger.

Infante, D. A. (1982). The argumentative student in the speech communication classroom: An investigation and implications. *Communication Education, 3,* 141–148.

Infante, D. A. (1987). Aggressiveness. In J. C. McCroskey & J. A. Daly (Eds.), *Personality and interpersonal communication* (pp. 157–192). Newbury Park, CA: Sage.

Infante, D. A., & Gordon, W. I. (1991). How employees see the boss: Test of an argumentative and affirming model of supervisors' communicative behavior. *Western Journal of Speech Communication, 55,* 294–304.

Infante, D. A., Chandler, T. A., & Rudd, J. E. (1989). Test of an argumentative skill deficiency model of interspousal violence. *Communication Monographs, 56,* 163–177.

Janis, I. L., & Feshbach, S. (1965). Effects of fear-arousing communications. *Journal of Personality and Social Psychology, 1,* 17–27.

Johnson, B. T., & Eagly, A. H. (1990). Effects of involvement on persuasion: A metaanalysis. *Psychological Bulletin, 106,* 290–314.

Kaufman, D. O., Stasson, M. F., & Hart, J. W. (1999). Are the tabloids always wrong or is that just what we think? *Journal of Applied Social Psychology, 29,* 1984–1997.

Kausel, E. E., Culbertson, S. S. Leiva, P. I., Slaughter, J. E., & Jackson, A. T. (2015). Too arrogant for their own good? Why and when narcissists dismiss advice. *Organizational Behavior and Human Decision Processes, 131,* 33–50.

Khoury, C., Struthers, C. W., Santelli, A. G., & Marjanovic, Z. (2012). The role of right wing authoritarianism on the repentance–forgiveness process. *Social Influence, 7,* 304–326.

Klingle, R. S. (2004). Compliance in medical contexts. In J. S. Seiter & R. H. Gass (Eds.), *Readings in persuasion, social influence and compliance gaining* (pp. 289–315). Boston, MA: Allyn & Bacon.

Knafo, A. (2003). Authoritarians, the next generation: Values and bullying among adolescent children of authoritarian fathers. *Analysis of Social Issues and Public Policy, 3*(1), 199–204.

Kraichy, D., & Chapman, D. S. (2014). Tailoring web-based recruiting messages: Individual differences in the persuasiveness of affective and cognitive messages. *Journal of Business Psychology, 29*, 253–268.

Krupnick, E. (2013, April 4). Target 'Manatee Gray' color on plus-size dress has customers irked. *Huffington Post*. Retrieved from: www.huffingtonpost.com/2013/04/04/target-manatee-gray-color_n_3013235.html on January 6, 2017.

Kunkel, D., Wilcox, B. L., Cantor, J., Palmer, E., Linn, S., & Dowrick, P. (2004). *Report of the APA task force on advertising to children*. Washington, DC: American Psychological Association.

Lee, S. Y., Gregg, A. P., & Park, S. H. (2013). The person in the purchase: Narcissistic consumers prefer products that positively distinguish them. *Journal of Personality and Social Psychology, 105*, 335–352.

Lehmann, S. (1970). Personality and compliance: A study of anxiety and self-esteem in opinion and behavior change. *Journal of Personality and Social Psychology, 15*, 76–86.

Liao, Q. V., & Fu, W. (2014). Age differences in credibility judgments of online health information. *ACM Transactions on Computer–Human Interactions, 21*, 2.

Lindstrom, M. (2011). *Brandwashed: Tricks companies use to manipulate our minds and persuade us to buy*. New York: Crown Business.

Linvill, D. L., Mazer, J. P., & Boatwright, B. C. (2016). Need for cognition as a mediating variable between aggressive communication traits and tolerance for disagreement. *Communication Research Reports, 33*, 363–369. doi:10.1080/08824096.2016.1224160

Ma, R., & Chuang, R. (2001). Persuasion strategies of Chinese college students in interpersonal contexts. *Southern Journal of Communication, 66*(4), 267–278.

Madlock, P. E., & Dillow, M. R. (2012). The consequences of verbal aggression in the workplace: An application of the investment model. *Communication Studies, 63*, 593–607.

Maki, A., & Raimi, K. T. (2017). Environmental peer persuasion: How moral exporting and belief superiority relate to efforts to influence others. *Journal of Environmental Psychology, 49*, 19–29.

Maslow, A. (1970). *Motivation and personality*. New York: Harper & Row.

Matthews, N. C. (2016). The influence of biological sex on perceived aggressive communication in debator–judge conflicts in parliamentary debate. *Western Journal of Communication, 80*, 38–59.

Mazer, J. P., & Stowe, S. A. (2016). Can teacher immediacy reduce the impact of verbal aggressiveness? Examining effects on student outcomes and perceptions of teacher credibility. *Western Journal of Communication, 80*, 21–37.

McAlister, A. R., & Cornwell, T. B. (2009). Preschool children's persuasion knowledge: The contribution of theory of mind. *Journal of Public Policy & Marketing, 28*, 175–185.

McGill, A. R., Johnson, M. D., & Bantel, K. A. (1994). Cognitive complexity and conformity: Effects on performance in a turbulent environment. *Psychological Reports, 75*, 1451–1472.

McGuire, W. J. (1968). Personality and attitude change: An information-processing theory. In A. G. Greenwald, T. C. Brock, & T. M. Ostrom (Eds.), *Psychological foundations of attitudes* (pp. 171–196). San Diego, CA: Academic Press.

McQuail, D. (1997) *Audience analysis*. Thousand Oaks, CA: Sage.

Mills, C. M., & Elashi, F. B. (2014). Children's skepticism: Developmental and individual differences in children's ability to detect and explain distorted claims. *Journal of Experimental Child Psychology, 124*, 1–17.

Morgenstern, M., Isensee, B., Sargent, J. D., & Hanewinkel, R. (2011). Exposure to alcohol advertising and teen drinking. *Preventive Medicine, 52*(2), 146–151. doi:10.1016/j.ypmed.2010.11.020

Myers, J. R., & Sar, S. (2013). Persuasive social approval cues in print advertising: Exploring visual and textual strategies and consumer self-monitoring. *Journal of Marketing Communications, 19*, 168–181. doi:10.1080/13527266.2011.581303

Nai, A., Schemeil, Y., & Marie, J. L. (2016). Anxiety, sophistication, and resistance to persuasion: Evidence from a quasi–experimental survey on global climate change. *Political Psychology.* Advance online publication. doi:10.1111/pops.12331

Nunnally, J. C., & Bobren, H. M. (1959). Variables concerning the willingness to receive communications on mental health. *Journal of Personality, 27*, 275–290.

Oates, C., Blades, M., & Gunter, B. (2002). Children and television advertising: When do they understand persuasive intent? *Journal of Consumer Behavior, 1*(3), 238–245.

Ogden, M. (2000, February 4). To succeed globally, think small in marketing efforts. *Kansas City Business Journal, 18*(22), 29.

Orji, R. (2016, May 4). Persuasion and culture: Individualism–collectivism and susceptibility to influence strategies. In R. Orji, M. Reisinger, M. Busch, A. Dijkstra, A. Stibe, & M. Tscheligi (Eds.), *Proceedings of the personalization in persuasive technology workshop*, Persuasive Technology, Salzburg, Austria.

Orji, R., Mandryk, R. L., & Vassileva, J. (2015). Gender, age, and responsiveness to Cialdini's persuasion strategies. In T. MacTavish, & S. Basapur (Eds.), *Persuasive Technology* (pp. 147–159). Heidelberg: Springer International.

Panic, K., Cauberghe, V., & De Pelsmacker, P. (2013). Comparing TV ads and advergames targeting children: The impact of persuasion knowledge on behavioral response. *Journal of Advertising, 42*, 264–273.

Penn, M. J., with Zalesne, E. K. (2007). *Microtrends: The small forces behind tomorrow's big changes.* New York: Twelve.

Perlini, A. H., & Hansen, S. D. (2001). Moderating effects of need for cognition or attractiveness stereotyping. *Social Behavior and Personality, 29*(4), 313–322.

Phillips, D. (1999, September). 'Tween beat: Targeting pre-teenage consumers. *Entrepreneur, 27*(9), 126.

Preiss, R. W., & Gayle, B. M. (1999, February). *Authoritarianism, dogmatism, and persuasion: A meta-analytic review.* Paper presented at the Annual Meeting of the Western States Communication Association, Vancouver, BC.

Rancer, A. S. (2004). Argumentativeness, verbal aggressiveness and persuasion. In J. S. Seiter & R. H. Gass (Eds.), *Readings in persuasion, social influence and compliance gaining* (pp. 113–131). Boston, MA: Allyn & Bacon.

Reinhard, M., & Messner, M. (2009). The effects of source likeability and need for cognition on advertising effectiveness under explicit persuasion. *Journal of Consumer Behavior, 8*, 179–191. doi:10.1002/cb.282

Rhodes, N., & Wood, W. (1992). Self-esteem and intelligence affect influenceability: The mediating role of message reception. *Psychological Bulletin, 111*, 156–171.

Rodero, E., Larrea, O., & Vázquez, M. (2013). Male and female voices in commercials: Analysis of effectiveness, adequacy for the product, attention and recall. *Sex Roles, 68*, 349–362.

Rokeach, M. (1960). *The open and closed mind.* New York: Basic Books.

Rosen, M. D. (1994, August). Don't talk to strangers. *Ladies Home Journal, 111,* 108, 109, 153, 154.

Saucier, D. A., & Webster, R. J. (2010). Social vigilantism: Measuring individual differences in belief superiority and resistance to persuasion. *Personality and Social Psychology Bulletin, 36,* 19–32. doi:10.1177/0146167209346170

Saucier, D. A., Webster, R. J., Hoffman, B. H., & Strain, M. L. (2014). Social vigilantism and reported use of strategies to resist persuasion. *Personality and Individual Differences, 70,* 120–125.

Schewe, C. D., & Meredith, G. (2004). Segmenting global markets by generational cohorts: Determining motivations by age. *Journal of Consumer Behavior, 4*(1), 51–63.

Sears, D. O. (1981). Life stage effects on attitude change, especially among the elderly. In S. B. Kiesler, J. N. Morgan, & V. K. Oppenheimer (Eds.), *Aging: Social change* (pp. 183–204). New York: Academic Press.

Seiter, J. S., & Gass, R. H. (2010). Aggressive communication in political contexts. In T. A. Avtgis & A. S. Rancer (Eds.), *Arguments, aggression, and conflict: New directions in theory and research* (pp. 217–240). New York: Routledge.

Sénémeaud, C., Mange, J., Fointiat, V., & Somat, A. (2014). Being hypocritical disturbs some people more than others: How individual differences in preference for consistency moderate the behavioral effects of the induced-hypocrisy paradigm. *Social Influence, 9,* 133–148. doi:1080/15534510.2013.791235

Serving ethnic markets. (1999, May–June). *Professional Candy Buyer, 7*(3), 76.

Sherif, M., & Sherif, C. W. (1967). Attitudes as the individual's own categories: The social-judgment approach to attitude and attitude change. In C. W. Sherif & M. Sherif (Eds.), *Attitude, ego-involvement, and change* (pp. 105–139). New York: John Wiley.

Sherif, C. W., Sherif, M., & Nebergall, R. E. (1965). *Attitude and attitude change: The social judgment-involvement approach.* Philadelphia, PA: W. B. Saunders.

Sherif, C. W., Kelly, M., Rodgers, H. L., Jr., Sarup, G., & Tittler, B. I. (1973). Personal involvement, social judgment and action. *Journal of Personality and Social Psychology, 27,* 311–328.

Shestowsky, D., & Horowitz, L. M. (2004). How the need for cognition scale predicts behavior in mock jury deliberations. *Law and Human Behavior, 28*(3), 305–337.

Smidt, K. E., & DeBono, K. G. (2011). On the effects of product name on product evaluation: An individual difference perspective. *Social Influence, 6,* 131–141.

Smith, A. N., Watkins, M. B., Burke, M. J., Christian, M. S., Smith, C. E., Hall, A., & Simms, S. (2013). Gendered influence: A gender role perspective on the use and effectiveness of influence tactics. *Journal of Management, 39,* 1156–1183. doi:10. 1177/0149206313478183

Snyder, M. (1974). Self-monitoring of expressive behavior. *Journal of Personality and Social Psychology, 30,* 526–537.

Snyder, M. (1979). Self-monitoring processes. In L. Berkowitz (Ed.), *Advances in experimental and social psychology* (Vol. 12, pp. 85–128). New York: Academic Press.

Snyder, M., & DeBono, K. G. (1989). Understanding the functions of attitudes: Lessons from personality and social behavior. In A. R. Pratkanis, S. J. Brecklet, & A. G. Greenwald (Eds.), *Attitude structure and function* (pp. 339–359). Hillsdale, NJ: Erlbaum.

Sojka, J. Z., & Deeter-Schmelz, D. R. (2008). Need for cognition and affective orientation as predictors of sales performance: An investigation of main and interaction effects. *Journal of Business Psychology, 22,* 179–190. doi:10.1007/s10869–008–9069-x

Teaching fear. (1986, March 10). *Newsweek,* p. 62.

Vanwesenbeeck, I., Walrave, M., & Ponnet, K. (2016). Children and advergames: The role of product involvement, prior brand attitude, persuasion knowledge and game attitude in purchase intentions and changing attitudes. *International Journal of Advertising.* doi:10.1080/02650487.2016.1176637

Waldron, V. R., & Applegate, J. L. (1998). Person-centered tactics during verbal disagreements: Effects on student perceptions of persuasiveness and social attraction. *Communication Education, 47,* 53–66.

Ward, D. A., Seccombe, K., Bendel, R., & Carter, L. F. (1985). Cross-sex context as a factor in persuadability sex differences. *Social Psychology Quarterly, 48,* 269–276.

White, M. J., & Gerstein, L. H. (1987). Helping: The influence of anticipated social sanctions and self-monitoring. *Journal of Personality, 55,* 41–54.

Williams-Piehota, P., Schneider, T. R., Pizarro, L. M., Mowad, L., & Salovey, P. (2003). Matching health messages to information processing styles: Need for cognition and mammography utilization. *Health Communication, 15*(4), 375–392.

Wiseman, R. L., Sanders, J. A., Congalton, K. J., Gass, R. H., Sueda, K., & Du, R. (2009). A cross-cultural analysis of compliance gaining: China, Japan, and the United States. In B. Hoffer and N. Honna (Eds.), *Intercultural communication: Beyond the canon* (pp. 186–212). San Antonio, TX: International Association for Intercultural Communication Studies.

Wooden, K. (1988, June). How sex offenders lure our children. *Reader's Digest,* pp. 149–154.

Wooden, K. (1995). *Child lures: What every parent and child should know about preventing sexual abuse and abduction.* Arlington, TX: Summit.

Wooden, K. (2014). *Child lures prevention: Think of it as a vaccine.* Retrieved from www.childluresprevention.com/research/vaccine.asp on December 20, 2016.

Wooden, K., Webb, R., & Mitchell, J. (2014). *A profile of the child molester.* Retrieved from www.childluresprevention.com/research/vaccine.asp on December 20, 2016.

CHAPTER 6

Conformity and Influence in Groups

B O, PEEP, SHEEP, AND THE HALE–BOPP COMET may sound like the makings of a good fairytale, but, as the saying goes, truth is stranger than fiction, and, unfortunately, the story of Bo and Peep's sheep is a true one. We refer to the people of the Heaven's Gate cult as sheep because who else but sheep would believe what these people were told—that they should commit mass suicide so they might shed their bodies and be whisked away by an alien spaceship that was flying around in the tail of the Hale–Bopp comet? Whether they believed it or not, they did what their leaders, Bo and Peep, told them to do. In 1997, sheriff's deputies found the corpses of 21 women and 18 men decomposing in a home in Rancho Santa Fe, California. All of the members of the cult had apparently ingested a fatal mixture of phenobarbital, applesauce, pudding, and vodka (Gleick, 1997).

As authors who are interested in the process of social influence, we can't help but wonder how and why people like those in the Heaven's Gate cult can be persuaded to such extremes. Clearly, several factors must have contributed to the largest mass suicide in U.S. history. The cult members—though reportedly bright and happy—must have been highly persuadable. Moreover, the leaders of the cult, Marshall Herff Applewhite and Bonnie Lu Nettles (known as Bo and Peep), were highly charismatic and trusted by their followers. But beyond the characteristics of the cult leaders and members, we believe that a strong group dynamic may have contributed to the suicide. Indeed, although from society's perspective the members of the cult were deviants, there seemed to be pressure within the cult to "fit in." For instance, the members of the cult reportedly looked the same, so much so that when the corpses were first discovered, they were believed to be men only. The cult members were described as having androgynous appearances; the women wore cropped hair, and many of the men, including the cult's leader, had been castrated. Finally, the cult members were known to dress the same, wearing what one person described as black pajamas. When the 39 corpses were found, each was dressed in black: black pants, black shirt, and brand-new black Nike shoes (Gleick, 1997).

We imagine that, if nothing else, being a member of a cult satisfies a need to belong. Cults often attract new members by providing seemingly loving environments for their new recruits. Along with this, however, comes pressure to fit in. With such pressure, it's easy to see how a cult member might have been sucked into the suicide. When you identify so strongly with people who are carrying out some action, the action not only seems more "right," it becomes necessary for you to participate if you want to be part of the group. This is true not only in cults, a topic we revisit later in this chapter, but in other social collectives as well. Families, peer groups, workplaces, even classrooms, exert strong pressure on their members to behave in certain ways. For that reason, this chapter examines the role of groups in the process of social influence. We begin by discussing the topic of conformity.

CONFORMITY AS PERSUASION: IN WITH THE CROWD

During a lecture by a sociology professor, in a classroom that held more than 100 people, an undergraduate student, known by both of your authors, removed his shirt, pants, shoes, and socks. Then, almost naked, he stood in the aisle, waiting to be noticed. The professor, who had been looking down at his notes, did not notice our friend until other people in the classroom began gasping and laughing. When the professor finally did look up, he was stunned. Undaunted, the nearly naked student looked down at himself and asked, "Does this count?"

Apparently, just before the student disrobed, the professor had been lecturing on the topic of norms and conformity. *Norms* are expectations held by a group of people about what behaviors or opinions are right or wrong, good or bad, acceptable or unacceptable, appropriate or inappropriate (Andrews, 1996). Once norms are understood, we feel pressure to conform to them. Of course, the professor had probably explained to our friend and his other students that some norms are explicit. *Explicit norms* are written or spoken openly. For example, road signs indicate how fast you are permitted to drive and game rules may send you to jail without collecting $200. Some norms, however, are *implicit* and not so openly stated. For example, we imagine that when you're a guest in someone's home, you don't put your feet on the dinner table even though you've never read a rule saying you shouldn't. Likewise—and this is what the sociology professor told his class—because we all conform to social norms, no one would take his or her clothes off in the middle of a classroom lecture. Of course, our friend, who prides himself on being a nonconformist, couldn't resist this challenge. The rest is history, and the professor now has a good story to tell whenever he lectures about norms and conformity.

In the Beginning: Early Research on Conformity Effects

Not everyone is like our friend, the student-stripper in the sociology class. As we've noted, in most cases, people know the norms and try to go along with the crowd. Perhaps the most compelling experiment on the effects of conformity was conducted by Solomon Asch (1956). Here's how his experiment worked: Asch gathered several (seven to nine) college students into a classroom and told them that they would be participating in an experiment about visual judgment. The students were asked to look at two large, white cards. As can be seen in Figure 6.1, a single vertical line appeared on the first card, and three vertical lines, each of different length, appeared on the second card. The students' task was simple: After observing both cards, they were asked to match lines—that is, each student was asked to report out loud, to the rest of the group, which of the three lines on the second card was the same length as the line on the other card. According to Asch (1966), the experiment began uneventfully but changed rapidly:

> The subjects announce their answers in the order in which they have been seated in the room, and on the first round every person chooses the same matching line. Then a second set of cards is exposed: Again the group is unanimous. The members appear ready to endure politely another boring experiment. On the third trial there is an unexpected disturbance. One person near the end of the group disagrees with all the others in his selection of the matching line. He looks surprised, indeed incredulous, about the disagreement.

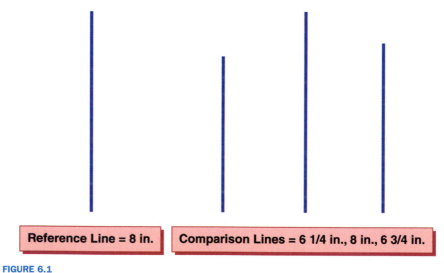

Reference Line = 8 in.   Comparison Lines = 6 1/4 in., 8 in., 6 3/4 in.

FIGURE 6.1
example of Visuals Used in Asch's experiment. Subjects are asked which of the three lines on the comparison card (right) match the line on the reference card (left).

FIGURE 6.2
Source: © Charles Barsotti/The New Yorker Collection/www.cartoonbank.com. All Rights Reserved.

On the following trial he disagrees again, while the others remain unanimous in their choice. The dissenter becomes more and more worried and hesitant as the disagreement continues in succeeding trials; he may pause before announcing his answer and speak in a low voice, or he may smile in an embarrassed way.

(p. 320)

What the dissenting student in Asch's study did not know was that all of the other students in the group were planted by Asch and told beforehand to give the wrong answers. In other words, Asch was really interested in what a person would do when he or she was giving correct answers that are contrary to the answers of a near-unanimous group decision. What he found was that conformity was common; under group pressure, 75 percent of the subjects gave the wrong answer in at least one of the trials.

In short, then, Asch's experiment illustrates the tremendous power of groups to exert influence. Even so, not all of Asch's subjects behaved in the same way. For instance, about 25 percent remained fairly independent, rarely conforming to the group's answers. Moreover, about 10 percent of the subjects agreed with the group on almost every trial. Thus, it is probably true that some individuals are more prone to conformity than others. In addition, some situations may produce more conformity than others, a topic we discuss next.

Variables Related to Conformity

Does Group Size Affect Conformity? The More the Scarier?

On the television show *Who Wants to Be a Millionaire?* contestants can make a bundle of money if they can answer a series of questions that become progressively more difficult. Of course, if they get stumped, the rules allow them to "poll the audience," asking those in the studio for advice on one, and only one, question. With that in mind, if you were a contestant on the show and had the choice of an audience with 5 people or 500 people, which audience would you want? What if your choice were between an audience of 499 and 500 people? Would the extra person make a very big difference and, if not, at what point does adding people to the audience become less relevant?

Regardless of whether they watch *Who Wants to Be a Millionaire?*, for some time researchers have been interested in the role that group size plays in persuasion. Two of many theories that make different predictions about the relationship between group size and persuasion are *social impact theory* (SIT) (Latané, 1981) and the *social influence model* (SIM) (Tanford & Penrod, 1984). The first, SIT, argues that the first person you add to a group has the most influence. Each additional member has some impact, but less than the person added before him or her. In contrast, SIM argues that the third and fourth people added to a group have the most impact because no minority is possible with only two people. In other words, it is easier to disagree with one person than it is to disagree with two or three people. After three or four people are added, however, the pressure to conform levels off.

Empirical results and meta-analyses on which is the better of these two perspectives are mixed (see Bond, 2005; Bond & Smith, 1996): Some studies support one perspective, some the other, and some neither. After reviewing the literature, we suspect that both models have found support because both may be accurate when you consider an additional variable—that is, when you are making a decision in a group, you are motivated by two things: You want to be right and you want to be liked (Campbell & Fairey, 1989; Deutsch & Gerard, 1955). Specifically, sometimes we conform to a group because the group has *informational influence*—that is, we have a desire to be right and we conform to the group because we think the group may be correct. However, sometimes we conform to a group because it has *normative influence*. This means that we conform in order to gain rewards (e.g., be liked) and avoid punishments (e.g., scorn) that are associated with agreement and disagreement.

What does this have to do with group size? According to Campbell and Fairey (1989), increasing the number of people in a group affects informational and normative processes differently. Specifically, when you want to be right, as in the millionaire example, the first person added has the most impact because each additional person's judgment is more likely to be redundant with others in the group. On the other hand, imagine you are just playing an "at home" version of *Who Wants to Be a Millionaire?* with some new neighbors. Your goal is not to win money, but just to fit in, be liked, and make some new friends. In this case, agreeing with the neighbors, especially when the number of them reaches two or three, is more likely, even if you think they are wrong. According to Bond (2005), normative influence is stronger when people respond in front of the group, while informational influence is stronger when people respond in private. That's not to say that these two forms of influence act independently. One study (Levitan & Verhulst, 2016), for example, found that *both* normative and informational influence can have long-lasting effects on people's political attitudes. (For more about group size and conformity, see Box 6.1.)

Security in Numbers: The Effect of More Than One Dissenter

Having an ally helps a person resist conforming to a group. For example, Allen and Levine (1971) found that a single subject is likely to conform when faced with four other people who disagree, but if one of those four sides with the subject, the subject continues to dissent. Interestingly, this seems to be the case even when the supporting partner's judgments are questionable. For example, Allen and Levine (1971) found that when trying to make judgments about visual stimuli, even a supporting partner who seemed visually impaired (e.g., wore thick glasses and seemed to have a hard time seeing) prevented subjects from conforming.

Emotional Reaction of the Majority: Foaming at the Mouth

Since most people are motivated to fit in, it makes sense that getting angry at them when they disagree should increase their motivation to conform. At least that's what one group of researchers thought (Heerdink, van Kleef, Homan, & Fischer, 2015). But they were wrong. Contrary to their hypothesis, when a majority group of members expressed anger, it led to anti-conformity, perhaps because the dissenter wanted to harm the group or restore freedom of choice (reactance). Bottom line? If you're trying to bring someone back into the fold, keep your cool.

Moral Conviction: Wrong Is Wrong?

Imagine this scenario: Enemy soldiers are approaching your neighborhood. You and your neighbors try to hide, but, suddenly, your baby starts crying. The only way to keep from being discovered is to smother your baby. Is it morally wrong to do so?

So far, we've seen that conformity influences the ways in which people answer factual questions (e.g., which lines are similar lengths?), but what about ethical questions like the one above? To find out, Kundu and Cummins (2013) asked research participants to respond, either alone or in groups of confederates, to the "smother-baby" question and others like it. Results indicated that participants were swayed by the opinions of others. Stated differently, moral judgments are vulnerable to group pressure too.

BOX 6.1 | Majority Rules: How to Influence When You're Alone in a Group

This chapter discusses the ways in which a majority of people can influence a minority. As many minority groups have illustrated throughout history, however, sometimes, the minority can influence the majority. This is especially true when the person in the minority is believed to have experience and expertise in whatever topic the group is discussing (Hart, Stasson, & Karau, 1999).

Even when the person in the minority is not an expert, however, it may be possible for him or her to influence the majority. According to a review of research by Tanford and Penrod (1984), two strategies that a minority member can try are (1) conforming with the group and then deviating and (2) consistently disagreeing with the group. The first tactic involves accumulating what might popularly be known as brownie points. Specifically, by going along with the group on most issues, you are more favorable in the group's eyes when you disagree. As a result, you may convince the group to go along with your point of view. In contrast, the second tactic involves disagreeing with the group consistently and competently. By doing this, whoever holds the minority point of view looks more confident and may get the group's attention (Moscovici & Faucheux, 1972; Moscovici, Lage, & Naffrechoux, 1969). Of course, these two tactics involve opposite behaviors, so if you're in the minority, don't try both; pick one tactic and stick to it. If you're able to convince even one member of the majority to join you, research suggests that others may follow suit (see Clark, 1999). Finally, recent research indicates that the majority are more willing to consider minority viewpoints if they expect future interactions (San Martin, Swaab, Sinaceur, & Vasiljevic, 2015). Considering that, you could always mention the likelihood of future interaction.

That said, there may be exceptions. Indeed, according to the *morality as motivated resistance hypothesis*, people with stronger moral convictions should be more resistant to majority influence than people with weaker convictions (Aramovich, Lytle, & Skitka, 2012). Thus far, research supports this hypothesis. For example, Aramovich and colleagues (2012) found that people with strong (versus weak) convictions against torture were more likely to express opposition to torturing suspected terrorists, even when their groups expressed support for such torture.

Indoctrination: Intense Initiations and Mindless Membership

The only time one of your authors was formally initiated into a group, his high school's Varsity Club, he had to wear a dress and sing Christmas carols in a shopping mall (and it wasn't even Christmas time). Of course, there are more severe initiations than this. In 2003, for instance, a group of Chicago high school girls viciously hazed some younger girls by kicking, strangling, and pelting them with feces, urine, fish entrails, and blood. The same year, three young football players in Bellmore, New York, were sodomized with broomsticks, golf balls, and pinecones during a hazing incident. And although previous literature indicates that 50 percent or more of college athletes and fraternity and sorority members have been involved in hazing (Waldron, 2015), students are not the only ones participating. In recent incidents, for example, two U.S. servicemen committed suicide after being repeatedly abused by fellow soldiers, and four Texas firefighters were suspended after binding a rookie with duct tape and dousing him with water (Hosansky, 2013).

As brutal as these rituals sound, some argue that such practices build cohesiveness by encouraging bonding among new recruits and rookies (see Hosansky, 2013). Interestingly enough, this may be true. Research suggests that we value a group more if our indoctrination into the group is severe and intense (e.g., Aronson & Mills, 1959). Not only that, once we value a group, we are likely to conform to it. As the introduction to this chapter illustrated, religious cults provide a frightening example of the high level of compliance that may result from intense levels of indoctrination. Indeed, a disturbing number of cult members have died in mass suicides that were encouraged by their leaders (see Box 6.2).

How do cults lure such people into their trap? Baron (2000) noted that indoctrination into cults occurs in four stages. First, in the *softening-up stage,* recruits, often targeted when vulnerable (e.g., following a divorce or death of a loved one), are befriended by a member and invited to meetings. There, recruits are showered with attention and praise from cult members, a technique referred to as "love bombing" (Richmond, 2004). Often, recruits are "squired" by enthusiastic group members or "messianic" leaders, deprived of sleep, and then confused. The idea here is to lure, then stress, the recruits. In the second stage, *compliance,* the recruits tentatively experiment with some of the behaviors requested by the cult, which may include changes in diet, sleep, and appearance. Though in this stage recruits may simply be paying lip service to the demands of the cult, by the third stage, *internalization,* the recruits begin to consider some of the demands and beliefs of the cult (e.g., all nonmembers are evil) to be more acceptable. Finally, in the *consolidation stage,* recruits become loyal to the cult and demonstrate their allegiance with costly behaviors such as abandoning their careers or academic goals, donating all their personal possessions to the cult, and recruiting new members.

BOX 6.2 | Modern-Day Cults: A Sad Chronology

1978: Reverend Jim Jones and 900 followers, including children, commit suicide in Jonestown, Guyana, by drinking cyanide-laced punch.

1991: A Mexican minister and 29 followers suffocate after he instructs them to keep praying and ignore toxic fumes filling the church.

1993: At least 80 Branch Davidians, followers of David Koresh, perish in a fire and shoot-out with the BATF at their compound in Waco, Texas.

1993: Using primitive weapons, 53 Vietnamese tribal villagers commit suicide in the belief that they will go straight to heaven.

1994: Sixty-seven members of the "Order of the Solar Temple" cult are found burned to death in the French Alps in Switzerland and in Quebec, Canada.

1997: Thirty-nine members of the "Heaven's Gate" cult, led by Marshall Applewhite, commit suicide in California. They die so they can join the Mother Ship following the Hale–Bopp comet.

2000: More than 900 members of a reclusive Christian doomsday cult in Africa are murdered by their leaders. Many are burned to death and many are buried in mass graves.

2003: Members of the Raelians (a cult founded by Claude Vorilhon), now known as "Rael," claim that with the assistance of Clonaid, a human cloning company, they have cloned two or more human infants. The claims have never been substantiated.

Identification and Conformity: You're My Kind of People

According to Kenneth Burke (1950), *identification* occurs when people achieve shared meaning. Burke argued that humans are motivated to communicate with one another to create identification. The notion of identification is important here because the more a person identifies with a group, the more power the group has to influence that person.

A group that has the power to influence us through the process of identification is known as a *reference group*. Of course, not all groups are reference groups. For example, you might get together with several other students to study for a test. It's unlikely that such a group would exert much influence on the way you think and behave on a daily basis. However, a group of people you admire and want to be like might have a strong impact on you, often without your even knowing it. Because we identify with reference groups, we tend to dress the way they dress, think the way they think, and act the way they act. With this in mind, it's not surprising that a considerable amount of research indicates that we tend to conform more to a group of people who are similar to us than to a group of people who are not (e.g., see Phua, 2013). Previous research, for example, found that university students were more likely to engage in high-risk sexual activity (i.e., unplanned, inebriated sex)

FIGURE 6.3
Cartoon by John Seiter.

(Holman & Sillars, 2012), and consume more alcohol (Reed, Lange, Ketchie, & Clapp, 2007) when their peers approved of such behavior. Similarly, students and police officers reported being less willing to help a victim of intimate partner violence when they believed their reference group would avoid doing so also (Baldry & Pagliaro, 2014).

Although fitting in and getting along can be a good thing, Seiter (1998) argued that too much identification can have negative consequences in a variety of contexts. For example, in intercultural contexts, *ethnocentrism,* or the belief that one's culture is the standard by which all others should be evaluated, occurs when members of a culture identify too strongly with their own culture. In small group contexts, *groupthink* (Janis, 1972) occurs when the members in a group are so concerned with achieving consensus and getting along with each other that they don't disagree when they should. In organizational communication contexts, too much identification can lead to what Tompkins and his colleagues (Bullis & Tompkins, 1989; Tompkins & Cheney, 1985) call *strong culture.* Strong cultures exist when employees identify so much with their organization that they conform to the organization's values and actions.

As you might imagine, ethnocentrism, groupthink, and strong culture can result in some seriously negative consequences. For instance, ethnocentrism can lead to hatred, discrimination, and violence toward members of another culture (Gudykunst & Kim, 1997). Moreover, groups and organizations characterized by groupthink and strong culture are notorious for bad decision making, because they involve collectives of people who are all thinking in the same way (Sims & Sauser, 2013). Seiter (1995), for example, showed how a lumber company with a strong culture had difficulty communicating with people outside the organization. That's because inside the company, everyone thought things were rosy, and, as a result, the organization found itself threatened in the face of environmentalist attacks. Clearly, organizations and groups need members who will occasionally "rock the boat," "blow whistles," and "play devil's advocate" (Locke et al., 2001; Redding, 1985). In fact, although such dissenters can be seen as troublemakers, they can also be admired contributors who promote innovation, creativity, and better decisions (Jetten & Hornsey, 2014). In short, then, it is apparent that identification, by enabling us to communicate, organize, and decrease division, can be a worthwhile goal. However, we must be moderate in promoting it because too much identification can be "too much of a good thing" (Seiter, 1998).

Communicator Characteristics and Conformity

In Chapter 5, we discussed in some detail the ways in which communicator characteristics are related to persuasion. Many of the same characteristics examined there have also been studied by researchers interested in the topic of conformity.

Sex Difference

In an analysis of a large number of studies, Bond and Smith (1996) concluded that females are more likely to conform than males. This seems to be the case regardless of when the studies were conducted (i.e., sex differences have not narrowed over time) or whether the participants in the studies were in the presence of the other group members. At least one study suggests that such differences may be due to confidence or lack thereof. Specifically, when performing tasks that favored males, females were less confident and conformed more than did males. For gender-neutral tasks, however, no differences in conformity were found (Cross, Brown, Morgan, & Laland, 2016).

Peer-suasion

The pressure to conform to peers begins early in life. Even preschoolers experience it (Haun & Tomasello, 2011). Even so, we suspect that most people associate peer pressure with the teen years, perhaps for good reason. Indeed, Knoll and her colleagues (2015) found that teens, compared to younger children and adults, were more likely to value the opinions of other teens than those of adults. According to McCoy (1991), one study conducted on more than 3,000 teenagers found that more than two-thirds of them felt substantial peer pressure to have sex, drink, and take drugs. Gordon (1986) found that peer pressure is the most important factor in determining whether teens begin smoking. Moreover, because teens so desperately want to be accepted by their peers, for those who do not believe that they fit in with groups that pressure them, the consequences can be severe. For instance, not fitting in can lead to depression, the number-one risk factor for teen suicide (Royte, 1994). That being said, we must keep in mind that peer pressure is not always a bad thing. In her Pulitzer Prize-winning book, *Join the Club*, for instance, Tina Rosenberg (2011) argued that peer pressure, which she calls "the social cure," can be used to transform the world for the better. As one example, she showed how groups of young nonsmokers with names such as "Rage Against the Haze" used peer pressure to cut the rate of teen smoking in half, something that government-led antismoking campaigns based on fear (e.g., smoking kills) were unable to do.

Personality

Several studies have identified various aspects of personality that are related to conformity. First, Burger (1987) found that people high in the desire to control events in their lives react negatively to group pressure and are, therefore, less likely to conform than people with a low desire for control. Second, high self-monitors, who pay close attention to social cues on appropriate behavior, are more likely to conform than low self-monitors (Snyder, 1987). Finally, Rose, Shoham, Kahle, and Batra (1994) found that people who are high in the need for affiliation and group identification conform more than people without such needs.

Culture

After surveying more than 100,000 people in 40 different cultures, Hofstede (1984) identified four different dimensions of values along which any culture can be placed. He labeled these dimensions *power distance, uncertainty avoidance, masculinity–femininity,* and *individualism–collectivism.* Lustig and Cassotta (1996) argued that each of Hofstede's dimensions can be applied to the topic of conformity.

First, people from cultures that score high on power distance value hierarchy and obedience to authority, whereas those who score low on power distance prefer equality and participative decision making. For that reason, Lustig and Cassotta (1996) argued that people from cultures with low power-distance scores (e.g., Israel, Australia, western European countries) are less likely to conform than those from cultures with high power-distance scores (e.g., the Philippines, Mexico, Venezuela, India, Singapore).

Second, people from some cultures avoid uncertainty and have little tolerance for ambiguity, whereas people from other cultures are more at ease with the unknown. Because ambiguous stimuli foster conformity more than unambiguous stimuli, Lustig and Cassotta (1996) argued that cultures that are uncomfortable with ambiguous situations (e.g., Greece, Portugal, Japan, Peru, Chile, Spain) should conform more than cultures that are comfortable with ambiguity (e.g., the United States, Singapore, India, England, Sweden).

Third, some cultures can be characterized as "masculine" because people in them value competition, strength, assertiveness, and achievement, whereas others can be characterized as "feminine" because people in them value cooperation, affection, intuition, and nurturance. As such, members from masculine cultures (e.g., Japan, Italy, Austria, Mexico, England, Venezuela) should conform less than members from feminine cultures (e.g., Scandinavian countries, Portugal, the Netherlands).

Finally, while people in individualistic cultures value personal goals and self-autonomy, those in collectivistic cultures emphasize the importance of group goals and harmony. For that reason, Lustig and Cassotta (1996) argued that individualists (e.g., people from the United States, England, Australia, Canada, Italy, Denmark) are less conforming than collectivists (e.g., people from Colombia, Korea, Peru, Taiwan, Pakistan, Chile). A meta-analysis by Bond and Smith (1996) supports this conclusion, finding conformity to be much higher among collectivists than individualists. In fact, even when they are encouraged to dissent, collectivists resist doing so more than individualists do (Curseu & ten Brink, 2016). That said, although collectivists seem to be especially susceptible to normative influence (Savani, Wadhwa, Ulchida, Ding, & Naidu, 2015; Oh, 2013), additional research found no difference between them and individualists when it came to conforming to informational influence (Oh, 2013).

Social Proof: Using the Sheep Factor to Persuade Others

"But, Mom, *everybody's* doing it," is a familiar childhood refrain. Even so, children are not the only ones who pattern their behavior after others. Much adult behavior is based on what Cialdini (1993) has termed *social proof*. Specifically, social proof is the tendency to view behaviors as more appropriate or correct when a lot of other people are engaging in such behaviors. According to Cialdini (1993), however, although using social proof can be a handy shortcut for deciding how to behave, it can also make us vulnerable to the persuasive attempts of others. This is because we are more likely to engage in a behavior when persuaders lead us to believe that a lot of other people are engaging in that behavior.

One of the authors once met a person who makes money by playing a guitar and singing in subways and on street corners. The person explained that, even before she starts singing, she throws some of her own money into the open guitar case. Why? When people pass by, they think others have contributed and are more likely to do the same. Not surprisingly, this subway minstrel is not the only one who uses the principle of social proof to persuade others. In fact, the success of "viral marketing" (also discussed in Chapter 1) is largely based on this principle. In his bestselling book *The Tipping Point*, for example, Malcolm Gladwell (2002) argued that in the same way a sick person can start an epidemic of the flu, so too can a small group of influential people launch a fashion trend or boost the popularity of a new product. The idea is that consumers will see products being used or talked about by others and follow suit. This strategy of relying on social proof or word of mouth has become known as *viral marketing* and is catching on. Did you know, for example, that companies are hiring "real people" to use their products? These "undercover" consumers are meant to provide proof that the product is effective or worthwhile. For example, Hebrew National hired "mom squads" to host hotdog barbeques (Goodman, 2001), and marketers for the energy drink Red Bull decided they didn't even need people to spread the word. Instead, they filled sidewalk trash cans and bar tables with empty cans of the stuff (Eisenberg, 2002).

Once again, the idea is the same; if people see or hear about others using a product, they're more likely to try the product themselves. Research supports this notion as well. For example, a study by Cody, Seiter, and Montagne-Miller (1995) found that when people are buying gifts for others, social proof is one of the most effective tactics that a salesperson can use. In fact, when salespersons told their customers that a particular product was "the most popular," "the best selling," or "selling faster than we can bring them in," customers spent more money than when the salespersons used other tactics, such as praising the customer, doing favors for the customer, and trying to demonstrate expertise and trustworthiness (Cody et al., 1995). Why? It may be that people are less certain about purchases when buying for others than when buying for themselves.

Not surprisingly, social media is a haven for social proof as well. Would it surprise you to learn, for example, that some bloggers earn $100,000 or more per year to promote certain brands? It's true. Those bloggers may seem ordinary enough, but beware—their brand choices are not always random (Wolverson, 2013).

From an organization's point of view, digital marketing can also be tricky. Indeed, although social media can garner a lot of attention, it can also backfire spectacularly. Consider what happened when a British government agency tried to drum up support for a $287 million research ship by allowing Internet users to suggest and vote on names. Do you suppose they ended up with a dignified name like "Shackleton," "Endeavor," or "Falcon"? Not a chance. It turns out that voters went with "Boaty McBoatface" instead. Similarly, imagine Taylor Swift's surprise when Internet voters chose a school for the deaf as a concert location, or Slovakian legislators' astonishment when the public voted to name a pedestrian bridge after the celebrity Chuck Norris (Rogers, 2016).[1]

Another method for sparking word-of-mouth marketing is a selling strategy known as *group buying*, which encourages individual customers to make purchases through buying groups in order to receive a discounted group rate (see Jing & Xie, 2011). For example, a company might sell a $100 item for $75 if 20 people sign up to buy the item. As a result, customers who want the discount spread the word, essentially becoming sales agents for the company. The Internet, of course, is a ripe environment for this approach, and it is not surprising that a number of group-buying websites, such as Groupon.com, have emerged. According to Chen and Lu (2015), group buying is effective for marketing products, especially when those products are endorsed by members of our reference groups.

That said, online customer reviews of products and services can also operate as social proof. Take, for example, the following reviews of vacation resorts adapted from Expedia.com (Book, Tanford, Montgomery, & Love, 2015, p. 13):

"We just got back yesterday and had the time of our lives! The resort was amazing . . ."

"We cannot wait to go back!"

"Let me give you the real '5 Star review'. If you like old, dirty and run down hotels—5 stars! If you like hard beds and bring your own air mattress—5 stars! If you like a cesspool for a swimming pool—5 stars!"

According to a study by Book and her colleagues (2015), reviews such as these function like traditional word of mouth, yet have the capability of reaching far more customers. If fact, such reviews can be more influential than prices, especially when they are unanimously positive or negative (Book et al., 2015). Not surprisingly, online reviews are particularly persuasive when they contain quality information (Filieri, 2015).

Social proof, of course, has the power to influence more than buying behavior, as illustrated in a study by Burger and Shelton (2011, p. 74). Specifically, these researchers posted two signs near elevators. One, using social proof, read, "More than 90 percent of the time, people in this building use the stairs instead of the elevator." The other sign said, "Taking the stairs instead of the elevator is a good way to get some exercise." Within two weeks, the number of people using the elevator instead of the stairs dropped 46 percent, but only in the social proof condition. No change was observed with the sign that merely encouraged exercise.

Although social proof is probably a universally effective persuasion tactic, it may be more effective when used in some cultures than others. Recall, for example, our earlier discussion about the distinction between individualistic and collectivistic cultures. According to Cody and Seiter (2001), because social proof is rooted in people's tendency to conform, it should be especially effective in collectivistic cultures where conformity is prevalent. This seems to be the case. For instance, Cialdini, Wosinska, Barrett, Butner, and Gornik-Durose (2001) conducted a study to see how well social proof worked in the United States (an individualistic culture) and Poland (a collectivistic culture). In the study, people from both cultures were asked to indicate how willing they would be to comply with three requests: once while considering that all their peers had complied with the request (high social proof), once while considering that half their peers had complied with the request (moderate social proof), and once while considering that none of their peers had complied (no social proof). Results of the study indicated that, in both cultures, as the level of social proof increased, so did compliance. This was especially true in Poland (Cialdini et al., 2001).

OSTRACISM: SHUNS AND GUNS

In 1976, on the campus where one of the authors teaches, a disturbed man shot and killed six students and one communication professor. In 1999, at Columbine High School in Colorado, two students, Eric Harris and Dylan Klebold, shot and killed 12 students and a teacher before committing suicide, and in 2007, Seung-Hui Cho killed 32 people on the Virginia Tech campus before committing suicide. More recently, in 2012, a gunman killed 20 children and 6 adults at Sandy Hook Elementary School in Newtown, Connecticut. Sadly, such school shootings are all too prevalent. They leave us shaking our heads and asking, "Why?" What would lead people to do such horrible things? One explanation is *ostracism*, the act of excluding and ignoring others (Carter-Sowell, Chen, & Williams, 2008). Indeed, according to Zadro and Williams's (2006) sources, the Columbine killers acted out as a form of retaliation after being shunned by their peers.

Up to this point, we have seen how people's desire to belong can lead them to conform to that group, even if they think the group is wrong. The study of ostracism underlines just how important this need can be and how desperate for attention ostracized people can become. By way of example, Carter-Sowell and colleagues (2008) noted that the "Bind, Torture, Kill" serial killer was so desperate for recognition that he wrote about it to the press: "How many do I have to kill, before I get my name in the paper or some national attention?" (p. 144).

Although the act of ostracism does not always lead to such violent incidents, research suggests that it can affect behavior in other ways. For instance, in order to gain the acceptance they seek, ostracized people may behave in more socially acceptable ways (Feinberg, Willer, & Schultz, 2014). As Carter-Sowell and colleagues (2008) argued, however, the need to fit in may render ostracized people easy marks for persuaders. To test this notion, Riva, Williams, Torstrick, and Montali (2014) conducted a study. In it, students played "Cyberball," a computer ball-tossing game with two other players, who, unbeknown to the students, were actually computer generated and programmed to ostracize the students by hardly ever tossing the ball to them. After about two minutes of virtual shunning, the students were approached by the experimenter, who handed them a camera and commanded them to go outside when temperatures were below 30° Fahrenheit to take 39 creative pictures. As suspected, the students who had been ostracized were significantly more obedient. Judges rated their pictures to be significantly more creative than those taken by non-ostracized students.

DEINDIVIDUATION, SOCIAL LOAFING, AND SOCIAL FACILITATION: GETTING LOST IN THE CROWD

In previous sections, we saw how people can be pressured to conform to a group. This, however, is not the only way that groups can influence an individual. In this section we examine how groups can affect a person's behavior by causing the person to lose his or her sense of self or by making the person feel less responsible for his or her actions.

What a Riot: An Examination of Deindividuation

Crowds influence people's behavior; once we get lost in them, we tend to do things that we would never do alone. If you don't believe us, ask our friend who was one of the 500,000 people at the Woodstock concert in 1969. She won't say whether she was one of the people running around naked, but she admits to doing things she wouldn't have done if she had not been lost in the crowd.

This tendency "to get lost in the crowd" was first labeled *deindividuation* by Festinger, Pepitone, and Newcomb (1952). Deindividuation is said to occur when being in a group causes people to become less aware of themselves and less concerned with how others will evaluate them (Diener, 1980). Because being in a large group makes a person both more aroused and anonymous, the person focuses less on himself or herself and behaves more impulsively.

Although running around naked at concerts may sound harmless enough, it is clear that deindividuation can have much more severe consequences. For example, one of the authors was a student at the University of Southern California when the Los Angeles riots broke out in 1992. Seeing firsthand the trashed storefronts and burnt buildings of the riot's aftermath made the potentially cruel nature of deindividuation all too real. The riots made it clear to everyone how powerful mob psychology can be: When one person starts wreaking havoc, others may be likely to follow. Consider, for example, the comments of a U.S. soldier trying to explain what caused him to kill innocent children and civilians during the My Lai massacre:

> I just went. My mind just went. And I wasn't the only one that did it . . . a lot of people were doing it, so I just followed suit. I just lost all sense of direction, of purpose. I just started killing. I just started killing any kinda way I could kill. It just came. I didn't know I had it in me.
>
> (Biton & Sim, cited in Epley & Gilovich, 1999, p. 578)

A classic study by Diener, Fraser, Beaman, and Kelem (1976) illustrates how deindividuation can lead to such antisocial behavior. The researchers suspected that if any night of the year would lead to deindividuation, it was Halloween. To be sure, children usually trick-or-treat in groups and, because they wear costumes, are more anonymous than usual. To see if deindividuation would affect children's behavior, these researchers gave 1,352 trick-or-treaters, who were either trick-or-treating alone or in groups, the opportunity to steal candy or money from 27 homes in Seattle. How did the experiment work? When trick-or-treaters came to the door, an experimenter greeted them, commenting on their costumes. The experimenter asked some of the children their names, and other children were allowed to remain anonymous. The experimenter then left the room after telling the trick-or-treaters they could take one of the candies that was in a bowl near the door (there was also a bowl full of nickels and pennies). Unbeknown to the children, a hidden observer watched how much candy (and money) the children really took, and here's what the observer saw: When children were trick-or-treating alone, 7.5 percent of them took more candy than they were supposed to. When they were in groups, however, the thievery increased substantially; 20.8 percent stole candy. Moreover, when the children remained anonymous, they stole more candy and money than they did when the experimenter asked their names. In short, deindividuation led the trick-or-treaters to a night of petty crime.

Perhaps the most disturbing research on deindividuation focused on violent behaviors perpetrated in groups. First, in one study, Mann (1981) examined more than 150 newspaper accounts of what happened when people threatened to kill themselves by jumping from buildings. Mann found that in some cases, people who had gathered on the streets below actually baited the potential jumpers, encouraging them to leap to their deaths. Can you guess what one of the factors was that caused observers to egg on jumpers? According to Mann, when the crowds contained more than 300 people, baiting was more common than it was in smaller crowds. This, of course, is consistent with the notion that larger crowds produce more deindividuation.

Second, in an even more disturbing study, Mullen (1986) examined the relationship between the size of lynch mobs and the severity of atrocities committed by such mobs. To do so, he analyzed more than 300 newspaper reports to determine the following: (1) the number of people in each lynch mob; (2) whether the lynchings included violent acts, such as hanging, shooting, burning, lacerating, and dismembering the victims; and (3) whether the lynchings happened quickly or were prolonged and torturous. Results of the study indicated that victims suffered more when the lynch mobs were larger. Mullen (1986) concluded that "these results support the contention that lynchers become less self-attentive, and thereby more likely to engage in acts of atrocity, as the lynchers become more numerous relative to the number of victims" (p. 191).

Considering these studies, an important question concerns how deindividuation might be attenuated. Because deindividuation results from low self-awareness, the answer may lie in making people more aware of themselves. According to Prentice-Dunn and Rogers (1982), however, there are two types of self-awareness and only one is related to deindividuation. First, *public self-awareness* refers to how we view ourselves as social objects and our concerns about such things as our appearance and the impression we are making on others. *Private self-awareness* refers to our focus on hidden aspects of ourselves such as our thoughts, feelings, and perceptions (see Buss, 1980). Prentice-Dunn and Rogers (1982) found that deindividuation is decreased only when a person's private self-awareness is increased. This suggests, then, that to attenuate deindividuation, the object is to get people focused on their own thoughts and feelings. Thus, rather than state that people will get in trouble for their actions or look bad for doing something, it may be better to have them reflect on their personal views on what is right and wrong. (For more on deindividuation in a specific context, see Box 6.3.)

Social Loafing: Not Pulling Your Own Weight

Have you ever had to push a stalled car or move a heavy piece of furniture with several other people? If so—be honest for a moment—did you give it your all? Or, because there were others to share the burden, did you slack off a bit? If you're at all like the average research participant, you probably did not work as hard as you could have. Indeed, research suggests that when working in groups, people may not try as hard as they do when working alone (e.g., Harkins, Latané, & Williams, 1980; Karau & Williams, 1993). In short, like a lot of other people, you may be a social loafer.

According to Karau and Williams (1993), "social loafing is the reduction in motivation and effort when individuals work collectively compared with when they work individually or coactively" (p. 681). What causes such loafing? There are several explanations, although we only have room to discuss the most prominent perspectives (for a review of others, see Guerin, 1999; Karau & Williams, 2001; Locke et al., 2001).

First, the *collective effort model* (Karau & Williams, 2001) argues that we tend to get lazy if we don't expect our efforts to lead to personally valued outcomes or if we don't think our effort will be instrumental in obtaining those outcomes. Thus, social loafing occurs because we don't think we will get the credit we are due or achieve the results we desire.

Second, the *free ride effect* suggests that when they can get away with it, people try to benefit from the efforts of others—that is, they slack off when others are working, when they are anonymous, and when they don't think their own efforts will be

BOX 6.3 | Computer-Mediated Conformity: When Group Members Flame the Same

From what you've read so far, you can see that being in the presence of a group can seriously affect your behavior. With that in mind, what do you suppose might happen if you were still able to communicate with a group but were removed physically from the group's presence? Liberation from social pressure? Freedom to do as you please without worrying about fitting in?

If that's what you were thinking, think again. Optimists once figured that email and the Internet might provide emancipation from group pressure, but empirical research suggests otherwise. For instance, a study by Williams, Cheung, and Choi (2000) found that people using Internet chat rooms are likely to conform to the unanimous incorrect judgments of a group of strangers, especially after being ostracized by a previous group. Moreover, Postmes, Spears, and Lea (2000) found that the same types of norms and conformity that occur in face-to-face groups evolve in computer-mediated groups as well.

With that said, you probably won't be surprised to learn that communicating via computer does not make you immune to negative behaviors often evidenced in groups. In fact, some studies (e.g., Jessup, Connolly, & Tansik, 1990) suggest that the anonymity afforded to people who communicate via computers makes uninhibited and inappropriate behavior (e.g., insulting others, using profanity) more likely than it is in face-to-face conversations. Such "flaming," as it is called in the world of computer users, has been blamed on deindividuation, which, as you already know, is fostered by anonymity.

The good news is that computer-mediated group communication does not necessarily lead to negative behavior, but rather positive or negative behavior depending on the norms of the group with which one is communicating (Spears, Lea, & Lee, 1990). Specifically, the social identity model of deindividuation effects (SIDE; Postmes, Spears, & Lea, 1998, 2000) argues that immersion in a group prompts greater conformity to the group's norms. Thus, if the group's norms are positive, you are more likely to engage in prosocial behaviors. If the group's norms are negative, you are more likely to "flame."

evaluated. Working in groups not only allows them to "hide in the crowd" without getting blamed for poor work but also enables them to reduce their own effort and still enjoy an equal share of the rewards (see Karau & Williams, 2001; Locke et al., 2001).

Finally, the *sucker effect* occurs when people suspect that others may be taking a free ride. Rather than be a "sucker" who does all the work, people slack off in order to match the level of work done by others (see Locke et al., 2001).

Whatever the reason for social loafing, one thing is clear: It, like deindividuation, can have disastrous effects. For example, in Richmond, California, in 2009, at least a dozen bystanders watched as a 15-year-old girl was beaten and gang-raped outside the building where her high school homecoming dance was being held. The ordeal lasted more than two hours before anyone summoned help. Likewise, social loafing has been observed in laboratory research. For instance, in a study by Latané and Darley (1970), subjects were led to believe that they were having a conversation over an intercom with other subjects in the study. Some believed they were talking with only one other person; others believed they were talking with five other people. In reality, there were no other subjects, just tape-recorded messages. At one point during the conversation, one of the "pretend subjects" began choking and gasping as if having a seizure. Did the supposed victim receive help? The answer is "it depends." When subjects thought they were in groups with five other people, only 30 percent of them helped. When the subject thought she or he was alone with the victim, 85 percent helped. The larger the group, the less likely people are to lend a hand.

Considering our discussion so far, you might be wondering how social loafing can be decreased. According to Karau and Williams (1993), social loafing can be reduced or overcome by:

> providing individuals with feedback about their own performance or the performance of their work group, monitoring individual performance or making such performance identifiable, assigning meaningful tasks, making tasks unique such that individuals feel more responsibility for their work, enhancing the cohesiveness of work groups, and making individuals feel that their contributions to the task are necessary and not irrelevant.
>
> (p. 700)

Furthermore, it may be easier to attenuate social loafing if you know the conditions under which it occurs. For instance, because loafing is more likely in larger groups, limiting the number of people in a group may be effective (Aggarwal & O'Brien, 2008). Moreover, earlier in this chapter, we talked about how we are more likely to conform to groups with which we identify. Knowing this, it's not surprising to find that people who identify with a group are not as likely to loaf as those who do not identify (Barreto & Ellemers, 2000). For those who do not identify, another approach is to make them accountable for their work. Evidence for the effectiveness of this approach is mixed, however. For instance, while Aggarwal and O'Brien (2008) found that university students were less likely to loaf on group projects when their peers evaluated them, Dommeyer (2007) did not. Lount and Wilk (2014) found that employees were less likely to loaf when their performance was posted publicly, but argued that it was because doing so triggered social comparison between workers, which, in turn, increased their motivation to work hard.

Another variable that influences the potential for loafing is the nature of the people involved in the task, suggesting that before you join a group, you should know whom you're joining. First, research indicates that people who are open to new experiences, conscientious, agreeable, and high in the need for cognition (see Chapter 5) are less likely to loaf than their counterparts (Klehe & Anderson, 2007; Smith, Kerr, Markus, & Stasson, 2001; Tan & Tan, 2008). Second, Pieterse and Thompson (2010) noted that *diligent isolates*, unlike social loafers, are people who increase their efforts and willingly work alone in an effort to rescue group projects. However, because they do not know how to delegate or have the social skills required for group projects, diligent isolates can be just as bad for group projects as social loafers. In fact, Pieterse and Thompson (2010) observed that the presence of diligent isolates promoted social loafing in other group members. Finally, the way in which people perceive themselves might influence the degree to which they loaf. Specifically, a study by Huguet, Charbonnier, and Monteil (1999) found that people who see themselves as uniquely superior to others are most likely to loaf when working collectively on an easy task (i.e., imagining different uses for a knife). This is because they perceive their contribution to such a task as redundant, dispensable, and unlikely to make others aware of their superior talents. However, these types of people tend to work extra hard on difficult tasks (i.e., imagining different uses for a doorknob) (Huguet et al., 1999) or when they perceive their teammates as being unequipped for handling the task (Plaks & Higgins, 2000). And why not? Such *social compensation*, as it is called in the literature, helps them maintain the belief that they are unique and reap possible rewards if their group does well (Huguet et al., 1999). What can we learn from such research? Consider this: If you ever ask a group to perform an easy task, watch out for people who think they're the cat's meow. If that sounds simple, consider one more thing: Most people see themselves as superior to the average person, a phenomenon known as *self-serving bias* (see Goethals, Messick, & Allison, 1991). Unfortunately, this probably means that when tasks are easy, there are a lot of loafers out there.

Social Facilitation: Would You Rather Be Alone?

The presence of other people does not always lead to loafing. In fact, it can have the opposite effect. Years ago, for example, when one of the authors was on his high school's track team, he ran "practice races" by himself, attempting to beat his best time. No matter how hard he tried, however, he could never match his performance in real races. He didn't know it then, but his faster times in real races were most likely the result of *social facilitation*, or rather, the tendency to perform better when other people are around (see Zajonc, 1965). The effect has been demonstrated time and time again, but before you decide to surround yourself with spectators the next time you write a research paper, consider this: The presence of others tends to improve performance on simple or well-rehearsed tasks while impairing performance on complex or unfamiliar tasks. Not only that, it can affect your health and bankroll. Did you know, for example, that as the number of diners increases, so does the amount of food consumed, especially when the people are friends and family (Cavazza, Graziani, & Guidetti, 2011; Herman, 2015)? Moreover, the energizing effects of being around other people might cause people to take greater risks. To illustrate, Rockloff, Greer, and Fay (2011) observed people playing computerized slot machines alone or alongside others. Results revealed that people played faster and longer in the presence of other gamblers than when alone. The implications, of course, are that large commercial gaming venues might accelerate the pace at which gamblers part with their dough.

HOW GROUPS AFFECT DECISION MAKING: TO RISK OR NOT TO RISK

Imagine that you're the parent of a small child, a daughter, with a serious heart condition. Because of the condition, your daughter has to refrain from any activity that might put too much strain on her. Your child's doctor, however, presents you with some interesting news: There's a new surgery your child can have that will make her completely healthy. There's a catch, however: The doctor tells you that there is a 1 percent chance your child will die from the surgery. What choice would you make? Would you allow the doctor to perform the surgery? If you thought "yes," imagine that the odds are different; instead of a 1 percent chance, what if there were a 50 percent chance your child would die?

Interestingly, research has shown that when selecting between alternatives like the preceding ones, groups and individuals make different decisions. The first study on this subject was conducted by Stoner (1961, cited in Brauer, Judd, & Gliner, 1995), who found that individuals made riskier decisions when they were in groups than they did when alone. In other words, while an individual might decide to allow the surgery when there was a 1 percent chance of death, a group might allow it when there was a 50 percent chance. Following Stoner's study, several other researchers confirmed these results, and soon this effect became known as the *risky shift phenomenon*. Not all studies, however, confirmed this phenomenon. In fact, some later studies found just the opposite effect. Sometimes groups made decisions that were *less* risky than those made by individuals (e.g., Myers & Arenson, 1972). How might such results be explained? According to Myers and Arenson (1972), instead of a risky shift phenomenon, what actually occurs is a *group polarization phenomenon*. In short, groups cause people to become more extreme in their decisions. Thus, if you are predisposed to making a slightly risky decision, being in a group may cause you to make a riskier decision; if you are predisposed to make a conservative decision, being in a group may cause you to make an even more conservative decision. As you might suspect, as decisions become more extreme, they might also become less accurate. Indeed, in one study (Palmer & Loveland, 2008), poor, good, and average lecturers were evaluated by individuals or by people who engaged in group discussions. Results showed that group discussion led to less accurate ratings of the lecturers.

Although there are many explanations for why group polarization occurs, two are most prominent (see Boster, 1990; Brauer et al., 1995; Pavitt, 1994). The first, *social comparison theory*, argues that we learn about ourselves by comparing ourselves to others. Because most people are average, when they compare their view to the views of others, they don't find much difference. Interestingly, however, because most people want to see themselves in a positive light, they don't want to be average; they want to be "better than average." Thus, according to this theory, when people learn that their position is the same as that of everyone else in the group, they shift their position so that it is more extreme. Because everyone tends to do this, group polarization occurs.

A second perspective, *persuasive arguments theory*, asserts that, before entering a group discussion, each member has one or more arguments that support his or her own position. If you consider all these arguments together, there will be more supporting one position than another (e.g., there may be more support for a risky decision than there is for a conservative one). Persuasive arguments theory asserts that the position that has the best and largest number of arguments supporting it is the position toward which members shift.

Several authors have argued that these theories are not contradictory (Boster, 1990; Isenberg, 1986; Pavitt, 1994). In other words, *both* social comparison and persuasive arguments might contribute to group polarization. In addition, Brauer and colleagues (1995) have argued that a third process might contribute to the extreme decisions made by groups. They noted that although social comparison and persuasive

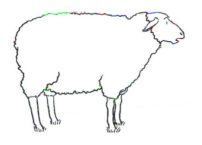 

FIGURE 6.5
Source: © Alex Gregory/
The New Yorker Collection/
www.cartoonbank.com.
All Rights Reserved.

"Sure, I follow the herd—not out of brainless obedience, mind you, but out of a deep and abiding respect for the concept of community."

arguments explanations both focus on interpersonal processes (e.g., what we hear from other group members), *intra*personal processes also may affect polarization. Specifically, they argued that when making decisions in groups, we not only hear from other group members, we state our own opinion and defend it several times. Such repetition, they argued, also moves us toward polarization.

Before concluding this section, we wish to point out that, like the other topics we've discussed in this chapter, group polarization can have disastrous effects. For instance, imagine being on the front lines in a hopeless battle. Who would you want deciding whether you should take a hill: one military leader or a group of them? How about if a decision were being made to start a war or launch a missile? Or imagine an innocent person accused of a crime. Would he or she be better off with or without a jury deciding on a verdict? You get the idea. As frequent members of groups, it is important to remember the effects that groups can have on us. Only then might we hope to be less vulnerable to their influence.

SUMMARY

In this chapter we examined several topics related to influence in groups. First, we discussed early research on conformity and saw that several perspectives explain why people tend to conform. In addition, several factors (i.e., group size, moral conviction, having an ally, the intensity of indoctrination, the degree to which we identify with a group, communicator characteristics, and culture) influence how likely we are to conform. We also saw that social proof can be a powerful persuasive tactic because it relies on people's tendency to conform. We then saw that the presence of others can lead to deindividuation, social loafing, and social facilitation. Finally, for various reasons, groups tend to make more extreme decisions than do individuals (group polarization).

NOTE

1. In all three cases, the organizations disregarded voters' wishes. The boat was named "Attenborough," the bridge was named "Freedom Cycling Bridge," and Taylor Swift didn't play the concert, but she and four other organizations donated $10,000 each to the school.

REFERENCES

Aggarwal, P., & O'Brien, C. L. (2008). Social loafing on group projects: Structural antecedents and effect on student satisfaction. *Journal of Marketing Education*, *30*, 255–264. doi:10.1177/0273475308322283

Allen, V. L., & Levine, J. M. (1971). Social support and conformity: The role of independent assessment of reality. *Journal of Experimental Social Psychology*, *4*, 48–58.

Andrews, P. H. (1996). Group conformity. In R. S. Cathcart, L. A. Samovar, & L. D. Henman (Eds.), *Small group communication* (7th ed., pp. 184–192). Madison, WI: Brown & Benchmark.

Aramovich, N. P., Lytle, B. L., & Skitka, L. J. (2012). Opposing torture: Moral conviction and resistance to majority influence. *Social Influence*, *7*, 21–34.

Aronson, E., & Mills, T. (1959). Effects of severity of initiation on liking for a group. *Journal of Abnormal and Social Psychology*, *59*, 177–181.

Asch, S. E. (1956). Studies of independence and conformity: A minority of one against a unanimous majority. *Psychological Monographs*, *70*, entire volume.

Asch, S. E. (1966). Opinions and social pressure. In A. P. Hare, E. F. Borgatta, & R. F. Bales (Eds.), *Small groups: Studies in social interaction* (pp. 318–324). New York: Alfred A. Knopf.

Baldry, A. C., & Pagliaro, S. (2014). Helping victims of intimate partner violence: The influence of group norms among lay people and the police. *Psychology of Violence*, *4*, 334–347. doi:10:1037/a0034844

Baron, R. S. (2000). Arousal, capacity, and intense indoctrination. *Personality and Social Psychology Review*, *4*(3), 238–254.

Barreto, M., & Ellemers, N. (2000). You can't always do what you want: Social identity and self-presentational determinants of the choice to work for a low-status group. *Personality and Social Psychology Bulletin*, *26*(8), 891–906.

Bond, R. (2005). Group size and conformity. *Intergroup Relations*, *8*, 331–354.

Bond, R., & Smith, P. B. (1996). Culture and conformity: A meta-analysis of studies using Asch's (1952b, 1956) line judgment task. *Psychological Bulletin*, *119*(1), 111–137.

Book, L. A., Tanford, S., Montgomery, R., & Love, C. (2015). Online traveler reviews as social influence: Price is no longer king. *Journal of Hospitality & Tourism Research*, Online First. doi:10.1177/1096348015597029

Boster, F. J. (1990). Group argument, social pressure, and the making of group decisions. In J. A. Anderson (Ed.), *Communication yearbook 13* (pp. 303–312). Newbury Park, CA: Sage.

Brauer, M., Judd, C. M., & Gliner, M. D. (1995). The effects of repeated expressions on attitude polarizations during group discussions. *Journal of Personality and Social Psychology*, *68*(6), 1014–1029.

Bullis, C. A., & Tompkins, P. K. (1989). The forest ranger revisited: A study of control practices and identification. *Communication Monographs*, *56*, 287–306.

Burger, J. M. (1987). Desire for control and conformity to a perceived norm. *Journal of Personality and Social Psychology*, *35*(2), 355–360.

Burger, J. M., & Shelton, M. (2011). Changing everyday health behaviors through descriptive norm manipulations. *Social Influence*, *6*, 69–77.

Burke, K. (1950). *A rhetoric of motives.* New York: Prentice Hall.

Buss, A. H. (1980). *Self-consciousness and social anxiety.* San Francisco, CA: W. H. Freeman.

Campbell, J. D., & Fairey, P. J. (1989). Informational and normative routes to conformity: The effect of faction size as a function of norm extremity and attention to the stimulus. *Journal of Personality and Social Psychology, 57*(3), 457–468.

Carter-Sowell, A. R., Chen, Z., & Williams, K. D. (2008). Ostracism increases social susceptibility. *Social Influence, 3*, 143–143.

Cavazza, N., Graziani, A. R., & Guidetti, M. (2011). Looking for the "right" amount to eat at the restaurant: Social influence effects when ordering. *Social Influence, 6*, 274–290.

Chen, Y., & Lu, H. (2015). We-commerce: Exploring factors influencing online group-buying intention in Taiwan from a conformity perspective. *Asian Journal of Social Psychology, 18*, 62–75. doi:10.1111/ajsp.12083

Cialdini, R. B. (1993). *Influence: The psychology of persuasion* (Rev. Ed.). New York: Morrow.

Cialdini, R. B., Wosinska, W., Barrett, D. W., Butner, J., & Gornik-Durose, M. (2001). The differential impact of two social influence principles on individualists and collectivists in Poland and the United States. In W. Wosinska, R. B. Cialdini, D. W. Barrett, & J. Reykowski (Eds.), *The practice of social influence in multiple cultures* (pp. 33–50). Mahwah, NJ: Erlbaum.

Clark, R. D. (1999). Effect of number of majority defectors on minority influence. *Group Dynamics: Theory, Research, and Practice, 3*(4), 303–312.

Cody, M. J., & Seiter, J. S. (2001). Compliance principles in retail sales in the United States. In W. Wosinska, R. B. Cialdini, D. W. Barrett, & J. Reykowski (Eds.), *The practice of social influence in multiple cultures* (pp. 325–341). Mahwah, NJ: Erlbaum.

Cody, M. J., Seiter, J. S., & Montagne-Miller, Y. (1995). Men and women in the marketplace. In P. Kalbfleisch & M. Cody (Eds.), *Gender, power and communication in human relationships* (pp. 305–329). Hillsdale, NJ: Erlbaum.

Cross, C. P., Brown, G. R., Morgan, T. J. H., & Laland, K. N. (2016). Sex differences in confidence influence patterns of conformity. *British Journal of Psychology.* doi:10.1111/bjop.12232

Curseu, P. L., & ten Brink, T. (2016). Minority dissent as teamwork related mental model: Implications for willingness to dissent and group creativity. *Thinking Skills and Creativity, 22*, 86–96. doi:10.1016/j.tsc.2016.09.002

Deutsch, M., & Gerard, H. B. (1955). A study of normative and informational social influences upon individual judgment. *Journal of Abnormal Social Psychology, 51*, 629–636.

Diener, E. (1980). Deindividuation: The absence of self-awareness and self-regulation in group members. In P. B. Paulus (Ed.), *The psychology of group influence* (pp. 209–242). Hillsdale, NJ: Erlbaum.

Diener, E., Fraser, S. C., Beaman, A. L., & Kelem, R. T. (1976). Effects of deindividuation variables on stealing among Halloween trick-or-treaters. *Journal of Personality and Social Psychology, 33*(2), 178–183.

Dommeyer, C. J. (2007). Using the diary method to deal with social loafers on the group project: Its effects on peer evaluations, group behavior, and attitudes. *Journal of Marketing Education, 29*, 175–188.

Eisenberg, D. (2002, September 2). It's an ad, ad, ad, ad world. *Time, 160*(10), 38–41.

Epley, N., & Gilovich, T. (1999). Just going along: Nonconscious priming and conformity to social pressure. *Journal of Experimental Social Psychology, 35*, 578–589.

Feinberg, M. W., Willer, R., & Schultz, M. (2014). Gossip and ostracism promote cooperation in groups. *Psychological Science, 25*, 656–664. doi:10.1177/0956797613510184

Festinger, L., Pepitone, A., & Newcomb, T. (1952). Some consequences of deindividuation in a group. *Journal of Abnormal Social Psychology, 47,* 382–389.

Filieri, R. (2015). What makes online reviews helpful? A diagnosticity-adoption framework to explain informational and normative influences in e-WOM. *Journal of Business Research, 68,* 1261–1270. doi:10.1016/j.busres.2014.11.0060148–2963

Gladwell, M. (2002). *The tipping point.* New York: Little, Brown.

Gleick, E. (1997, April 7). The marker we've been waiting for. *Time, 149*(14), 28–36.

Goethals, G. R., Messick, D. M., & Allison, S. T. (1991). The uniqueness bias: Studies of constructive social comparison. In J. Suls & T. A. Wills (Eds.), *Social comparison: Theory and research* (pp. 149–176). Hillsdale, NJ: Erlbaum.

Goodman, E. (2001, August 11). Advertising hits zany levels. *The Herald Journal, 92*(223), p. A4.

Gordon, N. P. (1986). Never smokers, triers and current smokers: Three distinct target groups for school-based antismoking programs. *Health Education Quarterly, 13,* 163–179.

Gudykunst, W. B., & Kim, Y. Y. (1997). *Communicating with strangers: An approach to intercultural communication* (3rd ed.). Reading, MA: Addison-Wesley.

Guerin, B. (1999). Social behaviors as determined by different arrangements of social consequences: Social loafing, social facilitation, deindividuation, and a modified social loafing. *The Psychological Record, 49,* 565–578.

Harkins, S. G., Latané, B., & Williams, K. (1980). Social loafing: Allocating effort or taking it easy? *Journal of Experimental Social Psychology, 16,* 457–465.

Hart, J. W., Stasson, M. F., & Karau, S. J. (1999). Effects of source expertise and physical distance on minority influence. *Group Dynamics: Theory, Research, and Practice, 3*(1), 81–92.

Haun, D. B. M., & Tomasello, M. (2011). Conformity to peer pressure in preschool children. *Child Development, 82,* 159–1767. doi:10.1111/j.1467–8624.2011.01666x

Heerdink, M. W., van Kleef, G. A., Homan, A. C., & Fischer, A. H. (2015). Emotional reactions to deviance in groups: The relation between number of angry reactions, felt rejection, and conformity. *Frontiers in Psychology, 6,* 1–12. doi:10.3389/fpsyg.2015.00830

Herman, C. P. (2015). The social facilitation of eating. A review. *Appetite, 86,* 61–73. doi:10.1016/j.appet.2014.09.016

Hofstede, G. (1984). *Culture's consequences: International differences in work-related values.* Beverly Hills, CA: Sage.

Holman, A., & Sillars, A. (2012). Talk about "hooking up": The influence of college student social networks on nonrelationship sex. *Health Communication, 27,* 205–216. doi:10.1080/10410236.2011.575540

Hosansky, D. (2013, February 8). Preventing hazing. *CQ Researcher, 23,* 133–156.

Huguet, P., Charbonnier, E., & Monteil, J. (1999). Productivity loss in performance groups: People who see themselves as average do not engage in social loafing. *Group Dynamics: Theory, Research, and Practice, 3*(2), 118–131.

Isenberg, D. J. (1986). Group polarization: A critical review and metaanalysis. *Journal of Personality and Social Psychology, 50,* 1141–1151.

Janis, I. L. (1972). *Victims of groupthink.* Boston, MA: Houghton Mifflin.

Jessup, L. M., Connolly, T., & Tansik, D. A. (1990). Toward a theory of automated group work: The deindividuating effects of anonymity. *Small Group Research, 21*(3), 333–348.

Jetten, J., & Hornsey, M. J. (2014). Deviance and dissent in groups. *Annual Review of Psychology, 65,* 461–485. doi:10.1146/annurev-psych-010213–115151

Jing, X., & Xie, J. (2011). Group buying: A new mechanism for selling through social interactions. *Management Science, 57,* 1354–1372. doi:10.1287/mnsc.1110.1366

Karau, S. J., & Williams, K. D. (1993). Social loafing: A meta-analytic review and theoretical integration. *Journal of Personality and Social Psychology, 65*(4), 681–706.

Karau, S. J., & Williams, K. D. (2001). Understanding individual motivation in groups: The collective effort model. In M. E. Turner (Ed.), *Groups at work: Theory and research. Applied social research* (pp. 113–141). Mahwah, NJ: Erlbaum.

Klehe, U., & Anderson, N. (2007). The moderating influence of personality and culture on social loafing in typical versus maximum performance situations. *International Journal of Selection and Assessment, 15,* 250–262.

Knoll, L. J., Magis-Weinberg, L., Speekenbring, M., & Blakemore, S. (2015). *Psychological Science, 26,* 583–592. doi:10.1177/0956797615569578

Kundu, P., & Cummins, D. D. (2013). Morality and conformity: The Asch paradigm applied to moral decisions. *Social Influence, 8,* 268–279. doi:10.1080/15534510.2012.727767

Latané, B. (1981). The psychology of social impact. *American Psychologist, 36,* 343–356.

Latané, B., & Darley, J. M. (1970). *The unresponsive bystander: Why doesn't he help!* New York: Appleton-Century-Crofts.

Levitan, L. C., & Verhulst, B. (2016). Conformity in groups: The effects of others' views on expressed attitudes and attitude change. *Political Behavior, 38,* 277–315. doi:10.1007/s11109–015–9312-x

Locke, E. A., Tirnauer, D., Roberson, Q., Goldman, B., Latham, M. E., & Weldon, E. (2001). The importance of the individual in an age of groupism. In M. E. Turner (Ed.), *Groups at work: Theory and research* (pp. 501–528). Mahwah, NJ: Erlbaum.

Lount, R. B., & Wilk, S. L. (2014). Working harder or hardly working? Posting performance eliminates social loafing and promotes social laboring in workgroups. *Management Science, 60,* 1098–1106. doi:10.1287/mnsc.2013.1820

Lustig, M. W., & Cassotta, L. L. (1996). Comparing group communication across cultures: Leadership, conformity, and discussion processes. In R. S. Cathcart, L. A. Samovar, & L. D. Henman (Eds.), *Small group communication* (7th ed., pp. 316–326). Madison, WI: Brown & Benchmark.

Mann, L. (1981). The baiting crowd in episodes of threatened suicide. *Journal of Personality and Social Psychology, 30,* 729–735.

McCoy, K. (1991, May). Help your child beat peer pressure. *Reader's Digest,* pp. 67–70.

Moscovici, S., & Faucheux, C. (1972). Social influence, conforming bias, and the study of active minorities. In L. Berkowitz (Ed.), *Advances in experimental social psychology* (Vol. 6, pp. 149–202). New York: Academic Press.

Moscovici, S., Lage, E., & Naffrechoux, M. (1969). Influence of a consistent minority on the responses of a majority in a color perception task. *Sociometry, 32,* 365–379.

Mullen, B. (1986). Atrocity as a function of lynch mob composition: A self-attention perspective. *Personality and Social Psychology Bulletin, 12*(2), 187–197.

Myers, D. G., & Arenson, S. J. (1972). Enhancement of dominant risk tendencies in group discussion. *Psychological Reports, 30,* 615–623.

Oh, S. H. (2013). Do collectivists conform more than individualists? Cross-cultural differences in compliance and internalization. *Social Behavior and Personality, 41,* 981–994. doi:10.2224/sbp.2013.41.6.981

Palmer, J. K., & Loveland, J. M. (2008). The influence of group discussion on performance judgments: Rating accuracy, contrast effects, and halo. *Journal of Psychology, 142,* 117–130.

Pavitt, C. (1994). Another view of group polarizing: The "reasons for" one-sided oral argumentation. *Communication Research, 21*(5), 625–642.

Phua, J. J. (2013). The reference group perspective for smoking cessation: An examination of the influence of social norms and social identification with reference groups on smoking cessation self-efficacy. *Psychology of Addictive Behaviors, 27*, 102–112. doi:10.1037/a0029130

Pieterse, V., & Thompson, L. (2010). Academic alignment to reduce the presence of "social loafers" and "diligent isolates" in student teams. *Teaching in Higher Education, 15*, 355–367. doi:10.1080/13562517.2010.493346

Plaks, J. E., & Higgins, E. T. (2000). Pragmatic use of stereotyping in teamwork: Social loafing and compensation as a function of inferred partner–situation fit. *Journal of Personality and Social Psychology, 79*, 962–974.

Postmes, T., Spears, R., & Lea, M. (1998). Breaching or building social boundaries? Side-effects of computer-mediated communication. *Communication Research, 25*(6), 689–715.

Postmes, T., Spears, R., & Lea, M. (2000). The formation of group norms in computer-mediated communication. *Human Communication Research, 26*(3), 341–371.

Prentice-Dunn, S., & Rogers, R. W. (1982). Effects of public and private self-awareness on deindividuation and aggression. *Journal of Personality and Social Psychology, 43*(3), 503–513.

Redding, W. C. (1985). Rocking boats, blowing whistles, and teaching speech communication. *Communication Education, 34*, 247–276.

Reed, M. B., Lange, J. E., Ketchie, J. M., & Clapp, J. D. (2007). The relationship between social identity, normative information, and college student drinking. *Social Influence, 2*, 269–294.

Richmond, L. J. (2004). When spirituality goes awry: Students in cults. *Professional School Counseling, 7*(5), 367–375.

Rockloff, M. J., Greer, N., & Fay, C. (2011). The social contagion of gambling: How venue size contributes to player losses. *Journal of Gambling Studies, 27*, 487–497. doi:10.1007/s10899–010–9220–2

Riva, P., Williams, K. D., Torstrick, A. M., & Montali, L. (2014). Orders to shoot (a camera): Effects of ostracism on obedience. *Journal of Social Psychology, 154*, 208–216. doi:10.1080/00224545.2014.883354

Rogers, K. (2016, March 21). Boaty McBoatface: What you get when you let the Internet decide. *New York Times.* Retrieved from: www.nytimes.com/2016/03/22/world/europe/boaty-mcboatface-what-you-get-when-you-let-the-internet-decide.html?_r=0 on Jan. 22, 2017

Rose, G. M., Shoham, A., Kahle, L. R., & Batra, R. (1994). Social values, conformity, and dress. *Journal of Applied Social Psychology, 24*(17), 1501–1519.

Rosenberg, T. (2011). *Join the club: How peer pressure can transform the world.* New York: Norton.

Royte, E. (1994, November–December). They seemed so normal. *Health, 8*, 76–80.

San Martin, A., Swaab, R. I., Sinaceur, M., & Vasiljevic, D. (2015). The double-edged impact of future expectations in groups: Minority influence depends on minorities' and majorities' expectations to interact again. *Organizational Behavior and Human Decision Processes, 128*, 49–60. doi:10.1016/j.obhdp.2015.03.002

Savani, K., Wadhwa, M., Uchida, Y., Ding, Y., & Naidu, N. V. R. (2015). When norms loom larger than the self: Susceptibility of preference–choice consistency to normative influence across cultures. *Organizational Behavior in Human Decision Processes, 129*, 70–79. doi:10.1016/j.obhdp.2014.09.001

Seiter, J. S. (1995). Surviving turbulent organizational environments: A case study of a lumber company's internal and external influence attempts. *Journal of Business Communication, 32*(4), 363–382.

Seiter, J. S. (1998). When identification is too much of a good thing: An examination of Kenneth Burke's concept in organizational, intercultural, and small group communication contexts. *Journal of the Northwestern Communication Association, 26*(1), 39–46.

Sims, R. R., & Sauser, W. I. (2013). Toward a better understanding of the relationships among received wisdom, groupthink, and organizational ethical culture. *Journal of Management Policy and Practice, 14,* 75–90.

Smith, B. N., Kerr, N. A., Markus, M. J., & Stasson, M. F. (2001). Individual differences in social loafing: Need for cognition as a motivator in collective performance. *Group Dynamics, 5*(2), 150–158.

Snyder, M. (1987). *Public appearances, private realities: The psychology of self-monitoring.* New York: W. H. Freeman.

Spears, R., Lea, M., & Lee, S. (1990). De-individuation and group polarization in computer-mediated communication. *British Journal of Social Psychology, 29,* 121–134.

Tan, H. H., & Tan, M. L. (2008). Organizational citizenship behavior and social loafing: The role of personality, motives, and contextual factors. *Journal of Psychology, 142,* 89–108.

Tanford, S., & Penrod, S. (1984). Social influence model: A formal integration of research on majority and minority influence processes. *Psychological Bulletin, 95*(2), 189–225.

Tompkins, P. K., & Cheney, G. E. (1985). Communication and unobtrusive control. In R. McPhee & P. Tompkins (Eds.), *Organizational communication: Traditional themes and new directions* (pp. 179–210). Beverly Hills, CA: Sage.

Waldron, J. J. (2015). Predictors of mild hazing, severe hazing and positive initiation rituals in sport. *International Journal of Sports Science & Coaching, 10,* 1089–1101.

Williams, K. D., Cheung, C. K. T., & Choi, W. (2000). Cyberostracism: Effects of being ignored over the Internet. *Journal of Personality and Social Psychology, 79,* 748–762.

Wolverson, R. (2013, April 15). The human billboard. *Time, 181* (14), 47–51.

Zadro, L., & Williams, K. D. (2006). How do you teach the power of ostracism? Evaluating the train ride demonstration. *Social Influence, 1,* 81–104.

Zajonc, R. B. (1965). Social facilitation. *Science, 149,* 269–274.

Language and Persuasion

WHEN WILLIAM SHAKESPEARE WROTE, "A rose by any other name would smell as sweet," he found an eloquent way to note that words and the things they represent have no necessary connection. Indeed, you can't change a flower's scent just by renaming it "armpit" or "manure." That being said, sometimes the names we give things affect how we react to those things. For example, because we attach meanings to words and names, we might react differently to a woman named Rose than we would to a man with the same name. As another illustration, consider the story of Adolf Hitler Campbell, a 3-year-old from Hunterdon County, New Jersey, whose parents were unable to get a supermarket to write the child's name on his birthday cake, presumably because of the connotations associated with such an infamous name. After meeting with resistance, the family, including Adolf's little sister, Joyce-Lynn Aryan Nation Campbell, hightailed it to Pennsylvania, where a Walmart employee was willing to produce their cake ("Three-year-old Hitler," 2008).

These examples illustrate an interesting property of language that is one of the main themes of this chapter. Specifically, because we associate meanings with words, words have the power to influence us. Indeed, the maxim "The pen is mightier than the sword" is correct. Words are the primary means of persuasion. They not only affect our perceptions, attitudes, beliefs, and emotions but they also create reality.

Because words are so important in the process of persuasion, the purpose of this chapter is to examine words and their effects on social influence. We begin by discussing the nature of symbols and of meaning, which are integral to understanding the relationship between language and persuasion.

SYMBOLS, MEANING, AND PERSUASION: THE POWER OF BABBLE

What is a *symbol?* A very basic definition is that a symbol is something that represents something else. Names are a good example. Your name represents who you are, just as the word *pig* represents an animal with a curly tail and slimy snout.

As noted above, one important characteristic of symbols is that they are arbitrary. In other words, symbols have no necessary connection to what they represent, although we sometimes seem to forget this. For example, S. I. Hayakawa (cited in Adler, Rosenfeld, & Towne, 1995) told the story of a little boy who thought that pigs were called pigs because they are so dirty. The word *pig*, however, has no direct connection to the curly-tailed animal, just as your name, although it may seem to fit, has no necessary connection to you—that is, when your parents were trying to decide what to call you, there was nothing written in stone that said you had to be given a certain name. You could just as easily have been called Binky or Unga Bunga. Don't laugh—the singer Frank Zappa named his children Moon Unit and Dweezil, and when tax authorities told a Swedish couple that they had to give their 5-year-old son a name or pay a fine, the couple named the child Brfxxccxxmnpcccclllmmnprxvclnmckssqlbb11116 ("The best and worst," 1996). As wrong as such names might seem, however, they're not. When it comes to finding representations of things, there's not one "right" word or symbol.

Because they are arbitrarily connected to what they represent, a second characteristic of symbols is that they are conventionalized, which means that if we want to use a symbol to communicate to someone else, we have to agree on the symbol's meaning. Without some measure of agreement on the meanings of words, communication and persuasion would be difficult, if not impossible. If you've ever tried to communicate with someone who speaks a different language, you know this is true.

Connotative and Denotative Meaning: That's Not How I See It

Up to this point, we've noted how important it is for communicators to agree on the meaning of the symbols they use. With that said, however, we are certain that, without telepathy, total agreement on the meaning of symbols is impossible. Of course, the degree to which people agree may depend on the type of meaning with which we're concerned. There are at least two meanings for every word. The first, the *denotative* meaning, is a word's direct, explicit dictionary definition.

The second type of meaning, *connotative*, refers to the thoughts and emotions associated with a word. As you might expect, the connotations associated with words vary widely from person to person. To illustrate, let's return to pigs. Although all of us might agree on the denotative meaning of the word *pig* (i.e., curly-tailed animal with snout), our attitudes associated with the word may be quite different. For instance, compared to a farmer's child who grew up sloppin' hogs, a person who grew up reading books or watching movies about cuddly, talking pigs, such as Wilbur from *Charlotte's Web* or Babe from the movie *Babe,* would probably have a different view of pigs. In contrast, the members of some religious groups, Jews and Muslims, are forbidden to eat pork, which is perceived as unclean. Not long ago, in fact, a woman in Israel was sentenced to 50 years for depicting Allah as a pig.

As persuaders, it is important to recognize that the meanings of words are subjective. As scholars in the field of communication are fond of saying, "Meanings are in people, not in words." Effective persuaders are aware of this and attempt to adapt their messages accordingly.

Ultimate Terms: Speak of the Devil

Although connotative meanings tend to be more subjective than denotative meanings, sometimes the connotations associated with certain words are shared by large groups of people (i.e., societies and cultures). As a result, such words can be powerfully persuasive tools for motivating people. This is especially true of what Richard Weaver (1953) labeled *ultimate terms,* which are words or phrases that are highly revered, widely accepted, and carry special power in a culture. According to Weaver, there are three types of ultimate terms. The first, *god terms,* carry the greatest blessing in a culture and demand sacrifice or obedience (see Foss, Foss, & Trapp, 1985; Hart, 1997). When Weaver wrote, he used terms such as *fact* and *progress* as examples of god terms. Modern-day god terms include *family values*, *critical thinking*, and *teachable moment*.

In contrast to god terms, Weaver argued that some terms, which he labeled *devil terms,* are perceived by a culture as associated with the absolutely abhorrent and disgusting. Examples of past devil terms include *communism, Nazi,* and *fascist* (Foss et al., 1985). Today, terms such as *dead-beat dad, racist, terrorist, child molester, sweat shop,* and *hate crime* might be considered devil terms. Because such terms represent what is evil or detestable to a culture, they can also be extremely persuasive (Hart, 1997).

Finally, Weaver labeled a third type, *charismatic terms*. Unlike god and devil terms, which are associated with something observable, charismatic terms, much like a charismatic person, have a power that in some ways is mysteriously given (Foss et al., 1985):

> "Freedom" and "democracy" are charismatic terms in our culture. We demand sacrifice in the name of these terms, yet the referents most of us attach to them are obscure and often contradictory. In fact, Weaver says, we may resist the attempt to define such terms, perhaps fearing that a term defined explicitly will have its charisma taken away.

(p. 66)

What becomes clear, then, is that although god, devil, and charismatic terms have power, their ability to persuade is not stable; the connotations associated with such terms may change over time. For instance, calling someone a communist today would not have the same impact as it did in the days of Senator Joseph McCarthy.

Considering the power of ultimate terms, it is not surprising that politicians spend considerable amounts of money discovering the "right" terms to use in their ads and speeches. By way of example, Lemann (2000) noted that politicians use focus groups in order to discover specific words that should and should not be used in campaigns. The people in such groups watch ads and speeches while moving dials from right to left, indicating when they like or dislike what they are hearing and seeing. As a result, politicians learn an entirely new vocabulary of god and devil terms. For example, based on his research with focus groups, Frank Luntz, a political consultant, advises his candidates to say

> "Department of Defense" instead of "Pentagon," "opportunity scholarships" instead of "vouchers," "tax relief" instead of "tax cuts," and "climate change" instead of "global warming." The terms "Washington" and "I.R.S.," Luntz says, always play as super-negative and should be attached to a policy you want to turn people against. "Prosperity" is super-positive. In general, words starting with an "r" or ending with an "-ity" are good—hence "reform" and "accountability" work and "responsibility" really works.
>
> (Lemann, 2000, p. 100)

Politicians might also use language to create other images. For instance, following the September 11 attacks on the World Trade Center and Pentagon, George W. Bush used words such as *evil, those people,* and *demons* to characterize people of Arab/Middle Eastern descent. Merskin (2004) argued that Bush's speeches were carefully constructed and that the use of such words creates an enemy image by dehumanizing the "other."

In addition to politicians, people in the business world are fond of using ultimate terms as persuasion devices. For instance, the word *empowerment* is a modern-day charismatic term on which marketers and advertisers have capitalized. Products and services that promise to *empower* people have become unavoidable. For instance, as a former suit salesman, one of the authors was regularly asked by customers where the "power ties" could be found or what was the "power color" for ties this year. The Hotel del Coronado in Southern California offers its guests "power walks" in the morning, and one of our colleagues told us about a seminar his sister attended that teaches its clients how to take "power naps." Finally, one of the authors was recently notified that he is a *Time* magazine "Power Subscriber." He can now read the news with gusto.

Other terms that seem to have appeal these days are *extreme, alternative,* and *indie.* Indeed, these words are popular now as "rebel" labels for things. There is, of course, alternative music and alternative clothes (e.g., baggy pants, visible boxer shorts, tattoos, piercings). There are also extreme sports, such as snowboarding, bungee jumping, skateboarding, and mountain biking. But does placing words in front of something necessarily make it cooler, or more "edgy"? Is "alternative golf" really alternative simply because the people playing it have man buns and wear tennis shoes (instead of golf shoes)? Does throwing some bacon and Monterey cheese on a Whopper really make it an "Xtreme burger," as Burger King claims?

What is clear from this discussion is that words, when widely accepted as representing what is good or evil in a culture, have incredible persuasive potential. As we've noted, being labeled a communist in the 1950s was hazardous. In the late 1600s, being labeled a witch in Salem, Massachusetts, was deadly. In the current political climate, labeling one's opponent as a socialist or fascist seems to be popular. A little later, we explore more thoroughly the power of such labeling. But first, we examine a topic related to ultimate terms.

Aphorisms and Familiar Phrases: That Rings a Bell

Aphorisms are sayings, maxims, and adages that offer advice. They may be time honored (e.g., "look before you leap") or more contemporary ("love is fleeting, herpes is forever"). They are found in economics, politics, religion, science, and everyday life. We see them on bumper stickers, political slogans, and advertising campaigns.

Aphorisms are persuasive because they are succinct, easily remembered, and appear to contain "truisms." And because they are pithy, they require far less explanation. For example, the political expression "A rising tide lifts all boats" captures the essence of "trickle-down economics," whereby economic policies that benefit the rich also benefit everyone else. Although some aphorisms may offer bad advice, Levine and Bleakley (2012) argue that aphorisms are undervalued in medicine. For example, simple adages, such as "An ounce of prevention is worth a pound of cure" and "What you don't know can hurt you," are efficient ways of explaining the value of preventive medicine. In a similar vein, Vernon (2008) highlighted the importance of aphorisms in modern politics. "In an age when the average attention span is apparently decreasing," he noted, "the sagacious sound-bite could yet become the solution to—rather than a symptom of—the tendency to dumb down" (p. 50). Texting, tweeting, and other social media seem ripe for persuasion in the form of aphorisms.

When are aphorisms most persuasive? Howard (1997) conducted a study to find out when familiar phrases are influential. Using the elaboration likelihood model (see Chapter 2) as a theoretical base, Howard suspected that familiar phrases would be most persuasive when people weren't able or motivated to scrutinize a message—that is, familiar phrases, Howard thought, would act as peripheral cues to persuasion. To test this idea, he had groups of students listen to radio commercials trying to persuade them to plan for retirement. The commercials contained either familiar phrases (e.g., "Don't put all your eggs in one basket") or literal phrases (e.g., "Don't risk everything on a single venture"). Half the students were able to carefully attend to the commercials, but the rest were distracted (i.e., they were asked to watch and record the nonverbal behavior of another person in the room). Results of the study indicated that the students who viewed commercials with familiar phrases were more persuaded than those who had not, but only when they were distracted. Those who were not distracted were persuaded (by strong arguments), regardless of whether familiar or literal phrases were used (Howard, 1997).

FIGURE 7.1
Cartoon from *The New Yorker* with doctor telling patient, "Good news. The test results show it's a metaphor."
Source: © Leo Cullum/ The New Yorker Collection/ www.cartoonbank.com. All Rights Reserved.

"Good news. The test results show it's a metaphor."

Metaphors: One and the Same

What is love? It depends, apparently, on whom you ask. Various singers, for instance, have called it "a losing game" (Amy Winehouse), "a battlefield" (Pat Benatar), "a rose" (Neil Young), "a tower" (U2), and "a piano dropped from a fourth-story window" (Ani DiFranco). In each of these cases, love was depicted through the use of metaphors, which are figures of speech that compare two things. In the process, aspects of one thing are transferred to the second (Sopory & Dillard, 2002). It turns out that singers are not the only ones who are fond of using metaphors. Persuaders like them too, perhaps for good reason. Indeed, metaphors are persuasive (e.g., see Chang & Yen, 2013; Sopory & Dillard, 2002; Thibodeau, 2016). Thus, when Tropicana calls its orange juice "Your daily ray of sunshine" and Skittles invites you to "taste the rainbow," they're not just being smart, they're clever foxes.

The Power of Labeling

Earlier, we stated that names such as Dweezil and Brfxxccxxmnpcccclllmmn-prxvclnmckssqlbb11116 are not wrong, but we might have misled you. As arbitrary symbols, they work just fine, but pragmatically, how would you like to be saddled with such a name? Perhaps you wouldn't mind, but, whatever the case, one thing is clear: The name you use affects the way people respond to you. In fact, we know a person who changes his name every decade because he says that people respond differently to him depending on whether he's a Richard, a Jay, or a Hank. And research supports the idea that our friend is not simply a kook. For instance, according to the sources of Adler and colleagues (1995), compared to names like Percival, Elmer, Isadore, and Alfreda, common names such as John, Michael, Karen, and Wendy are rated as more likable, active, and stronger. Moreover, when such names were placed on essays and evaluated by teachers, the more common names tended to receive higher grades than the less common ones. Finally, in a small study, a graduate student at MIT put 24 photos on the website www.hotornot.com. Interestingly, with different first names attached, the same photos were judged as more "hot" or more "not" (Strasser, 2005, p. E22).

It turns out that your name doesn't just affect how others behave or perceive you; it affects how you behave and perceive yourself as well. People, it seems, respond favorably to their own names. Several studies, for example, indicate that diners leave higher tips when food servers use their names than when they do not (Seiter, Givens, & Weger, 2016; Seiter & Weger, 2013). In one such study, food servers who had learned their customers' names (by reading them on credit cards as customers paid their bills) addressed those customers in one of several ways. Specifically, they addressed customers (1) by using their first names (e.g., "Thank you, Babbs."); (2) by using their titles plus last names (e.g., "Thank you, Mr. Jones."); (3) by being formal yet impersonal (e.g., "Thank you, sir/ma'am."); or by using no form of address (i.e., "Thank you."). Results of the study showed that diners left significantly higher tips in the first two conditions, with younger customers preferring to be addressed by their first names and older customers (age 54 and up) preferring to be addressed by their titles plus last names (Seiter & Weger, 2013). Similarly, research shows that people purchased more (Howard & Gengler, & Jain, 1995) and complied more quickly (Howard & Gengler, 1995) when their names were used than when their names were not used.

The power of labels extends far beyond the names that people are given (see Box 7.1). To be sure, the labels we use to describe people or things reflect our attitudes about them and affect others' reactions to the people and things labeled. For example, many years ago, children with divorced parents came from "broken homes." Talk about stigmatization! Nowadays, we say children belong to "single-parent" or "blended" families.

The notion that the labels we use affect our attitudes about what we label lies at the heart of criticisms aimed at sexist language. For example, if a professor refers to all of his male students as "men" or "sirs" and to all of his female students as "girls," "broads," or "dears," it not only says something about the professor's attitudes toward men and women but it also has the power to shape attitudes. Thus, when women are wrongly described in ways that make them seem inferior to men, people may begin to believe that women truly are inferior.

This is related to an idea that is commonly known as the *Sapir–Whorf hypothesis* (Sapir, 1949; Whorf, 1956). The "hard" version of the hypothesis is deterministic, arguing that language dictates thought. The "soft" version is that language influences or affects thought. We subscribe to the latter view. For example, some languages assign gender to nouns. In German, doctor (*der Doktor*) is masculine, whereas nurse (*die Krankenschwester*) is feminine. If a German girl asks, "What can I be when I grow up, mommy?" the mother may be more likely to say a doctor than a nurse. Meanwhile, although it doesn't shove, the language provides a nudge.

The same dynamics are at work when people use racist language, which perpetuates the illusion that one racial group is superior to another. Ethnic/cultural references carry vastly different meanings. For example, Americans with an African

BOX 7.1 | Just a Spoonful of Sugar (and a Well-Chosen Name) Makes the Medicine Go Down

In this chapter, we've shown that names affect how we react to people. As you might have suspected, they also influence our reaction to products. For example, did you know that people react more favorably to sweaters and jellybeans that are given ambiguous color names (e.g., Moody Blue, Alpine Snow, and Monster Green) than less ambiguous color names (e.g., blueberry blue) (Miller & Kahn, 2005)? Considering this: it's not surprising that a lot of attention goes into naming products. This may be especially true when naming prescription drugs.

Most of us refer to prescription drugs by their brand names. For example, we say "Prozac" rather than "fluoxetine" and "Valium" rather than "diazepam." We do this because we've been trained to by pharmaceutical manufacturers. Drug companies engage in "branding" when they air commercials and print ads urging us to "ask your doctor about _____." Is the Purple Pill right for you? Ask your doctor, but first go to the company's website for more online propaganda to offer your doctor.

Naming a drug is extremely important to how the drug is perceived by consumers/patients and, in turn, to the drug maker's bottom line (Kirkwood, 2003). The name has to be short (no more than three syllables), unique, easy to pronounce, easy to remember, and, importantly, it must convey the essence of what the drug does. But the name cannot be false or misleading, according to the FDA. Viagra, a pill for erectile dysfunction sufferers, is a classic case of the power of naming as it applies to drugs. The name Viagra was conjured up to convey two themes: vigor, virility, or vitality and power or force, such as the raw power of Niagara Falls. Yes, the Freudian association with a torrent of powerful water is intentional. Viagra sounds more manly than sildenafil citrate, its generic name, don't you think? Celebrex, an arthritis medicine, was so named because it suggests celebrating—celebrating one's freedom to move without pain.

Companies such as the Brand Institute and Name Base/Medibrand are paid $250,000 or more to come up with names for drugs that conjure up idealized associations. See if you can guess the positive associations pharmaceutical manufacturers are trying to create for the following drugs.

- Alleve: hint—it *alleviates* something, right? (and that something happens to be minor arthritis pain).

- Ambien: hint—it creates a soothing *ambience* (to help you sleep better).

- Claritin: hint—it *clarifies* things, like watery eyes and a runny nose due to allergies.

- Levitra: hint—it *levitates* something (need we say more?).

- Prevacid: hint—it *prevents* something (and that something has to do with the last four letters of its name. Sounds better than its generic name, lansoprazole, doesn't it?).

- Propecia: hint—it *propagates* something (like hair restoration).

The letters X and Z are popular in drug names because people think they sound scientific, hence names like Nexium, Paxil, Vioxx, Zanex, Zocor, and Zoloft. Now that you know how drugs are named, see if you can come up with effective names for hypothetical new drugs that would help Alzheimer's sufferers, diabetics, or kids with attention-deficit/hyperactivity disorder (ADHD).

heritage have been identified by terms such as *African American, black, Negro, colored,* and more derogatory terms as well. Such derogatory terms, whether racist or sexist, have the power to shape perceptions. One study, for example, found that referring to Mexican immigrants as "illegal aliens" (which connotes criminality) invoked greater prejudice than referring to them as "undocumented workers" (Pearson, 2010).

Finally, consider these names: "Citizens for the Environment," "National Wetlands Coalition," and "Greening Earth Society." Which would you say sounds the most environmentally friendly? Would it surprise you to learn that they're all names for anti-environmental think tanks? According to Bricker (2014), those names weren't accidental either. They were chosen on purpose to hide the organizations' true intent: to prevent environmental regulations. By pretending to be environmentally friendly, they were more effective at manipulating public opinion (Bricker, 2014). This practice of posing as a nonprofit group in order to exploit others has been called *astroturfing* or *astroturf activism* (Durkee, 2017).

Euphemisms and Doublespeak: Making the Worse Appear the Better and Vice Versa

In the fifth century BCE, a group of teachers known as Sophists created private schools in Athens, Greece. Students who wanted to learn from the Sophists were charged fees and were taught, among other subjects, oratory and persuasion. Soon, however, being a Sophist was so profitable that the occupation attracted a number of charlatans, who gave the Sophists a bad reputation (today, *sophistry* connotes deceitful or fallacious reasoning). In fact, Plato argued that the Sophists were more interested in lies than truths and more interested in dazzling audiences than in instructing them. Sophists, Plato argued, were skilled at making the "worse cause appear the better" (Corbett, 1971).

The practice of using words to make the worse appear the better (and vice versa) is still alive and well. Modern-day Sophists commonly use *doublespeak* (ambiguous or evasive language) and *euphemisms* (inoffensive terms substituted for offensive ones) to create messages with less sting. For example, in the business world, no one gets fired or laid off any more. Instead, companies engage in "downsizing," "right-sizing," or even "bright-sizing." Mercedes no longer sells used cars; it sells "pre-owned automobiles" (try asking the Mercedes dealer, "Was this car previously used, or simply owned?"). Other companies give their employees job titles that sound more important or grandiose than they really are. A garbage collector is now a "sanitation engineer." And, in Great Britain, legislation was introduced to substitute the stigmatized word *prostitute* with the phrase *person who sells sex persistently* (Stinchfield, 2007).

The use of doublespeak and euphemisms is rampant in other places as well. For example, the military refers to civilian casualties, killing enemy soldiers, and combat operations as "collateral damage," "servicing the target," and "peacekeeping missions," respectively. Flight attendants don't talk about crashing in the ocean, only "water landings" (Murphy, 2001). In the medical field, terms such as *assisted suicide, transsexual surgery,* and *cancer* might instead be labeled *hastening death* (or *death with dignity*), *gender reassignment,* and *a growth,* respectively. Media reports use words like "terrorism" and "terrorist" less and less often, relying instead on ambiguous terms such as "assailants," "militants," "extremists," and "attackers" (Matusitz, 2016). Politicians don't raise taxes or lie, they adopt "revenue enhancing measures" and "misremember." And one of our friends is not allowed to have parties in her high school classes so, instead, has "reinforcement for desirable behavior days." In the world of undertakers and funeral directors, people "pass away" rather than die, are "interred" rather than buried, and are called "cases" or "patients" rather than corpses. Instead of saying "No," parents are fond of saying "We'll see" or "Maybe later." And finally, in the abortion controversy, the words you use probably depend on the side you take. For example, *pro-life* is more value-laden than *anti-abortion* or *anti-choice*. *Pro-choice* avoids the term *abortion* altogether and sounds much nicer than *anti-life* or *anti-anti-abortion*.

In the midst of all this word spinning, researchers (McGlone & Batchelor, 2003) have identified two possible motives people might have for using euphemisms. First, people might use euphemisms because such words are less threatening and more respectful, therefore saving the "face" of audience members. Second, people might use euphemisms in order to be regarded as tasteful and sensitive, thereby saving their own "face." To test these competing explanations, McGlone and Batchelor (2003) asked students communicating with someone via computer to describe various photographs, including two that depicted the aftermath of a urinating dog and a defecating parrot. Some students were led to believe that their identity would later be revealed to the person they were communicating with, while others were not. Results showed that the first group of students was more prone to using euphemisms, suggesting that saving their own face seemed to be their priority. It turns out, however, that when trying to create favorable impressions by spinning words, not

BOX 7.2 | If You Can't Say Something Nice, Spin It

If you've ever been asked to serve as a reference for someone, you know that it can be a complex business. Because what you say may no longer be confidential, saying something negative can lead to all kinds of personal and legal tangles. With that in mind, Robert Thornton (2003) has created the *Lexicon of Inconspicuously Ambiguous Recommendations* (LIAR). Here are some examples of what to say about people, depending on their flaws:

If the person is inept: "I recommend this man with no qualifications whatsoever." (p. 33)

If the person is extremely lazy: "In my opinion, you will be very fortunate to get this person to work for you." (p. 5)

If the person is chronically absent: "A man like him is hard to find." (p. 19)

If the person is dishonest: "The man is simply an unbelievable worker." (p. 33)

If the person is a drunk: "We remember the hours he spent working with us as happy hours." (p. 20)

Although we don't actually recommend using this lexicon, we think it is an entertaining way to illustrate how tricky language can be.

just any euphemism will do. Indeed, a study by McGlone, Beck, and Pfeister (2006) found that because euphemisms with longer "careers" (e.g., "use the restroom," "go number two") are more familiar and draw less attention, people who use them are perceived more favorably than those who use newer, less familiar euphemisms (e.g., "make room for tea," "cast a pellet") (for more on doublespeak, see Box 7.2).

LANGUAGE INTENSITY, VIVIDNESS, AND OFFENSIVENESS

So far, we've examined the nature of symbols and how they relate to the notion of meaning and the process of persuasion. We now turn to a discussion of specific variables related to language and persuasion. Three of these include language intensity, vividness, and offensiveness. These three variables are closely related. For example, when studying intense language, some authors include reviews of research on profanity, which, of course, has the potential to be quite offensive. However, it is possible to use intense language without being offensive. Moreover, although some definitions imply that vividness is a component or outcome of intense language (e.g., see Hamilton & Stewart, 1993), others do not (e.g., see Bowers, 1964). Because these three topics are so closely related, we examine them together in this section. We then turn to a discussion of several theories that have been used to explain the relationship between intense language and persuasion.

##@!!!!##: Profanity and Persuasion

Even though profanity, like any symbol, is arbitrary, it clearly plays a role in the process of persuasion, mostly because such strong connotations are associated with swearing. Perhaps this is why ancient rhetoricians like Quintilian advised against using profanity (Rothwell, 1971). Because profanity is so common (Cameron, 1969),

FIGURE 7.2
DILBERT.

Source: © Scott Adams/Dist. by United Feature Syndicate, Inc.

some authors have asserted that it merits more attention as a form of persuasion. For instance, J. Dan Rothwell (1971) argued:

> Despite centuries of negative criticism, verbal obscenity has become a more frequent rhetorical device. It is successful in creating attention, in discrediting an enemy, in provoking violence, in fostering identification, and in providing catharsis. Its effects are governed by a variety of circumstances which need to be understood more fully. It has precipitated a police riot, brutal beatings, and even death. Hoping it will go away will not make it so. It is time to accept verbal obscenity as a significant rhetorical device and help discover appropriate responses to its use.
>
> (p. 242)

To explore more thoroughly people's perceptions of profanity, E. Scott Baudhuin (1973) gave students "swear word" booklets and asked the students to evaluate several words according to how offensive they were. Based on the students' perceptions, he found that the words could be categorized into one of three categories: religious, excretory, and sexual. Which type of profanity did students find most offensive? The results of the study indicated that sexual words received the most negative responses. Religious profanities were perceived to be the least offensive.

If profanity is perceived to be offensive, are people who use it perceived negatively and are they less persuasive? Several studies have been conducted to test this question and most, but not all (e.g., see Rassin & Van Der Heijden, 2005), indicate that if you want to be perceived as attractive, credible, and persuasive, you should clean up your language. For example, a study by Powell and his colleagues asked students to evaluate applicants who either did or did not cuss during a job interview. The researchers found that applicants with filthy mouths, regardless of their gender, were perceived as significantly less attractive than their counterparts (Powell et al., 1984). Similarly, Bostrom, Baseheart, and Rossiter (1973) found that, in general, using profanity damages a speaker's credibility. On the other hand, Scherer and Sagarin (2006) noted that society's stance about swearing has become more relaxed since many of these earlier studies were conducted. As such, they revisited the relationship between obscenity, credibility, and persuasion by having students listen to speeches in which a male speaker either did or did not use the word *damn*. Results showed that cussing had no effect on perceptions of the speaker's credibility, but when the speaker cussed, he was more persuasive than when he did not. Before you decide to become potty-mouthed the next time you're speaking, however, consider this: the students in this study were listening to speeches in favor of lowering tuition, a topic they presumably would be in favor of. In contrast, most of the classic studies on this topic asked participants to listen to topics they did not favor. In short, it may be that profanity is persuasive, but only under very specific conditions. Indeed, two studies found that perceptions of cussing depend on additional variables. Specifically, and not surprisingly, Johnson and Lewis (2010) found that people who cussed in formal settings were perceived as significantly less competent than people who cussed in less formal settings. Similarly, Johnson (2012) found that when cussing violated audience expectations in a positive way (e.g., people rated themselves as positively surprised by the cussing), ratings of the speaker's competence increased. Another study found that

college students had mixed reactions when their instructors cussed. While the majority of students reported neutral to positive emotions, many reacted negatively (Generous, Houser, & Frei, 2015).

Political Correctness

Obviously, using profanity is not the only way to be verbally offensive. Earlier we discussed the notion of political correctness, which, in many ways, is all about being nonoffensive. Indeed, political correctness refers to issues of inclusive speech and advocacy of nonracist, nonageist, and nonsexist terminology (Hoover & Howard, 1995).

Although political correctness is relevant to a wide range of contexts and topics, including issues of gender, race, ethnicity, age, socioeconomic status, and so forth, a study by Seiter, Larsen, and Skinner (1998) focused on political correctness as it related to speaking about people with disabilities. In the study, college students read one of four hypothetical scenarios, each involving a person seeking donations who portrayed people with disabilities as "normal" (e.g., "uses a wheelchair"), "heroic" (e.g., "handicapable"), "disabled" (e.g., "confined to a wheelchair"), or "pathetic" (e.g., "abnormal"). After reading the scenarios, participants rated the speakers on scales measuring credibility and persuasiveness. Results of the study showed that, compared to communicators who portrayed people with disabilities as "pathetic," communicators who portrayed such people as "normal," "heroic," and "disabled" were perceived as significantly more trustworthy and competent (Seiter et al., 1998). However, only communicators portraying people with disabilities as "heroic" and "disabled" were perceived as more persuasive than the communicator portraying such people as "pathetic." How did the authors interpret these results? Perhaps by trying *not* to portray people with disabilities as victims, the communicator

FIGURE 7.4
Source: © Robert Mankoff/
The New Yorker Collection/
www.cartoonbank.com

"Love it! 'People of smoke' instead of 'Smokers.'"

using "normal" language also did not demonstrate as urgent a need to help people with disabilities as the communicators using "disabled" and "heroic" language did (e.g., a child described as "being confined to a wheelchair," or one who is aggrandized, may be perceived as requiring more help than a child described as "using a wheelchair"). Whatever the case, the results of this study suggest that individuals seeking donations for people with disabilities face a dilemma: How can a person raise money to help people with disabilities while at the same time describing people with disabilities in a politically correct and dignified manner?

The Effects of Vividness: A Picture's Worth a Thousand Words

According to Nisbett and Ross (1980), vivid information captures and holds our attention and excites our imagination because it is "emotionally interesting, concrete and imagery-provoking, and proximate in a sensory, temporal, or spatial way" (p. 45). By way of example, it's more vivid to say "the glass crashed and shattered into pieces" than it is to say "the glass broke." Although previous research is somewhat inconsistent, a meta-analysis of over 40 studies found that vivid messages tend to be more persuasive than pallid ones (Blonde & Girandola, 2016). This is especially true when vividness helps receivers recall information.

Language Intensity

"You are shockingly stupid" versus "You are not real smart."

"The lumber industry is raping our forests" versus "The lumber industry is cutting down a lot of trees."

In the preceding pairs of phrases, which phrase has the strongest connotative meaning? Obviously, the first phrase in each pair. The terms *shockingly* and *raping* are more intense than terms found in the other phrases. Language that is intense is emotional, metaphorical, opinionated, specific, forceful, extreme, and evaluative. For that reason, perhaps, Bowers (1964) defined *language intensity* as "the quality of language which indicates the degree to which the speaker's attitude deviates from neutrality" (p. 215). Clearly, someone who compares "cutting down trees" to "rape" is far from neutral in his or her attitudes about the lumber industry. But is a person who uses such language persuasive? The best answer to that question may be "it depends." To be sure, several variables have been found that affect the persuasiveness of intense language. With that said, let's examine four different theories that attempt to explain when and why intense language does or does not persuade.

First, *reinforcement theory* assumes that people are motivated to avoid pain and seek pleasure. Bradac, Bowers, and Courtright (1979, 1980) assumed that the same is true when people are being persuaded. If a person generally agrees with the position advocated by a source, the person will find it rewarding and evaluate the source positively. The reverse is true if the person generally disagrees with the position advocated by the source. Language intensity is believed to enhance this effect. Specifically, if the listener generally agrees with the speaker, when the speaker throws some forceful language at the listener, the listener is even more motivated to agree. However, a listener who generally disagrees will react even more negatively than he or she normally would when the speaker uses intense language (Bradac et al., 1980).

A second perspective on language intensity is found in *language expectancy theory* (see Burgoon & Siegel, 2004). This theory assumes that we have expectations about what types of language are normal to use when trying to persuade other people. For example, we may not think it is normal for a speaker to use intense words such as *rape* and *shockingly*. According to language expectancy theory, when persuaders violate our expectations concerning normal language, those violations can either help or hurt the effectiveness of the persuasive message, depending on whether the violations are perceived in a positive or negative way. How violations are perceived depends on who is using the language. For instance, Burgoon and Siegel (2004) noted that highly credible sources are granted a "wider bandwidth" of acceptable communication than those with low credibility. As such, sources with low credibility are likely to be perceived in a negative way when they use language that is aggressive and intense. This, in turn, leads them to be less persuasive. The reverse is true for highly credible sources. For sources with non-established levels of credibility, using intense language may cause them to be perceived as less credible (Jensen, Averbeck, Zhang, & Wright, 2013).

Third, Hamilton and Stewart (1993) have extended *information processing theory* (McGuire, 1968, 1989) to explain the effects of intensity on persuasion. The theory argues that to be persuaded, you must first attend to and comprehend a persuasive message. If you attend to and comprehend the message, you then compare your own position on the message to the position that's being argued by the source. Ultimately, you may either accept or reject the source's position. According to Hamilton and Stewart (1993; also see Craig & Blankenship, 2011), language intensity affects this process by making a source's position on an issue seem more extreme compared to your own position. This can be good, up to a point. In general, some discrepancy between a persuader and a receiver's positions leads to increased attention and, therefore, more attitude change. However, as we noted in our discussion of social judgment theory in Chapter 5, too much discrepancy may lead a receiver to reject a message or to scrutinize a message so much that he or she fails to attend to all of the message's content. In addition, intense language tends to be more specific and vivid.

Finally, *communication accommodation theory* (Giles & Wiemann, 1987; Street & Giles, 1982) argues that when we communicate with others we adjust our style of speaking to their style in order to gain approval and increase communication efficiency. For example, we may try to talk the same way others talk so that they will like us better. Aune and Kikuchi (1993) conducted a study to see if this theory would predict the effectiveness of messages that either were or were not intense. In the study, speakers delivered intense and nonintense messages to people whose language style could be categorized as either intense or nonintense. Results of the study supported communication accommodation theory. Specifically, speakers using intense language were most persuasive with people who use intense language, whereas speakers using nonintense language were most persuasive with people who use nonintense language. Speakers who "matched" the style of their audience also were perceived as more credible.

POWERLESS LANGUAGE AND PERSUASION: UM'S THE WORD

As a student, one of the authors had two speech professors who did not like the utterance *um* too much. One called *ums* social burps. The other, when listening to speeches, smacked her pencil on a desk whenever the author said *um*. It was not fun, but it beat electrical shocks. In retrospect, the author supposes he should be grateful to these professors, because *ums*, as well as a number of other utterances, prevent people who use them from being persuasive. Why? Because such utterances create the perception of *powerlessness.* In case you want to avoid using them when you talk, here is a list of such speech mannerisms with some examples in italics (also see Bradley, 1981; Erickson, Lind, Johnson, & O'Barr, 1978; Lakoff, 1973, 1975; Lowenberg, 1982; Newcombe & Arnkoff, 1979; O'Barr, 1982):

- *Hesitations* (signal uncertainty or anxiety): "*Well,* I, *uh, you know, um,* would like to borrow a dollar."
- *Hedges* (qualify the utterance in which they occur): "I *guess I sort of* like you and *kind of* want to know you."
- *Intensifiers* (fortify the utterance): "I *really* believe that and agree with you *very* much."
- Polite forms (indicate deference and subordination): "*Excuse me, if you wouldn't mind too much, I'd appreciate* it if you'd *please* shut the door. *Thank you.*"
- *Tag questions* (lessens the force of a declarative sentence): "This is fun, *don't you think?* Much more fun than yesterday, *isn't it?*"
- *Disclaimers* (utterances offered before a statement that anticipate doubts, signal a problem, or ask for understanding): "I know this is a *really dumb question,* but . . . ?"
- *Deictic phrases* (phrases indicating something outside the speaker's vicinity): "That man *over there* is the one who stole my wallet."

As noted previously, a considerable amount of research indicates that using these powerless forms of speech can prevent you from being persuasive (Erickson et al., 1978; Newcombe & Arnkoff, 1979), even when you are using strong arguments (Hosman & Siltanen, 2011). However, the relationship between power and speech may depend on additional factors. Two are noteworthy.

First, the type of powerless language a person uses may influence how he or she is perceived. Specifically, one problem with some research on powerless language is that it has lumped together all of the powerless forms previously discussed. However, some research indicates that this may not be the best idea, because not all the forms may be detrimental to a speaker. For instance, in one study, Bradac and Mulac (1984) found that using polite forms actually enhanced speakers' credibility. Moreover, Durik, Britt, Reynolds, and Storey (2008) found that the use of colloquial-sounding hedges (e.g., "kind of," "sort of") undermined persuasive attempts, but the use of professional-sounding hedges (e.g., "probably," "may," "seem to") did not.

Second, the type of language that is most effective may depend on who is using it. For example, Blankenship and Craig (2007) found that when low credible sources used tag questions, the sources were less persuasive regardless of whether their messages contained strong or weak arguments. In contrast, when highly credible sources used tag questions, the sources were more persuasive, but only when their messages contained strong arguments. Why? Presumably, if you already believe a source is credible, tag questions get you to think more carefully about the message being presented. If the message is strong, you will be more persuaded by it (Blankenship & Craig, 2007).

In addition to sources' credibility, Carli (1990) found that sources' and receivers' sex affects the persuasiveness of language. Specifically, females were persuasive with men when they used powerless forms of speech but persuasive with females when using powerful speech. For male speakers, it did not matter what form of speech was used. This may mean that women, compared to men, need to be more sensitive about the style of speech they use when trying to be persuasive. Clearly, along with the topics we discussed earlier, the results of this study suggest that men have negative stereotypes about women who use powerful speaking styles.

SUMMARY

In this chapter, we examined the role of language in the process of persuasion. We began with an examination and definition of the term *symbol*. Symbols are arbitrary but have the power to shape perceptions and construct social reality. Symbols also have connotative and denotative meanings, both of which affect persuasion. For example, we examined ultimate terms, which, because of their strong connotations, have incredible persuasive power in a culture. We also examined the power of labels and how, oftentimes, through the use of euphemisms and doublespeak, persuaders attempt to lessen (or strengthen) the connotative impact of a word. Finally, we discussed several language variables that affect persuasion. By making their words more vivid, intense, offensive, and powerless/powerful, persuaders affect the way audiences respond to their messages.

REFERENCES

Adler, R. B., Rosenfeld, L. B., & Towne, N. (1995). *Interplay: The process of interpersonal communication* (6th ed.). Fort Worth, TX: Harcourt, Brace.

Aune, R. K., & Kikuchi, T. (1993). Effects of language intensity similarity on perceptions of credibility, relational attributions, and persuasion. *Journal of Language and Social Psychology, 12*(3), 224–237.

Baudhuin, E. S. (1973). Obscene language and evaluative response: An empirical study. *Psychological Reports, 32*, 399–402.

The best and worst of everything. (1996, December 29). *Parade Magazine*, pp. 6, 7, 10.

Blankenship, K. L., & Craig, T. Y. (2007). Language and persuasion: Tag questions as powerless speech or as interpreted in context. *Journal of Experimental Psychology, 43*, 112–118.

Blonde, J., & Girandola, F. (2016). Revealing the elusive effects of vividness: A meta-analysis of empirical evidence assessing the effect of vividness on persuasion. *Social Influence, 11*, 111–129. doi:10.1080/15534510.2016.1157096

Bostrom, R. N., Baseheart, J. R., & Rossiter, C. M. (1973). The effects of three types of profane language in persuasive messages. *Journal of Communication, 23*, 461–475.

Bowers, J. W. (1964). Some correlates of language intensity. *Quarterly Journal of Speech, 50*, 415–420.

Bradac, J. J., & Mulac, A. (1984). A molecular view of powerful and powerless speech styles: Attributional consequences of specific language features and communicator intentions. *Communication Monographs, 51*, 307–319.

Bradac, J., Bowers, J., & Courtright, J. (1979). Three language variables in communication research: Intensity, immediacy, and diversity. *Human Communication Research, 5*, 257–269.

Bradac, J., Bowers, J., & Courtright, J. (1980). Lexical variations in intensity, immediacy, and diversity: An axiomatic theory and causal model. In R. W. St. Clair & H. Giles (Eds.), *The social psychological contexts of language* (pp. 193–223). Hillsdale, NJ: Erlbaum.

Bradley, P. H. (1981). The folk-linguistics of women's speech: An empirical evaluation. *Communication Monographs, 48*, 73–90.

Bricker, B. J. (2014). Feigning environmentalism: Antienvironmental organizations, strategic naming, and definitional argument. *Western Journal of Communication, 78*, 636–652. doi:10.1080/10570314.2013.835065

Burgoon, M., & Siegel, J. T. (2004). Language expectancy theory: Insight to application. In J. S. Seiter & R. H. Gass (Eds.), *Readings in persuasion, social influence, and compliance gaining* (pp. 149–164). Boston, MA: Allyn & Bacon.

Cameron, P. (1969). Frequency and kinds of words in various social settings, or what in the hell's going on? *Pacific Sociological Review, 12*, 101–104.

Carli, L. L. (1990). Gender, language, and influence. *Journal of Personality and Social Psychology, 59*, 941–951.

Chang, C., & Yen, C. (2013). Missing ingredients in metaphor advertising: The right formula of metaphor type, product type, and need for cognition. *Journal of Advertising, 42*, 80–94. doi:10.1080/00913367.2012.7949090

Corbett, E. P. J. (1971). *Classical rhetoric for the modern student* (2nd ed.). New York: Oxford University Press.

Craig, T. Y., & Blankenship, K. L. (2011). Language and persuasion: Linguistic extremity influences message processing and behavioral intentions. *Journal of Language and Social Psychology, 30*, 290–310.

Durik, A. M., Britt, M. A., Reynolds, R., & Storey, J. (2008). The effects of hedges in persuasive arguments. *Journal of Language and Social Psychology*, 27, 217–234.

Durkee, M. J. (2017). Astroturf activism. *Stanford Law Review*, 69, 201–268.

Erickson, B., Lind, E., Johnson, A., & O'Barr, W. M. (1978). Speech style and impression formation in a court setting: The effects of "powerful" and "powerless" speech. *Journal of Experimental Social Psychology*, 14, 266–279.

Foss, S. K., Foss, K. A., & Trapp, R. (1985). *Contemporary perspectives on rhetoric*. Prospect Heights, IL: Waveland Press.

Generous, M. A., Houser, M. L., & Frei, S. S. (2015). Exploring college students' emotional responses to instructor swearing. *Communication Research Reports*, 32, 216–224. doi:10.1080/08824096.2015.1052901

Giles, H., & Wiemann, J. M. (1987). Language, social comparison, and power. In C. R. Berger & S. H. Chaffee (Eds.), *The handbook of communication science* (pp. 350–384). Newbury Park, CA: Sage.

Hamilton, M. A., & Stewart, B. L. (1993). Extending an information processing model of language intensity effects. *Communication Quarterly*, 41(2), 231–246.

Hart, R. P. (1997). *Modern rhetorical criticism* (2nd ed.). Boston, MA: Allyn & Bacon.

Hoover, J. D., & Howard, L. A. (1995). The political correctness controversy revisited. *American Behavioral Scientist*, 38(7), 963–975.

Hosman, L. A., & Siltanen, S. A. (2011). Hedges, tag questions, message processing, and persuasion. *Journal of Language and Social Psychology*, 30, 341–349.

Howard, D. J. (1997). Familiar phrases as peripheral persuasion cues. *Journal of Experimental Social Psychology*, 33, 231–243.

Howard, D. J., & Gengler, C. (1995). Motivating compliance with a request by remembering someone's name. *Psychological Reports*, 77, 123–129. doi:10.2466/pr0.1995.77.1.123

Howard, D. J., Gengler, C., & Jain, A. (1995). The name remembrance effect: A test of alternative explanations. *Journal of Consumer Research*, 22, 200–211.

Jensen, M. L., Averbeck, J. M., Zhang, Z., & Wright, K. B. (2013). Credibility of anonymous online product reviews: A language expectancy perspective. *Journal of Management Information Systems*, 30, 293–324. doi:10.2753/MIS0742–1222300109

Johnson, D. I. (2012). Swearing by peers in the work setting: Expectancy violation valence, perceptions of message, and perceptions of speaker. *Communication Studies*, 63, 136–151.

Johnson, D. I., & Lewis, N. (2010). Perceptions of swearing in the work setting: An expectancy violations theory perspective. *Communication Reports*, 23, 106–118.

Kirkwood, J. (2003, September 1). What's in a name? *The Eagle Tribune*. Retrieved on June 5, 2005, from: www.igorinternational.com/press/eagletrib-drug-names.php

Lakoff, G. (1973). Language and woman's place. *Language in Society*, 2, 45–79.

Lakoff, G. (1975). *Language and woman's place*. New York: Harper & Row.

Lemann, N. (2000, October 16, 23). The word lab: The mad science behind what the candidates say. *The New Yorker,* pp. 100–112.

Levine, D., & Bleakley, A. (2012). Maximising medicine through aphorisms. *Medical Education*, 46, 153–162. doi:10.1111/j.1365–2923.2011.04141.x

Lowenberg, I. (1982). Labels and hedges: The metalinguistic turn. *Language and Style*, 15, 193–207.

Matusitz, J. (2016). Euphemisms for terrorism: How dangerous are they? *Empedocles: European Journal for the Philosophy of Communication*, 7, 225–237. doi:10.1386/ejpc.7.2.225_1

McGlone, M. S., & Batchelor, J. A. (2003). Looking out for number one: Euphemism and face. *Journal of Communication*, 53, 251–264.

McGlone, M. S., Beck, G., & Pfiester, A. (2006). Contamination and camouflage in euphemisms. *Communication Monographs*, *73*, 261–282.

McGuire, W. J. (1968). Personality and susceptibility to social influence. In E. F. Borgotta & W. W. Lambert (Eds.), *Handbook of personality theory and research* (pp. 1130–1187). Chicago: Rand McNally.

McGuire, W. J. (1989). Theoretical foundations of campaigns. In R. E. Rice & C. K. Atkin (Eds.), *Public communication campaigns* (2nd ed., pp. 43–65). Newbury Park, CA: Sage.

Merskin, D. (2004). The construction of Arabs as enemies: Post September 11 discourse of George W. Bush. *Mass Communication and Society*, *7*(2), 157–175.

Miller, E. G., & Kahn, B. E. (2005). Shades of meaning: The effect of color and flavor names on consumer choice. *Journal of Consumer Research*, *32*, 86–92.

Murphy, A. G. (2001). The flight attendant dilemma: An analysis of communication and sensemaking during in-flight emergencies. *Journal of Applied Communication Research*, *29*(1), 30–53.

Newcombe, N., & Arnkoff, D. B. (1979). Effects of speech style and sex of speaker on person perception. *Journal of Personality and Social Psychology*, *37*, 1293–1303.

Nisbett, R., & Ross, L. (1980). *Human inference: Strategies and shortcomings in social judgment*. Englewood Cliffs, NJ: Prentice Hall.

O'Barr, W. M. (1982). *Linguistic evidence: Language, power, and strategy in the courtroom*. New York: Academic Press.

Pearson, M. R. (2010). How "undocumented workers" and "illegal aliens" affect prejudice toward Mexican immigrants. *Social Influence*, *5*, 118–132. doi:10.1080/15534511003593679

Powell, L., Callahan, K., Comans, C., McDonald, L., Mansell, J., Trotter, M. D., & Williams, V. (1984). Offensive language and impressions during an interview. *Psychological Reports*, *55*, 617–618.

Rassin, E., & Van Der Heijden, S. (2005). Appearing credible? Swearing helps! *Psychology, Crime & Law*, *11*(2), 177–182.

Rothwell, J. D. (1971). Verbal obscenity: Time for second thoughts. *Western Speech*, *35*, 231–242.

Sapir, E. (1949). *Culture, language and personality*. Berkeley, CA: University of California Press.

Scherer, C. R., & Sagarin, B. J. (2006). Indecent influence: The positive effects of obscenity on persuasion. *Social Influence*, *1*, 138–146.

Seiter, J. S., & Weger, H. (2013). Does a customer by any other name tip the same? The effect of forms of address and customers' age on gratuities given to food servers in the United States. *Journal of Applied Social Psychology*, *43*, 1592–1598. doi:10.1111/jasp.12110

Seiter, J. S., Larsen, J., & Skinner, J. (1998). "Handicapped" or "handi-capable"? The effects of language describing people with disabilities on perceptions of source credibility and persuasiveness. *Communication Reports*, *11*(1), 1–11.

Seiter, J. S., Givens, K. D., & Weger, H. (2016). The effect of mutual introductions and addressing customers by name on tipping behavior in restaurants. *Journal of Hospitality Marketing & Management*, *25*, 640–651. doi:10.1080/19368623.2015.1040140

Sopory, P., & Dillard, J. P. (2002). The persuasive effects of metaphor: A meta-analysis. *Human Communication Research*, *28*, 382–419. doi:10.1111/hcre.2002.28.issue-3

Stinchfield, K. (2007). *A synonym for streetwalker*. Retrieved on September 30, 2008, from: www.time.com/time/specials/2007/top10/article/0,30583,1686204_1690170_1690508,00.html

Strasser, T. (2005, June 2). A big flop in the name of love. *Los Angeles Times,* p. E22.

Street, R. L., Jr., & Giles, H. (1982). Speech accommodation theory: A social cognitive approach to language and speech behavior. In M. Roloff & C. R. Berger (Eds.), *Social cognition and communication* (pp. 193–226). Beverly Hills, CA: Sage.

Thibodeau, P. H. (2016). Extended metaphors are the home runs of persuasion: Don't fumble the phrase. *Metaphor and Symbol, 31,* 53–72. doi:10.1080/10926488.2016. 1150756

Thornton, R. J. (2003). *Lexicon of inconspicuously ambiguous recommendations.* Naperville, IL: Sourcebooks.

Three-year-old Hitler can't get name on cake. (2008, December 17). MSNBC.com. Retrieved on October 25, 2012, from: www.msnbc.msn.com/id/28269290/ns/us_ news-weird _news/t/-year-old-hitler-cant-get-name-cake/#.UIl-iBjlXzI

Vernon, M. (2008, March 17). The art of the aphorism: When are the empty words of political spin profound? *New Statesman, 137,* 50.

Weaver, R. M. (1953). *The ethics of rhetoric.* Chicago: Henry Regnery.

Whorf, B. L. (1956). *Language, thought, and reality.* New York: John Wiley.

Nonverbal Influence

SHELLEY'S BOYFRIEND WAS PROBABLY frowning as he watched one of this book's authors reach out and take Shelley's hand. At the time, the author was not thinking about Shelley's boyfriend, though; he was thinking about how pretty Shelley was. He remembers leaning toward her and gazing into her eyes. Her lips tightened into a grin as she squeezed the author's hand. He'd never talked to her before this and was nervous, but even so, he had no trouble finding words. They came out smooth and suggestive. "Pass the salt," he whispered. And, after swallowing hard and leaning even closer, he repeated those words—"Pass the salt, pass the salt"—again and again.

Don't get the wrong idea. Even after writing a book about persuasion, neither author is even close to Don Juan status. When one of us met Shelley years ago, he was a sophomore in college, where he, Shelley, and Shelley's boyfriend were taking an acting class. As part of an exercise, the instructor paired each of us students up with a stranger and asked us to convince the rest of the class that we were deeply and passionately in love. "Pass the salt," however, was the only phrase we were allowed to use.

In retrospect, the author is not sure how persuasive an actor he was, but he did learn something that day: The words "I love you" are not all they are cracked up to be. Sure, it's nice to hear those words, but if you can convey the same meaning with "pass the salt," who needs them? The point here is that, when we are trying to interpret meaning, there is a lot more involved than simply words. As the old saying goes, "It's not what a person says, it's *how* the person says it that's important," which is why it is crucial that we understand something about nonverbal communication—how we say things through the use of gestures, body movements, touch, spatial behavior, appearance, eye contact, and so forth. In this chapter, we are interested in focusing on one particular question about nonverbal communication—that is, in what way does nonverbal communication influence the process of persuasion?

According to Burgoon (1994), nonverbal communication plays an important role in the process of social influence for several reasons. First, we can use nonverbal behavior to create certain impressions of ourselves. If we are successful in making ourselves appear powerful, authoritative, credible, or attractive, we may also be more persuasive. (For a different twist on nonverbal behavior and impression management, see Box 8.1.) Second, through the use of nonverbal behaviors, people can establish intimate relationships. In other words, nonverbal cues, such as touch, can be influential in developing rapport. Third, nonverbal behaviors can heighten or distract attention from persuasive messages that are likely to reinforce learning. For example, a teacher can use nonverbal cues to get his or her students to pay more attention to a message, and a heckler can use such tactics to distract listeners. Fourth, through nonverbal cues, a person can be reinforced to imitate a model's behavior. Fifth, nonverbal cues can be used to signal a person's expectations and elicit behavior that conforms to those expectations. For example, a simple frown can inform a child that he or she is not behaving appropriately. And finally, nonverbal behaviors can be used to violate people's expectations so as to distract them. Later in the chapter, for instance, we'll see that standing too close to another person can, under some circumstances, make that person more compliant.

Of course, we don't have the space needed in one chapter to discuss every aspect of nonverbal communication. We have, therefore, chosen to focus on those areas that we find the most important and intriguing. We begin by discussing a model that suggests that the relationship between nonverbal behavior and persuasion is quite simple.

BOX 8.1 | Smirks and Sneers Behind Your Back: Influencing Impressions of Others

Impression management theory (see Goffman, 1959; Schlenker, 1980; Tedeschi & Reiss, 1981) suggests that people control their behaviors—particularly nonverbal behaviors—in order to create desired impressions of themselves (Leathers, 1997). If you want to be liked, for instance, you might smile. If you want to be intimidating, you might frown. Clearly, however, our nonverbal behavior can affect impressions other than those made about us. Seiter (2001), for example, argued that impression management theory should be expanded to include the ways in which we strategically attempt to control impressions made of others. Although such attempts might be aimed at making others appear better, Seiter maintained that sometimes our attempts to appear honest and desirable are undermined by others—that is, sometimes other people may attempt to make us appear undesirable and dishonest.

One context in which such attempts might occur is a political debate. Indeed, because candidates' versions of a story often differ, they may look for opportunities to make their opponents appear deceptive. For instance, in the last several presidential debates, where split screens allowed viewers to see both the speaker and nonspeaking debater simultaneously, candidates were criticized for their silent, yet derogatory, background behavior.

To see if such background behavior is effective in undermining an opponent, Seiter and his colleagues (Seiter, 1999, 2001; Seiter, Abraham, & Nakagama, 1998; Seiter & Weger, 2005; Seiter, Weger, Kinzer, & Jensen, 2009) conducted studies that asked students to watch one of four versions of a televised debate. One version used a single-screen presentation showing only the speaker, while the other three versions used a split-screen presentation in which the speaker's opponent displayed constant, occasional, or no nonverbal disbelief regarding the content of the speaker's message. In other words, in some versions of the tape, the nonspeaking debater was shown shaking his head, rolling his eyes, and frowning while his opponent was speaking. After watching the videos, students rated the debaters. Results indicated that, in general, when any background disbelief was communicated by the nonspeaking debater, the speaker's credibility improved (Seiter et al., 1998). However, when the audience was led to be suspicious of the debaters' truthfulness, moderate background behavior on the part of the nonspeaking debater made his speaking opponent appear more deceptive (Seiter, 2001). Be warned, however. If you're ever in a debate and are thinking about silently deriding your opponent, you'll probably hurt your own image in the process. To be sure, the studies also found that any derogatory background behavior led the nonspeaking debater to be perceived as more deceptive, less credible, less likable, and inappropriate (Seiter, 1999, 2001; Seiter et al., 2009; Seiter & Weger, 2005). Finally, if an opponent ever confronts you with such nonverbal behaviors, research generally suggests that you'll be perceived as most effective if you politely and directly ask him or her to stop (Weger, Seiter, Jacobs, & Akbulut, 2010, 2013).

THE DIRECT EFFECTS MODEL OF IMMEDIACY

People who study nonverbal behavior use the term *immediacy* to describe actions that communicate warmth, closeness, friendliness, and involvement with other people (Andersen, 2004). If, for instance, you smile, make a lot of eye contact, nod, and lean forward when talking to someone else, you are demonstrating some common immediacy cues. According to the *direct effects model of immediacy* (see Andersen, 2004; Segrin, 1993), there is a simple relationship between nonverbal behavior and social influence—that is, warm, involving, immediate behaviors lead to increased persuasion (Andersen, 2004). As you'll see in the remainder of this chapter, a considerable amount of research supports this model and the effectiveness of immediacy behaviors in a number of different contexts, including intercultural (Booth-Butterfield & Noguchi, 2000), medical (Kafetsios, Anagnostopoulos, Lempesis, & Valindra, 2014), educational (Mazer & Stowe, 2016), organizational (Teven, 2007), athletic (Turman, 2008), and interpersonal settings (e.g., Hinkle, 1999). However, some research presents a more complicated picture. As we turn now to a discussion of the different types of nonverbal behavior, you will see that demonstrating immediacy may generally be a good rule of thumb, but an awareness of other factors may be necessary to sort out the sometimes complex relationship between nonverbal behaviors and persuasion.

TYPES OF NONVERBAL COMMUNICATION

Before discussing specific forms of nonverbal behavior, we think it's important to point out that such behaviors are interdependent. By way of illustration, we should probably tell you that the "Shelley story" is not yet over. There's still the part about Shelley's boyfriend, Louis, who responded to the "pass the salt" line by attacking the author after class. With eyes wide and fists clinched, Louis called the author a "lousy something-or-other" and then slugged him. In response, the author merely chuckled, because he could see that Louis was only having fun; Louis was smiling, and the punch was only a playful "tap."

As it turns out, Louis's behavior was probably not all that uncommon. Indeed, like us, you may have seen people (probably men) play-fighting as a means of greeting one another. But how do we know that they are only playing? We know because we don't see *only* their punches or *only* their eyes; we see other cues that help us interpret their messages. In other words, although there are many types of nonverbal communication, they do not occur in isolation. Nonverbal behaviors occur simultaneously, and how we interpret one behavior can affect our interpretations of other behaviors. Thus, although we discuss each of the following codes separately, it is important to realize that each code rarely operates alone.

With that said, we now examine seven types of nonverbal communication that are important in the process of persuasion: kinesics, haptics, proxemics, chronemics, artifacts, physical appearance, and paralinguistics.

Kinesics: Head, Shoulders, Knees and Toes, Knees and Toes

The word *kinesics* was derived from the Greek term *kinein,* which means "to move" and refers to the study of eye contact, facial expressions, gestures, and body movements and posture. We start by taking a look at eye contact.

The Eyes Have It

Several years ago, one of the authors was involved in a study that investigated the influence strategies used by panhandlers when attempting to get money from strangers (Robinson, Seiter, & Acharya, 1992). As part of the study, 36 panhandlers were interviewed, and several claimed that, before even asking for money, the first thing they tried to do was establish eye contact with whoever was passing by. Without eye contact, the beggars argued, it was easier for their "targets" to ignore them and walk on by.

If eye contact helps beggars get more money, does it also help communicators to be more persuasive? Some evidence seems to support this notion. For example, Murphy (2007) found that people who looked more at their interaction partners while speaking and listening were perceived as more intelligent than those who did not. Moreover, in a meta-analysis of several studies on eye contact, Segrin (1993) found that in all but one study, gazing at listeners produced more compliance than averting gaze.

Conversely, communicators who do not use eye contact may have problems being persuasive. Guéguen and Jacob (2002), for example, found that people, especially females, were less likely to comply when persuaders quickly averted their glance than when they maintained eye contact. Similarly, three studies by Wirth, Sacco,

Hugenberg and Williams (2010) indicated that people who perceived averted eye gaze from others, compared to those who did not, felt more ostracized, more negative emotions (e.g., anger and sadness), and more temptation to perform aggressive behaviors. Finally, a study by Neal and Brodsky (2008) found that expert witnesses who maintained less eye contact with jurors and attorneys were perceived as less credible than witnesses who maintained more eye contact. Perhaps this is why law students are taught to block eye contact between witnesses and jurors during cross-examination while encouraging their witnesses to make eye contact with jurors during direct examination (Brodsky, 1991).

Before concluding this section, we should note that more eye contact is not always associated with greater persuasion. Indeed, some situations call for less eye contact. That's because a fixed gaze can be perceived as a challenge or threat. Stare at someone too long on a New York subway, and you might find someone saying, "Hey, you lookin' at me?" or "Whachu lookin' at?"

Finally, a classic study by Kleinke (1980) illustrates that the effectiveness of eye contact may depend on other factors, such as the legitimacy of the request you make. In the study, persuaders were instructed to approach people in an airport and ask them for money. Some of the targets were told that the money would be used to make an important phone call (a legitimate request), whereas others were told that the money would be used to pay for a candy bar or gum (an illegitimate request). It turned out that people who thought the persuader needed to make a phone call gave more money, but only when the persuader looked at them. Interestingly, however, eye contact actually decreased compliance when the persuader made an illegitimate request (see Table 8.1). Perhaps, as the researcher suggested, looking away while making an illegitimate request makes a person seem more humble or embarrassed, thereby increasing his or her persuasiveness by winning the sympathy of others (Kleinke, 1980).

About Face

Of all possible facial expressions, smiling has probably been studied the most. To be sure, research has shown that by smiling, waitresses earn more tips (Tidd & Lockard, cited in Guéguen & Fischer-Lokou, 2004), therapists are judged to be warmer and more competent (Leathers, 1997), job interviewees create positive impressions of themselves (Washburn & Hakel, 1973) and are more likely to get jobs (Forbes & Jackson, 1980), female hitchhikers get more rides (Guéguen & Fischer-Lokou, 2004), students accused of cheating are treated with greater leniency

TABLE 8.1 **Illustration of Kleinke's (1980) Results**

	Legitimate Request	Illegitimate Request
Eye contact	Persuadee complies with request	Persuadee does not comply with request
No eye contact	Persuadee does not comply with request	Persuadee complies with request

Source: Adapted from Kleinke (1980).

(LaFrance & Hecht, 1995), and teachers inspire students to pay more attention (Saigh, 1981). One study found that right after being smiled at, people were more willing to help a third person who dropped some computer disks on the ground (Guéguen & De Gail, 2003).

We do not, however, want to give you the impression that influence is always as easy as a smile. As noted in Chapter 4, persuaders need to come across as trustworthy and sincere. Not all smiles accomplish this goal, however. One study, for example, found that when smiles appear quickly, the smiling person is perceived as less trustworthy and attractive than when smiles have a slower onset (Krumhuber, Manstead, & Kappas, 2007). Besides that, smiling may not fit the situation. Consider, for instance, advertisements seeking donations for starving children. One study found that when 4- and 8-year-olds were pictured with sad facial expressions, they generated more sympathy and donations than when they were pictured with smiles (Baberini, Coleman, Slovic, & Västfjäll, 2015). Additionally, in situations where an angry or dominant demeanor would be most persuasive, positive and likable facial expressions could be counterproductive. For instance, one study found that, although smiling and nodding were more persuasive when used by people of equal status, dominant behaviors are more effective in established hierarchies (Mehrabian & Williams, 1969). Another found that while politically conservative audiences prefer leaders with dominant faces, politically liberal audiences prefer leaders with non-dominant ones (Laustsen & Petersen, 2016). And still another found that angry facial expressions led audiences to scrutinize messages and, consequently, to prefer stronger over weaker arguments (Calanchini, Moons, & Mackie, 2016).

The situational nature of facial expressions and other nonverbal behaviors is even more apparent if you consider *communication accommodation theory* (Giles & Wiemann, 1987), which we discussed in Chapter 7. According to the theory, rather than using any one type of nonverbal behavior, a persuader should try to build rapport with others by *mirroring* or *mimicking* their nonverbal cues. In other words, smile when people smile and frown when people frown. For example, in one study (Guéguen, 2009), 66 males interacted in speed-dating sessions with women who had been instructed beforehand either to mimic or not mimic the males' behavior (e.g., the mimickers stroked their faces or crossed their arms when the males did). Results indicated that women who mirrored the males' behavior, compared to those who did not, were chosen more often to give their contact information and were rated as being more sexually attractive. Another study found that negotiators who mirrored others' behavior were more likely to reach a deal than those who did not (Maddux, Mullen, & Galinsky, 2008).

Interestingly, it may also be the case that mimicking another person's behavior makes us more susceptible to that person's persuasive attempts. In one study, for example, people who mimicked the movements of a person presenting a product had more intention to buy the product than people who did not mimic the person (Stel, Mastop, & Strick, 2011). Another study showed that people who had been mimicked were more helpful and generous than those who had not been (van Baaren, Holland, Kawakami, & van Knippenberg, 2004).

From the Neck Down: Persuasion and Body Language

Some of the principles of persuasion that we discussed in relation to the eyes and the face also apply to communication with the body. For example, just as you can mirror a person's facial expressions, you can mirror his or her gestures and body movements. Moreover, consistent with the direct effects model of immediacy (discussed previously), people who lean forward when communicating tend to be more persuasive than those who do not. In addition to these findings, research shows that people are more persuasive when they are pictured using open body positions (i.e., when their arms and legs are positioned away from their bodies) rather than neutral or closed positions (McGinley, LeFevre, & McGinley, 1975). (Did you know that the way you move your body may also make you safer? See Box 8.2.)

Perhaps most of the research on body movement and persuasion, however, has focused on the use of gestures. Although various researchers have discussed a number of different gestures, Argyle (1988) argued that it is most useful to focus on three: emblems, illustrators, and self-touching.

Emblems

According to Ekman and Friesen (1969), *emblems* are nonverbal behaviors, usually hand movements, that have precise verbal meaning. Thus, emblems can substitute for words. Traffic cops, referees, baseball catchers, and scuba divers are well-known emblem users, but we all use them. Think of all the words for which we have gestures:

BOX 8.2 | Walk This Way: Are You Vulnerable to Attack?

From an early age, you were probably instructed to use crosswalks, to look both ways before crossing the street, and to walk rather than run around swimming pools. But did you know that walking safely might also depend on how you carry yourself? According to Gunns, Johnston, and Hudson (2002), victims of attack are not chosen randomly. These researchers suggest that, in the same way that vulnerable sheep in a herd are identified, isolated, and pounced on by wolves, some people, by virtue of their gait, may appear more vulnerable to would-be attackers. Consistent with this notion, a study by Wheeler, Book, and Costello (2009) found that males with higher psychopathic scores were better able to distinguish people who had been victimized from those who had not after viewing short video clips of those people walking. To shed light on the characteristics of different walking styles, Gunns and colleagues (2002) asked 30 males and 30 females to watch videotapes of more than 100 male and female walkers while rating how vulnerable to attack the walkers seemed. Analysis of the ratings and videotapes revealed that the typical "hard to attack" walker was characterized by a longer stride, a larger range of arm swing, higher energy, lower constraint, and a faster walk. Before concluding this segment, we want to be clear, as Wheeler and colleagues (2009) were, that people are not responsible for victimization because of how they walk. The attacker is always to blame. That said, knowing what perpetrators look for is a weapon you can use to defend yourself. In short, to appear less vulnerable, put some pep in your step!!!

hello, good-bye, come here, crazy, quiet or shush, peace, I don't know, good luck, think, and shame on you, not to mention the ever-popular middle finger gesture.

Emblems are an important part of communication and serve many functions, persuasion included. But what part do emblems play in social influence? Several scholars have argued that a prerequisite for persuasion is attention to and retention of a message (e.g., McGuire, 1968; Petty & Cacioppo, 1986), and it seems that by providing more visual information, emblems play a large role in fostering attention and retention in persuadees. Woodall and Folger (1981), for example, found that people recalled 34 percent of a verbal message when it was accompanied by an emblem compared to only 11 percent when other types of gestures were used.

Illustrators

Although emblems have meaning independent of verbal communication, *illustrators,* a second type of gesture, accompany speech (Ekman & Friesen, 1969). Like their name implies, illustrators illustrate, emphasize, or repeat what is being said. A child saying she loves you "this much" while spreading her arms wide is using an illustrator. Likewise, we can use illustrators to give directions, show our excitement, follow a rhythm, demonstrate a shape, and so forth.

Several studies indicate that the use of illustrators increases a speaker's persuasiveness. In one study, for instance, actors who used more forceful and rhythmic gestures were more persuasive than those who did not (Maslow, Yoselson, & London, 1971). In addition, some illustrators make speakers appear more effective and composed (Maricchiolo, Gnisci, Bonaiuto, & Ficca, 2009), which doesn't hurt when you are trying to be persuasive.

Self-Touching Behaviors (Adaptors)

Although emblems and illustrators seem to increase people's persuasiveness, the jury is still out on the effect of *self-touching behaviors* (e.g., scratching your arm, rubbing your cheek, picking your nose, stroking your hair), also known as *adaptors* (Ekman & Friesen, 1969). For example, while some research suggests that the use of adaptors was associated with less persuasion (Maslow et al., 1971; Mehrabian & Williams, 1969), other research shows the opposite (Maricchiolo et al., 2009). Even so, most research agrees that self-touching behaviors are often seen as a sign of anxiety and lack of composure (unless, perhaps, you are Britney Spears or Madonna). With that in mind, our best advice at this point is to avoid using adaptors if you want to be persuasive.

Haptics: Reach Out and Touch Someone

If touching yourself makes you less persuasive, does touching other people have the same effect? Many years ago, three researchers interested in the topic of *haptics* (or touch) conducted a simple yet classic study to explore this question. In the study, library clerks did one of two things when they handed library cards back to university students who were checking out books: Either they did not touch the students or they made light physical contact by placing a hand over the students' palms. After their cards were returned, students were asked to rate the quality of the library, and, interestingly, those who were touched evaluated the library much more favorably than those who were not (Fisher, Rytting, & Heslin, 1976).

The persuasive impact of touch has been demonstrated in other contexts as well. For example, touch has been found to increase the number of people who volunteered to score papers (Patterson, Powell, & Lenihan, 1986), sign petitions (Willis & Hamm, 1980), complete questionnaires (Vaidis & Halimi-Falkowicz, 2008), return money that had been left in a telephone booth (Kleinke, 1977), accept invitations to dance in nightclubs (Guéguen, 2007), provide phone numbers to prospective dating partners (Guéguen, 2007), and help someone pick up items that had been dropped (Guéguen & Fischer-Lokou, 2003). Similarly, when food servers touch diners appropriately, the servers earn higher tips (Hornick, 1992), and the diners are more likely to take servers' recommendations about what to order (Guéguen, Jacob, & Boulbry, 2007). Hornick (1992) found that touching bookstore customers on the arm caused them to shop longer (22.11 minutes versus 13.56 minutes), purchase more ($15.03 versus $12.23), and evaluate the store more positively than customers who had not been touched. Hornick (1992) also found that supermarket customers who had been touched were more likely to taste and purchase food samples than untouched customers.

One common way of touching people is through handshakes, and, as it turns out, the way you shake hands may influence the impressions people form of you. For instance, Bernieri and Petty (2011) found that people make judgments about whether others are conscientious and extroverted on the basis of handshakes. Not only that, the way you shake hands might help you get a job. Specifically, in one study, men and women who used desirable handshakes (i.e., firm clasps with a full grip while looking the other person in the eye) received higher ratings of employment suitability from interviewers than did men and women with less desirable, limp-fishy types of handshakes (Stewart, Dustin, Barrick, & Darnold, 2008).

Considering this research, it seems, then, that all the stuff we learned as kids about "the Midas touch" may not be such a fairytale. Touching people, when done appropriately, seems to be persuasive. Touch may put people in a good mood, making them more likely to comply with requests (Hornick, 1992). Another explanation is that people who touch create more favorable impressions of themselves and, therefore, are more persuasive (Hornick, 1992). Finally, people who touch may be more persuasive because, through touch, they augment their image of power (Patterson et al., 1986).

BOX 8.3 | If It Feels Good, Buy It: The Role of Touching Merchandise on Persuasion

When you are shopping, do you find yourself picking things up, feeling the texture of fabrics, and running your fingers over merchandise? If so, you may be what researchers have called high in the need for touch (NFT) (Peck & Childers, 2003a, 2003b; Peck & Wiggins, 2005). High NFTs get frustrated while shopping if they cannot touch things. Not all NFTs are the same, however. Some, called instrumental NFTs, use touch to evaluate products, while others, called autotelic NFTs, touch things because it is fun and pleasurable for them. With that in mind, autotelic NFTs are persuaded when there are pleasurable things to touch, even when those things are not relevant to what is being marketed (e.g., soft swatches of fabric on a pamphlet seeking donations for a nature center) (Peck & Wiggins, 2005) and regardless of whether they are involved in the issue being considered or not (Peck & Johnson, 2011). Instrumental NFTs, however, are persuaded only when what is being touched is relevant to what is being marketed (e.g., feathers and tree bark samples on a pamphlet seeking donations for a nature center) (Peck & Wiggins, 2005), and when their involvement in the issue is low (Peck & Johnson, 2011).

Whatever the reason for the persuasive impact of touch, one thing is clear: The use of touch for persuasive purposes is tricky because touch is so ambiguous. What one person may see as "warm," for example, another may view as a "power play." In fact, one study found that in competitive contexts, touching another person led to decreased cooperation, perhaps because it is perceived as an attempt to dominate (Camps, Tuteleers, Stouten, & Nelissen, 2013). What's more, what one person might interpret as "friendly," another may see as "flirtatious." The "brushing" of one employee against another could be interpreted as accidental or as a form of sexual harassment. Clearly, interpretations of touch depend on a vast array of factors, including context, gender, and culture. In most of the studies we've just discussed, touching generally occurred on the hands or arms. We suspect that too much touching or touching other parts of a person might actually backfire, making persuasion less likely. As potential persuadees, it is important to realize that even touches, such as those enacted in most of the studies we discussed, wield tremendous persuasive power. Such touches may be so subtle that we might not even be aware that they are being used for persuasive purposes. But do not be fooled. Touch is persuasive, as is the use of space—our next topic. (For more on the persuasive effects of touch, see Box 8.3.)

Keep Your Distance? Proxemics and Persuasion

The study of *proxemics,* or how we use space to communicate, covers a variety of topics, such as territoriality and dominance. In this chapter, however, we are less concerned with those topics and, instead, focus our discussion on the concept of *personal space,* which refers to what might be considered an invisible bubble that surrounds us. An obvious case in point is that a door-to-door salesperson should not stick his or her nose in a potential customer's face. However, there is some evidence that indicates that the opposite is the case: That is, violating a person's space may be more persuasive.

In a study by Baron and Bell (1976), for instance, diners in a cafeteria were approached by an experimenter and asked to volunteer for a survey for a period of 30 minutes to 2 hours and 30 minutes. The experimenter stood close to some diners (12–18 in.) and farther away from others (3–4 ft). Results of the study showed that diners volunteered to participate for longer periods of time when they were approached at closer distances.

How can we explain this finding? First, because people tend to stand closer to people they like (Argyle, 1988), persuadees may simply be reciprocating the liking by complying with the violator's requests (Baron & Bell, 1976). In addition, because people find spatial invasion uncomfortable, those invaded may perceive persuaders as more demanding, desperate, and needful (Baron & Bell, 1976).

As with other forms of nonverbal communication, some caution is advised when making generalizations about the role of proxemics in persuasion. Indeed, at least two studies indicate that closer distances may not encourage compliance. For instance, Smith and Knowles (1979) found that pedestrians who had their space invaded without justification were less likely to return a lost object than those who had not had their space invaded. Moreover, a study by Albert and Dabbs (1970) found that speakers were more persuasive the farther they were from other people (i.e., speakers were more persuasive when standing 4–5 or 14–15 ft from their audiences than they were when standing 1–2 ft from their audiences).

If the conflicting results of these studies seem confusing, you might be interested in a theory presented by Judee Burgoon (1978, 1992, 1994). It is called *expectancy violations theory,* and we think it provides a strong and elegant explanation for the ways in which space violations affect the process of social influence.

According to the theory, we all have expectations about how close other people should stand to us. When people violate those expectations and get either too close or too far away, we experience arousal and may become distracted. How we react to the violation, however, depends on several factors, perhaps the most important being the "reward value" of the violator. If he or she is attractive, has the power to reward or punish us, or is just plain likable, the violation is perceived as a pleasant surprise, and we are more likely to be persuaded. However, if the violator has low reward value, the violation will be perceived as negative, and compliance will be less likely. In addition, the theory states that if violations are so extreme that they are perceived as threatening, they also will decrease compliance.

The theory has received a considerable amount of support and implies several practical suggestions for those interested in persuading others. First, if you think the person you are trying to persuade sees you as attractive, powerful, or credible, it is best to stand a little farther or a little closer to that person than would be expected. Second, if you think you are perceived by someone as powerless and icky, you should maintain appropriate distances. Finally, never overdo it. If you stand too close or too far away, you will probably not be persuasive.

Chronemics: All Good Things to Those Who Wait?

In science, the concepts of space and time are often discussed together. However, in the study of persuasion, although considerable research has examined the topic of proxemics, little attention has been paid to *chronemics,* or the study of how time is used to communicate. Even so, we know that time can be an important commodity, especially in a culture like the United States.

A common expression in the military, especially among soldiers with lower ranks, is "hurry up and wait." Oftentimes, it seems that such soldiers are expected to be on time although their superiors can show up whenever they want to. The point is, the higher your status, the more power you have over other people's time.

This is true in other contexts as well. For instance, how much time have you spent waiting in doctors' offices? Do you have to make appointments to see some professors or to get interviewed for a job? And don't be fooled: If you are a subordinate and show up more than a few minutes late to a business meeting, do you think you'll be very persuasive? We suspect not.

Practically speaking, then, you might be wondering whether it is okay to be late if you have a lot of status. Our suggestion is "be careful." Indeed, a study mentioned in the work of Burgoon and colleagues (1996) found that people who arrive 15 minutes late are considered dynamic, but much less competent, composed, and sociable than people who arrive on time. Plus, we think making people wait is rude.

Time not only affects perceptions of people but it also can be used as a persuasive ploy. For instance, for people in a hurry, drive-through banking or fast-food restaurants may have appeal, as may establishments such as Jiffy Lube, LensCrafters, and 1-Hour Photo. When such services save you time, it's terrific. But beware. Just because an exercise video promises to transform your buns into steel in only three minutes a day, or a flyer claims you can earn $60,000 a year working at home in your spare time, or an audiotape claims it will teach you how to play guitar in two weeks doesn't mean that will really happen. Too often, people seek quick solutions to complicated problems. We want to buy a product, take a pill, or push a button, and make a problem go away. Persuaders prey on this quick-fix mentality.

In addition to ploys offering to save time, sometimes strategies are based on what Cialdini (1993) calls the principle of *scarcity*. According to Cialdini and others (e.g., Brehm, 1966; Brehm & Brehm, 1981), people love freedom, and when that freedom is threatened or limited, people experience something called *psychological reactance*, a concept we introduced in Chapter 3. For example, a shopper in a store may decide she likes a certain dress. If a salesperson explains to the customer that there is only one more dress like that in her size (i.e., the dress is *scarce*), the woman, who might have thought that she was free to buy the dress at any time, may now *react psychologically* by wanting the dress more than she did in the first place (Cialdini, 1993). As you well know, persuaders also attempt to use psychological reactance in their favor by making time scarce. For instance, by telling us that we must "act now" or that there is a "limited time offer," advertisers are relying on the principle of scarcity. By limiting our time, they hope to make us more likely to purchase their product or service.

The notion that "time is running out" has the potential to nudge us in other ways as well. For example, one of our favorite vintage studies (Pennebaker et al., 1979) tested country singer Mickey Gilley's (1975) prediction that "the girls get prettier at closing time" by asking bar patrons to rate the attractiveness of other patrons during various times in the evening. Results indicated that ratings of opposite-sex patrons increased near closing time, suggesting that people's standards change as the pickin's get slim (i.e., as time and potential partners become scarce). A recent replication of this study (Johnco, Wheeler, & Taylor, 2010) suggests that, although these results are due, in part, to alcohol consumption (known in popular culture as the "beer goggles" effect), scarcity remains a viable explanation for why people's standards for attractiveness change over time. Of course, if you haven't hooked up with a "10" by last call, you can always settle for two "5's."

Interestingly, perhaps because the psychological pressure created by scarcity is so uncomfortable, some persuaders have found that a "nonurgency" tactic is preferable. In other words, because people don't want to be rushed and pressured, sometimes coming across as if time is *not* an issue can be very persuasive. Starbucks and other coffee houses that offer free Wi-Fi encourage customers to stay. "No, no, no" sales also use this approach: A consumer buys a mattress, a big-screen TV, or an appliance and pays no money down, no interest, and no monthly payments until anywhere from 90 days to a year later. Products or services that advertise a "free 30-day trial offer" also facilitate sales by removing time pressures.

Finally, if customers get tired of waiting, there might be a creative solution. Consider, for example, how executives at a Houston airport responded when they got swamped with complaints about the long waits at baggage claim. Instead of reducing wait times, the executives routed flights to distant arrival gates, thereby forcing passengers to walk longer distances. As a result of keeping passengers busy, complaints virtually disappeared (Stone, 2012).

Artifacts and Physical Features of the Environment: Dress for Success

While talking about the notion of time, did we mention that an expensive watch with a gold wristband couldn't hurt your image much? Obviously, the clothes and makeup we wear, the cars we drive, the furniture we own, and other physical objects, also known as *artifacts,* can communicate a great deal about our credibility and status. In our society, material goods are viewed as an extension of oneself. Why else would color analysts be getting rich by telling people whether to wear summer, autumn, winter, or spring colored makeup? And why else would someone pay thousands of dollars for an Armani suit?

Speaking of suits, we know a good story about how artifacts can affect people's perceptions. Many years ago, one of the authors sold men's suits for commission. Because he obviously did not earn anything unless he sold merchandise, when given a choice, the author tried to help customers who appeared as if they would spend a lot of money. One day a customer entered the store wearing a greasy T-shirt, jeans, no socks, and filthy tennis shoes. Because at the time there were plenty of other people shopping, the author decided to pick a more "profitable-looking" customer on whom to wait. One of the new employees, however, decided to help the "greaseball." Much to the author's surprise, however, that greaseball ended up buying six very expensive suits. It turned out he was not a greaseball at all; he was a high-paid

"You're right. It does send a powerful message."

executive who had just lost all of his suits in a fire. He was restocking his wardrobe. Of course, the old saying "you can't judge a book by its cover" took on a whole new meaning that day.

Apparently, when it comes to making quick judgments like this, the author is not alone. Indeed, previous literature suggests that first impressions are not only powerful and enduring, they are often based on seemingly trivial appearance cues (see Burgoon, Buller, & Woodall, 1996). Research indicates, for example, that cues such as clothing (e.g., Gorham, Cohen, & Morris, 1999; Seiter & Dunn, 2000), grooming (e.g., Atkins & Kent, 1988), cosmetics (Johnson & Workman, 1991), hair length (Atkins & Kent, 1988), tattooing (Seiter & Hatch, 2005; Swami & Furnham, 2007), and body piercing (Seiter & Sandry, 2003) influence judgments about credibility, attractiveness, and whether or not to hire someone. In other words, if anything, such research indicates that such cues are not trivial at all and, in some contexts (e.g., when interviewing), may be more important than verbal cues (Goldberg & Cohen, 2004).

In addition to those discussed, other artifacts and features of the environment can be influential. For instance, power and status might be communicated through the size and location of a person's office. Large offices in corner spaces, for example, are often considered prestigious (Andersen, 1999). Not only that, one of our favorite studies (Teven & Comadena, 1996) illustrates that an office's appearance may be important as well. In the study, 97 students went one at a time to meet a professor in his office. On arriving for the meeting, however, they found no professor and were asked to wait 5 minutes for him. Some of the students waited in a disorganized and untidy office, whereas others waited in a clean and neatly arranged office. After the 5 minutes were up, the students were told that the professor could not make the meeting. Later, however, they saw the professor lecture and rated him on several scales. The results of the study showed that the professor's office had a significant influence on students' perceptions. Specifically, compared to students who visited the tidy office, those who visited the untidy one perceived the professor as less authoritative, less trustworthy, less open, less relaxed, less concerned about making a good impression, less animated, and less friendly. Interestingly, however, the "untidy" professor was seen as the most dynamic, perhaps because the disheveled office created the impression of a busy and energetic person (Teven & Comadena, 1996). Whatever the case, after reading this study, we'll be straightening up.

And apparently, we're not the only ones. Other people know about the importance of structuring the environment. For example, if you're thinking of buying a house, before you do, remember that those dandy model homes may not look the same once you're living in them. Why not? The furniture is downsized to make the rooms look larger (Martin, 2000). Plus, empty closets, refrigerators without kiddie art, and the absence of other household necessities make such homes look tidy and ever so inviting. The practice of "staging" homes by using decluttering and inexpensive improvements is now a big business.

Supermarkets are another example of how environments are arranged strategically (e.g., see Field, 1996; Meyer, 1997; Tandingan, 2001). Next time you're shopping, for instance, take a look around. You might notice that staples such as dairy, meat, and produce are in the back or on opposite sides of the store. Why? It forces shoppers to meander through the aisles where they'll be tempted to buy all kinds of other goodies. You'll also notice that chips, dips, and other products that "go together" are intentionally placed side by side, encouraging additional purchases. And it's no accident that children's products (e.g., Cap'n Crunch) are often placed on middle shelves so that they are at eye level to little precious who is seated in the shopping cart, whereas adult products (e.g., Grape Nuts) are at higher elevations. What's more, snack foods, which appeal to impulsive shoppers, are often located in checkout areas and at the ends of aisles where they're more likely to be snatched up. Clearly, such placement is adapted to particular audiences and aimed at making products noticeable to consumers.

In addition to the studies and tactics we've mentioned so far, considerable evidence shows that artifacts and physical features of the environment can not only make products more noticeable and people appear more (or less) credible, they can also lead to persuasion. Most of this research has focused on the impact of clothing. Lawrence and Watson (1991), for example, found that individuals asking for contributions to law enforcement and health-care campaigns earned more money when wearing sheriffs' and nurses' uniforms than when they did not. In another classic study, Bickman (1974) had young men dressed as either civilians or uniformed guards, approach pedestrians on the streets of New York and ask them to do one of three things. In one situation, pedestrians were shown a bag lying on the ground and were told, "Pick up this bag for me!" In another condition, the experimenter pointed at a man standing near a parked car and said, "This fellow is over-parked at the meter but doesn't have any change. Give him a dime!" In the final condition, a person standing at a bus stop was told, "Don't you know you have to stand on the other side of the pole? The sign says, 'No Standing.'" Results of the study showed that, in all three conditions, people complied more with the guard than they did with the civilians. In other words, something about a uniform tends to make us obedient.

Although meta-analyses indicate that fancy suits, uniforms, and high-status clothing are related to higher rates of compliance (Segrin, 1993), such apparel might not always be necessary for persuasion. In some cases, it may also be possible to influence people by wearing clothing that makes them identify with a persuader. Hensley (1981), for instance, found that well-dressed people were more persuasive in airports, but casually dressed people were more persuasive at bus stops.

In short, it appears that artifacts, particularly clothing, make a difference when trying to seek compliance. Of course, artifacts can also affect your appearance or attractiveness, which, in turn, can affect your persuasiveness. We now turn our discussion to this topic.

Physical Appearance: Of Beauties and Beasts

Beauty may only be skin deep, but it is persuasive. And the people out there trying to influence us know this. Beauty sells. For example, if Gisele Bündchen had a big nose and warts with hair growing out of them, do you think you'd have seen her face spread across the pages of makeup and lingerie ads? It seems, in fact, that the products being endorsed by attractive spokespersons do not even have to be connected with making us more attractive. Indeed, beautiful people are trying to sell us everything from milk, to law firms, to dog food.

Not surprisingly, plenty of research indicates that physical attractiveness is persuasive in contexts other than advertising (see Box 8.4). For instance, compared to their less-attractive counterparts, attractive people are judged to be happier, more

BOX 8.4 | Hot by Association: How Facebook Friends Affect Your Attractiveness

If you are one of the millions of people who use the social networking website Facebook, you might be interested to know that people may be judging you by the company you keep. It has been known for some time that judgments of attractiveness are relative. For example, when photos of average-looking people are shown beside photos of attractive and unattractive people, a contrast effect occurs: Average people are seen as more attractive when seen alongside unattractive people and less attractive when seen alongside attractive people. If, however, the people judging attractiveness are told that a relationship exists between the people in the photos, the opposite effect (assimilation) occurs: Average people are now seen as less attractive when paired with unattractive people and more attractive when paired with attractive people (Melamed & Moss, 1975). Knowing this, it probably won't surprise you to learn that, if you want to appear "hotter," it helps to have attractive friends on Facebook. Indeed, two studies found that Facebook users were perceived as more physically and socially attractive when they were associated with good-looking pals (Jaschinski & Kommers, 2012; Walther, Van Der Heide, Kim, Westerman, & Tong, 2008).

intelligent, friendlier, stronger, and kinder and are thought to have better personalities, better jobs, and greater marital competence (Knapp, 1992). Seiter and Dunn (2000) found that it did not matter whether a woman was made to appear attractive in a pristine way (e.g., conservative clothing, makeup, and jewelry) or attractive in a sexy way (e.g., revealing clothes, heavy makeup). In both cases, she was believed more when claiming to have been sexually harassed than when she was made to appear unattractive (e.g., blotchy skin, greasy hair, no makeup). Finally, Palmer and Peterson (2016) found that, when talking politics, attractive people (particularly poorly informed ones), are more likely than unattractive people to try persuading others. Not only that, they're perceived as better informed and more persuasive than unattractive people.

According to Palmer and Peterson (2016), these results may be due to a "halo effect," in which one positive characteristic of a person causes us to see everything about the person in a positive light. In other words, if the person is attractive, he or she must also be trustworthy, well informed, and so forth. Whatever the case, given the preceding findings, perhaps you are wondering what physical characteristics are related to attractiveness. Although we know that standards for beauty change over time (e.g., did you know that, in medieval times, pale and plump people were perceived as the most attractive?) and that beauty is supposedly in the eye of the beholder, research tells us that some of the following characteristics are related to perceptions and/or persuasiveness:

1. **Body shape**: Dwayne "The Rock" Johnson, Taylor Swift, and Jonah Hill represent the three basic body shapes. The first, a *mesomorph*, is muscular; the second, an *ectomorph* is thin; and the third, an *endomorph,* is round. Findings summarized by Argyle (1988) show that whereas mesomorphs are rated as, among other things, strong and adventurous, ectomorphs are seen as tense, pessimistic, and quiet, and

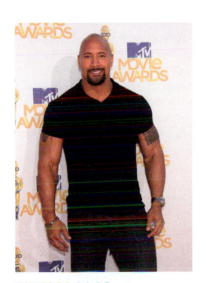  

FIGURES 8.3, 8.4, 8.5
Celebrities sporting different body shapes: Can you spot the mesomorph, ectomorph, and endomorph?
Sources: DFree/Shutterstock.com; Kathy Hutchins/Sutterstock.com; s_buckley/Shutterstock.com

endomorphs are seen as warm, sympathetic, agreeable, and dependent. Because of negative stereotypes, endomorphs tend to be perceived as less powerful, successful, attractive, and enthusiastic than those with different body shapes (Breseman, Lennon, & Schulz, 1999; Wade, Fuller, Bresnan, Schaefer, & Mlynarski, 2007). Moreover, endomorphs are less likely to get jobs, less likely to earn high salaries, and less likely to be accepted into colleges than thinner people with the same IQs (Argyle, 1988).

Even so, one study (Martins, Pliner, & Lee, 2004) indicated that perceptions based on body shape depend on other factors, specifically meal size. In the study, Canadian students reported their impressions of normal or overweight males and females who were portrayed as eating small or large meals. Overweight males eating large meals were perceived by all students as the least socially attractive, perhaps because they are thought to lack self-control (Martins et al., 2004). Interestingly, however, while female students perceived normal-weight females who ate small meals as the most socially attractive, male students rated normal-weight females who ate large meals as the most socially attractive. Why? The researchers suggested that males may perceive normal-weight females who eat heartily as more comfortable with themselves, more confident, and more honest (Martins et al., 2004). That being said, women may face a double standard when it comes to weight. A study by Judge and Cable (2011), for example, found that thin women earned significantly higher salaries than middleweight women, while thin men earned lower salaries than middleweight men. Being obese negatively affected the salaries of both men and women (Judge & Cable, 2011).

2. *Facial appearance*: According to Argyle (1988), faces are perceived as more attractive when they have wide cheekbones, narrow cheeks, high eyebrows, wide pupils, large smiles, noses that are not too long or too short, and eyes not too far apart or too close together. Baby-faced women are perceived as more attractive but immature by men (Berry & McArthur, 1986) and, whereas baby-faced people are cast into commercials that want to portray trustworthiness, mature-faced people are cast into commercials that want to emphasize expertise (Brownlow & Zebrowitz, 1990). Interestingly, because baby-faced speakers may look more honest (Masip, Garrido, & Herrero, 2004), they are more persuasive when their trustworthiness is questioned, while mature-faced speakers are more persuasive when their expertise is questioned (Brownlow, 1992). In addition, while being baby-faced seems to benefit female politicians, it works to male politicians' disadvantage (Lee, 2013).

That said, the most persuasive faces, perhaps, are ones that remind us of ourselves. Indeed, in one of our favorite studies (Richards & Hample, 2016), research participants saw photographs of a speaker. Unbeknown to the participants, the speaker's face was actually a composite of two faces that had been digitally morphed together. What's more, while some participants saw photos that merged the faces of two strangers, others saw photos that merged their own face with a stranger's. Compared to the first group of participants, those in the second group perceived the speaker to be more likable, credible, and persuasive. Why? According to the researchers, evolution benefits people who give preferential treatment to their kin. See the connection? People who look like us may be genetically similar. As such, we're prone to prefer them over dissimilar others, a concept known *nepotistic altruism* (Hamilton, 1964).

3. *Hair*: Do blondes, as the old saying goes, "have more fun?" We're not sure about that, but when it comes to another old saying—"Gentlemen prefer blondes"—research seems to agree. Indeed, in several studies the same women sported different hair colors, and, generally speaking, were favored by males when posing as blondes. By way of example, blonde hitchhikers (Guéguen & Lamy, 2009), waitresses (Guéguen, 2012b), and night clubbers (Guéguen, 2012a) received more rides, tips, and attention (Swami & Barrett, 2011, Study 1), respectively. On the other hand, although blondes received more help (Guéguen, 2012c) and were rated as more attractive (Sorokowski, 2008), they were also perceived as more needy and less competent than brunettes (Swami & Barrett, Study 2).

That said, research shows that hair of any color may be better than no hair at all. For instance, a study comparing hair loss among male governors and members of Congress to the general public found that elected politicians are more likely to have a full head of hair than would be expected of men their age (Sigelman, Dawson, Nitz, & Whicker, 1990). Before you conclude that more hair means more persuasion, however, consider a study by Guido, Peluso, and Moffa (2011), which examined the persuasive effects of beards. Based on research suggesting that men with beards tend to be perceived as less attractive but more trustworthy and competent than men with no facial hair (De Souza, Baião, & Otta, 2003), these researchers found that clean-shaven men were more persuasive when endorsing products related to attractiveness (i.e., underwear), while bearded guys were more persuasive when endorsing products related to trustworthiness and expertise (i.e., cellphones and toothpaste). Such research supports the *match-up hypothesis* (Kamins, 1990), which argues that persuasion is increased when endorsers are paired with products that emphasize characteristics of the endorsers.

4. *Height*: According to a meta-analysis of 45 studies (Judge & Cable, 2004), when it comes to a person's height, size matters. The analysis found that being taller, especially if you are male, is positively associated with ratings of leadership, performance, and social esteem. Not only that, the study reported that taller people earn significantly more money in their careers than do their shorter counterparts (Judge & Cable, 2004).

Paralinguistics and Persuasion: Pump Up the Volume?

Paralinguistics, or *vocalics,* is the study of vocal stimuli aside from spoken words. It includes such elements as pitch, rate, pauses, volume, tone of voice, silences, laughs, screams, sighs, and so forth. We know from prior research that the *way* in which persons speak affects how they are perceived as well as their ability to persuade. In one study, for instance, people who listened to high-pitched voices perceived the speaker as more attractive and extroverted than those who listened to low-pitched voices (Imhof, 2010). Similarly, Hinkle (2001) found that when managers spoke clearly and varied their tone, employees tended to like them better.

More recently, researchers have identified a quality of voice known as *vocal fry* or "creaky voice," which is characterized by drawing out the end of sentences with a low, croaking growl in the back of the throat (to hear it, Google "vocal fry" or think Britney Spears, Kim Kardashian, or Matthew McConaughey). According to Anderson and her colleagues (2014), vocal fry is increasingly common among young American females, and leads them, more so than males, to be perceived as less competent, less trustworthy, less attractive, and less hirable. Such findings suggest that women's voices may be subject to more criticism than men's, a double standard if you ask us.

In addition to pitch and quality, researchers have examined the effects of speaking rate. Previous studies, for example, indicate that faster speakers are perceived as more credible (Simonds, Meyer, Quinlan, & Hunt, 2006) and persuasive (Miller, Maruyama, Beaber, & Valone, 1976) than those who speak slower, perhaps because they appear more competent and knowledgeable. On the other hand, Buller and Aune (1988) found that for persuasion to occur, the optimal rate of speech may depend on both the encoding ability of the sender and the decoding ability of the receiver. Specifically, although good decoders were more likely to comply with speeches delivered at fast rates, poor decoders preferred slower rates. In a related study, Smith and Shaffer (1995) found that speeches delivered at faster rates hinder people's ability to scrutinize messages. Thus, consistent with the elaboration likelihood model (see Chapter 2), people who heard a speech delivered at a normal speed were persuaded when the speech contained strong arguments, whereas those who heard accelerated speeches were persuaded equally by strong and weak messages. That said, if you're at all like us, you've undoubtedly heard that old stereotype about "fast-talking" salespeople. You can't trust them, right? We're not sure about that, but one study found that those end-of-commercial disclaimers are less persuasive when delivered at fast-paced rather than normal-paced speeds (Herbst, Finkel, Allan, & Fitzsimons, 2012). If you ask us, they're also pretty irritating.

Finally, you might be interested to know that not all studies on vocalics focus exclusively on human speech. Indeed, for those of you who've been unfortunate enough to answer your telephone and find one of those eerie computer-synthesized voices selling some product on the other end, here's an interesting study. The study asked people to listen to persuasive messages spoken by either a natural human voice or a synthetic computerized voice and then measured how persuaded the people were. Surprisingly, the results indicated that the synthetic voice was just as persuasive as the human voice (Stern, Mullennix, Dyson, & Wilson, 1999). Even so, in real life, we bet those computers are easier to hang up on.

SUMMARY

In this chapter, we learned that persuasion is not as simple as what you say. How you say something may be just as, if not more, important. We also learned that there are many categories of nonverbal communication that affect the process of persuasion. In our examination of kinesics, for instance, we saw that people are generally more persuasive when they (1) make eye contact, (2) use facial expressions and body movements that signal relaxation and sociability, and (3) use more emblems and illustrators but fewer adaptors. Similarly, we noted that people tend to be more compliant when they are touched or approached at distances that violate their expectations, as long as the touch and distances are not perceived as being too inappropriate. Moreover, people can make themselves appear more credible, dominant, or powerful, and, in turn, affect their persuasiveness through the use of time, artifacts, or physical appearance. Those who control others' time, wear the right clothing at the right time, and are attractive tend to be more persuasive than their counterparts. Finally, various features of the voice, particularly its rate, influence how persuasive one tends to be.

REFERENCES

Albert, S., & Dabbs, J. M., Jr. (1970). Physical distance and persuasion. *Journal of Personality and Social Psychology, 15*, 265–270.

Andersen, P. A. (1999). *Nonverbal communication: Forms and functions.* Mountain View, CA: Mayfield.

Andersen, P. A. (2004). Influential actions: Nonverbal communication and persuasion. In J. S. Seiter & R. H. Gass (Eds.), *Readings in persuasion, social influence, and compliance gaining* (pp. 165–180). Boston, MA: Allyn & Bacon.

Anderson, R. C., Klofstad, C. A., Mayew, W. J., & Venkatachalam, M. (2014). Vocal fry may undermine the success of young women in the labor market. *PLoS One, 9*, e97506. doi:10.1371/journal.pone.0097506

Argyle, M. (1988). *Bodily communication* (2nd ed.). Madison, CT: International Universities Press.

Atkins, C. P., & Kent, R. L. (1988). What do recruits consider important during the employment interview? *Journal of Employment Counseling, 25*, 98–103.

Baberini, M., Coleman, C., Slovic, P., Västfjäll, D. (2015). Examining the effects of photographic attributes on sympathy, emotions, and donation behavior. *Visual Communication Quarterly, 22*, 118–128. doi:10.1080/15551393.2015.1061433

Baron, R. A., & Bell, P. A. (1976). Physical distance and helping: Some unexpected benefits of "crowding in" on others. *Journal of Applied Social Psychology, 6*, 95–104.

Bernieri, F. J., & Petty, K. N. (2011). The influence of handshakes on first impression accuracy. *Social Influence, 6*, 78–87.

Berry, D. S., & McArthur, L. Z. (1986). Perceiving character in faces: The impact of age-related craniofacial changes on social perception. *Psychological Bulletin, 100*, 3–18.

Bickman, L. (1974). The social power of a uniform. *Journal of Applied Social Psychology, 4*, 47–61.

Booth-Butterfield, M., & Noguchi, T. (2000). Students' perceptions of teachers' nonverbal behavior: Comparisons of American and international students' classroom response. *Communication Research Reports, 17*(3), 288–298.

Brehm, J. W. (1966). *A theory of psychological reactance.* New York: Academic Press.

Brehm, S. S., & Brehm, J. W. (1981). *Psychological reactance: A theory of freedom and control.* New York: Academic Press.

Breseman, B. C., Lennon, S. J., & Schulz, T. L. (1999). Obesity and powerlessness. In K. K. P. Johnson & S. J. Lennon (Eds.), *Appearance and power* (pp. 173–197). New York: Berg.

Brodsky, S. L. (1991). *Testifying in court: Guidelines and maxims for the expert witness.* Washington, DC: American Psychological Association.

Brownlow, S. (1992). Seeing is believing: Facial appearance, credibility and attitude change. *Journal of Nonverbal Behavior, 16*, 101–115.

Brownlow, S., & Zebrowitz, L. A. (1990). Facial appearance, gender, and credibility in television commercials. *Journal of Nonverbal Behavior, 14*, 51–60.

Buller, D. B., & Aune, R. K. (1988). The effects of vocalics and nonverbal sensitivity on compliance: A speech accommodation theory explanation. *Human Communication Research, 14*, 301–332.

Burgoon, J. K. (1978). A communication model of personal space violations: Explications and an initial test. *Human Communication Research*, *4*, 129–142.

Burgoon, J. K. (1992). Applying a comparative approach to nonverbal expectancy violation theory. In J. Blumler, K. E. Rosengren, & J. M. McLeod (Eds.), *Comparatively speaking: Communication and culture across space and time* (pp. 53–69). Newbury Park, CA: Sage.

Burgoon, J. K. (1994). Nonverbal signals. In M. L. Knapp & G. R. Miller (Eds.), *Handbook of interpersonal communication* (2nd ed., pp. 229–285). Thousand Oaks, CA: Sage.

Burgoon, J. K., Buller, D. B., & Woodall, W. G. (1996). *Nonverbal communication: The unspoken dialogue* (3rd ed.). New York: McGraw-Hill.

Calanchini, J., Moons, W. G., & Mackie, D. M. (2016). Angry expressions induce extensive processing of persuasive appeals. *Journal of Experimental Social Psychology*, *64*, 88–98. doi:10.1016/j.jesp.2016.02.004

Camps, J., Tuteleers, C., Stouten, J., & Nelissen, J. (2013). A situational touch: How touch affects people's decision behavior. *Social Influence*, *8*, 237–250. doi:10.1080/15534510.2012.719479

Cialdini, R. B. (1993). *Influence: Science and practice* (3rd ed.). New York: HarperCollins.

De Souza, A. A. L., Baião, V. B. U., & Otta, E. (2003). Perception of men's personal qualities and prospect of employment as a function of facial hair. *Psychological Reports*, *92*, 201–208.

Ekman, P., & Friesen, W. V. (1969). The repertoire of nonverbal behavior: Categories, origins, usage, and coding. *Semiotica*, *1*, 49–98.

Field, A. (1996, February). Outsmart your supermarket. *McCall's*, *123*, 114–115.

Fisher, J. D., Rytting, M., & Heslin, R. (1976). Hands touching hands: Affective and evaluative effects of an interpersonal touch. *Sociometry*, *39*, 416–421.

Forbes, R. J., & Jackson, P. R. (1980). Non-verbal behaviour and the outcome of selection interviews. *Journal of Occupational Psychology*, *53*, 65–72.

Giles, H., & Wiemann, J. M. (1987). Language, social comparison, and power. In C. R. Berger & S. H. Chaffee (Eds.), *The handbook of communication science* (pp. 350–384). Newbury Park, CA: Sage.

Gilley, M. (1975). Don't all the girls get prettier at closing time. In *The Best of Mickey Gilley* (Vol. 2). Columbia Records. New York: Broadcast Music.

Goffman, E. (1959). *The presentation of self in everyday life*. Garden City, NY: Anchor/Doubleday.

Goldberg, C., & Cohen, D. J. (2004). Walking the walk and talking the talk: Gender differences in the impact of interviewing skills on applicant assessments. *Group & Organization Management*, *29*(3), 369–384.

Gorham, J., Cohen, S. H., & Morris, T. L. (1999). Fashion in the classroom III: Effects of instructor attire and immediacy in natural classroom interactions. *Communication Quarterly*, *47*(3), 281–299.

Guéguen, N. (2007). Courtship compliance: The effect of touch on women's behavior. *Social Influence*, *2*, 81–97.

Guéguen, N. (2009). Mimicry and seduction: An evaluation in a courtship context. *Social Influence*, *4*, 249–255.

Guéguen, N. (2012a). Hair color and courtship: Blond women received more courtship solicitations and redhead men received more refusals. *Psychological Studies*, *57*, 369–375. doi:10.1007/s12646–012–0158–6

Guéguen, N. (2012b). Hair color and wages: Waitresses with blond hair have more fun. *Journal of Socio-Economics*, *41*, 370–372. doi:10.1016/j.socec.2012.04.012

Guéguen, N. (2012c). The sweet color of an implicit request: Women's hair color and spontaneous helping behavior. *Social Behavior and Personality*, 40, 1099–1102. doi:10.2224/sbp.2012.40.7.1099

Guéguen, N., & De Gail, M. (2003). The effect of smiling on helping behavior: Smiling and good Samaritan behavior. *Communication Reports*, 16(2), 133–140.

Guéguen, N., & Fischer-Lokou, J. (2003). Tactile contact and spontaneous help: An evaluation in a natural setting. *Journal of Social Psychology*, 143, 785–787.

Guéguen, N., & Fischer-Lokou, J. (2004). Hitchhikers' smiles and receipt of help. *Psychology Reports*, 94, 756–760.

Guéguen, N., & Jacob, C. (2002). Direct look versus evasive glance and compliance with a request. *Journal of Social Psychology*, 142, 393–396.

Guéguen, N., & Lamy, L. (2009). Hitchhiking women's hair color. *Perceptual and Motor Skills*, 109, 941–948. doi:10.2466/pms.109.3.941–948

Guéguen, N., Jacob, C., & Boulbry, G. (2007). The effect of touch on compliance with a restaurant's employee suggestion. *Hospitality Management*, 26, 1019–1023.

Guido, G., Peluso, A. M., & Moffa, V. (2011). Beardedness in advertising: Effects on endorsers' credibility and purchase intention. *Journal of Marketing Communications*, 17, 37–49.

Gunns, R. E., Johnston, L., & Hudson, S. M. (2002). Victim selection and kinematics: A point-light investigation of vulnerability to attack. *Journal of Nonverbal Behavior*, 26, 129–158.

Hamilton, W. D. (1964). The genetical evolution of social behavior. *Journal of Theoretical Biology*, 7, 1–16. doi:10.1016/022–5193(64)90038–4

Hensley, W. E. (1981). The effects of attire, location, and sex on aiding behavior: A similarity explanation. *Journal of Nonverbal Behavior*, 6, 3–11.

Herbst, K. C., Finkel, E. J., Allan, D., & Fitzsimons, G. M. (2012). On the dangers of pulling a fast one: Advertisement disclaimer speed, brand trust, and purchase intention. *Journal of Consumer Research*, 38, 909–919. doi:10.1086/660854

Hinkle, L. L. (1999). Nonverbal immediacy communication behaviors and liking in marital relationships. *Communication Research Reports*, 16, 16–26.

Hinkle, L. L. (2001). Perceptions of supervisor nonverbal immediacy, vocalics, and subordinate liking. *Communication Research Reports*, 18, 128–136.

Hornick, J. (1992). Tactile stimulation and consumer response. *Journal of Consumer Research*, 19, 449–458.

Imhof, M. (2010). Listening to voices and judging people. *International Journal of Listening*, 24, 19–33.

Jaschinski, C., & Kommers, P. (2012). Does beauty matter? The role of friends' attractiveness and gender on social attractiveness ratings of individuals on Facebook. *International Journal of Web Based Communities*, 8, 389–401. doi:10.1504/IJWBC.2012.048060

Johnco, C., Wheeler, L., & Taylor, A. (2010). They do get prettier at closing time: A repeated measures study of the closing-time effect and alcohol. *Social Influence*, 5, 261–271.

Johnson, K. K. P., & Workman, J. E. (1991). The role of cosmetics in impression formation. *Clothing and Textiles Research Journal*, 10(1), 630–667.

Judge, T. A., & Cable, D. M. (2004). The effect of physical height on workplace success and income: Preliminary test of a theoretical model. *Journal of Applied Psychology*, 89, 428–441.

Judge, T. A., & Cable, D. M. (2011). When it comes to pay, do the thin win? The effect of weight on pay for men and women. *Journal of Applied Psychology*, 96, 95–112.

Kafetsios, K., Anagnostopoulos, F., Lempesis, E., & Valindra, A. (2014). Doctors' emotion regulation and patient satisfaction: A social-functional perspective. *Health Communicaiton, 29*, 205–214. doi:10.1080/10410236.2012.738150

Kamins, M. A., (1990). An investigation into the match-up hypothesis in celebrity advertising: When beauty may be only skin deep. *Journal of Advertising, 19*, 4–13.

Kleinke, C. L. (1977). Compliance to requests made by gazing and touching experimenters in field settings. *Journal of Experimental Social Psychology, 13*, 218–223.

Kleinke, C. L. (1980). Interaction between gaze and legitimacy of request on compliance in a field setting. *Journal of Nonverbal Behavior, 5*, 3–12.

Knapp, M. L. (1992). *Nonverbal communication in human interaction* (3rd ed.). New York: Holt, Rinehart, Winston.

Krumhuber, E., Manstead, A. S. R., & Kappas, A. (2007). Temporal aspects of facial displays in person and expression perception: The effects of smile dynamics, head-tilt, and gender. *Journal of Nonverbal Behavior, 31*, 39–56.

LaFrance, M., & Hecht, M. A. (1995). Why smiles generate leniency. *Personality and Social Psychology Bulletin, 21*(3), 297–314.

Laustsen, L., & Petersen, M. B. (2016). Winning faces vary by ideology: How nonverbal source cues influence election and communication success in politics. *Political Communication, 33*, 188–211. doi:10.1080/10584609.2015.1050565

Lawrence, S., & Watson, M. (1991). Getting others to help: The effectiveness of professional uniforms in charitable fund raising. *Journal of Applied Communication Research, 19*, 170–185.

Leathers, D. G. (1997). *Successful nonverbal communication* (3rd ed.). Boston, MA: Allyn & Bacon.

Lee, Y. (2013). Babyfacedness, sex of face stimulus, and social context in face percepton and person evaluation. *Psychological Reports, 112*, 800–817. doi:10.2466/01.17. PRO.112.3.800–817

Maddux, W. W., Mullen, E. & Galinsky, A. D. (2008). Chameleons bake bigger pies and take bigger pieces: Strategic behavioral mimicry facilitates negotiation outcomes. *Journal of Experimental Social Psychology, 44*, 461–468.

Maricchiolo, F., Gnisci, A., Bonaiuto, M., & Ficca, G. (2009). Effects of different types of hand gestures in persuasive speech on receivers' evaluations. *Language and Cognitive Processes, 24*, 239–266.

Martin, E. J. (2000, December 3). Home's looks—both good and bad—can be deceiving. *Los Angeles Times,* p. K4.

Martins, Y., Pliner, P., & Lee, C. (2004). The effects of meal size and body size on individuals' impressions of males and females. *Eating Behaviors, 5*(2), 117–132.

Masip, J., Garrido, E., & Herrero, C. (2004). Facial appearance and impressions of credibility: The effects of facial babyishness and age on person perception. *International Journal of Psychology, 39*(4), 276–289.

Maslow, C., Yoselson, K., & London, H. (1971). Persuasiveness of confidence expressed via language and body language. *British Journal of Social and Clinical Psychology, 10*, 234–240.

Mazer, J. P., & Stowe, S. A. (2016). Can teacher immediacy reduce the impact of verbal aggressiveness? Examining effects on student outcomes and perceptions of teacher credibility. *Western Journal of Communication, 80*, 21–37. doi:10.1080/10570314. 2014.943421

McGinley, H., LeFevre, R., & McGinley, P. (1975). The influence of a communicator's body position on opinion change in others. *Journal of Personality and Social Psychology, 31*, 686–690.

McGuire, W. J. (1968). Personality and susceptibility to social influence. In E. G. Borgatta & W. W. Lambert (Eds.), *Handbook of personality theory and research* (pp. 1130–1187). Chicago: Rand McNally.

Mehrabian, A., & Williams, M. (1969). Nonverbal concomitants of perceived and intended persuasiveness. *Journal of Personality and Social Psychology, 13*, 37–58.

Melamed, L., & Moss, M. K. (1975). The effect of context on ratings of attractiveness of photographs. *Journal of Psychology, 90*, 129–136.

Meyer, M. (1997, August). Outsmart your supermarket and save. *Good Housekeeping, 225*, 147.

Miller, N., Maruyama, G., Beaber, R. J., & Valone, K. (1976). Speed of speech and persuasion. *Journal of Personality and Social Psychology, 34*, 615–624.

Murphy, N. A. (2007). Appearing smart: The impression management of intelligence, person perception accuracy, and behavior in social interaction. *Personality and Social Psychology Bulletin, 33*, 325–339.

Neal, T. M. S., & Brodsky, S. L. (2008). Expert witness credibility as a function of eye contact behavior and gender. *Criminal Justice and Behavior, 35*, 1515–1526.

Palmer, C. L., & Peterson, R. D. (2016). Halo effects and the attractiveness premium in perceptions of political expertise. *American Politics Research, 44*, 353–382. doi:10.1177/1532673X15600517

Patterson, M. L., Powell, J. L., & Lenihan, M. G. (1986). Touch, compliance and interpersonal affect. *Journal of Nonverbal Behavior, 10*, 41–50.

Peck, J., & Childers, T. L. (2003a). To have and to hold: The influence of haptic information on product judgments. *Journal of Marketing, 67*, 35–48.

Peck, J., & Childers, T. L. (2003b). Individual differences in haptic information processing: The "need for touch" scale. *Journal of Consumer Research, 30*, 430–442.

Peck, J., & Johnson, J. W. (2011). Autotelic need for touch, haptics, and persuasion: The role of involvement. *Psychology & Marketing, 28*, 222–239.

Peck, J., & Wiggins, J. (2005). It just feels good: Customers' affective response to touch and its influence on persuasion. *Journal of Marketing, 70*, 56–69.

Pennebaker, J. W., Dyer, M. A., Caulkins, R. S., Litowitz, D. L., Ackreman, P. L., Anderson, D. B., & McGraw, K. M. (1979). Don't the girls get prettier at closing time: A country and western application to psychology. *Personality and Social Psychology Bulletin, 5*, 122–125.

Petty, R. E., & Cacioppo, J. T. (1986). *Communication and persuasion: Central and peripheral routes to attitude change*. New York: Springer-Verlag.

Richards, A. S., Hample, D. (2016). Facial similarity mitigates the persuasive effects of source bias: An evolutionary explanation for kinship and susceptibility to influence. *Communication Monographs, 83*, 1–24. doi:10.1080/03637751.2015.1014822

Robinson, J. D., Seiter, J. S., & Acharya, L. (1992, February). *"I just put my head down and society does the rest." An examination of influence strategies among beggars*. Paper presented at the annual meeting of the Western Speech Communication Association, Boise, ID.

Saigh, P. A. (1981). Effects of nonverbal examiner praise on selected WAIS subtest performance of Lebanese undergraduates. *Journal of Nonverbal Behavior, 6*, 84–86.

Schlenker, B. R. (1980). *Impression management*. Monterey, CA: Brooks/Cole.

Segrin, C. (1993). The effects of nonverbal behavior on outcomes of compliance gaining attempts. *Communication Studies, 44*, 169–187.

Seiter, J. S. (1999). Does communicating nonverbal disagreement during an opponent's speech affect the credibility of the debater in the background? *Psychological Reports, 84*, 855–861.

Seiter, J. S. (2001). Silent derogation and perceptions of deceptiveness: Does communicating nonverbal disbelief during an opponent's speech affect perceptions of debaters' veracity? *Communication Research Reports*, *18*(4), 334–344.

Seiter, J. S., Abraham, J. A., & Nakagama, B. T. (1998). Split-screen versus single-screen formats in televised debates: Does access to an opponent's nonverbal behaviors affect viewers' perceptions of a speaker's credibility? *Perceptual and Motor Skills*, *86*, 491–497.

Seiter, J. S., & Dunn, D. (2000). Beauty and believability in sexual harassment cases: Does physical attractiveness affect perceptions of veracity and the likelihood of being harassed? *Communication Research Reports*, *17*(2), 203–209.

Seiter, J. S., & Hatch, S. (2005). Effects of tattoos on perceptions of credibility and attractiveness. *Psychological Reports*, *96*, 1113–1120.

Seiter, J. S., & Sandry, A. (2003). Pierced for success? The effects of ear and nose piercing on perceptions of job candidates' credibility, attractiveness, and hirability. *Communication Research Reports*, *20*(4), 287–298.

Seiter, J. S., & Weger, H. (2005). Audience perceptions of candidates' appropriateness as a function of nonverbal behaviors displayed during televised political debates. *Journal of Social Psychology*, *145*(2), 225–235.

Seiter, J. S., Weger, H., Kinzer, H. J., & Jensen, A. S. (2009). Impression management in televised debates: The effect of background nonverbal behavior on audience perceptions of debaters' likeability. *Communication Research Reports*, *26*, 1–11.

Sigelman, L., Dawson, E., Nitz, M., & Whicker, M. L. (1990). Hair loss and electability: The bald truth. *Journal of Nonverbal Behavior*, *14*, 269–283.

Simonds, B. K., Meyer, K. R., Quinlan, M. M., & Hunt, S. (2006). Effects of instructor speech rate on student affective learning, recall, and perceptions of nonverbal immediacy, credibility, and clarity. *Communication Research Reports*, *23*, 187–197.

Smith, R. J., & Knowles, E. S. (1979). Affective and cognitive mediators of reactions to spatial invasions. *Journal of Experimental Social Psychology*, *15*, 437–452.

Smith, S. M., & Shaffer, D. R. (1995). Speed of speech and persuasion: Evidence for multiple effects. *Personality and Social Psychology Bulletin*, *21*(10), 1051–1060.

Sorokowski, P. (2008). Attractiveness of blonde women in evolutionary perspective: Studies with two Polish samples. *Perceptual and Motor Skills*, *106*, 737–744. doi:10.2466/pms.106.3.737–744

Stel, M., Mastop, J., & Strick, M. (2011). The impact of mimicking on attitudes toward products presented in TV commercials. *Social Influence*, *6*, 142–152.

Stern, S. E., Mullennix, J. W., Dyson, C., & Wilson, S. J. (1999). The persuasiveness of synthetic speech versus human speech. *Human Factors*, *41*(4), 588–595.

Stewart, G. L., Dustin, S. L., Barrick, M. R., & Darnold, T. C. (2008). Exploring the handshake in employment interviews. *Journal of Applied Psychology*, *93*, 1139–1146.

Stone, A. (2012, Aug. 18). Why waiting in line is torture. *New York Times*. Retrieved from: www.nytimes.com/2012/08/19/opinion/sunday/why-waiting-in-line-is-torture.html on February 3, 2017.

Swami, V., & Barrett, S. (2011). British men's hair color preferences: An assessment of courtship solicitation and stimulus ratings. *Scandinavian Journal of Psychology*, *52*, 595–600. doi:10.1111/j.1467–9450.2011.00911.x

Swami, V., & Furnham, A. (2007) Unattractive, promiscuous and heavy drinkers: Perceptions of women with tattoos. *Body Image*, *4*, 343–352.

Tandingan, R. (2001, October 5). *Persuasion at the supermarket*. Retrieved from: www.uoregon.edu/~bfmalle/sp/romila3.html

Tedeschi, J. T., & Reiss, M. (1981). Identities, the phenomenal self, and laboratory research. In Tedeschi, J. T. (Ed.), *Impression management theory and social psychological research* (pp. 3–22). New York: Academic Press.

Teven, J. J. (2007). Effects of supervisor social influence, nonverbal immediacy, and biological sex on subordinates' perceptions of job satisfaction, liking, and supervisor credibility. *Communication Quarterly, 55*, 155–177.

Teven, J. J., & Comadena, M. E. (1996). The effects of office aesthetic quality on students' perceptions of teacher credibility and communicator style. *Communication Research Reports, 13*(1), 101–108.

Turman, P. D. (2008). Coaches' immediacy behaviors as predictors of athletes' perceptions of satisfaction and team cohesion. *Western Journal of Communication, 72*, 162–179.

Vaidis, D. C. F., & Halimi-Falkowicz, S. G. M. (2008). Increasing compliance with a request: Two touches are more effective than one. *Psychological Reports, 103*, 88–92.

van Baaren, R. B., Holland, R. W., Kawakami, K., & Knippenberg, A. (2004). Mimicry and prosocial behavior. *Psychological Science, 15*, 71–74.

Wade, T. J., Fuller, L., Bresnan, J., Schaefer, S., & Mlynarski, L. (2007). Weight halo effects: Individual differences in personality evaluations and perceived life success of men as a function of weight. *Personality and Individual Differences, 42*, 317–324.

Walther, J. B., Van Der Heide, B., Kim, S., Westerman, D., & Tong, S. T. (2008). The role of friends' appearance and behavior on evaluations of individuals on Facebook: Are we known by the company we keep? *Human Communication Research, 34*, 28–49.

Washburn, P. V., & Hakel, M. D. (1973). Visual cues and verbal content as influences on impressions formed after simulated employment interviews. *Journal of Applied Psychology, 58*, 137–141.

Weger, H., Seiter, J. S., Jacobs, K. A., & Akbulut, V. (2010). Perceptions of debater effectiveness and appropriateness as a function of decreasingly polite strategies for responding to nonverbal disparagement in televised political debates. *Argumentation and Advocacy, 47*, 39–54.

Weger, H., Seiter, J. S., Jacobs, K. A., & Akbulut, V. (2013). Responses to an opponent's nonverbal behavior in a televised debate: Audience perceptions of credibility and likeability. *Journal of Argumentation in Context, 2*, 179–203. doi:10.1075/jaic.2.2.01weg

Wheeler, S., Book, A., & Costello, K. (2009). Psychopathic traits and perceptions of victim vulnerability. *Criminal Justice and Behavior, 36*, 635–648.

Willis, F. N., & Hamm, H. K. (1980). The use of interpersonal touch in securing compliance. *Journal of Nonverbal Behavior, 5*, 49–55.

Wirth, J. H., Sacco, D. F., Hugenberg, K., & Williams, K. D. (2010). Eye gaze as relational evaluation: Averted eye gaze leads to feelings of ostracism and relational devaluation. *Personality and Social Psychology Bulletin, 36*, 869–882.

Woodall, W. G., & Folger, J. P. (1981). Encoding specificity and nonverbal cue context: An expansion of episodic memory research. *Communication Monographs, 48*, 39–53.

CHAPTER 9

Structuring and Ordering Persuasive Messages

THE STUDY OF PERSUASION and the study of rhetoric, if not one and the same, are closely related. Aristotle, for instance, defined *rhetoric* as "the faculty of discovering all the available means of persuasion." Although, in everyday parlance the term "rhetoric" is often used in conjunction with words such as "empty" or "meaningless," the connotations surrounding the term were not always so negative. The ancient Greeks and Romans, for example, considered rhetoric an essential ingredient in a good education. By the time the great Roman orator Cicero wrote about rhetoric, its study was divided into five parts. Four were called *inventio, elocutio, memoria,* and *pronuntiatio,* which focused on finding and inventing arguments, speaking with style, remembering arguments, and delivering speeches effectively. The last part, *dispositio,* focused on selecting the most important arguments and ideas and on the effective and orderly arrangements of those ideas and arguments (Corbett, 1971). Quintilian, another Roman rhetorician, noted the significance of strategically planning and organizing a persuasive message. As Corbett (1971) wrote:

> Quintilian hints at the more important concern of disposition when he says that it is to oratory what generalship is to war. It would be folly to hold a general to a fixed, predetermined disposition of his forces. He must be left free to distribute his troops in the order and proportion best suited to cope with the situation in which he may find himself at any particular moment. So he will mass some of his troops at one point on the battle line, thin them out at other points, keep other troops in reserve, and perhaps concentrate his crack troops at the most crucial area. Guided by judgment and imagination, the general stands ready to make whatever adjustments in strategy eventualities may dictate.
>
> (pp. 299–300)

When planning a persuasive message, we are often confronted with questions of strategy such as "What should I leave in, and what should I leave out?" "How should I arrange my arguments?" and "Should my strongest arguments come first or last?" However, in addition to questions concerning the order of arguments within persuasive messages, there is the issue of the sequencing of messages when more than one persuader is involved. For example, imagine that you are about to speak to a large audience and want to convince that audience to lower tuition at your school. You know that after you've spoken, another person will argue just the opposite: Tuition should be raised. Is there anything you can do to make your opponent's arguments less powerful? In this chapter we examine these issues.

IMPLICIT AND EXPLICIT CONCLUSIONS: LET ME SPELL IT OUT FOR YOU

According to Lee (2014), one of the most common approaches to advertising is based on the hope that consumers will draw their own inferences, which, in turn, will lead them to hold favorable attitudes toward a specific product. Consider, for example, the following ad:

> A commercial . . . begins when a perky young woman comes on the screen and says, "I've got a question. Pay attention, there will be a quiz later. People prefer their hamburgers at home and flame-broiled. Now, if McDonald's and Wendy's *fry* their hamburgers and Burger King *flame-broils* theirs . . . where do you think people should go for a hamburger?"
>
> (Sawyer, 1988, p. 159)

Because this advertisement relies on customers to draw their own inferences (in this case, "People should go to Burger King"), it uses what persuasion scholars refer to as an *implicit conclusions approach*. Had the spokesperson said, "People should go to Burger King," the ad would have used an *explicit conclusion* approach, in which case claims are directly stated by the person sending the message (e.g., "You should buy our product," or "Our product is simply the best").

One possible advantage of an implicit approach is that receivers may prefer their own conclusions (Kardes, Kim, & Lim, 1994). On the other hand, there are risks. For example, what if receivers are unable to draw the desired conclusions? Perhaps the content of the message is too complex. Or what if the situation doesn't lend itself to "filling in the blanks"? Some forms of entertainment are meant to be persuasive. When people are reading literature or watching television shows, for instance, can they be expected to actively draw conclusions? Or are they simply caught up in the drama, lost in a good book, and better off having conclusions drawn for them?

To find out, one study (Moyer-Guse, Jain, & Chung, 2012) aired an episode of a prime-time television drama (*Law & Order: SVU*) that focused on the issue of drunk driving. After viewing it, one group of participants watched an epilogue, featuring an actress from the show, who explicitly emphasized the dangers of drunk driving. Other participants watched the show or the epilogue, but not both. Results indicated that a combination of episode *and* epilogue was most persuasive. In other words, explicit messages worked best. This seems to be the case not only when it comes to narrative-based materials (e.g., literature and television), but also with persuasive speeches and arguments as well. Indeed, according to one review (Dillard, 2014), explicit messages are most persuasive because they provide clear directions to receivers.

That's not to say that implicit messages should be abandoned altogether. Indeed, given the right conditions, they can be especially effective. For instance, when messages are personally relevant to the receiver (e.g., Bubba is in the market for a new car when a Volkswagen ad pops up), implicit conclusions are more persuasive than explicit ones (Sawyer & Howard, 1991). Similarly, because people who are "high in the need for cognition" (see Chapter 6) are more likely to "fill in the blanks," they prefer implicit approaches to explicit ones (Martin, Lang, and Wong (2003/2004). Finally, when people are suspicious of persuaders' intentions, they tend to view an explicit-conclusion approach as pushy, rendering it less effective than an implicit approach (Martin & Strong, 2016).

GAIN-FRAMED VERSUS LOSS-FRAMED MESSAGES: KEEP ON THE SUNNY SIDE?

Imagine for a moment that one of those deadly swine or avian flu viruses has swept into your neighborhood and is predicted to kill 600 people unless immediate action is taken. If you were in charge and given the following choices, which action would you choose?

Action 1: guarantees that 200 of the 600 people will be saved.
Action 2: gives a 33.3 percent chance that all 600 people will be saved and a 66.6 percent chance that no one will be saved.

Got your answer?

If you are like the majority of people in a classic study conducted by Amos Tversky and Daniel Kahneman (1981), you picked Action 1. Interestingly, however, another group of people were presented with exactly the same scenario, with the options worded in a slightly different way:

Action 1: guarantees that 400 of the 600 people will die.

Action 2: gives a 33.3 percent chance that no one will die and a 66.6 percent chance that everyone will die.

Notice the difference? The first pair of actions looks on the brighter side by focusing on how many lives will be saved, while the second pair of actions portrays the glass half empty by focusing on how many will die. Persuasion scholars refer to messages like the first pair as *gain-framed* and messages like the second pair as *loss-framed*. And it turns out that such framing of messages can make a big difference. Indeed, the majority of people in the second group chose Action 2. This, then, led early researchers to conclude that, people are *risk averse;* they fear losses more than they prefer gains. As such, they are willing to take greater risks in order to avoid or recoup their losses (Tversky & Kahneman, 1981).

Subsequent research, however, suggests that, overall, there are no noticeable differences between the persuasiveness of loss-framed and gain-framed messages (see Dillard, 2014). That said, some conditions may favor one approach over the other. For instance, Nan (2012) found that *present-minded people*, who tend to focus on the short-term consequences of their decisions, responded more favorably to loss-framed messages. However, *future-minded people*, who consider long-term consequences of their decisions, were equally persuaded by loss- and gain-framed messages. Similarly, Hull and Hong (2016) found that people who are *high sensation seekers* (think bungee jumpers and skydivers) are more persuaded by loss-framed messages, while *low sensation seekers* are more persuaded by gain-framed messages. Another study found that, when people are in a good mood, loss-framed messages are most persuasive. This might be because positive moods help people cope with aversive, yet useful, information (Wirtz, Sar, & Ghuge, 2015). Finally, because people may perceive disease-detecting behaviors (e.g., mammography, HIV screening) as risky in the sense that such behaviors might reveal something that is feared, using loss-framed messages may be a more effective way to motivate people to follow through on preventive medical check-ups. A doctor, for instance, might tell a patient, "if you don't detect cancer early, you narrow your options for treatment." In contrast, because people may perceive disease-preventing behaviors (e.g., wearing sunscreen, exercising) as less risky, using gain-framed messages may be more effective. For instance, a doctor might offer a health-affirming message such as, "Eating a lot of veggies will help you maintain your good health." Recent research using meta-analysis suggests that, while gain-framed appeals are indeed more effective than loss-framed appeals when trying to promote dental hygiene (O'Keefe & Jensen, 2007), loss-framed appeals were more effective than gain-framed appeals for promoting breast cancer-detection behaviors (O'Keefe & Jensen, 2009).

QUANTITY VERSUS QUALITY OF ARGUMENTS: THE MORE THE MERRIER?

What are you going to have for your next dinner? If given the choice between an all-you-can-eat buffet and a fancy French restaurant, which would you pick? We imagine your answer depends on whether you like to fill your belly or reward your palate. Indeed, buffets usually offer lots of mediocre food, while a good French restaurant typically promises small portions of fine cuisine. What appeals to you more than likely depends on your priorities.

The same is probably true of persuasive messages. For some people, it is the *quantity* of arguments presented that counts. For them, a "kitchen sink" approach in which an advocate throws in every available argument works best. For other people, it is the *quality* of arguments that counts. For such people, the number of arguments is inconsequential. They require "gourmet" arguments. To illustrate this notion, we return briefly to Petty and Cacioppo's (1986) elaboration likelihood model (ELM), which we discussed in more detail in Chapter 2.

Recall that, according to the ELM, there are two routes to persuasion: the *peripheral route* and the *central route*. First, when people are persuaded by a message that they have carefully scrutinized, they are being persuaded via the central route (of course, after scrutinizing a message, they may also remain unpersuaded). Often, however, people do not scrutinize the persuasive messages. Instead, they rely on the peripheral route, which involves mental shortcuts and simple decision rules.

According to Petty and Cacioppo (1984), one type of peripheral cue may be the number of arguments that a persuader presents. These researchers reasoned that some people might decide that a persuasive message containing a lot of arguments must be a lot better than one that does not ("It must be a good argument! Look at all those reasons!"). Of course, not all people would be persuaded by a lot of weak arguments. People who carefully scrutinized the arguments, they hypothesized, would not be fooled. Results of one study (Petty & Cacioppo, 1984) supported this hypothesis. Specifically, when people were not involved in a topic, the quality of the arguments they heard did not matter. Quantity did, however. They tended to be persuaded by a lot of arguments, even if the arguments were weak. In contrast, when people were involved in the topic they were not taken in by a lot of weak arguments. They were persuaded only when strong arguments were used, especially when there were a lot of strong arguments (Petty & Cacioppo, 1984). The moral of this line of research, then, is the following: If you think your audience will scrutinize your message, use strong arguments, but if your audience does not seem involved in the topic, a smorgasbord of arguments may be quite effective.

THE USE OF EVIDENCE: THE PROOF'S NOT IN THE PUDDING

Different persuasive claims require different types of proof. One common form of proof is evidence. Evidence comes in many forms including narratives, personal anecdotes, statistics, quotations, testimonials, graphs and charts, and more. Physical evidence may be offered as well (e.g., lipstick on a collar, a "smoking gun" memo). As a general rule, evidence facilitates persuasion. A meta-analysis by Reinard (1988) demonstrates that as long as the evidence is relevant to the claim being made, evidence is almost always persuasive. As is the case with the quantity versus quality of arguments discussed above, the quantity of evidence matters more when receivers have low involvement, whereas the quality of evidence matters more when receivers have high involvement.

Evidence sometimes functions as a *peripheral cue*. For example, a prosecutor might pile up a "mountain" of evidence against a defendant. The sheer quantity of evidence may seem so great that jurors infer that the defendant must be guilty. However, evidence is put to best use when receivers rely on *central processing* (Reynolds & Reynolds, 2002). A meta-analysis by Stiff (1986) revealed a significant positive correlation between evidence use and attitude change, especially when receivers were involved in the topic or issue.

Another benefit of using evidence is that it tends to increase a source's perceived credibility (O'Keefe, 1998). Reinard (1988) found a *ceiling effect* for the persuasiveness of evidence. If a source already has very high credibility, evidence won't help. Most everyday persuaders, however, need all the help they can get. Unless you are the foremost expert in the world on an issue, go ahead and include high-quality evidence, and lots of it, in your persuasive message.

One question that has been raised is whether some types of evidence are more persuasive than others. For instance, two meta-analyses have shown that using *statistical proof* is more effective than using *anecdotal* or *narrative proof* (Allen & Preiss, 1997; Kim et al., 2012). Other studies (e.g., Braverman, 2008; Han & Fink, 2012; Hoeken & Hustinx, 2009) suggest that statistical evidence works best under some conditions (e.g., when making generalizations, when there is a lot of evidence, or when receiver involvement is high) while narrative proof works best in others (e.g., when narratives are vivid or when receiver involvement is low) (for additional considerations, see Box 9.1).

Although such studies are fascinating for academic reasons, Braddock and Dillard (2016) argued that they are only meaningful if we assume that narrative and statistical evidence are naturally opposed to one other, which they are not. Indeed, not only are narratives persuasive in and of themselves, "sometimes, characters in narratives speak

"In the case of the missing pork chop, all the facts, statistics, and evidence support the butcher's side, but we find the defendant adorable and his story irresistible."

FIGURE 9.1
A butcher and a dog are in court.
Source: Cartoon by John Seiter and Robert Gass.

BOX 9.1 | The Identifiable Victim Effect

A short time ago, in a small community where one of the authors lives, a 14-year-old girl was found lying in a dry canal, shot in the back of her head. The suspects, two teenage boys, had allegedly lured her to the secluded location with plans to murder her. And yet, she survived. As the girl clung to life, people hurried to raise money. The author was moved to contribute, partly because of the incident's proximity, but mostly because the girl became more than just a statistic. Her name, photo, and story not only appeared on TV and newspapers, it was posted in banks, grocery stores, and other places the author frequently visited.

Beyond its horrible nature, the ordeal illustrates a phenomenon known as the *identifiable victim effect* (IVE), which suggests that people are more willing to help specific, recognizable victims than anonymous, statistical victims (Jenni & Loewenstein, 1997; Schelling, 1968; Small, Lowenstein, & Slovic, 2007). Why? According to Lee and Feeley (2017), an identifiable victim evokes stronger emotional reactions than a statistical victim. According to a meta-analysis of over 40 studies, this is especially true when the victim is a photographed child suffering from poverty and/or bearing little responsibility for the need (Lee & Feeley, 2016).

in statistical arguments" (Braddock & Dillard, 2016, p. 448). As such, we think it's better to view different types of evidence as teammates rather than competitors. Specifically, if each type of evidence contributes to the persuasiveness of a message, why not include all of them in your message? Previous literature supports this approach. Reinard (1988), for instance, argued that a persuader might combine narrative and statistical evidence for maximum effect. He recommends starting with a narrative example and then following up with statistics to show that the example is not atypical. Moreover, a recent meta-analysis indicated that the persuasive effects of different types of evidence (i.e., assertive evidence, statistical evidence, and evidence source qualification) were additive, meaning that each contributed to the persuasiveness of a message (Kim et al., 2012). Go team!

REPETITION AND MERE EXPOSURE: YOU CAN SAY THAT AGAIN

Although earlier we saw that using a lot of arguments in a message can sometimes make you more persuasive, what happens if you use the *same* argument or message repeatedly? Stated differently, can repeating your message make you more persuasive? Several researchers have argued that *message repetition* can be an effective tactic, although there is some disagreement concerning why. One perspective that has received considerable attention by persuasion scholars is known as the *mere exposure effect* (Zajonc, 1968). According to Sawyer (1981), "This theory hypothesizes that familiar objects are more liked than less familiar ones, and that by merely being repetitively exposed, something initially unfamiliar will be looked upon more favorably" (p. 238). In other words, mere exposure theory suggests that we really do "acquire tastes," that things can "grow on us," and that "familiarity does *not* breed contempt." By way of example, previous research has found that people's faces are rated as more likable (Rhodes, Halberstadt, & Brajkovich, 2001) and attractive (Peskin & Newell, 2004) after repeated viewing, suggesting that the old saying "love at first sight" should be reconsidered. Research also suggests that the effect might generalize to other, similar faces. For instance, one study found that, compared to White participants who had not been exposed to images of Black and Asian people's faces, those who had been exposed reported greater liking for a different set of Black and Asian faces (Zebrowitz, White, & Wieneke, 2008).

In one of our favorite classic studies, Zajonc (1968) found that repeated exposure even made the Chinese language more likable to people who didn't know how to read or speak it. In the study, subjects saw pictures of Chinese characters anywhere from 1 to 25 times. Afterward, the subjects were asked to guess the meanings of the characters. Interestingly, the characters that were seen most often were "defined" in much more positive ways than were the characters that were seen less often. With this in mind, it's not surprising to us that politicians pepper front yards, telephone poles, bumpers, and just about anything they can get their hands on with their names and faces.

Although research has shown that mere and repeated exposure to songs, people, languages, and posters may increase likability, there has been some disagreement about whether repeating longer or more complex messages is persuasive. Several studies, for example, have found evidence for an inverted U-curve in which repetition is persuasive up to a point (about three repetitions), but after that, excessive repetition decreases a message's persuasiveness (e.g., see Reinhard, Schindler, Raabe, Stahlberg, & Messner, 2014). Why? Some researchers suggest that excessive repetition damages perceptions of source credibility (Reinhard et al., 2014). Others suggest that it leads to boredom or irritation (Petty & Cacioppo, 1979), which may depend, of course, on how creative the message is (Lehnert, Till, & Carlson, 2013). The authors, for example, are so tired of that tedious Energizer bunny that they wish it would "keep going and going" and never come back!!! And as long as we're complaining, is anybody else as tired as we are of those advertisements repeatedly popping up on their mobile devices? If so, they've apparently got company. Indeed, one study found that businesses can get away with sending two SMS advertisements a day. After that, the ads cease to be persuasive, perhaps because they're perceived as irritating (Rau, Zhou, Chen, & Lu, 2014).

Finally, some research (Claypool, Mackie, Garcia-Marques, McIntosh, & Udall, 2004) suggests that the way people respond to repetition depends on how personally relevant the message is to the audience. Earlier, for example, we discussed a study involving messages about comprehensive exams. For students who thought they might have to take the exams, the messages were personally relevant. The opposite was true of those who thought they would never take the exams.

Claypool and her colleagues found that when people were presented with a familiar message that was not personally relevant to them, they were likely to respond to the message nonanalytically (analogous to peripheral processing in the ELM). In other words, rather than actively think about the message, the people responded to it merely on the basis of previously stored information. As a result, repetition did not increase the persuasiveness of strong over weak arguments.

On the other hand, when the people were presented with a familiar message that was personally relevant to them, they were likely to process the message analytically (this is analogous to ELM's central route to persuasion). Because repetition provided them with more opportunities to scrutinize the message, strong messages were more persuasive than weak ones when they were repeated (Claypool et al., 2004). In short, like other studies we have seen so far, the research on repetition illustrates the importance of knowing your audience before trying to persuade it.

ORDER EFFECTS AND PERSUASION: FIRST THINGS FIRST

In the preceding sections, we've seen that strong arguments are not always the most persuasive and that people are generally more willing to hear a strong argument repeated rather than a weak one. Sometimes, however, it is not so easy to separate strong from weak arguments. In other words, persuasive messages often contain many arguments, some stronger than others. When that happens, whoever is delivering the persuasive message must decide how he or she should arrange the arguments. For example, imagine you're planning to give a persuasive speech. Should you begin with your strongest argument to create a favorable first impression? Or would it be better to dazzle your audience at the end of your speech so that the audience leaves feeling motivated? Of course, there's always a third option: You could compromise and put your strongest argument in the middle of your speech.

When strong arguments come first, a message is said to have an *anticlimax order*. When they come last, a message has a *climax order*. A message with a *pyramidal order* has strong arguments in the middle. But which order works best? Most research on this subject suggests that putting your strongest argument either first *or* last is the best strategy (e.g., Sikkink, 1956). Both seem to work better than sandwiching strong arguments in the middle of a speech, but beyond that, strong arguments seem effective at either the beginning or end of a message.

Of course, other variables may determine whether strong or weak arguments should go first or last. For example, Unnaba, Burnkrant, and Erevelles (1994) argued that the medium, or channel, by which a message is transmitted should determine whether strong arguments go first or last. Their study found that when groups were visually exposed to information about the characteristics of a book bag, their attitudes about the bag were the same whether they were exposed first to strong or weak arguments about the bag's quality. However, if they received auditory messages about the bag, they had more favorable attitudes when strong arguments came before weak arguments. Thus, when information is presented for people to hear, order is important.

PRIMACY AND RECENCY EFFECTS: THE FIRST SHALL BE LAST, AND THE LAST SHALL BE FIRST

Up to this point, we've been looking at how arguments should be selected and organized within a single speech. The issue of what goes first and what goes last extends beyond single speeches, however. It is also possible to consider whether *who*

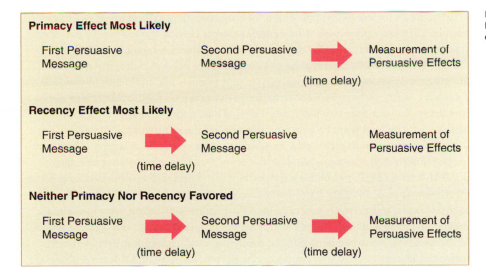

FIGURE 9.2
Primacy versus recency effects in persuasion.

goes first and *who* goes last affects the process of persuasion. Nowadays, it is quite common for political candidates to be involved in debates that are not very interactive. A coin is flipped, one candidate speaks, and then the other takes a turn. When that happens, is there any advantage to speaking first, or do all good things come to those who wait? As with research on climax and anticlimax, results in this area are mixed; some studies support a *primacy effect* (i.e., the first arguments presented have an advantage) but others support a *recency effect* (i.e., the later arguments presented have an advantage). However, several studies have investigated whether some circumstances favor primacy whereas others favor recency. We consider two such circumstances now.

First, a classic study by Miller and Campbell (1959) demonstrated that the passage of time determines whether primacy or recency prevails. Primacy, they found, works best when you hear two opposing messages, back to back, and then have to wait a while before deciding what to do about the messages. For instance, a primacy effect is likely when you hear one candidate speak right after another and then wait a week before voting for one of the candidates. Why should this scenario work to the advantage of the candidate who speaks first? According to Miller and Campbell (1959), with time we tend to remember information we receive first. In other words, first impressions may be lasting impressions.

However, Miller and Campbell (1959) found that the recency effect is more likely when you hear one message, wait some time before hearing the opposing message, and then decide immediately after the second message what you are going to do. For instance, a recency effect is likely if you hear one candidate give a speech and then, just before voting, hear the opposing candidate give a speech. Why, in this situation, should the second candidate prevail? The researchers argued that because we tend to forget information rapidly, we'll have forgotten most of the first message by the time we vote. However, voting immediately after hearing the second message should enable us to remember most of the candidate's message, giving him or her an advantage (see Figure 9.2).[1]

In addition to time delay, the content of a message may determine whether first messages are more persuasive than second messages or vice versa. For instance, some research indicates that material that is relatively unsalient, noncontroversial, uninteresting, and unfamiliar to the audience tends to produce a recency effect. However, salient, interesting, controversial, and familiar material tends to produce a primacy effect, perhaps because an audience starts with a high level of interest that decreases over time (see Furnham, 1986). Thus, if given the choice to speak first or last, you may want to base your decision on the nature of your material.

So far, we've seen that the order in which we are exposed to messages affects how we respond to such messages, but does the same hold true when we are sampling products? Nowadays, it's common for marketers to spend billions of dollars each year (Wadhwa, Shiv, & Nowlis, 2008) beckoning consumers with samples of products such as cheese, music, wine, and perfume. While some folks might sample one item, others, including a couple authors we know (ahem!), make meals through the process of "researching" multiple items. If you, too, are a multiple sampler, you might be interested in a series of studies conducted by Biswas, Grewal, and Roggeveen (2010). These researchers examined what would happen if people sampled and evaluated more than one product. Results of their initial studies found evidence for a recency effect. Specifically, when people sampled two equally desirable music clips, they preferred the clip they sampled second, but when they sampled two equally undesirable music clips, they preferred the one they had sampled first. The same results were found for beverage samplers. This, the authors argued, is because people have better recall for what they sampled last. As such, if whatever they sampled last seemed icky, they preferred the alternative. In contrast, if whatever they sampled last seemed delightful, they stuck with it.

Interestingly, however, the pattern of results changed depending on the product being sampled. Specifically, in one of their later studies, Biswas and colleagues (2010) found, as they had before, that people who sampled two equally desirable music clips preferred the second clip. Conversely, people who sampled two equally desirable scissors preferred the first pair of scissors. How can these results be explained? According to Biswas et al., *nonexperiential products*, such as scissors, are different from *experiential products*, such as food and music. This is because evaluations of experiential products depend on sensory reactions rather than informational components. Such sensory reactions are more immediate, thereby giving recently sampled products an advantage. In contrast, evaluations of nonexperiential products depend on informational components (e.g., the scissors' blade sharpness, material, shape). As such, when sampling them, consumers' short-term working memory can become crowded, making people less likely to notice the desirable qualities of the follow-up product. As a consequence, they tend to prefer the first product.

AN OUNCE OF PREVENTION: INOCULATION, MESSAGE-SIDEDNESS, AND FOREWARNING

Parents sometimes admonish their children by saying "and if your friends told you to jump off a cliff, would you do that, too?" Scolding kids for something they've already done, however, may just make them feel dumb. We're sure that parents would much rather prevent their children from doing "dumb stuff" in the first place. Likewise, governments have and still wish to prevent their citizens from adopting certain political viewpoints. For instance, did you know that citizens of the former Soviet Union were not supposed to play Monopoly, a clearly capitalistic game? Moreover, after World War II, there was widespread paranoia in the United States that Americans would be brainwashed by Communist propaganda. In short, although most of this book has been devoted to examining how people persuade other people, oftentimes a more immediate concern centers on how to *prevent* people from being persuaded. This section discusses research and theory on such preventive attempts. Because the term "prevention" often implies something happening *before* something else, we hope it's clear why we've included this topic in a chapter on order effects in persuasion. We begin by examining inoculation theory, a classic perspective developed by William McGuire (1964).

Inoculation Theory: Of Needles and Arguments

Inoculation theory might best be understood by using a biological analogy. Specifically, if you want to keep your body healthy, what should you do? One strategy is to eat your Wheaties and Flintstones vitamins, avoid fats and sugars, stay rested, and exercise. This is what is known as a *supportive strategy* or treatment. The rationale here is that a stronger body will be more effective at fending off diseases and viruses. A second way to stay healthy is through *inoculation*. Perhaps your rear end has forgotten all of those needles it encountered in your youth (e.g., DPT immunizations), but if you've ever had a flu shot or treated your dog or cat to a rabies booster, you're familiar with the reasoning behind such injections. The idea is that if you or Fido are exposed to a small dose of a disease virus, your bodies are better able to defend themselves against the virus later. This is because a dose that is too small to give you the disease often stimulates your body's defenses. Thus, if exposed to a stronger dose of the virus later, your body can overpower it.

According to McGuire (1964), this metaphor can also be applied to situations involving persuasion. For example, imagine you are a lawyer hired to defend someone who is accused of murder but who is innocent. You realize that after you have a chance to present your case, another lawyer will argue against you, presenting evidence that he or she hopes will help convict your client. With that in mind, what might you do? First, you could use a *supportive strategy*, making the jury's belief in your client's innocence as "healthy" as possible by spending a lot of time discussing reasons why the client is not guilty. On the other hand, you could use an *inoculation strategy*, which consists of two parts. The first, *threat*, warns jurors that a challenging argument is approaching. The second, *refutational preemption*, exposes jurors to weak doses of the approaching arguments and shows how such arguments might be refuted. The hope is that jurors exposed to weak doses of the opposition's argument will be less persuaded.

In a classic test of inoculation theory, McGuire and Papageorgis (1961) focused on the support and refutation of *cultural truisms*. A cultural truism is a belief whose truth is taken for granted. For example, the idea that "it is good to brush your teeth after every meal, if possible" is a cultural truism because it is generally accepted in our culture. According to McGuire and Papageorgis, however, cultural truisms should also be especially vulnerable when attacked. This is most likely because they have never been questioned. Returning to the biological metaphor for a moment, imagine that you were raised in a plastic bubble all your life, breathing only pure, germ-free air. What would happen if you stepped out of the bubble? Your body, having never been exposed to germs, would be especially vulnerable to them. Indeed, huge numbers of Native Americans died when missionaries exposed them to smallpox and other unfamiliar European viruses. According to McGuire and Papageorgis, the same thing can happen with cultural truisms. Unlike beliefs on such topics as capital punishment and the legalization of drugs, which may be challenged frequently, cultural truisms exist in what amounts to hermetically sealed bubbles; they've never been questioned, they've never required defense, and, therefore, they are sitting ducks when attacked. Even so, McGuire and Papageorgis (1961) argued that inoculation could help defend such beliefs.

To test this notion, these researchers exposed participants in their study to several messages that attacked cultural truisms (e.g., brushing your teeth too much damages the teeth's protective enamel). Two days before hearing the attacking messages, however, the participants were provided with one of two defenses against the attacks. One group of participants was equipped with a *supportive defense*—that is, they were presented with several arguments that supported the cultural truisms. A second group of participants received an *inoculation defense* against the attacking message; they heard weak messages attacking a cultural truism in addition to arguments that refuted the attacks. A third group of participants was not provided with any defense. After hearing the attacking messages, the participants rated the degree to which they believed the cultural truisms were true or false. Results of the study supported the researchers' expectations. Specifically, both the supportive and inoculation defenses were better than no defense at all at making participants more resistant to persuasion. Moreover, the group that had been inoculated was the most resistant to the attacking messages. A recent meta-analysis of more than 40 studies arrived at the same conclusion: Inoculation treatments are more effective than supportive treatments and nontreatments at conferring resistance to persuasion (Banas & Rains, 2010).

Research also suggests that inoculating people against one particular argument may make them resistant to other, different arguments (Papageorgis & McGuire, 1961; Parker, Rains, & Ivanov, 2016). This *"blanket of protection,"* as it has been called (Pfau, 1997), is analogous to getting penicillin for pneumonia, but, as a result, also being protected against strep throat, scarlet fever, and rheumatic fever. For example, imagine you hold the belief that a person should drink eight glasses of water a day. A counterargument might be that too much water neutralizes acids that you need for proper digestion. To get you to resist such a counterargument, we might inoculate you by providing weak doses and refutations of the "neutralize acid" argument. In doing so, the research shows that you will become more resistant to other, new arguments to which you weren't originally exposed. For instance, you will be more resistant to a message that says drinking too much water now can wear out your bladder and lead to incontinence in old age.

Why would such generalized immunization work? According to Papageorgis and McGuire (1961), inoculation causes people to think of more arguments that support their beliefs, thereby making subsequent attacking arguments less credible. Thus, once

BOX 9.2 | When Smoke Gets in Your Eyes: Inoculation Theory Applied

It's clear from our discussion of inoculation theory that inoculation works effectively with messages that attack cultural truisms in laboratory settings. But how does the theory pan out when tested in "real-life" settings? First, Pfau, Van Bockern, and Kang (1992) argued that inoculation might be a good approach to use if you want to prevent young adolescents from smoking cigarettes. According to these researchers' sources, more than 3,000 teenagers become smokers each day and, as a result, millions die of smoke-related diseases later in life. Because more than half of all smokers become "regulars" before high school, Pfau and colleagues (1992) conducted their study using seventh graders. The students were shown videos that (1) warned them that peer pressure might cause them to change their minds about smoking and (2) presented and refuted arguments that challenged the students' attitudes about smoking (e.g., smoking is cool). Results showed that inoculation helped students resist smoking, but only if the students had low self-esteem. Interestingly, however, a follow-up study two years later found just the opposite: Inoculation worked for students with high self-esteem but not for those with low self-esteem (Pfau & Van Bockern, 1994). Thus, inoculation may wear off for those with low self-esteem, but there may be a sleeper effect for those with high self-esteem. Whatever the case, the authors argue that inoculating children against smoking must occur between elementary school and high school. After that, resistance strategies do not seem to work (Pfau & Van Bockern, 1994).

Second, Pfau, Kenski, Nitz, and Sorenson (1990) examined inoculation in political campaigns. These researchers noted that negative advertisements, in which one politician attacks another, are becoming more common and that one-third to one-half of all political ads may be negative. With that in mind, what should politicians do? One possibility is to inoculate voters; another is to wait until they are attacked and then refute the attacks. To test which strategy works best, Pfau and colleagues sent messages to voters during the 1988 presidential campaign. Voters received messages attacking their preferred candidate. Some of the voters were inoculated before being exposed to the attack message. Other voters, after being exposed to the attack message, received a message that refuted it. Results of the study found that an inoculation strategy worked the best. Those voters who had been inoculated were the least affected by the attack message.

In short, research has shown inoculation theory to be robust in applied contexts. Of course, given our space, we have only been able to scratch the surface here, but we hope you can imagine the wide array of contexts where an inoculation approach shows promise. For instance, recent research has detailed the ways in which inoculation might be used to defend people against conspiracy propaganda (Banas & Miller, 2013), deceptive advertising (Mason & Miller, 2016), and inoculation itself (Banas & Miller, 2013).

a cultural truism has been defended, it is easier to defend against a later attack, even if the arguments attacking it are different from the original arguments.

Over time, inoculation theory has been refined. Researchers have discovered a number of variables that influence resistance to persuasion, including the audience's level of involvement with a topic (Pfau et al., 2004), and the degree to which psychological reactance (e.g., telling people that their freedom to hold a current attitude will be challenged) can give a boost to inoculation effects (Miller, Ivanov, Sims, Compton, Harrison, Parker, Parker, & Averbeck, 2013). Although we do not have space enough to discuss such research here, if you are hungry for more on inoculation theory, check out Box 9.2.

One-Sided Versus Two-Sided Messages: Both Sides Now

In the previous section, we saw that either supportive or inoculation treatments can be effective at making people resistant to persuasion. With that in mind, you might be wondering if a *combination* of supportive and inoculation treatments might work even better. A considerable amount of past research has examined this issue by trying to determine whether a *one-sided message,* presenting arguments in favor of a single proposition, is more or less persuasive than a *two-sided message,* which presents arguments in favor of one proposition and considers opposing arguments as well. In other words, when trying to persuade an audience to accept your arguments and reject your opponent's arguments, is it best to address your opposition or ignore them?

The first empirical study to investigate this issue was conducted by Hovland, Lumsdaine, and Sheffield (1949), at the request of the War Department during World War II. The study's purpose was to determine the best way to convince U.S. soldiers that the war in Japan would last a considerable amount of time. The researchers asked their subjects to listen to one of two messages. One presented arguments that supported the war with Japan and argued that the war would be a long one. The other message included the same arguments as the first, in addition to a brief description of opposing arguments. Results of the study found that the effectiveness of one- or two-sided arguments depended on two factors: education level and initial attitude. First, the one-sided message was more effective for persuading subjects with little education, whereas the two-sided message was more effective for persuading subjects who had at least a high school education. Second, when the subjects initially agreed with the argument presented, they were more persuaded by the one-sided argument. Just the opposite was true of subjects who initially disagreed with the argument presented.

Although the large number of studies examining the effects of one- and two-sided messages has produced some contradictory findings, work by Daniel O'Keefe (1999) and Mike Allen (1998) has demonstrated that such findings are not contradictory when you consider the type of two-sided messages that have been used in past studies. Specifically, they argue that some studies have used two-sided messages that are *nonrefutational.* In these messages, opposing arguments are mentioned but not argued against. However, some studies have used two-sided messages that are *refutational,* such as those used in the inoculation studies discussed earlier. In these messages, opposing arguments are not only mentioned but also shown to be inferior to the position advocated by the speaker.

These researchers suspected that *two-sided messages* that are refutational would be much more persuasive than those that merely mention opposing arguments. In fact, they suspected that two-sided arguments that did not refute opposing arguments might make a speaker less persuasive than would *one-sided arguments*. Hence, the contradictions of past research.

To test their idea, these researchers (Allen, 1998; Allen et al., 1990; O'Keefe, 1999) examined a large number of previous studies on message-sidedness, this time taking into account both types of two-sided messages. What they found confirmed their hypothesis: Two-sided messages were more persuasive than one-sided messages, as long as the two-sided messages were refutational. When they were not refutational, they were less persuasive than one-sided messages (see Table 9.1). Moreover, speakers

TABLE 9.1 Hierarchy of Effectiveness for Message-Sidedness

Type of Message	Effectiveness
Two-sided refutational message	Most effective (20% more effective than a one-sided message)
One-sided message	Second most effective (20% more effective than a two-sided nonrefutational message)
Two-sided nonrefutational message	Least effective

who used two-sided refutational messages were more credible than those who used one-sided messages (O'Keefe, 1999), which makes sense. Indeed, such speakers may not only seem more informed, they may seem more trustworthy because they are sharing the opposing side's point of view. Consistent with this notion, Eisend (2010) found that speakers boosted their credibility when they presented two-sided messages, as long as they were perceived to be doing so voluntarily. This, of course, makes sense. If a spokesperson for a cigarette company disclosed all the negative side effects that might result from smoking, and we knew the spokesperson was required to do so by law, why should we trust him or her? Whatever the case, the practical implications of this research are clear: When delivering a message, present the opponent's perspective, but make sure you "go all the way" by refuting your opponent's position. It will make you appear more credible and help you be more persuasive. This is particularly true when your audience is ambivalent about the issue (Cornelis, Cauberghe, & De Pelsmacker, 2013).

Forewarning: You'd Better Watch Out

In the classic film *A Few Good Men,* Kevin Bacon and Tom Cruise play lawyers who are prosecuting and defending two Marines accused of murder. At the beginning of the trial, Bacon's character, the prosecutor, tells the jury to beware; the defense attorney, he warns, "will try a little misdirection. He's going to astonish you with stories of rituals and dazzle you with official-sounding terms like 'Code Red.'" A similar tactic was used in the 2000 presidential campaign, when Al Gore warned voters that George W. Bush would try to scare them about issues such as Medicare. In each of these cases, the warnings were not effective (both Bacon and Gore lost), but considerable research indicates that *forewarning* an audience of a persuasive message can be an effective way of making the audience resistant to that message. Of course, this line of research is related to inoculation, although the two tactics are distinct; whereas inoculation refutes and exposes people to a weakened dose of the attacking message, forewarning only makes people aware of a possible *counterattitudinal* attack.

According to Papageorgis (1968), there are two types of forewarning messages. First, you can simply warn people that they will hear a message intended to persuade them. Second, you can warn people by telling them about the topic and position taken in the persuasive message. Research indicates that both tactics are moderately effective at inducing resistance to persuasion (see Benoit, 1998). Even so, the process by which each tactic works may be different. For instance, when people are warned about a topic and position, it permits them to arm themselves with counterarguments before the attack. If forewarning about a persuasive topic and position works by making people *counterargue*, Freedman and Sears (1965) thought that the amount of time between the warning and the persuasive speech might be an important variable moderating the effect of forewarning. They hypothesized that people who were given more time between the warning and the persuasive message would be able to think of more counterarguments and should, therefore, be more resistant to persuasion than those who were given little time. To test this hypothesis, the researchers told high school students that they would hear a message arguing that teenagers were a menace on the road and should not be allowed to drive. After being warned, some of the students were exposed to the message immediately, while others did not hear the message for 2 or 10 minutes. Results of the study confirmed the hypothesis; the high schoolers who waited 10 minutes were most resistant to the message. Those who were exposed to the message immediately were least resistant.

Despite these findings, some scholars have questioned the notion that forewarning leads to counterarguing and then resistance. Meta-analyses by Benoit (1998), Quinn and Wood (2004), and Wood and Quinn (2003), for instance, found that the presence of a delay between a warning and a message did not matter. Thus, there is some question as to whether counterarguing is really necessary for developing resistance.

To examine this issue further, Romero, Agnew, and Insko (1996) conducted a study. These researchers argued that if forewarning leads people to counterargue, then we should notice two things. First, people who are more motivated to counterargue should be more affected by forewarning than those who are not. Second, people who have the ability to counterargue should be more affected by forewarning than those who do not have the ability.

To test this notion, Romero and colleagues (1996) forewarned college students who either did or did not have the motivation or ability to counterargue with a persuasive message. The researchers motivated some of the students to counterargue by making the topic of the message more personally relevant to them. Specifically, they told some of the students that the message they were about to be exposed to argued that they all should be required to take comprehensive exams before graduation. The remaining students were told that the comprehensive exams would not be required for 10 years, long after they had left the university. Thus, this second group of students was not that motivated to counterargue. In addition, the researchers hindered some students' ability to counterargue by distracting them. Specifically, after they were warned, some students simply waited 3 minutes before being exposed to the message about comprehensive exams. Other students, however, were distracted during the 3 minutes with difficult letter and number puzzles. Thus, their ability to counterargue was hampered. Results of the study confirmed the researchers' suspicions; compared to students without the motivation and ability to counterargue, the students who found the topic personally relevant and who were not distracted by puzzles were more resistant to the persuasive message (for more on distraction and persuasion, see Box 9.3). In short, it seems that forewarning of topic and position made people more resistant by encouraging counterarguing.

That said, while 3 minutes without distraction helped people who had been forewarned, some evidence suggests that the effects of forewarning can wear off over longer periods of time. One study, for example, warned a group of older adults to be wary of a particular telephone scam. Later, these same adults were contacted via telephone with the same mock scam. Interestingly, those who were contacted 2 weeks after being warned were generally able to defend themselves, but those who were contacted 4 weeks later were not (Scheibe et al., 2014).

An additional line of forewarning research is based on the *strength model of self-control* (see Baumeister, Vohs, & Tice, 2007). According to this model, in the same way that our muscles get tired from exertion, our mental resources become depleted when we work hard to regulate our behavior. As a result of such depletion, our willpower suffers. If you've ever been to a dinner party while trying to diet, you may understand just how exhausting self-control can be. And if you're at all like us, by the end of such meals, you've been spotted shoveling dessert into your face by the handful. But what if you'd been warned before arriving to the party that your favorite dessert was on the menu? Would you be better able to resist it? According to Janssen, Fennis and Pruyn (2010), such warnings are effective because, when exposed to them, we conserve our mental resources so we can mobilize them when needed later. To illustrate, these researchers conducted several studies. In them, some participants were mentally tuckered out (e.g., they gave speeches about themselves but were not allowed to use the word "I"), while others were not. In addition, some participants were warned that they would eventually be exposed to persuasive

BOX 9.3 | Distraction and Persuasion

Did you know that it is not unheard of for people working on political campaigns to send hecklers to their opponents' speeches? The practice is known as bracketing (Pinocchio index, 1996). It almost certainly is designed to fluster the heckled candidate. What bracketers may not be aware of, however, is that heckling may actually benefit the heckled speaker. Indeed, a study by Beatty and Kruger (1978) found that when an audience identifies with a heckled speaker, the speaker is more persuasive and is perceived as more credible. But how is it possible that the effects of heckling can be exactly opposite to those intended? According to one perspective, distraction, whether caused by hecklers, flashing lights, eating, static, loud noises, or other things, prevents people from scrutinizing a counterattitudinal message. And if they cannot scrutinize the message, people are more likely to be persuaded by it.

Although considerable research supports this explanation (e.g., Festinger & Maccoby, 1964; Keating & Brock, 1974; Osterhouse & Brock, 1970), Buller (1986) and Buller and Hall (1998) examined several studies and found more support for a different perspective. Specifically, learning theory (McGuire, 1969) argues that to be persuaded, people must first comprehend a message. Because distraction hinders comprehension, distraction also should decrease the persuasiveness of a message. Buller and Hall's work supports this notion by indicating that distraction generally reduces the effectiveness of a persuasive message. This may depend, however, on the type of distraction being examined. For instance, in addition to distraction that is external to a communicator (such as hecklers and loud noises), a second type of distraction can be initiated by the communicator. For example, you might be distracted by someone who stands too close or who uses intense language. According to Buller and Hall, when a distraction is initiated by a communicator, our reaction depends not so much on comprehension or counterarguments as on the communicator's credibility. Specifically, when distracted by a highly credible source, we tend to be more persuaded; when distracted by a less credible source, we tend to be less persuaded. Thus, if you are a highly credible source and want to be persuasive, feel free to distract your audience.

messages asking them to volunteer their time or money for charitable causes. Results showed that mentally depleted participants, compared to nondepleted participants, were more persuadable unless they had been forewarned. Apparently, the forewarned participants conserved their mental energy, enabling them to counterargue effectively and, in turn, to resist influence.

It may be the case, however, that counterarguing is not the only factor mediating the effectiveness of forewarning. To be sure, a study by Jacks and Devine (2000) found that, for some people, forewarning heightened not only counterarguing but also irritation—that is, some people, when warned that specific attitudes they held would be attacked, became more agitated and angry. This, in turn, led them to be more resistant to attacks (Jacks & Devine, 2000).

Although warning people about a topic and position provides them with an opportunity to think of and rehearse counterarguments, it is clear that the other type of warning—a warning about persuasive intent—does not. Indeed, if people don't know what the topic will be, how can they think of counterarguments? But if counterarguing is not responsible for the effectiveness of this type of warning, what is? As noted in Chapter 8, Brehm (1966) and Brehm and Brehm (1981) argued that when people feel that their freedom to behave or think in a certain way is restricted, they experience *psychological reactance* and attempt to restore their freedom. If you've ever tried reverse psychology on a child, you are familiar with how psychological reactance works. For instance, some time ago, one of the authors was having trouble getting his preschooler to pack up his toys, leave his pals, and get in the car to go home. The child, of course, thought he had the freedom to choose: stay with his pals or get in the car. However, when dad pretended he was leaving without his son, the child gathered his toys and hurried into the car. Why? His freedom to choose the ride home was being taken away. He was reacting to the loss of freedom.

According to some writers (see Fukada, 1986; Hass & Grady, 1975), this phenomenon occurs when you are warned that someone intends to persuade you. It's like a comedian who tells you that he or she will make you laugh before telling a joke. We like to feel free to laugh or to be persuaded, and if we feel that freedom is in jeopardy, we experience *psychological reactance*; we don't laugh or we resist persuasion. To illustrate this principle, Fukada told one group of people that they would be exposed to a message intended to make them afraid and to change their attitude. Another group did not receive the warning. Later, both groups received a message that tried to persuade them to be tested for syphilis. Results indicated that the warned group not only experienced more psychological reactance, it was also less persuaded than the unwarned group.

Before concluding this section, we should note that not all research indicates that forewarning increases resistance to persuasion. Indeed, a meta-analysis by Wood and Quinn (2003; see also Quinn & Wood, 2004) found that, in some cases, forewarning shifts attitudes toward the impending message. It all depends on the motives of the audience. Specifically, as we have seen, when people want to defend their existing attitudes, forewarning is effective at increasing resistance. On the other hand, sometimes warnings threaten people's self-concepts by suggesting that they may be gullible or vulnerable to influence. Rather than resist, people may shift their attitude toward the future appeal in order to reduce its impact. In other cases, people may be concerned about the impressions they are leaving on others. For instance, they may not want to appear pigheaded to their peers. In these cases, warnings may move them to a more neutral, easily defensible position that helps them leave a good impression (Quinn & Wood, 2004).

Whatever the case, because forewarning has the potential to make people more resistant to persuasion, you might be wondering what you should do if you ever want to persuade an audience that has been warned or is aware of your intent to persuade them. With that question in mind, Benoit (1998) offered the following advice:

> In these cases, the persuader may wish to attempt to compensate for the inhibiting effects of forewarning. The persuader could stress a lack of bias, emphasize that the audience's best interests were considered (and not just the persuader's own selfish interests), explain that both sides of the issue were carefully considered before a position was taken, or simply ask the audience to keep an open mind. At the very least, persuaders should moderate their expectations for success, keeping in mind that their persuasive task is more difficult when the audience is forewarned.
>
> (pp. 147–148)

SUMMARY

In this chapter, we examined the topic of message selection and organization. First, we saw that, depending on the characteristics of the audience, it's sometimes better for a persuader to tell the audience what to believe, but at other times it's best to let the audience members draw their own conclusions. Second, we saw that the ways in which messages are framed affect how they are reacted to. Third, we saw that when selecting arguments to use for persuasion, quality arguments matter with audiences that will scrutinize the message, but quantity works for less discerning audiences. Fourth, we discussed the role of evidence in the process of persuasion. Fifth, we examined message repetition and noted the conditions under which it increases and decreases persuasion. Sixth, we looked at the ways in which arguments might be ordered or arranged in a speech and indicated that the most effective order depends on several variables. Similarly, our examination of primacy and recency effects showed that when two people are giving opposing speeches, under some circumstances the first speaker may have the advantage, while under others the last speaker may have the advantage. Finally, we explored the ways in which people may be more resistant to persuasion, either by being inoculated with a weak dose of an opposing argument, by presenting two-sided refutational messages, or by being warned about the possibility of an attacking argument.

NOTE

1. Miller and Campbell (1959) also found that if there is a time delay between both messages, and between the second message and the measurement of attitude, neither primacy nor recency works better. Moreover, if there are no time delays between messages and the measurement of attitudes, neither primacy nor recency works better.

REFERENCES

Allen, M. (1998). Comparing the persuasive effectiveness of one- and two-sided messages. In M. Allen & R. W. Preiss (Eds.), *Persuasion: Advances through meta-analysis* (pp. 87–98). Cresskill, NJ: Hampton Press.

Allen, M., Hale, J., Mongeau, P., Berkowitz-Stafford, S., Stafford, S., Shanahan, W., Agee, P., Dillon, K., Jackson, R., & Ray, C. (1990). Testing a model of message sidedness: Three replications. *Communication Monographs*, *57*, 275–291.

Allen, M., & Preiss, R. W. (1997). Comparing the persuasiveness of narrative and statistical evidence using meta-analysis. *Communication Research Reports*, *14*, 125–131.

Banas, J. A., & Miller, G. (2013). Inducing resistance to conspiracy theory propaganda: Testing inoculation and metainoculation strategies. *Human Communication Research*, *39*, 184–207. doi:10.1111/hcre.12000

Banas, J. A., & Rains, S. A. (2010). A meta-analysis of research on inoculation theory. *Communication Monographs*, *77*, 281–311.

Baumeister, R. F., Vohs, K. D., & Tice, D. M. (2007). The strength model of self-control. *Current Directions in Psychological Science, 16*, 351–355. doi:10.1111/j.14678721.2007.00543.x

Beatty, M. J., & Kruger, M. W. (1978). The effects of heckling on speaker credibility and attitude change. *Communication Quarterly*, *26*(2), 46–50.

Benoit, W. L. (1998). Forewarning and persuasion. In M. Allen & R. Preiss (Eds.), *Persuasion: Advances through meta-analysis* (pp. 139–154). Cresskill, NJ: Hampton Press.

Biswas, D., Grewal, D., & Roggeveen, A. (2010). How the order of sampled experiential products affects choice. *Journal of Marketing Research*, *47*, 508–519.

Braddock, K., & Dillard, J. P. (2016). Meta-analytic evidence for the persuasive effect of narrative on beliefs, attitudes, intentions, and behaviors. *Communication Monographs*, *83*, 446–467. doi:10.1080/03637751.2015.1128555

Braverman, J. (2008). Testimonials versus informational persuasive messages: Moderating effect of delivery mode and personal involvement. *Communication Research*, *35*, 666–694.

Brehm, J. W. (1966). *A theory of psychological reactance*. New York: Academic Press.

Brehm, S. S., & Brehm, J. W. (1981). *Psychological reactance: A theory of freedom and control*. New York: Academic Press.

Buller, D. B. (1986). Distraction during persuasive communication: A meta-analytic review. *Communication Monographs*, *53*, 91–114.

Buller, D. B., & Hall, J. R. (1998). The effects of distraction during persuasion. In M. Allen & R. W. Preiss (Eds.), *Persuasion: Advances through meta-analysis* (pp. 155–173). Cresskill, NJ: Hampton Press.

Claypool, H. M., Mackie, D. M., Garcia-Marques, T., McIntosh, A., & Udall, A. (2004). The effects of personal relevance and repetition on persuasive processing. *Social Cognition*, *22*, 310–335.

Cornelis, E., Cauberghe, V., & De Pelsmacker, P. (2013). Two-sided messages for health risk prevention: The role of argument type, refutation, and issue ambivalence. *Substance Use & Misuse*, *48*, 741–752. doi:10.3109/10826084.2013.787093

Corbett, E. P. J. (1971). *Classical rhetoric for the modern student* (2nd ed.). New York: Oxford University Press.

Dillard, J. P. (2014). Language, style and persuasion. In P. E. Nathan (Ed.), *The Oxford handbook of language and social psychology* (pp. 177–187). New York: Oxford University Press.

Eisend, M. (2010). Explaining the joint effect of source credibility and negativity of information in two-sided messages. *Psychology & Marketing*, 27, 1032–1049. doi:10.1002/mar.20372

Festinger, L., & Maccoby, N. (1964). On resistance to persuasive communications. *Journal of Abnormal and Social Psychology*, 68, 359–366.

Freedman, J. L., & Sears, D. O. (1965). Warning, distraction, and resistance to influence. *Journal of Personality and Social Psychology*, 1, 262–266.

Fukada, H. (1986). Psychological processes mediating the persuasion inhibiting effect of forewarning in fear arousing communication. *Psychological Reports*, 58, 87–90.

Furnham, A. (1986). The robustness of the recency effect: Studies using legal evidence. *Journal of General Psychology*, 113(4), 351–357.

Garcia-Marques, T., & Mackie, D. M. (2001). The feeling of familiarity as a regulator of persuasive processing. *Social Cognition*, 19, 9–34.

Han, B., & Fink, E. L. (2012). How do statistical and narrative evidence affect persuasion? The role of evidentiary features. *Argumentation & Advocacy*, 49, 39–58.

Hass, R. G., & Grady, K. (1975). Temporal delay, type of forewarning, and resistance to influence. *Journal of Experimental Social Psychology*, 11, 459–469.

Hoeken, H., & Hustinx, L. (2009). When is statistical evidence superior to anecdotal evidence in supporting probability claims. *Human Communication Research*, 35, 491–510. doi:10.1111/j.1468–2958.2009.01360.x

Hovland, C. I., Lumsdaine, A., & Sheffield, F. (1949). *Experiments on mass communication*. Princeton, NJ: Princeton University Press.

Hull, S. J., & Hong, Y. (2016). Sensation seeking as a moderator of gain- and loss-framed HIV-test promotion message effects. *Journal of Health Communication*, 21, 46–55. doi:10.10810730.2015.1033113

Jacks, J. Z., & Devine, P. G. (2000). Attitude importance, forewarning of message content, and resistance to persuasion. *Basic and Applied Social Psychology*, 22(1), 19–29.

Janssen, L., Fennis, B. M., & Pruyn, A. T. H. (2010). Forewarned is forearmed: Conserving self-control strength to resist social influence. *Journal of Experimental Social Psychology*, 46, 911–921. doi:10.1016/j.jesp.2010.06.008

Jenni, K., & Loewenstein, G. (1997). Explaining the identifiable victim effect. *Journal of Risk and Uncertainty*, 14, 235–257. doi:10.1023/A:1007740225484

Kardes, F. R., Kim, J., & Lim, J. S. (1994). Moderating effects of prior knowledge on the perceived diagnosticity of beliefs derived from implicit versus explicit product claims. *Journal of Business Research*, 29, 219–224.

Keating, J. P., & Brock, T. C. (1974). Acceptance of persuasion and the inhibition of counterargumentation under various distraction tasks. *Journal of Experimental Social Psychology*, 10, 301–309.

Kim, S., Allen, M., Gattoni, A., Grimes, D., Herrman, A. M., Huang, H., Kim, J., Lu, S., Maier, M., May, A., Omachinski, K., Omori, K., Tnzek, K., Turkiewicz, K. L., & Zhang, Y. (2012). Testing the additive model for the effectiveness of evidence on the persuasiveness of a message. *Social influence*, 7, 65–77.

Lee, D. H. (2014). The impact of inference generation on belief formation. *Journal of Business Research*, 67, 2064–2071. doi:10.1016/j.jbusres.2014.04.014

Lee, S., & Feeley, T. H. (2016). The identifiable victim effect: A meta-analytic review. *Social Influence*. Advance online publication. doi:10.1080/15534510.2016.1216891

Lee, S., & Feeley, T. H. (2017). The identifiable victim effect: Using an experimental-causal-chain design to test for mediation. *Current Psychology*. Advance online publication. doi:10.1007/s12144-017-9570-3

Lehnert, K., Till, B. D., & Carlson, B. D. (2013). Advertising creativity and repetition: Recall, wearout and wearin effects. *International Journal of Advertising*, 32, 211–211. doi:10.2501/IJA-32-2-211-231

Martin, B. A. S., Lang, B., & Wong, S. (2003/2004). Conclusion explicitness in advertising: The moderating role of need for cognition (NFC) and argument quality (AQ) on persuasion. *Journal of Advertising*, 32(4), 57–65.

Martin, B. A. S., & Strong, C. A. (2016). The trustworthy brand: effects of conclusion explicitness and persuasion awareness on consumer judgments. *Marketing Letters*, 27, 473–485. doi:10.1007/s11002–014–9343–9

Mason, A. M., & Miller, C. H. (2016). Potentially deceptive health nutrition-related advertising claims: The role of inoculation in conferring resistance. *Health Education Journal*, 75, 144–157. doi:10.1177/0017896915569365

McGuire, W. J. (1964). Inducing resistance to persuasion: Some contemporary approaches. In L. Berkowitz (Ed.), *Advances in experimental social psychology* (pp. 191–229). New York: Academic Press.

McGuire, W. J. (1969). The nature of attitudes and attitude change. In G. Lindzey & E. Aronson (Eds.), *The handbook of social psychology* (2nd ed., pp. 136–314). Reading, MA: Addison-Wesley.

McGuire, W. J., & Papageorgis, D. (1961). The relative efficacy of various types of prior belief-defense in producing resistance to persuasion. *Journal of Abnormal and Social Psychology*, 62, 327–337.

Miller, C. H., Ivanov, B., Sims, J., Compton, J., Harrison, K. J., Parker, K. A., Parker, J. L., & Averbeck, J. M. (2013). Boosting the potency of resistance: Combining the motivational forces of inoculation and psychological reactance. *Human Communication Research*, 39, 127–155. doi:10.1111/j.1468–2958.2012.01438.x

Miller, N., & Campbell, D. T. (1959). Recency and primacy in persuasion as a function of the timing of speeches and measurements. *Journal of Abnormal and Social Psychology*, 59, 1–9.

Moyer-Guse, E., Jain, P., & Chung, A. H. (2012). Reinforcement or reactance? Examining the effect of an explicit persuasive appeal following an entertainment-education narrative. *Journal of Communication*, 62, 1010–1027. doi:10.1111/j.1460–2466.2012.01680.x

Nan, S. (2012). Relative persuasiveness of gain-versus loss-framed human papillomavirus vaccination messages for the present- and future-minded. *Human Communication Research*, 38, 72–94.

O'Keefe, D. J. (1998). Justification explicitness and persuasive effects: A meta-analytic review of the effects of varying supportive articulation in persuasive messages. *Argumentation and Advocacy*, 35, 61–75.

O'Keefe, D. J. (1999). How to handle opposing arguments in persuasive messages: A meta-analytic review of the effects of one-sided and two-sided messages. In M. E. Roloff (Ed.), *Communication yearbook 22* (pp. 209–249). Thousand Oaks, CA: Sage.

O'Keefe, D. J., & Jensen, J. D. (2007). The relative persuasiveness of gain-framed loss-framed messages for encouraging disease prevention behaviors: A meta-analytic review. *Journal of Health Communication*, 12, 623–644.

O'Keefe, D. J., & Jensen, J. D. (2009). The relative persuasiveness of gain-framed and loss-framed messages for encouraging disease detection behaviors: A meta-analytic review. *Journal of Communication*, 59, 296–316. doi:10.1111/j.1460–2466.2009.01417.x

Osterhouse, R. A., & Brock, T. C. (1970). Distraction increases yielding to propaganda by inhibiting counterarguing. *Journal of Personality and Social Psychology*, 15, 344–358.

Papageorgis, D. (1968). Warning and persuasion. *Psychological Bulletin*, 70, 271–282.

Papageorgis, D., & McGuire, W. J. (1961). The generality of immunity to persuasion produced by pre-exposure to weakened counterarguments. *Journal of Abnormal and Social Psychology, 62,* 475–481.

Parker, K. A., Rains, S. A., & Ivanov, B. (2016). Examining the "blanket of protection" conferred by inoculation: The effects of inoculation messages on the cross-protection of related attitudes. *Communication Monographs, 83,* 49–68. doi:10.1080/03637751.2015.1030681

Peskin, M., & Newell, F. N. (2004). Familiarity breeds attraction. Effects of exposure on attractiveness of typical and distinctive faces. *Perception, 33,* 147–157.

Petty, R. E., & Cacioppo, J. T. (1979). Effects of forewarning of persuasive intent and involvement on cognitive responses and persuasion. *Personality and Social Psychology Bulletin, 5,* 173–176.

Petty, R. E., & Cacioppo, J. T. (1984). The effects of involvement on responses to argument quantity and quality: Central and peripheral routes to persuasion. *Journal of Personality and Social Psychology, 46,* 69–81.

Petty, R. E., & Cacioppo, J. T. (1986). *Communication and persuasion: Central and peripheral routes to attitude change.* New York: Springer-Verlag.

Pfau, M. (1997). Inoculation model of resistance to influence. In G. A. Barnett & F. J. Boster (Eds.), *Progress in communication sciences: Advances in persuasion* (Vol. 13, pp. 133–171). Greenwich, CT: Ablex.

Pfau, M., & Van Bockern, S. (1994). The persistence of inoculation in conferring resistance to smoking initiation among adolescents: The second year. *Human Communication Research, 20,* 413–430.

Pfau, M., Van Bockern, S., & Kang, J. G. (1992). Use of inoculation to promote resistance to smoking initiation among adolescents. *Communication Monographs, 59,* 213–230.

Pfau, M., Kenski, H. C., Nitz, M., & Sorenson, J. (1990). Efficacy of inoculation strategies in promoting resistance to political attack messages: Application to direct mail. *Communication Monographs, 57,* 1–12.

Pfau, M., Compton, J., Parker, K. A., Wittenberg, E. M., An, C., Fergusun, M., Horton, H., & Malyshev, Y. (2004). The traditional explanation for resistance versus attitude accessibility: Do they trigger distinct or overlapping processes of resistance? *Human Communication Research, 30,* 329–360.

Pinocchio index. (1996, September 3). *Time,* p. 22.

Quinn, J., & Wood, W. (2004). Forewarnings of influence appeals: Inducing resistance and acceptance. In S. Eric (Ed.), *Resistance and persuasion* (pp. 193–213). Mahwah, NJ: Erlbaum.

Rau, P. P., Zhou, J., Chen, D., & Lu, T. (2014). The influence of repetition and time pressure on effectiveness of mobile advertising messages. *Telematics and Informatics, 31,* 463–476. doi:10.1016/j.tele.2013.10.003

Reinard, J. C. (1988). The empirical study of the persuasive effects of evidence: The status after fifty years of research. *Human Communication Research, 15,* 3–59.

Reinhard, M., Schindler, S., Raabe, V., Stahlberg, D., & Messner, M. (2014). Less is sometimes more: How repetition of an antismoking advertisement affects attitudes toward smoking and source credibility. *Social Influence, 9,* 116–132. doi:10.1080/15534510.2013.790839

Reynolds, R. A., & Reynolds, J. L. (2002). Evidence. In J. P. Dillard & M. Pfau (Eds.), *The persuasion handbook: Developments in theory and practice* (pp. 427–444). Thousand Oaks, CA: Sage.

Rhodes, G., Halberstadt, J., & Brajkovich, G. (2001). Generalization of mere exposure effects to averaged and composite faces. *Social Cognition, 19,* 57–70.

Romero, A. A., Agnew, C. A., & Insko, C. A. (1996). The cognitive mediation hypothesis revisited: An empirical response to methodological and theoretical criticism. *Personality and Social Psychology Bulletin, 22,* 651–665.

Sawyer, A. G. (1981). Repetition, cognitive responses, and persuasion. In R. E. Petty, T. M. Ostrom, & T. C. Brock (Eds.), *Cognitive responses in persuasion* (pp. 237–261). Hillsdale, NJ: Erlbaum.

Sawyer, A. G. (1988). Can there be effective advertising without explicit conclusions? Decide for yourself. In S. Hecker & D. W. Stewart (Eds.), *Nonverbal communication in advertising* (pp. 159–184). Lexington, MA: Lexington Books.

Sawyer, A. G., & Howard, D. J. (1991). Effects of omitting conclusions in advertisements to involved and uninvolved audiences. *Journal of Marketing Research, 28,* 467–474.

Scheibe, S., Notthoff, N., Menkin, J., Ross, L., Shadel, D., Deevy, M., Carstensen, L. L. (2014). Forewarning reduces fraud susceptibility in vulnerable consumers. *Basic and Applied Social Psychology, 36,* 272–279. doi:10.1080/01973533.2014.903844

Schelling, T. C. (1968). The life you save may be your own. In S. Chase (Ed.), *Problems in public expenditure analysis* (pp. 127–176). Washington, DC: Brookings Institute.

Sikkink, D. (1956). An experimental study of the effects on the listener of anticlimax order and authority in an argumentative speech. *Southern Speech Journal, 22,* 73–78.

Small, D. A., Loewenstein, G., & Slovic, P. (2007). Sympathy and callousness: The impact of deliberative thought on donations to identifiable and statistical victims. *Organizational Behavior and Human Decision Process, 102,* 143–153. doi:10.1016/ j.obhdp.2006.01.005

Stiff, J. B. (1986). Cognitive processing of message cues: A meta-analytic review of the effects of supporting information on attitudes. *Communication Monographs, 53,* 75–89

Tversky, A., & Kahneman, D. (1981). The framing of decisions and the psychology of choice. *Science, 211,* 453–458.

Unnaba, H. R, Burnkrant, R. E., & Erevelles, S. (1994). Effects of presentation order and communication modality on recall and attitude. *Journal of Consumer Research, 21,* 481–495.

Wadhwa, M., Shiv, B., & Nowlis, S. M. (2008). A bite to whet the reward appetite: The influence of sampling on reward-seeking behaviors. *Journal of Marketing Research, 45,* 403–413.

Wirtz, J. G., Sar, S., & Ghuge, S. (2015). The moderating role of mood and personal relevance on persuasive effects of gain- and loss-framed health messages. *Health Marketing Quarterly, 32,* 180–196. doi:10.1080/07359683.2015.1033936

Wood, W., & Quinn, J. (2003). Forewarned or forearmed? Two meta-analytic syntheses of forewarning of influence appeals. *Psychological Bulletin, 129,* 119–138.

Zajonc, R. B. (1968). Attitudinal effects of mere exposure. *Journal of Personality and Social Psychology Monographs, 9*(2, Part 2), 1–27.

Zebrowitz, L. A., White, B., & Wieneke, K. (2008). Mere exposure and racial prejudice: Exposure to other-race faces increases liking for strangers of that race. *Social Cognition, 26,* 259–275.

Compliance Gaining

A POLICE OFFICER pulls a driver to the side of the road and says, "Sir, your car was swerving all over the place. I'd like you to blow into this breathalyzer, please."

"I apologize," the driver replies, "but I'm asthmatic and can't blow into anything without having an asthma attack."

"Alright. Let's head down to the station for a urine sample."

"I don't think so, officer. Given my diabetes, who knows what that might do to my blood sugar?"

"You'll have no choice but to take a blood test, then."

"Afraid not," the driver says. "You see, I'm a hemophiliac and even the slightest prick of a needle could make me bleed to death."

"Fine! Step out of your car, close your eyes, and walk in a straight line."

"Sorry, officer."

"What now?"

"I'm too drunk to do that."

We like this old joke not just because we think it's funny, but also because it illustrates one of the main themes in this chapter. Specifically, when faced with a situation involving persuasion, there's more than one way to skin a cat. Indeed, just as the police officer uses a variety of approaches—some more polite than others—to influence the driver, and just as the driver resists the officer in an assortment of ways, real-life persuaders often come up with any number of different approaches for persuading or thwarting the persuasive attempts of others. What types of strategies are available to people who are seeking or resisting compliance? What specific approaches are people most likely to use? Do the approaches people use vary across situations?

All of these issues have been explored by researchers who study what is often labeled *compliance gaining*, the topic of this chapter. Before we discuss how this important subject has been investigated and what has been found, let's begin with a few definitions.

ACTIONS SPEAK THE LOUDEST: A DEFINITION OF COMPLIANCE GAINING

We once knew a guy who liked to say, "I don't care if you hate me, as long as you're nice to me." We think that this maxim is a fine illustration of the distinction between thoughts and actions that undergirds the primary difference between compliance and other forms of persuasion. As we mentioned in Chapter 2, it is useful to distinguish between the terms *persuasion* and *compliance*. Persuasion, an umbrella term, is concerned with changing beliefs, attitudes, intentions, motivations, and behaviors. Compliance is more restrictive, typically referring to changes in a person's overt behavior. For example, a mother might tell her 10-year-old son, "Take out the trash." If the child says, "I don't want to," the mother might respond, "I don't care what you want. Take out the trash!" In this case the mother is not concerned with belief or attitude change. She doesn't care if the child likes taking out the trash, believes in recycling, and so on. She just wants compliance, or behavior change (i.e., the trash emptied). In short, research examining compliance gaining generally focuses on persuasion aimed at getting others to do something or to act in a particular way.

We should also note that compliance gaining differs from more traditional notions of persuasion in other important ways. First, for the most part, studies of compliance gaining have concentrated on influence in interpersonal and/or face-to-face contexts rather than in one-to-many contexts. Beyond that, two lines of compliance-gaining research can be identified. The first has concerned itself with determining which strategies are most effective at persuading receivers, a topic we'll get to in Chapter 11. The second line has focused more on "senders" rather than "receivers." Specifically, such research has attempted to identify the broad array of strategies available to people who want to influence others. What's more, such studies have examined which strategies people are most likely to *select and use* when trying to persuade others. As such, a better title for this chapter might be "compliance seeking," even though we'll stick with the more traditional term "compliance gaining." We start by discussing how this type of research got started.

IN THE BEGINNING: THE ROOTS OF COMPLIANCE-GAINING RESEARCH

Imagine you are a parent with a son whose room is a pigsty. What would you do to get him to clean up? Can you think of several different approaches? If not, consider the work of two sociologists, Gerald Marwell and David Schmitt (1976), who might help add a few tactics to your repertoire. Specifically, after examining past research and theory in the areas of power and influence, these two researchers developed a taxonomy of 16 different tactics that might be used to gain compliance (these tactics are presented in Table 10.1). Afterward, they told people to imagine themselves in four scenarios (i.e., requesting a tutor, doing more studying, making a purchase, and seeking a promotion) and asked the people how likely they would be to use each of the 16 tactics in each of the scenarios. Finally, based on their responses, Marwell and Schmitt grouped the tactics in terms of their commonalities, ultimately identifying five basic types of compliance-gaining strategies:

- *Rewarding activity:* involves seeking compliance in an active and positive way (e.g., making promises).
- *Punishing activity:* involves seeking compliance in an explicitly negative way (e.g., making threats).
- *Expertise:* involves attempts to make a person think that the persuader has some special knowledge (e.g., trying to appear credible).
- *Activation of impersonal commitments:* involves attempts to appeal to a person's internalized commitments (e.g., telling the person he or she will feel bad about him/herself if he/she does not comply).
- *Activation of personal commitments:* relies on appeals to a person's commitment to others (e.g., pointing out that the person is indebted and should, therefore, comply to repay the favor).

Calvin and Hobbes　　　　by Bill Watterson

FIGURE 10.1
Source: Calvin and Hobbes © (1995) Watterson, Disttributed by Universal Press Syndicate. Reprinted with permission. All Rights Reserved.

TABLE 10.1 Marwell and Schmitt's Compliance-Gaining Tactics, with Examples of How You Might Get Your Son, Beaufort, to Clean His Room

1. **Promising a reward:** You tell a person you will reward him/her if he/she complies with your request. For example, you offer to buy Beaufort an ice-cream cone if he cleans his room.

2. **Threatening a punishment:** You tell a person you will punish him/her if he/she does not comply with your request. For example, you threaten to give away Beaufort's Wii system if he doesn't tidy up.

3. **Using positive expertise:** Because you know what's best or "how things are," you tell a person that he/she will benefit by complying with your request. For example, you tell Beaufort that, based on your experience, you know that clean, organized people are those who succeed in life.

4. **Using negative expertise:** Because you know what's best or "how things are," you tell a person that he/she will be negatively affected if he/she does not comply with your request. For example, you tell Beaufort that, based on your experience, you know that people who are slobs do not succeed in life.

5. **Promoting liking:** You get a person to like you before asking him/her to comply with your request. For example, you act cheerful and give Beaufort a lot of attention before asking him to clean his room.

6. **Using reciprocity:** Before seeking compliance, you give a person something he/she wants or needs. For example, you buy Beaufort a video game he's always wanted and then ask him to clean his room.

7. **Administering punishment:** You keep punishing a person and don't stop until he/she complies with your request. For example, you forbid Beaufort to use his Wii system and explain that he won't be allowed to use it until he keeps his room clean for a month.

8. **Creating indebtedness:** You tell a person that he/she owes you compliance because of something you previously did for him/her. For example, you tell Beaufort that you are a good parent who bends over backward to provide the things he wants and needs, so he owes it to you to keep his room clean.

9. **Generating moral obligation:** You tell a person that it would be immoral for him/her not to comply with your request. You tell Beaufort that people who are disorganized and dirty are morally bad.

10. **Promoting positive esteem:** You tell a person that complying will improve his/her self-esteem. For example, you tell Beaufort that having a clean room will make him feel good about himself.

11. **Promoting negative esteem:** You tell a person that not complying will hurt his/her self-esteem. For example, you tell Beaufort that having a filthy and untidy room will make him feel bad about himself.

12. **Using positive altercasting:** You note that admirable people would comply with your request, and suggest that, to be like such people, this person should comply with your request. For example, you tell Beaufort that good boys like him naturally want to keep their rooms clean and tidy (for more on this strategy, see Box 10.1).

13. **Using negative altercasting:** You note that people with negative qualities would not comply with your request, and suggest that, to avoid being like such people, this person should comply with your request. For example, you tell Beaufort that only bratty little boys have dirty rooms, so he should clean his room.

14. **Being altruistic:** You tell the person how much his/her assistance would help you. For example, you tell Beaufort that you are overwhelmed with work and that he could help you a great deal if he kept his room clean so you didn't have to do it for him.

15. **Using positive admiration:** You tell the person that people he/she admires will hold him/her in higher regard if he/she complies. For example, you tell Beaufort that his older brother, Timmy (who Beaufort idolizes), will be proud of him if he keeps his room clean.

16. **Using negative admiration:** You tell the person that people he/she admires will hold him/her in lower regard if he/she doesn't comply. For example, you tell Beaufort that his older brother, Timmy (who Beaufort idolizes), will be ashamed of him if he keeps his room messy.

Based upon Marwell & Schmitt (1967). (Note: Marwell and Schmitt's terminology differs somewhat from our own.)

BOX 10.1 | Only a Jerk Would Refuse: An Examination of the Altercasting Tactic

As noted in Table 10.1, negative altercasting, when used as a compliance-gaining tactic, involves projecting a person into an unflattering role and then expecting the person to comply in order to avoid fitting into that role. For example, if someone collecting donations said, "Only a heartless person would refuse to feed hungry children," he or she would be using negative altercasting. Before you decide to try the tactic on your own, consider this: Research suggests that people who use it are perceived as less competent than people who use more prosocial tactics, such as liking (Johnson, 1992). Not only that, they may be less persuasive. In one study (Turner, Banas, Rains, Jang, Moore, & Morrison, 2010), for instance, researchers tucked unmailed, stamped letters under the windshield wipers of several thousand parked vehicles. Along with the letters were messages employing one of three compliance-gaining techniques: (1) positive altercasting ("I found this next to your car. A good person would mail it [that is, if it's not yours.]"), (2) negative altercasting ("I found this next to your car. Only a bad person wouldn't mail it [that is, if it's not yours]."); and direct request ("I found this next to your car. Mail it [that is, if it's not yours]."). Results showed that negative altercasting did not work well. To be sure, significantly more letters were returned in the direct request and positive altercasting conditions than in the negative altercasting condition (Turner et al., 2010). Perhaps that's because people believe that only a jerk would use the negative altercasting tactic.

Marwell and Schmitt's (1967) study showed that there are a wide range of tactics available to persuaders. The study was important because it became the springboard for compliance-gaining research that followed. Even so, as is often the case with research on human communication, the study made compliance gaining appear simpler than it really is. We will see later in this chapter the ways in which this study was criticized and improved on. First, however, we turn to a discussion of some of the factors that affect the selection of compliance-gaining strategies.

SITUATION: THE "IT DEPENDS" OF COMPLIANCE-GAINING BEHAVIOR

Long before this chapter was written, one of the authors was faced with two different situations requiring persuasion. In the first, the author's then 2-year-old son tried to provoke a food fight at the dinner table by throwing a chunk of roast beef, gravy and all at his older brother. There was quite a splat. The 2-year-old then proceeded to reach for a second chunk, at which point the author intervened, explaining that any more "beef bombs" would result in a time-out (i.e., 2 minutes of sitting alone in the bedroom). Fortunately, the next hunk of beef found its way into the kid's mouth.

In the second situation, the same author needed to ask his boss to hurry up and look over some paperwork that needed the boss's signature. The deadline for the paperwork was nearing. Although threatening the boss with something like a time-out had appeal, quite obviously, doing so would have been inappropriate. Instead, the author tapped lightly on the boss's door, smiled, and asked ever so politely whether the boss had "had a chance to look over that paperwork yet?"

The point is that even though we can isolate a specific number of compliance-gaining strategies, not all strategies are appropriate in all situations. To be sure, even when trying to persuade the same person, different contexts require different strategies. For instance, trying to keep a 2-year-old from repeatedly playing near electrical outlets may require a different strategy than trying to get the same child to eat asparagus. Obviously, selecting a compliance-gaining strategy depends a lot on the situation.

For quite some time now, communication scholars have argued that compliance-gaining behavior can vary greatly from one situation to the next. By way of example, research by Cody, Woelfel, and Jordan (1983) showed that, when trying to decide which compliance-gaining strategy to use, there are seven situational dimensions that affect those decisions:

- *Dominance:* The level of control or power in a relationship. For example, because a boss generally has more power to influence a subordinate than vice versa, a boss's strategies may differ from a subordinate's.
- *Intimacy:* The level of emotional attachment or knowledge one has of a partner's affect. For example, because they are more intimate and more concerned with the relationship, spouses may use different strategies than strangers.
- *Resistance:* The degree to which the persuader thinks a strategy will be resisted. For example, strategies that are more likely to be resisted will probably not be used as readily as those that are less likely to be resisted. (For more information on resisting compliance, see Box 10.2.)
- *Personal benefits:* The extent to which the self or the other is benefited by compliance. For example, strategies that are perceived to produce the greatest benefits are most likely to be used.
- *Rights:* The extent to which a persuader thinks a request is warranted. For example, a persuader may believe that complaining about a barking dog and losing sleep is justified, but complaining about someone else's hairstyle is not.
- *Relational consequences:* The degree to which a strategy will have long-term or short-term effects on the persuader's relationship with the persuadee. For example, a threat that may lead to divorce may be less likely than one that merely leads to an argument.
- *Apprehension:* The degree to which a persuader perceives nervousness in the situation. For example, situations filled with anxiety may lead to different strategies than those without anxiety.

It is clear, then, that compliance-gaining behavior depends a great deal on the situation in which it is used. In fact, research shows that these situational dimensions not only affect decisions to use strategies but also decisions to avoid them (Hample & Dallinger, 2002). In the following sections, we discuss some research findings on several of these situational dimensions.

Seeking Compliance From Strangers and Intimates

In what is now considered a classic study, Gerald Miller, Frank Boster, Michael Roloff, and David Seibold (1977) examined the effects of intimacy on compliance-gaining behavior. These researchers imagined that compliance gaining in interpersonal relationships differ from compliance gaining in noninterpersonal relationships. Specifically, because people in interpersonal relationships know their partners well, they can tailor their messages to appeal to their partners' specific wants, needs, interests, and so forth. The same is not true in noninterpersonal relationships, where little is known about the other person. In addition, Miller and colleagues (1977) thought that the type of compliance-gaining strategy a person decided to use would depend on whether a situation had short-term or long-term consequences.

BOX 10.2 | Just Say No? A Look at Strategies for Resisting Compliance and Resisting Resistance

In our opinion, a lot of advertising makes persuasion seem pretty simple. For example, Nike's classic "Just do it" campaign suggested that we should forget all about reasoning and weighing pros and cons. On the other side of the coin, you might be familiar with the once popular slogan for keeping kids off of drugs; "Just say 'no,'" it advised. But is resisting compliance really all that easy? Whatever the case, some research shows that just saying "no" is not the only option available to us when trying to resist the compliance-gaining attempts of others. For instance, a study by McLaughlin, Cody, and Robey (1980) identified four possible strategies you might use to resist persuasion:

1. **Nonnegotiation**: You overtly refuse to comply (you say, "No").
2. **Identity management**: You resist by manipulating images of the other person (you say, "I would never make such an awful request").
3. **Justifying**: You justify noncompliance by pointing to negative outcomes (you say, "If I comply with your request I might lose my job").
4. **Negotiation**: You engage in an alternative behavior that you propose (rather than turn off the stereo, you offer to turn it down).

Rather than look at resistance strategies, perhaps a more important issue centers on situations in which people find themselves wanting to resist compliance. One prevalent example occurs when people are pressured into having sex. Indeed, according to Impett and Peplau's (2003) sources, between 26 and 40 percent of men and 50 and 65 percent of women report that they've agreed to have sex even though they did not want to. With this in mind, and considering contemporary issues associated with the spread of HIV and the prevalence of date rape, researchers have examined strategies that can be used to resist sexual advances. An interesting study by Byers and Wilson (1985) examined men's and women's perceptions of the different ways in which women refuse sexual advances by men. In the study, subjects watched a videotape of a man and woman engaged in romantic physical behavior. At some point in the tape, the woman refuses to go any further by (1) simply saying, "No"; (2) saying "No" and offering an excuse (i.e., "someone's coming over"); or (3) saying "No" and offering an explanation (i.e., "we don't know each other well enough"). Results of the study showed that most of the males in the study would comply with all of the requests, but several said they would be reluctant to do so. Moreover, both male and female subjects interpreted the simple "No" and the "No, with explanation" as meaning the man should stop his advances but interpreted the "No" with an excuse as meaning that the man should try making more advances later that day.

One possible problem with messages meant to resist sexual advances centers on the stereotype that "when women say 'no,' they really mean 'yes.'" Muehlenhard and Hollanbaugh (1988), for

Continued

example, found that nearly 40 percent of women in their study claimed to have said "no" when they meant "yes" because they did not want to appear promiscuous, wanted to show concern for religious issues, and so forth. Perper and Weis (1987) argued that such token resistance can cause problems by encouraging males not to take "no" for an answer. With this in mind, when faced with such situations, it is important to say what you mean. Indeed, research shows that direct, verbal messages, compared to indirect messages, are the best for avoiding sexual advances (Christopher & Frandsen, 1990). A possible problem, however, is that sexual rejection messages that are moderately direct are perceived to be more comfortable and "face saving" than very direct messages (Metts, Cupach, & Imahori, 1992).

It is apparent from this discussion so far that resistance strategies, in and of themselves, may not be as important as how people respond to those resistance strategies. For instance, research indicates that people who have met with noncompliance tend to follow up with more direct strategies than they did initially (Harris, Monahan, & Hovick, 2014). Moreover, in some situations, noncompliance is likely to be met with physical aggression (deTurck, 1987). So, what happens if your resistance meets with resistance? If you ever find yourself confronted by a person who wants you to comply when you don't want to, it might help to know this: Research suggests that forceful verbal and physical resistance is related to the decreased likelihood of being raped (Senn, Eliasziw, Hobden, Newby-Clark, Barata, Radtke, & Thurston, 2017; Tark & Kleck, 2014). What's more, although some scholars have suggested that resistance may be dangerous because it might provoke rapists to become more violent, Tark and Kleck (2014) found that additional injuries besides rape following resistance are rare.

To test their hypotheses, these researchers asked people how likely they would be to use each of Marwell and Schmitt's (1967) strategies to persuade others in four different situations:

1. *Noninterpersonal; short-term consequences:* You want to get a car dealer, whom you barely know, to give you a $1,000 trade-in on your old car.
2. *Noninterpersonal; long-term consequences:* You want your new neighbors, who are planning to cut down a shade tree that adds value to your home, to leave the tree standing.
3. *Interpersonal; short-term consequences:* You have a close relationship with a man or woman and want to cancel a date with him or her in order to visit an old acquaintance who is passing through town.
4. *Interpersonal; long-term consequences:* You have a close relationship with a man or woman and want to persuade him or her to move to another geographical location so you can take a better job.

Results of this study showed that the situation strongly affected strategy choice. In general, people preferred "friendly," socially acceptable strategies (e.g., liking) in all the situations but said they were more likely to use different tactics in different situations. For instance, threat tactics were more likely in short-term, non-interpersonal contexts. Finally, in noninterpersonal situations, people picked a greater variety of strategies, perhaps because, without knowing much about the person they were trying to persuade, more trial and error was necessary (Miller et al., 1977).

Previous research suggests that intimates, compared to strangers, are perceived to be more effective in their compliance-gaining attempts. Dennis (2006), for example, found that people expected intimates, rather than non-intimates, to be more effective when trying to persuade them to engage in healthy behaviors, especially when their intimate others used strategies showing that they cared (e.g., "I don't want your weight to bother you. You should eat better."). For some types of health-related behavior, other strategies were perceived to be effective as well. For instance, when trying to get their romantic partners to stop smoking, intimate others were perceived to be effective when using threat (e.g., "I don't know if I can handle being with you when you smoke.") and liking (e.g., "I'd like kissing you more if your mouth didn't taste like an ashtray") strategies (Dennis, 2006).

Thus, the choice and perceived effectiveness of compliance-gaining strategies may differ depending on whether a relationship is interpersonal or noninterpersonal. But are all interpersonal relationships the same? One of our favorite studies shows that they are not. Specifically, Witteman and Fitzpatrick (1986) argued that husbands and wives can be categorized into three different couple-types: *Traditionals, Separates*, and *Independents*. They explained that:

> Traditionals hold conventional values about the relationship. These values emphasize stability as opposed to spontaneity. Traditionals exhibit interdependence, both physically and psychologically, and tend not to avoid conflict. Separates hold ambivalent views on the nature of relationships, report having the least interdependence, and avoid open marital conflict. Independents hold fairly non-conventional relational values and maintain some interdependence, yet not with respect to some of the physical and temporal aspects of their lives. Also Independents report some assertiveness and tend to engage in conflict.
>
> (p. 132)

Because couples differed in the ways they interacted, Witteman and Fitzpatrick suspected that couples also would differ in the ways they sought compliance. Results of a study confirmed these expectations. First, Traditionals sought compliance by discussing what they expected to be the positive and negative outcomes of a proposed course of action. They tended to be open and used their relationship as a basis of power. Separates, however, did not attempt to identify with their partners or to use their relationship to seek compliance. Instead, Separates focused on the negative consequences of noncompliance and tried to constrain the behavior of their spouses. Finally, Independents, compared to other couple types, used a wider variety of power bases when seeking compliance. They also tended to discount and refute their partners more than other couple types, indicating that Independent couples debate one another relatively intensely.

While it is clear, then, that our use of compliance-gaining strategies depends on the type and degree of intimate relationship in which we are involved, research also suggests that our compliance-seeking behaviors are affected by the particular circumstances we face in our relationships. As one example, if the person with whom you are involved starts thinking about leaving you, are there particular strategies you might use to save the relationship? Research by Buchanan, O'Hair, and Becker (2006) identified four overall strategies that people reported using while attempting to hang on to their spouses. *Commitment*, the most common strategy, includes tactics such as being more loving and caring, being submissive ("I'll do anything to save this relationship."), and asking your partner to commit to the relationship. *Alignment*, the second most common strategy, includes tactics like demonstrating to other people that your partner is taken (e.g., by holding hands), punishing your partner's threats of infidelity, and trying to make your partner want you sexually. *Negativity*, the third strategy, includes tactics such as degrading your partner, making your partner jealous (e.g., by threatening to be unfaithful), and concealing your partner from others. *Harm*, the last and least frequent strategy, includes tactics such as threatening or being violent toward someone who might come between you and your partner (Buchanan et al., 2006).

Power, Legitimacy, and Politeness

Our earlier illustration about trying to influence a child versus a boss makes it clear that power plays a large role in the selection of compliance-gaining strategies. In what is now considered a seminal work, French and Raven (1960) argued that there are five bases of power that people can draw upon to influence others:

1. A person with *reward power* has control over some valued resource (e.g., promotions and raises).
2. A person with *coercive power* has the ability to inflict punishments (e.g., fire you).
3. *Expert power* is based on what a person knows (e.g., you may do what a doctor tells you to do because he or she knows more about medicine than you do).
4. *Legitimate power* is based on formal rank or position (e.g., you obey someone's commands because he or she is the vice president in the company for which you work).
5. People have *referent power* when the person they are trying to influence wants to be like them (e.g., a mentor often has this type of power).

Regardless of the type of power that's at work, one thing remains clear: Power affects compliance-gaining behavior. For example, although managers are more successful when using consultation, inspirational appeals, rational persuasion, and nonpressure tactics (Yukl, Kim, & Falbe, 1996), because they often believe that their power adds legitimacy to their requests, they may not provide justifications or explanations when seeking compliance. Their influence strategies, therefore, may tend to be more direct than the influence strategies used by their less powerful subordinates (see Hirokawa & Wagner, 2004). Moreover, regardless of the messages they use when seeking compliance, research has shown that people with power tend to be more persuasive than those without it (Levine & Boster, 2001).

With that said, is there any hope for people who possess little power? To address this question, several researchers (e.g., Baxter, 1984; Craig, Tracy, & Spisak, 1986; Wilson & Kunkel, 2000) have applied Brown and Levinson's (1987) *politeness theory* to the study of compliance-gaining behavior.

FIGURE 10.2
The use of coercive
power in the workplace.
Source: BIZARRO © by
Dan Piraro. Reprinted by
permission.

According to *politeness theory,* all people are motivated to maintain two kinds of face: positive and negative. We maintain *positive face* when others like, respect, and approve of us. We maintain *negative face* when we do not feel constrained or impeded by others. According to Brown and Levinson (1987), when making a request of someone else, both types of faces may be challenged. First, the request may constrain the other person's freedom, thereby challenging his or her negative face. By way of illustration, asking someone to pick you up at the airport is challenging because it keeps a person from doing something else that he or she might rather be doing. Second, the request may imply that the other person is being taken advantage of, thereby challenging his or her positive face. For example, in our opinion, the stereotypical sports slob who shouts to his wife, "Bring me another beer!" does not convey much respect.

So, how does the issue of power fit into the picture? According to Brown and Levinson (1987), a person is less likely to comply if his or her face is threatened. Thus, to keep from threatening a person's positive or negative face, we try to be polite when making requests. Moreover, when trying to persuade someone who is more powerful than us, we may be extra polite because it is not as likely that our requests will be perceived as legitimate. Research so far has supported this conclusion. For example, in one study, Leslie Baxter (1984) found that compared to less powerful others (i.e., group members), more powerful others (i.e., group leaders) were less polite when making requests. Similarly, two studies found that when students tried to persuade their instructors to change grades or paper deadlines, their compliance-gaining strategies were overwhelmingly positive (Golish, 1999; Golish & Olson, 2000). Not only that, Levine and Boster (2001) found that when people with little power tried to persuade others, positively framed messages were the only ones that met with much success. Finally, Jenkins and Dragojevic (2013) found that face-threatening messages caused people to derogate both the message and the source, leading to less persuasion.

Considering the preceding studies, you might be wondering which types of strategies are polite and which are not. Most would agree that threats are not as polite as hints. However, threats may be more efficient than hints. To test this notion, Kellermann and Shea (1996) asked people to rate how polite and efficient they perceived several different strategies to be. Interestingly, threats, although impolite, were not considered efficient, and hints, although inefficient, were not considered polite. Perhaps the best way to get compliance is by using direct requests (i.e., explicitly ask for what you want); such requests were among the most efficient strategies and were not considered impolite (Kellermann & Shea, 1996). Consistent with this notion, one study found that speaking debaters who were confronted with nonverbal disparagement from their opponents were perceived as most effective and appropriate when they politely and directly requested that their opponents stop displaying such disparaging behaviors (Weger, Seiter, Jacobs, & Akbulut, 2010).

While considering the topic of politeness, keep in mind that persuasion is a two-way street. As such, people not only threaten others' face when making requests, they do so when refusing others' requests as well (see Johnson, 2007). By way of example, it would be one thing for Olga to tell Xenia, "I can't take you to the airport because my driver's license was revoked when I was arrested for drunk driving" (a threat to Olga's positive face) and quite another to tell Xenia, "Yeah, right. You're not worth the time, gas, or wear and tear on my vehicle" (a threat to Xenia's positive face). Johnson (2007) has shown that the nature of refusals (i.e., do they threaten the requester's, the target's, or both the requester's and target's positive and/or negative face) affect perceptions about whether the refusal is effective or appropriate.

It is apparent from our discussion so far that behavior designed to gain or resist compliance depends, to a large extent, on several contextual and relational dimensions. (To learn about compliance-gaining behavior in a *specific* context, see Box 10.3.) The context, however, is not the only factor that affects compliance-gaining behavior. In the next section we explore the impact of individual differences on interpersonal influence.

WHO ARE YOU? INDIVIDUAL CHARACTERISTICS AND COMPLIANCE-GAINING BEHAVIOR

Up to this point we've talked about the whats and whens of compliance gaining. We've shown that past research has pointed to a number of situational dimensions (e.g., interpersonal/noninterpersonal, short-term/long-term consequences) that influence strategy choice. According to Hunter and Boster (1987), however, there is but one factor that determines what types of compliance-gaining strategies will be used in a given situation. These researchers argued that when trying to decide what

BOX 10.3 | Take Two Aspirin and Call Me in the Morning: Compliance Gaining Between Doctors and Patients

One of the authors attended a dinner party at which the conversation turned to health-related matters. Several of the guests explained how they fooled their physicians to make it appear that their blood pressure was normal. One said she raised her arms above her head for five minutes beforehand. Another said he made sure he was dehydrated when visiting his doctor. "But why would you want to deceive your doctor about your blood pressure?" the author asked. "Why wouldn't you want to?" one of them replied.

This story illustrates how attitudes can pose serious concerns for people in the medical profession. Indeed, physicians not only face patients who shade the truth about their health, they are also confronted with the task of persuading patients to comply with requests to take medication, return for regular checkups, modify their behaviors, and so forth. When one considers the personal and economic costs of not complying with doctors' requests, the study of persuasion in medical contexts is of obvious significance.

According to Burgoon and Burgoon (1990), compliance gaining in medical contexts is unique because, unlike most other compliance-gaining situations, patients visit physicians voluntarily, pay for physicians' compliance-gaining directives, perceive physicians as experts, and believe that compliance will benefit themselves rather than the physician. Unfortunately, however, Klingle's (2004) and Burgoon, Birk, and Hall's (1991) sources indicate that patient noncompliance is the most significant problem facing medicine today and that patient noncompliance is as high as 62 percent with prescribed drug regimens, 50 percent with medical appointment keeping, and 92 percent with health promotion and lifestyle changes.

For these reasons, researchers have attempted to determine not only what types of compliance-gaining strategies physicians use but also what types of strategies are the most effective. For example, a review of literature by Burgoon and Burgoon (1990) found that physicians prefer to use strategies that appeal to authority, knowledge, and expertise, and tend to avoid threatening and antisocial strategies. Indeed, Schneider and Beaubien (1996) found that positive expertise, legitimacy, and liking (see strategies discussed earlier) accounted for 83.5 percent of all the compliance-gaining strategies used by doctors on patients. Physicians report that their strategies tend to become more verbally aggressive, however, when patients have not complied with previous requests and have more severe medical problems (Burgoon & Burgoon, 1990).

In addition to issues about strategy use, researchers have also tried to determine what types of strategies are most effective. Some research, for instance, has found that patients are more likely to comply with doctors who express similarity (i.e., indicate that they share things in common with the patient) and are more satisfied with doctors who communicate a willingness to listen, express affection, are composed, are similar, formal, and nondomineering (Burgoon, Pfau, Parrott, Birk, Coker, & Burgoon, 1987). Some research suggests that there are gender differences in strategy effectiveness (Klingle, 2004). Male doctors can get away with using more negative strategies than can female doctors. In addition, research indicates that both female and male doctors who vary their strategies are more effective than doctors who employ the same strategy repeatedly. Finally, in situations involving terminal illness, family members are more likely to consent to donating the patient's organs when compliance-gaining messages communicate additional emotional support to the family (Anker & Feeley, 2011).

strategy we will use, we try to determine what the emotional impact of the message will be. For example, if you tried to persuade your friend to study more, the friend might become angry and resentful. However, the friend could be grateful that you cared enough to say something. According to Hunter and Boster, we prefer using strategies that have a positive emotional impact.

But how do we decide which strategies will have a positive emotional impact and which will have a negative emotional impact? Hunter and Boster (1987) argued that each of us has a perceptual "threshold" that helps us make decisions about what strategies are acceptable and what strategies are not. Threatening someone, for example, may exceed the threshold, whereas promising something may not. Strategies that do not cross the threshold are more likely to be used.

A major implication of this model, of course, is that these thresholds are idiosyncratic, varying from one person to the next. Biff, for example, may be perfectly comfortable threatening others, whereas Babbs may not. Obviously, then, individual differences are important in determining the types of compliance-gaining messages that are used. For that reason, considerable research has examined several "sender" characteristics that affect strategy choice. Some of these characteristics include Machiavellianism (O'Hair & Cody, 1987), dogmatism (Roloff & Barnicott, 1979), self-monitoring (Smith, Cody, Lovette, & Canary, 1990; Snyder, 1979), type A personality (Lamude & Scudder, 1993), verbal aggressiveness and argumentativeness (Boster, Levine, & Kazoleas, 1993; Infante, Trebing, Shepard, & Seeds, 1984; Infante & Wigley, 1986), gender (Dallinger & Hample, 1994; deTurck & Miller, 1982; Fitzpatrick & Winke, 1979; Harris et al., 2014), culture (Burgoon, Dillard, Doran, & Miller, 1982; Hirokawa & Mirahara, 1986; Lu, 1997; Sellnow, Liu, & Venette, 2006), and age (Haslett, 1983). Because many of these characteristics were detailed in Chapter 5, we use the rest of this section to discuss the work of O'Keefe (1988, 1990), who argued that people produce different compliance-gaining messages because they think differently about communication. O'Keefe called these different beliefs about communication *design logics* and argued that they are threefold:

1. *Expressive design logic:* A person with this design logic believes that communication is a process by which people merely express what they think and feel. Such people fail to realize that communication can be used to achieve other goals and, therefore, "speak from the gut," dumping whatever they think and feel without any regard for what might be appropriate in a given situation. For that reason, such people's messages tend to be "primitive." For instance, a person with an expressive design logic might say something like the following: "You **##**$*@ jerk. You've had it. I'm going to get you fired for this!"
2. *Conventional design logic:* A person with this design logic believes that communication is a game played cooperatively, according to social conventions and procedures. Thus, people using this logic express their thoughts and feelings, but believe that they also must follow rules for appropriate social behavior in a given situation. For instance, a person with a conventional design logic might say something like the following: "You missed our meeting today and I don't appreciate this irresponsibility. If you miss one more meeting, you're fired."
3. *Rhetorical design logic:* A person with a rhetorical design logic believes that communication's purpose is to negotiate character, attitude, selves, and

situations. The process involves repeatedly solving and coordinating problems, consensus, and harmony. Thus, someone with this logic pursues multiple goals, tends to be proactive, and uses rational arguments. Here's an example:

> You have been coming back late from lunch and we need to reach some kind of understanding about this. I don't want to have to force you to follow the rules, but I will if I have to. But surely you can appreciate why we have rules and what function they serve. I know if you just think about the situation you will see how your behavior could be creating a problem in this office.
>
> (O'Keefe, 1988, p. 103)

Research has found that messages reflecting a rhetorical design logic are rated as more competent, favorable, and persuasive than messages reflecting the other design logics (Bingham & Burleson, 1989; O'Keefe & McCornack, 1987; Scott, Caughlin, Donovan-Kicken, & Mikucki-Enyart, 2013). What's more, compared to people with expressive design logics, those with rhetorical design logics feel more effective in their persuasive attempts. One study, for example, found that people with rhetorical design logics felt more confident that they could do or say something to intervene when they see others engaged in high-risk behavior (e.g., "a guy–girl hookup" in which a drunk and reluctant female is heading toward a possible sexual encounter with a male (White & Malkowski, 2014)).

THE STUDY OF COMPLIANCE-GAINING GOALS: EYES ON THE PRIZE

In addition to creating typologies of compliance-gaining strategies, researchers have also examined the ways in which people's goals influence how they seek compliance. Simply defined, goals are states of affairs we want to attain or maintain often through persuasion (see Wilson, 1997). The following sections examine the ways in which goals are important when trying to understand compliance gaining.

How Goals Bring Meaning to Compliance-Gaining Situations: What's It All About, Alfie?

Years ago, one of the authors heard a story about two men scooping mud and straw into wooden molds.

> A passerby asked one of the men what he was doing.
> "Scooping mud and straw into this mold," the man told him.
> "What are you doing?" the passerby asked the second man, who seemed much happier than the first.
> "I'm part of a team making a beautiful cathedral," came the reply.

We like this story because it illustrates how goals can help people define situations. Clearly, the first man's goal (scooping mud) makes his situation seem dismal compared to the second man's. Our point here is that goals give meaning to situations, including situations that involve compliance gaining. According to Wilson and Kunkel (2000), "Individuals interpret compliance gaining episodes based on their understanding of specific influence goals" (p. 197). In a summary of literature, Kellermann (2004) identified several common compliance-gaining goals that appear meaningful to people. These included goals to provide guidance; get advice, a favor, permission, or information; share time; initiate, escalate, or end a relationship; fulfill an obligation; get a date; change an opinion; and stop an annoying habit (Kellermann, 2004).

How might these different influence goals affect perceptions of a situation and, in turn, the ways in which compliance is sought? By way of example, imagine that you have two different influence goals. One is to ask someone a favor. The other is to get someone who owes you a favor to repay you in some way. According to Cai and Wilson (2000), requests such as these create entirely different situations for persuaders and, as a result, may lead to different compliance-seeking behavior. Clearly, this notion relates to our earlier discussion of politeness and compliance gaining. For instance, because asking favors may impose on another person, when asking favors, you may be less direct, provide the target with a "way out," and provide a lot of reasons for your imposition. However, if you're seeking compliance from someone who owes you a favor, you might be more direct and less polite in your compliance attempts, perhaps even making the target feel guilty if he or she does not comply.

Research by Cai and Wilson (2000) suggests that different types of requests, such as these, present similar concerns for persuaders in all cultures, though cultural differences may occur when making such requests. For instance, on one hand, asking a favor may lead you to feel indebted, regardless of your cultural background. On the other hand, because they are more concerned with saving face, people from Japan, compared to those from the United States, may worry more about imposing on others. As a result, the Japanese may be less direct and especially polite when seeking favors (Cai & Wilson, 2000). Moreover, because in-group favoritism is more prevalent in collectivistic, compared to individualistic cultures, managers from collectivistic cultures (e.g., China) may be more likely to use less polite tactics (e.g., threat) when influencing subordinates they perceive to be different from themselves (i.e., out-group members), and more likely to use pro-social tactics (e.g., ingratiation) when influencing in-group members (Sheer, 2012).

Primary and Secondary Goals: Wanting and Eating Your Cake

If we told you that the most effective strategy for getting something was to make threats, would you start threatening people every time you wanted something?

"Loan me 20 bucks, or I'll break your nose!"

"If you want to keep your job, get me some coffee!"

"Keep it up, and you can stand in the corner for the next hour."

"Let me get a tattoo, or I'll run away from home!"

We suspect that, for most of you, the answer to this question would be "no." But why? If threats really were so effective, why not throw them around a little? Because, you might be thinking to yourself, if I made threats every time I wanted something, I might not have many friends. Plus, you probably wouldn't like yourself too much. And if the other party still refused, you might be forced to follow through with the threat.

In the previous section, we discussed several different types of influence goals. In this section, we note that influence goals are not the only ones affecting compliance gaining. Indeed, most of the time we are concerned with pursuing multiple goals at the same time. Kellermann (1992), for example, argued that when seeking compliance, people are constrained by concerns for both efficiency (achieving their goal without wasting time and other resources) and appropriateness (accomplishing their goal in a socially acceptable and respectful way). Similarly, in his *goals–plans–action theory,* James Dillard (2004, 2008) argues that people pursue different types of goals when they are trying to influence someone. These goals are important because they determine the types of strategies that people plan to use when trying to gain compliance. To identify these goals, Dillard and colleagues (Dillard, Segrin, & Harden, 1989) asked students to imagine themselves in a compliance-gaining situation and to state why they would or wouldn't use particular influence strategies in that situation. Results of the study indicated that one primary goal, to influence the other person, is the most important in determining the type of strategy that a person uses. For example, a person may decide not to use a strategy because he or she thinks it won't work or because it is irrelevant.

In addition, Dillard (2008) identifies several secondary goals that influence people's choices in compliance-gaining situations. First, *identity goals* are concerned with maintaining one's moral standards and principles for living. Thus, people might decide to ignore a strategy that seems immoral. Second, *interaction goals* are concerned with creating a good impression and behaving in appropriate ways. For instance, people motivated by this goal might refuse to use a strategy that would make them look bad. Third, *resource goals* are concerned with maintaining a relationship and increasing personal rewards. Thus, using a strategy that would end a friendship would not be likely. Finally, *arousal goals* are concerned with maintaining levels of arousal (e.g., nervousness) within an acceptable range. Thus, people with this goal would not use a strategy that would make them too anxious (Dillard, 2008; Dillard et al., 1989).

According to the goals–plans–action theory (Dillard, 2008), then, primary and secondary goals have different degrees of compatibility. Based on the relationships among all the goals involved, a person develops *plans,* which are possible methods or approaches for dealing with the complex structure of goals. In order to generate and then put plans into action, people seeking compliance must consider possible strategies and tactics, which can be a complicated business. One study, for example, examined how people create messages aimed at persuading loved ones suffering from depression to seek professional help. Results indicated that, oftentimes, a focus on secondary goals (e.g., saving both parties' face) led to the design of non-optimal messages (Wilson, Dorrance Hall, Gettings, & Pastor, 2015).

Of course, a number of variables might affect goals, plans, and actions in the process of seeking compliance. Consider, for example, relational certainty. It turns out that some people are far more certain than others when it comes to knowing whether they or their partners want to pursue a relationship. Given this, Knobloch (2006) surmised that, when asking someone for a date, things would go more smoothly for people who experienced little relational ambiguity than for those who experienced a lot of it. Specifically, those with less certainty are more likely to worry about competing goals such as damaging a friendship. Not only that, when planning and using their compliance-gaining messages, uncertainty may make people less sure about what to say. It might also get in the way of them saying it effectively. To test these ideas, research participants were observed requesting hypothetical dates from people they were attracted to in real life. The participants were asked to leave phone messages, requesting dates from people they knew and were attracted to. Some were more certain about their relationships than others. Results of the study confirmed the researcher's suspicions: Relational certainty was associated with requests for dates that were judged to be more fluent, affiliative, and effective. Here are two examples of requests from the study (Knobloch, 2006, p. 273). We hope it is obvious which was produced by the person with more relational certainty:

> "Hey babe, it's Kevin. I was just calling to see if you had any plans tonight, 'cause I wondered if I could take you out to dinner or something. So, just give me a call whenever you get the message. Bye."

> "Hey, Emily, uh, this is Bob. Um, yeah, just wondering what you were up to tonight. Uh, haven't talked to you in . . . in a little while, so, uh, yeah, I think there's some stuff we need to talk about. So, um, if I don't end up talking to you, I guess I'll talk to you on the Internet later. We'll see ya."

In short, then, compliance-gaining situations are not as simple as they may seem. People not only generate and select tactics that they think will help them gain compliance but do so in the face of multiple constraints, including competing goals and other factors.

PROBLEMS FACING COMPLIANCE RESEARCH: TROUBLE IN PARADISE

Up to this point, the things we have said about compliance gaining probably seem fairly simple; when trying to persuade people, we have a number of strategies at our disposal, and the strategies we use are determined in part by the situation, our personal characteristics, and our goals. Despite this rather straightforward description, however, there has been a lot of confusion and argument about research methods that have been used to draw such conclusions. Without straying too far into the weeds, we believe it is important to mention at least a couple of concerns here.

To illustrate one issue, imagine that you could listen to any song right now. What would it be? Can you think of three songs? Your choice of songs is open ended. Depending on how much music you listen to, coming up with your three favorites off the top of your head might not be all that easy. Now imagine you are on iTunes and looking at a list of the top 20 songs, from which you must pick 3. Your choice of songs is limited.

What does all of this have to do with compliance-gaining research? If you stop to think about it, the Marwell and Schmitt (1967) study we discussed earlier is not entirely different from our iTunes example. Only, instead of asking their research participants to select from a list of song titles, Marwell and Schmitt asked people to select from a list of pre-established compliance-seeking strategies. The problems with such an approach, however, have been pointed out by numerous researchers (e.g., Cody, McLaughlin, & Jordan, 1980; Wiseman & Schenck-Hamlin, 1981). First, by way of illustration, let's return to the iTunes example. Let's say your favorite Beyoncé song did not appear on the list, so you settle for a song by Rihanna instead. Obviously, your choice has been constrained by the songs that are on the top 20 list. You can't pick a song that's not available. Researchers who provide their subjects with lists of compliance-gaining strategies constrain their subjects' choices in the same way. You can't pick a strategy if it isn't on the list.

Second, imagine you notice a song that you hadn't remembered but would have selected had it come to mind. In other words, seeing the song title made you more likely to choose it. In the same way, strategies selected from a list can artificially "cue" participants. When participating in a study, it's possible that we see a strategy on a list and think, "Oh yeah, that seems like a good one." But in real life, the strategy would not have occurred to us. Thus, the list makes some strategies seem more popular than they truly are.

Finally, imagine you hate country music but are with a group of friends who love the stuff. To fit in, you download some Carrie Underwood tunes. Researchers have argued that the same type of thing can happen when participating in research. Specifically, in order to "fit in" or "look good," we may not report what we would do in real life but rather what makes us look the most socially desirable. Thus, although Astrid may go around threatening people in real life, she may tell researchers that she uses more prosocial compliance-gaining tactics. Having a list of tactics to choose from may make this *social desirability bias* more likely to occur.

In an attempt to overcome these problems, some researchers have scrapped "selection" in favor of "construction" procedures (e.g., Wiseman & Schenck-Hamlin, 1981). The argument goes like this: If people are presented with a situation requiring persuasion and are asked to describe the strategy they would use (i.e., construct the strategy from scratch rather than select it from a list), the strategy will better reflect true behavior, not misrepresent strategies that are not typically used, and be less prone to social desirability bias.

As neat as this sounds, research indicates little difference in the results of studies using these two techniques (Boster, 1988; Plax, Kearney, & Sorensen, 1990). What may be of even greater importance, though, are the findings of a study by Dillard (1988). To determine which of several methods for assessing compliance-gaining behavior was the best,[1] Dillard asked people to rate, on paper, how likely they would be to use 16 different compliance-gaining messages in persuasive situations. He then observed these people in actual compliance-gaining situations but found that, regardless of the method he used to assess compliance-gaining behavior, there was no correspondence between the paper–pencil measures and actual behavior. In other words, what people *said* they would do was not the same as what they actually *did*.

When we consider the implications of this study, it reminds us of a story we once heard about a man who exits a cab late at night and sees a drunk on his hands and knees, snooping around a street light. The man asks, "Is anything wrong?" to which the drunk replies, "Yeah, I lost my keys." The man says, "Did you lose them here?" The drunk answers, "Naw, I lost them over there in the dark, but the light is much better here." In the same vein, Dillard's (1988) study illustrates that investigators have been looking very hard at compliance gaining, but perhaps not in the right way.

CHAPTER 11

Sequential Persuasion

"IF YOU'RE A DOOR-TO-DOOR salesperson," we're told by a friend who once made his living selling encyclopedias, "half your job is getting into people's houses. Once you're inside," he informed us, "they're yours, all yours."

According to our friend, most door-to-door salespeople have sneaky ways of getting their feet into your doorway. Some mention your neighbors by name. Some ask for a glass of water. Our pal had a whole spiel based largely on deception. He's not proud of it now, he admitted, but when he greeted customers, he was trained to look like anything but a salesperson.

"After introducing myself," he told us, "I promised I was not going to try to sell them anything. I was just in the neighborhood conducting surveys. I asked them if they would give me their opinions about their family's educational needs and told them that, if they did, I would repay them with 'educational materials.' That usually got me inside."

Once our friend was in the door, he asked his customers to respond to a phony "opinion survey" (e.g., "Do your kids use the library?" "Do your kids go to the library after dark?") and then showed them a set of encyclopedias that he was "willing to give them, for promotional reasons, if they promised to keep the set up to date." How could they do that? Simply by purchasing one yearbook per year for the next 10 years.

Many of the customers agreed to this seemingly unbelievable offer. What they did not realize was that the amount of money they paid for the yearbooks actually covered the cost of the encyclopedias and then some. They'd been "schmoozed" into buying something they thought they were getting for free.

This example, together with the strategies discussed in Chapter 9, shows that oftentimes persuasion is not as simple as making a single request or giving one speech. Persuasion, quite frequently, is a process that requires a number of steps. Indeed, before making his pitch, our friend had to get himself into the customer's house. And for reasons we discuss later, by getting customers to agree to the survey, our friend probably increased his chances of making a sale.

In this chapter, we extend concepts from Chapter 9 by discussing the topic of "sequential persuasion," which examines social influence as a "multi-step" process. Similarly, this chapter extends concepts from Chapter 10 because sequential persuasion, for the most part, encompasses a number of tactics that are aimed at gaining compliance (i.e., getting people to behave in a particular way). We explore research that shows how people increase their persuasiveness, often at the expense of others, by saying or doing something before, or sometimes after, making their request. We begin with a strategy known as *pregiving*.

PREGIVING: THE OLD "I'LL-SCRATCH-YOUR-BACK-IF-YOU'LL-SCRATCH-MINE" APPROACH

Many years ago, when most cameras still used film, one of the authors received a package in the mail. The package contained two unused rolls of film and a letter explaining that the film was a gift. The letter went on to explain how, after using the film, the author could mail it to the company to be processed. And the funny thing is, the author did, even though the cost of the processing was more expensive than taking the film to a local developer. Why was the author persuaded to spend more money? Because the ploy used by the processing company is a well-known and effective tactic of persuasion known as pregiving. *Pregiving* entails trying to get someone to comply by doing favors or giving gifts in advance. When supermarkets offer free samples of foods to taste, they are employing this strategy. And when service personnel are especially helpful (e.g., a food server boxes leftovers for you), they are using this approach (Seiter & Weger, in press).

A classic study done by Dennis Regan (1971) showed how effective the pregiving strategy can be. In the study, first-year students at Stanford University who had been asked to participate in an experiment on "aesthetics" were seated in a room with another student. What the students had not been told was that the other student was a confederate who had been planted there by the researcher. After a few minutes, the confederate left the room. When he returned, he was either empty-handed or was carrying two Coca-Colas. If he was empty-handed, he simply sat back down. But if he had sodas, he offered one to the research subject and said, "I bought one for you too."

Seems nice enough, but there's a catch; later, the plant informed the subject that he was selling raffle tickets for a new high school gym and would appreciate it if the subject would do him a favor by buying some tickets. Not surprisingly, the results of the study revealed that subjects who had been given a soda ahead of time bought almost twice as many raffle tickets as those who had been given nothing.

Real-world persuaders are also known to put the pregiving tactic to use. For example, in touristy areas of big cities (the Louvre in Paris, the Dome of the Rock in Jerusalem, the Alamo in San Antonio, the Parthenon in Athens), panhandlers have figured out a tricky way to get donations from unsuspecting tourists. The panhandlers wait a block or two from a well-known tourist attraction. When tourists walk by, clearly headed for the attraction, the panhandlers catch up with them, walk in stride, and proceed to "guide" the tourists to their destination. Once there, the panhandlers ask for a donation for the unrequested and unneeded service rendered.

The pregiving tactic works in other contexts as well. For instance, as a suit salesperson, one of the authors was trained to ask customers if they would like to have their jackets pressed while they were shopping. Very few refused the favor, and even those who did were cheerfully surprised at the offer. What they did not understand was that there was a hidden rationale behind the gesture; not only was it an effective means of getting customers to spend more time shopping, but when it came to purchasing a suit, who better to buy from than the nice salesperson who had already done them a favor?

Two final examples of the pregiving strategy are, to us, perhaps the most disturbing. First, the next time a man asks if he can buy you a drink, women beware; a study by George, Gournic, and McAfee (1988) found that if women allow men to buy them drinks, both men and women perceive the women to be more sexually available than if the drinks are refused.[1] Second, in another study (Happ, Melzer, & Steffgen, 2016), experimenters posing as interviewers gave passersby a free package of chocolates before asking them to divulge confidential information such as computer passwords. Remarkably, 47.9 percent of participants revealed their passwords to complete strangers. That's compared to the (still remarkable) 29.8 percent who did the same without the incentive. Bottom line? That old warning—"never take candy from strangers"—is worth paying attention to.

Why Is the Pregiving Tactic Persuasive?

Common explanations for why pregiving works or doesn't work include liking, physical attraction, perceived ulterior motives, gratitude, impression management, and internalized social norms (see Burger, Sanchez, Imberi, & Grande, 2009; Goei, Roberto, Meyer, & Carlyle, 2007; Hendrickson & Goei, 2009). The *liking explanation* suggests that people who do or give something are perceived as kind and good. As a result, they are well liked, and, in turn, more persuasive. Similarly, the *physical attraction explanation* suggests that doing favors leads people to be seen as more attractive, which, in turn, leads them to be more persuasive. The *perceived ulterior motives explanation* suggests that when a favor is seen as a tool of manipulation, it is less likely to lead to compliance. Indeed, Groves, Cialdini, and Couper (1992) argued that pregiving actually decreases compliance when it is perceived as a bribe or a pressure tactic. The *gratitude explanation* suggests that receiving a favor leads to positive emotional states (i.e., feelings of gratitude) that motivate benevolent behavior. In other words, people comply because the favor creates a spirit of thankfulness and benevolence. The last two explanations, *impression management* and *internalized social norm*, are based on *the norm of reciprocity* (or *indebtedness*), which, if you recall from Chapter 10, states that it is desirable to repay what another person has provided us (Cialdini & Goldstein, 2004). More specifically, the impression management explanation suggests that repaying favors is desirable because it keeps you from looking like an ungrateful freeloader. The internalized social norm explanation suggests that repaying favors is desirable because it makes people feel good about themselves when they do the right thing.

Although all of these explanations have received support, the studies that test them side by side favor some explanations over others. For example, in a study by Burger and colleagues (2009), after receiving or not receiving a favor (an unexpected bottled water), research participants were asked to complete and return a survey. Half the participants were told that the person who had done them the favor would be collecting the surveys personally, while the other half were told that they could leave the surveys in a clearly labeled drop-off box. Results indicated that participants who had received the favor were more likely to complete the surveys regardless of how they returned the surveys. This, of course, supported the internalized social norm explanation over the impression management explanation. To be sure, who cares about impressing a drop-off box?

A second study conducted by Goei and his colleagues (Goei et al., 2007) tested the liking, gratitude, and indebtedness explanations. Support was found for the liking and gratitude explanations but depended on whether the person seeking compliance benefited from gaining compliance. Specifically, when the person doing a favor was seeking compliance for something that would personally benefit him or her (e.g., the person could win $50 by selling a lot of raffle tickets), the gratitude explanation was superior. If, however, the person doing the favor did not personally benefit from compliance (e.g., he or she was selling raffle tickets for a good cause), the liking explanation was superior.

Finally, a study by Hendrickson and Goei (2009) found support for the gratitude, liking, and physical attraction explanations, at least when a favor was done by a person of low status. Regardless of which explanation holds true in a given situation, pregiving is a robust strategy that works well across cultures and persuasive contexts.

FOOT IN THE DOOR: THE "GIVE-ME-AN-INCH-AND-I'LL-TAKE-A-MILE" TACTIC

Some time ago, one of the authors and a friend were leaving a shopping mall when they were approached by a woman. She was about 30 years old, nicely dressed, and had a small child with her.

"Excuse me," she said to the author, "would you please tell me what time it is?" The author obliged.

"I was wondering if you could also spare a few dollars?" the woman added. She claimed that her car had run out of gas, she had forgotten her purse, and, if the author would give her his address, she would be happy to return the money to him.

Once again, the author obliged, giving her three or four dollars. He never heard from the woman again. The author's friend, however, saw the same woman several weeks later, using the same scam but at a different mall.

In retrospect, there were probably several things that made the woman successful in her attempt to gain compliance. The fact that she was well dressed made her story seem more believable. She gave a plausible reason for needing the money. And having a small child with her probably created more sympathy. Interestingly, however, having nice clothes, good reasons, and a small child may not have been the only keys to her success. A considerable amount of research shows that the woman might have increased her chances of compliance by asking for the time *before* she asked for money (hmm, maybe there is a good reason then for not giving a stranger "the time of day").

The tactic we have just described is often referred to as the *foot-in-the-door strategy,* hereafter called FITD. The tactic involves making a small request first and then making a second, larger request. Of course, it is the second, larger request that most interests the persuader. The first, small request is merely a setup. For instance, the encyclopedia salesperson we talked about earlier used this tactic when he asked people if they would answer a short survey before he asked for a sale. He didn't really care about their responses to the survey; he simply wanted to soften them up. For reasons we discuss later, when people comply with a smaller request, it often makes them more likely to comply with a second, larger request.

The first study to demonstrate the effectiveness of the FITD strategy was conducted by Jonathan Freedman and Scott Fraser (1966) at Stanford University. These researchers were interested in finding out if they could get housewives to agree to a very large request. Specifically, they asked housewives to allow a team of five or six men into their homes for two hours. The men, they were told, would have complete freedom in the house to go through the cupboards and storage spaces in order to classify all of the household products that were there. Before being approached with this request, however, some of the women were set up with a smaller initial request. That is, three days before making the large request, the researchers called some of the housewives and asked if they would participate in a survey about household products (e.g., "What brand of soap do you use?"). Surprisingly, about 50 percent of the housewives who agreed to answer the survey also agreed to let complete strangers rifle through their houses. However, when the researchers had not approached housewives with a smaller request first, only about 25 percent of the housewives agreed to the subsequent larger request (Freedman & Fraser, 1966).

Why Is a Foot in the Door So Persuasive?

The FITD tactic appears to be a robust tactic that is effective given the right conditions (Burger, 1999). But what makes it so persuasive? The most common explanation for the effectiveness of the FITD tactic is based on Bem's (1972) *self-perception theory* (see DeJong, 1979; Freedman & Fraser, 1966). According to this theory, people come to know about their attitudes, emotions, and other internal states by inferring them from their own behavior (Bem, 1972). For example, if you notice yourself eating a lot of Nutrageous candy bars, you are likely to come to the conclusion that you have a favorable attitude toward chocolate. In other words, you use your behavior to infer your attitude.

As an explanation for the FITD effect, self-perception theory says this: When you agree to comply with a small request, you see yourself as an altruistic person who is likely to help. Once you form that impression, you are motivated to behave in a manner consistent with that impression. Thus, when a larger request is made, you are more likely to comply.

Although some research points to the viability of self-perception theory as an explanation for the effectiveness of the FITD tactic, other evidence is not so optimistic. For example, Gorassini and Olson (1995) conducted a study that measured how helpful people perceived themselves to be after complying with a first, small request. They found that although people's self-ratings of helpfulness were affected by compliance with the small request, those changes did not always predict people's compliance with a second, larger request. Moreover, compliance with a second, larger request often occurred without people perceiving themselves as being more helpful. Dillard (1990) argued that results of studies such as these show that more theorizing about the FITD tactic is necessary.

A meta-analysis by Burger (1999), however, suggests that self-perception *does* affect how much people comply with FITD requests. All research may not indicate this, however, because self-perception is probably not the only process involved. Specifically, Burger noted that other psychological processes operating in an FITD situation may overwhelm whatever impact self-perception has. As a result, not all studies will support a self-perception account of the FITD's effectiveness. By way of example, people may be less willing to comply with a request if they think most other people would reject the request. Thus, as Burger (1999) notes, "it appears that whatever push self-perception gives toward agreement with the target request can be overwhelmed by telling the individual that few people go along with such requests" (p. 323). In short, self-perception probably plays a role in the FITD's effectiveness, but the tactic's success depends on a lot of other factors (see Cialdini & Goldstein, 2004). We discuss some of these next.

When Does a Foot in the Door Work?

Research tells us that some of the following conditions play an important role in determining the effectiveness of the FITD tactic:

1. *Size of the initial request.* Is getting a person to comply with any request enough to get the person to comply with later requests? Research shows that the initial request should be neither too large nor too small. Seligman, Bush, and Kirsch (1976) argued that "the first request must be of sufficient size for the foot in the door technique to work" (p. 519). However, the initial request cannot be so large that it is rejected. Thus, the persuader must strike a balance between making a large enough initial request to trigger the FITD effect but not so large that it is declined. For instance, asking for a penny so you might later get a larger donation probably would not work because the penny might be perceived as

inconsequential. However, asking the average person for $1,000 to begin with might be a reach. In short, the persuader wants to use the largest possible request that will be accepted.

2. *Prosocialness of the request.* In a review of several studies, Dillard, Hunter, and Burgoon (1984) found that the FITD tactic is more effective when used for prosocial causes than it is when used for self-serving reasons. With this in mind, the FITD tactic would probably be more useful to social workers trying to raise money to help the homeless than it would be for commissioned salespeople.

3. *External incentives to comply.* Meta-analyses by Burger (1999) and Dillard and colleagues (1984) indicated that people are less susceptible to the FITD tactic if they are offered external incentives for complying with the first request. Most researchers use self-perception theory to explain these effects. For example, if you received a gift for agreeing to listen to a timeshare sales pitch, you would not form an impression of yourself as someone who is willing to comply readily with requests. You are only complying because you have a material reason for doing so. Thus, because the pregiving strategy (discussed earlier) uses external incentives, it may not be a good idea to use it and the FITD strategies together (see Bell, Cholerton, Fraczek, Rohlfs, & Smith, 1994; Weyant, 1996).

4. *Who makes the requests.* For the FITD strategy to work, the same person needn't make both the initial and the follow-up requests. Indeed, it is often the case that a person who complies with a request by one person will also comply with a second request, even when the second request is made by a different person. In fact, research by Chartrand, Pinckert, and Burger (1999) found that when a different person made the second request, compliance was more likely than when the same person made both requests. This was especially true when there was no time delay between the first and second requests (Chartrand et al., 1999).

5. *Labeling.* Imagine that just after you donated blood to the Red Cross, a nurse tells you how generous you are and thanks you. Or better yet, imagine that the nurse gives you a pin or bumper sticker that says, "I Care Enough to Donate Blood." A review of studies by Burger (1999) reported that this type of labeling increases the odds that you will comply with larger follow-up requests (e.g., to donate blood every month for a year). This finding, of course, is consistent with self-perception theory—that is, if someone labels you as someone who is helpful, you may begin to see yourself that way and, as a result, act in accordance with your self-perception. (For a different spin on social labeling, see Box 11.1.)

6. *Preference for consistency.* You may remember from Chapter 3 that most people strive for consistency in their behaviors and attitudes. How does this relate to the FITD tactic? If you agree to an initial request, you should be motivated to behave consistently by also agreeing to a second request. This is especially true if the two requests are similar (see Burger, 1999). According to Cialdini, Trost, and Newsom (1995), some people have a greater need for such consistency than others. As might be expected, those with a higher need for consistency are more influenced by the FITD tactic than are those who are not (Cialdini et al., 1995). This is especially true when people with a higher need for consistency are reminded of how important consistency is (Guadagno, Asher, Demaine, & Cialdini, 2001).

7. *Self-concept clarity.* Did you know that some people have a clearer picture of their self-concept than others? These folks are said to have "high self-concept clarity." Interestingly, research shows that these folks are more susceptible to the FITD tactic than are people with a fuzzier idea of self (Burger & Guadagno, 2003). Why? It turns out that people with high self-concept clarity are more likely to change their self-concepts. As such, after complying with an initial request, they are more likely than people with low self-concept clarity to see themselves as helpful and, in turn, comply with a second request (Burger & Guadagno, 2003).

BOX 11.1 | I'm So Hungry I Could Eat a Horse: The Darker Side of Labeling

Up to now, we've seen that labeling people in a positive way ("you're so helpful!") may lead them to perceive themselves in a positive way, which, in turn, may make them more likely to comply with requests for help. But what do you suppose would happen if people were labeled in a negative way? Is it possible that they would be more likely to comply with requests for help in order to restore their damaged self-esteem? A study by Nicolas Guéguen (2001) tested this possibility in a devilish way. More than 100 pedestrians on a busy street in France were approached individually by three women who were part of the study. The first woman asked each unsuspecting target, "Excuse me . . ., my bag is heavy and I would like to buy a magazine. . . . Would you mind keeping an eye on my bag while I go and get it?" (p. 745). If the pedestrians agreed, they were left with a bag, which contained a package on top labeled "Horse meat." Twenty seconds later, half of the pedestrians were approached by the second woman, who looked at the bag and said, "It is really appalling to eat horse meat. When I think that it is thanks to the horse that we have evolved so much. You should be ashamed." (p. 745). Without waiting, the second woman left, the first woman returned with her magazine, thanked the pedestrians, and left with her bag of meat. Finally, the third woman approached the pedestrians and asked one of two things. Half of the pedestrians were asked to sign a petition favoring the proper treatment by the government of abandoned animals. The other half were asked to sign a petition favoring the limitation of traffic in the city center. Results of the study showed that pedestrians who received the negative label were significantly more likely to sign the petition, but only if asked to sign the petition about the treatment of animals. This, of course, makes sense: Having been shamed for eating pony parts, the second petition allowed pedestrians to buck the negative label and declare their unbridled love for horses.

THE DOOR-IN-THE-FACE TACTIC: "ASK FOR THE STARS"

One of our students used to work selling jewelry in a large department store. She tells us that her approach to sales was very different from that of the other salespeople with whom she worked. Most of them, she tells us, started by showing their customers the "bottom of the line" merchandise. To increase their sales, they then moved to more expensive merchandise, demonstrating that "more money" meant "higher quality." However, our student started by showing her customers the most expensive merchandise first. Typically, they did not purchase what they were first shown but, even so, our student claims that while she worked at that store, her sales were always higher than anyone else's.

Actually, we are not surprised by our student's success as a salesperson. Whether she knew it or not, she was using a tactic of persuasion that researchers have known to be effective for many years. Often called the *door-in-the-face technique,* or DITF, this tactic is just the opposite of the FITD strategy. It works by first making a request so large that it is turned down, then following it up with a second, smaller request. Of course, just as with the FITD tactic, compliance with the second request is what the persuader has been aiming for all along.

The first empirical study of the DITF tactic was conducted by Robert Cialdini and his colleagues (Cialdini et al., 1975). To visualize the study, imagine what you would do if someone approached you, identified herself as a representative of a youth-counseling program, and asked if you'd be willing to chaperone a group of juvenile delinquents on a one day visit to the zoo. If you were like most of the people in the study (83 percent), you would refuse the request. It turns out, however, that people were much more responsive to the request if something happened beforehand. Specifically, when people were asked to volunteer two hours per week counseling juvenile delinquents for a minimum of two years, and then asked to chaperone the delinquents on the zoo trip, they were three times more likely to serve as chaperons. In other words, people were more likely to do a smaller favor (zoo chaperon) after refusing to do a large favor (counseling twice a week for up to two years) first.

Since the 1975 study of Cialdini and colleagues, the effectiveness of the DITF tactic has been demonstrated again and again (see reviews by Cialdini & Guadagno, 2004; Dillard et al., 1984; Feeley, Anker, & Aloe, 2012; Feeley, Fico, Shaw, Lee, & Griffin, 2017; Fern, Monroe, & Avila, 1986; O'Keefe & Hale, 1998, 2001). But rather than examine those studies, we turn now to a discussion of *why* the DITF tactic is thought to be so effective.

Why Is a Door in the Face So Persuasive?

A number of explanations for the persuasiveness of the DITF tactic have been proposed and tested, with some faring better than others.

1. *The perceptual contrast effect* (Cialdini, 1993) suggests that people are likely to comply with a second, smaller request because, compared to the initial, larger request, the second request seems much smaller than it normally would have (e.g., a $500 diamond ring seems inexpensive compared to the $3,000 rings but expensive compared to the $100 rings).
2. The *self-presentation explanation* (Pendleton & Batson, 1979) suggests that when people reject an initial request, they become concerned that they will be perceived negatively and thus comply with a second request in order to make themselves look better.
3. *Reciprocal concessions* (Cialdini et al., 1975) suggests that, when a persuader employing the DITF tactic makes a concession by following up with a smaller request, we may be motivated to reciprocate the favor by complying with the second request.
4. *The legitimacy explanation* (see Feeley et al., 2017) suggests that making concessions can signal that a persuader has a greater need for compliance

FIGURE 11.1
The door in the face
tactic gone awry.

Source: Calvin and Hobbes
© (1985) Watterson.
Distributed by Universal
Press Syndicate. Reprinted
with permission. All Rights
Reserved.

(i.e., the persuader is making a genuine request), which, in turn, engenders a greater obligation to help the persuader.

5. The *guilt-based account* (O'Keefe & Figgé, 1997) argues that refusing an initial, prosocial request leads persuadees to experience guilt, which they attempt to reduce by agreeing to a second request.

6. The *social responsibility position* (Tusing & Dillard, 2000) suggests that we think it is socially responsible to help people who deserve it. As such, we're more likely to comply when follow-up messages ask for our help.

Based on analyses of multiple experiments, the social responsibility (Feeley et al., 2012) and reciprocal concessions (Feeley et al., 2017) explanations have found the most support. That said, according to Feeley and his colleagues (2017), perceptual contrast, guilt, and the legitimacy of requests probably contribute to the tactic's effectiveness.

When Does a Door in the Face Work?

Research tells us that some of the following conditions play an important role in determining the effectiveness of the DITF tactic:

1. *Size of the initial request.* For the DITF strategy to work, the first request must be large enough to guarantee rejection by the persuadee but not so large as to appear incredible (Cialdini et al., 1975). But is there a right size for the initial request? A study by Even-Chen, Yinon, and Bizman (1978) addressed this question and concluded that the initial request must be large for the door in the face to work. However, they noted that the request must not be so large that it evokes anger, resentment, or incredulity in the persuadee (Even-Chen et al., 1978).

2. *Type of compliance sought.* A meta-analysis by Feeley and colleagues (2012) found that the DITF tactic is not effective when used for self-serving reasons but can increase compliance when used for altruistic purposes. Moreover, the tactic works better when seeking volunteers (e.g., to participate in research) than when seeking monetary donations, and for obtaining verbal, rather than behavioral, compliance. Finally, the DITF tactic is more effective than a single request when compliance is more difficult to achieve (Feeley et al., 2012).

3. *Elapsed time between first and second requests.* Several reviews of studies on the DITF (Dillard et al., 1984; Feeley et al., 2012; Fern et al., 1986) argue that compliance is increased when the delay between the two requests is short. By way of example, Guéguen, Jacob, and Meineri (2011) found that restaurant patrons who had refused invitations to order dessert were likely to accept invitations to order tea or coffee, especially when the follow-up invitation occurred immediately after the refusal rather than three minutes later.

4. *Can a different person make the second request?* Researchers who support the reciprocal concessions explanation (discussed earlier) like to point out that the DITF strategy does not work if the first and second requests are made by different people. Indeed, if a door-to-door salesperson offers you a vacuum cleaner for $500, and a different salesperson offers you the appliance for $300, you might perceive a contrast but not a concession. However, if the same salesperson made both offers, you might be more likely to reciprocate the concession and comply with the second offer.

THE THAT'S-NOT-ALL TACTIC: SEEKING COMPLIANCE BY SWEETENING THE DEAL

Remember our friend who sold encyclopedias? We began the chapter by telling you how he used to weasel his way into houses with the foot-in-the-door tactic. But that's not all he did to sell his books. He also used what he calls the "but wait, that's-not-all" strategy. Here's how it worked: After presenting the books and before asking for the sale, he showed his customers several other items they could receive for free (an atlas, a dictionary, a thesaurus) *if* they agreed to buy the encyclopedias. Perhaps you've observed this strategy used in other contexts. For instance, haven't we all seen those commercials for food and vegetable slicers and dicers? Typically, after a demonstration, you're asked, "How much would you pay for this?" Then you're presented with an add-on knife. How much would you pay now? How about if a carrot cleaner were added? Well, you get the idea, so "call now!"

To see whether this tactic was effective, Jerry Burger (1896) conducted several studies. In one, the tactic was used on customers at a bake sale. When customers asked about the price of a cupcake, they were told one of two things. Some customers were told that a cupcake and two cookies sold for 75 cents. Other customers, however, were not told about the cookies right away—a few seconds after they'd been told that the cupcakes sold for 75 cents each, it was explained that the price included the cost of two cookies. Results of the study showed that the "that's-not-all" tactic sold more cupcakes. Specifically, although only 40 percent of the customers who had been presented cookies and cupcakes at the same time made a purchase, 73 percent of the "that's-not-all" customers made a purchase.

Why does this tactic work so well? According to Burger (1986), the "that's-not-all" tactic's effectiveness may be because of the norm of reciprocity and contrast effect (discussed earlier in this chapter). First, because the seller has sweetened the deal by adding on items, the customer may feel obligated to buy the product, thereby *reciprocating* the seller's action. Second, in *contrast* to the original deal, the revised deal may seem much better than it would have without the comparison.

But wait, there's more: Before concluding this discussion, we should note that the "that's-not-all" tactic can include more than adding on items to make a deal look better; it can also involve lowering the price of an item. For example, Burger (1986) found that more people bought cupcakes when the price was dropped from $1 to 75 cents than when the price was simply stated as 75 cents. You might have noticed that, in this form, the "that's-not-all" tactic is a lot like the door in the face approach. The difference is that, when using the door in the face approach, the persuader waits for the initial request to be rejected before following up with a lesser request. Persuaders using the "that's-not-all" tactic do not wait for the initial request to be rejected before sweetening the deal. Some evidence indicates that of the two techniques, the "that's-not-all" tactic is the more persuasive (Burger, 1986). (For a look at how these two tactics and others might be used together, see Box 11.2.) Even so, salespeople or others wishing to use this tactic need to be careful. Some evidence suggests that it might backfire if the salesperson's initial request is too large (Burger, Reed, DeCesare, Rauner, & Rozolis, 1999). It's not difficult to imagine why. For example, if a salesperson asked you to buy a chocolate chip cookie for $5 and then lowered the price to 75 cents, you'd probably be suspicious that the initial price was purposely inflated and that the salesperson was trying to pull a fast one. (For more drawbacks on a related influence approach, see Box 11.3.)

BOX 11.2 | Doors and Feet: An Extension and Combination of Tactics

If given a choice of sequential request techniques to use, which works best? Some research has addressed this question. For instance, Chan and Au (2011) found that Chinese children completed more academic work when teachers used the door-in-the-face technique (e.g., "Complete 100 questions," then "Just complete 20 questions.") than when they used the foot-in-the-door technique (e.g., "Complete 5 questions," then "Complete 20 questions."). However, rather than pitting techniques against one another, perhaps a better approach, when possible, is to use them together. Indeed, research has found that combinations of sequential tactics can be effective (Goldman & Creason, 1981; Goldman, Creason, & McCall, 1981; Goldman, Gier, & Smith, 1981; Souchet & Girandola, 2013). For example, two doors in the face or two feet in the door made people more compliant than a single door or foot. Further research by Goldman (1986) found that the door-in-the-face and foot-in-the-door techniques also can be combined. Here's how it works: First, people are presented with a very large request that they are almost sure to reject (e.g., "Would you call 150 people and ask them questions about the zoo?"). Second, people are presented with a moderate request that serves as a foot in the door. Because this request follows the very large request, however, it can be more difficult than the initial request that is typically used in the foot-in-the-door approach (e.g., "Would you participate in a 25-minute survey about the zoo?" versus "Would you answer three or four questions about the zoo?"). Finally, people are asked to comply with the request that the persuaders wanted them to comply with all along (e.g., "Would you stuff and address 75 envelopes with information about the zoo?"). Results of Goldman's (1986) study found that this combination approach was more persuasive than either tactic alone.

THE LOW-BALL TACTIC: CHANGING THE DEAL

If you've ever bought a car from a dealership, there's a chance you've seen the *low-ball tactic* in action. Here's how it works. First, the salesperson makes you a deal that looks too good to refuse. Perhaps the car you want is offered for several hundred dollars less than any place else you've shopped. Excited, you accept the offer. But then, a number of things might go wrong. For instance, the salesperson might inform you that the quoted price did not include an expensive option (e.g., air conditioning) that you thought was included. Or, the salesperson might check with his or her manager for approval and later report that the deal was rejected. Why? The dealership would lose money if the car were sold so cheap. In short, the original offer is taken back, and you are asked to pay a much higher price for the car.

Slimy? You bet. But also very effective. Indeed, two meta-analyses of multiple experiments found that the low-ball tactic increased compliance significantly (Burger & Caputo, 2015; Pascual, Carpenter, Guéguen, & Girandola, 2016). By way of example, in one study, Cialdini and colleagues (Cialdini, Cacioppo, Bassett, & Miller, 1978) wanted to see if they could get undergraduate students to wake up

---

BOX 11.3 | Cheapening Your Product by Sweetening the Deal: The Drawbacks of Including Free Gifts With Purchases

Not long ago, one of the authors, intending to buy a Valentine's Day gift for his wife, ended up at a cosmetics counter in a local department store. After sniffing at a dozen samples he'd dabbed on his arms, he settled on some perfumed lotions. It wasn't until he'd paid and was leaving the counter that the salesperson called after him, explaining she'd forgotten that those particular lotions came with a free gift—a little handbag with an orange ribbon. The author didn't think much of the handbag—after all, it was just a freebie, probably something that was out of style or didn't sell—but he didn't mention that when he presented it, alongside the lotions, as a gift to his wife. To his surprise, she was thrilled. In fact, she made a bigger fuss over that bag than those darned expensive lotions. At the time, the author chalked up the differences between his and his wife's perceptions to his lack of appreciation for handbags. But then he came across a study suggesting that he was not alone; apparently, other people react the same way to free gifts. Indeed, in one study (Raghubir, 2004), research participants were asked to evaluate the desirability of a pearl bracelet. Half were told that the bracelet was a free gift accompanying the purchase of another item, while the other half were presented the bracelet as a stand-alone product. Results showed that the second group was willing to pay more for the bracelet than the first group. Similarly, another study showed that, compared to bundling items and selling them together, marketing them in "buy-one, get-one-free" offers led to a value-discounting effect—the free, add-on item was perceived as less valuable than when it was bundled with something else (Raghubir, 2005).

This research, of course, has implications for businesses that include their regular merchandise or services as free promotional items from time to time. By doing so, such businesses may cause their customers to perceive those items or services as less desirable. With that in mind, Raghubir (2004) suggests that customers should be informed of how valuable the gift is. For example, rather than say that a handbag is a "free gift," a salesperson should say something like, "You'll also receive this $50 handbag, with our compliments."

early. Here's what happened: Some students were simply asked to participate in a "thinking" experiment at seven in the morning. Others, however, were asked to participate but were not told when the experiment would take place. If they agreed to participate, they were told the time of the experiment and asked if they were still willing to participate. In other words, the second group of students was lowballed. Results of the study showed that although only 31 percent of the non-lowballed students agreed to participate, 56 percent of the lowballed students agreed.

As unethical as the low-ball tactic seems, it is used far more often than might be expected. Credit card issuers, for instance, are known for tempting customers with low introductory "teaser" rates. The problem is that these rates may double or even triple in a few months. Rates on some adjustable mortgages do this too; a few years at a very reasonable rate, then—BAM!—a balloon payment is due.

Why Lowballing Works

According to Burger and Caputo (2015), the effectiveness of the low-ball tactic can be explained by three psychological processes, which include commitment to the action, commitment to the person, and self-presentation. To illustrate the first, let's use the automobile customer as an example. Specifically, when the customer agrees to the initial offer, he or she becomes psychologically committed to the idea of owning the car. Thus, even when the reasons for buying the car change, the customer has a hard time altering his or her decision and commitment (Cialdini et al., 1978).

Second, Burger and Petty (1981) suggested that people fall victim to the tactic because agreeing with the initial request creates a commitment to the requester. In other words, people agree to a second, more costly request because they feel obligated to make good on their promises. In support of this hypothesis, Burger and Petty (1981) found that the low-ball tactic works only when the same person who made the first request also makes the less attractive request. It does not work when a different person makes the less attractive request.

The third explanation, self-presentation, suggests that people want to be seen in a favorable light. As such, they comply with requests to avoid looking bad (e.g., like "welshers" who don't keep their commitments). If that's the case, Guéguen and Pascual (2014) wondered how people might respond if asked to comply with requests that were associated with illegal behavior—the idea being that people should be less motivated to look good in the eyes of "deviant" persuaders. To find out, cigarette-smoking pedestrians were approached in one of two ways. In the low-ball condition, a researcher said, "I see that you are smoking a cigarette and I wonder if you could give me a light for my cigarette." If the pedestrians agreed, the researcher lowballed them by pulling out a large cannabis joint, which was illegal to smoke in the study's location. In another condition, a researcher produced the cannabis joint before asking for a light. What were the results? Lowballed pedestrians complied more than pedestrians who were not lowballed, leading Guéguen and Pascual (2014) to conclude that, compared to commitment, self-presentation is a weaker explanation for the effectiveness of the low-ball tactic.

"SORRY, WE DON'T HAVE ANY MORE OF THOSE IN YOUR SIZE, BUT . . .": THE BAIT-AND-SWITCH TACTIC

The next time you see a big sale advertised, be careful. If you aren't, you may fall victim to a persuasion tactic that some authors (Joule, Gouilloux, & Weber, 1989; Marchand, Joule, & Guéguen, 2015) call "the lure."

> This tactic . . . is frequently used when goods are put on sale. For example, a beautiful pair of shoes marked 40% off is displayed quite conspicuously in a store window. The enticed consumer enters the store with the intention of taking advantage of this exceptional offer, but the salesperson informs him that they are out of the shoe in his size. Just when the disappointed customer is ready to leave the store, he is shown a new pair that resembles the shoes on sale but that is being sold at the regular price.
>
> (p. 742)

The travel industry uses the same ploy, which is more commonly known as the *bait-and-switch tactic*. For instance, a company might advertise an inexpensive vacation package as part of a promotion. However, as many prospective travelers discover, very few of these seats or packages are available, and they are often sold out by the time people have committed themselves to the idea of a vacation. The only solution is to go home and mope or buy a more expensive option.

Research by Joule and colleagues (1989) indicates that the bait and switch is an effective strategy for gaining compliance. In one study, these researchers got several students to sign up to participate in a rather interesting and well-paying experiment. When the students showed up for the experiment, however, they were told that it had been canceled. Even so, these students, compared to those who were not lured, were more willing to participate in another experiment that was less interesting and unpaid.

The low-ball and bait-and-switch tactics are similar in that both lead the customer on before pulling the rug out. How do the two differ? With the low-ball technique, the customer is still buying the product he or she wanted, but at a higher cost. There are "strings attached" to the deal or "fine print" that drives up the cost. With the bait-and-switch, the customer is buying a different product altogether, often at a higher price or of lower quality. The product she or he wanted is sold out or out of stock.

THE DISRUPT-THEN-REFRAME AND PIQUE TECHNIQUES: I'M SO CONFUSED

If we offered to sell you five Nutrageous candy bars for 400 pennies, would you buy them? It would be a bargain.

Before you decide to buy anything after being presented an offer like this, be careful. You might be falling for a sequential compliance tactic known as the *disrupt-then-reframe technique* (DTR). According to Davis and Knowles (1999), the DTR rests on the assumption that certain requests (e.g., asking for charitable donations) create a conflict within persuadees. Specifically, persuadees want to help but are also resistant to the expense or effort required to do so. The DTR overcomes this problem by disrupting the persuadees' resistance. How? According to Davis and Knowles, certain confusion techniques (e.g., non sequiturs, requests stated in a peculiar way) can be used to divert people's minds from maintaining resistance. Once that is accomplished, reframing the request with a positive spin (e.g., "It's a bargain") works to engage the persuadees' underlying desire to help.

To test the effectiveness of this technique, Davis and Knowles (1999) examined door-to-door salespeople who were trying to sell greeting cards in order to earn money for a worthy charity. The salespeople presented different messages to potential buyers. Some customers received a straightforward sales pitch—"The cards are $3. It's a bargain"—whereas others were presented with a slightly peculiar pitch (i.e., the DTR technique)—"The cards are 300 pennies . . . that's $3. It's a bargain." Results of the study indicated that when salespersons used the DTR technique, they sold significantly more cards than when they used the more straightforward approach (Davis & Knowles, 1999). A meta-analysis of several studies suggests that this technique is effective, particularly when seeking donations in nonprofit contexts (Carpenter & Boster, 2009).

A related approach, called the *pique technique* is simpler (and sounds more poetic) than the DTR. It also involves making a peculiar request. For example, in the first examination of the technique (Santos, Leve, & Pratkanis, 1994), a woman posing as a vagrant asked passersby for "a quarter," "any change," or, more oddly, for "17 cents" or "37 cents." Results indicated that the more unusual requests (i.e., 17 and 37 cents) were more persuasive, perhaps because they, like the DTR, disrupt people's refusal scripts. A recent meta-analysis indicates that the pique technique is especially persuasive when smaller amounts of money are requested, when accompanied by a legitimate reason for making the request, and when used in France (Lee & Feeley, 2017).

LEGITIMIZING PALTRY CONTRIBUTIONS: EVEN A PENNY WILL HELP

A technique known as *legitimizing paltry contributions* (LPC for short) involves letting people know that very small donations would be acceptable. By way of example, in the first examination of the LPC technique, Cialdini and Schroeder (1976) found that adding the phrase "even a penny will help" to a request for donations increased the percentage of donations that people made to the American Cancer Society. Similarly, the phrase "even a single marble will make him/her happy" led more people to donate toys to children from needy families (Guéguen, Martin, & Meineri, 2013).

Originally, the approach was considered an effective way to fend off excuses like "I can't afford that right now" or "I don't have the money for that." A recent meta-analysis (Bolkan & Rains, 2015), however, suggests that the LPC is effective for two alternative reasons. Specifically, the impression management (self-presentation) explanation suggests that people who refuse tiny requests might worry that they'll be perceived as heartless cheapskates. Meanwhile, the "requester need" explanation suggests that people are more willing to donate because they feel that someone willing to accept exceptionally tiny donations must be especially desperate for help.

Previous research suggests that LPC is an effective way of amassing a large number of donations and may be even more effective when combined with other influence techniques (e.g., social proof) (Russell & Boster, 2016; Shearman & Yoo, 2007).

That said, although LPC garners a larger number of donations, research is inconsistent on whether the technique lowers the amount of money donated per person (see Bolkan & Rains, 2015 versus Lee, Moon, & Feeley, 2016). Either way, Bolkan and Rains (2015) noted that the technique would still be effective when all-or-none behavior is requested. For instance, someone requesting a signed petition might say, "even one signature will help" (Bolkan & Rains, 2015).

THE EVOKING FREEDOM TECHNIQUE: ". . . BUT YOU ARE FREE TO ACCEPT OR REFUSE"

If you hate being pressured to comply, the *evoking freedom technique* (a.k.a. *but you are free technique)* might appeal to you. If you've ever heard someone say something like "Feel free to say no" or "I'm asking, not insisting," he or she might have been using this technique. In the first study to examine it (Guéguen & Pascual, 2000), pedestrians were approached by an experimenter and asked, "Excuse me . . . can I ask for some change to take the bus, please?" Only 10 percent of pedestrians complied. However, when the experimenter added the phrase "but you are free to accept or to refuse," not only did compliance rates jump to 47.5 percent, the average donation was twice as large. Since then, a growing body of research indicates that the technique is effective in a large number of contexts (Carpenter, 2013; Guéguen, Joule, Halimi-Falkowicz, Pascual, Fischer-Lokou, & Dufourcq-Brana, 2013). One common explanation for the technique's effectiveness is that it reduces psychological reactance. Specifically, because people react negatively when their freedom is restricted (Brehm, 1966), declaring them "free" leads them to experience less reactance (Carpenter & Pascual, 2016; Meineri, Dupre, Guéguen, & Vallee, 2016).

FEAR-THEN-RELIEF AND HAPPINESS-THEN-DISAPPOINTMENT PROCEDURES: THE EMOTIONAL ROLLER COASTERS OF SOCIAL INFLUENCE

If you are a fan of detective novels and movies, you're undoubtedly familiar with the way the "good cop/bad cop" interrogation operates. First, the "bad cop" mistreats the suspect, humiliating, yelling at, and threatening to do harm. Next, the "good cop" enters the interrogation room, asks the bad cop to chill out, and then woos the suspect into confessing with little more than a cup of coffee and a dose of respect. Based on this scenario, Dolinski and Nawrat (Dolinski, 2007; Dolinski & Nawrat, 1998) identified the *fear-then-relief procedure*. The assumption underlying the procedure is that fear/relief confuses people, which, in turn, leads them to act rather mindlessly (Dolinski, 2016). Additionally, complying with requests can help them cope with their confusion (Dolinski, Dolinska, & Bar-Tal 2017). As such, they become prone to influence attempts. Previous research indicates that the procedure is effective (e.g., see Dolinski, 2007; Dolinski & Szczucka, 2012). For example, studies that have scared people (e.g., by blowing police whistles at jaywalkers or leaving "tickets" on illegally parked vehicles) and then relieved them (by having the people see that police weren't the ones blowing the whistles or that the tickets were really just leaflets), have found that those people are typically more compliant (e.g., willing to complete surveys) than people who have not undergone the procedure. Research also suggests that the persuasive effect of see-sawing emotions is not just confined to fear-then-relief. Indeed, one study found that a *happiness-then-disappointment procedure* (e.g., finding a note that had originally looked like money) also led people to comply more with later requests (Nawrat & Dolinski, 2007).

Before concluding this section, we think it's important to reiterate that a number of ethical concerns surround the use of influence tactics, perhaps even more so when persuasion involves unpleasant emotions such as fear. Remember, just because a tactic is effective does not mean it is ethical. Given the importance of these topics, we will have more to say about emotions and ethics in Chapters 13 and 16.

SUMMARY (AND THEN SOME)

This chapter featured some of the most prominently researched sequential tactics. Pregiving involves making a persuadee feel indebted so that he or she will be more compliant. The foot-in-the-door tactic involves making a small request and following up with a large one. The foot-in-the-mouth tactic works by getting people to admit to feeling terrific and then trying to get them to behave in a way consistent with their declaration. The door-in-the-face tactic involves making a large request and following up with a smaller one. The that's-not-all tactic seeks compliance by making deals more attractive before persuadees agree to them. When using the low-ball tactic, persuadees are asked to agree with an attractive request but are expected to agree with a less attractive request later. Similarly, the bait-and-switch technique lures people with merchandise that is attractive in order to get them to buy substitute merchandise that is less attractive. The disrupt-then-reframe and pique tactics divert people from resisting requests. The legitimization-of-paltry-favors approach minimizes excuses for making a donation. The fear-then-relief procedure uses changes in emotion to disorient and then persuade people. The dump-then-chase technique occurs when persuaders persist in their influence attempts by addressing obstacles to compliance.

We realize that we've covered a heap of strategies this chapter. Even so, we can't help but wish there was more space. Indeed, plenty of additional tactics are waiting to be explored. In case you're interested, Box 11.4 provides the briefest of glimpses to get you started.

BOX 11.4 | But Wait, There's More: A Laundry List of Additional Tactics

1. **The Foot-in-the-Mouth Effect**: Donation seekers are especially successful if they ask people how they are feeling, acknowledge the response, and then request compliance (Howard, 1990; Meineri & Guéguen, 2011). Thus, when a phone solicitor asks, "How are you?," you might be putting your foot in your mouth by replying, "Great!"

2. **The Dump-and-Chase:** Persuaders who "won't take no for an answer" and continue to chase compliance by responding to obstacles are using this tactic. "Too expensive?" they might reply. "Let's talk about our layaway plan . . ." According to some research (Boster, Shaw, Hughes, Kotowski,

Continued

Davis, B. P., & Knowles, E. S. (1999). A disrupt-then-reframe technique of social influence. *Journal of Personality and Social Psychology*, 76(2), 192–199.

DeJong, W. (1979). An examination of self-perception mediation of the foot-in-the-door effect. *Journal of Personality and Social Psychology*, 37, 2221–2239.

Dillard, J. P. (1990). Self-inference and the foot-in-the-door technique: Quantity of behavior and attitudinal mediation. *Human Communication Research*, 16, 422–447.

Dillard, J. P., Hunter, J. E., & Burgoon, M. (1984). Sequential-request persuasive strategies: Meta-analysis of foot-in-the-door and door-in-the-face. *Human Communication Research*, 10, 461–488.

Dolinski, D. (2007). Emotional see-saw. In A. R. Pratkanis (Ed.), *The science of social influence: Advances and future progress* (pp. 137–153). New York: Psychology Press.

Dolinski, D. (2016). *Techniques of social influence.* New York: Routledge.

Dolinski, D., & Nawrat, R. (1998). "Fear-then-relief" procedure for inducing compliance. Beware when the danger is over. *Journal of Experimental Social Psychology*, 34, 27–50.

Dolinski, D., & Szczucka, K. (2012). Fear-then-relief-then argument: How to sell goods using the EDTR technique of social influence. *Social Influence, 7*, 251–267. doi:10.1080/15534510.2012.669987

Dolinski, D., Dolinska, B., & Bar-Tal, Y. (2017). Cognitive structuring and its cognitive-motivational determinants as an explanatory framework of the fear-then-relief social influence strategy. *Frontiers in Psychology*, 8, 1–5. doi:10.3389/fpsyg.2017.00114

Even-Chen, M., Yinon, Y., & Bizman, A. (1978). The door in the face technique: Effects of the size of the initial request. *European Journal of Social Psychology*, 8, 135–140.

Feeley, T. H., Anker, A. E., & Aloe, A. M. (2012). The door-in-the-face persuasive message strategy: A meta-analysis of the first 35 years. *Communication Monographs*, 79, 316–343.

Feeley, T., Fico, A. E., Shaw, A. Z., Lee, S., & Griffin, D. J. (2017). Is the door-in-the-face a concession? *Communication Quarterly*, 65, 97–123. doi:10.1080/01463373.2016.1187186

Fern, E. F., Monroe, K. B., & Avila, R. A. (1986). Effectiveness of multiple request strategies: A synthesis of research results. *Journal of Marketing Research, 23*, 144–152.

Freedman, J. L., & Fraser, S. C. (1966). Compliance without pressure. *Journal of Personality and Social Psychology*, 4, 195–202.

George, W. H., Gournic, S. J., & McAfee, M. P. (1988). Perceptions of postdrinking female sexuality. *Journal of Applied Social Psychology*, 18, 1295–1317.

Goei, R., Roberto, A., Meyer, G., & Carlyle, K. (2007). The effects of a favor and apology on compliance. *Communication Research*, 34, 575–595.

Goldman, M. (1986). Compliance employing a combined foot-in-the-door and door-in-the-face procedure. *Journal of Social Psychology*, 126, 111–116.

Goldman, M., & Creason, C. R. (1981). Inducing compliance by a two-door-in-the-face procedure and a self-determination request. *Journal of Social Psychology*, 114, 229–235.

Goldman, M., Creason, C. R., & McCall, C. G. (1981). Compliance employing a two feet-in-the-door procedure. *Journal of Social Psychology*, 114, 259–265.

Goldman, M., Gier, J. A., & Smith, D. E. (1981). Compliance as affected by task difficulty and order of tasks. *Journal of Social Psychology*, 114, 75–83.

Gorassini, D. R., & Olson, J. M. (1995). Does self-perception change explain the foot-in-the-door effect? *Journal of Personality and Social Psychology*, 69, 91–105.

Groves, R. M., Cialdini, R. B., & Couper, M. P. (1992). Understanding the decision to participate in a survey. *Public Opinion Quarterly*, 56, 475–495.

Guadagno, R. E., Asher, T., Demaine, L., & Cialdini, R. B. (2001). When saying yes leads to saying no: Preference for consistency and the reverse foot-in-the-door effect. *Personality and Social Psychology Bulletin, 27*, 859–867.

Guéguen, N. (2001). Social labeling and compliance: An evaluation of the link between the label and the request. *Social Behavior and Personality, 29*, 743–748.

Guéguen, N. (2016). "You will probably refuse, but . . .": When activating reactance in a single sentence increases compliance with a request. *Polish Psychological Bulletin, 47*, 170–173. doi:10.1515/ppb-2016–0019

Guéguen, N., & Pascual, A. (2014). Low-ball and compliance: Commitment even if the request is a deviant one. *Social Influence, 9*, 162–171. doi:10.1080/15534510.2013. 798243

Guéguen, N., Jacob, C., & Meineri, S. (2011). Effects of the door-in-the-face technique on restaurant customers' behavior. *International Journal of Hospitality Management, 30*, 759–761.

Guéguen, N., Martin, A., & Meineri, S. (2013). "Even a single marble will make him/her happy . . .": Further evidence and extension of the legitimizing paltry contribution technique on helping. *Social Influence, 8*, 18–26. doi:10.1080/15534510.2012.689692

Guéguen, N., Joule, R., Halimi-Falkowicz, S., & Marchand, M. (2013). Repeating "yes" in a first request and compliance with a later request: The four walls technique. *Social Behavior and Personality, 41*, 199–202. doi:10.2224/sbp.2013.41.2.199

Guéguen, N., Joule, R., Halimi-Falkowicz, S., Pascual, A., Fischer-Lokou, J., & Dufourcq-Brana, M. (2013). I'm free but I'll comply with your request: Generalization and multidimensional effects of the "evoking freedom" technique. *Journal of Applied Social Psychology, 43*, 116–137. doi:10.1111/j.1559–1816.2012.00986.x

Happ, C., Melzer, A., & Steffgen, G. (2016). Trick with treat: Reciprocity increases the willingness to communicate personal data. *Computers in Human Behavior, 61*, 372–377. doi:10.1016/j.chb.2016.03.026

Hendrickson, B., & Goei, R. (2009). Reciprocity and dating: Explaining the effects of favor and status on compliance with a date request. *Communication Research, 36*, 585–608.

Howard, D. (1990). The influence of verbal responses to common greetings on compliance behavior: The foot-in-the-mouth effect. *Journal of Applied Social Psychology, 20*, 1185–1196.

Joule, R. V., Gouilloux, F., & Weber, F. (1989). The lure: A new compliance procedure. *Journal of Social Psychology, 129*, 741–749.

Lee, S., & Feeley, T. H. (2017). A meta-analysis of the pique technique of compliance. *Social Influence*. Advance online publication. doi:10.1080/15534510.2017.1305986

Lee, S., Moon, S., & Feeley, T. H. (2016). A meta-analytic review of the legitimization of paltry favor compliance strategy. *Psychological Reports, 118*, 748–771. doi:10.1177/ 0033294116647690

Meineri, S., & Guéguen, N. (2011). "I hope I'm not disturbing you, am I?" Another operationalization of the foot-in-the-mouth paradigm. *Journal of Applied Social Psychology, 41*, 965–975.

Marchand, M., Joule, R., & Guéguen, N. (2015). The lure technique: replication and refinement in a field setting. *Psychological Reports, 116*, 275–279. doi:10.2466/17.21. PR0.116k11w0

Meineri, S., Dupre, M., Guéguen, N., & Vallee, B. (2016). Door-in-the-face and but-you-are-free: Testing the effect of combining two no-pressure compliance paradigms. *Psychological Reports, 11*, 276–289. doi:10.1177/0033294116657064

Nawrat, R., & Dolinski, D. (2007). "See-saw of emotions" and compliance: Beyond the fear-then-relief rule. *Journal of Social Psychology, 147*, 556–571.

O'Keefe, D. J., & Figgé, M. (1997). A guilt-based explanation of the door-in-the-face influence strategy. *Human Communication Research*, 24, 64–81.

O'Keefe, D. J., & Hale, S. L. (1998). The door-in-the-face influence strategy: A random-effects meta-analytic review. In M. E. Roloff (Ed.), *Communication yearbook 21*(1–33). Thousand Oaks, CA: Sage.

O'Keefe, D. J., & Hale, S. L. (2001). An odds-ratio-based meta-analysis of research on the door-in-the-face influence strategy. *Communication Reports*, 14(1), 31–38.

Pascual, A., Carpenter, C. J., Guéguen, N., & Girandola, F. (2016). A meta-analysis of the effectiveness of the low-ball compliance-gaining procedure. *Revue européenne de psychologie appliquée*, 66, 261–267. doi:10.1016/j.erap.2016.004

Pendleton, M. G., & Batson, C. D. (1979). Self-presentation and the door-in-the face technique for inducing compliance. *Personality and Social Psychology Bulletin*, 5, 77–81.

Raghubir, P. (2004). Free gift with purchase: Promoting or discounting the brand? *Journal of Consumer Psychology*, 14, 181–186.

Raghubir, P. (2005). Framing a price bundle: The case of "buy/get" offers. *Journal of Product and Brand Management*, 14, 123–128.

Regan, D. T. (1971). Effects of a favor and liking on compliance. *Journal of Experimental Social Psychology*, 7, 627–639.

Russell, J., & Boster, F. J. (2016). Mediation of the legitimization of paltry favors technique: The impact of social comparison and nature of the cause. *Communication Reports*, 29, 13–22. doi:10.1080/08934215.2015.1080850

Santos, M. D., Leve, C., & Pratkanis, A. R. (1994). Hey buddy, can you spare seventeen cents? Mindful persuasion and the pique technique. *Journal of Applied Social Psychology*, 24, 755–764. doi:10.1111/j.1559-1816.1994.tb00610.x

Seiter, J. S., & Weger, H. (in press). The principle of reciprocity in hospitality contexts: The relationship between tipping behaviors and food servers' approaches to handling leftovers. *Journal of Hospitality & Tourism Research*.

Seligman, C., Bush, M., & Kirsch, K. (1976). Relationship between compliance in the foot-in-the-door paradigm and size of first request. *Journal of Personality and Social Psychology*, 33, 517–520.

Shearman, S. M., & Yoo, J. H. (2007). "Even a penny will help!": Legitimization of paltry donation and social proof in soliciting donation to a charitable organization. *Communication Research Reports*, 24, 271–282.

Souchet, L., & Girandola, F. (2013). Double foot-in-the-door, social representations and environment: application for energy savings. *Journal of Applied Social Psychology*, 43, 306–315. doi:10.1111/j.1559–1816.2012.01000.x

Tusing, K. J., & Dillard, J. P. (2000). The psychological reality of the door-in-the-face: It's helping, not bargaining. *Journal of Language and Social Psychology*, 19(1), 5–25.

Weyant, J. M. (1996). Application of compliance techniques to direct-mail requests for charitable donations. *Psychology & Marketing*, 13(2), 157–170.

Deception

WHEN ONE OF YOUR AUTHORS was 5 or 6 years old, he cut the hair off several of his sister's Barbie dolls. He was a proud little vandal, and savvy enough to realize that an interrogation was inevitable. To prep, he practiced angelic expressions in front of a mirror and then moseyed innocently around the house until his mother, provoked by her daughter's shrieks, found him. "Look me in the eye and tell me you didn't do it," his mom said, holding your author gently by his shoulders. "It wasn't me," the author replied. He stared straight at her . . . and then burst into tears.

Deception, he learned the hard way, is no cakewalk. Likewise, detecting lies, more often than not, is more difficult than this story makes it seem. Indeed, humans, in general, tend to be far less accurate than they believe when trying to detect deception. Some research shows that the average person can detect a liar with about the same accuracy as someone flipping a coin (Bond & DePaulo, 2006), whereas other research presents an even less optimistic view. For example, when accuracy rates for truthful and deceptive messages are examined separately (rather than together, as in most studies), people's detection accuracy is above 50 percent for truths, but well below 50 percent for lies. Levine and his colleagues (Levine, 2014; Levine & Kim, 2010; Levine, Park, & McCornack, 1999) call this the *veracity effect*.

The fact that people are not very accurate at detecting deception is unfortunate when you consider the practical and professional contexts within which accurate detection would be desirable (e.g., for jurists, consumers, law officers, negotiators, customs inspectors, job interviewers, secret service agents, and so forth; see Box 12.1). Clearly, there are practical advantages to improving detecting abilities, and this

BOX 12.1 | Something Phishy Is Going On: Beware of Internet Deception

Some time ago, one of the authors received an email greeting him as "Dear Bank of the West Customer." The email told him that because of too many failed login attempts, his banking account had been locked and could be unlocked only by following a link to a website where he could provide his ATM card number and PIN. Fortunately, he didn't take the bait, unlike others who have been hooked—line and sinker—by what are known as "phishing" or "spoofing" scams. Such scams try to lure you to a website where you provide personal or financial information, which, in turn, enables the con artists to commit identity theft or credit card fraud. Some, known as spear-phishing attacks, target specific victims and people with high net worth, often with intimate knowledge about the victim. In one study, spear phishing fooled one-third of the targets into clicking on an embedded link (Luo, Zhang, Burd, Seazzu, 2013). To prevent yourself from being filleted by such scams, beware of unfamiliar websites. Use only website addresses you have used before. If you receive an email that seems to be snooping for personal info, be especially wary. If you are suspicious, contact the legitimate company directly. Finally, if you've been hooked, contact the police and file a complaint with the FBI's Internet Crime Complaint Center (www.ic3.gov/default.aspx).

observation leads us to the following questions: Are there any reliable cues that can be used to detect deception? If so, what are they? Are some people better at lying than others? Can some people detect deceit more accurately than others? Are there factors that can improve people's ability to detect a liar?

These are some of the questions we address in this chapter. But, before doing so, we would like to make a point. You might ask, "Why is a chapter on deception in a book on persuasion?" We respond that *deception is a form of persuasion*. Even from the standpoint of pure cases of persuasion, deception involves an intentional attempt to get someone to believe what the liar knows to be false. As Miller (cited in Miller & Stiff, 1993) argued: "Deceptive communication strives for persuasive ends; or, stated more precisely, deceptive communication is a general persuasive strategy that aims at influencing the beliefs, attitudes, and behaviors of others by means of deliberate message distortion" (p. 28).

With this basic understanding of deception as persuasion under our belt, we now turn to a more in-depth discussion of some common conceptualizations of deception. The rest of the chapter examines research on the enactment and perception of deception.

WHAT IS DECEPTION? LIES AND DAMN LIES

In this section, we examine what deception entails conceptually. To answer the "conceptual question," scholars have attempted to outline several types of communication that might be considered deceptive. Many attempts to do so have focused on liars' motivations for telling lies.

Although some motivations for lying are self-evident, others are less obvious. For example, various researchers have posited all of the following reasons for lying (see Barnett et al., 2000; Camden, Motley, & Wilson, 1984; DePaulo, Ansfield, Kirkendol, & Boden, 2004; Lindskold & Walters, 1983; Seiter, Bruschke, & Bai, 2002).

- *Lie to benefit other:* Because she knows that her husband does not want to be disturbed, Babbs tells a door-to-door salesman that her husband is not home.
- *Lie to affiliate:* Buffy wants to spend some time with her father, so she tells him she needs help with her homework even though she is capable of doing it herself.
- *Lie to avoid invasion of privacy:* Muffy tells a co-worker that she is younger than she really is because she believes her age is no one's business but her own.
- *Lie to avoid conflict:* Biff tells his neighbor, who has called to complain about Biff's barking dog, that he cannot talk at the moment because dinner's on the table.
- *Lie to appear better:* To impress a date, Rex tells her that he was captain of his debate team when, in reality, he was treasurer of the Slide Rule Club (for more on this motivation, see Box 12.2).
- *Lie to protect self:* Trudy breaks her mother's vase but tells her the cat did it.
- *Lie to benefit self:* Favio tells his parents he needs extra money for textbooks so that he can buy tickets to a Lady Gaga concert.
- *Lie to harm other:* Barney's in a bad mood so he points in the wrong direction when a motorist asks him directions.

In addition to looking at people's motivations for lying, another approach to conceptualizing deception is to examine the types of strategies people use when lying. For example, Burgoon, Buller, Ebesu, and Rockwell (1994) distinguished three deception strategies: *distortion* (or equivocation), *omissions* (or concealment), and *falsification* (outright falsehoods). Yet other researchers have come up with other categories of deception (e.g., see Hopper & Bell, 1984).

In addition to looking at different types of deception, a final way of conceptualizing deception was proposed in *information manipulation theory* (McCornack, 1992; McCornack, Morrison, Paik, Wisner, & Zhu, 2014).[1] This theory argues that when we are talking with others, we typically assume that they will be cooperative, providing us information that is not only truthful but also informative, relevant, and clear. We're not always right, however. Indeed, people violate our assumptions by manipulating the information they communicate to us. First, they might not provide the *quantity* of information that we assume they will (i.e., they tell the truth, but not the *whole* truth). Second, they might violate our assumptions about the *quality* of information provided (i.e., what they tell us is not at all true). Third, they might manipulate information through *manner violations*, communicating messages that are vague and ambiguous. Finally, people can engage in *relation violations* by presenting messages that are not relevant. According to the theory, some violations (e.g., quantity) are predicted to occur more frequently than others (e.g., relation). That said, people can alter the quantity, quality, relation, and manner of messages all at the same time or in different

Box 12.2 | Can I Believe Anything That Comes Out of Your Mouse? Deception and Online Dating

If you or anyone you know has searched for love on any of the dozens of online dating sites available, beware. Apparently, people's motivation to create desirable impressions when trying to attract prospective partners is so powerful that they'll resort to some serious truth stretching in the process. In one study (Toma & Hancock, 2010), for example, researchers invited 80 online daters to their lab. Among other things, the researchers weighed and measured the daters to see if any funny business was going on, and found out that it was. Specifically, 81 percent of the daters lied in their profiles about their height, age, or weight, with men lying more than women about their height and women lying more than men about their weight. Moreover, independent judges considered about one third of the daters' online photographs to be deceptive representations of the daters' current appearance. In short, if you think "seeing is believing," think again.

BOX 12.3 | Information Manipulation Theory: Examples of Deceptive Dimensions of Messages

Gabriella has been babysitting several children for her neighbor, Betty Jones. The youngest child, Morgan (age 2), although usually well behaved, has been a handful all night. To top off a difficult evening, while Gabriella was cooking dinner and helping the other children, Morgan crawled behind the family's new leather couch and scribbled all over the back of it with a permanent marker. Although Gabriella scrubbed the couch with soap and water, she couldn't get the stains out. Later, after Gabriella has put the children to bed, Betty Jones returned home and inquired, "How did the night go?"

Examples of responses that:

1. Are clear, direct, and truthful: "Tonight was not good, Mrs. Jones. Morgan acted up most of the night. I don't know what got into him. As I was making dinner and helping the girls with their homework, he wrote all over the back of the couch with a Sharpie. I tried to get it off, but it was no use. I'm sorry if I didn't watch him as closely as I should have."

2. Violate assumptions about the quantity of information that should be provided: "Morgan was a little naughty, but it was no big deal."

3. Violate assumptions about the quality of information that should be provided: "The kids were perfect angels, especially Morgan. We did puzzles. We played games. We laughed. What fun!"

4. Violate assumptions about the manner of information that should be provided: "Oh, you know. We kept busy with this and that. We did some neat stuff . . . We definitely cleaned house tonight!"

5. Violate assumptions about the relevance of information that should be provided: "I don't mean to be rude, but I really need to be getting home, Mrs. Jones. It's late and I have homework to do."

combinations. In other words, there is an infinite variety in forms of deception (McCornack, Levine, Solowczuk, Torres, & Campbell, 1992). To give you an idea, examples of the ways in which people manipulate information along each of these dimensions are presented in Box 12.3.

Having laid the groundwork for examining deception, we now discuss what happens during the process of deception—that is, what goes on while deception is being enacted, and how is deception detected?

TELLING LIES: THE ENACTMENT OF DECEPTION

If all liars had noses like Pinocchio, deception detection would not be a problem. Unfortunately, spotting lies is not that simple. In fact, even empirical research has been inconsistent when trying to identify the types of behaviors that we can expect out of liars. (Some of the behaviors that have been associated with deception are listed in Box 12.4).

Theoretical Frameworks

Despite these inconsistencies, however, several theories of deception have been proposed that attempt to provide an understanding of the types of behaviors that are typical of liars. One such framework, known as the *four-factor model,* was proposed by Zuckerman and Driver (1985). Another, known as *interpersonal deception theory,* was proposed by Burgoon and Buller (2004). The following sections discuss each of these perspectives.

The Four-Factor Model

Rather than simply list all the things that people do when telling lies, the four-factor model tries to explain the underlying processes governing deceptive behavior. In other

FIGURE 12.1
"I knew the suspect was lying because of certain telltale discrepancies between his voice and nonverbal gestures. Also his pants were on fire."

Source: © Robert Mankoff/ The New Yorker Collection/ www.cartoonbank.com. All Rights Reserved.

BOX 12.4 | How Do Liars Behave?

A meta-analysis is a summary of several studies. Such an analysis attempts to resolve inconsistencies in research. Several of these analyses (i.e., DePaulo, Stone, & Lassiter, 1985; Kraut, 1980; Sporer & Schwandt, 2007; Vrij, 2000; Zuckerman & Driver, 1985) have examined cues that were associated with deception across a number of studies, but the largest analysis, combining the results of 1,338 estimates of 158 deception cues, was conducted by DePaulo and her colleagues (DePaulo et al., 2003). Based on this analysis, a number of cues were found to be associated with deception. Keep in mind, though, that all of these cues must be prefaced with the caveat, in general:

- **Talking time**: Liars' responses are shorter than truth tellers' responses.
- **Details**: Liars provide fewer details than do truth tellers.
- **Pressing lips**: Liars press their lips (as if holding back) more than truth tellers.
- **Making sense**: Compared to truth tellers, liars' stories are rated as more discrepant and ambivalent and as having less plausibility and logical structure.
- **Lack of immediacy**: Both verbally and vocally, liars seem evasive and impersonal, linguistically distancing themselves from their listeners and from the contents of their presentations (e.g., using passive vs. active voice).
- **Uncertainty**: Liars are rated as sounding more uncertain than truth tellers.
- **Raising chin**: Liars raise their chins more than truth tellers, perhaps to try to appear more certain about their stories.
- **Repetition**: Liars repeat themselves more than do truth tellers.
- **Cooperation**: Liars are rated as less cooperative in their conversations than are truth tellers.
- **Negative statements**: Liars' responses contain more negative expressions and complaints than do truth tellers' responses.
- **Pleasantness**: Liars' faces are less pleasant than are truth tellers' faces.
- **Nervousness**: Overall, liars appear more nervous than truth tellers.
- **Vocal tension and pitch**: Compared to truth tellers, liars' voices are more tense, and liars speak in a higher pitch.
- **Pupil dilation**: Liars' pupils are more dilated than are truth tellers' pupils.
- **Fidgeting**: Liars fidget more than truth tellers.
- **Spontaneous corrections**: Truth tellers spontaneously correct themselves more than do liars.
- **Admitted lack of memory**: Truth tellers admit not remembering things more than do liars.
- **Related external associations**: Compared to truth tellers, liars are more likely to mention events or relationships peripheral to the key event they are discussing.

Although the meta-analysis by DePaulo and colleagues (2003) examined some verbal behaviors, it focused primarily on nonverbal behaviors. Given that, some researchers have wondered whether a reliable set of verbal cues to deception might be uncovered. According to Ali and Levine (2008), however, although verbal indicators of deception appear to exist, they have not been consistent from situation to situation or from study to study.

words, rather than tell us *what* people do when lying, the model tries to tell us *why* people behave differently when lying. According to the model, the four factors that influence behavior when lying are arousal, attempted control, felt emotions, and cognitive effort.

First, the model assumes that people are more aroused or anxious when telling lies than when telling the truth. This is also the principle on which the polygraph operates. Of course, we know that results from polygraphs are inadmissible in courts because they are not 100 percent accurate. Why? Because a sociopath, for instance, who feels no remorse for murder certainly won't get anxious when lying. Even so, not all people are sociopaths. We know that many people do feel anxious when they lie. Perhaps they fear getting caught. Perhaps telling the lie reminds them of information they want hidden. Perhaps they are simply motivated to succeed in the deceptive task. Whatever the case, we know that such arousal can lead to certain behaviors during deception. Poker players, for example, are said to wear sunglasses because their pupils dilate when they get a good hand. Similarly, pupil dilation can be a reliable indicator of deception (DePaulo et al., 2003). What other cues to arousal accompany deception? A few that researchers have investigated include speech errors, speech hesitations, word-phrase repetitions, increased adaptors (e.g., finger fidgeting), eye blinks, vocal pitch, and leg movements.

Second, because people do not want to get caught telling lies, the four-factor model argues that they try to control their behaviors. This seems to be the case both before and during deception. For example, Hartwig, Granhag, and Strömwall (2007) found that when planning to be interrogated, liars strategized more than truth tellers by planning to remain calm and pleasant. Moreover, Vrij (2000) reported that during deception, liars tend to limit their movement to keep from looking nervous. Similarly, according to Ekman and Friesen's (1969, 1974) *sending capacity hypothesis,* when people tell lies, they try to control their behaviors but, in the process, pay more attention to some cues than others. Because it is difficult to monitor everything they do, liars try to control behaviors that communicate the most information, such as facial expressions and the words they use. But, while busy monitoring their faces and words, they tend to forget about parts of their body that communicate little information such as their legs and feet. So, according to the sending capacity hypothesis, those parts of the body that communicate little information reveal the most when people are lying. In other words, because people are concentrating so much on their faces and words, deception "leaks" in other places. At least some research tends to support this notion. First, Caso, Vrij, Mann, and De Leo (2006) found that, even when they were taught how to avoid looking deceptive, research participants were more effective at controlling their words than their nonverbal behavior. Moreover, one study found that people who watched liars' heads and faces (higher sending capacity) were less accurate at detecting deception than people who watched liars' bodies (lower sending capacity) (Ekman & Friesen, 1974). Finally, in a summary of more than 30 studies in which judges tried to detect others' deception from either single channels (i.e., only the face, body, tone of voice, or words of the liar) or from particular channel combinations, DePaulo and colleagues (1985) found that in all conditions in which judges relied on facial cues, detection accuracy was lower.

you'd do if a close friend asked you how you liked her new hairstyle. Imagine also that you thought the hairstyle looked hideous. In such situations, rather than creating a truthful yet tactful message that would preserve your relationship and spare your friend's feelings, it might be less cognitively taxing and less stressful to simply tell your friend that you loved her hair. In short, the underlying differences between truths and lies may not be as simple as some models make them out to be (McCornack, 1997).

What do we think of such criticisms? Recall from Chapter 1 that the complex nature of persuasion provides one of the most compelling reasons for studying it. When research seems confusing or contradictory, oftentimes it's because the research is approaching the study of persuasion too simplistically. With that in mind, we believe that the preceding criticisms should not be ignored by those who study deception. They are important because they suggest that deceptive behaviors are far more complex than many of us originally imagined. However, while such criticisms should be applauded, we do not think that they render assumptions from the four-factor model and interpersonal deception theory useless. Instead, they suggest that these assumptions apply to some but not all deceptive encounters. Telling different types of lies may lead to different types of behavior (see Seiter et al., 2002). For example, fabricating lies may require more mental effort than telling the truth, but only when lies are narrative or spontaneous in nature (see Vrij, 2014; Vrij, Kneller, & Mann, 2000). Moreover, the notion that deception leads to arousal may apply less to fibs and white lies than to more serious forms of deception, such as cheating on a spouse or denying a crime. Even then, what qualifies as a "serious" form of deception is subject to interpretation. For example, previous research indicates that a person's cultural background not only influences how acceptable that person perceives a lie to be (Mealy, Stephan, & Urrutia, 2007; Seiter et al., 2002), but also the emotions (e.g., guilt and shame) that person expects to experience after telling a lie (Seiter & Bruschke, 2007). In short, our assumptions about deceptive behavior may need to be more qualified or complex in nature. For instance, in Box 12.3, we list several cues to deception. It turns out that under certain conditions, the list gets longer. With that in mind, we turn to a discussion of factors affecting successful deception.

What Makes a Liar Persuasive?

Previous research suggests that some people are better at "pulling the wool over our eyes" than others. For instance, research by Bond and DePaulo (2008) and Levine and his colleagues (Levine, Serota, et al., 2010; Levine, 2016) indicates that while some people are especially *transparent*, leaking the fact that they are lying, others have an honest *demeanor* and, consequently, are typically seen as being truthful even when they are lying. In this section, we discuss the ways in which characteristics of the liar—in addition to characteristics of the lie being told and the deceptive situation—affect the process of deception.

The "Wool Pullers"

The boy who cried wolf should have quit while he was ahead. Or, before he got eaten, he should have at least taken a personality test. If he had, our guess is that he would have scored high on a test that measures a trait known as *Machiavellianism*. The Machiavellian personality is not interested in interpersonal relationships, manipulates others for selfish purposes, and has little sense of social morality (Christie & Geis, 1970; Geis & Moon, 1981). Machiavellian personalities are truly "wolves in sheep's clothing." Not only do they lie and intend to cheat more often than their counterparts (i.e., low Machiavellians) (Brewer, & Abell, 2015; Jonason, Lyons, Baughman, & Vernon, 2014), they appear more innocent while doing so. Indeed, a classic study by Braginsky (1970) backs up this claim. In the study, high and low Machiavellian children tasted bitter crackers and then were offered a nickel for each cracker they could get their little chums to eat. The results of the study showed that the high Machiavellian children were not only the most successful in their persuasive attempts, but were also seen as more innocent and honest than the low Machiavellian children.

In addition to Machiavellianism, a person's social skills influence how successful he or she is at deceiving others. For example, high self-monitors, people who use situational information to behave more appropriately, tend to be more skilled at deception than low self-monitors (Elliot, 1979; Miller, deTurck, & Kalbfleisch, 1983). Moreover, people skilled at communicating basic emotions are particularly good at convincing others to believe their deceptive messages (Riggio & Friedman, 1983), whereas those who are apprehensive in their communication tend to leak more deceptive cues (see O'Hair, Cody, & Behnke, 1985). Similarly, people who are expressive and socially tactful (Riggio, Tucker, & Throckmorton, 1987); socially skilled (Riggio, Tucker, & Widaman, 1987); competent communicators (Feeley, 1996); and attentive, friendly, and precise in their communication (O'Hair, Cody, Goss, & Krayer, 1988) are more successful at deceiving others than those who do not possess such skills.

Finally, who do you suppose is better at not being detected when lying—males or females? The results of two meta-analyses found that males tend to be more successful at lying than females (Kalbfleisch, cited in Burgoon, Buller, Grandpre, & Kalbfleisch, 1998; Zuckerman, DePaulo, & Rosenthal, 1981). Even so, a review of literature by Burgoon and colleagues (1998) suggests that such gender differences are small, perhaps because the deceptive strategies of men and women both have shortcomings. Specifically, when they are lying, men tend to restrict their nonverbal behavior. Although this may prevent them from leaking deceptive cues, if they overdo it, they run the risk of appearing deceptive. Women, however, try to appear more involved in conversations. As a result, this greater activation may cause them to leak more arousal cues and appear more nervous than usual (Burgoon et al., 1998).

Are Some Lies Easier to Tell Than Others?

Imagine that Babbs, a 15-year-old high school sophomore, has a curfew of 9 p.m. It's Thursday, a school night, but Babbs is on the dance floor, partying it up when she suddenly notices the time: 11 p.m! Knowing that her parents usually go to bed around 8 p.m., she hopes they'll be asleep but, on arriving home, she finds herself face to face with her parents, who have been waiting up for her. "Where have you been?" they demand to know, at about the same time Babbs decides that she had better start lying her pants off if she doesn't want to spend the next two weeks in solitary confinement.

How successful do you think Babbs will be? According to previous research (e.g., O'Hair, Cody, & McLaughlin, 1981; Vrij, 2014), behavior during deception depends, to a large extent, on whether the liar is telling a prepared lie or a spontaneous lie. To be sure, think about some of the components of the four-factor model we discussed earlier. When telling a prepared lie, compared to a spontaneous lie, Babbs should be less aroused, have more control, and should not find lying as cognitively difficult. Not surprisingly, research on deceptive cues supports this idea; in general, spontaneous lies are accompanied by more cues associated with deception than are prepared lies. And, because prepared liars make a more credible impression, they are more difficult to detect than spontaneous liars (deTurck & Miller, 1985; Littlepage & Pineault, 1979; Strömwall, Granhag, & Landström, 2007).

Spontaneity, though, is not the only dimension of a lie that seems to affect deceptive success. Indeed, research also has shown that the length and the content of a lie influences how well a person can tell it. Longer lies, for instance, are more difficult to tell than short ones (Kraut, 1978). And concerning content, in a study by Thackray and Orne (1968), subjects played the role of an espionage agent who attempted to conceal both his or her identity and certain code words he or she had learned. The results of the study showed that subjects were more successful when telling lies about personally relevant information (i.e., their identity) than when telling lies about neutral information (i.e., code numbers). Similarly, one study (Warren, Schertler, & Bull, 2009) found that people detected emotional lies (e.g., liars describing Hawaiian landscapes while watching videos of grisly surgeries) more successfully than they detected unemotional lies (liars describing surgeries while watching landscape videos). This finding is consistent with a meta-analysis showing that deceivers displayed fewer nods and illustrators when lying about facts and feelings than when lying about facts only (Sporer & Schwandt, 2007). Finally, a meta-analysis by DePaulo and colleagues (2003) found that when lying about transgressions, people took longer to respond, talked faster, blinked more, and fidgeted less than truth tellers.

Deceptive Situations and Deceptive Success

The context in which a lie is told can influence how successful the liar is. Several situational features have been found to influence deception success. One is motivation. Certainly, there are times when you are simply more motivated to lie successfully than others. A fisherman, for example, may not care so much when someone discovers that his trophy "bass" was really a guppy. A playboy husband cheating on his wife, however, might have more at stake if his affair were discovered. So who, then, is the better liar: the fisherman or the cheat?

To address this question, recall the four-factor model, which suggests that liars attempt to control their behavior to avoid being detected. As you might suspect, this attempt to control behavior increases as people's motivation to lie successfully increases. Consequently, as people become more motivated to lie successfully, their behavior becomes more rigid and over-controlled, a phenomenon known as the *motivational impairment effect* (DePaulo & Kirkendol, 1989). In short, being overly motivated may cause you to be especially detectable.

To further illustrate the role of motivation in the process of deception, Frank and Ekman (1997) gave 20 males $10 each for participating in their research. As part of the study, the males were provided with an opportunity to commit a "mock" crime— they would either steal or not steal $50 from a briefcase. Before given the opportunity, the participants were told that if they took the money and were able to convince an interrogator that they were innocent, they could keep the $50. If, however, they were caught lying, they would be punished. Specifically, if caught, they would be forced to forfeit both the stolen $50 and their initial $10 participation fee. Worse yet, they would be required to sit on a cold, metal chair inside a cramped, darkened room, where they would have to endure anywhere from 10 to 40 randomly sequenced, 110-decibel startling blasts of white noise over the course of an hour. Needless to say, the liars in this study were motivated to succeed. Unfortunately for them, results of the study showed that telling such high-stakes lies made them consistently detectable to certain types of people (if you were worried about how they fared in the "torture chamber," rest assured, the researchers didn't follow through on their threat). In short, telling high-stakes lies motivates people to succeed and, as a result, makes them more detectable.

DETECTING DECEPTION: I CAN SEE RIGHT THROUGH YOU

Just as persuaders need someone to persuade, liars need someone to lie to. In the preceding pages we discussed deception from the liar's perspective. In this section, we examine the opposite side of the coin: deception detection. One framework, proposed by Seiter (1997), suggests that we treat deception detection a lot like reaching a verdict in a trial (see also Henningsen, Valde, & Davies, 2005). Whichever verdict we reach (i.e., the person is lying or the person is telling the truth) depends on how we integrate a vast array of verbal and nonverbal information (e.g., Biff is twitching), past knowledge (e.g., Biff doesn't like Gummi Bears), and inferences (e.g., Biff is nervous). Sometimes the information we observe is contradictory (e.g., Biff seems nervous but tells a plausible story), and, sometimes new information causes us to discount our earlier perceptions. This illustrates how complex and idiosyncratic the process of deception detection can be. In other words, the information that one person uses to detect deception may be quite different from the information that another uses. With that as a backdrop, we turn now to a discussion of factors that affect the detection process.

Factors That Influence Detection

Truth Bias: Presuming That People are Honest

Suppose what would happen if everyone in the world always suspected that everyone else was lying. Cooperation would become impossible. So instead, people tend to assume that other people are being honest. In other words, we go through life with a *"truth bias,"* mostly believing what other people tell us. This notion forms the basis of Levine's (2014) *truth-default theory*. According to the theory, the truth bias is adaptive and functional because most of the time people are being honest. When they're being deceptive, however, the truth bias makes detecting them less likely.

"Look Me in the Eye": Stereotypes and Intuitions About Deception

What kinds of things do you look for to detect deception? When we ask our students this question, the most common response we get is "eye contact." When people are lying, our students suggest, they won't look you in the eye or they look up and to the right.

If you've ever thought the same thing about lying and eye contact, you and our students are not alone. According to Lock's (2005) sources, research in more than 60 countries indicates that, from Afghanistan to Zimbabwe, people report that eye contact is one of the most common behaviors they use for detecting deception. Here's the catch, though: Generally, research has shown that liars do not avoid eye contact (DePaulo, et al., 2003; Sporer & Schwandt, 2007), and in some situations engage in more deliberate eye contact than truth do tellers (Mann, Vrij, Shaw, Leal, Ewens, Hillman, Granhag, & Fisher, 2013). Likewise, evidence that people look in certain directions when lying—a hypothesis derived from neurolinguistic programming—is weak at best (Mann, Vrij, Nasholm, Warmelink, Leal, & Forrester, 2012). What's more, many of the other behaviors people say they use to detect deception are not reliable indicators of deception (e.g., see Granhag, Giolla, Sooniste, Stromwell, & Lui-Jonsson, 2016; Hart, Hudson, Fillmore, & Griffith, 2006).

Given that, you might be thinking that such stereotypes are to blame for our generally less-than-stellar ability to detect deception. If so, think again. Although this notion, known as the *wrong subjective cue hypothesis* (see Hartwig & Bond, 2011), prevailed for decades, recent research suggests that people tend to be unaware of the cues they actually rely on to detect deception. In other words, people *say* they look for one set of cues, but they actually use a different set of cues. In one meta-analysis, for instance, Hartwig and Bond (2011) found that rather than relying on lack of eye contact and other stereotypical cues, people tend to look for signs of ambivalence, uncertainty, and indifference to detect deception. What's more, the latter group of cues was more reliable, suggesting that people's intuitions about deceptive cues are less flawed than the stereotypical cues they report using. As such, Hartwig and Bond (2011) note that one possible avenue for improving detection might be to promote (and improve) more automatic, intuitive processing of messages. This, they suggest, might occur if people receive feedback about the accuracy of their judgments often enough to develop useful intuitions about deceptive behaviors.

Training People to Be Effective Lie Detectors

Training people to be better at spotting lies, however, could prove to be tricky business. Indeed, an analysis of 30 studies indicated that training people to spot verbal and nonverbal cues to deception improved their detection accuracy, but the effect was small (Hauch, Sporer, Michael, & Meissner, 2016). Not only that, two studies found that training might actually backfire (Akehurst, Bull, Vrij, & Köhnken, 2004; Kassin & Fong, 1999)—that is, people who had been trained to spot cues to deception, compared to those who had not, were significantly *less* accurate at spotting lies.

That said, if you're thinking that deception detection is a hopeless endeavor, don't surrender just yet. Instead, keep in mind that when experts are allowed to actively question suspects, accuracy rates get much higher (Levine, Clare, Blair, McCornack, Morrison, & Park, 2014; Luke, Hartwig, Joseph, Brimbal, Chan, Dawson, Jordan,

Donovan, & Granhag, 2016). With that in mind, a more promising approach might be to focus on improving people's interrogation techniques, a topic we'll return to later in this chapter.

Humans as Polygraphs

Just as some people are better at deceiving others, are some people more skillful at detecting deception? Some research seems to indicate that this is the case. For example, earlier we mentioned that some, but not all people, were fairly consistent when trying to detect high-stakes lies. What, then, you might wonder, distinguishes these people from more gullible folks? Is there some type of trait or individual difference that separates effective from ineffective deception detectors? If so, research has not identified it. Although some studies have identified individual differences such as involvement (Forrest & Feldman, 2000), self-monitoring (Brandt, Miller, & Hocking, 1980b; Geizer, Rarick, & Soldow, 1977), and sex (DePaulo, Zuckerman, & Rosenthal, 1980; Rosenthal & DePaulo, 1979) as characteristics that may help or hinder successful deception detection, one meta-analysis examining over 140 studies (Bond & DePaulo, 2008) found that when large numbers of studies are examined side by side, individual differences do not appear to play a significant role in deception detection. Such differences do, however, predispose some people to be more suspicious and others to be more trusting, which, in turn, may make them less accurate when trying to distinguish lies from truths. We will examine these biases later in the chapter. For now, though, we should mention that Bond and DePaulo (2008) do not completely rule out the possibility that individual differences may affect deception detection in the real world. For example, they suggest that individual differences in people's ability to analyze nonverbal behaviors some time after an interaction might lead to more accuracy.

Familiarity, Biases, and Deception Detection

Does knowing a person help us detect his or her deception? Several researchers have asked this question but, for quite some time, results of such studies seemed mixed. For instance, in five studies (Brandt, Miller, & Hocking, 1980a, 1980b, 1982; Feeley & deTurck, 1997; Feeley, deTurck, & Young, 1995), people rated communicators' veracity after either watching or not watching videotapes of the communicators' normal, truthful behavior. The results of these studies showed that people who were familiar with the communicators' previous, truthful behaviors were more accurate in their judgments than those who were unfamiliar. Similarly, Comadena (1982) found that spouses could detect each other's deception better than friends could. However, Miller and colleagues (1981) found that when judging lies about emotional information, friends were more accurate than either strangers or spouses, and two studies (Al-Simadi, 2000; Seiter & Wiseman, 1995) found that people who tried to detect the deception of people from their own ethnic or cultural group (e.g., those with whom they would presumably be the most familiar) were less accurate than people who tried to detect the deception of people from ethnic or cultural groups other than their own.[2]

Although such results may seem inconclusive, interpersonal deception theory (Buller, Stiff, & Burgoon, 1996; Burgoon & Buller, 2008) suggests that they may not be when you consider the possible effects of familiarity on deception. The theory argues that familiarity is a double-edged sword: In some ways, it may help you to be a better deception detector; in other ways, it might hinder your ability to detect deception. First, because of certain biases, the better you know someone, the less effective you are at detecting his or her lies. Specifically, McCornack and Parks (1986) found that familiarity increased a person's confidence about judging veracity which, in turn, led to a *truth bias* (see above). The results of their study and others (Stiff, Kim, & Ramesh, 1992) support this idea by showing that the truth bias was positively associated with familiarity and negatively associated with detection accuracy. In other words, people were less accurate when judging familiar others because they thought the others were always honest and trustworthy. In positive relationships based on trust, a truth bias is likely. However, in "negative" relation-ships, a *lie bias* (i.e., the perception that people are being dishonest) becomes more likely (McCornack & Levine, 1990). Whatever the case, both the truth and lie biases make you less accurate when judging veracity because they prevent you from distinguishing truths from lies.

Although truth and lie biases make you less accurate at detecting the deception of familiar others, the knowledge you've gained about familiar others can also make you more accurate at detecting them (Buller, Stiff, & Burgoon, 1996). Specifically, because you have more background information about familiar others, you might be more likely to notice contradictions in what they say (e.g., your significant other has told you that he or she has never been to San Francisco but later says, "The view from the Golden Gate Bridge is fantastic"). Moreover, because you have more knowledge about the way a familiar other typically behaves, you may be more likely to detect his or her deception when the behavior suddenly changes (e.g., your significant other, who is normally calm, becomes very nervous whenever he or she talks about espionage agents). Finally, when you know another person well, you may be more likely to recognize idiosyncratic behaviors that that person only enacts while lying (Anderson, Ansfield, & DePaulo, 1999). In short, then, familiarity can both help and hinder accurate deception detection. Familiarity is related to biases that decrease accuracy and knowledge that increases accuracy.

Suspicion

According to interpersonal deception theory (Buller, Stiff, & Burgoon, 1996; Burgoon & Buller, 2004, 2008), as a deceptive interaction is unfolding, people may become suspicious of being lied to and, in turn, may behave in certain ways because of it. In some cases, they may hide their suspiciousness. For example, at least two studies show that when we suspect that someone is lying to us, we alter our behavior so we don't look suspicious (Buller, Strzyzewski, & Comstock, 1991; Burgoon, Buller, Dillman, & Walther, 1995). Specifically, suspicious people tend to use shorter responses, take longer to answer, and manage their body movements more. In other situations, however, our behaviors may reveal our suspicion and, in turn, may affect our partner's behavior. Indeed, if someone who is lying to us thinks we are suspicious, the liar may try even harder to be convincing. Previous research has supported this notion, demonstrating that deceivers' verbal and nonverbal behavior changes during the course of interactions, often becoming indistinguishable from truthful behavior well into the interaction (see, Burgoon & Buller, 2004; Burgoon & Qin, 2006; White & Burgoon, 2001). On the other hand, one study found that interviewers who displayed a supportive demeanor during an interrogation encouraged truth tellers, but not liars, to provide more details (Mann et al., 2013).

Although it is apparent that suspiciousness plays a role in both senders' and receivers' behaviors, does it affect people's ability to judge veracity? Research suggests the answer to this question is no. In other words, there appears to be a weak relationship between suspicion and the ability to discriminate lies from truths. To help understand why, imagine that a person is making a number of statements and you are trying to decide which of the statements are true and which are false. The *opposing effects model* (Kim & Levine, 2011) suggests that suspicion decreases the truth bias. As such, being suspicious makes you more accurate when judging lies and less accurate when judging truths. Such opposing effects cancel each other out, making little difference in your overall ability to tell truths from lies. In short, suspicion helps you spot lies but misjudge truths.

Probing and Deception Detection

In the previous section we learned that when trying to detect deception, people sometimes try to alter their behavior so they don't look suspicious. But sometimes, probing a potential liar for more information may be necessary. To be sure, if a liar won't talk, it's difficult to find contradictions or inconsistencies in his or her story. Interestingly, however, most research indicates that probing suspects for more information (e.g., "Tell me more about where you were when the book bag was stolen") does *not* increase the accuracy with which you can detect that suspect's deception (Buller et al., 1991). Perhaps even more interesting is the fact that probing a suspect for more information causes third parties to perceive the suspect as more honest (Buller et al., 1991). This phenomenon has been called the *probing effect* by those who study deception (e.g., Levine & McCornack, 1996a, 1996b).

Although scholars agree that the probing effect occurs, there is some disagreement on what causes it. (For a more detailed debate, see Buller, Stiff, & Burgoon, 1996; Levine & McCornack, 1996a, 1996b.) For instance, several authors argue in favor of the *behavioral adaptation explanation,* which in a nutshell asserts that when probing occurs, liars realize they are suspected of lying and alter their behavior to be more believable. Levine and McCornack (1996a), however, assert that this explanation is flawed and in one study found evidence that contradicts it (Levine & McCornack, 2001). In the study, liars were videotaped being probed. Afterward, research participants watched one of two versions of the videotaped liars. Both versions showed exactly the same footage of the liars, but one had the probes edited out. Interestingly, participants who watched the videos in which probes were deleted perceived liars to be significantly less honest than those who saw the probed liars. Thus, Levine and McCornack (2001) showed that the probing effect occurred, but not because liars changed their behaviors.

What, then, is responsible for the probing effect? According to Levine and McCornack (2001), when trying to tell if someone is lying, judges often rely on shortcuts rather than on scrutinizing the behavior of the suspect. One shortcut judges rely on is called the *probing heuristic* (Levine & McCornack, 2001). Here's how it works. Imagine you're watching a suspect and trying to decide if he or she is lying or telling the truth. Also imagine that the suspect is being probed. Rather than scrutinize the suspect's words and behaviors, you use a shortcut. Specifically, you think to yourself: "It's mighty difficult and nerve racking to lie while being probed, so, given the choice, people being probed will choose to tell the truth." Based on such thinking, you decide that people being probed are also being honest. Your judgment has nothing to do with the suspect's behavioral adaptation but rather a simple shortcut that saves you the effort of scrutinizing the suspect's behavior (Levine & McCornack, 2001).

Before concluding this section, we should note that others have questioned whether behavioral adaptation happens. For example, in contrast to behavioral adaptation, Ekman (1985) suggests that an opposite phenomenon may occur: When suspected of deceit, a *truthful* communicator may become anxious. This, in turn, may cause a detector to commit what Ekman calls the *Othello error*—that is, the detector wrongly assumes that the anxious behavior is indicative of deception. A study by Henningsen, Cruz, and Morr (2000) supported this notion by finding that people who were perceived as nervous were also perceived as deceptive.

Eliciting Cues to Deception: Puttin' the Squeeze On

Earlier in this chapter, we suggested that one possible way to improve deception detection is by training people to spot reliable cues to deception. A second, and, according to Hartwig and Bond (2011), perhaps more promising strategy, is less passive in nature. Specifically, rather than simply observing a person's verbal and nonverbal cues, this approach actively attempts to increase behavioral differences between liars and truth tellers, thereby making them easier to distinguish from one another. Let's examine two techniques for doing so.

The Imposing-Cognitive Load Approach: Too Much to Think About

The *imposing-cognitive load approach* (see Vrij et al., 2011) is based on the assumption that lying is more mentally taxing than telling the truth (see above). As such, if you increase cognitive demands further, liars, who have fewer cognitive resources, will struggle more than truth tellers. By way of example, Vrij, Mann, Fisher, Leal, Milne, and Bull (2008) asked liars and truth tellers to provide an account in either chronological or reverse chronological order. It turns out that liars who told the story backward were more detectable than those who told it from front to back, presumably because of increased cognitive load. Another study found that describing an event in different ways (i.e., verbally and pictorially) was more difficult for liars than for truth tellers. As such, liars were less consistent between descriptions (Leins, Fisher, & Vrij, 2012).

Strategic Questioning: Designed to Trip You Up

A second approach suggests that specific types of interrogation questions may be particularly useful for detecting deceit. Consider, for example, the *strategic use of evidence (SUE) technique* (Granhag & Hartwig, 2008; Hartwig et al., 2005). In it, interrogators who possess certain evidence about a case do not reveal that evidence, hoping instead that suspects will say something to contradict it. Later, the interrogator pounces, revealing the evidence and asking the suspect to explain the contradiction. Recent research indicates that revealing evidence late in the interrogation, rather than early or gradually, is most effective. Indeed, revealing evidence early or gradually allows a suspect to adapt. What's more, revealing evidence gradually causes innocent suspects to appear guilty (Sorochinski, Hartwig, Osborne, Wilkins, Marsh, Kazakov, & Granhag, 2014).

A compatible approach suggests that deception detectors are more accurate when they consider *context-sensitive information* (Levine, Blair, and Clare, 2014). To illustrate, imagine that a middle-aged woman whom you know nothing about has just told you Nutrageous bars are her favorite type of candy. And then imagine a tiny, 5-year-old girl tells you that she has just been signed as the new quarterback for the Denver Broncos, her favorite football team. Assuming both people are lying, which would be easier to detect? Obviously, if you know anything about the typical size and demographics of professional football players, the little girl should be easier to detect. Indeed, according to Blair, Levine, and Shaw (2010), when given meaningful information about context (e.g., professional football players are usually large males), the typical 50 percent detection rates we told you about at the beginning of this chapter increase drastically.

In fact, one series of studies (Levine et al., 2014) increased accuracy rates to over 70 percent! In the studies, students tried to win cash prizes while playing a trivia game with a teammate. Unbeknown to the students, however, their teammates were really part of the study. What's more, the teammates encouraged the students to cheat, which many of them did. Later, the students were interrogated using several questions that were strategically designed to garner diagnostically useful information about whether they were lying or telling the truth. For example:

1. "When I interview your partner, what will they say about cheating?" (The rationale for asking this question: Liars, compared to truth tellers, should be less confident that their teammates will exonerate them).

2. "For the answers you got right, explain how you got the right answer?" (Rationale: Cheaters, compared to noncheaters, should feel the need to justify their performance).

3. "If someone did cheat, what should happen to them?" (Rationale: Cheaters, compared to noncheaters, should be more likely to suggest leniency).

Given such research, it is clear that interrogation strategies can be vital when trying to detect deception.

SUMMARY

Deception is a multifaceted and complex communication phenomenon that has been broadly conceptualized. In this chapter we explored some of these conceptualizations. We also learned that although people are not very good at detecting deception, some factors improve their accuracy. Other factors (e.g., the truth bias), however, can impede detection accuracy. We also examined some of the behaviors that distinguish truthful from deceptive individuals and some of the frameworks that explain such differences. Finally, we discussed various approaches for eliciting cues to deception.

NOTES

1. Although there are two versions of information manipulation theory, for our purposes, we treat them as one.
2. Results of research on inter- and intra-ethnic deception detection are mixed. Though the two studies already mentioned (i.e., Al-Simadi, 2000; Seiter & Wiseman, 1995) found that interethnic detection is more accurate than intraethnic detection, other studies have found the opposite (e.g., Bond & Atoum, 2000; Bond, Omar, Mahmoud, & Bosner, 1990).

REFERENCES

Akehurst, L., Bull, R., Vrij, A., & Köhnken, G. (2004). The effect of training professional groups and laypersons to use criteria-based content analysis to detect deception. *Applied Cognitive Psychology, 18*(7), 877–891.

Ali, M., & Levine, T. (2008). The language of truthful and deceptive denials and confessions. *Communication Reports, 21*, 82–91.

Al-Simadi, F. A. (2000). Detection of deceptive behavior: A cross-cultural test. *Social Behavior and Personality, 28*(5), 455–462.

Anderson, D. E., Ansfield, M. E., & DePaulo, B. M. (1999). Love's best habit: Deception in the context of relationships. In P. Philippot & R. S. Feldman (Eds.), *The social context of nonverbal behavior: Studies in emotion and social interaction* (pp. 372–409). New York: Cambridge University Press.

Barnett, M. A., Bartel, J. S., Burns, S. R., Sanborn, F. W., Christensen, N. E., & White, M. M. (2000). Perceptions of children who lie: Influence of lie motive and benefit. *Journal of Genetic Psychology, 161*(3), 381–383.

Blair, J. P., Levine, T. R., & Shaw, A. S. (2010). Content in context improves deception detection accuracy. *Human Communication Research, 36*, 423–442.

Bond, C. F., & Atoum, A. O. (2000). International deception. *Personality and Social Psychology Bulletin, 26*(3), 38–395.

Bond, C. F., & DePaulo, B. M. (2006). Accuracy of deception judgments. *Review of Personality and Social Psychology, 10*, 214–234.

Bond, C. F., & DePaulo, B. M. (2008). Individual differences in judging deception: Accuracy and bias. *Psychological Bulletin, 134*, 477–492.

Bond, C. F., Omar, A., Mahmoud, A., & Bosner, R. N. (1990). Lie detection across cultures. *Journal of Nonverbal Behavior, 14*, 189–204.

Braginsky, D. D. (1970). Machiavellianism and manipulative interpersonal behavior in children. *Journal of Experimental Social Psychology, 6*, 77–99.

Brandt, D. R., Miller, G. R., & Hocking, J. E. (1980a). The truth deception attribution: Effects of familiarity on the ability of observers to detect deception. *Human Communication Research, 6*, 99–108.

Brandt, D. R., Miller, G. R., & Hocking, J. E. (1980b). Effects of self-monitoring and familiarity on deception. *Communication Quarterly, 22*, 3–10.

Brandt, D. R., Miller, G. R., & Hocking, J. E. (1982). Familiarity and lie detection: A replication and extension. *Western Journal of Speech Communication, 46*, 276–290.

Brewer, G., & Abell, L. (2015). Machiavellianism and sexual behavior: Motivations, deception and infidelity. *Personality and Individual Differences, 74*, 186–191. doi:10.1016/j.paid.2014.10.028

Burgoon, J. K., & Buller, D. B. (2004). Interpersonal deception theory. In J. S. Seiter & R. H. Gass (Eds.), *Readings in persuasion, social influence, and compliance gaining* (pp. 239–264). Boston, MA: Allyn & Bacon.

Buller, D. B., & Burgoon, J. K. (1996). Interpersonal deception theory. *Communication Theory, 6*(3), 203–242.

Buller, D. B., Stiff, J. B., & Burgoon, J. K. (1996). Behavioral adaptation in deceptive transactions: Fact or fiction: Reply to Levine and McCornack. *Human Communication Research, 22*(4), 589–603.

Buller, D. B., Strzyzewski, K. D., & Comstock, J. (1991). Interpersonal deception: I. Deceivers' reactions to receivers' suspicions and probing. *Communication Monographs, 58,* 1–24.

Buller, D. B., Burgoon, J. K., White, C., & Ebesu, A. S. (1994). Interpersonal deception: VII. Behavioral profiles of falsification, concealment and equivocation. *Journal of Language and Social Psychology, 13,* 366–395.

Burgoon, J. K., & Buller, D. B. (2008). Interpersonal deception theory: Purposive and interdependent behavior during deception. In L. A. Baxter & D. O. Braithwaite (Eds.), *Engaging theories in interpersonal communication: Multiple perspectives* (pp. 227–239). Los Angeles, CA: Sage.

Burgoon, J. K., & Qin, T. (2006). The dynamic nature of deceptive verbal communication. *Journal of Language and Social Psychology, 25,* 76–96.

Burgoon, J. K., Buller, D. B., Dillman, L., & Walther, J. B. (1995). Interpersonal deception: IV. Effects of suspicion on perceived communication and nonverbal behavior dynamics. *Human Communication Research, 22*(2), 163–196.

Burgoon, J. K., Buller, D. B., Ebesu, A. S., & Rockwell, P. (1994). Interpersonal deception: V. Accuracy in deception detection. *Communication Monographs, 61,* 303–325.

Burgoon, J. K., Buller, D. B., Grandpre, J. R., & Kalbfleisch, P. (1998). Sex differences in presenting and detecting deceptive messages. In D. J. Canary & K. Dindia (Eds.), *Sex differences and similarities in communication: Critical essays and empirical investigations of sex and gender in interaction* (pp. 351–372). Mahwah, NJ: Erlbaum.

Camden, C., Motley, M. M., & Wilson, A. (1984). White lies in interpersonal communication: A taxonomy and preliminary investigation of social motivations. *Western Journal of Speech Communication, 48,* 309–325.

Caso, L., Vrij, A., Mann, S., & De Leo, G. (2006). Deceptive responses: The impact of verbal and nonverbal countermeasures. *Legal and Criminological Psychology, 11,* 99–111.

Christie, R., & Geis, G. (1970). *Studies in Machiavellianism.* New York: Academic Press.

Comadena, M. E. (1982). Accuracy in detecting deception: Intimate and friendship relationships. In M. Burgoon (Ed.), *Communication yearbook 6* (pp. 446–472). Beverly Hills, CA: Sage.

DePaulo, B. M., & Kirkendol, S. E., (1989). The motivational impairment effect in the communication of deception. In J. C. Yuille (Ed.), *Credibility assessment* (pp. 51–70). Belgium: Kluwer.

DePaulo, B. M., Stone, J. I., & Lassiter, G. D. (1985). Deceiving and detecting deceit. In B. R. Schlenker (Ed.), *The self and social life* (pp. 323–370). New York: McGraw-Hill.

DePaulo, B. M., Zuckerman, M., & Rosenthal, R. (1980). Humans as lie detectors. *Journal of Communication, 30,* 129–139.

DePaulo, B. M., Ansfield, M. E., Kirkendol, S. E., & Boden, J. M. (2004). Serious lies. *Basic and Applied Social Psychology, 26*(2–3), 147–167.

DePaulo, B. M., Lindsay, J. J., Malone, B. E., Muhlenbruck, L., Charlton, K., & Cooper, H. (2003). Cues to deception. *Psychological Bulletin, 129*(1), 74–118.

deTurck, M. A., & Miller, G. R. (1985). Deception and arousal: Isolating the behavioral correlates of deception. *Human Communication Research*, *12*, 181–201.

Ekman, P. (1985). *Telling lies*. New York: W. W. Norton.

Ekman, P., & Friesen, W. V. (1969). Nonverbal leakage cues to deception. *Psychiatry*, *32*, 88–106.

Ekman, P., & Friesen, W. V. (1974). Detecting deception from the body or face? *Journal of Personality and Social Psychology*, *54*, 414–420.

Elliot, G. C. (1979). Some effects of deception and level of self-monitoring on planning and reacting to a self-presentation. *Journal of Personality and Social Psychology*, *37*, 1282–1292.

Feeley, T. H. (1996, November). *Conversational competence and perceptions of honesty in interpersonal deception*. Paper presented at the annual meeting of the Speech Communication Association, San Diego, CA.

Feeley, T. H., & deTurck, M. A. (1997). Case-relevant vs. case-irrelevant questioning in experimental lie detection. *Communication Reports*, *10*(1), 35–46.

Feeley, T. H., & Young, M. J. (1998). Humans as lie detectors: Some more second thoughts. *Communication Quarterly*, *46*(2), 109–126.

Feeley, T. H., deTurck, M. A., & Young, M. J. (1995). Baseline familiarity in lie detection. *Communication Research Reports*, *12*(2), 160–169.

Forrest, J. A., & Feldman, R. S. (2000). Detecting deception and judge's involvement: Lower task involvement leads to better lie detection. *Personality and Social Psychology Bulletin*, *26*(1), 118–125.

Frank, M. G., & Ekman, P. (1997). The ability to detect deceit generalizes across different types of high-stake lies. *Journal of Personality and Social Psychology*, *72*(6), 1429–1439.

Geis, G. L., & Moon, Y. Y. (1981). Machiavellianism and deception. *Journal of Personality and Social Psychology*, *41*, 766–775.

Geizer, R. S., Rarick, D. L., & Soldow, G. F. (1977). Deception judgment accuracy: A study of person perception. *Personality and Psychology Bulletin*, *3*, 446–449.

Granhag, P. A., & Hartwig, M. (2008). A new theoretical perspective on deception detection: On the psychology of instrumental mind-reading. *Psychology, Crime and Law*, *14*, 189–200. doi:10.1080/10683160701645181

Granhag, P. A., Giolla, E. M., Sooniste, T., Stromwell, L., & Liu-Jonsson, M. (2016). Discriminating between statements of true and false intent: The impact of repeated interviews and strategic questioning. *Journal of Applied Security Research*, *11*, 1–17. doi:10.1080/19361610.2016.1104230

Hart, C. L., Hudson, L. P., Fillmore, D. G., & Griffith, J. D. (2006). Managerial beliefs about the behavioral cues of deception. *Individual Differences Research*, *4*, 176–184.

Hartwig, M., & Bond, C. F., Jr. (2011). Why do lie-catchers fail? A lens model meta-analysis of human lie judgments. *Psychological Bulletin*, *137*, 643–659.

Hartwig, M., Granhag, P. A. & Strömwall, L. A. (2007). Guilty and innocent suspects' strategies during police interrogations. *Psychology, Crime, and Law*, *13*, 213–227.

Hartwig, M., Granhag, P. A. & Strömwall, L. A., & Vrij, A. (2005). Detecting deception via strategic disclosure of evidence. *Law and Human Behavior*, *29*, 469–484. doi:10.1007/s10979–005–5521-x

Hauch, V., Sporer, S. L., Michael, S. W., & Meissner, C. A. (2016). Does training improve the detection of deception? A meta-analysis. *Communication Research*, *43*, 283–343. doi:10.1177/009365021453974

Henningsen, D. D., Cruz, M. G., & Morr, M. C. (2000). Pattern violations and perceptions of deception. *Communication Reports*, *13*, 1–9.

Henningsen, D. D., Valde, K. S., & Davies, E. (2005). Exploring the effect of verbal and nonverbal cues on perceptions of deception. *Communication Quarterly, 53*(3), 359–375.

Hopper, R., & Bell, R. A. (1984). Broadening the deception construct. *Quarterly Journal of Speech, 70,* 288–302.

Jonason, P. K., Lyons, M., Baughman, H. M., & Vernon, P. A. (2014). What a tangled web we weave: The dark triad traits and deception. *Personality and Individual Differences, 70,* 117–119. doi:10.1016/j.paid.2014.06.038

Kassin, S. M., & Fong, C. T. (1999). "I'm innocent!": Effects of training on judgments of truth and deception in the interrogation room. *Law and Human Behavior, 23*(5), 499–516.

Kim, R. K., & Levine, T. R. (2011). The effect of suspicion on deception detection accuracy: Optimal level or opposing effects? *Communication Reports, 24,* 51–62.

Kraut, R. E. (1978). Verbal and nonverbal cues in the perception of lying. *Journal of Personality and Social Psychology, 36,* 380–391.

Kraut, R. E. (1980). Humans as lie detectors: Some second thoughts. *Journal of Communication, 30,* 209–216. doi:10.1111/j.1460-2466.1980.tb02030.x

Leins, D. A., Fisher, R. P., & Vrij, A. (2012). Drawing on liars' lack of cognitive flexibility: Detecting deception through varying report modes. *Applied Cognitive Psychology, 26,* 601–607. doi:10.1002/acp.2837

Levine, T. R. (2014). Truth-default theory (TDT): A theory of human deception and deception detection. *Journal of Language and Social Psychology, 33,* 378–392. doi:10.1177/0261927X14535916

Levine, T. R. (2016). Examining sender and judge variability in honesty assessments and deception detection accuracy: Evidence for a transparent liar but no evidence of deception-general ability. *Communication Research Reports, 33,* 188–194. doi:10.1080/08824096.2016.11896629

Levine, T. R., Blair, J. P., & Clare, D. D. (2014). Diagnostic utility: Experimental demonstrations and replications of powerful question effects in high-stakes deception detection. *Human Communication Research, 40,* 262–289. doi:10.1111/hcre.12021

Levine, T. R., Clare, D. D., Blair, J. P., McCornack, S., Morrison, K., & Park, H. S. (2014). Expertise in deception detection involves actively prompting diagnostic information rather than passive behavioral observation. *Human Communication Research, 40,* 442–462. doi:10.1111/hcre.12032

Levine, T. R., & Kim, R. K. (2010). Some considerations for a new theory of deceptive communication. In M. S. McGlone & M. L. Knapp (Eds.), *The interplay of truth and deception: New agendas in communication* (pp. 17–34). New York: Routledge.

Levine, T. R., & McCornack, S. A. (1996a). A critical analysis of the behavioral adaptation explanation of the probing effect. *Human Communication Research, 22*(4), 575–588.

Levine, T. R., & McCornack, S. A. (1996b). Can behavioral adaptation explain the probing effect? Rejoinder to Buller et al. *Human Communication Research, 22*(4), 604–613.

Levine, T. R., & McCornack, S. A. (2001). Behavioral adaptation, confidence, and heuristic-based explanations of the probing effect. *Human Communication Research, 27,* 471–502.

Levine, T. R., & McCornack, S. A. (2014). Theorizing about deception. *Journal of Language and Social Psychology, 33,* 431–440. doi:10.1177/0261927X14536397

Levine, T. R., Park, H. S., & McCornack, S. A. (1999). Accuracy in detecting truths and lies: Documenting the "veracity effect." *Communication Monographs, 66*(2), 125–144.

Levine, T. R., Serota, K. B., Shulman, H., Clare, D. D., Park, H. S., Shaw, A. S., Shim, J. C., & Lee, J. H. (2010). Sender demeanor: Individual differences in sender believability have a powerful impact on deception detection judgments. *Human Communication Research*, *37*, 377–403.

Lindskold, S., & Walters, P. S. (1983). Categories for the acceptability of lies. *Journal of Social Psychology*, *120*, 129–136.

Littlepage, G. E., & Pineault, M. A. (1979). Detection of deceptive factual statements from the body and the face. *Personality and Psychology Bulletin*, *5*, 325–328.

Lock, C. (2005). Psychologists try to learn how to spot a liar. Retrieved September 30, 2005, from: www.sciencenews.org/articles/20040731/bob8.asp

Luke, T. L., Hartwig, M., Joseph, M., Brimbal, L., Chan, G., Dawson, E., Jordan, S., Donovan, P., & Granhag, P. A. (2016). Training in the strategic use of evidence technique: Improving deception detection accuracy of American law enforcement officers. *Journal of Police and Criminal Psychology*, *31*, 270–278. doi:10.1007/s11896–015–9187–0

Luo, X., Zhang, W., Burd, S., & Seazzu, A. (2013). Investigating phishing victimization with the heuristic-systematic model: A theoretical framework and exploration. *Computers & Security*, *38*, 28–38. doi:10.1016/j.cose.2012.12.003

Mann, S., Vrij, A., Nasholm, E., Warmelink, L., Leal, S., & Forrester, D. (2012). The direction of deception: Neuro-linguistic programming as a lie detection tool. *Journal of Police and Criminal Psychology*, *27*, 160–166. doi:10.1007/s11896–011–9097–8

Mann, S., Vrij, A., Shaw, D. J., Leal, S., Ewens, S., Hillman, J., Granhag, P. A., & Fisher, R. P. (2013). Two heads are better than one? How to effectively use two interviewers to elicit cues to deception. *Legal and Criminological Psychology*, *18*, 324–340. doi:10.1111/j.2044–8333.2012.02055x

McCornack, S. A. (1992). Information manipulation theory. *Communication Monographs*, *59*, 1–16.

McCornack, S. A. (1997). The generation of deceptive messages: Laying the groundwork for a viable theory of interpersonal deception. In J. O. Greene (Ed.), *Message production: Advances in communication theory* (pp. 91–126). Mahwah, NJ: Erlbaum.

McCornack, S. A., & Levine, T. R. (1990). When lovers become leery: The relationship between suspicion and accuracy in detecting deception. *Communication Monographs*, *57*, 219–230.

McCornack, S. A., & Parks, M. R. (1986). Deception detection and relational development: The other side of trust. In M. L. McLaughlin (Ed.), *Communication yearbook 9* (pp. 377–389). Beverly Hills, CA: Sage.

McCornack, S. A., Levine, T. R., Solowczuk, K., Torres, H. I., & Campbell, D. M. (1992). When the alteration of information is viewed as deception: An empirical test of information manipulation theory. *Communication Monographs*, *59*, 17–29.

McCornack, S., Morrison, K., Paik, J. E., Wisner, A. M., & Zhu, X. (2014). Information manipulation theory 2: A propositional theory of deceptive discourse production. *Journal of Language and Social Psychology*, *33*, 348–377. doi:10.1177/0261927x14534656

Mealy, M., Stephan, W., & Urrutia, I. C. (2007). The acceptability of lies: A comparison of Ecuadorians and Euro-Americans. *International Journal of Intercultural Relations*, *31*, 689–702.

Miller, G. R., & Stiff, J. B. (1993). *Deceptive communication*. Newbury Park, NJ: Sage.

Miller, G. R., deTurck, M. A., & Kalbfleisch, P. J. (1983). Self-monitoring, rehearsal, and deceptive communication. *Human Communication Research*, *10*, 97–117.

Miller, G. R., Bauchner, J. E., Hocking, J. E., Fontes, N. E., Kaminski, E. P., & Brandt, D. R. (1981). ". . . and nothing but the truth": How well can observers detect deceptive testimony? In B. D. Sales (Ed.), *Perspectives in law and psychology. Vol. II: The jury, judicial, and trial process* (pp. 145–179). New York: Plenum.

O'Hair, D., Cody, M. J., & Behnke, R. R. (1985). Communication apprehension and vocal stress as indices of deception. *Western Journal of Speech Communication, 49,* 286–300.

O'Hair, D., Cody, M. J., & McLaughlin, M. L. (1981). Prepared lies, spontaneous lies, Machiavellianism, and nonverbal communication. *Human Communication Research, 7,* 325–339.

O'Hair, D., Cody, M. J., Goss, B., & Krayer, K. J. (1988). The effect of gender, deceit orientation and communicator style on macro-assessments of honesty. *Communication Quarterly, 36,* 77–93.

Riggio, R. E., & Friedman, H. S. (1983). Individual differences and cues to deception. *Journal of Personality and Social Psychology, 45,* 899–915.

Riggio, R. E., Tucker, J., & Throckmorton, B. (1987). Social skills and deception ability. *Personality and Social Psychology Bulletin, 13,* 568–577.

Riggio, R. E., Tucker, J., & Widaman, K. F. (1987). Verbal and nonverbal cues as mediators of deception ability. *Journal of Nonverbal Behavior, 11,* 126–143.

Rosenthal, R., & DePaulo, B. M. (1979). Sex differences in eavesdropping on nonverbal cues. *Journal of Personality and Social Psychology, 37,* 273–285.

Seiter, J. S. (1997). Honest or deceitful? A study of persons' mental models for judging veracity. *Human Communication Research, 24*(2), 216–259.

Seiter, J. S., & Bruschke, J. C. (2007). Deception and emotion: The effects of motivation, relationship type, and sex on expected feelings of guilt and shame following acts of deception in the United States and Chinese samples. *Communication Studies, 58,* 1–16.

Seiter, J. S., & Wiseman, R. (1995). Ethnicity and deception detection. *Journal of the Northwest Communication Association, 23,* 24–38.

Seiter, J. S., Bruschke, J. C., & Bai, C. (2002). The acceptability of deception as a function of perceivers' culture, deceiver's intention, and deceiver–deceived relationship. *Western Journal of Communication, 66*(2), 158–180.

Sporer, S. L., & Schwandt, B. (2007). Moderators of nonverbal indicators of deception: A meta-analytic synthesis. *Psychology, Public Policy, and Law, 13,* 1–34.

Stiff, J. G., Kim, H. J., & Ramesh, C. (1992). Truth biases and aroused suspicion in relational deception. *Communication Research, 19,* 326–345.

Sorochinski, M., Hartwig, M., Osborne, J., Wilkins, E., Marsh, J., Kazakov, D., & Granhag, P. A. (2014). Interviewing to detect deception: When to disclose the evidence. *Journal of Police and Criminal Psychology, 29,* 87–94. doi:10.1007/s11896–013–9121–2

Strömwall, L. A., Granhag, P. A., & Landström, S. (2007). Children's prepared and unprepared lies: Can adults see through their strategies? *Applied Cognitive Psychology, 21,* 457–471.

Thackray, R. I., & Orne, M. T. (1968). Effects of stimulus employed and the level of subject awareness on the detection of deception. *Journal of Applied Psychology, 52,* 234–239.

Toma, C. L., & Hancock, J. T. (2010). Lying for love in the modern age: Deception in online dating. In M. S. McGlone & M. L. Knapp (Eds.), *The interplay of truth and deception: New agendas in communication* (pp. 147–164). New York: Routledge.

Vrij, A. (2000). *Detecting lies and deceit: The psychology of lying and the implications for professional practice.* Chichester, UK: John Wiley.

Vrij, A. (2014). Interviewing to detect deception. *European Psychologist, 19,* 184–194. doi:10.1027/1016–9040/a000201

Vrij, A., Kneller, W., & Mann, S. (2000). The effect of informing liars about criteria-based content analysis on their ability to deceive CBCA-raters. *Legal and Criminological Psychology*, *5*, 57–70.

Vrij, A., Granhag, P. A., Mann, S., & Leal, S. (2011). Outsmarting the liars: Toward a cognitive lie detection approach. *Current Directions in Psychological Science*, *20*, 28–32.

Vrij, A., Mann, S. A., Fisher, R. P., Leal, S., Milne, R., & Bull, R. (2008). Increasing cognitive load to facilitate lie detection: The benefit of recalling an event in reverse order. *Law and Human Behavior*, *32*, 253–265.

Warren, G., Schertler, E., & Bull, P. (2009). Detecting deception from emotional and unemotional cues. *Journal of Nonverbal Behavior*, *33*, 59–69.

White, C. H., & Burgoon, J. K. (2001). Adaptation and communicative design: Patterns of interaction in truthful and deceptive conversations. *Human Communication Research*, *27*(1), 9–37.

Zuckerman, M., & Driver, R. E. (1985). Telling lies: Verbal and nonverbal correlates of deception. In A. W. Siegman and S. Feldstein (Eds.), *Multichannel integrations of nonverbal behavior* (pp. 129–147). Hillsdale, NJ: Erlbaum.

Zuckerman, M., DePaulo, B. M., & Rosenthal, R. (1981). Verbal and nonverbal communication of deception. In L. Berkowitz (Ed.), *Advances in experimental social psychology* (pp. 2–59). New York: Academic Press.

Motivational Appeals

IF REAL LIFE WERE A CARTOON, the salesperson who showed up at the home of one of the authors could have been Elmer Fudd. The author needed rain gutters on his house. On the advice of a neighbor, he contacted a company located a good 40 miles from where he lived to come out and provide an estimate. The salesperson, a paunchy fellow in his mid-40s, arrived in a beat-up clunker. He looked tired and disheveled as he got out. He fumbled with his clipboard, calculator, and an armload of gutter samples as he made his way up the sidewalk.

"Find the place okay?" the author asked.

"The diwections wuh gweat," the salesperson answered, "but the twaffic was tewwible, and I got a ticket on the way."

"That's too bad," the author replied.

"I didn't have my seat belt on," the salesperson lamented, "because it's bwoken, and it costs $300 to fix. I can't affawd it wight now."

Owing to the salesperson's unkempt appearance, his speech impediment, and his sad tale, the author felt sympathetic. Even though the salesperson's estimate was slightly higher than those of several local businesses, the author signed a contract. How could he do otherwise? The salesperson had come all that way—risked his life, in fact—to provide an estimate. He'd gotten a ticket for his trouble. The way the author saw it, the difference in the salesperson's price from that of the local competitors was probably less than the cost of the ticket. And the guy obviously needed the sale.

Or did he? After the salesperson drove away, the author began wondering if it were all a ruse. What if the salesperson told every potential customer he'd gotten a ticket? What if his seat belt worked just fine? What if he faked or exaggerated the speech problem to elicit sympathy and help make the sale? The author never did find out whether the "sad sack" character was genuine or a guise, but the rain gutters have worked splendidly.

Whether the salesperson's strategy was honest or not, it's clear that his success was based, to a large extent, on pity. His sad story plucked at the author's heartstrings. And in the end, the author was willing to pay more because he felt sorry for the fellow. The salesperson's appeal to pity, if it were designed as such, represents but one example of a *motivational appeal,* the topic of this chapter. Motivational appeals may be generally defined as external inducements, often of an emotional nature, that are designed to increase an individual's drive to undertake some course of action. By external inducements, we mean incentives that exist apart from the substance of a message itself. Such external inducements typically seek to alter people's moods, feelings, or emotions as a means of persuasion.

INTRINSIC VERSUS EXTRINSIC MOTIVATION

Motivational appeals can be thought of as attempts to jump-start an individual's drive to do something. They provide an external incentive for performing some action. *Intrinsic motivation* is drive that comes from within (Deci, 1975; Deci & Ryan, 1978). If you "live to work," your motivation for doing your job is internal. *Extrinsic motivation* is instilled by some outside factor (Petri, 1991). If you "work to live," your motivation for going to work each day is external. All the motivational appeals we discuss here can be thought of as extrinsic in nature. Motivational appeals are found everywhere. Daily entreaties include anxiety, fear, guilt, health, honor, humor, patriotism, pity, pride, sex, warmth, and more. One might be tempted to think that all emotional appeals are ethically suspect. However, as Corbett and Conners (1999) advise, "there is nothing necessarily reprehensible about being moved to action through emotion; in fact, it is perfectly normal" (p. 206). We begin with an examination of emotional appeals in marketing.

EMOTION AND PERSUASION: OH, WHAT A FEELING!

Emotions and the ELM

Emotions tend to exert more influence when receivers rely on peripheral processing, as opposed to central processing (Greifeneder, Bless, & Pham, 2011). However, central processing and peripheral processing can coexist, a phenomenon known as *parallel processing*. A patient, for example, might perceive that her doctor was offering rational arguments for taking her medication and demonstrating empathy for her as well.

Emotions sometimes precede thinking. In such cases, a person's emotional state may bias subsequent thinking (Petty & Briñol, 2015). For example, if an art patron were in a foul mood before attending an art exhibit, the patron might decide the display was "a pile of rubbish" and the artist was a "buffoon." Sometimes emotions follow thinking, in which case they tend to validate the thought process used (Petty & Briñol, 2015). For instance, a traveler who planned a trip carefully, might become elated as the date of departure neared.

Emotional Marketing

Marketers often design ad campaigns to elicit emotions such as fear, love, and regret in consumers (Achar, So, Agrawal, & Duhachek, 2016). According to *attachment theory*, people develop emotional ties to specific brands (Thomson, MacInnis, & Park, 2005). Apple products are a case in point. Mac, iPhone, and iPad owners share an emotional connection with their devices unlike that of their counterparts who use non-Apple products. Such emotional attachments enable marketers to engage consumers, making them passionate about, and loyal to, their brands.

In an episode of the popular television series *Mad Men*, advertising guru Don Draper clearly grasps this concept. His clients, from Kodak, want Draper to create an ad campaign that touts the technology of the new "wheel" on their slide projector. Draper advises them to drop the "glittering lure" of technology and establish a deeper emotional connection with consumers. Nostalgia, Draper stresses, is the key.

> In Greek, nostalgia literally means the pain from an old wound. A twinge in your heart, far more powerful than memory alone. This device . . . is a time machine. It goes backwards and forwards. It takes us to a place where we ache to go again. It's not called the wheel. It's called the carousel. It lets us travel the way a child travels. Around and around and back home again. To a place where we know we are loved.
>
> (Weiner & Veith, 2007)

His pitch invokes the nostalgia he wants consumers to feel. The concept of a carousel establishes a sentimental bond between the consumer and the product.

Don Draper isn't the only one who understands the power of emotional marketing. Persuaders in the real world have acknowledged the effectiveness of motivational appeals for years. Traditional thinking on this topic suggested that such appeals are effective in some contexts but not in others. Specifically, traditionalists suggested that decisions, such as buying gasoline, a microwave, or detergent are more *utilitarian* in nature and are prompted by practical concerns (Babin, Darden, & Griffin, 1994). Other decisions, such as purchasing clothing or music, are more *hedonic* in nature and are driven more by pleasure seeking (Khan, Dhar, & Wertenbroch, 2005). Some decisions, like buying a car, are a mixture of both. A two-seater convertible may seem fun, but what if there are five people in the family?

More recently, however, thinking has shifted in favor of a greater role for emotion compared to reason. Livingston (2007), for instance, argued that "people buy for emotional reasons, and then justify their purchases with logic" (p. 16). By way of example, Adler, Iacobelli, and Gutstein (2016) found that positive emotional appeals outperformed positive rational appeals in an online persuasion context. Similarly, Geuens, De Pelsmacker, and Faseur (2011) found that emotional ads outperformed nonemotional ads for both hedonic *and* utilitarian products. Some go so far as to say that all consumer purchases are dictated by emotion rather than reason (Robinette & Brand, 2001).

While we agree that emotions play an important role in persuasion, we don't believe that emotions rule all our decisions. A wealth of studies show that highly involved receivers favor high-quality arguments and evidence, or what Petty and Cacioppo (1986) call *central processing*. What's more, the distinction between logic and emotion is not altogether clear, as we point out next.

LOGICAL AND EMOTIONAL APPEALS: A FUZZY DISTINCTION

People often think of "logical" and "emotional" appeals as opposites. This distinction dates back to Aristotle, who classified *logos* (logic, reasoning) and *pathos* (passion, emotion) as separate, distinct forms of influence (Aristotle, trans. 1932). This way of thinking, however, represents something of an artificial dichotomy. Whether a message is perceived as logical or emotional has as much to do with the person *perceiving* the message as it does with the message itself (Becker, 1963). In fact, researchers (Evans, Barston, & Pollard, 1983; Oakhill & Garnham, 1993; Reuchelle, 1958) have learned that when people agree with a message, they tend to perceive it as being more logical or rational in nature. When they disagree with a message, they tend to think of it as being more emotional in nature.

In an advertising context, Akbari (2015) found that rational appeals were more effective for low-involvement products (sunscreen), while emotional appeals were more effective for high-involvement products (laptops). This finding was borne out in a meta-analysis (Hornik, Ofir, & Rachamim, 2016) that showed emotional appeals are generally more effective than rational appeals. In addition, positive emotional appeals (humor, for example) were generally more effective than negative appeals (fear, guilt). Purely emotional ads, however, may capture consumers' attention, without persuading them.

FEAR APPEALS: IF YOU DON'T STOP DOING THAT, YOU'LL GO BLIND

"If you cross your eyes, they'll stay that way." "Don't run with scissors, you'll poke your eye out." "Don't stuff beans up your nose, they'll sprout." What child hasn't heard these or similar admonitions from a parent? When he was a little tyke, one of the authors put beans up his nose anyway. While having them removed at the doctor's office, he had to endure his mother's "I told you so" lecture.

Fear appeals are not only a staple of child-rearing, they are also prevalent in the workplace, in public health messages, advertising, and elsewhere. Advertisements for dandruff shampoos, deodorants, mouthwashes, and acne medications, for example, are often predicated on the fear of social ostracism. Pharmaceutical ads tell us to ask our doctor if a new prescription pill is right for us. Then those ads go on to describe a litany of side effects that sound worse than the original illness.

Some commentators charge that America has become a culture based on fear (Altheide, 2002; Gardner, 2009; Glassner, 1999). Whether to sell products, garner votes, or increase ratings, persuaders use scare tactics to increase our anxiety about all sorts of things. We're afraid of exotic diseases such as Ebola, mad cow, and West Nile. We stress out about school shootings, child abductions, homeland security, and road rage. The world is a scary place.

When designed properly, fear appeals can be highly effective. Reviews of the fear appeal literature have shown that inducing fear can bring about changes in attitudes, intentions, and behavior (Boster & Mongeau, 1984; Cho & Witte, 2004; Higbee, 1969; Mongeau, 1998; Ruiter, Abraham, & Kok, 2001; Sutton, 1982; Witte & Allen, 2000). But how and when do fear appeals work best? Two well-known models explain. We discuss these next.

The Stage Model: Scared Stiff

Natascha de Hoog and her colleagues (2007, 2008) developed a dual process model, known as the *stage model*, that explains how fear level or intensity works. According to the model, when a person is exposed to a fear-arousing message, the person engages in *threat appraisal* to assess the *perceived severity* of the threat and her or his *perceived vulnerability* to the threat. The stage model posits four possible threat conditions, based on the combination of low versus high severity and low versus high vulnerability to a threat (see Figure 13.1).

If both severity and vulnerability are seen as low, a person will tend to ignore the threat or rely on peripheral processing. For example, Simone, who lives in Manhattan, might know that bee stings hurt (mild severity), but if she's not allergic to them and doesn't spend much time trekking in meadows (low vulnerability), she might think, "No big deal. I'll worry about it if it happens."

If a person perceives that a threat is severe, but vulnerability is low, the person will engage in moderate cognitive processing, mostly to make sure that the threat is assessed accurately. For example, Dieter, who lives in Stuttgart, might believe that Ebola is a deadly disease (high severity), but that there is little or no risk of contracting it in Germany (low vulnerability). He might be motivated to support eradication efforts in Africa, though, and health screening to prevent travelers from infected areas entering Germany. A converse scenario, with low severity, but high vulnerability, would also prompt moderate central processing. For example, Dieter is mindful of pickpockets on public transit, so he holds his backpack on his lap.

When perceived severity and perceived vulnerability are both high, *defense motivation* kicks in and the person utilizes central processing (see Figure 13.1). Under defense motivation, a person actively scrutinizes the message and evaluates strategies for minimizing the harm. For example, suppose Alain lives in Nice, which was the

FIGURE 13.1
Stage model of
fear-arousing
communication.

Vulnerability to Threat		Severity of Threat	
		Low	High
	Low	Heuristic processing Accuracy motivation	Systematic processing Accuracy motivation
	High	Systematic processing Accuracy motivation	Systematic processing Defense motivation

target of a horrific terrorist attack in 2016. In that incident, a truck plowed into a crowd on Bastille day killing 86 people and injuring 434 more. As a resident of the French city, Alain might perceive that he and other residents are highly vulnerable to another deadly attack. In the high-severity/high-vulnerability condition, the person would examine the message carefully, not just to be clear about the threat, but to identify specific strategies for avoiding or minimizing the threat. The latter process is referred to as *coping appraisal.*

A person using coping appraisal would ask "What can I do to avoid having this happen to me?" In Alain's case, he would likely assess ways of reducing his risk during another attack. He could, of course, move to another city that is less likely to be targeted. He could also avoid places where large crowds congregate. "Why make myself a target?" he might reason. He might be vigilant about possible methods of attack; explosives, assault weapons, or vehicle ramming. He might increase his situational awareness by noting exits or avenues of escape in case of an emergency. He might still drink coffee at outdoor cafés, but not sit street side or near glass windows.

The Extended Parallel Process Model: Nothing to Fear but Fear Itself

When are people likely to use coping strategies? When are they more likely to panic? Although the stage model excels at explaining how threat level or intensity functions, we think another model is better at explaining how people actually respond to threats. Kim Witte's *extended parallel processing model* (EPPM) addresses these concerns (Maloney, Lapinski, & Witte, 2011; Witte, 1992, 1994). According to the model, when a person encounters a fear-arousing message, the person can respond in one of three ways. Let's say a Japanese student, Mayumi, is thinking of visiting South Africa. Her friends, however, have expressed concerns about contracting a disease there. First, she might ignore the message altogether, believing she is not at risk. Mayumi might think to herself, "I've traveled a lot and I've never gotten seriously ill."

Second, if Mayumi perceives that she is at risk, she can try to avoid the danger. She would use *danger control*, by focusing on constructive ways of preventing or minimizing the threat. For example, there are vaccines that prevent hepatitis A and typhoid, two diseases that are found in South Africa. Malaria is also a risk, so she might wear insect repellent or avoid being outdoors at night.

Third, Mayumi might fixate on her fear, which is a non-constructive response known as *fear control*. Fear control essentially involves "worrying about worry." Such a reaction can result in panic. If she decided to visit South Africa anyway, but spent every moment riddled with fear, she would be engaged in fear control.

In the EPPM, danger control is a far more effective response because it focuses on the solution. Fear control, conversely, is counterproductive because it focuses on managing one's fear. A persuader's goal in using fear appeals, then, should be to arouse fear in a manner that triggers danger control rather than fear control.

Returning to our example, for danger control to occur, Mayumi must believe there is a clear course of action that she can take to avoid the threat. This element of the EPPM is called *perceived efficacy*. Perceived efficacy has two components. The first, *response efficacy*, has to do with whether there are effective steps for avoiding the harm. For example, Mayumi might reason that by staying current on immunizations and taking reasonable precautions, she can avoid contracting a disease. The second, *self-efficacy*, has to do with whether she, personally, is capable of taking those steps. If Mayumi is allergic to some vaccines, or she will be visiting rural areas with no potable water, or she will be sleeping outdoors at night, she may not believe she can avoid hepatitis A, typhoid, or malaria.

Both response efficacy and self-efficacy are important components of perceived efficacy. If both are present, a person is more likely to engage in danger control. If either is missing, the person is more likely to resort to fear control. Indeed, a meta-analysis (Casey, Timmermann, Allen, Krahn, & Turkiewicz, 2009) demonstrated this very result: High-response efficacy and self-efficacy correlated significantly with greater condom use. At the point where "perceptions of threat begin to outweigh perceptions of efficacy . . . people begin to shift from danger control to fear control" (Maloney, Lapinski, & Witte, 2011, p. 210).

According to the stage model, then, fear appeals that heighten the perceived severity of, and vulnerability to, a threat, are most likely to succeed. According to the EPPM, identifying specific actions, that the target audience can perform, is essential too. An excellent summary of fear's effectiveness based on these and other models was provided by Tannenbaum, Hepler, Zimmerman, Saul, Jacobs, Wilson, and Albarracin (2015). After reviewing 128 different studies on fear appeals, they concluded, "fear appeals are particularly effective when the communication depicts relatively high amounts of fear, includes an efficacy message, stresses severity and susceptibility, recommends one-time only behaviors, and targets audiences that include a larger percentage of female message recipients" (p. 1198).

We would be remiss if we didn't acknowledge that there are serious ethical concerns surrounding the use of fear appeals. We address these in Chapter 16. For the time being, suffice it to say that a persuader should exercise caution in using fear appeals. Nevertheless, if the harmful consequences are real or genuine, we would suggest it is not only acceptable for a persuader to employ fear appeals, but also that the persuader has an obligation to use them.

The beans, by the way, did not sprout.

NEGATIVE EMOTIONS: WOE IS ME, SHAME ON YOU

Persuaders often seek to stir negative emotions in people. Pity, guilt, and shame are three such negative emotions that can be leveraged to a persuader's advantage. Appeals involving these emotions are often interrelated. Becheur and Valette-Florence (2014), for example, found that a combination of guilt and shame was more effective than guilt alone in persuading young people, ages 18–25, to limit their alcohol consumption. As another example, charitable organizations regularly air television spots portraying starving children or abused pets. The ads induce pity for the kids or animals and guilt in viewers for not donating. "For just a few cents per day," the ads claim, "you can make a difference." Is it possible for nonprofits to use a different approach? Absent pity ploys, guilt trips, and shaming, will people still donate?

One study suggests it may not be possible to have it both ways. Eayres and Ellis (1990) asked males and females to evaluate 10 posters for charitable causes that used different appeals. Some posters depicted people with mental disabilities in a negative light (dependent, incapable), whereas others portrayed them in a positive light (valued, capable). The researchers found that the negative depictions were most likely to induce participants to donate money. Participants were less likely to donate if the posters featured positive portrayals. As the researchers noted, "this tends to validate the supposition that in order to produce a successful poster in charity terms it is necessary to play on people's feelings of guilt and pity" (p. 356). Interestingly, the participants were more willing to become actively involved in, and donate time to, charitable causes that were featured positively in the posters. This bodes well for charities seeking increased voluntarism, but not for ones seeking monetary contributions.

On the subject of guilt itself, some researchers have found that invoking feelings of guilt in another person can facilitate compliance (O'Keefe, 2002). Inducing guilt made people more likely to comply with a subsequent request (Freedman, Wallington, & Bless, 1967; Hibbert, Smith, Davies, & Ireland, 2007; Lindsey, 2005; Lindsey, Yun, & Hill, 2007). Surprisingly, they were more likely to comply even if the person making the request, or the person benefiting from the request, was not the source of their guilt. However, other research (Bessarabova, Turner, Fink, & Blustein, 2015) found that inducing guilt can be counterproductive. Stronger guilt appeals may produce *psychological reactance*, which refers to resistance to a perceived threat to one's freedom. According to Bessarabova et al., internally generated guilt is more effective than externally induced guilt.

A second caution regarding guilt appeals is that the target of the appeal may seek to avoid further interaction with the source, to avoid further embarrassment or minimize the risk of a confrontation. Guilt appeals should, therefore, be designed to emphasize the positive self-feelings that come from doing the right thing, rather than focusing on further loss of face.

There is a dark side to guilt appeals as well. Unscrupulous persuaders can use guilt appeals to extract money from people who are in mourning, as we point out in Box 13.1.

Along the same lines, several investigations have examined people's emotional reactions to others who possess varying maladies or stigmas. How people react to

BOX 13.1 | Funeral Home Persuasion

"You can't take it with you . . . but you don't have to give it all to the mortuary!"

Funerals are expensive. In the USA the price of a typical funeral is $8,000–11,000 (Miller, 2016, www.parting.com). A funeral is a "distress purchase" that is often made under emotional duress. Unfortunately, consumers are quite naive about funeral home practices. What's more, the process of negotiating the price of a funeral comes at the worst possible time: when thinking is impaired by the loss of a loved one. We may feel it is crass to engage in hard bargaining over prices (Gentry, Kennedy, Paul, & Hill, 1995), but this is exactly why some unscrupulous funeral home directors try to take advantage of us. They know that a person who is grieving is an easy mark.

Not all, or even most, mortuaries prey on those who are grieving, but some clearly do (Wasik, 1995). To increase your consumer awareness, and to arm you against the unscrupulous practices employed by some funeral homes, we offer the following list of dos and don'ts when making funeral arrangements. The suggestions apply to a traditional burial. If cremation, burial at sea, or some other option is chosen, not all the suggestions will apply.

1. **Do try to be as rational as possible**. Grieve for the deceased with all your heart, but negotiate the price of the funeral with your head. A funeral home is a for-profit enterprise. You need to be a savvy consumer when negotiating the arrangements and the price.

2. **Don't give in to guilt appeals, such as** "Don't you think he/she deserves genuine brass handles on his/her coffin?" The amount you love someone isn't measured by the amount you spend on that person's funeral. You can always spend more on that person later. For example, you could make a donation in the deceased's name to a worthwhile charity or social cause.

3. **Do conduct price comparisons**, just as you would when buying a car or making any other major purchase. Websites such as Parting.com and FuneralDecision.com allow consumers to shop online. Telephone mortuaries and ask for quotes over the phone. The FTC now requires funeral homes to provide prices by phone. Ask what a complete funeral would cost, including embalming, casket, burial, flowers, and so on. If you don't feel up to making the calls, ask a trusted friend.

4. **Do ensure that everything you are promised is itemized in writing**. The FTC now requires mortuaries to provide itemized prices. Don't take the funeral director's word for it if he or she says, "leave it to us, we'll take care of everything."

5. **Do shop around for prices on caskets**. Funeral homes mark up casket prices astronomically. You can save thousands of dollars by purchasing a casket factory-direct from a manufacturer, or even Costco, and having it delivered to the funeral home. Federal law requires funeral homes to accept a casket purchased elsewhere and prohibits the imposition of "handling fees."

6. **Don't pay for unnecessary frills**. Rather than paying for brass handles, silk ruffles, or carved wood panels, consider personalizing the casket with family photos, poetry, or artwork. Decide what is within your budget and have the funeral director accommodate your needs. If the price isn't right, use outside vendors to provide additional services.

7. **Don't pay more than you must for basic services**. These include transporting the remains, embalming, a casket, interment, and a plot. Try calling around to see if the same services can be

obtained more cheaply elsewhere. Cremation is a cheaper option than burial (no casket required, no plot or mausoleum, no gravestone or marker). To learn about what fees funeral homes may and may not charge legally, see www.consumer.ftc.gov/articles/0301-funeral-costs-and-pricing-checklist

8. **Don't prepay for a plot, casket, or other services without discussing the contract with an attorney or accountant**. Prepaid plans might seem like a good idea, but most consumer groups advise against them. If you change your mind about where you want to be buried, or how you want to be disposed of, it may be impossible to alter the contract or obtain a refund. You also lose the potential interest your money could earn in a bank account (see item 10).

9. **Do consider opening a "Totten" trust, a payable on-demand account at a bank or savings institution for the cost of a funeral**. The trust is revocable, so it can be moved, altered, or closed completely (Jaffe, 1996).

10. **Do make use of helpful information sources**. You can locate excellent advice and information on planning a funeral at www.funerals.org, www.clarkhoward.com

others' stigmas (obesity, paraplegia, blindness, AIDS, etc.) depends on the causal inferences they make about those stigmas (Blaine & Williams, 2004; Weiner, Perry, & Magnusson, 1988). For example, these researchers analyzed college students' emotional reactions to people with varying stigmas (obesity, drug addiction, etc.), based on how controllable the students thought the stigma was. Students expressed more feelings of guilt and sympathy if the stigma was uncontrollable (e.g., obesity ascribed to a glandular dysfunction) and more feelings of anger and reluctance to help if the stigma was controllable (e.g., obesity due to overeating). Thus, persuaders seeking to use emotional appeals such as pity or guilt for fundraising or other purposes need to ensure that the beneficiaries are *not* perceived as having a physical or social malady that they brought on themselves.

HUMOROUS APPEALS: STOP ME IF YOU'VE HEARD THIS ONE

You might not think of comedians as being particularly persuasive, but *Time* magazine's list of the 100 most influential people in 2017 included three comics: Samantha Bee, Leslie Jones, and Jordan Peele (*Time*, 2017). An Egyptian comedian, Bassem Youssef, who is referred to as the "John Stewart of Egypt," hosted a top-rated political satire show that lampooned the Egyptian government. He was arrested repeatedly for skewering powerful elites and eventually fled to the USA where he is now living in exile. In China, Zhou Libo, another comedian, used humor to draw attention to government corruption. In Paris in 2015, Al Queda terrorists gunned down the editor and staff members of the satirical magazine, *Charlie Hebdo*. Why? Because the magazine published cartoons critical of Islam.

Why do authoritarian governments and religious extremists fear comedians? Political satire is subversive. Beyond the laughs, comedians offer social commentary. "Good comics," say Cohen and Richards (2006) "are playing an important function

FIGURE 13.2
Source: Jerry King,
www.CartoonStock.com

*"I've hired this musician to play a sad melody while
I give you a sob story why I didn't do my homework.
It's actually quite effective."*

in society by holding up a mirror and forcing us to confront realities that we would prefer to ignore" (para. 2).

The use of humor in persuasion is pervasive, and not just the political kind. Humorous advertisements account for 24 percent of all advertising in the USA (Laroche, Nepomuceno, Huang, & Richard, 2011). Internet memes rely heavily on humor to offer pithy social and political commentary. Humor is common in the boardroom, the courtroom, the classroom, interpersonal conversations, and even the pulpit. Using humor to influence is like skinning a cat; there's more than one way. A humorous appeal can consist of a pun, satire, an anecdote, innuendo, irony, a metaphor, slapstick, or just a plain old joke, as in "an armadillo walks into a bar . . ." Humor can be directed at oneself, which is known as *self-disparaging humor,* or at others. All in all, Berger (2011) identified 45 different types of humor.

Humor as an Indirect Form of Influence: All Kidding Aside

Typically, jokes themselves don't persuade. Humor tends to operate in a more roundabout manner using the peripheral route to persuasion. Two well-established ways in which humor assists persuasion are by *capturing attention* and *increasing liking* for the source (Eisend, 2011; Gulas & Weinberger, 2006; Nabi, Moyer-Gusé, & Byrne, 2007; Weinberger & Gulas, 1992). This explains why comedians like Ellen DeGeneres, Tina Fey, Jim Gaffigan, and Jerry Seinfeld are popular endorsers. A meta-analysis of humor in advertising revealed that humor was highly effective in increasing attention and positive feelings toward a brand (Eisend, 2009).

A third way in which humor may facilitate persuasion is by serving as a *distraction* (Nabi, Moyer-Gusé, & Byrne, 2007; Strick, Holland, van Baaren, & van Knipperberg, 2012). Specifically, because the cognitive effort required to comprehend a joke trades off with the mental energy needed to analyze the substance of a message, humor tends to suppress *counterarguing* (Young, 2008). For example, one study found that participants who read a series of jokes told by late-night comedians were less inclined to scrutinize the statements carefully, compared to a control group of participants who read nonhumorous versions of the same statements. This suggests that a persuader facing a hostile audience could use humor to "soften up" the crowd.

A fourth way in which humor may aid a persuader is by serving as a form of *social proof*, which involves modeling our behavior after the actions or reactions of others (see Chapter 6). The use of "laugh tracks" or live audience laughter on television sitcoms illustrates this principle. Researchers have found that the perceived funniness of low- to medium-quality jokes can be enhanced by including canned laughter (Cupchik & Leventhal, 1974; Leventhal & Cupchik, 1975, 1976). Speakers often use "shills" or "plants" in an audience to initiate laughter or applause to help sway audience members.

Finally, the use of humor might affect perceptions of a source. One meta-analysis, for example, found that overall, humor tends to reduce perceptions of a source's credibility (Eisend, 2009). That said, humorous sources are perceived as being more socially attractive (Murnstein & Burst, 1985; Wanzer, Booth-Butterfield, & Booth-Butterfield, 1996) and more competent communicators (Wanzer et al., 1996). Our advice, then, would be to employ humor judiciously, tailoring your message to the audience, the situation, and your goals.

Self-Disparaging Humor: LOLing at Yourself

Should you ever make yourself the brunt of a humorous appeal? On one hand, it might seem that putting yourself down, even lightheartedly, would damage your image. On the other hand, it might seem that the ability to poke fun at yourself would bolster your image. Again, the answer depends on the type of image you are aiming to create. The ability to laugh at yourself demonstrates that you are friendly and good-natured (Graham, Papa, & Brooks, 1992). Presidential candidates often appear on late-night comedy shows. By showing a lighter side, they hope to seem more natural, genuine, and spontaneous.

Actual studies on self-disparaging humor have yielded mixed results (Chang & Gruner, 1981). Hackman (1988) revealed that self-disparaging humor led to lower ratings of speaker competence. Our advice is to avoid self-disparaging humor if you think you have low credibility to begin with or if you need to bolster your credibility in the competence dimension. If you have moderate to high credibility to begin with, then making light of some of your human frailties might make you appear more genuine and good-natured.

But Is Humor Persuasive?

Earlier attempts to determine whether the use of humor enhanced persuasion produced inconsistent results (Gulas & Weinberger, 2006; Skalski, Tamborini, Glazer,

& Smith, 2009; Weinberger & Gulas, 1992). This is understandable, given that humor takes many forms. And let's face it, some jokes are funnier than others. A recent meta-analysis, however, suggests that humor enhances at least two measures of persuasion: attitudes toward a brand and purchase intentions (Eisend, 2009). Although humor may be effective, it doesn't appear to be superior to other appeals, such as fear and pride (Verma, 2009). An additional study (Nabi, Moyer-Gusé, & Byrne, 2007) also found that humorous appeals may benefit from a *sleeper effect*— that is, humor may grow on people over time, leading to more persuasion later on.

Maximizing Humor's Potential

Some advice for maximizing humor's persuasive potential seems in order. First, if you aren't good at telling jokes, don't. Another suggestion is to use *related humor*, which integrates the humor into the content of the message. *Unrelated humor*, such as a stand-alone joke, is not as effective (Gulas & Weinberger, 2006; Weinberger & Gulas, 1992; Weinberger & Spotts, 1989). Another suggestion is to add gravitas toward the end of a humor-laden message. Let the audience know your message is not all fun and games. Stress the seriousness of the point you are trying to make through your use of humor (Nabi, Moyer-Gusé, & Byrne, 2007).

Another important piece of advice is *don't overdo it*. Too much humor may cause listeners to discount the message as little more than a joke (Gruner, 1967; Nabi et al., 2007). After all, if you don't appear to take your own message seriously, why should others? Similarly, the use of inappropriate humor can decrease perceptions of credibility (Derks, Kalland, & Etgen, 1995; Munn & Gruner, 1981).

PRIDE AND PATIOTISM: TURNING RED, WHITE, AND BLUE INTO GREEN

In the summer of 2016, Budweiser beer temporarily renamed itself, *America*. Skittles offered packages with red, white, and blue candies. M&Ms followed suit with its own patriotic palette. If the trend continues, Schultz (2016) observed, "Buyers might have to salute each time they walk into a grocery store."

Politicians are fond of wrapping themselves in the flag, standing next to veterans at public events, and declaring theirs to be the greatest nation on earth (whatever nation that happens to be). Does flag waving work? The answer is yes, quite well. Several investigations suggest that patriotic ploys are effective, when used appropriately. Seiter and Gass (2005), for example, compared the tips earned by food servers who wrote a patriotic message ("United We Stand") on patrons' checks with a more traditional message ("Have a Nice Day"). Food servers who used the patriotic slogan earned significantly higher tips.

Even brief exposure to a patriotic emblem can sway people. Those who saw an American flag on a survey of voter attitudes shifted their attitudes in a more conservative direction. Voting intentions also leaned more toward the right after a single exposure to the flag (Carter, Ferguson, & Hassin, 2011). Why? As a patriotic symbol, the flag may be more closely associated with the Republican than the Democratic party (Kalmoe & Gross, 2016). Han (1988) found that patriotism had a positive effect on consumers' intentions to purchase domestic as opposed to foreign

brands, but didn't necessarily alter their perceptions of brand quality or reliability. Pedic (1990) discovered that nationalistic ads were more effective than non-nationalistic ads, but only if the receivers were themselves nationalistic.

In America, patriotic appeals have a lot going for them. Even so, recent evidence suggests that the effectiveness of flag waving may be wearing off (Wellner, 2002). In the USA, there has been pushback against Trump's anti-immigration policies. Shepard Fairey's series of pro-diversity posters, entitled "We the People" illustrates this trend (see Figure 13.3).

Not only that, patriotic appeals can backfire, as Samuel Johnson's famous remark that patriotism is the "last refuge of scoundrels" warns. Companies can still use American branding successfully, but if a persuader appears to be "cashing in" on patriotic ploys or using patriotism as a wedge issue, then receivers may reject the message or the source.

FOR MATURE AUDIENCES: SEX APPEALS

Television is replete with sexual appeals. So are print ads. One analysis found that half of all print ads depict women as sex objects (Stankiewicz & Rosselli, 2008). And then there's the Internet. There's more sex on the Web than flies on a cowpie. "Sex sells," goes the advertising adage.

Although the use of sexual appeals has been a fixture of advertising for decades, two things have changed. First, the use of more overt sexual appeals has increased (Malik, 2016). Second, increasingly younger audiences are being targeted. Media is sexualizing children at younger and younger ages (American Psychological Association, 2010; Hill, 2011).

Historically, females have been depicted as sex objects in advertising (Snigda & Venkatesh, 2011), a situation decried by feminists and other media critics. Grounded in *objectification theory,* females are more likely to be seen as objects or things. Accordingly, females are more likely than males to be portrayed as passive, submissive, and subordinate (Mager & Helgeson, 2011). Women also are depicted as being disembodied, silenced, and occupying less space than men (Conley & Ramsey, 2011; Eisend, 2010). Not surprisingly then, women respond less favorably to sex appeals than men (Black & Morton, 2017).

Despite the media's obsession with sex appeals, studies show that simply increasing the amount of sexual imagery does not make a message more persuasive. As Ma and Gal (2016) warn, "in general, research has found that sex in advertising does not improve brand recall or sales effectiveness" (p. 479).

The sexual objectification of males is also well underway (Sexualization of men, 2016). For example, the Magic Mike franchise, starring Channing Tatum, rides the current wave of toned dudes. David Beckham is hunky in H&M's underwear ads. Duckett (cited in Brown, 2016) emphasized that "the trend for using hyper-athletic male models and celebrities in advertising has grown significantly in recent years, giving rise to the term 'hunkvertising'" (para. 7). And while one in six males under 24 reported being more self-conscious about their bodies, more than half of males said they pay little attention to male advertising physiques (Brown, 2016). Men, therefore, have far less reason to worry about women ogling them than women do from the "male gaze."

How Sex Sells

How do sex appeals work? Typically, the unspoken message in ads employing sexual appeals is either (1) if you use product "X" you will look, act, or feel more sexy or (2) if you use product "X" other sexy people will be attracted to you. Of course, such ads rarely make explicit cause–effect claims about the benefits of the product. Rather, the product is paired with sexually laden imagery. Through this associative process (see Chapter 3) the receiver comes to identify the product with sexiness or sensuality.

Caveats and Cautions

Although it is true that sexual appeals can be effective, there are also cautions regarding their use (see, for example, Sengupta & Dahl, 2008). First, despite their prevalence, sex appeals are not always effective. A study conducted in a pharmaceutical sales context found that a female sales representative who showed cleavage was no more persuasive than a female salesperson who did not (Glick, Chrislock, Petersik, Vijay, & Turek, 2008). Context means a lot, however. A study conducted in France found that males were much more likely to approach a female in a bar if she had large breasts (Guéguén, 2007). Who says research has to be boring? The conclusion might seem obvious. The point is that sex appeals may not function the same way in professional settings as they do in social settings. A boardroom is not a barroom.

Second, in some cases the targeted audience may resent the use of sexual appeals. For example, sexual stimuli are frequently included in ads aimed at women. Yet if women perceive the ads as sexist, the ads may backfire. Nowadays, an advertiser

must walk a fine line between creating ads that are considered sexy and ads that are considered sexist.

A third liability in using sex appeals is that they may function as a *distraction*, inhibiting receiver recall. If a consumer is salivating over a sexy model in a magazine ad, his or her attention may be diverted from the product being advertised. Several studies have shown this to be the case (Bushman & Bonacci, 2002; Judd & Alexander, 1983; Malik, 2016; Steadman, 1969). Advertisers face something of a dilemma here: A sexual appeal that is too mild may not stand out in the crowd, yet a sexual appeal that is too strong may serve as a distraction.

A fourth downside to using sex appeals is that they may produce undesirable social consequences. Objectification of women in media can lead to *self-objectification*, whereby females begin viewing themselves as objects (Snigda & Venkatesh, 2011). This, in turn, may result in lower self-esteem, negative body image, and eating disorders (Conley & Ramsey, 2011; Kilbourne, 1999). We don't fault the media entirely for the current obsession that people have with their bodies. We do think, however, that advertisers, the movie industry, and the fashion industry must shoulder some of the blame for exploiting people's insecurities about their looks.

WARMTH APPEALS: STRAIGHT FROM THE HEART

"Nothing says lovin' like something from the oven, and Pillsbury says it best." Some advertisements convey a warm, cozy feeling. They emphasize family, friends, and a sense of belonging. They make us feel sentimental or nostalgic about life. Such ads are based on *warmth*. Aaker and Bruzzone (1981) identify warmth as one of a half-dozen basic dimensions people use to describe advertisements. The use of warmth in advertising is quite common (Aaker, Stayman, & Hagerty, 1986). A little more than one in five prime-time commercials include warmth as an advertising theme (Aaker & Stayman, 1990). State Farm's "Like a good neighbor . . . State Farm is there" campaign is based on this theme, as is Olive Garden's "When you're here, you're family" slogan. So are ads for Hallmark cards, "Poppin' Fresh," the Pillsbury doughboy, and Snuggle fabric softener, which features a cuddly teddy bear. Insurance companies, airlines, health-care providers, restaurants, and hotel chains all use warmth to convey images of folksiness, hominess, friendliness, and familiarity (see Goldman & Papson, 1996).

So how do they work? Primarily through association. A product or service is associated with the image of being warm, caring, or friendly. When we think of that product or service we get a warm-fuzzy feeling.

Warmth appeals aren't limited to television advertising. One study found that parental warmth was more effective in influencing adolescents' eating habits than the use of negative pressure (Lessard, Greenberger, & Chen, 2010). Real-estate listings often use words like *charming*, *cozy*, or *rustic* to describe houses that are for sale. Restaurants boast of "home-style" cooking. Frozen foods claim to be based on "authentic family recipes" that are "made the old-fashioned way." In interpersonal encounters, warmth can be conveyed through actions that generate a sense of friendship, bonding, or camaraderie. The Walmart "greeter" is a living embodiment of a warmth appeal. When a food server introduces himself or herself by name and smiles, the food server is also conveying warmth.

"If they don't like our proposal I'll show them the kittens. Everybody likes kittens."

FIGURE 13.5
Source: © Peter C. Vey/
The New Yorker Collection/
www.cartoonbank.com.
All Rights Reserved.

Warmth appeals can be quite effective, but their success depends on their believability. The warm-fuzzy images being portrayed must come across as sincere for the appeal to work (Aaker & Stayman, 1989). As Aaker and Stayman (1990) note, the appeal "need[s] to avoid creating the perception of an ad's being phony, pointless, or contrived; such perceptions could interfere with the emotional response" (p. 59). Warmth appeals, then, are a persuader's friend. They offer a positive approach to using motivational appeals by engendering warm, happy feelings in receivers.

INGRATIATION: POLISHING THE APPLE

You may know it as "brownnosing," "sucking up," or "boot-licking," but *ingratiation* is the term researchers use for flattery as a motivational inducement. Ingratiation has been thoroughly studied in organizational settings (see Deluga & Perry, 1994; Liden & Mitchell, 1988; Tal-Or, 2010). Indeed, Westphal and Shani (2016) report that "ingratiation is perhaps the most widely studied form of interpersonal influence behavior in the organization literature" (p. 481). Will flattery get you everywhere? An overall assessment of the research to date suggests that ingratiation works—and works well (Gordon, 1996). For instance, a study by Watt (1993) found that ingratiators were perceived by their supervisors as being more competent, more motivated, and more qualified for leadership positions than their noningratiating counterparts. Another study (Wayne, Kacmar, & Ferris, 1995) found that the use of ingratiation tactics by subordinates resulted in higher satisfaction for the supervisor and co-workers. In fact, one study quantified the advantage enjoyed by ingratiators over noningratiators. In a study of 152 pairs of managers and employees, Deluga (cited in Kelleher, 1997) found that ingratiators enjoyed a 5 percent edge over noningratiators in getting favorable evaluations. Ziemke and Brodksy (2015) found that the use of ingratiation by defense attorneys during their closing arguments increased their perceived attractiveness, likability, and credibility. Two studies in organizations—one conducted in restaurants (Seiter, 2007), the other in hair styling salons (Seiter & Dutson, 2007)—found that food servers and hair stylists earned significantly higher tips when they complimented (ingratiated) their customers than when they did not.

Researchers know that ingratiation works, but just how does it work? What is the secret behind its success? There are three interrelated explanations for ingratiation's effectiveness (Dubrin, cited in Kelleher, 1997). First, ingratiatory behavior tends to increase *liking* ("I love that outfit on you!"). Second, ingratiatory behavior can create perceptions of *similarity* ("You love polka music? Hey, I do too!"). Third, ingratiation can work through *social labeling*. The use of positive social labels ("You sure are in a good mood today," "You are so thoughtful") can produce changes in the target's self-concept that, in turn, lead to changes in the target's behavior (Kraut, 1973). The person being ingratiated thus lives up to the positive label bestowed on her or him.

How many kinds of ingratiation are there? Edward Jones (1963), who authored the first major work on ingratiation, identified three basic categories of ingratiation. The first is *other enhancement,* such as paying compliments or engaging in flattery. A derivative of this technique is to have a third party deliver the compliment, so that it seems more genuine ("Biff speaks highly of you. He says you are the nicest boss he's ever had"). The second technique is *opinion conformity*. This involves agreeing with the target's statements, ideas, and views. A variation on this technique is to initially disagree, then subsequently yield, creating the impression the target has changed your mind ("Okay, you've convinced me, Godiva chocolates taste better than See's chocolates"). A third approach is *self-presentation*. This involves bragging or otherwise displaying one's attributes to increase the target's evaluation of oneself ("Gee, I'd love to play golf with you, but I'm helping at the homeless center this weekend"). Some scholars include *performing favors* as a fourth type of ingratiation (Zin, Ngah, Ismail, Tajuddin, Abdullah, & Salleh, 2010). So you see, there is more than one way to engage in brownnosing.

But, you might ask, wouldn't the other person *know*, or at least suspect, that the ingratiator was trying to curry favor? If so, can ingratiation backfire? The answer is yes, although some studies find that shameless ingratiation still works, though perhaps not as well (e.g., Chan & Sengupta, 2010).

Research on the "slime effect" suggests that inept ingratiators are seen as unlikable and are suspected of ulterior motives (Vonk, 1998). In one study, for example, food servers who delivered compliments to large parties in one fell swoop ("You all made good choices!") received lower tips than food servers who complimented smaller parties, thereby seeming more sincere (Seiter & Weger, 2010).

That said, some ingratiators are more skilled at disguising their motives. Westphal and Shani (2016), for instance, found that effective ingratiators self-regulate their thought process to focus on the positive characteristics of another person, rather than on his or her negatives. Successful ingratiators also rely on more subtle forms of flattery, such as turning a compliment as a question—e.g., "Ralph, you're always dressed sharp. Do you think I should wear black or brown shoes with a blue suit?"

Considering such manipulative tactics, you might be thinking that ingratiation is an unethical influence strategy. We tend to agree, but not in all cases. If the ingratiator *believes* in the praise he or she is offering, we see no ethical problem in focusing on the positive side of things. Indeed, if the praise is genuine, this strategy offers the prospect for a "win–win" communication encounter. We discuss the ethical implications of ingratiatory behavior in more detail in Chapter 16.

FIGURE 13.6
Beetle Bailey.

MIXED EMOTIONS: OTHER APPEALS AND COMBINATIONS OF APPEALS

There are many other types of motivational appeals that we do not have space to cover here. Some of these include appeals to honor, youth, beauty, shame, freedom, and the environment. Almost any human drive or emotion can serve as the basis for a motivational appeal.

Motivational appeals also can be used in combination. A threat of punishment can be coupled with a promise of reward, for example. A prosecutor might tell a defendant, "If you cooperate, I'll cut you a deal. If you don't, I'll throw the book at you." The "good cop/bad cop" technique used in police interrogations also combines positive and negative appeals (Inbau, Reid, & Buckley, 1986; Kassin & McNall, 1991). One study found that adding humor to a fear appeal about skin cancer reduced defensiveness by providing a "margin of safety" to the audience (Mukherjee & Dubé, 2012).

Guilt is commonly coupled with pity in charity fund-raisers ("If you don't help, who will?"). In a twist involving "strange bedfellows," the animal rights group known as PETA (People for the Ethical Treatment of Animals) has collaborated with *Penthouse* magazine for the past few years to produce an anti-fur advertisement. The ads feature sexy supermodels who proclaim they would rather go naked than wear fur, thus combining a sex appeal with a guilt appeal. Evidence suggests that when people experience mixed emotions, they don't recall them clearly (Aaker, Drolet, & Griffin, 2008). For example, riding a roller coaster might evoke positive (e.g., excitement, exhilaration) and negative (e.g., fear, apprehension) emotions. Over time, though, the person would tend to remember the ride as mostly exciting and enjoyable or mostly scary and unpleasant.

We see definite advantages in combining appeals. If one appeal proves ineffective, another may still work. And there is always the prospect that combinations of appeals will have an additive effect—that is, the combination of appeals may work better than they would individually. A danger in combining appeals is that they may appear contradictory or cancel one another out. Combining humor with pity, for instance, might create the appearance that a persuader was insensitive or disingenuous. Some research suggests that inducing conflicting emotions (happiness and sadness) may be better suited for Asian American than Anglo-American receivers (Williams & Aaker, 2002). In selecting motivational appeals, then, a persuader must be judicious.

SUMMARY

Motivational appeals are external inducements used to increase another's drive to do something. The use of motivational appeals is an omnipresent phenomenon. Attempts at casting logical and emotional appeals as opposites are suspect. Although motivational appeals aren't necessarily rational, neither are they irrational. Eight types of motivational appeals were discussed: fear, pity, guilt, humor, patriotism, sex, warmth, and ingratiation. These represent only a fraction of the appeals available to persuaders. Experimental studies have shown some of these to be highly effective in facilitating persuasion, whereas others have been shown to be less effective. It also was suggested that motivational appeals can be successfully combined if certain precautions are followed.

REFERENCES

Aaker, D. A., & Bruzzone, D. E. (1981). Viewer perceptions of prime-time television advertising. *Journal of Advertising Research, 21*(5), 15–23.

Aaker, D. A., & Stayman, D. M. (1989). What mediates the emotional response to advertising? The case of warmth. In P. Cafferata & A. M. Tybout (Eds.), *Cognitive and affective responses to advertising* (pp. 287–303). Lexington, MA: Lexington Books.

Aaker, D. A., & Stayman, D. M. (1990). A micro approach to studying feeling responses to advertising: The case of warmth. In S. J. Agres, J. A. Edell, & T. B. Dubitsky (Eds.), *Emotion in advertising: Theoretical and practical explorations* (pp. 53–68). New York: Quorum Books.

Aaker, J., Drolet, A., & Griffin, D. (2008). Recalling mixed emotions. *Journal of Consumer Research, 35,* 268–278. doi:10.1086/588570

Aaker, D. A., Stayman, D. M., & Hagerty, M. R. (1986). Warmth in advertising: Measurement, impact, and sequence effects. *Journal of Consumer Research, 12*(4), 365–381.

Achar, C., So, J., Agrawal, N., & Duhachek, A. (2016). What we feel and why we buy: The influence of emotions on consumer decision-making. *Current Opinion in Psychology, 10,* 166–170. doi:10.1016/j.copsyc.2016.01.009

Adler, R.F., Iacobelli, F., & Gutstein, Y. (2016). Are you convinced? A Wizard of Oz study to test emotional vs. rational persuasion strategies in dialogues. *Computers in Human Behavior, 57,* 75–81. doi:10.1016/j.chb.2015.12.011

Akbari, M. (2015). Different impacts of advertising appeals on advertising attitude for high and low involvement products. *Global Business Review, 16*(3), 478–493. doi:10.1177/0972150915556993

Altheide, D. L. (2002). *Creating fear: News and the construction of crisis.* Hawthorne, NY: Aldine DeGruyter.

American Psychological Association. (2010). *Report of the APA Task Force on the Sexualization of Girls.* Retrieved on May 17, 2012, from: www.apa.org/pi/women/programs/girls/report-full.pdf

Aristotle. (1932). *The rhetoric* (L. Cooper, Trans.). Englewood Cliffs, NJ: Prentice Hall.

Babin, B. J., Darden, W. R., & Griffin, M. (1994). Work and/or fun: Measuring hedonic and utilitarian shopping value. *Journal of Consumer Research, 20*(4), 644–656.

Becheaur, I., & Valette-Florence, P. (2014). The use of negative emotions in health communication messages: Study on the effects of fear, guilt, and shame. *Recherche et Applications en Marketing, 29*(4), 89–109. doi:10.1177/205157071455262

Becker, S. L. (1963). Research on emotional and logical proofs. *Southern Speech Journal, 28*(3), 198–207.

Berger, A. A. (2011). *Ads, fads, and consumer culture* (4th ed.). Lanham, MD: Rowman & Littlefield.

Bessarova, E., Turner, M.M., Fink, E.L., & Blustein, N.B. (2015). Extending the theory of reactance to guilt appeals. *Zeitschrift für Psychologie, 223,* 215–224. doi:10.1027/2151-2604/a000223

Black, I. R., & Morton, P. (2017). Appealing to men and women using sexual appeals in advertising: In the battle of the sexes, is a truce still possible? *Journal of Marketing Communications, 23*(4), 331–350. doi:10.1080/13527266.2015.1015108

Blaine, B., & Williams, Z. (2004). Belief in the controllability of weight and attributions to prejudice among heavyweight women. *Sex Roles, 51,* 79–84.

Boster, F. J., & Mongeau, P. A. (1984). Fear-arousing persuasive messages. In R. N. Bostrum & B. H. Wesley (Eds.), *Communication yearbook 8* (pp. 330–375). Beverly Hills, CA: Sage.

Brown, J. (2016, January 27). The sexualization of men in advertising. *AskMen*. Retrieved on May 31, 2017 from: http://uk.askmen.com/news/fashion/the-sexualisation-of-men-in-advertising.html

Bushman, B. J., & Bonacci, A. M. (2002). Violence and sex impair memory for television ads. *Journal of Applied Psychology*, 87(3), 557–564.

Carter, T. J., Ferguson, M. J., & Hassin, R. R. (2011). A single exposure to the American flag shifts support toward Republicanism up to 8 months later. *Psychological Science*, 22(8), 1011–1018.

Casey, M. K., Timmermann, L., Allen, M., Krahn, S., & Turkiewicz, K. L. (2009). Response and self-efficacy of condom use: A meta-analysis of this important element of AIDS education and prevention. *Southern Communication Journal*, 74(1), 57–78.

Chan, E., & Sengupta, J. (2010). Insincere flattery actually works: A dual attitudes perspective. *Journal of Marketing Research*, 47, 122–133.

Chang, M., & Gruner, C. R. (1981). Audience reaction to self-disparaging humor. *Southern Speech Communication Journal*, 46, 419–426.

Cho, H., & Witte, K. (2004). A review of fear appeal effects. In J. S. Seiter & R. H. Gass (Eds.), *Readings in persuasion, social influence, and compliance gaining* (pp. 223–238). Boston, MA: Allyn & Bacon.

Cohen, R., & Richards, R. (2006). When the truth hurts, tell a joke: Why America needs its comedians. Retrieved on May 30, 2017 from: www.humanityinaction.org/knowledgebase/174-when-the-truth-hurts-tell-a-joke-why-america-needs-its-comedians

Conley, T. D., & Ramsey, L. R. (2011). Killing us softly? Investigating portrayals of women and men in contemporary magazine advertisements. *Psychology of Women Quarterly*, 35(3), 467–478.

Corbett, E. P. J., & Connors, R. J. (1999). *Classical rhetoric for the modern student* (4th ed.). Oxford, NY: Oxford University Press.

Cupchik, G. C., & Leventhal, H. (1974). Consistency between expressive behavior and the evaluation of humorous stimuli: The role of sex and self-observation. *Journal of Personality and Social Psychology*, 30, 429–442.

Deci, E. L. (1975). *Intrinsic motivation*. New York: Plenum.

Deci, E. L., & Ryan, R. (1978). *Intrinsic motivation and self-determination in human behavior*. New York: Plenum.

de Hoog, N., Stroebe, W., & de Wit, J. B. F. (2007). The impact of vulnerability to and severity of a health risk on processing and acceptance of fear-arousing communications: A meta-analysis. *Review of General Psychology, 11*(3), 258–285.

de Hoog, N., Stroebe, W., & de Wit, J. B. F. (2008). The processing of fear-arousing communications: How biased processing leads to persuasion. *Social Influence, 3*, 84–113. doi:10.1080/ 15534510802185836

Deluga, R. J., & Perry, J. T. (1994). The role of subordinate performance and ingratiation in leader–member exchanges. *Group Organization Management, 19*(1), 67–86.

Derks, P., Kalland, S., & Etgen, M. (1995). The effect of joke type and audience response on the reaction to a joker: Replication and extension. *Humor, 8*(4), 327–337.

Eayres, C. B., & Ellis, N. (1990). Charity advertising: For or against people with a mental handicap? *British Journal of Social Psychology*, 29, 349–360.

Eisend, M. (2009). A meta-analysis of humor in advertising. *Journal of the Academy of Marketing Science*, 37 (191–203).

Eisend, M. (2010). A meta-analysis of gender roles in advertising. *Journal of the Academy of Marketing Science*, 38, 418–440. doi:10.1007/s11747–009–0181-x

Eisend, M. (2011). How humor in advertising works: A meta-analytic test of alternative models. *Marketing Letters*, 22(2), 115–132.

Evans, J. St., B. T., Barston, J. L., & Pollard, P. (1983). On the conflict between logic and belief in syllogistic reasoning. *Memory and Cognition, 11*, 295–306.

Freedman, J. L., Wallington, S., & Bless, E. (1967). Compliance gaining without pressure: The effect of guilt. *Journal of Personality and Social Psychology, 7*, 117–124.

Gardner, D. (2009). *The science of fear*. New York: Penguin.

Gentry, J. W., Kennedy, P. K., Paul, K., & Hill, R. P. (1995). The vulnerability of those grieving the death of a loved one: Implications for public policy. *Journal of Public Policy and Marketing, 14*(1), 128–142.

Geuens, M., De Pelsmacker, P., & Faseur, T. (2011). Emotional advertising: Revisiting the role of product category. *Journal of Business Research, 64*(4), 418–426.

Glassner, B. (1999). *The culture of fear: Why Americans are afraid of the wrong things*. New York: Basic Books.

Glick, P., Chrislock, K., Petersik, K., Vijay, M., & Turek, A. (2008). Does cleavage work at work? Men, but not women, falsely believe cleavage sells a weak product. *Psychology of Women Quarterly, 32*, 326–335.

Goldman, R., & Papson, S. (1996). *Sign wars: The cluttered landscape of advertising*. New York: Guilford Press.

Gordon, R. A. (1996). Impact of ingratiation on judgments and evaluations: A meta-analytic investigation. *Journal of Personality and Social Psychology, 71*(1), 54–70.

Graham, E. E., Papa, M. J., & Brooks, G. P. (1992). Functions of humor in conversation: Conceptualization and measurement. *Western Journal of Communication, 56*, 161–183.

Greifeneder, R., Bless, H., & Pham, M. T. (2011). When do people rely on affective and cognitive feelings in judgment? A review. *Personality and Social Psychology Review, 15*, 107–141. doi:10.1177/10888 68310367640

Gruner, C. R. (1967). Effect of humor on speaker ethos and audience information gain. *Journal of Communication, 17*(3), 228–233.

Guéguén, N. (2007). Women's bust size and men's courtship solicitation. *Body Image, 4*, 386–390.

Gulas, C. S., & Weinberger, M. G. (2006). *Humor in advertising: A comprehensive analysis*. Armonk, NY: M.E. Sharpe.

Hackman, M. Z. (1988). Reactions to the use of self-disparaging humor by informative public speakers. *Southern Speech Communication Journal, 53*, 175–183.

Han, C. M. (1988). The role of consumer patriotism in the choice of domestic music versus foreign products. *Journal of Advertising Research, 28*, 25–32.

Hibbert, S., Smith, A., Davies, A., & Ireland, F. (2007). Guilt appeals: Persuasion knowledge and charitable giving. *Psychology & Marketing, 24*(8), 723–742.

Higbee, K. L. (1969). Fifteen years of fear-arousal: Research on threat appeals. *Psychological Bulletin, 72*, 426–444.

Hill, J. A. (2011). Endangered childhoods: How consumerism is impacting youth and identity. *Media, Culture, & Society, 33*(3), 347–362.

Hornik, J., Ofir, C., & Rachamim, M. (2016). Quantitative evaluation of persuasive appeals using comparative meta-analysis. *Communication Review, 19*(3), 192–222. doi:10.1080/10714421.2016.1195204

Inbau, F. E., Reid, J. E., & Buckley, J. P. (1986). *Criminal interrogations and confessions* (3rd ed.). Baltimore, MD: Williams & Wilkins.

Jaffe, C. A. (1996, October 16). Shopping for your funeral makes financial sense. *Los Angeles Times*, pp. D3, D9.

Jones, E. (1963). *Ingratiation*. New York: Appleton-Century-Crofts.

Judd, B. B., & Alexander, M. W. (1983). On the reduced effectiveness of some sexually suggestive ads. *Journal of the Academy of Marketing Science, 11*, 156–168.

Kalmoe, N.P., & Gross, K. (2016). Cueing patriotism, prejudice, and partisanship in the age of Obama: Experimental tests of U.S. flag imagery in presidential elections. *Political Psychology, 37*(6), 883–899. doi:10.1111/pops.12305

Kassin, S. M., & McNall, K. (1991). Police interrogations and confessions. *Law and Human Behavior, 15,* 233–251.

Kelleher, K. (1997, February 24). Flattery will get you . . . everywhere. *Los Angeles Times,* pp. E1–E2.

Khan, U., Dhar, R., & Wertenbroch, K. (2005). A behavioral decision theory perspective on hedonic and utilitarian choices. In S. Ratneshwar & D. G. Mick (Eds.), *Inside consumption: Consumer motives, goals, and desires* (pp. 144–165). New York: Routledge.

Kilbourne, J. (1999). *Deadly persuasion: Why women and girls must fight the addictive power of advertising.* New York: Free Press.

Kraut, R. E. (1973). The effects of social labeling on giving to charity. *Journal of Experimental Social Psychology, 9,* 551–562.

Laroche, M., Nepomuceno, M. V., Huang, L., & Richard, M. O. (2011). What's so funny? The use of humor in magazine advertising in the United States, China, and France. *Journal of Advertising Research, 51*(2), 404–416.

Lessard, J., Greenberger, E., & Chen, C. (2010). Adolescents' response to parental efforts to influence eating habits: When parental warmth matters. *Journal of Youth Adolescence, 39,* 73–83. doi:10.1007/s10964–008–9376–6

Leventhal, H., & Cupchik, G. C. (1975). The informational and facilitative effects of an audience upon expression and evaluation of humorous stimuli. *Journal of Experimental Social Psychology, 11,* 363–380.

Leventhal, H., & Cupchik, G. C. (1976). A process model of humor judgment. *Journal of Communication, 26*(3), 190–204.

Liden, R., & Mitchell, T. (1988). Ingratiatory behaviors in organizational settings. *Academy of Management Review, 13,* 572–587.

Lindsey, L. L. M. (2005). Anticipated guilt as behavioral motivation: An examination of appeals to help unknown others through bone marrow donation. *Human Communication Research, 31,* 453–481.

Lindsey, L. L. M., Yun, K. A., & Hill, J. B. (2007). Anticipated guilt as motivation to help others: An examination of empathy as a moderator. *Communication Research, 34*(4), 468–480.

Livingston, S. (2007, November 26). Emotional intelligence. *Adweek, 48*(43), 16.

Ma, J., & Gal, D. (2016). When sex and romance conflict: The effects of sexual imagery in advertising on preference for romantically linked products and services. *Journal of Marketing Research, 53*(4), 479–496. doi:10.1509/jmr.14.0374

Mager, J., & Helgeson, J. G. (2011). Fifty years of advertising images: Some changing perspectives on role portrayals along with enduring consistencies. *Sex Roles, 64,* 238–252. doi:10.1007/s11199–010–9782–6

Malik, G. (2016). Impact of sexual content in advertising on purchasing behavior of customers: An empirical analysis. *International Journal of Asian School of Business Management, 9*(1), 47–56.

Maloney, E. K., Lapinski, M. K., & Witte, K. (2011). Fear appeals and persuasion: A review and update of the extended parallel processing model. *Social and Personality Psychology Compass, 5*(4), 206–219. doi:10.1111/j.1751–9004.2011.00341.x

Miller, J. T. (2016, October 17). This is how much an average funeral costs. Retrieved on May 28, 2017 from: www.huffingtonpost.com/entry/how-much-does-a-funeral-cost_us_5804c784e4b0f42ad3d264de

Mongeau, P. (1998). Another look at fear-arousing appeals. In M. Allen & R. W. Preiss (Eds.), *Persuasion: Advances through meta-analysis* (pp. 53–68). Cresskill, NJ: Hampton Press.

Mukherjee, A., & Dubé, L. (2012). Mixing emotions: The use of humor in fear advertising. *Journal of Consumer Behavior*, *11*, 147–161. doi:10.1002/cb389

Munn, W. C., & Gruner, C. R. (1981). "Sick" jokes, speaker sex, and informative speech. *Southern Speech Communication Journal*, *46*, 411–418.

Murnstein, B. L., & Burst, R. G. (1985). Humor and interpersonal attraction. *Journal of Personality Assessment*, *49*, 637–640.

Nabi, R. L., Moyer-Gusé, E., & Byrne, S. (2007). All joking aside: A serious investigation into the persuasive effect of funny social issue messages. *Communication Monographs*, *74*, 29–54.

Oakhill, J., & Garnham, A. (1993). On theories of belief bias in syllogistic reasoning. *Cognition*, *46*, 87–92.

O'Keefe, D. J. (2002). Guilt as a mechanism of persuasion. In J. P. Dillard & M. Pfau (Eds.), *The persuasion handbook: Developments in theory and practice* (pp. 329–344). Thousand Oaks, CA: Sage.

Pedic, F. (1990). Persuasiveness of nationalistic advertisements. *Journal of Applied Social Psychology*, *20*, 724–728.

Petri, H. (1991). *Motivation: Theory, research, and application* (3rd ed.). Belmont, CA: Wadsworth.

Petty, R.E., & Briñol, P. (2015). Emotion and persuasion: Cognitive and meta-cognitive processes impact attitudes. *Cognition and Emotion*, *29*(1), 1–26. doi:10.1080/02699931.2014.967183

Petty, R. E., & Cacioppo, J. T. (1986). *Communication and persuasion: Central and peripheral routes to attitude change*. New York: Springer-Verlag.

Reuchelle, R. C. (1958). An experimental study of audience recognition of logical and intellectual appeals in persuasion. *Speech Monographs*, *25*(1), 49–58.

Robinette, S., & Brand, C. (2001). *Emotion marketing: The Hallmark way of winning customers for life*. New York: McGraw-Hill.

Ruiter, R. C., Abraham, C., & Kok, G. (2001). Scary warnings and rational precautions: A review of the psychology of fear appeals. *Psychology and Health*, *16*, 613–630.

Schultz, E.J. (2016). Patriotic packaging. *Advertising Age*, *87*(11), p. 4.

Seiter, J. S. (2007). Ingratiation and gratuity: The effect of complimenting customers on tipping behavior in restaurants. *Journal of Applied Social Psychology*, *37*(3), 478–485.

Seiter, J. S., & Dutson, E. (2007). The effect of compliments on tipping behavior in hair styling salons. *Journal of Applied Social Psychology*, *37*(9), 1999–2007.

Seiter, J. S., & Gass, R. H. (2005). The effect of patriotic messages on restaurant tipping. *Journal of Applied Social Psychology*, *35*, 1–10.

Seiter, J. S., & Weger, H., Jr. (2010) The effect of generalized compliments, sex of server, and size of dining party on tipping behavior in restaurants. *Journal of Applied Social Psychology*, *40*, 1–12. doi:10.1111/j.1559–1816.2009.00560.x

Sengupta, J., & Dahl, D. W. (2008). Gender-related reactions to gratuitous sex appeals in advertising. *Journal of Consumer Psychology*, *18*, 62–78.

Sexualization of men—not women—in film has worsened. (2016). *The Economist*, retrieved on July 21, 2017 from: www.economist.com/blogs/prospero/2016/04/inequality-screen

Skalski, P., Tamborini, R., Glazer, E., & Smith, S. (2009). Effects of humor on presence and recall of messages. *Communication Quarterly*, *57*(2), 136–153.

Snigda, S., & Venkatesh, S. (2011). Impact of female sexual objectification in advertising on women. *Advances in Management*, *4*(12), 10–13.

Stankiewicz, J. M., & Rosselli, F. (2008). Women as sex objects and victims in print advertisements. *Sex Roles*, *58*, 579–589.

Steadman, M. (1969). How sexy illustrations affect brand recall. *Journal of Advertising Research*, *9*, 15–19.

Strick, M., Holland, R.W., van Baaren, R.B., & van Knippenberg, A. (2012). Those who laugh are defenseless: How humor breaks resistance to influence. *Journal of Experimental Psychology: Applied*, *18*(2), 213–223. doi:10.1037/a0028534

Sutton, S. R. (1982). Fear-arousing communication: A critical examination of theory and research. In J. R. Eisner (Ed.), *Social psychology and behavioral medicine* (pp. 303–337). London: John Wiley.

Tal-Or, N. (2010). Indirect ingratiation: Pleasing people by associating them with successful others and by praising their associates. *Human Communication Research*, *36*, 163–189. doi:10.1111/j.1468-2958.2010.01372.x

Tannenbaum, M. B., Hepler, J., Zimmerman, R. S., Saul, L., Jacobs, S., Wilson, K., & Albarracin, D. (2015). Appealing to fear: A meta-analysis of fear appeal effectiveness and theories. *Psychological Bulletin*, *141*(6), 1178–1204. doi:10.1037/a0039729

Thomson, M., MacInnis, D. J., & Park, C. W. (2005). The ties that bind: Measuring the strength of consumers' emotional attachments to brands. *Journal of Consumer Psychology*, *15*(1), 77–91.

Time (2017, April 20). The 100 most influential people. Retrieved on May 29, 2017 from: http://time.com/4745798/time-100-2017-full-list/

Verma, S. (2009). Do all advertising appeals influence consumer purchase decision: An exploratory study. *Global Business Review*, *10*(1), 33–43.

Vonk, R. (1998). The slime effect: Suspicion and dislike of likeable behavior toward superiors. *Journal of Personality and Social Psychology*, *74*, 849–864.

Wanzer, M. B., Booth-Butterfield, M., & Booth-Butterfield, S. (1996). Humor and social attraction: Are funny people more popular? An examination of humor orientation, loneliness, and social attraction. *Communication Quarterly*, *44*(1), 42–52.

Wasik, J. F. (1995, September/October). Fraud in the funeral industry. *Consumer's Digest*, *34*, 53–59.

Watt, J. D. (1993). The impact of frequency of ingratiation on the performance evaluation of bank personnel. *Journal of Psychology*, *127*(2), 171–177.

Wayne, S. J., Kacmar, K., & Ferris, G. R. (1995). Coworker response to others' ingratiation attempts. *Journal of Managerial Issues*, *7*(3), 277–289.

Weinberger, M. G., & Gulas, C. S. (1992). The impact of humor in advertising: A review. *Journal of Advertising*, *21*(4), 35–59.

Weinberger, M. G., & Spotts, H. E. (1989). Humor in U.S. versus U.K. TV and advertising. *Journal of Advertising*, *18*(2), 39–44.

Weiner, W. & Veith, R. (Writers), & Weiner, W. (Director). (first broadcast October 18, 2007). The wheel [television series episode, season 1, episode 13]. In W. Weiner (Producer) *Mad Men*. Los Angeles, CA: AMC.

Weiner, B., Perry, R. P., & Magnusson, J. (1988). An attributional analysis of reactions to stigmas. *Journal of Personality and Social Psychology*, *55*, 738–748.

Wellner, A. S. (2002, September). The perils of patriotism. *American Demographics*. Retrieved August 24, 2005, from: www.lexis-nexis.com

Westphal, J.D., & Shani, G. (2016). Psyched-up to suck-up: Self-regulated cognition, interpersonal influence, and recommendations for board appointments in the corporate elite. *Academy of Management Journal*, *59*(2), 479–509. doi:10.5465/amj.2014.0010

Williams, P., & Aaker, J. (2002). Can mixed emotions peacefully exist? *Journal of Consumer Research, 28*, 636–649.

Witte, K. (1992). Putting the fear back into fear appeals: The extended parallel process model. *Communication Monographs, 59*, 329–349.

Witte, K. (1994). Fear control and danger control: A test of the extended parallel process model. *Communication Monographs, 61*(2), 113–134.

Witte, K., & Allen, M. (2000). A meta-analysis of fear appeals: Implications for effective public health campaigns. *Health Education and Behavior, 27*(5), 591–615.

Young, D. G. (2008). The privileged role of the late-night joke: Exploring humor's role in disrupting argument scrutiny. *Media Psychology, 11*, 119–142.

Ziemke, M. H., & Brodsky, S. L. (2015) To flatter the jury: Ingratiation during closing arguments. *Psychiatry, Psychology, and Law, 22*(5), 688–700. doi:10.1080/13218719.2014.965296

Zin, S. M., Ngah, N. E., Ismail, R., Tajuddin, N. H., Abdullah, I. H., & Salleh, A. (2010). The effects of ingratiation on employee career success. *Canadian Social Science, 6*(6), 161–167.

CHAPTER 14

Visual Persuasion

WANT TO CAPTURE AN AUDIENCE'S ATTENTION? Try taking off your clothes. You wouldn't be the first to use this approach. People for the Ethical Treatment of Animals (PETA) use this strategy to protest wearing leather and fur. Their "Naked Truth" campaign features attractive models and celebrities, sans clothing, with the caption "I'd rather go naked than wear fur." Not to be outdone, Spencer Tunick, a performance artist/photographer convinced 18,000 people in Mexico City to strip naked for a photo shoot. He sees mass nudity as a form of collective defiance against social norms. Nudity, however, is not reserved for protesters and artists. When a German supermarket offered free groceries to the first 100 naked shoppers, more than 200 people showed up (Zimmerman, 2012). The promotion worked! We suspect that the male shoppers avoided the frozen food aisle.

Hang on. Before you give your next class presentation in the buff, we should warn you that while nudity may be a great attention getter, your "visual aids" may serve as a distraction during the rest of your presentation. Moreover, you may encounter a good deal of audience resentment. Lots of folks tend to react negatively to nudity (Christy & Haley, 2008). With that said, and, now that we have your attention, we'd like to examine the role of images in persuasion.

IMAGE IS EVERYTHING

We are living in an increasingly visual society. Gurri, Denny, and Harms (2010) underscored this trend, commenting that "Many more images than ever before are available, and many more people are paying a disproportionate amount of attention to them" (p. 101). Fewer people are reading newspapers and books. More people are watching movies and TV. As Metros (2008) observed:

> politicians wage campaigns not on issues, but through their visual persona; wars are televised live through the eyes of embedded journalists; criminal trials have become 24/7 international spectator events; newspapers have had to reduce text to pack their pages with charts, graphics, and photos to compete for market-share; and even radio directs its listeners to Web sites to illustrate the spoken word.
>
> (p. 109)

In television commercials, magazine ads, and billboards, images are primary and words are secondary. Politicians worry about "bad optics," such as being on vacation when a crisis unfolds. The Internet is chock-full of images. Facebook, Instagram, YouTube, and other social media are saturated with images. Internet memes are ever popular. Selfies are all the rage. And it is not only mass media that rely on visual cues. Protest marches, sit-ins, demonstrations, rallies, and picketing are highly visual acts that are intended to persuade.

In this chapter, we examine some of the important ways in which images shape beliefs, attitudes, and behaviors. First, we consider the importance of visual stimuli and how images persuade. Next, we examine art as a form of persuasion, cinematic influence, images in advertising, and photojournalism as a form of persuasion.

OVERLOOKED AND UNDER-APPRECIATED

"Visual images," writes Taewon Suh (1999), "have become a predominant means of transmitting information in the twentieth century and may be even more so in the next century" (p. 3). Yet, despite the increasing importance of visual persuasion, the topic has been under-studied in the field of communication. Traditionally, the study of persuasion has focused on influence attempts that take place within the world of words. Messaris (1997) underscored this point when he noted:

although the study of persuasive communication has a history of more than two millennia, the focus of this scholarly tradition has tended overwhelmingly to be on verbal strategies. With a few notable exceptions, the systematic investigation of visual persuasion is still in its infancy.

(p. vii)

THE POWER OF IMAGES: A THOUSAND WORDS

Images are powerful. They can move us in ways that words cannot. Their potency stems partly from their perceived "realness," or the idea that seeing is believing. As Gurri, Denny, and Harms (2010) noted, "with visual media, however, the illusion is created that we are gazing out a window at the real world" (p. 102). The power of images also arises from their emotional force. Joffe (2008) emphasized the advantages of images over words when she noted that "the most salient distinction between the relative effects of textual/verbal versus visual messages concerns their emotive impact" (p. 84). The grim photo of a Sudanese infant starving to death (see Figure 14.1) demonstrates this capacity. The ghoulish image won a Pulitzer Prize in 1993.

Despite the traditional emphasis on words, studies have revealed a *picture superiority effect* for images. Pictures are more easily recognized and recalled than words (Hockley, 2008; Pelli, Farell, & Moore, 2013; Stenberg, 2006). Medina (2014) reports, for example, that people remember only about 10 percent of what they hear three days hence, compared to 65 percent recall when pictures are included. Images also cross languages and cultures more easily.

FIGURE 14.1
Source: Photo: Kevin Carter 1993 Getty Images.

HOW IMAGES PERSUADE

What is it about images and other visual stimuli that make them so persuasive?
We take up this question here. In doing so, we rely heavily on Paul Messaris's (1997)
conceptualization of the role of images in persuasion. He suggests that images
persuade in three basic ways: through *iconicity, indexicality,* and *syntactic
indeterminacy.*

Iconicity: Bearing a Resemblance

One way that images persuade is by functioning as *icons*, which simply means that
they stand for and resemble the things they represent. An image can sum up a concept.
The stick figure on a "pedestrian crossing" sign is an icon. An emoji is an icon for an
emotion. A caricature of a politician drawn by an editorial cartoonist is also iconic.
The Statue of Liberty, Uncle Sam, and the bald eagle are all icons of America. It
doesn't matter whether they are accurate representations or not (silhouettes of
pedestrians on a crossing sign lack hands and feet) as long as people understand what
they represent. This is, perhaps, the most important property of images: to summarize
ideas and concepts. As Messaris (1997) noted, "If there is one property that most
clearly distinguishes pictures from language and other modes of communication, that
property is iconicity" (p. 3).

A good illustration of the iconic nature of images can be found in Philip Morris's
Marlboro man. The Marlboro man is immediately recognizable around the world.
He is a mythical American hero. He represents the Old West. He symbolizes an
idealized image of the cowboy—a rugged, self-reliant individual. He's always pictured
outdoors, on the range. Without even seeing the brand-name or the slogan, most
people can spot the Marlboro man in an instant. And boy, can he sell cigarettes!
Marlboro cigarettes are the most popular brand in the world (de Guzman, 2007).
For this reason, the Marlboro man has been called "the most universally recognized,
consistently profitable, and aesthetically appealing image in the advertising world"
(Selling tobacco, 1990, p. 84). Now that's an icon.

As part of their iconic nature, images also can be selective. Lighting, camera angle,
perspective, distance, cropping, and editing all figure into what a viewer sees. Ads for
Weightwatchers and Nutrisystem, for example, can choose which "before" and
"after" photos to show.

Another iconic function of images is that they can violate the reality they represent
(Messaris, 1997). An image can make something look real that isn't. For example, a
busy mother who has her hands full doing the laundry, cooking dinner, cleaning
house, and taking care of the kids could be pictured with four arms rather than two.
An ad for a pain reliever might show someone suffering from a splitting headache,
whose head actually appears to be splitting in two. Images can thus simulate a reality
that doesn't exist.

Indexicality: Seeing Is Believing

A second way in which images persuade is through *indexicality* (Messaris, 1997).
This refers to the ability of images, in particular photos and video, to document that
an event happened or that something took place. For example, photos of Iraqi
detainees being abused by U.S. soldiers at Abu Ghraib prison or images of Syrian

children killed by U.S. drone missile strikes function as "proof" to many in the Middle East that the United States does not value Muslim lives.

Indexical images often function as a form of sign reasoning or circumstantial evidence. For example, a high school yearbook photo might document who was in the glee club. An image of a zipper-shaped scar down the center of a person's chest is evidence the person had open heart surgery. Airline passenger "shaming" photos verify that some travelers, like the slob in seat 15A with his bare foot on your arm rest, are disgusting reprobates. A poignant example of indexicality involves police shootings that have been recorded by witnesses on smartphones or dashboard cameras. Such footage contributed to the rise of the Black Lives Matter movement.

A recent study (Cornelis & Peter, 2017) demonstrated that consumers consider the veracity of images when evaluating products. Female respondents rated photos of models with labels stating that "the model in this ad has been retouched" versus "the model in this ad has *not* been retouched" versus no label. The photos labeled as not retouched were perceived as more authentic and increased purchase intentions.

The documentary aspect of images, however, also can be misleading. Pictures are not always faithful representations of reality. Gunning (2004) refers to the common misconception that "the camera never lies" as the *truth claim* of photography. In this regard, Messaris (1997) cautioned, "photographs, of course, can lie. The picture of a model in a fashion ad can be made more attractive through airbrushing, and voter interviews or product demonstrations can be staged" (p. xvii). A controversy over what images do or do not prove involved the size of the crowd at Trump's presidential inauguration. Although Trump declared his audience was the largest in history, the National Park Service released photos that challenged that claim. You can judge for yourself at www.nps.gov/aboutus/foia/foia-frd.htm (scroll halfway down the page to inaugural photos).

Staged events also call the veracity of images into question. Let's say we are watching the news and we see a political candidate, shirtsleeves rolled up, wearing a hardhat, while touring a factory. The image emphasizes the candidate's "plain folks" appeal. He or she identifies with ordinary workers. But would the candidate have rolled up his or her sleeves, donned a hardhat, and toured the factory in the absence of any camera crews? The cameras are recording an event that might not take place in their absence.

We've all seen news footage of angry citizens in foreign lands burning the American flag to protest U.S. foreign policies. It seems fair to ask, however, whether the cameras are there because the protesters are burning the flag or the protesters are burning the flag because the cameras are there. A critical viewer should, therefore, question the indexicality of visual records of events. Media events can be staged. Hey, some people think the moon landing was faked! We don't, but the presence of cameras and film crews can alter people's behavior. Photographs and videotapes can be digitally altered to create the appearance that events occurred when, in fact, they did not, or did not occur in the way they are pictured.

Syntactic Indeterminacy: Don't Look for Logic in Images

A third way in which images persuade is through *syntactic indeterminacy*. This simply means that, unlike words, pictures cannot convey precise relationships between things. Messaris (1997) thus noted, "what visual syntax lacks, especially in comparison to verbal language, is a set of explicit devices for indicating causality, analogy, or any other relationships other than those of space or time" (pp. xvii–xviii). The problem is that images lack logical operators—that is, they can't explicitly state cause–effect, if–then, either–or relationships, or other logical connections between people, objects, and events. As an example, a picture can show what a person's abdominal muscles looked like before using the new "Monster Ab-Cruncher." Another picture can show what the person's abdominal muscles look like afterward. However, pictures themselves can't specify a cause–effect relationship.

The fact that images can't convey logical relationships, such as "A causes B," "A is analogous to B," or "either A or B will happen," is both a blessing and a curse. The blessing is that pictures can be used to equate one thing with another, via association. Images can be juxtaposed to imply an association without actually saying so. This can work to a persuader's advantage. For example, researchers found that a picture of 14 sugar cubes stacked next to a can of Coke was more effective at reducing intentions to consume sugary soft drinks than a text-only label stating that the same Coke can contained 35 grams of sugar (Adams, Hart, Gilmer, & Lloyd-Richardson, 2014).

A persuader can also foster subtle associations through images without making the associations explicit in words. For example, an advertiser can equate a product with being cool, or sexy, or conferring social status simply by pairing the product with cool, sexy, or classy images.

The curse is that images can never suggest the precise nature of relationships, so it is up to the observer to guess what the relationship is. A car commercial might depict a happy family carrying kayaks from their hybrid SUV to a river. Rather than make the consumer want a hybrid SUV, as the advertiser intends, the sequence of images may make the consumer want to go camping, or buy a kayak, or spend more time with the family instead. This is not a serious drawback, however, for two reasons. First, advertisers have decades of practice at manipulating lighting, camera angle, color, and other aspects of images to achieve the results they want. Second, advertisers use words when they want to make a point explicitly and pictures when they want to make a point implicitly. Thus, they enjoy the best of both worlds.

Now that you have a better understanding of how images persuade, we can turn our attention to some of the intriguing and important ways visual stimuli affect us. We begin by examining art as a visual form of influence.

THE ART OF PERSUASION INCLUDES ART AS PERSUASION

The use of art to further political and religious ends dates to ancient civilizations. Greek friezes and frescoes taught citizens moral lessons involving Greek gods and Greek mythology. In the Middle Ages, organized religions sponsored art to further religious ends. The Catholic Church commissioned thousands of works of art to promote Catholicism. As only one example, Michelangelo's painting of the finger of God reaching out to man that adorns the ceiling of the Sistine Chapel endorses a biblical view of creation.

The Paintbrush Is Mightier than the Sword

Governments, especially totalitarian governments, have used art as a form of political propaganda (Clark, 1997). Under Stalin, the Soviet Union declared all art to be subservient to the interests of the state. "Socialist Realism" became the officially recognized standard for art, and its purpose was to advance the political and social ideals of communism. All art projects were commissioned by the government. Not surprisingly, paintings and posters from this era featured members of the proletariat working side by side in factories and on farms. Such iconic representations idealized communism. Clark (1997) explains how such politicized art modeled behavior for the masses:

> in paintings, novels, and films, Socialist Realism created a parallel world peopled by heroes and heroines who personified political ideals. As tireless labourers, courageous Red Army soldiers, diligent schoolchildren, or dedicated Party activists, they demonstrated exemplary behaviour and the attitudes of perfect citizens.
>
> (p. 87)

Similarly, under Mao, China produced a great deal of art aimed at promoting Communist ideology. When the Communists assumed power in 1949, posters and murals contributed to the deification of Chairman Mao. Graphic arts also were used to mobilize and indoctrinate the people during the Cultural Revolution. Posters

FIGURE 14.2
This poster from the Chinese cultural revolution portrays an idealized view of agrarian life.

Source: Reprinted by permission. AP / Dita Alangkara.

学习好经验 建设新山区

showed smiling, cherubic children, peasants, and soldiers all harvesting bumper crops together—a tribute to the agricultural achievements of the revolution.

Meanwhile, in the Western world, art was not only sponsored by governments but was directed against governments as well. Eugène Delacroix's well-known painting *Liberty Leading the People* (1830) now hangs in the Musée du Louvre in Paris. The painting shows a mythical lady liberty, rifle in one hand and French flag in the other, leading French citizens in a charge during the French Revolution. Through its iconicity, the painting both endorses and romanticizes the revolution. Diego Rivera's *History of Mexico* (1929–1935), a large mural painted on the walls of the National Palace in Mexico City, depicts the domination of Mexico's peasants first by Spanish conquistadors, then the Catholic Church, then the Mexican army, and finally by wealthy landowners. The painting reveals the struggle of the downtrodden against oppression, a struggle that culminated in the Mexican Revolution. These are but two examples of socially and politically inspired art.

Art and Social Change: I Must Protest

As we noted in Chapter 1, not all art is created for art's sake. Art serves more than an aesthetic or decorative function. Contemporary artists have strong opinions on political and social issues, and they express them in and through their work. Bertolt Brecht's oft-cited quip that "art is not a mirror to reflect reality, but a hammer with which to shape it" (as cited in McLaren & Leonard, 1993, p. 80) sums up this view.

A contemporary manifestation of this perspective can be found in protest art or the art of social activism. Such art critiques society and promotes social change (Hobbs & Woodard, 1986; Lippard, 1984). This activity typically occurs in public spaces. For example, a bronze sculpture, called *Fearless Girl*, was unveiled in a highly public space near Wall Street in 2017 in honor of International Women's Day. The girl stands with her hands on her hips, head held high, facing down a sculpture of a charging bull that was already in place. The statue immediately sparked a public debate. Admirers said *Fearless Girl* sent a powerful message about the need for gender diversity in corporate America. Congresswoman Carolyn Maloney of New York declared, "this statue has touched hearts across the world with its symbolism of the resiliency of women" (O'Connor, 2017, para. 3).

Critics, however, complained that the sculpture represented faux feminism, since it was commissioned by a Wall Street investment firm promoting a gender diverse fund called SHE. Arturo Di Modica, the sculptor who created the charging bull, complained that his sculpture had been hijacked. He demanded that *Fearless Girl* be relocated. The juxtapositioning of one icon opposite another suggested an adversarial relationship between the girl and the bull. Mayor de Blasio countered with the tweet shown in Figure 14.3.

Fearless Girl achieved her purpose by provoking a public debate about gender representation in the boardroom. Activist artists seek to engage the public in their art and increase the public's social consciousness. As Felshin (1995) notes, such artists are "attempting at the very least to 'change the conversation' to empower individuals and communities, and ultimately to stimulate social change" (p. 26). For example, a popular graffiti artist, known as Banksy, stencils images onto walls and buildings in public places at night (Pryor, 2007). One of his works depicts Dorothy and Toto, from the *Wizard of Oz*. Her basket is being searched by an officer in riot gear wearing

FIGURE 14.3
Screen capture of
de Blasio's Tweet on
Fearless Girl statue.

FIGURE 14.3
Screen capture of de Blasio's Tweet on *Fearless Girl* statue.

latex gloves. The image suggests that society's paranoia over security has gone too far. Duncombe (2016) identifies a number of goals and functions of activist art, including altering perceptions, building community, causing disruption, fostering dialogue, promoting political change, and transforming the environment. We focus on two such functions here, involving increased awareness.

Awareness Through Interpretation

How do activist artists go about persuading? One method is by increasing *awareness through interpretation*. Activist art might consist of an exhibit that is odd, disturbing, or peculiar. The artist seeks to pique the viewer's curiosity and pull him or her in. In the process of trying to understand the work, the viewer's awareness is increased. Interpretation requires active thinking or central processing, which, as we learned earlier, is more likely to trigger lasting attitude change.

For instance, Suzanne Lacy re-created an earlier work, called *Three Weeks in May*, again in 2012, this time called *Three Weeks in January* (www.suzannelacy.com/three-weeks-in-january/). As part of a collaboration with SafeLA.org and other groups, she sought to increase public awareness of sexual assault. On a huge map of Los Angeles, she stenciled the word "rape," in red block letters, at the locations where rapes had been reported, from January 12 to February 1, 2012. Before long, the map was peppered with red stencils. The exhibit provided a graphic revelation of the scope and severity of the problem.

Awareness Through Participation

Yet another approach is to increase *awareness through participation*. Such art is collaborative or interactive. As Felshin (1995) comments, "participation is a catalyst for social change" (p. 12). By way of example, Wafaa Bilal created an interactive installation, called *Domestic Tension*, in a Chicago art gallery (Bilal & Lydersen, 2008). Bilal, an Iraqi artist living in political asylum in the United States, occupied a Plexiglas room for one month. During this time, people went online and shot at him using a robotically controlled paintball gun. This went on 24 hours a day. They shot him in the head when he fell asleep and in the groin when he stood up. More than 60,000 shots were fired at him by strangers from more than 120 countries. Over time, some sympathetic viewers formed a "human shield" by trying to aim the gun away from Bilal. Others hacked in to the system to make the gun fire more rapidly. By the project's end, the room was drenched in paint and Bilal was suffering from posttraumatic stress disorder.

So what did viewers' participation mean? Clearly, many people had no qualms about shooting a person online. Others were confronted with their own morality in choosing to shoot, or not to shoot, another human being. The project laid bare cultural, ethnic, and religious tensions between Westerners and Middle Easterners. By allowing virtual strangers to shoot him, Bilal focused attention on how desensitized modern societies are to violence. Killing has become robotic, clinical, and—as in his project—carried out from afar. When innocent civilians are killed by drone missiles, they are simply labeled "collateral damage." People living comfortably in stable societies are blithely unaware of the suffering of people in conflict zones.

Another example of collaborative art is the AIDS Memorial Quilt, founded by Cleve Jones (Jones & Dawson, 2000). The quilt, also known as the NAMES Project, is a folk-art project commemorating those who died of AIDS. It comprises thousands of 3 ft. × 6ft. panels, each dedicated to the memory of a specific person. The quilt was first displayed on the Washington Mall in 1987, and again in 1992 and 1996. It became the largest community art project in the world. Portions of the quilt are now part of traveling displays that are shown throughout the world. The panels are preserved in an archive (www.aidsquilt.org/about/the-aids-memorial-quilt).

The AIDS Memorial Quilt persuades on multiple levels. We often hear statistics about AIDS, but the quilt puts a human face on these numbers. Every panel is a handmade testimonial to a specific individual's life. When people see the quilt they understand, in concrete rather than abstract terms, the toll taken by the disease. The very choice of making a quilt was a persuasive one. Cleve Jones was attracted to the idea of quilting because it is a traditional American folk art. Quilts conjure up images of home and family. AIDS, however, was thought of as a promiscuous gay male disease. The quilt served as a means of countering that image. As Jones and Dawson (2000) note:

There was hope we could beat the disease by using the quilt as a symbol of solidarity, of family and community; there was hope that we could make a movement that would welcome people—men and women, gay and straight, of every age, race, faith, and background.

(p. 108)

The AIDS Memorial Quilt increased the public's awareness of the disease. It also brought people together. Loved ones who didn't know how to grieve found an outlet in creating a panel. This was truly participatory art. Students who have seen the quilt reported that the experience reduced their homophobia and increased their desire to practice safe sex. This fact alone demonstrates the quilt's persuasiveness as a work of art.

Activist art is often controversial. Indeed, that is its purpose. It is precisely because art has the capacity to arouse people's interest, attention, and ire that it is influential. A primary goal of activist artists is to raise the public's consciousness on a variety of social and political issues (Felshin, 1995; Hobbs & Woodard, 1986; Lippard, 1984; Von Blum, 1976, 1994). Art can challenge the existing social order. It can make

FIGURE 14.4
The AIDS Memorial Quilt, also known as the NAMES Project, is an example of folk art, activist art, and a social movement all in one.

Source: NAMES project/AIDS Memorial Quilt. Reprinted by permission.

people angry. It can offend. At the same time it can heighten people's awareness. It can make people question their assumptions. It can change the way they see things. It can make them reconsider long-held beliefs. In doing so, art persuades.

CINEMATIC PERSUASION: SEX, DRUGS, AND POPCORN

Upon receiving an award from the American Museum of the Moving Image, Steven Spielberg remarked that cinema "is the most powerful weapon in the world" (cited in Fuller, 1995, p. 190). There are several factors at work that lend films their power to persuade.[1] First, there is the potential for mass suggestion. Millions of people are exposed to movies in the United States and abroad. In fact, movies are one of America's leading exports. Thus, movies reach vast audiences. Second, movies are told in a *narrative* form—that is, as stories. Stories possess an aura of believability not found in other mediums for communication. When we watch a movie, we engage in a "willing suspension of disbelief." In order to follow the story, we must lose ourselves in the imaginary world of the film. In so doing, we give up some of our ability to think and reason. Third, the power of films to persuade is aided by the fact that when people sit down in a theater they don't expect to be persuaded, they expect to be entertained. Therefore, they tend to let down their guards and become more open to suggestion. We believe this is one of the reasons that *product placement*—the practice of inserting brand-name items into movie scenes—is so prevalent. Lastly, films are carefully crafted works. Considerable planning and attention to detail go

"What kind of moviemaking do we want to reinforce?"

FIGURE 14.5
"What kind of moviemaking do we want to reinforce?"
Source: © William Haefeli, www.cartoonbank.com. All Rights Reserved.

into the making of a film. Something as simple as a close-up or a swell in the music can enhance the intensity of emotion on the big screen. Thus, motion pictures represent finely crafted messages. Few real-world persuaders, such as salespeople, attorneys, or politicians, have the luxury of lavishing so much time and attention on their persuasive messages.

Acting Out: How Movies Persuade

Movies persuade in multiple ways and on multiple levels. Some of the influential features are unique to particular genres of film. Docudramas, such as *JFK* or *Titanic*, for instance, may convince viewers that a subjective interpretation of events is an objective recounting of the facts (Simpson, 2008). Dramas and romantic comedies may model traditional or nontraditional gender roles. Violent movies, such as *Pulp Fiction*, *Kill Bill*, and *Natural Born Killers*, may desensitize people to violent or aggressive behavior. We examine some of the most important ways that films persuade here.

Exporting Values Abroad

The first of the ways in which films persuade is that American movies export *Western values*. As one commentator noted, "Hollywood films are America's biggest cultural export, consumed by billions around the globe" (Hey, 2001, p. 4). People in remote areas of the world know who Sylvester Stallone is, based on the film character *Rocky*. They know who Julia Roberts is from her role in *Pretty Woman*. American films embody Western values. Rocky was the blue-collar guy who made his dream come true. Julia Roberts was the prostitute with a heart of gold.

Not everyone is happy about the values promoted by American movies. Some view the movie industry as a form of cultural imperialism (Crane, 2014). As Su (2016) observes, "American popular culture in general, and Hollywood films in particular, explicitly and actively advocate American values and the American way of life, thereby threatening other national and local cultures" (p. 46). Foreign audiences often resent the infusion of Western values such as promiscuity, violence, and drug use into their own culture (many in the United States aren't too thrilled with these values either). Others resent the emphasis on materialism and conspicuous consumption. At the same time, movies can advance positive values such as freedom, human rights, and equality. The point is that movies tacitly endorse Western values that may or may not be shared by people in other cultures.

On the positive side, movies can promote prosocial values. Movies often champion the underdog. In *Hunger Games*, *Rudy*, and *Slumdog Millionaire*, the underdog perseveres and, ultimately, wins. Other films, such as *Finding Nemo*, *My Left Foot*, and *Theory of Everything* feature those with disabilities in a favorable light. *Forrest Gump* demonstrated that values such as honesty and compassion can triumph over mental and physical limitations. Fate threw hardships in his way, but Forrest showed us that it is how we deal with adversity that determines who we are. More recently, animated Disney movies, such as *Brave, Mulan,* and *Frozen* have abandoned the "damsel in distress" refrain in favor of assertive, independent roles for female protagonists. Films like *Akeelah and the Bee*, *Hidden Figures*, and *The Princess and the Frog* offer positive, uplifting roles for African American females.

Promoting Popular Culture

A second way in which movies persuade is by *promoting popular culture* both at home and abroad. Fashions, hairstyles, habits, lifestyles, and slang terminology are often emulated by moviegoers (Chansanchai, 2001; Unterberger, 2001). If you are old enough, or into retro fashion, you may recall the popularity of white, three-piece suits following the release of the disco film *Saturday Night Fever*, starring John Travolta. *Donnie Darko* and *The Crow* inspired "Goth" culture. Katniss Everdeen's braided hair in *Hunger Games* popularized the side plait. Edward Cullen's upswept hair in *Twilight* made him a heartthrob among brooding, moody teens. After seeing Mark Wahlberg, Taylor Lautner, or Chris Hemsworth on the big screen, many guys hit the gym to work on their abs and pecs. As a function of their iconicity, movies have a way of idealizing and romanticizing trends and lifestyles. Cinema, then, is a major vehicle for the dissemination of fads, fashions, and trends.

Modeling Behavior: Social Proof

A third way in which movies persuade is by *modeling behaviors*. People may gauge what constitutes appropriate behavior in social situations by taking a movie character's lead. Albert Bandura's *social cognitive theory* maintains that adolescents observe behaviors that are modeled in the media and then imitate those behaviors in real life (Bandura, 1986, 1989). For example, young teens who watch movies about dating and relationships, such as *Mean Girls*, *American Pie*, and *Superbad*, may take their cue about how to deal with love and relationships based on behaviors they see in movies (Behm-Morawitz & Mastro, 2008). At a subconscious level, people may enact scripts they've learned from movies as well.

Characters in movies also model risky, unsafe, or violent behaviors. This can have the effect of legitimizing such behaviors. Movie characters rarely wear seat belts. They often engage in unprotected sex. They frequently smoke, use drugs, get drunk, and drive recklessly. Oh, and they kill lots of people. Regardless of whether these activities are intentional, their prevalence in movies tends to glamorize them. The actions of the characters in movies may be seen as placing a stamp of approval on those behaviors. For example, there is strong evidence that adolescents who see a lot of smoking on the big screen are more likely to light up. A study by Heatherton and Sargent (2009) reported that teens with high exposure to smoking in movies were three times more likely to smoke than those with low exposure. The same applies to unprotected sex. More than 80 percent of PG and PG-13 rated movies include some sexual content. Exposure to sexual content increases the likelihood of unprotected sex (O'Hara, Gibbons, Gerrard, Li, & Sargent, 2012). Yet 98 percent of movies with sex scenes make no mention of safe sex (Gunasekera, Chapman, & Campbell, 2005).

Cultivation Theory: It's a Mean, Scary World

A fourth way in which movies persuade is by fostering beliefs about a world fraught with danger. Other studies have examined the effects of a steady diet of violence on TV. Would it surprise you to learn that gun violence in the top PG-13 rated movies was greater than in the top R-rated films? Such is the case (Cha, 2017). *Cultivation theory* maintains that the more violence people watch on TV, the more likely they are to develop an exaggerated belief in a *mean, scary world* (Gerbner, Gross, Morgan, & Signorielli, 2002). In addition to developing a jaded view of the world, viewing violence tends to increase aggression and antisocial behavior in people. "Fifty years of research on the effects of TV violence," notes John Murray (2008), "leads to the inescapable conclusion that viewing media violence is related to increases in aggressive attitudes, values, and behaviors" (p. 1212). With respect to cinema's influence on behavior, Oliver Stone, who directed *Natural Born Killers*, commented, "Film is a powerful medium. Film is a drug. It goes into your eye. It goes into your brain. It stimulates, and that's a dangerous thing" (cited in Leiby, 1995, p. G1).

Viewer Identification

A fifth way in which movies persuade is by promoting viewer identification. Moviegoers may idolize a particular actor or actress or a specific character played by that actor or actress. Perhaps you know a few Kristen Stewart or Johnny Depp "wannabes." Young adults may discover "possible selves" from seeing movies or may derive a sense of validation from a character (Greenwood & Long, 2015).

Sometimes the story of the character overlaps with the viewer's own experience, causing the viewer to identify with the character in the film. If you've ever felt like an outcast, a nerd, the underdog, or misunderstood, you might identify with movies such as *Napoleon Dynamite*, *Ghost World*, *My Big Fat Greek Wedding*, *Happy Times*, or *Pretty in Pink*. In this way, movies establish a common bond with viewers.

Viewer identification can take place even if a viewer's experience doesn't directly overlap with that of a character in a movie. None of us have met an extraterrestrial (okay, *most* of us haven't), but we can still identify with a movie such as *E.T.*, because all of us have had to say goodbye to someone we love. None of us are green ogres, but we can identify with Shrek because we've all felt like outsiders from time to time.

Perpetuating Stereotypes

A final way in which cinema shapes public perceptions is by fostering and perpetuating stereotypes. Hollywood frequently typecasts minorities, women, overweight people, the elderly, and other groups into limited roles (Benshoff & Griffin, 2009). This may create the impression that these are the only roles these groups are capable of performing. Although the number of parts for minorities has increased, the roles often involve the same predictable stereotypes. Middle Easterners, for example, are frequently cast as terrorists (Shaheen, 2009). When they aren't terrorists, they are often playboys or cab drivers. Hispanics are often depicted as drug dealers or gang-bangers. While the situation has improved, many roles for Hispanics remain tied to cultural stereotypes. Asians also tend to occupy stereotypic roles in films. If Hollywood is to be believed, every Asian is skilled in martial arts. They are often undersexed and romantically awkward (Whitty, 2001). As with other minorities, things are changing, but slowly.

In a similar vein, African Americans have been historically typecast (Entman & Rojecki, 2001). African American males fit the mold of athlete, drug dealer, or musician (Waxman, 2000). African American women tend to be relegated to stereotypic roles such as beautiful wife, beautiful girlfriend, or beautiful prostitute. African Americans also are typecast as the funny sidekick in "buddy" movies. Eddie Murphy, Martin Lawrence, Chris Rock, and Chris Tucker have all played such parts. These, too, are narrowly defined roles. The situation has improved. Halle Berry, Jamie Foxx, Denzel Washington, and Forest Whitaker have all won Oscars for best actress or actor. Their success may convince filmmakers and the movie-going public that African Americans can be taken seriously on screen. In 2016, the dearth of African American Oscar nominees sparked a #OscarsSoWhite movement, with numerous black stars boycotting the Academy Awards ceremony.

When it comes to stereotypic roles, women fare no better. With few exceptions women must be thin and beautiful to land starring roles (Benshoff & Griffin, 2009). In action-adventure movies, women are depicted as powerful and objects of desire (McClearen, 2015). Women also tend to be confined to traditional roles: mother, wife, mistress, girlfriend. This isn't particularly surprising, given that fewer than 10 percent of screenplays are written by women, and fewer than 6 percent of movies are directed by women (Maher, 2009). Admittedly, there are some women in nontraditional roles. Nevertheless, roles for women, especially older women, remain limited.

If there is a silver lining, it is that younger moviegoers tend to be more tolerant, if not completely color-blind (Welkos, 2001). This is evidenced by the box-office success of recent multiethnic, multicultural movies, such as *Joy Luck Club*, *Moana*, *Slum Dog Millionaire*, *the Big Sick*, and *The Help*. Because youth culture includes more African Americans, Asian Americans, and Hispanic Americans, filmmakers are producing more multiethnic movies to meet the demands of a new generation of viewers.

IMAGES IN ADVERTISING: AND NOW A WORD FROM OUR SPONSORS

"Advertising," write Woodward and Denton (1999), "is undoubtedly the most pervasive form of persuasion in our society" (p. 286). When we think of pure cases of persuasion, advertising immediately comes to mind. Over $200 billion per year is spent on advertising in the United States, with an increasing share going to digital advertising (Statista, 2017). Various estimates suggest that the average person is exposed to more than 3,000 advertising messages per day (Dupont, 1999; Simons, 2001; Woodward & Denton, 1999). Some estimates are even higher. One estimate places daily media exposure at 15.5 hours per day (Walsh-Childers, 2017). If all the money spent on advertising were divvied up, it would work out to about $800 per person in the United States and $40 per person in all other countries combined (Berger, 2011). Most of us are "armchair" experts in advertising, having watched so many commercials during our lives. Indeed, the average American spends about one hour per day watching television commercials (Salter, 2009). That works out to more than two years of commercial viewing over an average lifespan.

Advertisements, whether on television, in a magazine, online, or some other medium, feature images. The visual components of such ads are often key to their effectiveness. Visually oriented ads work their magic in a variety of ways. We don't have enough space to examine all the ways here, so we focus on four of the most important ones.

Visual Extravaganzas: Now You've Got My Attention

One challenge that advertisers face in trying to convince consumers to buy their products is *media clutter*. There are so many ads competing for consumers' attention that it is difficult for a message to stand out in the crowd. Commercials must grab and hold viewers' attention. Thanks to CGI, it is now possible for advertisers to create and manipulate images in ways previously not possible. A plain-vanilla commercial simply won't hold up to an eye-popping extravaganza, especially when viewers have low involvement with the topic or issue.

Anti-Ads: You Can't Fool Me

Another challenge facing advertisers is that consumers are increasingly cynical about advertising. They don't trust Madison Avenue. But that skepticism is the very premise on which *anti-ads* are based. Anti-advertising, or "subvertising" as it is sometimes called, caters to consumers who distrust the media. Anti-ads mock advertising itself (Axelton, 1998; Beato, 1999). They denounce traditional advertising to gain acceptance by consumers.

Many anti-ads are spoofs on commercial advertising (see www.adbusters.org). Others are designed to sell actual products and services. Geico spoofed insurance comparison ads by conducting a mock insurance "taste test." Consumers who sampled a glass of Geico said "mmm, yum," while consumers who taste-tested a competing brand of auto insurance said "ugh, yuck!"

An antismoking commercial also offers an example of an anti-ad. The spot shows two cowboys in a downtown setting, one playing guitar and the other singing. The singing cowboy, however, is singing through a hand-held device pressed against his neck (an electro larynx). He's had a laryngectomy. He sings, "You don't always die from tobacco, sometimes you just lose a lung. Oh, you don't always die from tobacco, sometimes they just snip out your tongue." This ad mocks the rugged cowboy mystique associated with Marlboro cigarettes.

In essence, anti-ads are telling viewers, "Hey, you're on to us. You're too smart to be fooled." But of course, that strategy is itself a ploy designed to appeal to jaded consumers. Such an approach creates the perception that the advertiser respects the viewer's intelligence. Advertisers are constantly finding ways to reinvent themselves. As consumers have grown more skeptical, advertisers have found ways to adapt to, and capitalize on, their skepticism. Anti-ads or subvertising thus mark another evolutionary phase in advertising.

Image-Oriented Advertising: Materialism as Happiness

In addition to using vivid imagery and anti-advertising, advertisers also seek to create positive associations between their brands and idealized images or lifestyles. This approach is known as *image-oriented* or *image-based advertising* and it is the bread and butter of modern advertising campaigns. Image-oriented ads rely on the syntactic indeterminacy of images. Remember, images don't contain logical operators, so they can't make clear-cut claims. That turns out to be a plus, however, because by pairing a product with a favorable image, an advertiser can equate the two without actually saying so in words. Messaris (1997) underscored this feature, stating that "this ability to imply something in pictures while avoiding the consequences of saying it in words has been considered an advantage of visual advertising since the first days of its development as a mass medium" (p. xix).

Let's consider some examples of this in action. Oil companies don't want you to think about tar-covered birds on an oil-stained beach when you envision petroleum products. They want you to associate oil companies with pro-environmental attitudes. Hence, Chevron's "People do" advertising campaign, which portrays Chevron as a guardian of endangered species.

Image-oriented ads portray a brand as the embodiment of an idealized lifestyle. Equating the brand with an idealized lifestyle creates identification with that brand. When we buy that brand we are buying into that lifestyle. Some brands are *luxury brands*, prestigious, yet within reach of many consumers (Ralph Lauren, Mercedes). Some are *aspirational brands*; few people can afford them, but they hope to own them one day (Armani, Rolls Royce). Still others are *authentic or genuine brands* (Gilmore & Pine, 2007; Rosica, 2007). These brands are unpretentious. In a marketplace filled with fake, phony products, consumers value what seems real. A smaller brand with a story to tell may be more desirable than a mass-produced commodity. Organic foods, handmade goods, and artisanal beers fall into this category. With a little practice, you should be able to watch a TV commercial or view a magazine ad and decipher the favorable image or association the advertiser is trying to manufacture. Some of the most common associations are as follows:

- *Social status and elitism:* Ads for luxury cars and expensive watches often associate owning these products with prestige and success. Ads for expensive wines, luggage, jewelry, and other upscale goods often imply that the products are symbols of taste and refinement.
- *Sex or romance:* Ads for perfume, lingerie, and hair-care products often equate the products with sexiness, allure, and romance. The association established by many perfume ads is that if you wear that fragrance you'll be more sexy, or other sexy people will be attracted to you.
- *Cause-related:* Some brands have a cause to promote. Consumers aren't just buying a product or service, they are also helping to feed starving children, save rainforests, or protect endangered species (Adkins, 1999; Pringle & Thompson, 1999). TOMS shoes and (Product) Red exemplify this approach. Ben & Jerry's promotes social change as well by donating a percentage of their profits to social causes.
- *Power, speed, and strength:* Ads for tools, trucks, SUVs, computers, and nutritional supplements often equate buying a product with conferring power on the user. Dodge trucks are "Ram tough." Chevy trucks are built "Like a rock." You, too, can have rock-hard abs or buns of steel. If you've got the newest, fastest computer, you are a "power user."
- *Youth culture:* A number of products are marketed by associating products with youth culture, rebelliousness, and an alternative lifestyle. Soft drinks, clothing, fast food, skateboards, small electronics, makeup, and many other goods and services appeal to what is hip, trendy, or cool. These commercials are often shot with handheld cameras and employ rapid editing techniques to simulate the look of "reality TV."
- *Safety, security:* Ads for banking, insurance, and retirement accounts try to foster images of being safe and secure. Consumers want peace of mind and a sense of stability when it comes to their finances and retirement.

- *Sense of place, belonging:* Ads for foods, restaurants, furniture, and other household goods often strive to create a sense of hominess. The advertisers want you to get a warm, comfortable, familiar feeling when you think of their products.

These are only some of the important values and lifestyles to which advertisers attempt to link their brands. When you watch a commercial or read a print ad, you should examine the associations the advertiser is trying to establish. For decades, cigarette ads fostered the association that smoking was cool. More recently, antismoking ads have associated smoking with being uncool. Both approaches rely on the underlying assumption that "being cool" is what really counts in life. Is it? When evaluating a commercial or print ad, ask yourself three important questions:

1. What image or lifestyle is being associated with the product?
2. Is that image or lifestyle truly desirable? Is that the image I'm really seeking or the lifestyle to which I truly aspire?
3. Would buying the product actually grant me the image or lifestyle equated with the product? If so, how?

Shock Ads: Edgy Images as Persuasion

Some pro-life videos feature grisly images of late-term abortions in which the fetus has been dismembered prior to extraction. The images are intended to be repulsive. Is it acceptable to use gory images to persuade? Kelland and Macleod (2015) note that anti-abortionists view such gruesome images as revealing the truth about the practice of abortion. Only by showing such images, anti-abortionists argue, can the immorality of the practice be revealed. Images of abortion, pro-life proponents claim, are analogous to images of the Holocaust. They must be seen to be believed.

In contrast, pro-choice proponents argue that grisly photos are misleading, because a small percentage of abortions are late-term. Shocking photos, pro-choice advocates maintain, ignore the circumstances of a woman who opted for a late-term abortion, such as rape, incest, severe birth defects, or a threat to the woman's life. The contested nature of pro-life imagery illustrates the tension between images that appeal to the head or the heart (Kelland & Macleod, 2015).

Images also figure heavily into the form of advertising known as *shock ads*. Shock ads, or "shockvertising" as it has also been called, push the boundaries of taste and propriety (Lazar, 2003; McCarthy, 2000). The goal is to sell products by being edgy. Some shock ads are vulgar, some erotic, some humorous, and others nauseating. Some adopt an "in your face" style of advertising.

The Montana Meth Project ran a series of public service announcements graphically depicting the consequences of meth use. One depicted a boyfriend who "pimped out" his girlfriend to support their meth habit (www.youtube.com/watch?v=E-iEA6-I1xU). A billboard showed a young woman with a thousand-yard stare and the caption "15 bucks for sex isn't normal, but on meth it is." The effectiveness of the MMP has been questioned, however (Anderson, 2010; Marsh, Copes, & Linnemann, 2017).

Even shock ads can go too far. In the United Kingdom, hundreds of readers complained when they found a full-page ad showing a newborn infant with a cockroach in its mouth. The ad was sponsored by Barnardo's, a children's charity group, and was designed to draw attention to the plight of children living in poverty. The ad was banned by Britain's Advertising Standards Authority.

Given their widespread use, do shock ads really work? A study by Dahl, Frankenberger, and Manchanda (2003) suggests they do. These researchers concluded that "shocking content in an advertisement significantly increases attention, benefits memory, and positively influences behavior" (p. 1). Other studies also support the effectiveness of shock ads (Scudder & Mill, 2009). But shock ads must walk a fine line. If they aren't shocking enough, they won't provoke the public dialogue and publicity they seek. If they are overly shocking, they may prompt a consumer rebellion. Furthermore, consumers may build up a tolerance to shocking images. One commentator warned that shock ads were analogous to drug addiction; a larger and larger dose is required to achieve the desired effect until consumers eventually overdose on the strategy (Black, cited in Klara, 2012).

PHOTOJOURNALISM AS PERSUASION: THE CAMERA DOES LIE

Even without any accompanying text, photographs tell their own persuasive stories. Because there are entire courses offered in photojournalism, we won't attempt to explore the whole field here. What we wish to emphasize is that still photographs can make powerful statements. They can affect people's perceptions of events. They also can reach people on an emotional level in ways that words alone cannot. As Zumwalt (2001) noted, "There is tremendous potential in a photograph to inflame emotions" (p. B12). Because photographs don't require literacy or familiarity with a particular language, they also are more universally understood than messages that rely on words. Photographic images also can distort reality, as we shall see.

Many well-known photos serve as iconic representations of events or eras in history (Hariman & Locaites, 2007). In all likelihood, you've seen Joe Rosenthal's famous 1945 photo of U.S. Marines raising the Stars and Stripes at Iwo Jima. The picture symbolizes the determination of the United States to win the war in the Pacific. You may have seen John Filo's photo of a female student at Kent State University in 1970, kneeling over the body of a fellow student who was slain by the National Guard. That picture symbolized the schism between the protest movement and the government, as well as the generation gap of the late 1960s. You may have seen the photograph taken by Nick Ute in 1972 of a naked, 9-year-old Vietnamese girl, running down the road, with napalm burns from the bombs that had just been dropped on her village. The photo epitomized the feelings of many Americans that the United States was involved in an unjust war in Vietnam.

Photos can sum up social problems or controversies. They can document events in ways that words cannot. This is where the old saying, "a picture is worth a thousand words" applies. Owing to their iconicity, photographs can cement themselves in the public's mind. They function as touchstones that capture entire events in our collective conscience. The fact that so many cellphones now have cameras has elevated the role of amateur photographers. Photos can be uploaded instantly to Facebook, Twitter, and other social media.

Playing Tricks With the Camera: Photographic Deception

An important point to keep in mind about photographic images is that they aren't objective, impartial representations of things. The *truth claim* implied by a photograph can be misleading. All photographs are mediated by the photographer. Someone must aim the camera. Photographs give us the photojournalist's point of view, which is simply that—one point of view. The photographer decides which events to capture on film, and which aren't worth preserving. The photographer decides on the distance, camera angle, lighting, shutter speed, and so on. The photographer decides which pictures to develop, how to edit or crop them, and which prints to offer for public consumption.

For example, photojournalists and news editors make decisions about which photos of war zones to publish and how gory or sanitized those images are. McEntee (2015) found that more graphic war photos (showing human carnage) evoked greater empathy than less graphic photos (showing building rubble). She contended that news outlets function as gatekeepers, deciding what the public sees, thereby shaping public opinion about conflict zones.

Some well-known historical and recent examples of photographic deception serve to illustrate how easily this medium can be manipulated. On June 27, 1994, *Time* magazine darkened O. J. Simpson's mug shot on one of its covers, making him appear more sinister and menacing. In the year 2000, a brochure for the University of Wisconsin–Madison was doctored by adding an African American student into a photo of fans cheering at a football game. The manipulation was done to make the campus seem more ethnically diverse. Kim Kardashian once "broke the Internet" with a photo of a champagne glass balanced on her behind. But when a non-airbrushed photo of Kim Kardashian's derriere surfaced on the Web, fans realized all her other photos were digitally altered (Cacich, 2017). She lost 100,000 Instagram followers in a week. Wait, her fans were unaware that she had some physical and digital sculpting done? Not to worry, with 99 million followers she can afford the loss.

Outside of photojournalism, photos also are not carbon copies of reality either. Political attack ads often show a politician at his or her worst. Fashion magazines show models at their best. When people join online dating services, they often alter their profile photographs to appear more attractive (Hancock & Toma, 2009). These examples underscore the point that seeing is not necessarily believing. Just because someone claims to have captured an image on film doesn't necessarily mean the image is genuine and unaltered. Box 14.1 offers some useful suggestions on how to avoid being duped by photos and other visual media.

BOX 14.1 | On Your Guard: Remaining Vigilant Against Visual Deception

Images, whether in the form of television commercials, cinema, magazine ads, photojournalism, Web pages, or other media, function as powerful tools for influence. They give us a vicarious sense of "being there." For this reason, we must remain wary of visual communication designed to persuade us. We've all seen supermarket tabloids with doctored photos claiming "Martian now on Supreme Court" or some other such nonsense. We know these images can't be trusted. But images may be manipulated by others as well. Politicians may manipulate images for propaganda purposes. Images may be manipulated by lawyers to make a defendant seem innocent or guilty ("If it doesn't fit, you must acquit."). Images may be used by the media to increase ratings ("Stay tuned, film at 11!") and by advertisers to sell goods ("Get the body you want now!"). With this in mind, we offer the following tips and advice when evaluating persuasive images.

1. Try to improve your *visual literacy*—that is, the ability to critically analyze and evaluate visual communication (Felton, 2008). As Messaris and Moriarty (2005) note, "visual literacy can . . . be seen as a potential antidote to attempted manipulation of the viewer in TV, print, and Web-based advertising; visual journalism; and other forms of pictorial entertainment, information, or persuasion" (p. 482).

2. Don't succumb to the adage "Seeing is believing." The camera does lie (Brugioni, 1999). What you are seeing may well be a manipulated image. When you see a fashion model on a magazine cover, for example, don't assume she or he looks that good in real life. The cover photo has probably been digitally altered to remove blemishes, whiten teeth, highlight hair color, etc.

3. Be especially wary of images on the Internet. Anyone can digitally alter an image on a home computer nowadays using Photoshop and mobile apps. If you are unsure whether to trust an image or not, try checking out some useful Web-based resources that identify hoaxes. Using Google, you can conduct a reverse image search (see www.youtube.com/watch?v=p5e9wTdAuIA. www.Tineye.com also does reverse searches. We like www.snopes.com (check out their photo gallery link); factcheck.org, and Skeptical Enquirer, at www.csicop.org. For celebrity gossip, Gossip.com is useful.

4. When watching so-called reality shows on TV, remember they may bear little resemblance to reality. Reality shows are carefully engineered productions. Guests or contestants typically try out for the show and are carefully vetted. This selection process allows producers to cast contestants for maximum dramatic effect. Footage can be edited so that a contestant seems braver, cleverer, more devious, more hostile, or more psycho than she/he really is. Hosts may encourage or reward certain types of behavior while discouraging others. You don't really think that every guest on the Jerry Springer show threw a chair on his or her own initiative, do you?

5. When viewing documentaries, keep in mind that they do not objectively recount events. They advocate a point of view. Documentaries often use techniques such as re-enactment (recreating scenes for which no original footage is available), substituted or modified footage (film of something similar or related, but not the same thing), time compression (cramming years or even centuries into a one-and-a-half-hour-long movie), and composite characters (combining several different people into one). While all these techniques may make the story easier to follow and the narrative more compelling, they come at the expense of impartiality. Some exemplars of this genre, such as Michael Moore's *Fahrenheit 9/11* and Morgan Spurlock's *Supersize Me*, have been dubbed "mockumentaries" or "*shockumentaries*" because the director's bias is so intense.

6. Beware of images in diet ads, cosmetic surgery ads, supplement ads, and infomercials. Take a typical ad for a weight loss product: Notice that the person in the "Before" photo usually has a bland expression, poor posture, pasty skin, unkempt hair, unflattering clothes, and unflattering lighting. In comparison, the person shown in the "After" picture is usually smiling, has an upright posture, stylish hair, a tan and/or makeup, and flattering lighting. Does the ad say both photos are unretouched? Does the fine print acknowledge "Results may vary" or "Results not typical?" If a diet ad claims a user lost 30 pounds in two weeks, but you can see the person's hair is much longer in

the "After" photo, then you would know that more than two weeks had passed between photos. Testimonials and the photos that accompany them are always subject to the "hasty generalization" fallacy.

7. The context and captioning of images can have an important impact as well. Following the aftermath of Hurricane Katrina, newspapers printed two photos of survivors wading in the flood water. One Associated Press photo showed an African American male clutching a six-pack of Pepsi with the caption "A young man walks through chest deep flood water after looting a grocery store " (Ralli, 2005). Another AFP/Getty photo, showed a white couple and carried the caption, "two residents wade through chest deep water after finding bread and soda from a local grocery store." The captioning implied a clear double-standard: Blacks were looting, but white folks were acting out of necessity.

SUMMARY

In this chapter, we've examined a variety of ways in which visual stimuli, including but not limited to images, facilitate persuasion. We have not touched on all the ways in which visual cues persuade. Yet the principles we've discussed about how images persuade through iconicity, indexicality, and syntactic indeterminacy apply to other forms of visual communication as well. Our society is becoming increasingly visually oriented. More people now get their news from television than from newspapers. More people now watch movies than read books. Persuaders are capitalizing on this trend by enlisting images in support of their persuasive endeavors. Based on what you've learned in this chapter, you should be able to watch a television commercial, see a movie, or read a print ad with a sharper eye toward the strategic choices made by the persuader. In short, we hope you will be a wiser consumer of visual persuasion.

NOTE

1. Most of our comments about cinematic persuasion apply equally to television shows. Television shows, however, typically have smaller budgets and tighter production schedules. Hence, they are less polished works. Nevertheless, many TV series have altered attitudes and behavior in the same ways as films.

REFERENCES

Adams, J. M., Hart, W., Gilmer, L., & Lloyd-Richardson, E. E. (2014). Concrete images of sugar content in sugar-sweetened beverages reduces attraction and selection of those beverages. *Appetite*, *83*, 10–18. doi:10.1016/j.appet.2014.07.027

Adkins, S. (1999). *Cause related marketing: Who cares wins*. Oxford, UK: Reed Educational.

Anderson, M. (2010). Does information matter? The effectiveness of the Meth Project on meth use among youths. *Journal of Health Economics*, *29*(5), 732–742. doi:10.1016/j.jhealeco.2010.06.005

Axelton, K. (1998, March). Ads with attitude: Can you afford to use anti-advertising? *Entrepreneur Magazine*. Retrieved on September 5, 2005, from: http://entrepreneur. com/magazine/entrepreneur/1998/march/15326.html

Bandura, A. (1986). *Social foundations of thought and action: A social cognitive theory*. Englewood Cliffs, NJ: Prentice-Hall.

Bandura, A. (1989). Social cognitive theory. In R. Vasta (Ed.) *Annals of child development, 6. Six theories of child development* (pp. 1–60). Greenwich, CT: JAI Press.

Beato, G. (1999, May/June). Does it pay to subvertise? The critics of corporate propaganda co-opt its best weapon. *Mother Jones*. Retrieved on September 5, 2005, from: www.motherjones.com/commentary/columns/1999/05/beato.html

Behm-Morawitz, E., & Mastro, D. E. (2008). Mean girls? The influence of gender portrayals in teen movies on emerging adults' gender-based attitudes and beliefs. *Journalism & Mass Communication Quarterly*, 85(1), 131–146.

Benshoff, H. M., & Griffin, S. (2009). *America on film: Representing race, class, gender, and sexuality at the movies* (2nd ed.). Malden, MA: Blackwell.

Berger, A. A. (2011). *Ads, fads, and consumer culture* (4th ed.). Lanham, MD: Rowman & Littlefield.

Bilal, W., & Lydersen, K. (2008). *Shoot an Iraqi: Art, life, and resistance under the gun*. San Francisco, CA: City Lights.

Brugioni, D. A. (1999). *Photo fakery: The history and techniques of photographic deception and manipulation*. Dulles, VA: Brassey's.

Cacich, A. (2017, April 28). Kim Kardashian's unairbrushed butt photos cost her 100,000 Instagram followers! Retrieved on June 14, 2017 from: www.lifeandstylemag.com/ posts/kim-kardashian-unairbrushed-butt-photos-instagram-131152/photos/kim-butt-82518

Cha, A. E. (2017). Gun violence in PG-13 movies soars: Are 'superhero' movies to blame? *The Washington Post*. Retrieved on June 13, 2017 from: https://search-proquest-com.lib proxy.fullerton.edu/docview/1857569457?accountid=9840

Chansanchai, A. (2001, August 19). Starring in school: Teens are taking back-to-school fashion cues from five stylish celebrities. *The Baltimore Sun*, p. 5N.

Christy, T. P., & Haley, E. (2008). The influence of advertising context on perceptions of offense. *Journal of Marketing Communications*, 14(4), 271–291.

Clark, T. (1997). *Art and propaganda in the twentieth century*. New York: Harry N. Abrams.

Cornelis, E., & Peter, P. C. (2017). The real campaign: The role of authenticity in the effectiveness of advertising disclaimers in digitally enhanced images. *Journal of Business Research*, 77, 102–112. doi:10.1016/j.jbusres.2017.03.018

Crane, D. (2014). Cultural globalization and the dominance of the American film industry: Cultural policies, national film industries, and transnational film. *International Journal of Cultural Policy*, 20(4), 365–82.

Dahl, D. W., Frankenberger, K. D., & Manchanda, R. V. (2003). Does it pay to shock? Reactions to shocking and nonshocking advertising among university students. *Journal of Advertising Research*, 43(3), 1–13.

De Guzman, N. F. (2007, July 31). Special feature: The power of advertising; where there's smoke, there's Marlboro. *Business World*. Retrieved on June 27, 2012, from the Lexis-Nexis Academic search engine.

Duncombe, S. (2016). Does it work? The æffect of activist art. *Social Research: An International Quarterly*, 83(1), 115–134. Retrieved November 1, 2017 from: Project MUSE, muse.jhu.edu/article/620873

Dupont, L. (1999). *Images that sell: 500 ways to create great ads*. Sainte-Foy, Quebec: White Rock.

Entman, R. M., & Rojecki, A. (2001). *The black image in the white mind: Media and race in America.* Chicago: University of Chicago Press.

Felshin, N. (Ed.). (1995). *But is it art? The spirit of art as activism.* Seattle, WA: Bay Press.

Felton, P. (2008, November/December). Visual literacy. *Change,* 60–63.

Fuller, L. K. (1995). Hollywood is holding us hostage: Or, why are terrorists in the movies Middle-Easterners? In Y. R. Kamalipour (Ed.), *The U.S. media and the Middle East: Image and perception* (pp. 187–197). Westport, CT: Greenwood Press.

Gerbner, G., Gross, L., Morgan, M., & Signorielli, N. (2002). Growing up with television: The cultivation perspective. In J. Bryant & D. Zillmann (Eds.), *Media effects: Advances in theory and research* (2nd ed., 17–41). Hillsdale, NJ: Erlbaum.

Gilmore, J. H., & Pine II, B. J. (2007). *Authenticity: What consumers really want.* Boston, MA: Harvard Business School Press.

Greenwood, D., & Long, C.R. (2015). When movies matter: Emerging adults recall memorable movies. *Journal of Adolescent Research, 30*(5), 625–650. doi:10.1177/0743558414561296

Gunasekera, H., Chapman, S., & Campbell, S. (2005). Sex and drugs in popular movies: An analysis of the top 200 films. *Journal of the Royal Society of Medicine, 98*(10), 464—470.

Gunning, T. (2004). What's the point of an index? Or, faking photographs? *NORDICOM Review, 5*(1/2), 39–49.

Gurri, M., Denny, C., & Harms, A. (2010). Our visual persuasion gap. Parameters: *U.S. Army War College, 40*(1), 101–109.

Hancock, J. T., & Toma, C. L. (2009). Putting your best face forward: The accuracy of online photographs. *Journal of Communication, 59,* 367–386. doi:10.1111/j.1460–2466.2009.01420.x

Hariman, R., & Locaites, J. L. (2007). *No caption needed: Iconic photographs, public culture, and liberal democracy.* Chicago: University of Chicago Press.

Heatherton, T. F., & Sargent, J. D. (2009). Does watching smoking in movies promote teenage smoking? *Current Directions in Psychological Science, 18*(2), 63–67.

Hey, S. (2001, November 12). So will the Brits play the baddies? *The London Independent,* p. 4.

Hobbs, R. H., & Woodard, F. (Eds.). (1986). *Human rights/human wrongs: Art and social change.* Iowa City, IA: University of Iowa Museum of Art.

Hockley, W. E. (2008). The picture superiority effect in associative recognition. *Memory & Cognition, 36*(7), 1351–1359.

Joffe, H. (2008). The power of visual material: Persuasion, emotion, and identification. *Diogenes, 217,* 84–93. doi:10.1177/0392192107087919

Jones, C., & Dawson, J. (2000). *Stitching a revolution.* San Francisco, CA: HarperCollins.

Kelland, L., & Macleod, C. (2015). When is it legitimate to use images in moral arguments? The use of foetal imagery in anti-abortion campaigns as an exemplar of an illegitimate instance of a legitimate practice. *Philosophy and Social Criticism, 4*(2), 179–195. doi:10.1177/0191453714556691

Klara, R. (2012, February 20). Advertising's shock troops. *Adweek, 53*(7), 26–27.

Lazar, D. (2003, December). Shockvertising. *Communication Arts, 45*(7), 198–201.

Leiby, R. (1995, December 3). Movie madness: Does screen violence trigger copy-cat crimes? *The Washington Post,* p. G1.

Lippard, L. R. (1984). *Get the message? A decade of art for social change.* New York: E. P. Dutton.

Maher, K. (2009, February 4). What do women want? Surely not this: Can anything stop the inane decline of the chick flick? *The Times* (London), pp. T2, 14–15.

Marsh, W., Copes, H., & Linnemann, T. (2017). Creating visual differences: Methamphetamine users' perceptions of anti-meth campaigns. *International Journal of Drug Policy*, *39*, 52–61. doi:10.1016/j.drugpo.2016.09.001

McCarthy, M. (2000, June 20). 'Shockvertising' pushes envelope, risks backlash. *USA Today*, p. 6B.

McClearen, J. (2015). Unbelievable bodies: Audience readings of action heroines as a post-feminist visual metaphor. *Continuum: Journal of Media & Cultural Studies*, *29*(6), 833–846. doi:10.1080/10304312.2015.1073683

McEntee, R. S. (2015). Shooting straight: Graphic versus non-graphic war photographs. *Visual Communication Quarterly*, *22*(4), 221–236. doi:10.1080/15551393.2015. 1105103

McLaren, P., & Leonard, P. (1993). *Paulo Freire: A critical encounter*. New York: Routledge.

Medina, J. J. (2014). *Brain rules: 12 principles for surviving and thriving at work, home, and school*. Seattle, WA: Pear Press.

Messaris, P. (1997). *Visual persuasion: The role of images in advertising*. Thousand Oaks, CA: Sage.

Messaris, P., & Moriarty, S. (2005). Visual literacy theory. In K. Smith, S. Moriarty, G. Barbatsis, & K. Kenney (Eds.), *Handbook of visual communication* (pp. 481–502). Mahwah, NJ: Lawrence Erlbaum Associates.

Metros, S. E. (2008). The educator's role in preparing visually literate students. *Theory into Practice*, *47*, 102–109.

Murray, J. P. (2008). Media violence: The effects are both real and strong. *American Behavioral Scientist*, *51*(8), 1212–1230.

O'Connor, R. (2017, March 27). The Fearless Girl statue will stay on Wall Street until 2018. *The Independent*. Retrieved on June 11, 2017 from: www.independent.co.uk/arts-entertainment/art/news/fearless-girl-charging-bull-wall-street-new-york-broadway-2018-bronze-statue-stand-up-a7651471.html

O'Hara, R. E., Gibbons, F.X., Gerrard, M., Li, Z., & Sargent, J. D. (2012). Greater exposure to sexual content in popular movies predicts earlier sexual debut and risk taking. *Psychological Science*, *23*(9), 984–993. doi:10.1177/095679761143552

Pelli, D. G., Farell, B., & Moore, D. C. (2013). The remarkable inefficiency of word recognition. *Nature*, *423*(6941), 752–756.

Pringle, H., & Thompson, M. (1999). *Brand spirit: How cause-related marketing builds brands*. Chichester, UK: John Wiley.

Pryor, F. (2007, February 8). On the trail of artist Banksy. BBC News. Retrieved on May 15, 2009, from: http://news.bbc.co.uk/2/hi/entertainment/6343197.stm

Ralli, T. (2005, September 5). Who's a looter? In storm's aftermath, pictures kick up a different kind of tempest. *The New York Times*, p. 6.

Rosica, C. (2007). *The authentic brands: How today's top entrepreneurs connect with customers*. Paramus, NJ: Noble Press.

Salter, B. (2009, March 26). 8 hours a day spent on screens, study finds. *New York Times*, p. B-6.

Scudder, J. N., & Mill, C. B. (2009). The credibility of shock advocacy: Animal rights attack messages. *Public Relations Review*, *35*, 162–164.

Selling tobacco: Defending the rights of the Marlboro man. (1990, April 21). *The Economist*, *315*, p. 84.

Shaheen, J.G. (2009). *Reel bad Arabs*. Northampton, MA: Olive Branch Press.

Simons, H. W. (2001). *Persuasion in society*. Thousand Oaks, CA: Sage.

Simpson, K. E. (2008). Classic and modern propaganda in documentary film. *Teaching of Psychology*, *35*(2), 103–108.

Statista (2017). Media advertising spending in the United States from 2015 to 2020 (in billion U.S. dollars). Retrieved on June 14, 2017 from: www.statista.com/statistics/272314/advertising-spending-in-the-us/

Stenberg, G. (2006). Conceptual and perceptual factors in the picture superiority effect. *European Journal of Cognitive Psychology, 18*(6), 813–847.

Su, W. (2016). *China's encounter with global Hollywood*. Lexington, KY: University of Kentucky Press.

Suh, T. (1999). Visual persuasion. *Communication Research Trends, 19*(3), 1–15.

Unterberger, L. (2001, July 16). Mimicking a movie star. *The Milwaukee Sentinel Journal*, p. 4E.

Von Blum, P. (1976). *The art of social conscience*. New York: Universe Books.

Von Blum, P. (1994). *Other visions, other voices: Women political artists in greater Los Angeles*. Lanham, MD: University Press of America.

Walsh-Childers, K. (2017). *Mass media and heath: Examining media impact on individuals and the health environment*. New York: Routledge.

Waxman, S. (2000, December 21). 1999 saw more roles for minorities in film, TV. *The Washington Post,* p. C7.

Welkos, R. W. (2001, July 2). Multiethnic movies ringing true with youths. *Los Angeles Times,* p. A1.

Whitty, S. (2001, August 26). Who are the Asians on screen? New stereotypes no better than old. *The San Diego Union Tribune,* p. F2.

Woodward, G. C., & Denton, R. E. (1999). *Persuasion and influence in American life* (3rd ed.). Prospect Heights, IL: Wadsworth.

Zimmerman, N. (2012, June 22). Supermarket offers free groceries to first 100 naked shoppers. www.gawker.com. Retrieved on July 7, 2012 from: http://gawker.com/5920613/supermarket-offers-free-groceries-to-first-100-naked-shoppers

Zumwalt, J. (2001, November 13). How a powerful image can shape a war. *Los Angeles Times,* p. B12.

Esoteric Forms of Persuasion

PREVIOUS CHAPTERS HAVE DEALT with fairly "mainstream" types of persuasion. In this chapter, we examine more esoteric forms of persuasion. The topics we discuss in this section often receive short shrift or are neglected entirely by other texts. Yet we find that these are among the most interesting topics to students and laypersons. We include them here partly because they are so intriguing, partly because there are important research findings, and partly to debunk some of the myths and superstitions surrounding these topics. The topics we'll examine are color, subliminal persuasion, backward masking or reverse speech, neurolinguistic programming, music as persuasion, and the role of smell in persuasion.

COLOR AS PERSUASION: THE GRASS IS ALWAYS GREENER

Sheriff Joe Arpaio of Arizona was known as "America's toughest sheriff." Besides making male prisoners work on chain gangs, he also required them to wear pink underwear—that is, until an appeals court overturned the practice. Wrote one justice, "it is a fair inference that the color is chosen to symbolize a loss of masculine identity" (Williams, 2012, p. AA-2). Whether one agrees with Arpaio's methods or not, clearly color was being used as an instrument of power and control.

In this section, we examine some of the ways in which color influences people. The meanings we assign to color are based, in part, on biology and, in part, on culture and socialization (Genschow, Reutner, & Wänke, 2012). In nature, for example, red often serves as a warning, or *aposematism*, signifying toxicity. In human society, red often signifies danger as well. Ignore a red stop sign or a red traffic light, for example, and you do so at your own risk.

Color Coded at Birth: Dyed in the Wool

Color exerts an enormous influence on our lives—and not just in our choice of undies. Take clothing colors, for instance. In much of the United States and Western Europe, newborn girls are swaddled in pink, boys in blue. Thus, gender differentiation, through color, begins in infancy (Paoletti, 2012). In old Westerns, the good guys wear white hats, the bad guys black. Good and evil are thus differentiated by color. Business executives often wear "power" colors to signify their status. Brides traditionally wear white to symbolize their purity. Schools adopt uniforms to minimize clothes consciousness and focus students' attention on learning. Soldiers and hunters wear camouflage clothing to evade detection. Scientists wear white lab coats, at least on TV, to convey their expertise. Gang members display their gangs' colors to mark their turf. Sports fans wear color-coordinated clothing, or even face paint, to express their identification with their team.

Colorful Associations: A Blonde Walks Into a Bar . . .

In Chapter 3, we discussed the importance of attitudinal associations. We also have strong associations with colors. In politics, for instance, states are referred to as red or blue based on their political leanings. Likewise, we often classify occupations according to colors of collars: white, blue, and sometimes pink or green. The meanings attached to such colors shape our beliefs, attitudes, and behaviors. For example, companies boast about their green initiatives—which, not coincidentally, makes for good PR. A recent study shows this strategy is effective. Seo and Scammon

(2017) asked college students to evaluate a product, based only on its packaging. All versions included a label expressing support for the Sierra Club's environmental work. What differed was the color of the packaging: Green, red, blue, yellow, or gray. Products with green or blue packaging were rated more positively than the other colors.

The associations we have with colors are highly contextual. At a funeral, wearing black conveys grief or sorrow. At a nightclub, however, wearing black may suggest class or elegance. Red may signify sin in one context (red light district, scarlet woman) or reverence in another (the Pope's red shoes, red vestments). The meanings associated with colors are also culture bound. Traditionally, brides in America have worn white gowns, while brides in China have worn red gowns. That has changed, though, with more Chinese brides adopting the Western white wedding gown (Labrecque, Patrick, & Milne, 2013).

Seeing Red

To better illustrate how associations with colors can affect attitudes and behavior, let's examine the color red in a specific context: Grading students' papers. Has a teacher ever returned a paper to you that was "bleeding" with red ink? Did it make you feel like a dunce? If so, you are not alone. Studies on the *red pen effect*, as it is known, have prompted many school districts to encourage teachers to avoid marking papers in red, which is associated with failure, in favor of purple or some other color. You may scoff, but as it turns out, the color red significantly affects students and teachers alike. Studies show that even brief exposure to the color red before or during a challenging intellectual task can activate thoughts of failure and hinder performance (Elliot, Maier, Binser, Friedman, & Pekrun, 2009; Elliot, Maier, Moller, Friedman, & Meinhardt, 2007; Lichtenfeld, Maier, Elliot, & Pekrun, 2009). What's more, using a red pen affects the grader, too. Evaluators who graded essays using red pens identified significantly more mistakes than evaluators who used blue pens. Red pens thus predisposed the evaluators to grade more harshly (Rutchick, Slepian, & Ferris, 2010). Our advice: Give your instructor a purple pen when you submit your next paper. If you are a teacher, manager, or other evaluator, consider using a less pejorative color to minimize defensiveness. Even positive feedback in red may be ignored.

Color and Branding: Big Blue, Red Bull, and Pink (Victoria's Secret)

Not only do corporations use logos to identify their brands, they also rely on color. Color is "a central aspect of a brand's visual identity" (Labrecque, Patrick, & Milne, 2013, p. 193). To illustrate, if you were told that a laptop was white, could you guess the brand? A Mac, no doubt. Color serves as an identifier for many brands, such as McDonald's (golden arches), Coke (red), and Rabobank (orange and blue). According to one source, color can increase brand recognition by 80 percent (Goldstein, 2011). Philanthropic causes also use color to gain recognition. Livestrong's yellow wristbands and the Susan G. Komen Foundation's pink ribbons are cases in point.

In some instances, a color becomes synonymous with a brand, such as UPS's ubiquitous Pullman brown trucks or Reese's Pieces' orange, yellow, and brown wrappers. What's more, the distinctive colors of a particular brand are often trademarked. T-Mobile's specific shade of magenta is a trademarked color. So is Tiffany's distinctive robin-egg blue. Owens-Corning even trademarked the shade of

FIGURE 15.1
An author aboard his
trusty John Deere
tractor.
Source: Photo by Debora
Seiter.

pink used in its fiberglass insulation. One of the ever-gullible authors bought a
John Deere tractor largely because he liked its venerable green and yellow color,
which is trademarked (see Figure 15.1). Companies protect their brand colors, too.
Cadbury won a lawsuit for trademark infringement when Nestlé also tried to market
a chocolate bar with a purple wrapper (Clark, 2011). A similar suit was filed by high
heel designer, Christian Louboutin, whose pricey shoes have distinctive red soles,
against Yves Saint Laurent.

Color and Emotion: Mood Indigo

We often refer to emotions by color. You might hear someone say, "I'm feeling blue,"
"He's seeing red," "She was green with envy," or "I'm tickled pink." A meta-analysis
revealed that different colors can and do affect our emotional state (Jalil, Yunus, &
Said, 2012). Individual color preferences, quite obviously, are a major determinant
in whether a given color is viewed favorably or unfavorably. Generally speaking,
warm colors such as red, orange, and yellow tend to be more stimulating, while cool
colors, such as blue, green, and purple tend to be more calming. As Gobé (2009)
explains, "Colors with long wavelengths are arousing (e.g., red is the most stimulating
color that will attract the eye faster than any other) and colors with short wavelengths
are soothing (e.g., blue, which actually lowers blood pressure, pulse, and respiration
rates)" (p. 80).

Consistent with this generalization, males rated a female wearing a red blouse as
more sexually attractive than the same female wearing a blue blouse (Elliot & Niesta,
2008; Niesta Kayser, Elliot, & Feltman, 2010). Similarly, waitresses wearing red
lipstick, as compared with pink, brown, or no lipstick, earned higher tips, but only

from male customers (Guéguen & Jacob, 2012). In addition, observers rated rooms with warm colors as more exciting and cool colors as more restful (Yildirim, Hidayetoglu, & Capanoglu, 2011). Want your new store to encourage hustle and bustle? Use warm colors. Want it to foster a sense of relaxation? Go with cool colors.

Women in White, Men in Blue

Uniform colors also evoke different emotional responses in people. Suppose you were a little kid about to get a vaccination. Would the nurse's uniform color affect your anxiety level? It just might. One study found that blue uniforms were perceived by kids as more calming than white uniforms (Albert, Burke, Bena, Morrison, Forney, & Krajewksi, 2013). For adult patients, nurses in white uniforms were perceived as more competent, professional, and efficient, whereas nurses wearing printed patterns were perceived as more caring, attentive, and approachable (Kucuk, L., Çömez, T., Kaçar, S., Sümeli, F., & Taşkiran, Ö, 2015; Skorupski & Rea, 2006). Thus, one color of scrubs might be better suited for an emergency room (ER) and another color or pattern for an intensive care unit (ICU).

Let's consider another type of uniform. Imagine you've just been pulled over by a police officer. Would the color of the officer's uniform affect your emotional state? Research shows that all-black uniforms are the most intimidating (Johnson, 2005). Black is authoritative, commanding more respect and attention (Nickels, 2008). However, a uniform consisting of a light-blue shirt and navy pants was judged to be more warm, friendly, and honest than all black (Johnson, 2005). Which image is most important for cops to project? Uniform colors may affect police officers' behavior too. Johnson (2013) found that police departments with dark uniforms were significantly more likely to use deadly force than departments with lighter uniforms.

Color and Behavior: Hue Made Me Do It

Color influences consumer ratings of products and product purchases. Color is one of the first cues that we perceive about products, often before we can touch, smell, or taste them. The use of color in product packaging therefore matters a great deal (Lichtlé, 2007). A color–product mismatch can turn off consumers. Would you buy Pepto Bismol if it were grey? Would you like Tidy Bowl if it made your toilet water red? We suspect not. Color also can be used to prime consumer reactions. In one study, participants were given orange or green pens to evaluate two soft drinks, one in an orange container (Fanta orange), the other in a green container (Sprite). Pen color functioned as a peripheral cue, such that ratings for Fanta were higher when using an orange pen and higher for Sprite when using a green pen (Berger & Fitzsimons, 2008).

Some of the ways in which color affects behavior are a bit weird. Take snacking, for example. When snacks are served on red plates or drinks in red cups, people tend to consume less (Genschow, Reutner, & Wänke, 2012). Why? Partly due to biology and partly due to social conditioning, red evokes avoidance reactions. As noted earlier, red is associated with danger, risk, and hazards. This finding may seem trivial until you consider the current epidemic of childhood obesity in the United States and elsewhere. If simple measures such as serving meals on red plates or trays can help reduce food intake, they are worth considering by parents, school districts, and health agencies.

The Color–Aggression Link: Men in Black

A host of studies have examined whether uniform color affects sports performance. Does donning a black uniform make an athlete think, "I'm *bad*"? An early study (Frank & Gilovich, 1988) found that NFL and NHL teams with black uniforms racked up more penalties. The finding was attributed, in part, to greater aggression by players and, in part, to selective perception by referees. Other studies have questioned the *color–aggression link*, finding no differences (Caldwell & Burger, 2011). A larger study, however, confirmed the link. Data from 25 NHL seasons (52,098 games) revealed that players wearing black uniforms were penalized more often, about two minutes of penalty time per game on average, than players wearing white (Webster, Urland, & Correll, 2012). There may a "chicken–egg" question involved as well. Do black uniforms make teams more aggressive or do more aggressive teams choose to wear black uniforms?

Color is not the "be all and end all" of persuasion. Nevertheless, color has an important supporting role to play on the stage of persuasion. Color can facilitate or inhibit influence attempts through associations, by activating attitudes or stereotypes, by evoking moods and emotional responses, and by altering behavior.

SUBLIMINAL INFLUENCE: HIDDEN MESSAGES OR HOKUM?

A good deal of misinformation surrounds the topic of subliminal influence. Most Americans believe subliminal messages are not only common in advertising but that they are highly effective as well (Broyles, 2006). Public belief in subliminal persuasion dates to the 1950s, when James Vicary claimed to have flashed the words "Eat popcorn" and "Drink Coca-Cola" on a movie screen. Allegedly, popcorn sales increased by almost 58 percent and Coke sales by 18 percent (Rogers, 1992–1993). Thus was born an urban myth. Vicary never achieved the results he claimed. His so-called experiment was merely a publicity stunt.

The Laboratory Versus the Real World

The fact of the matter is that subliminal effects have been documented clearly and convincingly in controlled laboratory conditions but almost never in real-world settings. The examples found in the real world tend to be isolated cases rather than organized attempts at "mind control." Most cases involving the use of subliminals appear to be pranks. Some Disney movies, for example, contain embedded images, but these appear to be acts of mischief by individual artists and animators rather than a corporate conspiracy (see, for example, www.snopes.com/disney/films/films.asp). Mind you, these cases only demonstrate that subliminal messages exist, not that they work.

What Is and Isn't Subliminal

Let's begin by clearing up some confusion surrounding the term *subliminal*. Literally, the term means below (*sub*) the threshold (*limen*) of human consciousness. Thus, a subliminal stimulus is one that is processed without conscious awareness. This is in contrast to *supraliminal* messages that are consciously processed. An image that is flashed so quickly that a person can't consciously register it is subliminal. An image that is fleeting yet recognizable is supraliminal. Subtle is not the same as subliminal. This distinction is important, because product placements in movies and TV shows are *not* subliminal. Advertisers *want* you to notice their products and/or logos.

Subliminal Advertising: Much Ado About Nothing

In the 1970s and 1980s, "pop psychology" books and magazine articles made it seem as if every ice cube in a magazine ad contained a hidden phallic symbol. Brian Wilson Key championed this view with his popular but unscientific books on subliminal advertising (Key, 1972, 1976, 1980). We've looked at the particular ads in question and, although we can discern some of the symbols and shapes Key mentions, we find his approach somewhat akin to staring at clouds. If one looks long enough and hard enough, one is bound to see a rubber ducky, the Virgin Mary, or some other vaguely discernible shape.

Embedded Images

More rigorous studies were carried out from the mid-1970s through the mid-1990s, many of which focused on *embedded images*. Embedded images are buried or hidden within an advertisement. Researchers, however, were unable to substantiate any of the grandiose claims about hidden images making people want things or buy things (Gable, Wilkens, & Harris, 1987).

Studies examining embedded sexual imagery have found some effects, but only in controlled laboratory settings. For example, Gillith and Collins (2016) found that subliminal exposure to unclothed versus clothed opposite sex images increased the desire to have sex. This was measured, however, only by whether participants (mostly males) were more likely to choose a condom or a pen as a reward for participating. Another investigation (Wernicke, Hofter, Jordan, Fromberger, Dechent, & Müller, 2017) using fMRI (neural imaging) identified some brain activity associated with subliminal sexual stimuli, but the findings were inconclusive.

Results like these led Trappey (1996) to conclude in his meta-analysis that "the results show no significant positive or negative effect . . . subliminal advertising does little to influence consumer behavior" (p. 527). After reviewing 50 years' worth of research on subliminal advertising, Broyles (2006) similarly announced that "subliminal advertising just is not effective" (p. 405). More recent books, such as Bullock's *The Secret Sales Pitch* (2004), also have been faulted for making unsubstantiated claims about subliminal ads (Broyles, 2006). In 2011, Jeff Warrick aired a documentary entitled *Programming the Nation?*, which relied on dated, anecdotal evidence of subliminal advertising (Catsoulis, 2011).

Proof of Existence Is Not Proof of Effectiveness

A key point to bear in mind is that the mere existence of subliminal messages does not prove their effectiveness. Let's assume, for the sake of argument, that there are subliminal messages in some Disney movies. In what way are they influential? Where is the proof that they have any effect on viewers, other than providing fodder for conspiracy theorists? If they are more than isolated pranks, how would they advance Disney's business model of providing family-friendly entertainment?

Subliminal Priming: That Rings a Bell

There is scant evidence that subliminal influence works in advertising. In laboratory studies, however, a method known as *subliminal priming* has enjoyed considerable success (Bargh, 2002; Kouider & Dehaene, 2007). A meta-analysis of masked prime studies found strong support for the technique (Van den Bussche, Van den Noortgate, & Reynvoet, 2009). So compelling is the evidence for priming that Brintazzoli, Soetens, Deroost, and Van den Bussche (2012) declared, "the existence of unconscious subliminal perception is no longer questioned in an experimental context" (p. 824).

Methods vary, but a typical priming technique is as follows. First, participants view a *masked prime*. The mask is simply a string of characters covering up a word. For example, the characters #### could be used to mask the word *salt*. Second, the mask is removed and the *subliminal prime* is presented. Thus, the word *salt* might appear for 30 milliseconds, too quickly to be consciously perceived. Third, a *target word* that is consciously visible, for example, the word *pepper*, replaces the prime. Participants who are primed by the word *salt* tend to recognize the word *pepper* faster than participants who are not primed.

Importance of a Prior Need or Drive

For priming to work, however, it appears that a prior need or drive state must exist (Strahan, Spencer, & Zanna, 2002; Verwijmeren, Karremans, Bernritter, Stroebe, & Wigboldus, 2011). That is, for a subliminal prime about food to work, a person must be hungry. For a subliminal prime about a beverage to be effective, a person must be thirsty. The need or drive state increases receptivity to priming. In a controlled setting, for example, participants were exposed to subliminal images of happy or angry faces (Winkielman, Berridge, & Wilbarger, 2005). Then they sampled a lemon-lime-flavored drink. After reporting how thirsty they were, the participants were instructed to drink as much as they wanted. Participants exposed to the happy faces consumed much more of the new drink than those exposed to the angry faces, but only—and this is the key—if they were already thirsty. The amounts consumed by nonthirsty participants, whether exposed to happy or angry faces, did not differ significantly. Priming thus appeared to act as a trigger, but only for those whose thirst needed to be quenched.

Other studies have found similar results. Bermeitinger, Goelz, Johr, Neumann, Ecker, and Doerr (2009) asked participants to complete a task requiring high concentration. Half were well rested; the other half were tired. Before completing the task, participants in each group were subliminally primed with logos for a sugar pill called Dextro. Primed participants, who were also tired, consumed far more sugar pills than those who were not tired. The investigators concluded that "subjects' choice of a specific product is influenced by subliminally presented information only if there is a motivational state congruent with the subliminally presented stimulus" (p. 325).

Not So Fast: Limitations of Subliminal Priming

Although priming has been demonstrated in controlled laboratory settings, we wish to emphasize the practical limitations of this technique. Participants in laboratories are free from other distractions. They are instructed to pay close attention to the priming messages. The target words immediately follow the primes. The effects of priming are also fleeting. As Brintazzoli and colleagues (2012) cautioned, "the short-lived nature of the influence of subliminal information casts serious doubt on its effectiveness in everyday life and advertising" (p. 825). What's more, the minor effects of priming in laboratory studies can be nullified simply by informing participants of the presence of a subliminal message and warning them not to be influenced (Verwijmeren, Karremans, Bernritter, Stroebe, & Wigboldus, 2013). The real world is a very different environment, one chock-full of media clutter. A myriad of supraliminal stimuli vie for our attention. People don't always pay close attention to messages. We are aware of no studies demonstrating any commercial success at using subliminal priming.

By the way, do you suddenly feel smarter or like this book even more? The reason we ask is because we included a "subliminal" message at the top of p. 369. It is in very small type. Did you see it? Did it consciously register? Did it work?

Subaudible Messages: The Power of Suggestion

How would you like to lower your blood pressure, improve your memory, lose weight, release your body's natural healing forces, stop procrastinating, and win the lottery? These are just *some* of the claims that have been made on behalf of subliminal self-help audiotapes and CDs. The problem is that they don't work (Benoit & Thomas, 1992; Greenwald, Spangenberg, Pratkanis, & Eskenazi, 1991; Mitchell, 1995; Spangenberg, Obermiller, & Greenwald, 1992; Staum & Brotons, 1992). Other than provide soothing sounds, hiding reaffirming messages in ambient music accomplishes nothing. Believing can, in and of itself, produce changes in people, but such changes are the result of a *placebo effect* and have nothing to do with the content of the tapes or CDs themselves. A placebo effect follows the age-old notion that "thinking makes it so."

Backward Masking and Reverse Speech: Turn Me On, Dead Man

Can satanic, backward-masked lyrics cause impressionable teens to commit suicide? That is what the plaintiffs in a lawsuit filed against Ozzy Osbourne's record label claimed. The suit charged that backward-masked lyrics on the *Blizzard of Ozz* album drove a teen to commit suicide (Harmon, 1995). A similar suit was filed by the parents of two teens who committed suicide after listening to backward-masked lyrics on Judas Priest's *Stained Class* album (Goleman, 1990; Phillips, 1990). In both cases, the judges ruled in favor of the defendants, citing the lack of any causal connection between the reversed lyrics and the teens' deaths. The authors have listened to both albums and have experienced no suicidal tendencies. Justin Bieber tunes, however, are another story! All kidding aside, there are no credible studies showing that listening to reversed speech produces any effects. As Smith (2011) noted, "Psychological studies have produced no evidence that listeners are influenced, consciously or unconsciously, by the content of backward messages" (p. 539).

It is possible to infer meanings from reversed speech, but these may be a matter of coincidence. Vokey (2002), for example, noted that the phrase "Jesus loves you," when played backward, sounds like "we smell sausage" (p. 248). Some rock songs do contain backward-masked lyrics (the Beatles' song "Revolution 9" and Pink Floyd's "Goodbye Blue Sky," for example) but, as is the case with subliminal messages, their mere *presence* doesn't prove their *effectiveness*. Scientific studies of

"Now, that's product placement!"

backward masking have failed to demonstrate any effects on listeners (Kreiner, Altis, & Voss, 2003; Langston & Anderson, 2000; Swart & Morgan, 1992; Vokey & Read, 1985).

What Advertisers Really Do

Advertisers are not really interested in subliminals, subaudible messages, or reverse speech. What advertisers seek to do is to connect their products with favorable images and idealized lifestyles. Product placement is one way of accomplishing this. Placements in movies and TV exceed $6 billion dollars per year (PQ Media, 2015). According to Morgan (2005) "between 15–30 products are inserted into every half hour of television programming" (p. 62). Morgan Spurlock's (2011) documentary *The Greatest Movie Ever Sold* lampoons this trend.

Placements may be blatant or subtle, but they are in no sense subliminal. Some product placements operate at a low level of awareness, but they remain a form of supraliminal persuasion. In sum, we believe consumers have little to fear from subliminal advertising at this time.

NEUROLINGUISTIC PROGRAMMING: THE EMPEROR'S NEW CLOTHES

Did you know that by uttering a few magical words, you can get anyone to do your bidding? Some folks would like you to believe in such hocus-pocus. They claim that they can teach you, in a few easy steps, how to hypnotize people with your words. Some claim their techniques will help you get dates, overcome phobias, cure depression, improve spelling, alleviate colds and flu, and enlarge your breasts or penis.

Don't reach for your wallet just yet. What these folks are peddling is based on *neurolinguistic programming*, or NLP, which is a mix of linguistics, psychology, and hypnotism (Gow, Reupert, & Maybery, 2006). The original theory, developed by Richard Bandler and John Grinder (1975, 1979), lies somewhere between pop psychology and junk science. It is popular with authors of self-help books, such as Tony Robbins, and others on the lecture circuit. Despite the extravagant claims, there is scant evidence that NLP works. Indeed, although one meta-analysis (Zaharia, Reiner, & Schütz, 2015) found positive results when using NLP to reduce phobias, the authors acknowledged that "there is a major lack of high-quality data from observational, experimental studies or randomized trials on this field" (p. 361). What's more, most credible experts, e.g., those who don't stand to profit by writing, speaking, or training about the subject, denounce NLP as a form of pseudoscience (Corballis, 1999; Gumm, Walker, & Day, 1982; Heap, 1988, 2008; Sharpley, 1984, 1987; Thaler Singer & Lalich, 1996).

The basic idea behind NLP is that a person's inner, unconscious mind determines how he or she responds to persuasive messages. All persuaders have to do is use a few clever linguistic strategies and—presto!—they can "program" another person's responses. Certain words and nonverbal behaviors allegedly have hypnotic power and evoke a subconscious reaction in people, or so the theory goes. They do this by activating a person's *primary representational system* (PRS), which is reflected in the five senses.

For example, a salesperson who sensed that a consumer was "visually" oriented, based on the consumer's language style, mannerisms, and gaze, could adapt a message to emphasize visual features about a product—e.g., "As you can see . . ." "take a look . . ." "watch this . . ." A salesperson who perceived a customer was "auditory" would adjust the sales pitch by saying "I hear you . . ." "it sounds like this is what you're after . . ." But how, you might wonder, does a salesperson know if a customer is primarily visual or auditory? According to NLP, a customer who looks up and to the left (memory) or right (invention) is accessing visual information; a customer who looks horizontally left (memory) or right (invention) is accessing auditory information (see Lankton, 1980).

Although NLP's proponents assert that certain words and phrases have hypnotic power, their claims are suspect. The theory itself is nebulous and the evidence for its effectiveness is largely anecdotal. We agree that people respond reflexively to certain words, such as *free* or *sale*. That is a long way from saying, however, that specific words, phrases, and nonverbal cues have hypnotic power. By way of example, in one study, the investigators compared an indirect message using NLP with a direct message without NLP (Dixon, Parr, Yarbrough, & Rathael, 2001). They found that the direct message without NLP was significantly more effective than the indirect message employing NLP. As the investigators concluded, "Neurolinguistic programming may not be an effective device for improving the persuadability of messages" (p. 549).

In our view, NLP is much like the emperor's new clothes—people believe in it because others seem to believe in it. The underlying assumptions of NLP so annoyed one expert in neuroscience that he declared it "neurobabble" (Miller, 1986).

MUSIC AS PERSUASION

Have you ever heard an advertising jingle and then been unable to get the tune out of your head the rest of the day? Are you able to sing along to tunes like "Break me off a piece of that ____ ____ bar," or, "I'm stuck on ____ ____ 'cause ____ ____ stuck on me"? If so, you're not alone. In fact, advertising agencies spend big bucks developing "earworms" like these. What's more, 86 percent of prime-time television commercials include some form of music (Allan, 2008). And when you stop to consider the role of music in persuasion, it's easy to see why. Indeed, music facilitates persuasion in a variety of ways that we examine next.

Music as a Central and Peripheral Cue

Song lyrics persuade. The lyrics to the famous McDonald's song "You deserve a break today" offer a case in point. When song lyrics persuade, they may do so through what Petty and Cacioppo (1986a, 1986b) call the central route to persuasion—that is, the song lyrics are thought about and reflected on by listeners. This was the case with anti-war protest songs in the 1960s. It may be the case with rap and hip-hop lyrics today.

Music also can persuade via the peripheral route to persuasion. Peripheral processing occurs when listeners hear, but don't actively attend to, the music. You may, for example, prefer to study with music playing (or blaring) in the background. Background music can affect a person's mood or emotions, without the person's full awareness.

Music in Advertising and Sales

Music and Branding: What's That Song?

Music is often used to bolster a brand's image by creating favorable associations. As Danny Turner, the head of Mood Media, the company formerly known as Muzak, emphasized, "major brands realize that to move forward . . . positive, emotional connections have to be made—and there's no better way to do that than music" (cited by Lazarus, 2017, p. C1). Chevy's "Like a rock . . ." song, for example, reinforces a rugged image for its pickup trucks. The congruity of a song with a brand, known as *musical fit*, affects consumers' perceptions of a product or service (North, Sheridan, & Areni, 2016; Zander, Apaolaza-Ibáñez, & Hartmann, 2010). Coca-Cola, for example, has been particularly successful at pairing pop songs with its brand image of joy, happiness, and love (Sanchez-Porras & Rodrigo, 2017). A Nielsen study found that TV commercials with music outperformed those without in four key areas; creativity, empathy, emotive power, and information power (2015).

Brand endorsements now appear regularly in song lyrics (Gloor, 2014). One study found that 30 percent of all songs, and 73 percent of rap songs in particular, included brand mentions (Craig, Flynn, & Holody, 2017). For example, Busta Rhymes's hit "Pass the Courvoisier" is credited with increasing sales of the cognac brand by 30 percent (Emling, 2004; Schemer, Matthes, Wirth, & Textor, 2008). In another song,

Run-DMC love their Adidas. Lady Gaga's song "Telephone" mentions at least eight brands, including Miracle Whip, Virgin Mobile, and Polaroid. Some of these are paid endorsements, but many are not. Such endorsements appear to enhance brand identity, even if consumers know that the artist was paid for the brand mention (Van Vaerenbergh, 2017).

Mere Exposure Effect: Hearing Is Believing

Another way that music helps to sell products is through the *mere exposure effect* (Wang & Chang, 2004; Zajonc, 1968), which we discussed in Chapter 9. Repeated exposure to an unfamiliar stimulus increases liking for the stimulus over time. If a commercial includes a popular song or a likable jingle, repeated airings of the spot will facilitate liking for the product (Hargreaves, 1984; Obermiller, 1985). This is only true up to a point, however. Excessive repetition of a song or jingle can become annoying.

Music as a Mnemonic Device

Music also functions as a *mnemonic device* in advertising (Yalch, 1991). A mnemonic device is simply a memory aid that facilitates recall. Can you remember which insurance company goes with "We are _____, Bum Puh Dum Bum, Bum Bum Bum"? Hint: J. K. Simmons is the spokesman. Some tunes help the consumer to spell out the product's name and thus remember it. The Oscar Mayer bologna song is an example. Other jingles surround the product's name with positive associations. Can you fill in the company name for the tune "Like a good neighbor, _____ _____ is there"? If you are familiar with these commercials, you probably came up with the brand names. According to North, Mackenzie, Law, and Hargreaves (2004), the right kind of music can increase brand recall by as much as 96 percent. To be effective, jingles must be simple. This is because the words in a jingle tend to be processed phonetically (e.g., as mere sounds) rather than semantically (as meanings).

Background Music: Shop Till You Drop

Retailers rely heavily on background music. Some stores, such as Abercrombie & Fitch, Starbucks, and Victoria's Secret, provide their own in-store music. Background music has been shown to affect mood (Bruner, 1990; Nielsen, 2015; Wiesenthal, Hennessy, & Totten, 2003), regulate shopping pace (Ding & Lin, 2011; Garlin & Owen, 2006), improve sports performance (Boutcher & Trenske, 1990; Elliott, Carr, & Savage, 2004), lower anxiety in healthcare settings (Pelletier, 2004; Rudin, Kiss, Wetz, & Sottile, 2007), and enhance task performance (Mayfield & Moss, 1989; Miller & Schyb, 1989). In one of our favorite studies, researchers played either French or German music in a wine shop and kept track of which wines sold the most. The sobering findings were that French wine sold better when French music was playing, while German wine sold better while German music was playing (North, Hargreaves, & McKendrick, 1999). The shoppers' affective responses to the background music thus influenced their purchase decisions.

In their meta-analysis, Roschk, Loureiro, and Breitsohl (2017) concluded that background music significantly increases pleasure, satisfaction, and purchase intentions. Of course, one would expect the results to be modest, given that background music is only one of many environmental cues. Because background music is now so pervasive, some suggest that *habituation* may occur, whereby people become desensitized to background music over time (Kämpfe, Sedlmeier, & Renkewitz, 2010).

Music Videos and Persuasion: Is Hip-Hop Harmful?

A great deal has been written about the influence of music videos on the attitudes and behaviors of young people. Today, a typical music video is essentially a three-minute commercial for the artist, the brands that he or she endorses, and the lifestyle he or she espouses. There is little doubt that music videos influence fashions, trends, slang, sexual mores, and model social behavior. The question is how much they do so and how beneficial or detrimental the social proof found in music videos is.

Concerned parents and media critics have roundly criticized music videos for glorifying materialism and wealth (Kalis & Neuendorf, 1989), for being overly sexual (Hansen & Hansen, 1990; Kistler & Lee, 2012), and for promoting sexism (Barongan & Hall Nagayama, 1995; Peterson & Pfost, 1989). Indeed, as Wright and Qureshi (2015) reported, "1/3 of popular songs contain explicit sexual content and 2/3 of these references are degrading" (p. 228). The *general aggression model* (GAM) posits that music can prime aggressive behavior by activating negative thoughts or scripts in listeners (Anderson & Bushman, 2002). Support for the GAM is well-documented (Anderson, Carnagey, & Eubanks, 2003). A reverse effect has also been found, however, such that songs with pro-equality lyrics generate more favorable attitudes toward women (Böhm, Ruth, & Schramm, 2016; Greitmeyer, Hollingdale, & Traut-Mattausch, 2015).

With regard to musical genres, rap and hip-hop, in particular, have been singled out for criticism (Dunbar, Kubrin, & Scurich, 2016). "Rap music," one group of scholars notes, "has been blamed for youth violence, the rise of gangs and gang-related crime, drug use, and violence against women" (Reyna, Brandt, & Tendayi, 2009, p. 362). Some critics have warned that frequent exposure to rap and hip-hop is associated with illicit drug use, alcohol abuse, and misogyny (Adams & Fuller, 2006; Chen, Miller, Grube, & Waiters, 2006; Parker-Pope, 2007).

In response, defenders argue that rap and hip-hop music give a voice to the disenfranchised and serve as a medium for urban empowerment (Reyna et al., 2009). Proponents argue that some music videos make important socio-political statements and that others simply mirror the crass materialism and rampant sexism of the larger society. Rap and hip-hop artists respond that the mainstream media paint a distorted picture of rap and that the language and images used reflect the harsh realities of inner-city life (Brown & Campbell, 1986; Chambers & Morgan, 1992; Cummings & Roy, 2002; Tiddle, 1996). Dyson (1993), for example, classifies rap music as a form of resistance that empowers African Americans. He stresses that rap combines social protest, musical creation, and cultural expression all at the same time. Lynch (2003) states that hip-hop brings people from different races and cultures together.

Whether one perceives the messages in music videos as positive or negative, it is difficult to deny that such music serves to shape attitudes, beliefs, intentions, motivations, and behaviors. This is particularly true for adolescents who are heavy viewers of music videos (Council on Communications and Media, 2009). One must be cautious about making direct causal inferences, however, between what juveniles see or hear and their subsequent behavior. There are plenty of alternative sources for modeling behavior.

Weaponizing Music: What a Buzz Kill

Is subjecting someone to awful music akin to waterboarding? How much Miley Cyrus music can one human being take? It was reported that the U.S. military used music as a form of "torture lite" during the war in Iraq (Connor, 2008). One of the songs was Barney the Dinosaur's "I Love You, You Love Me." Amnesty International is investigating the use of music in interrogations.

Music has also been used as a deterrent. In 2009, the U.S. Border Patrol commissioned a CD, *Migra Corridos*, comprising popular Mexican ballads warning of the dangers of crossing the border illegally. The U.S. Border Patrol did not reveal that it was behind the CD, songs from which were played on several dozen Mexican radio stations (Surdin, 2009). Should music be used like barbed wire to repel people?

There have been reports that classical music was used to drive away the homeless, panhandlers, and gang members from fast-food restaurants and convenience stores (Hirsch, 2012). One officer commented, "If you're a tough guy and you like rock or rap, you're not going to sit there and listen to Tchaikovsky" (Holt, 1996, p. 2). In what has been termed the "Manilow Method," the town of Rockdale, near Sydney, initiated a campaign to discourage teens from congregating at a park late at night. Music by Barry Manilow was played over loudspeakers from 9 p.m. until midnight (Hirsch, 2007). We have to wonder, did the town pay Mr. Manilow any royalties?

Cautions: Face the Music

Before you get a hankering to use music to persuade others, bear in mind the following caveats. First, for music to be persuasive, there must be a good fit; the type of music must match the particular product, brand, purpose, and audience for which it is intended. Second, music shouldn't overpower the verbal content of a message. In a sales setting, for example, quieter music allows for more interaction between the salesperson and the customer. Third, music will probably have little effect on highly involved receivers who tend to concentrate on the substance of the message anyway. Music is best used on low-involved receivers who will process the message peripherally (Park & Young, 1986). In most cases, music functions as a useful supplement to verbal persuasion. Rarely can music be used as a substitute for verbal persuasion.

AROMA AND PERSUASION

Although few texts discuss the subject, smell plays an important role in the process of persuasion. Selling smells is a big business. Sales of fragrances and perfumes are expected to grow to $51 billion by 2022 (Global Industry Analysts, 2016). Think of all the fragrances you can buy to make you feel better; you can douse yourself in cologne or perfume, scent your car's interior, and place air fresheners throughout your home. You can use scented deodorants, soaps, and laundry detergent, as well as scented dishwashing liquid and toilet paper. In addition to personal uses of fragrances, the use of ambient (background) fragrances in the workplace and in retail settings is beginning to play an increasingly prominent role. In this section, we examine the role of fragrances and aromas as forms of influence.

Perfume: Romance in a Bottle

The fragrance industry is one in which a product often "wins by a nose." But is it the actual fragrance that sells or the associations that are paired with it? Scent alone isn't what sells perfume. The promise of romance sells perfume. The marketing themes associated with fragrances revolve around images of romance, intrigue, sensuality, and, of course, sex. "Between madness and infatuation," a Calvin Klein ad proclaims, "lies obsession" (for Obsession perfume). The slogan for FCUK's fragrance was far less subtle. "Scent to Bed," the ads proclaimed.

Love Stinks

Through images and innuendo, fragrance ads create the impression that using their products will increase your sexual attractiveness. But do perfumes make any actual difference? Do they help attract dates, win over lovers, or make one feel better about oneself? Empirical research on this question is mixed, with some studies showing that fragrances increase attraction and others showing they do not (Baron, 1983; Cann & Ross, 1989).

An interesting study that casts doubt on the allure of perfumes was conducted by Hirsch (cited in Stolberg, 1994). Male medical students were recruited as subjects for the study. Blood pressure monitors were attached to the volunteers' genitals while they smelled a variety of fragrances, including Chanel No. 5 and Obsession. The

FIGURE 15.3
"It's the smell of money."

FIGURE 15.4
A fragrance designer for Givaudan-Roure Corp. plies his trade.

Source: Photo by Joe Tabacca.

results? The only smell that consistently increased blood pressure, the measure of sexual arousal used in the study, was that of cinnamon buns! The results seem to reinforce the adage that the way to a man's heart is, after all, through his stomach. As with the preceding study, these results may also be questioned. Let's face it, having an apparatus attached to one's genitals doesn't approximate a real-world setting for arousal (not for most folks, anyway). In such a clinical environment, the participants may not have responded as they otherwise would.

Bear in mind that scent is only *one* factor in the overall attractiveness equation. Other factors include such things as physical appearances, personalities, and common interests, to name but a few. One would be foolish, indeed, to believe that fragrance alone could serve as the basis for a meaningful, lasting relationship.

Ambient Aromas: Something Special in the Air

Although there is little research on the relationship between fragrance and attraction, there is a sizable body of research on the ways in which ambient aromas affect people. We consider three such ways here: Mood or emotion, task performance, and shopping behavior.

Aromas and Moods: Am I Blue?

Background fragrances have been shown to have a calming effect on patients in healthcare settings. For example, vanilla and heliotropin (similar to baby powder) reduced anxiety in patients undergoing an MRI scan (Redd & Manne, 1991; Stolberg, 1994). Researchers have found that scents can influence people's emotional states in nonmedical settings as well. For example, investigators asked college students to write a brief essay about a childhood memory. Half the students composed their essays in a room with a mild floral scent. The other half wrote in an unscented room. The students in the scented condition used happy, positive terms three times more often than their counterparts in the unscented condition. What's more—and this is the part of the study we love—students in both groups were then instructed to direct a mime to act out their childhood memory. Some 75 percent of the students in the scented condition touched the mime while giving directions, compared to only 15 percent in the unscented condition (Welsh, 2011).

Another of our favorite studies (Hanisch, 1982), because of its unusual method, examined whether pleasant fragrances could reduce arachnophobia (fear of spiders) among females. The researcher dangled a spider at varying distances from the participants' faces. Part of the time, the participants were exposed to a pleasant, unfamiliar scent. Part of the time they were not. The pleasant fragrance reduced anxiety and allowed the spider to be placed closer to the participants' faces than the no-fragrance condition. The researcher didn't mention whether the spider liked the fragrance or not.

Aromas and Task Performance: Smell That Productivity

One area in which scents have been shown to have an effect is task performance. Several studies have shown that mild fragrances can improve the speed, accuracy, and efficiency with which people complete tasks (Hirsch, cited in Stolberg, 1994; Rotten, 1983; Sugano & Sato, 1991; Warm, Parasuraman, & Dember, 1990). For example, Baron and Kalsher (1998) found that a pleasant ambient fragrance improved driving performance on a simulated driving task. Moreover, Baron (1997) found that shoppers in a mall were more than twice as likely to help a stranger in the presence of pleasant ambient aromas (roasting coffee or baking cookies).

Scent Marketing: Follow Your Nose

Branded fragrances are increasingly being used to promote brand identity. Abercrombie & Fitch was among the first to market its own fragrance, called *Fierce* (Smiley, 2014). Other brands soon followed suit. Cadillac, Lincoln, Marriott, United Airlines, and Verizon all have branded fragrances. As of 2017, Ikea was poised to launch its own fragrance. Early reports hint at the smell of cinnamon buns. We haven't gotten a whiff yet, but we think the true essence of Ikea should be redolent of the tears, bitterness, and frustration that comes with trying to assemble one of their products. Finally, in a bizarre twist of fragrance, the fast-food chain KFC created fried-chicken scented sunscreen. What better way to fight sunburn than to wade into shark-infested waters smelling like meat?

Ambient Aromas and Consumer Behavior

Retail stores are increasingly using ambient odors to motivate shoppers. But does pumping fragrances into the air make customers buy more? A meta-analysis of aroma studies found that background fragrances resulted in increased arousal, pleasure, satisfaction, and intention to purchase (Roschk, Loureiro, & Breitsohl, 2017). Other research has shown that pleasant ambient aromas can increase shopping time (Knasko, 1989; Teerling, Nixdorf, & Koster, 1992) and improve product evaluations (Bosmans, 2006).

That said, researchers seem to agree that purchasing decisions are too complex to be influenced solely by smell, and not all studies find aromas to be persuasive. For instance, one study conducted in a shopping mall found no effects for background smells (Teller & Dennis, 2012). Not only that, one study shows that if consumers get wind of the fact that ambient aromas are being manipulated as a marketing ploy, they will become more skeptical toward the brand, the store, or the product in question (Lunard, 2012).

Caveats and Qualifications

Before you rush out to buy a case of room air-fresheners to make you feel better, study harder, and work more efficiently, keep the following in mind: First, there are large variations in individual preferences for smells. A scent that works on one person may not work on another. One of the authors, for example, likes the smell of a skunk from afar. Second, as was the case with subliminal research, some of the effects reported in these studies may be attributed to a placebo effect. The participants' expectations that smells affect behavior might account for the changes observed. Third, the repetitive use of scents can lead to counterconditioning such that an initially pleasant scent comes to be perceived as unpleasant. The smell of vanilla, for example, has been shown to be relaxing. But if it is introduced every time a child receives a vaccination, the smell may become aversive. Finally, there may be ethical as well as health-related concerns involved in using fragrances to influence people. People can close their eyes or look away from an image that offends them. They can't stop breathing or turn off their noses, however. We address ethical questions arising from the use of fragrances in Chapter 16.

SUMMARY

In this chapter, we examined several esoteric forms of persuasion: Color, subliminal messages, subaudible messages, backward masking or reverse speech, neurolinguistic processing, music as persuasion, and smell as persuasion. Despite the public's belief in subliminal persuasion, subliminal effects have only been demonstrated in highly controlled laboratory settings. At present, subliminal priming is not commercially viable. Embedded words and images, subaudible messages, and backward masking have not been shown to influence people. Neurolinguistic processing is a popular, but unproven phenomenon. Music was shown to be an important component of persuasion. Music facilitates persuasion in a variety of ways such as reinforcing advertising images, serving as a mnemonic device, and influencing receivers' moods. Though overlooked by most persuasion researchers, smell was also shown to be a useful tool for persuasion if the right conditions are met. Ambient fragrances can enhance moods, improve task performance, and influence consumer behavior.

REFERENCES

Color

Albert, N. M., Burke, J., Bena, J. F., Morrison, S. M., Forney, J., & Krajewksi, S. (2013). Nurses' uniform color and feelings/emotions in school-aged children receiving health care. *Journal of Pediatric Nursing*, 28(2), 141–149. doi:10.1016/j.pedn.2012.03.032

Berger, J., & Fitzsimons, G. (2008). Dogs on the street, Pumas on your feet: How cues in the environment influence product evaluation and choice. *Journal of Marketing Research*, 45, 1–14.

Caldwell, D. F., & Burger, J. M. (2011). On thin ice: Does uniform color really affect aggression in professional hockey? *Social Psychology and Personality Science*, *2*(3), 306–310.

Clark, N. (2011, November 16). Cadbury wins right to the colour purple. *The Independent* (London), p. 54. Retrieved on June 6, 2012 from Lexis-Nexis Academic search engine.

Elliot, A. J., Maier, M. A., Binser, M. J., Friedman, R., & Pekrun, R. (2009). The effect of red on avoidance behavior. *Personality and Social Psychology Bulletin*, *35*, 365–375.

Elliot, A. J., & Niesta, D. (2008). Romantic red: Red enhances men's attraction to women. *Journal of Personality and Social Psychology*, *95*, 1150–1164.

Elliot, A. J., Maier, M. A., Moller, A. C., Friedman, R., & Meinhardt, J. (2007). Color and psychological functioning: The effect of red on performance attainment. *Journal of Experimental Psychology: General*, *136*, 154–168.

Frank, M. G., & Gilovich, T. (1988). The dark side of self- and social perception: Black uniforms and aggression in professional sports. *Journal of Personality and Social Psychology*, *54*(1), 74–85.

Genschow, O., Reutner, L., & Wänke, M. (2012). The color red reduces snack food consumption and soft drink intake. *Appetite*, *58*, 699–702. doi:10.1016/j.appet.2011.12.023

Gobé, M. (2009). *Emotional branding: The new paradigm for connecting brands to people*. New York: Allworth Press.

Goldstein, T. (2011). Brand packaging: Solving the mystery of shelf impact. Retrieved on June 4, 2012 from: www.brandingstrategyinsider.com/branding_and_colors/

Guéguen, N., & Jacob, C. (2012). Lipstick and tipping behavior: When red lipstick enhances waitress tips. *International Journal of Hospitality Management*, *31*, 1333–1335. doi:10.1016/j.ijhm.2012.03.012

Jalil, N. A, Yunus, R. M., & Said, N. S. (2012). Environmental colour impact upon human behavior: A review. *Procedia: Social and Behavioral Sciences*, *35*, 54–62.

Johnson, R. R. (2005). Police uniform color and citizen impression formation. *Journal of Police and Criminal Psychology*, *20*(2), 58–66.

Johnson, R. R. (2013). An examination of police department uniform color and police–citizen aggression. *Criminal Justice and Behavior*, *40*(2), 228–244. doi:10.1177/0093854812456644

Kucuk, L., Çömez, T., Kaçar, S., Sümeli, F., & Taşkiran, Ö. (2015). Psychiatric patients' perspective: Nursing uniforms. *Archives of Psychiatric Nursing*, *29*(6), 383–387. doi:10.1016/j.apnu.2015.06.016

Labrecque, L. I., Patrick, V. M., & Milne, G. R. (2013). The marketers' prismatic palette: A review of color research and future directions. *Psychology and Marketing*, *30*(2), 187–202. doi:10.1002/mar.20597

Lichtlé, M.-C. (2007). The effect of an advertisements' colour on emotions evoked by an ad and attitude towards the ad. *International Journal of Advertising*, *26*(1), 37–62.

Lichtenfeld, S., Maier, M. A., Elliot, A. J., & Pekrun, R. (2009). The semantic red effect: Processing the word red undermines intellectual performance. *Journal of Experimental Social Psychology*, *45*, 1273–1276. doi:10.1016/j.jesp.2009.06.003

Nickels, E. (2008). Good guys wear black: Uniform color and citizens impressions of police. *Policing: An International Journal of Police Strategies & Management*, *31*(1), 77–92. doi:10.1108/13639510810852585

Niesta Kayser, D., Elliot, A. J., & Feltman, R. (2010). Red and romantic behavior in men viewing women. *European Journal of Social Psychology*, *40*(6) 901–908. doi:10.1002/ejsp.757

Paoletti, J. B. (2012). *Pink and blue: Telling the boys from the girls in America*. Bloomington, IN: Indiana University Press.

Rutchick, A. M., Slepian, M. L., & Ferris, B. D. (2010). The pen is mightier than the word: Object priming of evaluative standards. *European Journal of Social Psychology, 40,* 704–708. doi:10.1002/ejsp.753

Seo J. Y., & Scammon, D. L. (2017). Do green packages lead to misperceptions? The influence of package color on consumers' perceptions of brands with environmental claims. *Marketing Letters,* OnlineFirst, 1–13. doi:10.1007/s11002–017–9420-y

Skorupski, V. V. J., & Rea, R. E. (2006). Patients' perceptions of today's nursing attire: Exploring dual images. *Journal of Nursing Administration, 36,* 393–402.

Webster, G. D., Urland, G. R., & Correll, J. (2012). Can uniform color color aggression? Quasi-experimental evidence from professional ice hockey. *Social Psychological and Personality Science, 3*(3), 274–281. doi:10.1177/1948550611418535

Williams, C. J. (2012, March 8). Ruling in jail dress code: New trial ordered in death of Arizona inmate forced to wear pink underwear. *Los Angeles Times,* p. AA-2.

Yildirim, S., Hidayetoglu, M., & Capanoglu, A. (2011). Effects of interior colors on mood and preference: Comparisons of two living rooms. *Perceptual and Motor Skills, 112*(2), 509–524.

Subliminals

Bargh, J. A. (2002). Losing consciousness: Automatic influences on consumer judgment, behavior, and motivation. *Journal of Consumer Research, 29*(2), 280–285.

Benoit, S. C., & Thomas, R. L. (1992). The influence of expectancy in subliminal perception experiments. *Journal of General Psychology, 119*(4), 335–341.

Bermeitinger, C., Goelz, R., Johr, N., Neumann, M., Ecker, U. K. H., & Doerr, R. (2009). The hidden persuaders break into the tired brain. *Journal of Experimental Social Psychology, 45,* 320–326.

Brintazzoli, G., Soetens, E., Deroost, N., & Van den Bussche, E. (2012). Conscious, but not unconscious, logo priming of brands and related words. *Consciousness and Cognition, 21,* 824–834.

Broyles, S. J. (2006). Subliminal advertising and the perpetual popularity of playing to people's paranoia. *Journal of Consumer Affairs, 40,* 392–406.

Bullock, A. (2004). *The secret sales pitch: An overview of subliminal advertising.* San Jose, CA: Norwich.

Catsoulis, J. (2011, August 19). Powers of hidden persuasion. *New York Times,* p. 4.

Gable, M., Wilkins, H., & Harris, L. (1987). An evaluation of subliminally embedded sexual stimuli. *Journal of Advertising, 16*(1), 26–30.

Gillith, O., & Collins, T. J. (2016). Unconscious desire: The affective and motivational aspects of subliminal sexual priming. *Archives of Sexual Behavior, 45*(1), 5–20. doi:10.1007/s10508–015–0609-y

Goleman, D. (1990, August 14). Research probes what the mind senses unaware. *New York Times,* pp. B7–B8.

Greenwald, A. G., Spangenberg, E. R., Pratkanis, A. R., & Eskenazi, J. (1991). Double-blind tests of subliminal self-help audiotapes. *Psychological Science, 2,* 119–122.

Harmon, A. (1995, October 1). High-tech hidden persuaders. *Los Angeles Times,* pp. A1, A28–29.

Key, W. B. (1972). *Subliminal seduction: Ad media's manipulation of a not so innocent America.* Englewood Cliffs, NJ: Prentice Hall.

Key, W. B. (1976). *Media sexploitation.* Englewood Cliffs, NJ: Prentice Hall.

Key, W. B. (1980). *Clam-plate orgy: And other subliminal techniques for manipulating your behavior.* Englewood Cliffs, NJ: Prentice Hall.

Kouider, S., & Dehaene, S. (2007). Levels of processing during non-conscious perception: A critical review of visual masking. *Philosophical Transactions of the Royal Society of London. Series B, Biological Sciences, 362*(1481), 857–875.

Kreiner, D. S., Altis, N. A., & Voss, C. W. (2003). A test of the effect of reverse speech on priming. *Journal of Psychology, 137*(3), 224–232.

Langston, W., & Anderson, J. C. (2000). Talking back [wards]: A test of the reverse speech hypothesis. *Skeptic, 8* (3), 30–35.

Mitchell, C. W. (1995). Effects of subliminally presented auditory suggestions of itching on scratching behavior. *Perceptual and Motor Skills, 80*(1), 87–96.

Morgan, M. (2005). Review of the book *The psychology of entertainment media*. Blurring the lines between entertainment and persuasion. *Mass Communication & Society, 8*(1), 61–74.

Phillips, C. (1990, July 16). Trial to focus on issue of subliminal messages in rock. *Los Angeles Times*, pp. F10–F11.

PQ Media. (2015). Media update: US product placement revenues up 13% in 1H15; pacing for 6th straight year of accelerated growth as value of TV, digital & music integrations surge (press release). Retrieved from: www.pqmedia.com/about-press-20150615.html

Rogers, S. (1992–1993). How a publicity blitz created the myth of subliminal advertising. *Public Relations Quarterly, 37*(4), 12–17.

Smith, J. (2011). Turn me on, dead media: A backward look at the re-enchantment of an old medium. *Television & New Media, 12*(6), 531–551. doi:10.1177/1527476410 397754

Spangenberg, E. R., Obermiller, C., & Greenwald, A. G. (1992). A field test of subliminal self-help audiotapes: The power of expectancies. *Journal of Public Policy and Marketing, 11*(2), 26–36.

Spurlock, M., (Director), Spurlock, M., & Chilnick, J. (Writers). (2011). *The greatest movie ever sold*. [DVD]. Culver City, CA: Sony Pictures Home Entertainment.

Staum, M. J., & Brotons, M. (1992). The influence of auditory subliminals on behavior: A series of investigations. *Journal of Music Therapy, 29*(3), 130–185.

Strahan, E. J., Spencer, S. J., & Zanna, M. P. (2002). Subliminal priming and persuasion: Striking while the iron is hot. *Journal of Experimental Social Psychology, 556–568.*

Swart, L. C., & Morgan, C. L. (1992). Effects of subliminal backward-recorded messages on attitudes. *Perceptual and Motor Skills, 75*(3, Part 2), 1107–1113.

Trappey, C. (1996). A meta-analysis of consumer choice and subliminal advertising. *Psychology & Marketing, 13*(5), 517–530.

Van den Bussche, E., Van den Noortgate, W., & Reynvoet, B. (2009). Mechanisms of masked priming: A meta-analysis. *Psychological Bulletin, 135*(3), 452–477.

Verwijmeren, T., Karremans, J. C., Stroebe, W., & Wigboldus, D. H. J. (2011). The workings and limits of subliminal advertising: The role of habits. *Journal of Consumer Psychology, 21*, 206–213.

Verwijmeren, T., Karremans, J.C., Bernritter, S.F., Stroebe, W., & Wigbolduss, D.H.J. (2013). Warning: You are being primed! The effect of a warning on the impact of subliminal ads. *Journal of Experimental Social Psychology, 49*, 1124–1129. doi:10.1016/j.jesp.2013.06.010

Vokey, J. R. (2002). Subliminal messages. In J. R. Vokey and S. W. Allen (Eds.), *Psychological sketches* (6th ed., pp. 223–246). Lethbridge, Alberta: Science Link.

Vokey, J. R., & Read, J. D. (1985). Subliminal messages: Between the devil and the media. *American Psychologist, 40*(11), 1231–1239.

Warrick, J. (Producer and Director). (2011). *Programming the nation?* Ignite Productions. International Film Circuit, USA.

Wernicke, M., Hofter, C., Jordan, K., Fromberger, P., Dechent, P., & Müller, J.L. (2017). Neural correlates of subliminally presented visual sexual stimuli. *Consciousness and Cognition, 49*, 35–52. doi:10.1016/j.concog.2016.12.011

Winkielman, P., Berridge, K. C., & Wilbarger, J. L. (2005). Unconscious affective reactions to masked happy versus angry faces influence consumption behavior and judgments of value. *Personality and Social Psychology Bulletin, 31*(1), 121–135.

NLP

Bandler, R., & Grinder, J. (1975). *The structure of magic: A book about language and therapy*. Palo Alto, CA: Science and Behavior Books.

Bandler, R., & Grinder, J. (1979). *Frogs into princes*. Moab, UT: Real People Press.

Corballis, M. C. (1999). Are we in our right minds? In S. Sala (Ed.), *Mind myths: Exploring popular assumptions about the mind and brain* (pp. 25–41). New York: John Wiley.

Dixon, P. N., Parr, G. D., Yarbrough, D., & Rathael, M. (1991). Neurolinguistic programming as a persuasive communication technique. *Journal of Social Psychology, 126*(4), 545–550.

Gow, K., Reupert, A., & Maybery, D. (2006). NLP in action: Theory and techniques in teaching and learning. In S. M. Hogan (Ed.), *Trends in learning research* (pp. 99–118). New York: Nova Science.

Gumm, W. B., Walker, M. K., & Day, H. D. (1982). Neurolinguistic programming: Method or myth? *Journal of Counseling Psychology, 29*(3), 327–330.

Heap, M. (1988). Neurolinguistic programming: An interim verdict. In M. Heap (Ed.), *Hypnosis: Current clinical, experimental, and forensic practices* (pp. 268–280). London: Croom Helm.

Heap, M. (2008). The validity of some early claims of neuro-linguistic programming. *Skeptical Intelligencer, 11*, 1–8.

Lankton, S. (1980). *Practical magic*. Cupertino, CA: Meta.

Miller, L. (1986, April). Megabrain: New tools and techniques for brain growth. *Psychology Today, 20*, 70–72.

Sharpley, C. F. (1984). Predicate matching in NLP: A review of research on the preferred representational system. *Journal of Counseling Psychology, 31*(2), 238–248.

Sharpley, C. F. (1987). Research findings on neuro-linguistic programming: Non-supportive data or an untestable theory? *Journal of Counseling Psychology, 34(1)*, 103–107.

Thaler Singer, M., & Lalich, J. (1996). *Crazy therapies: What are they? Do they work?* San Francisco, CA: Jossey Bass.

Zaharia, C., Reiner, M., & Schütz, P. (2015). Evidence-based neuro linguistic psychotherapy: A meta-analysis. *Psychiatria Danubina, 27*(4), 355–363.

Music

Adams, T. M., & Fuller, D. B. (2006). The words have changed but the ideology remains the same: Misogynistic lyrics in rap music. *Journal of Black Studies, 36*(6), 938–957. doi:10.1177/0021934704274072

Allan, D. (2008). A content analysis of music placement in prime-time television advertising. *Journal of Advertising Research, 48*, 404–417. doi:10.2501/S0021849908080434

Anderson, C. A., & Bushman, B. J. (2002) Human aggression. *Annual Review of Psychology, 53*, 27–51. doi:10.1146/annurev.psych.53.100901.135231

Anderson, C. A., Carnagey, N. L., & Eubanks, J. (2003). Exposure to violent media: The effects of songs with violent lyrics on aggressive thoughts and feelings. *Journal of Personality and Social Psychology, 84*, 960–971. doi:10.1037/0022-3514.84.5.960

Barongan, C., & Hall Nagayama, G. C. (1995). The influence of misogynous rap music on sexual aggression against women. *Psychology of Women Quarterly, 19*(2), 195–207.

Böhm, T., Ruth, N., & Schramm, H. (2016). "Count on me": The influence of music with prosocial lyrics on cognitive and affective aggression. *Psychomusicology: Music, Mind, and Brain, 26*(3), 279–283. doi:10.1037/pmu0000155

Boutcher, S. H., & Trenske, M. (1990). The effects of sensory deprivation and music on perceived exertion and affect during exercise. *Journal of Sport and Exercise Psychology, 12*(2), 167–176.

Brown, J. D., & Campbell, K. (1986). Race and gender in music videos: The same beat but a different drummer. *Journal of Communication, 36*, 94–106.

Bruner, G. C., II (1990). Music, mood, and marketing. *Journal of Marketing, 54*, 94–104.

Chambers, G., & Morgan, J. (1992, September 12). Droppin' knowledge: A rap roundtable. *Essence*, 83–120.

Chen, M. J., Miller, B. A., Grube, J. W., & Waiters, E. D. (2006). Music, substance use, and aggression. *Journal of Studies on Alcohol, 67*(3), 373–381.

Connor, A. (2008, July 10). Torture chamber music. *BBC Magazine*. Retrieved on July 10, 2008, from: http://news.bbc.co.uk/2/hi/uk_news/magazine/7495175.stm

Council on Communications and Media. (2009). Impact of music, music lyrics, and music videos on children and youth. *Pediatrics, 124*, 1488–1495. doi:10.1542/peds.2009-2145

Craig, C., Flynn, M. A., & Holody, K. J. (2017). Name dropping and product mentions: Branding in popular music lyrics. *Journal of Promotion Management, 23*(2), 258–276. doi:10.1080/1049691.2016.1267679

Cummings, M. S., & Roy, A. (2002). Manifestations of Afrocentricity in rap music. *Howard Journal of Communications, 13*(1), 59–76.

Ding, C. G., & Lin, C. H. (2011). How does background music tempo work for online shopping? *Electronic Communication Research and Applications*, published online November 2011. doi:10.1016/j.elerap.2011.10.002

Dunbar, A., Kubrin, C. E., & Scurich, N. (2016). The threatening nature of "rap" music. *Psychology, Public Policy, and Law, 22*(3), 280–292. doi:10.1037/law0000093

Dyson, M. E. (1993). *Reflecting black: African-American cultural criticism*. St. Paul, MN: University of Minnesota Press.

Elliott, D., Carr, S., & Savage, D. (2004). Effects of motivational music on work output and affective responses during sub-maximal cycling of a standardized perceived intensity. *Journal of Sport Behavior, 27*(2), 134–147.

Emling, S. (2004, May 23). Hip-hop fans: "I'll have what he's having." *Atlanta Journal Constitution,* 1A.

Garlin, F. V., & Owen, K. (2006). Setting the tone with the tune: A meta-analytic review of the effects of background music in retail settings. *Journal of Business Research, 59*, 755–764.

Gloor, S. (2014), Songs as branding platforms? A historical analysis of people, places, and products in pop music lyrics. *Journal of the Music and Entertainment Industry Educators Association, 14*(1), pp. 39–60.

Greitemeyer T., Hollingdale J., Traut-Mattausch E. (2015). Changing the track in music and misogyny: Listening to music with pro-equality lyrics improves attitudes and behavior toward women. *Psychology of Popular Media Culture, 4*(1), 56–67

Hansen, C. H., & Hansen, R. D. (1990). The influence of sex and violence on the appeal of rock music videos. *Communication Research, 17*, 212–234.

Hargreaves, D. J. (1984). The effects of repetition on liking for music. *Journal of Research in Music Education, 32*, 35–47.

Hirsch, L. (2007). Weaponizing classical music: Crime prevention and symbolic power in the age of repetition. *Journal of Popular Music Studies, 19*(4), 342–358.

Hirsch, L. E. (2012). *Music in American crime and punishment.* Ann Arbor, MI: University of Michigan Press.

Holt, D. (1996, April 24). Fighting crime with violins. *Dallas Morning News,* 31A.

Kämpfe, J., Sedlmeier, P., & Renkewitz, F. (2010). The impact of background music on adult listeners: A meta-analysis. *Psychology of Music, 39*(4), 424–448.

Kalis, P., & Neuendorf, K. A. (1989). Aggressive cue prominence and gender participation in MTV. *Journalism Quarterly, 66*(1), 148–154, 229.

Kistler, M. E., & Lee, M. J. (2010). Does exposure to sexual hip-hop music videos influence the sexual attitudes of college students? *Mass Communication and Society, 13*, 67–86. doi:10.1080/15205430902865336

Lazarus, D. (2017, July 7, 2017). Whatever happened to Muzak? It's now Mood, and it's not elevator music. *Los Angeles Times,* p. C-1, C4.

Lynch, T. (2003). Hip-hop's bad rap is undeserved. *Broadcasting & Cable, 133*(51), 20.

Mayfield, C., & Moss, S. (1989). Effects of music tempo on task performance. *Psychological Reports, 65*(3, Part 2), 1283–1290.

Miller, L. K., & Schyb, M. (1989). Facilitation and interference by background music. *Journal of Music Therapy, 26*(1), 42–54.

Nielsen (2015, July 7). I second that emotion: The emotive power of music in advertising. Retrieved on July 7, 2017 from: www.nielsen.com/us/en/insights/news/2015/i-second-that-emotion-the-emotive-power-of-music-in-advertising.html

North, A. C., Hargreaves, D. J., & McKendrick, J. (1999). The influence of in-store music on wine selections. *Journal of Applied Psychology, 84*(2), 271–276.

North, A. C., Sheridan, L. P., & Areni, C. S. (2016). Music congruity effects on product memory, perception, and choice. *Journal of Retailing, 92*, 83–85. doi: org/10.1016/j.retai.2015.06.001

North, A. C., Mackenzie, L. C., Law, R. M., & Hargreaves, D. J. (2004). The effects of musical and voice "fit" on responses to advertisements. *Journal of Applied Social Psychology, 34*(8), 1675–1708.

Obermiller, C. (1985). Varieties of mere exposure: The effects of processing style and repetition on affective response. *Journal of Consumer Research, 12*(1), 17–30.

Park, C. W., & Young, S. M. (1986). Consumer response to television commercials: The impact of involvement and background music on brand attitude formation. *Journal of Marketing Research, 23*, 11–24.

Parker-Pope, T. (2007, November 6). For clues on teenage sex, experts look to hip-hop. *New York Times,* 5.

Pelletier, C. L. (2004). The effect of music on decreasing arousal due to stress: A meta-analysis. *Journal of Music Therapy, 41*(3), 192–214.

Peterson, D. L., & Pfost, K. S. (1989). Influence of rock videos on attitudes of violence against women. *Psychological Reports, 64*, 319–322.

Petty, R. E., & Cacioppo, J. T. (1986a). *Communication and persuasion: Central and peripheral routes to attitude change.* New York: Springer-Verlag.

Petty, R. E., & Cacioppo, J. T. (1986b). The elaboration likelihood model of persuasion. In L. Berkowitz (Ed.), *Advances in experimental social psychology* (Vol. 19, pp. 123–205). New York: Academic Press.

Reyna, C., Brandt, M., & Tendayi, G. V. (2009). Blame it on hip-hop: Anti rap attitudes as a proxy for prejudice. *Group Processes Intergroup Relations, 12*(3), 361–380.

Roschk, H., Loureiro, S. M. C., & Breitsohl, J. (2017). Calibrating 30 years of experimental research: A meta-analysis of the atmospheric effects of music, scent, and color. *Journal of Retailing*, *93*(2), 228–240. doi:10.1016/j.jretai.2016.10.001

Rudin, D., Kiss, A., Wetz, R. V., & Sottile, V. M. (2007). Music in the endoscopy suite: A meta-analysis of randomized controlled studies. *Endoscopy*, *39*(6), 507–510.

Sanchez-Porras, M. J., & Rodrigo, E. M. (2017). Emotional benefits of Coca-Cola advertising benefits. *Procedia—Social and Behavioral Sciences*, *237*, 1444–1448. doi:10.1016/j.sbspro.2017.02.227

Schemer, C., Matthes, J., Wirth, W., & Textor, S. (2008). Does "passing the Courvoisier" always pay off? Positive and negative evaluative conditioning effects of brand placements in music videos. *Psychology & Marketing*, *25*(10), 923–943.

Surdin, A. (2009, March 15). South of the border: Popular ballads about the perils of immigration have a surprising heritage: Made in—and by—the United States of America. *Washington Post*, p. E-1. Retrieved on June 22 from the Lexis-Nexis Academic search engine.

Tiddle, C. (1996, December 2). Tales from 'hood need to be told. *Los Angeles Times*, p. F3.

Wright, C., & Qureshi, E. (2015). The relationship between sexual content in music and dating and sexual behaviors of emerging adults. *Howard Journal of Communications, 26*, 227–253. doi:10.1080/10646175.2015.1014982

Van Vaerenbergh, Y. (2017). Consumer reactions to paid versus unpaid brand name placement in song lyrics. *Journal of Product & Brand Management*, *26*(2), 151–158. doi:10.1108/JPBM-05-2016-1167

Wang, M.-W., & Chang, C. (2004). The mere exposure effect and recognition memory. *Cognition and Emotion*, *18*(8), 11055–1078.

Wiesenthal, D. L., Hennessy, D. A., & Totten, B. (2003). The influence of music on mild driver aggression. *Transportation Research, Part F: Traffic Psychology and Behaviour*, *6*(2),125–134.

Yalch, R. F. (1991). Memory in a jingle jungle: Music as a mnemonic device in communicating advertising slogans. *Journal of Applied Psychology*, *76*, 268–275.

Zajonc, R. B. (1968). Attitudinal effects of mere exposure. *Journal of Personality and Social Psychology Monograph Supplement*, *9*(2, Pt. 2), 1–28.

Zander, M. F., Apaolaza-Ibáñez, V., & Hartmann, P. (2010). Music in advertising: Effects on brand and endorser perception. In R. Terlutter, S. Diehl, & S. Okazaki (Eds.), *Advances in advertising research* (Vol. 1, pp. 127–140). Wiesbaden, Germany: Gabler Verlag.

Smell

Baron, R. A. (1983). "The sweet smell of success?": The impact of pleasant artificial scents (perfume and cologne) on evaluations of job applicants. *Journal of Applied Psychology*, *68*, 709–713.

Baron, R. A. (1997). The sweet smell of . . . helping: Effects of pleasant ambient fragrance on prosocial behavior in shopping malls. *Personality and Social Psychology Bulletin*, *23*, 498–503.

Baron, R. A., & Kalsher, M. J. (1998). Effects of a pleasant ambient fragrance on simulated driving performance: The sweet smell of . . . safety? *Environment & Behavior*, *30*(4), 532–552.

Bosmans, A. (2006). Scents and sensibility: When do (in)congruent ambient scents influence product evaluations? *Journal of Marketing*, *70*(3), 32–43.

Cann, A., & Ross, D. A. (1989). Olfactory stimuli as context cues in human memory. *American Journal of Psychology*, *102*, 91–102.

Global Industry Analysts (2016, November). Growing popularity of premium, niche, and innovative fragrances and perfumes to outline growth in global fragrances and perfumes market. Retrieved on July 22, 2017 from: www.strategyr.com/Market Research/Fragrances_and_Perfumes_Market_Trends.asp

Hanisch, E. (1982). The calming effect of fragrances and associated remembrances. drom report, *The nose: Part 2*, pp. 18–19.

Knasko, S. C. (1989). Ambient odor and shopping behavior. *Chemical Senses*, *14* (94), 718.

Lunard, R. (2012). Negative effects of ambient scents on consumers' skepticism about retailers' motives. *Journal of Retailing and Consumer Services*, *19*, 179–185. doi:10.1016/j.jretconser.2011.11.007

Redd, W. H., & Manne, S. L. (1991). *Fragrance administration to reduce patient anxiety during magnetic resonance imaging in cancer diagnostic work-up*. Report to the Fragrance Research Fund (now the Olfactory Research Fund).

Roschk, H., Loureiro, S. M. C., & Breitsohl, J. (2017). Calibrating 30 years of experimental research: A meta-analysis of the atmospheric effects of music, scent, and color. *Journal of Retailing*, *93*(2), 228–240. doi:10.1016/j.jretai.2016.10.001

Rotten, J. (1983). Affective and cognitive consequences of malodorous pollution. *Basic and Applied Social Psychology*, *38*, 213–228.

Smiley, M. (2014, December 9). Dollars & scents: From clothes to cars to banks, brands seek distinction through fragrance. *Advertising Age*. Retrieved on July 8, 2017 from: http://adage.com/article/cmo-strategy/smell-money-marketers-sell-scent/296084/

Stolberg, S. (1994, June 29). Trying to make sense of smell. *Los Angeles Times*, pp. A1, A20, A21.

Sugano, H., & Sato, H. (1991). Psychophysiological studies of fragrance. *Chemical Senses*, *16*, 183–184.

Teerling, A., Nixdorf, R. R., & Koster, E. P. (1992). The effect of ambient odours on shopping behavior. *Chemical Senses*, *17*, 886.

Teller, C., & Dennis, C. (2012). The effect of ambient scent on consumers' perception, emotions, and behavior: A critical review. *Journal of Marketing Management*, *28*, 14–36. doi:10.1080/0267257X.2011.560719

Warm, J. S., Parasuraman, R., & Dember, W. N. (1990). *Effects of periodic olfactory stimulation on visual sustained attention in young and older adults*. Progress Report No. 4 to the Fragrance Research Fund (now the Olfactory Research Fund).

Welsh, J. (2011, June 16). Smell of success: Scents affect thoughts, behaviors. www.Livescience.com. Retrieved on June 24, 2012, from: www.livescience.com/14635-impression-smell-thoughts-behavior-flowers.html

The Ethics of Persuasion

"THE MOST DANGEROUS ANIMAL in the world," it has been said, "is a freshman with one semester of psychology." If that is true, then the second most dangerous creature must surely be a freshman with one persuasion class under his or her belt. If you give a child a toy hammer, the child will invariably find that every object he or she encounters needs pounding (Kaplan, 1964). In much the same vein, it is not uncommon for a student who has completed a course in persuasion to think that every communication encounter requires a test of her or his newfound skills. At best, this can be annoying to the recipients of the influence attempts.

At worst, it can damage or destroy relationships if the persuader is perceived as being unethical. Like a hammer, persuasion is a useful tool. But one shouldn't use it to pound on others.

For this reason and others, we consider in this chapter the ethics of influence attempts. Although this is the last chapter of the text, it is by no means the least important. We decided to place this chapter at the end so we could discuss ethical concerns raised throughout the book. We make no bones about trying to teach you how to become a more effective persuader, as well as a more discriminating consumer of persuasive messages. Hence, we feel morally obliged to offer some prescriptions and proscriptions on the ethical uses of persuasion. Before you go out and attempt to wield your persuasive skills on unsuspecting roommates, absent-minded professors, unwitting family members, unfortunate co-workers, or hapless strangers, we want to make sure that you understand the importance of respecting others' dignity, of showing concern for others' welfare, and, as they say in comic books, "of using your powers for good instead of evil." Quite seriously, we believe that the power to persuade carries with it a corresponding duty to persuade ethically. We don't claim to have a "corner" on the ethics market. Feel free to disagree with any of our guidelines, as you choose. Your time will be well spent thinking through the bases for your own ethical standards and in coming to terms with what you consider to be moral and immoral influence attempts.

IS PERSUASION IN GENERAL UNETHICAL?

A frequent charge leveled against persuasion is that it is unethical. Some people equate persuasion with manipulation and see it as a one-sided approach to communication. Communication, they argue, should emphasize cooperation, trust, and shared agreement. We believe this view of communication is noble but overly idealistic. What happens when people don't agree? What happens when their goals contradict? Enter the need for persuasion. Persuasion is what people rely on when things aren't "hunky dory" or "peachy keen."

We argued in the first chapter that persuasion is not a dirty word. But persuasion *is* used to do the "dirty work" of convincing others when disagreements develop. Attempts at convincing others, however, are not necessarily one-sided. Persuasion can be, and often is, two-sided. Persuasion can, and often does, result in mutually satisfactory solutions. Persuasion is not the antithesis of cooperation. Persuasion can be based on trust and mutual respect. In a relationship based on equality, for example, each party is free to influence the other.

As we noted in Chapter 1, persuasion performs a number of positive, prosocial functions. To the extent that some persuaders are unethical, it makes even more sense to learn how unethical influence attempts work and why they succeed. We don't deny that persuasion can be used in manipulative ways. Persuasion is a tool. Tools can be misused. In such cases, however, one should blame the tool's user, not the tool. By way of analogy, when someone uses the English language to belittle or demean another person, no one suggests that we should do away with language. Why, then, when persuasion is used unethically, do people blame persuasion rather than the persuader? Granted, some persuasive tools, such as fear appeals, hold greater potential for abuse, in the same way that a saw is more dangerous than a tape measure. Stronger safeguards need to be taken when using such persuasive tools, even when their use is for the receiver's own good.

THE MOTIVES COLOR THE MEANS

Consistent with our tool analogy, James McCroskey commented that "the means of persuasion themselves are ethically neutral" (McCroskey, 1972, p. 269). Contrasting this view, Jacksa and Pritchard (1994) adopt the position that "virtually any act of communication can be seen from a moral point of view" (p. 12). We believe that ethics and persuasion are closely intertwined. We maintain, however, that the moral quality of an influence attempt is derived primarily from the *motives* or ends of the persuader, and only secondarily from the means of persuasion that are employed. In our view, the means of persuasion take on the moral character of the persuader's ends.

To illustrate, imagine that three persuaders each employ one of three influence strategies: deception, fear appeals, or ingratiation. Is it possible to determine which persuader is the most ethical or least ethical, merely by knowing the strategy each employs? We think not. We don't see how an ethical evaluation of the strategies could be made without any knowledge of the purposes for which the strategies would be used. In Table 16.1, we list these three strategies (in column 1), along with two contrasting sets of motives (in columns 2 and 3). Notice that when paired with the first set of "good" motives, the use of the strategies appears justified. However, when paired with the second set of "evil" motives, the strategies appear highly unjustified.

TABLE 16.1 The Motives Color the Means

Strategy or Means	"Good" Motive or End	"Evil" Motive or End
Use of deception	Trying to conceal a surprise birthday party from the person in whose honor the party is being given	Trying to swindle an elderly person out of his or her life savings
Use of fear appeals	Trying to convince a child never to accept a ride from a stranger	Threatening to demote an employee for refusing a superior's sexual advances
Use of ingratiation	Trying to cheer up a friend who is depressed about a poor grade on a test	Lavishing attention on a dying relative in order to inherit the relative's money

Thus, in our view, the ethical quality of a persuader's motives tends to "rub off" on the persuasive strategy employed. The strategy itself is essentially neutral or amoral, until such time as it is paired with a particular motive or end. At that point, the entire influence attempt (motive and strategy) takes on a moral/immoral dimension.

In our view, a persuader's motives color the means of persuasion that are used, as the following examples illustrate.

ETHICS, CULTURE, AND THE ISSUE OF CENTRAL VERSUS PERIPHERAL PROCESSING

We readily admit that some persuasive strategies may seem more ethically defensible than others. For example, the use of reasoned argument might seem more ethically justifiable than the use of flattery or charm. The use of facts and statistics might appear more defensible than the use of emotional appeals. This highlights a general preference among Western societies for logical, rational thought, consistent with what Petty and Cacioppo (1986) call central processing. You may recall from our discussion of the elaboration likelihood model in Chapter 2 that the central route to persuasion involves actively thinking about issues, reflecting on information, and scrutinizing the content of messages. The peripheral route, however, is based on factors such as source credibility, imagery, or social cues. In U.S. culture, the central route is generally the preferred route for persuasion.

Not all cultures place the same emphasis, however, on rational, linear thinking. Other cultures value different ways of knowing, favor other means of gaining adherence to ideas, and prefer other methods of securing behavioral compliance. As one example, some Asian cultures emphasize the importance of fitting in, of conforming to group norms, and of not "rocking the boat." In such cultures, greater emphasis tends to be placed on *indirect* strategies of influence (such as hinting or stressing the importance of following group norms) than on *direct* strategies (arguing, open disagreement). The preference for indirect strategies reflects the importance of such cultural values as avoiding confrontation and preventing the loss of face (Ting-Toomey, 1988, 1994; Ting-Toomey & Kurogi, 1998; Wiseman et al., 1995).

Within Western culture there are also exceptions to the general preference for "rational" persuasion. A person who comes across as being overly logical or emotionless, such as the character Mr. Spock of *Star Trek* fame, may be viewed as "cold," "calculating," or "heartless." Similarly, the character of Dr. House, played by Hugh Laurie, displayed brusqueness with patients, indifference toward colleagues, and an acerbic tone with everyone. He was more interested in solving medical problems than the feelings of his patients. The ability to display compassion, convey empathy, and respond to the entreaties of others based on these same emotions is considered a desirable quality. Thus, even though it may seem that some forms of influence are more ethically defensible than others, this depends to some extent on cultural and situational factors.

ETHICAL QUESTIONS THAT CAN'T BE ANSWERED THROUGH THE STUDY OF PERSUASION

We've argued that the moral character of a persuasive act is derived primarily from the persuader's motives. Persuasion research, however, tends to focus almost exclusively on the means of persuasion (strategies and tactics) rather than on the motives of persuaders. For this reason, persuasion research is ill equipped to answer questions about what are good or evil ends. Take any current social controversy—for example, abortion, assisted suicide, gay marriage, and so forth. The study of persuasion cannot tell a persuader what side of the controversy to be on. The study of persuasion can't enlighten persuasion researchers as to what causes are good or bad, or what values are right or wrong. Persuasion researchers tend to defer to moral philosophers, religious leaders, the judicial system, and other ethical arbiters to make such determinations.

As far as specific strategies are concerned, many professional organizations have established codes of ethics. Newspaper journalists, television news anchors, and radio commentators, for example, are bound by codes of conduct established by their national organizations or government agencies. A print journalist, for instance, should not publish a story without verifying the information via two independent sources. Even the Word of Mouth Marketing Association (WOMMA) has adopted a code of ethics (see http://womma.org/ethics). On the Web, however, anything goes. There are no clear-cut guidelines. Bloggers can post anything they want. Legislation regarding hate speech and cyberbullying on the Web is evolving.

Perhaps persuasion researchers should give greater consideration to the possible uses of the strategies and tactics they are busy investigating. Bear in mind, though, that it is difficult for a researcher to know how a particular tool of influence will be used. If a persuasive tool can be used for good *or* evil ends, what is a persuasion researcher to do? In Box 16.1, we identify some well-known approaches to ethics that you might study in a course on ethics. In practice, individuals tend to follow a combination of the approaches identified in Box 16.1, making most of us ethical relativists. A complete discussion of the field of ethics and moral philosophy is beyond the scope of this text. Fortunately, several excellent works are available if you wish to learn more about ethics and communication (Christians, Rotzoll, & Fackler, 1991; Duffy & Thorson, 2015; Jacksa & Pritchard, 1994; Johannesen, 1983; Johannesen, Thayer, & Hardt, 1979; Nilsen, 1966; Rivers, Christians, & Schramm, 1980).

The inability of persuasion researchers to distinguish good from bad applications of persuasion is similar to the situation facing other researchers in other fields. Consider the controversy surrounding the cloning of human embryos. The topic of cloning is fraught with moral implications. Scientists conducting this sort of research are aware that their research has ethical overtones. For the most part, however, they tend to focus on scientific questions related to cloning, as opposed to moral questions. After all, neither politicians nor clergy agree on the answers to the moral questions.

Persuasion researchers are similar to other researchers in this respect: They are simply interested in learning more about how persuasion works. Their focus is not on whether a particular strategy or tactic should be used. Nor is their focus on what causes should or should not be furthered using persuasion. We don't deny that persuasion researchers should take heed of the ethical implications of the strategies and tactics they are investigating. We merely wish to point out that persuasion researchers are more interested in pursuing knowledge for its own sake than on discovering techniques for mind control. We readily admit, however, that like Dr. Frankenstein in Mary Shelley's novel, persuasion researchers—and all other researchers for that matter—are ethically responsible for the knowledge they uncover and pass along.

BOX 16.1 | Approaches to Ethics

- **Ends versus means:** An ethical controversy centering on whether the means or method of influence is justified by the desirability of the outcome. Can a persuasive outcome be so good or desirable that the use of force or coercion is justified to achieve it?

- **Consequentialism/teleological ethics:** An ethical approach emphasizing consequences or outcomes. A persuader should weigh the benefits and drawbacks of his or her actions. Those actions that produce the greatest balance of good over bad are ethical.

- **Deontological systems/duty ethics:** An ethical approach that focuses on moral imperatives, rather than specific consequences. A person has a duty to adhere to rules of moral conduct. One may be morally obliged to take some actions, regardless of their consequences.

- **Amoralism (or Machiavellianism):** This ethical approach authorizes whatever a persuader can get away with, constrained only by laws, or fear of social ostracism. The self-interest of the persuader is all that matters; others better watch out for themselves. Suckers deserve what they get. They should learn from their mistakes.

- **Situational ethics/relativism:** This ethical approach maintains that there are no moral absolutes. There are no ethical maxims. It isn't possible to follow a moral code that applies to all cultures, persons, times, and places. There are always exceptions to every rule. There can be good or bad forms of persuasion, but whether they are good or bad depends on the situation, the parties involved, the nature of the issue, and other related factors.

- **Universalism:** This ethical approach maintains that there are universal, immutable "dos" and "don'ts." Morals and values can be translated into enduring codes of conduct. Some actions are right or wrong for all people, places, and times. For example, torture is always wrong. Certain universal human rights must be honored. There are "hard" and "soft" versions of universalism, meaning that some perspectives are more absolute than others.

- **Egalitarianism (also known as the "Golden Rule"):** This approach to ethics involves doing unto others as you would have them do unto you. Treat other people as you would have them treat you. A more modern derivative of this principle is, "What goes around comes around."

- **Free market ethics:** This ethical approach is based on the metaphor of the free market or capitalism: caveat emptor, let the buyer beware. There should be little or no prior restraint on persuasive messages. This approach places greater responsibility on receivers to critically evaluate persuasive messages.

- **Utilitarianism (John Stuart Mill):** This is a teleological approach, based on the greatest good for the greatest number of people. The Star Trek version of this principle involves balancing "the needs of the many with the needs of the one."

- **Virtue ethics:** This perspective focuses on the character of the person, as opposed to specific moral rules or moral actions. A person should strive to be virtuous, to have good character. Instead of relying on a list of dos and don'ts, one should ask oneself, "What kind of person do I want to be?"

OUR APPROACH: CHARACTERISTICS OF ETHICAL INFLUENCE

The authors claim no special expertise in the field of ethics. We certainly don't possess the moral credentials of a Mother Teresa or the Dalai Lama. We feel obliged, nonetheless, to offer our own set of guidelines and recommendations for ethical persuasion. Just as we believe the power to persuade entails a responsibility to persuade ethically, we also believe that teaching others how to persuade entails an obligation to teach them how to do so ethically. Our views don't emanate from a single ethical perspective, so we can probably best be described as *situationalistic* or *relativistic* in our approach (see Box 16.1). We don't expect you to accept our advice as gospel. But we do hope you'll think about our guidelines and recommendations carefully. We believe that the more you think about the ethical dimensions involved in persuasion, the more conscientious you will tend to be as a persuader.

Ethics and Our Model of Persuasion

Recall that in our model of persuasion (see Chapter 2), we distinguished between pure and borderline cases of persuasion. Recall also from our model that there are five criteria that distinguish pure cases of persuasion from borderline cases. Pure cases of persuasion are those that are intentional; they occur with the receiver's conscious awareness, involve free choice on the part of the receiver, take place through language or symbolic action, and involve two or more persons. We believe that the first four of these criteria hold important ethical implications for persuaders.

Intentionality

A number of scholars subscribe to the view that only intentional influence attempts count as persuasion. From an ethical standpoint, however, this view is problematic. We maintain that such a view lets persuaders "off the hook" for the unintended consequences of their persuasion. A persuader whose efforts result in harmful, unforeseen consequences can avoid responsibility by saying, "That's not what I intended." A persuader whose influence attempts reach the wrong audience can say, "That's not where I was aiming." Studies have shown that unintended messages, such as an overheard ethnic slur, can damage a person's reputation in the eyes of other persons (Greenberg & Pyszczynski, 1985; Kirkland, Greenberg, & Pyszczynski, 1987). Thus, we think that persuaders should be held accountable for the unintended consequences of their persuasion.

Conscious Awareness

Pure cases of persuasion, according to our model, occur with the conscious aware-–ness of the participants. Borderline cases of persuasion, however, require no such realization on the part of the participants. We maintain that persuasion that takes place with the conscious awareness of all the parties involved is far more ethical than persuasion that does not. If a person knows that he or she is the target of an influence attempt, he or she can take active steps to resist the attempt or counter with an attempt of his or her own.

Free Choice/Free Will

Pure cases of persuasion, according to our model, are those that allow participants to make free, informed decisions about whether they wish to comply with persuasive messages. Borderline cases of persuasion, however, involve coercion in varying degrees. We believe, quite obviously, that persuasive attempts that allow persons to make free choices are ethically superior to those that do not. Free choice includes the ability to question others' influence attempts, to counter with influence attempts of one's own, and to resist complying with others' attempts. As a general rule, we believe the more freedom one has to say "No," the more ethical a given influence attempt is. This also explains why conscious awareness, discussed previously, is an important ingredient in ethical persuasion. A person cannot *choose* to comply with an influence attempt if the person is unaware that he or she is the target of an influence attempt.

Language and Symbolic Action

According to our model, pure cases of persuasion center on the use of language (the spoken or printed word) and symbolic actions (protest marches, sit-ins, etc.). Borderline cases of persuasion include persuasion via nonverbal or behavioral means. Using physical attractiveness or behavioral modification to alter another's behavior would both constitute instances of borderline persuasion. We believe that persuasion that takes place through language or symbol usage is generally more ethical than persuasion via nonverbal or behavioral means. Our preference for the former is based on the fact that language-based influence attempts are generally more easily recognized and more readily understood. Nonverbal appeals, however, are less recognizable as persuasive attempts.

Of course, it is possible for persuaders to let receivers know that they will be the targets of nonverbal influence attempts or behavioral modification techniques. Sit-ins and protest marches, for example, are fairly obvious instances of nonverbal persuasion. If the recipient is made aware that nonverbal or behavioral strategies will be employed, we see little ethical difference between language-based and nonlanguage-based persuasion.

Persuaders as Lovers

In a widely acclaimed essay, Wayne Brockriede (1974) suggested that arguers can be classified into three different types, based on their regard for the other person. "Seducers," he argued, use trickery, deceit, charm, flattery, and beguilement to achieve their ends. Seducers do not view others as equals but as unwitting victims. "Rapists," the second category identified by Brockriede, use threats, force, and coercion in an effort to win their arguments. They resort to browbeating, personal attacks, threats, and ultimatums to get their way. Like seducers, rapists view others as inferior. Others are treated as objects rather than equals. "Lovers," the third of Brockriede's categories, respect one another's dignity and base their relationships on equality. They don't treat each other as victims or objects but rather as partners. They are open and receptive to one another's arguments and look for mutually satisfactory solutions to their differences.

We believe that Brockriede's characterization of these three styles of argument applies equally well to persuasive encounters. We draw upon and extend his approach here by ascribing what we believe to be three essential attributes or qualities of "persuaders as lovers." The first quality is *respect*. Ethical influence attempts tend to reaffirm the other person's sense of self-worth. Persuaders who use ethical strategies and tactics tend to demonstrate respect for one another's dignity. In contrast, unethical influence attempts tend to express disdain for others. The target of an unethical influence attempt is viewed as a "mark," a "sucker," or a "patsy."

The second quality is *equality*. Influence attempts are most ethical when the parties enjoy equal status in a relationship. This is because in unequal relationships, status or power differences are more likely—whether intentionally or unintentionally—to impinge on the choice-making ability of the lower-status person. The person enjoying more status or power may find it difficult to resist using "carrots" or "sticks" to gain compliance. The person occupying the lower-status position may find it difficult to believe that the person with higher status will not resort to rewards or punishments.

We believe that ethical influence attempts are possible even when there are power disparities, but only if the more powerful party allows communication to take place, on an equal footing. In organizational communication, for example, the very concepts of "downward" and "upward" communication suggest inequality. To minimize such inequality, a superior could make it clear that he or she was suggesting, not ordering. The superior also would have to be open to having her or his mind changed as well. These same requirements—suggesting, not ordering and remaining open to influence—would apply to parental influence as well.

The third quality is *tolerance*. Each party to a persuasive encounter must be patient with the other, giving the other a chance to make his or her case. Each party should also be open to the other's point of view, making persuasion a two-way street. If a person wishes to influence another, we maintain that he or she also must be willing to be influenced. Turn-taking plays an important role in this process. Persuaders need to be willing to hear one another out. A person who enters a persuasive encounter with the mind-set, "I will persuade, but I will not be persuaded," is not displaying tolerance for the other person or the other person's point of view. Taken together, we believe that these three qualities have the potential to make persuasive encounters more ethical and more pleasant.

Bunglers, Smugglers, and Sleuths

Robert Cialdini, whom many consider to be the father of modern compliance-gaining research, suggests that persuaders can be categorized into three different types (Cialdini, 1999). *Bunglers,* the first type, squander their prospects for influence by selecting ineffective strategies and tactics. As the name implies, they bungle their chances for success. Bunglers aren't so much unethical as they are inept. *Smugglers,* the second type, know exactly what they are doing but rely on unethical influence tactics. Smugglers, for example, wouldn't hesitate to use deception as a compliance-gaining technique if they thought it would produce immediate results. *Sleuths,* the third type, are more knowledgeable about how influence works than bunglers, and they are more ethical in their choice of strategies and tactics than smugglers. According to Cialdini, sleuths function like detectives who study a persuasive situation, searching for clues about the most ethical and effective means of influence. For Cialdini, then, the sleuth is the ideal persuader. He maintains that both individuals and groups (marketers, advertisers, corporations) should be sleuth-like in their influence attempts. The problem, he says, is that persuaders don't always recognize the long-term advantages of sleuth-like influence. "The systematic use of misleading influence tactics," he maintains, "ultimately becomes a psychologically and financially self-damaging process" (Cialdini, 1999, p. 94). For example, the owner of a car lot who encourages the salespeople to use ethically suspect tactics to sell cars may sell a few more cars in the short run. In the long run, however, employee morale will suffer, repeat business will taper off, and eventually, the "bottom line" will suffer. If not for the sake of the persuadee, then, Cialdini suggests that ethical influence is ultimately in the persuader's best interest as well.

ETHICAL ISSUES ARISING FROM PREVIOUS CHAPTERS

Having offered some of our own guidelines for ethical persuasion, we now turn our attention to some of the ethical issues introduced elsewhere in this text. A number of ethical questions regarding persuasive strategies and tactics emanate from the preceding chapters. Here we examine some of those key questions and explore possible answers.

Ethics and Credibility

A number of ethical questions center on the use of source credibility as a tool for persuasion (see Chapter 4). Among the key questions on the ethical uses of credibility are the following:

1. Is it unethical for a celebrity endorser to promote a product or service he or she does not actually use or about which he or she lacks expertise?
2. Do we expect too much from politicians, professional athletes, and celebrities? To what extent should they be held accountable for errors in judgment, gaffes, and faux pas?
3. Does the use of authority become an abuse of authority if receivers place too much faith or reliance in a particular source? For example, can a TV evangelist hold too much sway over his or her followers, thereby clouding their judgment and independent thinking?

When celebrities endorse products they don't actually use, the problem tends to be self-correcting. The celebrity can be sued for breach of contract. This happened to Charlize Theron, an endorser for Raymond Weil watches, when she was photographed in public wearing another brand. Jessica Simpson and Teri Hatcher were sued for similar infractions. Sometimes endorsement deals can backfire when the products don't work. The Kardashians, for example, were named in a $5 million lawsuit for making "false, misleading, and unsubstantiated" claims about Quick-Trim, a weight loss product that they claimed helped them shed pounds (Kotz & Haupt, 2012, para. 1). A similar lawsuit targeted Shaquille O'Neal for touting the benefits of wearing a Power Balance bracelet, which used "holograms" to optimize the body's energy flow (Malinowski, 2011).

From time to time, sources say or do things that damage their own credibility. Such gaffes can haunt candidates, athletes, and celebrities. Olympic swimmer, Ryan Lochte, for instance, found himself in hot water after falsely claiming that he was robbed at gunpoint during the 2016 Olympics in Rio. It not only cost him multiple sponsorships, but hung his sponsors out to dry as well. Indeed, Fong and Wyer (2012) found that a scandal involving a celebrity endorser resulted in more negative attitudes toward the endorsed product and decreased purchase intentions. Twitter now makes it easier than ever for a source to put a virtual foot in his or her mouth. Consider, for example, former Congressman and chronic "sexter," Anthony Weiner, who might be considered the poster boy for regrettable tweets. The old adage "think before you speak" should now be amended to "and before you tweet."

Because credibility tends to function as a peripheral cue, a reliance on credibility as the principal means of persuasion tends to short-circuit thoughtful deliberation. We believe that persuasive appeals that emphasize central processing are generally superior to those that emphasize peripheral processing. The former are ethically preferable, we believe, because they enable receivers to analyze messages, scrutinize evidence, and generally think for themselves.

We believe that a reliance on source credibility, at the expense of thoughtful reflection, is ethically suspect. In cases where credibility is used to enhance the persuasiveness of a message, we believe a qualified source should be used. By "qualified," we mean a source possessing expertise in the area in which she or he is offering advice or making recommendations. Serena Williams, for example, knows a great deal about tennis, so her endorsement of a tennis racket brand would be meaningful. She's not an expert on vacuums, however, so her recommendation of a brand of vacuum cleaner would possess no more validity than that of the average person.

Ethics and Communicator Characteristics

We noted in Chapter 5 that some receivers are particularly vulnerable to influence attempts. Young children, for example, have difficulty distinguishing what toys featured in television commercials can and cannot do. Patients with terminal illnesses are highly vulnerable to hucksters peddling "miracle" cures. Elderly citizens, some of whose mental faculties are diminished, are highly susceptible to scams perpetrated by con artists. And some new immigrants are uniquely vulnerable, because of their naiveté, language barriers, or both. Concerns such as these invite several ethical questions on persuasion aimed at specialized audiences:

1. What ethical safeguards should be followed when attempting to persuade children?
2. What ethical responsibilities does a persuader have when attempting to persuade highly vulnerable audiences?

With respect to the first question, we strongly believe that special care must be taken when persuading children, especially young ones. According to a policy statement of the American Academy of Pediatrics "research has shown that young children—younger than eight years—are cognitively and psychologically defenseless against advertising" (2009, p. 2563). They often cannot distinguish ads from programs and fail to grasp disclaimers attached to ads. Although a variety of private and public agencies already regulate mass media messages aimed at children, advertisers have been criticized for a number of unfair practices. As Treise, Weigold, Conna, and Garrison (1994) commented:

advertising to children promotes the use of products, such as sweets, that are harmful to children (Gore, 1989), manipulates and disappoints children with exaggerated claims; creates conflicts with parents over purchases; has the potential to influence children to experiment with alcoholic beverages and/or drugs (Atkin, 1987); and creates confusion over product and commercial distinctions (Kunkel, 1988; Englehardt, 1987).

(p. 60)

Of particular concern is children's exposure to media violence. As the American Academy of Pediatrics (2009) cautioned, "Exposure to violence in media, including television, movies, music, and video games, represents a significant risk factor to the health of children and adolescents (American Academy of Pediatrics, 2009, p. 1495). Exposure to media violence increases children's social and physical aggression (Gentile, Mathieson, & Crick, 2011; Murray, 2008). What is surprising is that even advertising aimed at children includes as much or more violence than advertising aimed at adults (Jones, Cunningham, & Gallagher, 2010).

In addition to following those strictures that are already in place, we would advise those seeking to influence youngsters to follow three basic guidelines. First, they should ensure that they have a parent or legal guardian's permission before attempting any persuasion. For example, before you decide to convince the next-door neighbor's child (spoiler alert) that Santa Claus and the Easter Bunny are myths, check with the parent(s) first. Persuading without such permission not only usurps parental autonomy but invites lawsuits as well. Second, they should communicate using words and concepts that children can understand. Persuasive messages should be geared to the developmental level of the age group being targeted. Third, they should make sure they have the children's best interests at heart. Whose interest was R. J. Reynolds promoting by using the now-discontinued "Joe Camel" campaign? Critics charged that the use of the cartoonlike character was a transparent attempt to attract underage smokers (Bromberg, 1990). In our view, public awareness messages that target children for their sake (e.g., antidrug spots or stranger-danger messages) are less ethically suspect than for-profit advertisements that target children in order to make money.

With respect to the second question, there are clearly cases in which vulnerable groups are targeted by persuaders. As just one example, people who live in inner-city areas are subjected to more billboards promoting cigarettes and alcohol than people who live in more affluent, suburban areas. The poorer the neighborhood, the more billboards (Kwate & Lee, 2006).

We believe that many of the concerns involving highly vulnerable groups or individuals can be allayed by adhering to the aforementioned values of mutual respect, relational equality, and mutual tolerance. Part of the task of persuading vulnerable receivers involves displaying interpersonal or intercultural sensitivity. This includes the ability to empathize with others' feelings and points of view. Part of the task also involves avoiding the temptation to prey on others' fears, weaknesses, or vulnerabilities. The motto *caveat emptor* ("let the buyer beware") may make sense when one is dealing with fully functioning, informed consumers. When applied to vulnerable groups, however, the motto simply becomes an excuse for taking advantage.

Ethics and Deception

The study of deception and deception detection constitutes one of the most ethically sensitive areas of persuasion research. A number of ethical issues were addressed in Chapter 12. Of these, the overriding questions will be reexamined here: Is deception ever justified? Or, stated somewhat differently, is honesty always the best policy? How concerned should consumers be about online deception, including deception on social media?

Although some may believe that lying is always wrong, we believe that there are numerous situations in which telling "white lies" is beneficial for relationships. Such social rituals as complimenting another's clothing, praising your mother-in-law's cooking, or telling the host of a party that you had a good time seem like fairly harmless uses of deception to us. Even where candor is called for, we believe there is an important difference between being honest and being *brutally* honest.

Our view is that although deception is sometimes socially justified, one should examine the motives of the persuader by asking, "In whose interest is the lie being perpetrated?" Self-serving lies, we believe, are the least ethical. Lies told for the benefit of another, we maintain, are the most ethical. Research suggests that others hold this view as well. A study by Seiter, Bruschke, and Bai (2002), for example, asked people from China and the United States to rate the acceptability of various types of lies. Participants from both cultures tended to agree: They rated lies told for selfish reasons as unacceptable and lies told to benefit others as generally acceptable. In evaluating deception, one should also keep in mind that outright falsehoods and misrepresentations constitute only one type of deception. Deception can also include withholding information or purposeful ambiguity. The latter types of deception, we suggest, are more ethically defensible than "bald-faced" lies. A person might be "diplomatic," for example, to spare another the pain or loss of face that being blunt might cause. Both withholding of information and purposeful ambiguity thus can be used to benefit another.

A final note on the "honesty is the best policy" approach is that it works only if some of the preceding conditions for ethical persuasion exist—for example, if there is mutual respect, a relationship based on equality, and tolerance for one another's views. If these conditions do not exist, then being honest may simply result in the honest person being fired, punished, or ridiculed.

With regard to the second question on deception online, we believe there is some cause for concern. One reason is because social media are less regulated than traditional media, so consumers enjoy fewer protections. Another reason is that many people lack online media literacy. They are not as wary of peer-to-peer persuasion, word-of-mouth, and third-party endorsements as they should be. Online deception takes place in a variety of ways. One form is known as *native advertising* (Taylor, 2017). The "native" feature is that the ads are chameleon-like. They blend in with the social platforms in which they appear. For example, a native ad might have the look and feel of a Facebook or Instagram post. Suppose you were shopping for a handknit sweater for your dog. If you searched on Etsy for "dog sweater," the top row of items found would be paid or promoted ads. As another example, BuzzFeed's series of "Dear Kitten" videos for Friskies cat food, were viewed millions of times and, according to BuzzFeed, made viewers 57 percent more likely to buy that brand (BuzzFeed, 2014).

Native advertising is deceptive. Since native ads imitate the sites on which they appear, users may not recognize them for what they are. The Better Business Bureau has declared native advertising a deceptive practice, unless clear labeling is provided (Ikonen, Luoma-aho, & Bowen, 2017). The Federal Trade Commission adopted guidelines requiring all native ads to include disclosures such as "paid advertisement." A study by Media Radar, however, found that 37 percent of native advertisers failed to follow the FTC's labeling rules (Fletcher, 2017).

A related technique involves *sponsored content*. Compared to native advertising, sponsored content is more informational and less commercial in nature—hence the emphasis on content. What appears to be a legitimate news story, blog, or entertaining video showcases a particular person or organization as an *opinion leader* in a field (Herrman, 2016). For example, Vani Hari, a self-proclaimed food activist, who goes by the moniker the "Food Babe," blogs about healthy eating. She maligns major brands like Chick-fil-A, Panera, and Subway, while collecting reimbursements from smaller, cottage brands that she endorses (Schultz, 2014). She also sells her own juice cleanses and sugar detox guides, even though she holds no degree in nutrition or food science. As another example, to promote its fantasy role-play game, *Middle Earth: Shadow of Mordor*, Warner Brothers paid gaming enthusiasts to post online videos of themselves enthusiastically playing the game, without disclosing the payments. The FTC filed a complaint with Warner Brothers and a settlement was reached (FTC, 2016). FTC guidelines require that any for-profit arrangement between an opinion leader and a brand must be disclosed. The guidelines are routinely flouted, though, by including obscure acknowledgments such as #sp (for sponsored product) or #partner in Facebook or Instagram posts.

Ethics of Using Threats as a Compliance-Gaining Strategy

In Chapter 10, we discussed a number of strategies and tactics related to compliance gaining. Among the strategies identified were threats of punishment. As a general rule, studies have shown that using threats achieves greater compliance than not using them (Gass & Canary, 1988; Heisler, 1974; Nevin & Ford, 1976; Tittle & Rowe, 1973). Their effectiveness notwithstanding, there are serious ethical questions regarding the use of threats. Hence, we focus here on the ethics of using threats as a means of persuasion: Is the use of threats of punishment ever ethically justifiable and, if so, under what circumstances?

Every attempt to persuade involves ethical questions. To a greater extent than with other influence strategies, however, we believe the use of threats should raise red flags in the persuader's mind. There are numerous reasons for this. First, we believe threats are unethical inasmuch as their effectiveness hinges on creating a state of psychological distress in receivers. Second, threats tend to be exploitative of power or status differences in relationships. Third, issuing and carrying out threats tends to diminish the morale and self-esteem of the recipient. Fourth, a reliance on threats is damaging and destructive to relationships. In the long run, threats do more harm than good. Fifth, the use of threats can foster resentment or trigger aggression toward the threatener. If you rely on threats, you'd better watch your back. Sixth, threats must be carried out from time to time, an unpleasant prospect for both the threatener and the recipient. Seventh, the threatener is modeling a negative form of behavior for others to follow, thereby teaching others to rely on threats as well. Can you tell we're not too fond of threats?

When, if ever, then, should a persuader use threats? Our advice is that threats, although sometimes unavoidable, should never be the strategy of first resort. They should be used only when prosocial alternatives are unavailable or have failed and only when they are clearly in the best interests of the receiver or society. As an illustration, imagine that a spouse or an intimate partner is destroying himself or herself through alcohol abuse. The partner has pleaded with him or her to join Alcoholics Anonymous or to seek some other form of help, all to no avail. We believe that the partner would be justified in threatening, "I'm leaving you if you don't get help." Making such a threat, and following through on it if necessary, might well be in the long-term interests of both people.

Despite exceptions such as these, a reliance on threats produces so many undesirable social consequences that we think their use is rarely justified. A persuader who is contemplating the use of threats should, therefore, ask him- or herself if that is the only way to achieve an objective and if the objective is even worth achieving if threats must be used. Too often, we suspect that the use of threats represents reflex behavior on the part of the threatener. A reliance on threats can become habitual. If persuaders would reflect on their strategy selection more, they would recognize that prosocial alternatives are usually available and are more conducive to promoting and preserving relationships.

Ethics and Fear Appeals

Gloom and doom scenarios abound. Some commentators suggest that we have become a "culture of fear" (Glassner, 1999; Ropeik & Gray, 2002; Siegel, 2005). We are bombarded with media reports of dangers lurking everywhere (Altheide, 2002). The research we reviewed in Chapter 13 shows that fear appeals can be quite effective. Yet considerable caution should be used when employing fear appeals to promote constructive responses (e.g., danger control) rather than panic (e.g., fear control). We therefore posit two questions related to the ethics of using fear appeals.

1. Is it ethical to promote a "culture of fear"?
2. Is the use of fear appeals ever ethically justified and, if so, under what conditions or circumstances?

Many persuaders have a vested interest in scaring us. Politicians want our votes. The media wants ratings. "If it bleeds, it leads," goes the journalistic adage. Pharmaceutical manufacturers want to sell us prescription drugs. But is the use of such scare tactics justified? Take the case of rare, exotic diseases for example. In the last half dozen years, the public has been warned about the Zika virus, Ebola or hemorrhagic fever, swine flu or H1N1 flu, mad cow disease or BSE, West Nile, SARS, the "flesh-eating" virus or necrotizing fasciitis, and Asian bird flu. As of 2016, however, no American had contracted Zika within the continental USA. One person in Salt Lake City died of Zika, but that person had traveled to a high-risk country. Similarly, only one person died from Ebola in the USA, and that patient contracted the disease in Liberia. In contrast, chicken pox kills about 100 people a year in the United States. Chicken pox, however, just doesn't seem as scary as Zika or Ebola, so it garners little media attention.

There is a whole industry dedicated to scaring people about exotic diseases. Consider, for example, books such as *Plague* (Orent, 2004), *The Coming Plague* (Garrett, 1994), *Betrayal of Trust: The Collapse of Global Public Health* (Garrett, 2000), and *Secret Agents: The Menace of Emerging Infections* (Drexler, 2002). Scary, exotic diseases sell books. Tired of the same old scary diseases? Here are some exotic diseases you may not have heard of: fatal familial insomnia (death from lack of sleep), maple syrup urine disease (yup, MSUD makes your urine smell like maple syrup, but it can also cause brain damage and death), and brain worms (technically known as neurocysticercosis). Not to fear, perhaps some enterprising author will write a *Maple Syrup Urine Disease for Dummies* book in the near future.

Other persuaders profit from the public's fear of crime. We are assailed by stories of car-jackings, school shootings, freeway shootings, home invasion robberies, homegrown terrorists, serial killers, and child molesters. Yet, as a matter of fact, violent crime rates in the United States are near their lowest levels in three decades (FBI, 2013; Gramlich, 2017). Consider child kidnappings as a case in point. Parents have a heightened fear of abduction-murders in the wake of high-profile cases such as those of Polly Klaas and Amber Hagerman. Terrible as they may be, however, child-abduction murders are extremely rare. The actual risk of a child being kidnapped and killed in the United States is roughly 1 in 1.3 million (Ropeik, cited in Wilson et al., 2005). In comparison, the risk of a child dying from the flu is 1 in 130,000, a much greater risk. We don't mean to belittle parents for worrying about their kids' well-being, but a parent who gets his/her child a microchip but doesn't get his/her child a flu shot is giving in to irrational fear.

New media and social media make fearmongering easier than ever. We've been warned about cyberbullying, cybertracking, cyberstalking, and other cyber fears. Social media, however, are neither fact-checked nor carefully edited. Moreover, a single tweet, text, or post can go viral in no time. For example, following media chatter about face-eating zombies, the Centers for Disease Control felt compelled to issue a public statement saying there was no impending "zombie apocalypse" (Campbell, 2012). Similarly, after claims that a mermaid's body had been discovered, the National Oceanographic and Atmospheric Agency (NOAA) issued a disclaimer saying "no evidence of aquatic humanoids has ever been found" (Lynch, 2012, p. A12). Should we be concerned that the federal agencies have not denied the existence of vampires or werewolves?

We can't stop the fearmongers from practicing their trade. What we can do is urge you to use central rather than peripheral processing when evaluating fear appeals. Keep the numbers in perspective (Ropeik & Gray, 2002; Siegel, 2005; Simhan, 2004). When driving, be concerned about road rage (about 40 deaths per year), but be much more concerned about wearing your seat belt (9,200 preventable fatalities per year, according to the NHTSA) (Advocates for Highway and Auto Safety, 2005). When at the beach, worry about the risk of a shark attack (about three deaths per year in the United States), but worry far more about the risk of skin cancer from overexposure to the sun (about 8,000 deaths per year in the United States). Fret a little over exotic diseases, such as West Nile virus (100 deaths in the United States in 2004), but bear in mind that you have roughly the same chance of dying from a lightning strike (around 100 deaths per year in the United States) and a greater risk of drowning in a bathtub

(more than 300 cases in the United States annually). Don't worry about zombies or mermaids at all.

Turning to the second question of whether and when fear appeals are ever justified, we maintain that if the dangers alluded to in a fear appeal are real or genuine, then we believe it is not only acceptable but desirable to evoke fear. People should be informed about dangers and hazards to which they are exposed. Two guidelines should be observed when using fear appeals. The first is that specific recommendations for avoiding the harmful consequences must be included in the appeal. The specific recommendations must tell receivers how to cope with the dangers identified.

The second recommendation is that the persuader should include concrete recommendations that tell receivers what they should do. In our judgment, fear appeals should never be used if the alleged harms are exaggerated or, worse yet, fabricated. Nor should fear appeals be used if receivers are given no recourse for avoiding the harms. What is the point in scaring people if there is nothing they can do about it?

Ethics and Emotional Appeals

Some people take the view that emotional appeals, which tug at receivers' heartstrings, are unjustified precisely because they appeal to emotion rather than to reason. Persuasion, they say, should aim higher, at the mind, not the heart, and certainly not below the belt. In response to this concern, we raise the following ethical questions:

1. Is playing on others' emotions ethically justifiable?
2. Are some types of emotional appeals better, or more ethically defensible, than others?

Our answer to the first question is a qualified "Yes." Recall from Chapter 13, however, that the distinction between logical and emotional appeals represents something of an artificial dichotomy anyway. People tend to perceive messages they agree with as "logical" or "rational" and messages they disagree with as "emotional." To the extent that logical and emotional appeals can be differentiated, we believe they work perfectly well side by side. We see nothing wrong with using emotional appeals, as long as their use complements, rather than contradicts or substitutes for, other more thoughtful approaches to persuasion. We do not think emotional appeals should constitute the sole means of persuasion, nor do we believe emotional appeals should be used if they contradict sound reasoning and evidence. As we mentioned earlier, our preference is for central processing of persuasive messages. To the extent that emotional appeals are used to promote peripheral processing, at the expense of central processing, we believe their use is undesirable.

An example of persuasion that combines emotional and rational appeals effectively is Whirlpool's Care Counts program, which provides washers and dryers to schools so kids have clean clothes to wear (www.youtube.com/watch?v=oxbipSM8GmA). The video begins with gloomy statistics indicating that students who drop out of school face higher unemployment, require greater government assistance, and are more likely to be incarcerated. Next, testimonials from children report that they are embarrassed or ashamed to go to school wearing dirty clothes. "We have a washer and dryer at home," says one little girl, "It's just that our electricity was shut off." Whirlpool to the rescue. Pairs of washers and dryers were provided free of charge to 17 schools. Kids could bring their clothes to school to be laundered. Testimonials from teachers say the program improved attendance, class participation, and grades. Finally, statistics are presented, showing that over 90 percent of kids improved their attendance and at-risk kids attended nearly two weeks more than the previous year. The video has an emotional, "feel good" ending.

Despite potential limitations of the program (e.g., other, more significant barriers to school attendance), Whirlpool's program is a positive example of what is known as *corporate social responsibility* (CSR), in this case, by giving back to the community in the form of washers and dryers. Since the program is being expanded to more than 60 schools, it appears to be more than window dressing.

In answer to the second ethical question, we tend to believe that negative, divisive appeals are less ethically defensible than positive, prosocial appeals. When you think of emotional appeals, you may envision "negative" sorts of appeals, such as appeals to pity, shame, or guilt. Bear in mind, however, that emotional appeals have a positive side as well. Emotional appeals can be inspiring or uplifting. They can motivate us to try harder, to excel, to give our all. We hardly think that coaches, teachers, politicians, and clergy who provide emotional encouragement are behaving unethically. To the contrary, we believe that positive emotional appeals have a legitimate role to play in the persuasion process and that they function as useful complements to the use of reasoning and evidence.

Ethics and Ingratiation

Everyone claims to hate brownnosers, unless the brownnosing is directed at them, that is. In his seminal work on the subject, Jones (1963) defined ingratiation, the polite term for brownnosing, as an "illicit" form of strategic behavior (see Chapter 13). Thus, it would seem that ingratiation operates through unethical means. We thus explore the question: Is ingratiation an unethical practice or simply an honest acknowledgment of the way things work?

We sometimes tend to think of ingratiation as a form of deception—that is, we envision the ingratiator as being disingenuous in his or her use of flattery. But what if the ingratiator *believes* in the praise he or she bestows on another? We see no problem with the use of praise or compliments if the persuader genuinely believes in what she or he is saying. In fact, this is one of the ethical questions that allows us to draw a "bright line" between what we consider to be ethical and unethical persuasion. Sincere compliments, we maintain, are ethical, and insincere compliments unethical. Genuine praise offers the prospect of a win–win communication encounter. Both parties benefit. When a persuader pays a compliment and means it, he or she is demonstrating respect for the other person, and respect, we contend, is one of the essential ingredients of ethical influence attempts.

Ethics and Visual Persuasion

If a picture is worth a thousand words, as the saying goes, then is a misleading image equivalent to a thousand misleading words? Images are a powerful form of influence, as we noted in Chapter 14. Images are immediate and visceral. They evoke strong emotions. But images can be misleading too. When it comes to photographic evidence, determining what is real or fake can be difficult. There are multiple cases, for example, of prize-winning photographers who have been caught Photoshopping images, contrary to photojournalistic standards (Cooke, 2016; Laurent, 2017). Thus, we raise the question: What social responsibilities accompany the use of images and other forms of visual persuasion?

Size matters. Optics matter too. You may recall the brouhaha over the crowd size at Trump's inauguration in 2017 compared to Obama's in 2009. A similar controversy emerged when the *New York Times* tweeted comparison photos of Donald Trump greeting the 2017 Super Bowl champion New England Patriots on the steps of the White House, versus Barack Obama greeting the Patriots team that won the Super Bowl in 2015. The photos showed a noticeably smaller turnout for Trump than his predecessor. What the *New York Times* failed to mention, however, was that in 2015 the coaching staff was standing on the steps alongside the players, whereas in 2017 the coaching staff were not on the steps, but on the south lawn (Kerr-Dineen, 2017).

We believe that persuaders have a responsibility for fact-checking the accuracy of documentary images before publishing them in traditional media or circulating them on social media. For the Super Bowl photos in question, the whole point of the tweet was to compare turnout. Shouldn't the source, then, have checked to see if there were coaches, not just players, in both pictures? It didn't take long for viewers and the Patriot's front office to complain that the 2017 photo excluded 40 members of the coaching staff.

Patriots' turnout for President Obama in 2015
vs. Patriots' turnout for President Trump
today: nyti.ms/2o4Kwj7

1:25 PM - 19 Apr 2017

FIGURE 16.2
Tweet with comparison
photos from *The New
York Times*.

As a consumer of images, we believe that you bear some responsibility for fact-checking the accuracy of images before sharing, forwarding, or retweeting them, too. Some useful Web-based resources for checking the veracity of images include www.snopes.com (check out their photo gallery link); factcheck.org, and Skeptical Enquirer, at www.csicop.org. Using Google, you can conduct a reverse image search (see www.youtube.com/watch?v=p5e9wTdAulA).

Nowadays optics matter as much or more than words. As Zimmer (2010, para. 3) noted, "When politicians fret about the public perception of a decision more than the substance of the decision itself, we're living in a world of optics."

Ethics and Subliminal Influence

Unlike many other people, we aren't troubled by the use of subliminal messages. Why? Because, frankly, we don't believe they work outside of highly controlled laboratory settings. All of the research to date suggests that subliminal priming is not commercially viable. Thus, it is more as a matter of principle than out of genuine concern that we raise the ethical question: Should subliminal messages be allowed, and, if so, should they be regulated by the government or some other institution?

We feel much the same about the first part of this question as we do about the use of voodoo dolls. We'd prefer that people *not* stick pins in dolls that resemble us, but we aren't much bothered by it if they do. As we noted in Chapter 15, subliminal priming works, but the effects are difficult to produce and highly transitory. At present, priming cannot make people do something they do not want to do, although under the right circumstances, it can reinforce an existing goal, need, or value. The practice of "embedding," or hiding, images in advertisements has proven fruitless, as has the practice of planting subaudible oral messages. Other than disliking subliminals as a matter of principle, then, we believe there is little to fear from their actual use. If unscrupulous persuaders want to bombard us with subliminal messages, so much the better. The time and energy they waste on their fruitless endeavor may distract them from using other, more effective techniques of persuasion on us.

SUMMARY

We have argued in this chapter that persuasion is not an inherently unethical activity. To the contrary, we believe that persuasion can be used to advance all manner of positive, prosocial interests. Persuasion is a powerful tool that can be used for the noblest and basest of motives. Humankind's ability to persuade is thus both a blessing and a curse. Our view is that the moral quality of a given persuasive act is based primarily on the motives of the persuader and only secondarily on the strategies and tactics used by the persuader.

Based on our model of persuasion, we've argued that pure persuasion is more ethically defensible than borderline persuasion. That is, persuasion that is intentional, that occurs with the receiver's conscious awareness, that involves free choice, and that takes place through language or symbolic action is more ethically defensible than persuasion that takes place via other means. Furthermore, we offered three qualities that we consider to be characteristic of ethical persuasion—respect, equality, and tolerance.

Finally, we examined a number of ethical questions associated with particular topics and issues related to persuasion. We attempted to answer these questions as best we could—without dancing around the issues on one hand and without claiming to have a corner on truth and ethics on the other hand. Above all, we urge you to contemplate the bases for your own ethical beliefs and not to let anyone else, including us, tell you what is right or wrong. The cause of ethics will be better served if you figure out for yourself what you ought, and ought not, do as a persuader.

We've told you about a number of tools of influence in these pages. Many of them have proven to be highly effective. Unfortunately, we can't give you a conscience to go with them (the publisher said it would be too expensive). We have to trust that you will let your conscience be your guide. When pondering which persuasive strategies you should use, think not only about the persuasive ends you are seeking but also about the kinds of relationships you want to have with other people. Long-term relationships, we're convinced, should never be sacrificed for short-term compliance. Mutual influence requires give and take, not just take, take, take. If you put people first and persuasion second, we think you'll be more successful in the long run than if you put persuasion first and people second.

REFERENCES

Advocates for Highway and Auto Safety. (2005, September). *Buckling up*. Retrieved September 28, 2005, from: www.saferoads.org/issues/fs-stand.htm

Altheide, D. L. (2002). *Creating fear: News and the construction of crisis*. New York: Aldine de Gruyter.

American Academy of Pediatrics (2009) Policy statement: Media violence. *Pediatrics*, *124*(5), 1495–1503. doi:10.1542/peds.2009–2146

Brockriede, W. (1974). Arguers as lovers. *Philosophy and Rhetoric*, *5*, 1–11.

Bromberg, M. S. (1990). Critics fume at cigarette marketing. *Business and Society Review*, *73*, 27–28.

BuzzFeed. (2014, December 8). Adweek names BuzzFeed "hottest" in native advertising. Retrieved on July 12, 2017 from: www.buzzfeed.com/buzzfeedawards/adweek-names-buzzfeed-hottest-in-native-advertising?utm_term=.od724MNwM#.ejERnADLA

Campbell, A. (2012, June 1). Zombie apocalypse: CDC denies existence of zombies despite cannibal incidents. *Huffington Post*. Retrieved on July 15, 2012, from: www.huffingtonpost.com/2012/06/01/cdc-denies-zombies-existence_n_1562141.html

Christians, C. G., Rotzoll, K. B., & Fackler, M. (1991). *Media ethics: Cases and moral reasoning* (3rd ed.). New York: Longman.

Cialdini, R. B. (1999). Of tricks and tumors: Some little-recognized costs of dishonest use of effective social influence. *Psychology & Marketing, 16*(2), 91–98.

Cooke, A. (2016, May 12). The case of Steve McCurry: What is "truth" in photography? *Fstoppers*. Retrieved on July 15, 2017 from: https://fstoppers.com/editorial/case-steve-mccurry-what-truth-photography-129505

Drexler, M. (2002). *Secret agents: The menace of emerging infections*. New York: Penguin Books.

Duffy, M., & Thorson, E. (Eds.). (2015). *Persuasion ethics today*. New York: Routledge.

FBI. (2013). Uniform Crime Reports: Crime in the United States. Retrieved from: https://ucr.fbi.gov/crime-in-the-u.s/2013/crime-in-the-u.s.-2013/violent-crime/violent-crime-topic-page/violentcrimemain_final

Fletcher, P. (2017, March 19). Report: Nearly 40% of publishers ignore FTC's native advertising rules. *Forbes*. Retrieved on July 13, 2017 from: www.forbes.com/sites/paulfletcher/2017/03/19/nearly-40-percent-of-publishers-ignore-ftcs-native-advertising-rules/#5b44d0c867db

Fong, C. P. S., & Wyer, Jr., R. S. (2012). Consumers' reactions to a celebrity endorser scandal. *Psychology & Marketing, 29*(11), 885–896. doi:10.1002/mar.20571

FTC. (2016, July 11). Warner Brothers settles FTC charges that it failed to adequately disclose it paid online influencers to post gameplay videos. Retrieved on July 13, 2017 from: www.ftc.gov/news-events/press-releases/2016/07/warner-bros-settles-ftc-charges-it-failed-adequately-disclose-it

Garrett, L. (1994). *The coming plague: Newly emerging diseases in a world out of balance*. New York: Penguin Books.

Garrett, L. (2000). *Betrayal of trust: The collapse of global public health*. New York: Hyperion.

Gass, R. H., & Canary, D. J. (1988, May). *An experimental examination of threat of punishment and promise of reward on motivation*. Paper presented at the annual meeting of the International Communication Association, New Orleans.

Gentile, D. A., Mathieson, L. C., & Crick, N. R. (2011). Media violence associations with the form and function of aggression among elementary school children. *Social Development, 20*(2), 213–232. doi:10.1111/j.1467–9507.2010.00577.x

Glassner, B. (1999). *The culture of fear: Why Americans are afraid of the wrong things*. New York: Basic Books.

Gore, A. (1989. Children's TV Act of 1989 (Hearing before the U.S. Senate Subcommittee on Communications, No. 101–221). Washington, DC: U.S. Government Printing Office.

Gramlich, J. (2017, February 21). 5 facts about crime in the U.S. *Pew Research Center*. Retrieved on July 13, 2017 from: www.pewresearch.org/fact-tank/2017/02/21/5-facts-about-crime-in-the-u-s/

Greenberg, J., & Pyszczynski, T. (1985). The effect of an overheard ethnic slur on evaluations of the target: How to spread a social disease. *Journal of Experimental Social Psychology, 21*, 61–72.

Heisler, G. (1974). Ways to deter law violators: Effects of levels of threat and vicarious punishment on cheating. *Journal of Consulting and Clinical Psychology, 42*(4), 577–582.

Herrman, J. (2016, July 24). How sponsored content is becoming king on Facebook. *New York Times*, p. B1.

Ikonen, P., Luoma-aho, V., & Bowen, S. A. (2017). Transparency for sponsored content: Analysing codes of ethics in public relations, marketing, advertising and journalism. *International Journal of Strategic Communication, 11*(2), 165–178. doi:10.1080/1553118X.2016.1252917

Jacksa, J. A., & Pritchard, M. S. (1994). *Communication ethics: Methods of analysis* (2nd ed.). Belmont, CA: Wadsworth.

Johannesen, R. L. (1983). *Ethics and human communication* (2nd ed.). Prospect Heights, IL: Waveland Press.

Johannesen, R. L., Thayer, L. O., & Hardt, H. (1979). *Ethics, morality, and the media: Reflections on American culture*. New York: Hastings House.

Jones, E. (1963). *Ingratiation*. New York: Appleton-Century-Crofts.

Jones, T., Cunningham, P. H., & Gallagher, K. (2010). Violence in advertising: A multi-layered content analysis. *Journal of Advertising, 39*(4), 11–36. doi:10.2753/JOA0091-3367390402

Kaplan, A. (1964). *The conduct of inquiry*. New York: Thomas Crowell.

Kerr-Dineen, L. (2017, April 20). The truth behind the *New York Times*' Patriots photo that went viral. *USA Today*. Retrieved on July 15 from: http://ftw.usatoday.com/2017/04/new-england-patriots-donald-trump-white-house-new-york-time-crowd-size-visit-picture-truth

Kirkland, S. L., Greenberg, J., & Pyszczynski, T. (1987). Further evidence of the deleterious effects of overheard derogatory ethnic labels: Derogation beyond the target. *Personality and Social Psychology Bulletin, 13*(2), 216–227.

Kotz, D., & Haupt, A. (2012, March 5). The dangers of Kardashian-endorsed Quicktrim. *U.S. News and World Report*. Retrieved on July 14, 2012, from: http://health.usnews.com/health-news/diet-fitness/articles/2012/03/05/the-dangers-of-kardashian-endorsed-quicktrim-2

Kwate, N. O. A., & Lee, T. H. (2006). Ghettoizing outdoor advertising: Disadvantage and ad panel density in Black neighborhoods. *Journal of Urban Health: Bulletin of the New York Academy of Medicine, 84*(1), 21–31.

Laurent, O. (2017, May 4). Souvid Datta: "I foolishly doctored images." *Time*. Retrieved on July 15, 2017 from: http://time.com/4766312/souvid-datta/

Lynch, R. (2012, July 7). NOAA dashes dreams of mermaids. *Los Angeles Times*, p. A12.

Malinowski, E. (2011, January 26). Basketball stars sued over energy-bracelet endorsement. *Wired*. Retrieved on July 14, 2012, from: www.wired.com/playbook/2011/01/nba-lawsuit-power-balance/all/

McCroskey, J. C. (1972). *An introduction to rhetorical communication* (2nd ed.). Englewood Cliffs, NJ: Prentice-Hall.

Murray, J. (2008). Media violence: The effects are both real and strong. *American Behavioral Scientist, 51*(8), 1212–1230. doi:10.1177/0002764207312018

Nevin, J. R., & Ford, N. M. (1976). Effects of a deadline date and veiled threat on mail survey responses. *Journal of Applied Psychology, 61*, 116–118.

Nilsen, T. R. (1966). *Ethics of speech communication*. Indianapolis, IN: Bobbs-Merrill.

Orent, W. (2004). *Plague: The mysterious and terrifying future of the world's most dangerous disease*. New York: Simon & Schuster.

Petty, R. E., & Cacioppo, J. T. (1986). *Communication and persuasion: Central and peripheral routes to attitude change*. New York: Springer-Verlag.

Rivers, W. L., Christians, C. G., & Schramm, W. (1980). *Responsibility in mass communication* (3rd ed.). New York: Harper & Row.

Ropeik, D., & Gray, G. (2002). *Risk: A practical guide for deciding what's really safe and what's really dangerous in the world around you.* New York: Houghton Mifflin.

Schultz, E.J. (2014, July 4). Activist or capitalists? How the "Food Babe" makes money. *Advertising Age.* Retrieved on July 13, 2017 from: http://adage.com/article/news/activist-capitalist-food-babe-makes-money/294032/

Seiter, J. S., Bruschke, J., & Bai, C. (2002). The acceptability of deception as a function of perceivers' culture, deceiver's intention, and deceiver–deceived relationship. *Western Journal of Communication*, 66(2), 158–180.

Siegel, M. (2005). *False alarm: The truth about the epidemic of fear.* New York: John Wiley.

Simhan, R. (2004, August 24). Fears and facts: Most people worry about high-profile hazards but ignore common—and often deadlier—dangers. *Sacramento Bee,* p. E1.

Taylor, C. R. (2017, March). Native advertising: The black sheep of the marketing family. *International Journal of Advertising*, 36(2), pp. 207–209. doi:10.1080/02650487.2017.1285389

Ting-Toomey, S. (1988). Intercultural conflict styles: A face-negotiation theory. In Y. Y. Kim & W. Gudykunst (Eds.), *Theories in intercultural communication* (pp. 213–235). Newbury Park, CA: Sage.

Ting-Toomey, S. (1994). *The challenge of facework: Cross-cultural and interpersonal issues.* Ithaca, NY: SUNY Press.

Ting-Toomey, S., & Kurogi, A. (1998). Facework competence in intercultural conflict: An updated face negotiation theory. *International Journal of Intercultural Relations*, 22, 187–225.

Tittle, C. R., & Rowe, A. R. (1973). Moral appeal, sanction, threat, and deviance: An experimental test. *Social Problems*, 20(4), 488–498.

Treise, D., Weigold, M. F., Conna, J., & Garrison, H. (1994). Ethics in advertising: Ideological correlates of consumer perceptions: Special issue on ethics in advertising. *Journal of Advertising*, 23(3), 59–69.

Wilson, B. J., Martins, N., & Marske, A. L. (2005). Children's and parents' fright reactions to kidnapping stories in the news. *Communication Monographs*, 72, 46–70.

Wiseman, R. L., Sanders, J. A., Congalton, K. J., Gass, R. H., Sueda, K., & Ruiqing, D. (1995). A cross-cultural analysis of compliance gaining: China, Japan, and the United States. *Intercultural Communication Studies*, 5(1), 1–17.

Zimmer, B. (2010, March 4). Optics. *New York Times Magazine.* Retrieved on July 14, 2017 from: www.nytimes.com/2010/03/07/magazine/07FOB-onlanguage-t.html

Author Index

Subject Index